Birds

Rare and Endangered Biota of Florida
Ray E. Ashton, Jr., Series Editor

Florida Committee on Rare and Endangered Plants and Animals

Ray E. Ashton, Jr.
FCREPA Chair (1989–91)
and Series Editor
Applied Technology
and Management, Inc.
2770 NW 43rd Street
Gainesville, FL 32606

Daniel F. Austin, Co-Chair
Special Committee on Plants
Department of Biological Sciences
Florida Atlantic University
Boca Raton, FL 33431

James W. Beever III
FCREPA Chair (1993–94)
Florida Game and
  Fresh Water Fish Commission
306 Little Grove Lane
North Fort Myers, FL 33917

Mark Deyrup, Co-Chair
Special Committee on Invertebrates
Archbold Biological Station
Route 2, Box 180
Lake Placid, FL 33852

Richard Franz, Co-Chair
Special Committee on Invertebrates
Florida Museum of Natural History
University of Florida
Gainesville, FL 32611

Carter R. Gilbert
Chair, Special Committee on Fishes
Florida Museum of Natural History
University of Florida
Gainesville, FL 32611

Stephen R. Humphrey
Chair, Special Committee on Mammals
Florida Museum of Natural History
University of Florida
Gainesville, FL 32611

Dr. Herbert W. Kale II
(deceased)
FCREPA Chair (1985–86)
Chair, Special Committee on Birds
Florida Audubon Society

Paul Moler
FCREPA Chair (1991–92)
Chair, Special Committee
  on Reptiles and Amphibians
Wildlife Research Laboratory
Florida Game and
  Fresh Water Fish Commission
4005 S. Main Street
Gainesville, FL 32601

James A. Rodgers, Jr.
Co-Chair, Special Committee on Birds
Wildlife Research Laboratory
Florida Game and
  Fresh Water Fish Commission
4005 S. Main Street
Gainesville, FL 32601

Henry T. Smith
Co-Chair, Special Committee on Birds
Florida Park Service
Florida Department of Environmental Protection
13798 S.E. Federal Highway
Hobe Sound, FL 33455

I. Jack Stout
FCREPA Chair (1987–88)
Department of Biological Sciences
University of Central Florida
Orlando, FL 32816

Dr. Daniel B. Ward
FCREPA Chair (1983–84)
Co-Chair, Special Committee on Plants
Department of Botany
University of Florida
Gainesville, FL 32611

Rare and Endangered Biota of Florida

VOLUME V. BIRDS

EDITED BY
JAMES A. RODGERS, JR.,
HERBERT W. KALE II,
& HENRY T. SMITH

Co-Chairs, Special Committee on Birds
Florida Committee on Rare and Endangered
Plants and Animals

UNIVERSITY PRESS OF FLORIDA
Gainesville, Tallahassee, Tampa, Boca Raton,
Pensacola, Orlando, Miami, Jacksonville

This volume was made possible in part by a grant from Save the Manatee Club

01 00 99 98 97 96 6 5 4 3 2 1

Library of Congress Cataloging-in-Publication Data
(Revised for vol. 4)

Rare and endangered biota of Florida

    Includes bibliographical references and indexes.
    Contents: v. 1. Mammals / edited by Stephen R. Humphrey—v. 2. Fishes /
edited by Carter R. Gilbert—[etc.]—v. 5. Birds / edited by James A. Rodgers,
Jr., Herbert W. Kale II, & Henry T. Smith
    1. Rare animals—Florida.   2. Endangered species—
Florida.   3. Rare plants—Florida.   4. Endangered plants—
Florida.   I. Ashton, Ray E.
QL84.22.F6R37   1992   591.52'9'09759   91-36368
ISBN 0-8130-1127-2 (v. 1: alk. paper)
ISBN 0-8130-1128-0 (v. 1: pbk: alk. paper)

The University Press of Florida is the scholarly publishing agency of the State
University System of Florida comprised of Florida A&M University, Florida
Atlantic University, Florida International University, Florida State University,
University of Central Florida, University of Florida, University of North
Florida, University of South Florida, University of West Florida.

Orders for books published by all member presses should be addressed to
University Press of Florida, 15 NW 15th St., Gainesville, FL 32611.

In Memoriam

Herbert W. Kale II, 1931–1995

This volume in the Rare and Endangered Biota of Florida series is dedicated to Herbert W. Kale II. Herb was the editor of the original 1978 bird volume, co-editor of this current volume, and Chair of the Special Committee on Birds, Florida Committee on Rare and Endangered Plants and Animals. His legacy in avian and environmental conservation in Florida will continue long into the future. Herb was that special type of person who cared about little brown birds.

Herb holding a Snail Kite nestling. Photograph taken on May 2, 1972 by Paul W. Sykes, Jr., in an Indian River County marsh where kites formerly bred.

Contents

Species of Special Concern

Status Undetermined

Foreword

The initial six-volume Rare and Endangered Biota of Florida series has enjoyed enormous popularity (each volume was reprinted at least once, most two or three times). It has served as the definitive reference compendium on endangered and threatened species in Florida and is widely recognized as among the most authoritative and comprehensive such works in the nation. I am proud the Florida Game and Fresh Water Fish Commission was integrally involved in that initial work, and likewise proud that we were involved in producing this revised series.

In the forewords to the initial volumes, my predecessors, Dr. O. E. Frye, Jr., and Colonel Robert M. Brantly acknowledged the momentum of endangered species conservation to that point, and how the series was a significant contribution in that regard, but admonished that we must not rest on our laurels—much remained to be done. Although much has indeed been done in the interim, I am disappointed that we have not approached the level of progress I had hoped we would attain by now. As the species accounts herein clearly demonstrate, many Florida species are perilously near extinction, and many of the factors leading to that dire circumstance are still with us. The composition of the current official state lists—40 endangered, 27 threatened, and 50 special concern animals, along with 199 endangered and 283 threatened plants—is compelling evidence in and of itself that our progress has been relatively minor (by comparison, there were 31 endangered and 54 threatened species in 1978). There are several reasons for this much-less-than-hoped-for progression, but primarily it has been related to insufficient funding at both the state and federal levels. And without proper funding, the necessary manpower and other resources cannot be emplaced to address many critical needs. So we face the dilemma of either addressing the needs of only a few species so as to maximize effect, or spreading our resources thinly among many species, minimizing the effects on an individual basis.

This is not to say, however, that we have not made some substantial strides forward in the last decade or so. Through an innovative translocation strategy, we have reestablished in Florida the previously extirpated Perdido Key beach mouse and significantly expanded the range of the Choctawhatchee beach mouse; because of stringent protection and rigorous application of "Habitat

Management Guidelines for the Bald Eagle in the Southeast Region," Florida's bald eagle nesting population has grown to nearly 700 pairs (as of the 1992–93 nesting season); the brown pelican and Pine Barrens tree-frog have been delisted because of increasing populations and/or because our research efforts have provided new insight into those species' true status; nearly 50 manatee sanctuaries have been established in which boat speeds are restricted during the winter congregation period; our research over the past two decades has resulted in more knowledge about endangered species biology, habitat needs, etc., than during all previous time cumulatively; considerable endangered species habitat has been secured through CARL, (Conservation and Recreation Lands), Save Our Coasts, Save Our Rivers, Save Our Everglades, and other land acquisition programs; and various information/education programs have resulted in a significant increase in public awareness and support for endangered species conservation. These few examples demonstrate what can be done with adequate resources and commitment, but in fact represent only the proverbial drop in the bucket in light of the total needs.

I hope this revised series reinvigorates our resolve and commitment to endangered and threatened species conservation and we will be able to cite a multitude of such examples by the time a third revision is necessary. These volumes provide an authoritative and comprehensive database from which to embark on such a course, and I congratulate and personally thank each researcher, writer, editor, and individual whose committed efforts have culminated in this exemplary work.

Allan L. Egbert, Executive Director
State of Florida Game and Fresh Water Fish Commission

Preface

"Thirty years ago Florida was one of the most extraordinary states in the Union, but being flat and quite park-like in character (a large part of the country consisted of open pinelands) it was an easy state for man to ruin, and he has ruined it with worthless efficiency." This quote from Thomas Barbour's *That Vanishing Eden, A Naturalist's Florida,* written in 1944, is ever more appropriate today. He continues his lament—"A large part of Florida is now so devastated that many of her friends are disinclined to believe that she ever could have been the Paradise which I know once existed." Barbour was talking about the loss of natural habitat in Florida from 1915 to the early 1940s. Imagine what he would think today!

Within the FCREPA volumes, the emphasis is on specific plants and animals that the committee considers to be endangered, threatened to become endangered, or species of special concern (those species apparently in danger but about which we need more information). However, as one reads through the species accounts, there is a continuing theme of habitat loss or alteration by man. Since Barbour's days of study in Florida, the loss and degradation of natural habitats have accelerated beyond human comprehension. We are faced with the possible reality that the only thing which will cause a decline in the loss is that there will soon be no land left to develop.

We are also faced with the fact that we actually know very little about the fauna and flora of this state. When challenged to protect a species or develop regulations to prevent extinction, we are inevitably confronted with the fact that we know little about their life histories, let alone what is needed to preserve a population through biological time. We are also faced with the dilemma that there probably is not enough time or money to allow us to study these organisms, let alone experiment with management techniques. Our ecological knowledge of interactions and biological communities is even less. Yet we do know that once certain biological needs are not met, we lose another species and another community. The biological communities of this state are being compromised time and again by all levels of government, simply to serve the hunger for growth and development.

We are the first generation to realize that not only do we have local or regional environmental concerns but we now have to be aware of serious global degradations of our air and water. Global warming, acid rain, increased ultraviolet radiation, and degradation of our oceans are making us realize for the first time that our species may well be jeopardizing itself as well as the lowly gopher tortoise and tree snail. We are realizing that the world's biodiversity and the biological engine that drives many of the necessities of all life are being used up or changed by our overpopulated species. If we know so little about individual species and communities, how can we be prepared to understand the complexities of the biosphere, let alone the cause and effect of our actions.

Alarms have sounded in the minds of many people around the world, including Florida. The first step toward a solution to all of this is acknowledging that we are causing problems. Loss of uplands not only means loss of wildlife but also that we affect our water supplies, river systems, and ultimately the health of our coastal systems. Our state agencies are in the fledgling stages of creating regulations on development and the organized effort of protecting biological diversity and natural communities. Hopefully these agencies and the people of Florida will begin to recognize that we must increase our efforts to protect our environment and the creatures who inhabit it, not just to use for recreation but for the sake of preserving the machinery that makes our lives as living things possible.

It is these concerns that have been the driving force behind the volunteer biologists who have unselfishly spent so many long hours putting together the information in these volumes. We hope that through the information provided here more biologists will turn their thoughts from the test tube to the laboratory in the field, funding agencies will realize the need for this basic knowledge, and government agencies will begin to think more on the biological community level and not the species or individual organism level. Most important, we hope that these volumes serve to educate the citizens of Florida so that we may all recognize the need to learn more and work together to make prudent decisions about our "Vanishing Eden."

Ray E. Ashton, Jr.
Series Editor

A Brief History of FCREPA

The Florida Committee on Rare and Endangered Plants and Animals, FCREPA, was founded in 1973. The original group of 100 scientists, conservationists, and concerned citizens was organized by James Layne, Peter Pritchard, and Roy McDiarmid. The chairs of the Special Committees on Terrestrial Invertebrates, Marine Invertebrates, Plants, Reptiles and Amphibians, Fish, Birds, Mammals, and Liaison made up the first Endangered Species Advisory Board to the Florida Game and Fresh Water Fish Commission. These special committees were made up of concerned biologists who were living and/or working in the state of Florida. The first FCREPA meeting was called for biologists to discuss and evaluate the status of Florida's wildlife and to determine which species should be considered for special classification and concern. From this conference, five volumes—the Rare and Endangered Biota of Florida series—were produced. These were edited by Peter Pritchard of the Florida Audubon Society and Don Wood of the Florida Game and Fresh Water Fish Commission. Section editors for the first series included Roy McDiarmid, reptiles and amphibians; Herb Kale, birds; James Layne, mammals; Carter Gilbert, fish; Howard Weems, terrestrial invertebrates; Joe Simon, marine invertebrates; and Dan Ward, plants. Before its completion, the invertebrate volumes were combined under the editorship of Richard Franz.

Following the production of the FCREPA volumes by the University Press of Florida in 1976, FCREPA continued to meet and support a special section of papers at the annual meeting of the Florida Academy of Sciences. The affiliation of FCREPA was organized under the guidance of Dan Ward, director of the herbarium at the University of Florida.

In the fall of 1986, it became obvious that the original publications were becoming dated and the demand for the publication was great (the volumes had been reprinted repeatedly). Then chair, Herbert Kale, vice president of the Florida Audubon Society, convened the second FCREPA conference at the youth camp in the Ocala National Forest. The committees on each group met and deliberated on the status of the species in their charge. It was decided at that meeting to rewrite the FCREPA series since considerable changes in our knowledge and in the state of the natural environment in Florida made much of the information produced more than 13 years before out of date.

Editors for each of the volumes called together those knowledgeable individuals and potential contributors to the future volumes to discuss the status of the taxa covered in their volume. Their recommendations on the status (and the criteria used) of various species were discussed by everyone present at the 1986 meeting.

Under the direction of Jack Stout, University of Central Florida, and each of the section chairs and editors, the arduous task of preparing the new manuscripts was undertaken. Each section chair served as compiler and editor for each volume. Individual species accounts were prepared by biologists who were among the most qualified to write about the status of that species.

Ray Ashton, vertebrate zoologist, Water and Air Research, Inc. was appointed by the section chairs as managing editor of the series in 1988. Four years of preparation and coordination, fund raising, and gentle prodding of the volunteer editors and contributors have produced the second FCREPA series.

Without the thousands of volunteer hours given by many outstanding Florida biologists, and the support from the Florida Game and Fresh Water Fish Commission, Save the Manatee Club, and Florida Power and Light Company, this effort would not have been possible. Royalties from the sales of these volumes and donations to the FCREPA effort are used to keep all the volumes in print and to fund future work.

Ray E. Ashton, Jr.
Series Editor

Definitions of Status Categories

Categories used to designate the status of the organisms included in the Florida list of rare and endangered species are defined below. In the case of species or subspecies whose ranges extend outside the state, the category to which the form is assigned is based on the status of its population in Florida. Thus, a plant or animal whose range barely reaches the state ("peripheral species") may be classified as endangered, threatened, or rare as a member of the Florida biota, although it may be generally common elsewhere in its range.

In the following definitions, "species" is used in a general sense to include (1) full taxonomic species, (2) subspecies (animals) or varieties (plants), and (3) particular populations of a species or subspecies that do not have formal taxonomic status. This use of the term agrees with that of the Endangered Species Act of 1973.

Recently extinct.—Species that have disappeared from Florida since 1600 through extinction.

Recently extirpated.—Species that have disappeared from Florida since 1600 but still exist elsewhere.

Endangered.—Species in danger of extinction or extirpation if the deleterious factors affecting their populations continue to operate. These are forms whose numbers have already declined to such a critically low level or whose habitats have been so seriously reduced or degraded that without active assistance their survival in Florida is questionable.

Threatened.—Species that are likely to become endangered in the state within the foreseeable future if current trends continue. This category includes: (1) species in which most or all populations are decreasing because of overexploitation, habitat loss, or other factors; (2) species whose populations have already been heavily depleted by deleterious conditions and, while not actually endangered, are nevertheless in a critical state; and (3) species that may still be relatively abundant but are being subjected to serious adverse pressures throughout their range.

Rare.—Species that, although not presently endangered or threatened as defined above, are potentially at risk because they are found only within a restricted geographic area or habitat in the state or are sparsely distributed over a more extensive range.

Species of special concern.—Species that do not clearly fit into one of the preceding categories yet warrant special attention. Included in this category are: (1) species that, although they are perhaps presently relatively abundant and widespread in the state, are especially vulnerable to certain types of exploitation or environmental changes and have experienced long-term population declines; and (2) species whose status in Florida has a potential impact on endangered or threatened populations of the same or other species outside the state.

Status undetermined.—Species suspected of falling into one of the above categories for which available data are insufficient to provide an adequate basis for their assignment to a specific category.

Major Habitats of Florida

The basic wetlands and terrestrial community descriptions below follow those of Brad Hartman, presented in the most recent FCREPA mammal and amphibian/reptile volumes, edited by Stephen R. Humphrey and Paul Moler, respectively, and expanded upon in the invertebrate volume, edited by Richard Franz and Mark Deyrup. The aquatic community descriptions were extensively modified from the FCREPA fish volume, edited by Carter R. Gilbert.

Major Terrestrial and Wetland Habitats
1. Coastal Strand
2. Dry prairies
3. Pine flatwoods
4. Sand pine scrub
5. Longleaf pine-xerophytic oak woodlands
   (Sand and Clay Hills)
6. Mixed hardwood-pine
7. Hardwood hammocks
8. Tropical hammocks
9. Freshwater marshes and wet prairies
10. Scrub cypress
11. Cypress swamps
12. Hardwood swamps

Coastal and Nearshore Habitats
13. Mangrove swamps
14. Coastal marshes
15. Coral reefs

Freshwater Habitats
16. Rivers
17. Creeks
18. Springs
19. Ditches, sloughs, and ponds
20. Lakes

Major Terrestrial and Wetland Habitats

1. Coastal Strand

The coastal strand includes beaches and the vegetation zones of beaches and adjacent dunes or rock. This vegetation type is most commonly associated with shorelines subjected to surf and high winds, but may sometimes be found bordering calmer bays and sounds.

The vegetation of the beaches and foredunes is characterized by pioneer plants able to establish themselves in the shifting sand. Typical species include railroad vines, beach cordgrass, and sea oats. Inland from the foredune, saw palmetto and dwarf scrubby oaks are found and, in southern Florida, sea grape and other tropical vegetation as well. The vegetation tends to change from grassy to woody from the foredune inland to the more protected back dunes, and the composition of the vegetation of these back dunes is often similar to that of sand pine scrub habitat found inland on old dunes.

Strand communities are adapted to the severe stresses of shifting sands, a highly saline environment, and high winds. In some instances, salt spray plays a role similar to fire in other ecosystems by retarding succession indefinitely at a grass or shrubby stage.

Historically, impacts to coastal strand plant communities (sometimes the total loss of the community) have resulted from beachfront residential development; invasion by exotic vegetation, primarily Australian pine; and accelerated erosion of beaches due to maintenance of inlets or nearby residential and tourist development.

2. Dry Prairies

Dry prairies are vast, treeless plains, often intermediate between wet grassy areas and forested uplands. Scattered bayheads, cypress ponds, or cabbage palm hammocks often occur in prairie areas. The largest areas of dry prairies occur north and west of Lake Okeechobee.

This community is dominated by many species of grasses such as wire-grass and broomsedge. Palmettos are the most common shrubby plant over large areas, with fetterbush, staggerbush, and dwarf blueberry common in places. A number of sedges and herbs are also found on the dry prairies.

Relatively little has been published on the ecology of dry prairies. They have often been compared to flatwoods minus the overstory trees, and the similar vegetative ground cover would seem to justify this idea.

Fire is important in determining the nature of the vegetation and its suitability for different species of wildlife. Winter burning associated with cattle operations may have shifted this community from grasses and forbs to saw palmetto. Absence of fire may result in shrubby communities, while frequent growing season fires yield a more herbaceous environment.

Large areas of native dry prairies have been converted to improved pasture, and this trend is continuing. Eucalyptus plantations have also been established on some former dry prairie sites, although this does not appear to be a continuing trend. Expansion of citrus production southward is probably responsible for most dry prairie loss at this time.

3. Pine Flatwoods

Pine flatwoods are characterized by one or more species of pine as the dominant tree species and occur on level areas. The soils of flatwoods are sandy with a moderate amount of organic matter in the top few centimeters and an acid, organic hardpan 0.3-1.0 m (1-3 ft) beneath the surface.

Three major types of flatwoods occur in Florida: **longleaf pine flatwoods** found on well-drained sites and characterized by longleaf pine as the dominant overstory tree; **slash pine flatwoods** with slash pine as the dominant overstory species and usually in areas of intermediate wetness; and **pond pine flatwoods** with the pond pine as the dominant tree species and typically occurring in poorly drained areas. South Florida slash pine tends to replace both slash pine and longleaf pine in central to southern peninsular Florida.

Southern slash pine forest is found on the sand flatlands and rocklands of extreme southern Florida, and is characterized by an overstory of the South Florida variety of the slash pine. This association often has tropical components in its understory.

Considerable overlap in understory plants exists among the three major types of flatwoods, with many species found in all three communities. Generally, however, gallberry and saw palmetto dominate the understory in slash pine flatwoods; wiregrasses, blueberries, and runner oaks are especially prevalent in longleaf pine flatwoods; and several of the bay trees are characteristic of pond pine areas. Flatwoods also often include intermingled cypress domes, bayheads, and small titi swamps.

Pine flatwoods are the most widespread of major plant communities, occurring throughout the relatively level Pleistocene marine terraces in both peninsular and panhandle Florida. Their suitability for growing pine trees has resulted in vast areas being incorporated into industrial forests. Changes in both fire and moisture regimes have resulted in changes in plant species composition and wildlife values. In south Florida, residential development is rapidly eliminating this plant community (and all other upland communities).

4. Sand Pine Scrub

Sand pine scrub is a plant community found almost exclusively on Florida relict dunes or other marine features. Sand pine scrub communities occur along the coasts on old dunes, in the Ocala National Forest, and along the

Lake Wales Ridge extending through Polk and Highlands counties. The soil is composed of well-washed, sterile sands.

This community is typically two-layered, with sand pine occupying the top layer and various scrubby oaks and other shrub species making up a thick, often clumped, understory. Little herbaceous groundcover exists, and large areas of bare sand occur frequently. Groundcover plants, when present, frequently include gopher apple and Florida bluestem grass. Deermosses are often common. Typical understory plants include myrtle oak, inopina oak, sand live oak, Chapman's oak, rosemary, scrub holly, and silkbay.

Where sand pines are absent, this community is often referred to as evergreen oak scrub. **Scrubby flatwoods** is a scrub-like association often occurring on drier ridges in typical flatwoods or near coasts. The understory species of this vegetation type are similar to those of sand pine scrub, but the sand pine is replaced by slash pine or longleaf pine.

The sand pine scrub is essentially a fire-based community. Ground vegetation is extremely sparse and leaf fall is minimal, thus reducing the chance of frequent ground fires so important in the sandhill communities. As the sand pines and scrub oaks mature, however, they retain most of their branches and build up large fuel supplies in the crowns. When a fire does occur, this fuel supply, in combination with the resinous needles and high stand density, ensures a hot, fast-burning fire. Such fires allow for regeneration of the sand pine community and associated oak scrub, which would otherwise pass into a xeric hardwood community.

Sand pine scrub and its ecologically important variations are seriously threatened. Residential development and especially citrus production have eliminated much of this plant community. In addition, isolation from fire has resulted in succession to xeric hardwood hammock with a relatively closed canopy, thereby reducing its value to most endemic plants and animals.

5. Longleaf Pine–Xerophytic Oak Woodlands (Sand and Clay Hills)

Sandhill communities (the longleaf pine–turkey oak association being one major subtype of this community) occur on well-drained, white to yellowish sands.

Longleaf pines form a scattered overstory in mature natural stands. In many areas, xeric oaks such as turkey oak, bluejack oak, southern red oak, and sand post oak, which were originally scattered or small understory trees, now form the overstory as the result of cutting of the pines and prevention of fire. In some areas of southern peninsular Florida, South Florida slash pine replaces longleaf pine in the overstory. Although tree species diversity in sandhills is low, there is a wide variety of herbaceous plants such as wiregrass, piney woods dropseed, golden aster, partridge pea, gopher apple, bracken fern, and paw paw, which provide fairly complete groundcover.

Sandhills were second in area only to flatwoods in Florida's predevelopment landscape, occurring widely throughout the panhandle and the northern half of the peninsula. Fire is a dominant factor in the ecology of this community. The interrelationships of the sandhill vegetation types, particularly the longleaf pine–wiregrass relationship, are dependent on frequent ground fires. The longleaf pine is sensitive to hardwood competition, and wiregrass plays a major role in preventing the germination of hardwood seeds while ensuring that there is sufficient fuel buildup on the floor of the community to carry a fire over large areas.

Very little longleaf pine sandhill remains. Commercial foresters have attempted to convert large areas to slash pine with poor success, but have had better success converting sandhills to a closed canopy monoculture of sand pine. In many cases the wiregrass groundcover has been destroyed, making restoration of this community type problematic. Large areas have been converted to improved pasture or citrus. The well-drained soils make attractive development sites, and the majority of sandhill community in peninsular Florida in private ownership has either been developed, is being developed, or is platted and subdivided for future development.

6. Mixed Hardwood–Pine

The mixed hardwood–pine community of John H. Davis (General Map of the Natural Vegetation of Florida, 1967) is the southernmost extension of the piedmont southern mixed hardwoods, and occurs in the clay soils of the northern panhandle.

Younger growth may be primarily pine, with shortleaf and loblolly pine predominant. As succession proceeds, the various hardwoods become dominant and constitute the natural climax vegetation of much of the area, especially wetter, yet well-drained sites. The overstory is characterized by a high species diversity and includes American beech, southern magnolia, white oak, sweetgum, mockernut hickory, pignut hickory, basswood, yellow poplar, white ash, and spruce pine. The understory includes many young overstory species plus dogwood, red mulberry, hop hornbeam, blue beech, and sweetleaf.

Historically, fire played a role in the function of this community by limiting its expansion into higher, better-drained sites. Later, agriculture served a similar function and limited this community to slopes and creek bottoms. The best examples, with the most diversity of tree species, tend, therefore, to occur in creek bottoms or on moist but well-drained slopes.

Residential subdivisions and other aspects of urbanization and conversion to loblolly pine plantations and agriculture are resulting in continued losses of this plant community. Locally significant losses result from stream or river impoundments, clay mining, and highway construction.

7. Hardwood Hammocks

The hardwood hammock community constitutes the climax vegetation of many areas of northern and central Florida. Hardwoods occur on fairly rich, sandy soils and are best developed in areas where limestone or phosphate outcrops occur. Hardwood forests are similar to the mixed hardwood and pine of the panhandle, but generally lack the shortleaf pine, American beech, and other more northern species, have a lower overstory species diversity, and tend to have a higher proportion of evergreen species. Southern magnolia, sugar-berry, live oak, laurel oak, American holly, blue beech, and hop hornbeam are characteristic species of this association. Variations in the species composition of hardwood hammocks are partially due to differences in soil moisture.

Major variations of this vegetative association include coastal hammocks, live oak–cabbage palm hammocks, and maritime hammocks. **Coastal hammocks** are relatively wet hardwood communities that occur in narrow bands along parts of the Gulf and Atlantic coasts and often extend to the edge of coastal marshes. **Live oak–cabbage palm hammocks** often border larger lakes and rivers and are scattered throughout the prairie region of central Florida. Either the oak or palm may almost completely dominate in any one area. **Maritime hammocks** occur behind sheltering beachfront dunes and are often dominated by live oak.

Notable examples of hardwood hammocks are in public ownership, but residential development is widespread in better-drained hammocks within the ever-increasing range of urban centers. Historically, large areas of coastal hardwood hammocks have been site-prepared and planted to pine for pulp-wood production. The current rate of loss due to this land use has apparently declined. Hammocks continue to be lost to agricultural conversion, although the near-surface limestone of many hammocks sometimes makes them unattractive for agriculture.

8. Tropical Hammocks

Tropical hammocks are found on many of the tree islands in the Everglades and on many of the Florida Keys. Remnants of these habitats occur north to Palm Beach on the east coast and Sarasota on the west coast.

Tropical hammocks typically have very high plant diversity, containing over 35 species of trees and almost 65 species of shrubs and small trees. Typical tropical trees are the strangler fig, gumbo limbo, mastic, bustic, lancewood, the ironwoods, poisonwood, pigeon plum, and Jamaica dogwood. Vines, air plants and ferns are often abundant. Tropical hammocks of the Florida Keys contain a number of plants that are extremely rare in the United States, including mahogany, lignum vitae, and thatch palms.

The tropical hardwood forest is the successional climax for much of the uplands of extreme south Florida. Because of susceptibility to frequent fires, this association is largely confined to islands or slightly wetter areas, but may invade drier areas if fire is removed for any length of time.

Tropical hammocks have been largely lost to residential development in most areas of southern Florida. Relatively large areas remain on north Key Largo, where intensive efforts to buy or regulate this community have occurred.

9. Freshwater Marshes and Wet Prairies

Freshwater marshes are herbaceous plant communities occurring on sites where the soil is usually saturated or covered with surface water for one or more months during the growing season.

Wet prairies are characterized by shallower water and more abundant grasses, and usually fewer of the tall emergents, such as bulrushes, than marshes. This category also includes the wet to dry marshes and prairies found on marl areas in south Florida.

Upwards of 15 separate types of marshes or wet prairies have been described in Florida. Major ones include sawgrass marshes; flag marshes dominated by pickerel weed, arrowhead, fire flags, and other nongrass herbs; cattail marshes; spike rush marshes; bulrush marshes; maidencane prairies; grass, rush, and sedge prairies; and switchgrass prairies dominated by taller grasses. Any single marsh may have different sections composed of these major types, and there is also almost complete intergradation among the types.

Fire and water fluctuations, the two major ecosystem managers of Florida, are important in the maintenance of marshes and wet prairies. Fire, especially when combined with seasonal flooding, serves to stress plants not adapted to these conditions and reduces competition from more upland species.

Historic major marsh systems include the Everglades, Upper St. Johns River, Kissimmee River floodplain, and Lake Apopka/Oklawaha marshes. Drainage for agriculture has been the dominant factor in marsh losses. Existing wetland regulatory programs and a relatively small amount of agriculturally suitable major marsh systems remaining in private ownership have reduced past rates of loss of these large systems. Major wetland acquisition and restoration projects are underway in the examples cited. Ephemeral, isolated, smaller marshes are more vulnerable to both agricultural and urban development and drainage or use as stormwater holding basins.

10. Scrub Cypress

Scrub cypress areas are found on frequently flooded rock and marl soils in south Florida. The largest areas occur in the Big Cypress region of eastern Collier County and northern Monroe County.

Scrub cypress forests are primarily marshes with scattered, dwarfed pond cypress. Much of the vegetation is similar to other relatively sterile marshes with scattered sawgrass, beakrushes, St. John's-wort and wax myrtle occurring commonly. Bromeliads, as well as orchids and other epiphytes, are often abundant on the cypress trees.

Most scrub cypress in the Big Cypress is in public ownership and does not appear threatened.

11. Cypress Swamps

Cypress swamps are usually located along river or lake margins or interspersed through other habitats such as flatwoods or dry prairies. In addition, they also occur as strands along shallow, usually linear drainage systems. These swamps have water at or above ground level for a considerable portion of the year.

Bald cypress is the dominant tree along lake and stream margins and may be the only tree that occurs in significant numbers in these locations. Other trees that are found within bald cypress swamps include water tupelo, ogeechee tupelo, and Carolina ash. Pond cypress occurs in cypress heads or domes that are typically found in flatwoods or dry prairies. Associated trees and shrubs include slash pine, blackgum, red maple, wax myrtle, sweetbay, and button-bush. Other plants include various ferns, epiphytes, poison ivy, greenbrier, and lizard's tail, with arrowhead, pickerel weed, sawgrass, and other marsh plants often found in the open water within cypress domes or strands.

Cypress swamps occur in submerged or saturated soils. Fire is an additional factor in drier cypress heads or domes. These factors are important in reducing competition and preventing the community from advancing to one dominated by evergreen hardwood trees (the bayhead community). There has apparently been a shift from cypress to hardwood swamps in areas where heavy harvesting of cypress has occurred in the past and the surviving hardwoods subsequently prevented cypress regeneration.

Bald cypress swamps are reasonably well protected by wetland regulations and the high cost of converting them to other land uses. Pond cypress swamps, while extremely widespread, have less protection because of their smaller size and more isolated nature. Cypress heads and ponds are susceptible to draining associated with industrial pine management, dredging for open water sites in residential development, and increased flooding when used to store stormwater runoff.

12. Hardwood Swamps

Deciduous hardwood swamps are found bordering rivers and lake basins where the forest floor is saturated or submerged during part of the year. Other names for this community include floodplain forest, bottomland hardwoods, and river swamp.

The wettest portions of these forests usually overlap with bald cypress swamps and consist largely of water tupelo, Carolina ash, and ogeechee tupelo. In slightly higher areas this community is characterized by such hardwoods as pop ash, pumpkin ash, red maple, overcup oak, sweetgum, and water hickory. On terraces or other higher portions of the floodplain, the overstory includes a variety of more mesic species such as spruce pine, swamp chestnut oak, and diamond-leaf oak. Understory trees and shrubs include dahoon holly, buttonbush, blue beech, and hop hornbeam. Groundcover is sparse in most of these swamps.

· Two distinctive additions to this major category are **bay swamps** (bayheads or baygalls) and **titi swamps.** The former are broadleaf evergreen swamps occurring in shallow drainage ways and depressions, particularly in pine flatwoods. Loblolly bay, red bay, and sweet bay are the major tree species. Water levels are relatively stable, and the soil is usually an acidic peat. Titi swamps are dominated by one or more of three titi species and occur on strands or depressions in flatwoods or along the borders of some alluvial swamps in north Florida.

The periodic flooding of the river swamps is a dominant factor in the functioning of the system, and different communities will become established if these fluctuations are eliminated. All species within this community must be able to withstand or avoid the periodic stresses imposed by high water.

Hardwood swamps share common threats with cypress swamps. The wetter and the more contiguous with open waters, the stronger the regulatory protection. Bay swamps are occasionally mined for peat or lost in phosphate-mining operations and receive comparatively less wetland regulation protection than other wetlands. The rate of loss is unknown.

Coastal and Nearshore Habitats

13. Mangrove Swamps

Mangroves occur along low wave-energy shorelines on both coasts south from Cedar Keys on the Gulf and St. Augustine on the Atlantic. Some of the best examples of mangrove forests are located in the in Ten Thousand Islands area of southwest Florida.

Three species of mangroves dominate the composition of mangrove swamps.

The red mangrove, with its stilt root system, is typically located on the outer-most fringe with the most exposure to salt water. Further inland, but usually covered by water at high tides, are the black mangroves, with white mangroves yet farther inland. Buttonwood trees are often found above the reach of salt water. Other plants commonly found among the mangroves include saltwort, glasswort, and a variety of other salt marsh species.

The mangrove community contributes to the productivity of bordering estuaries. Leaf fall from the mangroves provides food or substrate for countless organisms, ranging from bacteria to large fish such as the striped mullet. Detritus-feeding organisms support much of the estuarine trophic structure in mangrove areas including such gamefish as snook, tarpon, and spotted sea trout.

Mangrove swamps are largely in public ownership and the remainder are reasonably well protected by wetland regulations, although losses due to ma-rina and residential developments occur on a relatively small scale.

14. Coastal Marshes

Coastal marshes occur on low wave-energy shorelines north of the range of the mangroves, and are also interspersed with mangroves in many areas. Salt marshes may also extend into tidal rivers and occur as a narrow zone between the mangroves and freshwater marshes in the southern areas of the state.

Many areas within salt marshes are dominated by one plant such as saltgrass, smooth cordgrass, or blackrush. The species existing in any one area depends largely on the degree of inundation by tides.

Smooth cordgrass typically occupies the lower areas and often borders tidal creeks and pools. Blackrush occurs over vast areas, particularly along the Gulf coast, and is inundated less frequently, while the highest areas of the marsh are vegetated by saltgrass or such succulents as saltwort, glasswort, and sea ox-eye daisy.

The functioning of salt marshes centers primarily on tides and salinity. The harsh conditions associated with daily inundation, desiccation, and high salini-ties contribute to a low plant and animal species diversity. Those organisms that have adapted to this environment can be very productive, however. Tides also provide a close ecological relationship with adjacent estuaries.

Coastal marshes have been affected primarily by waterfront residential de-velopment. Current wetland regulatory programs appear to be successful in preventing major losses of this community for the time being, although scat-tered losses continue.

15. Coral Reefs

In Florida, reef corals occur primarily on an arc-shaped shallow water lime-stone shelf, approximately 240 km long and about 7 km wide in extreme south

Florida. Known as the Florida Reef Tract, this shelf is bounded on the seaward side by the straits of Florida and on the shore side by the Florida Keys and south Florida. The Florida Reef Tract consists of the Outer Reefs on the seaward edge, the Patch Reef behind them, and the numerous channels that dissect the reef structure. The Outer Reefs with the greatest variety of coral species protect the Patch Reefs from wave action of the open ocean. Some corals also occur in deep reefs off Broward County.

Reef corals are sensitive to the encroachment of silt and sand, and sometimes die as a result of being smothered by excessive amounts of sediment. Because of this, coral growth is suppressed in some parts of the reef tract. Key Largo, which acts as a barrier to sediments from Florida Bay, protects the northeastern portions of the reef tract, making it the most favorable area for coral growth.

Freshwater Habitats

16. Rivers *

Thirteen major rivers occur in Florida, five of which have drainage basins greater than 3000 sq. mi. (Apalachicola, 17,600 sq. mi; Suwannee, 9,640 sq. mi; Choctawhatchee, 4,384 sq. mi; St. Johns, 3,066 sq. mi; and Escambia, 3,817 sq. mi.) (Livingston 1991). The largest rivers in the Florida panhandle originate in Alabama and/or Georgia (Escambia, Choctawhatchee, and Apalachicola rivers). Other smaller rivers (Black, Yellow, Shoal, Chipola, and Ochlockonee rivers) originate mostly in Florida with minor portions of their drainages in adjoining states. The Apalachicola River, the largest river system that enters Florida, has its origin in the mountainous area of northern Georgia. The St. Johns River is the longest river that lies entirely within the state (318 mi.). This river and the southern Withlacoochee River are among the few rivers of the world that flow north. The St. Marys and Suwannee rivers originate in the Okefenokee Swamp on the Florida-Georgia state line but flow in opposite directions.

The drainages in south Florida are dominated by the Kissimmee-Okeechobee-Everglades system (Livingston and Fernald 1991). Few natural streams exist in south Florida because natural drainages have been severely altered by canal construction and intensive water management since before the turn of the century. Many of these canals had opened directly into the sea in the past, allowing salt water to penetrate inland during the dry season. Now, many of these canals have salinity-control structures built near their mouths to prevent this intrusion.

The main rivers along the southwest coast of Florida include the Caloosahatchee, Peace, Alafia, Manatee, Little Manatee, Myakka, and Hillsborough rivers. Most of these rivers are badly degraded from phosphate mining, agriculture, and urban runoff.

*See map page xxxii.

Gilbert (1992) provides an excellent description of Florida rivers, notably (1) stagnant, (2) slow-flowing and deep, and (3) larger calcareous streams. The nature of these rivers is dependent on color, bottom type, amount of vegetation, and chemical composition.

17. Creeks

Permanent creeks are similar to the larger rivers in general characteristics, except for size. Gilbert (1992) provides an excellent description of sand-bottomed creeks and silt-bottomed creeks. He considered the amount of vegetation important in his description.

18. Springs

Most large springs in Florida are artesian in nature. They generally flow from flooded cave systems in Eocene and Miocene limestones. As many as 27 springs are considered first-magnitude, with flow rates that average over 6 billion gallons per day. Spring water usually is high in calcium and magnesium, and maintains temperatures that reflect the average annual surface temperature of the region (69-72°F in north Florida). Upon emergence from the ground, the water is low in oxygen. This condition rapidly changes as the water passes through dense vegetation downstream from the spring. The water of Florida springs is crystal clear, cool, and definitely alkaline in nature. Because of large quantities of phosphates in the water, springs and spring runs are among the most productive aquatic habitats in the state.

19. Ditches, Sloughs, and Ponds

A large portion of Florida's surface freshwater collects in ditches, sloughs, and ponds. Many ditches and sloughs are clogged with vegetation that restricts water flow. Roadside ditches are a common sight throughout Florida, many created when road beds were constructed or for mosquito control.

Ponds in Florida are usually localized pools that seldom have surface outlets. Gilbert recognized sinkhole ponds, fluctuating ponds, temporary woodland ponds, sporadic ponds, and alligator ponds. Most of these water bodies tend to be small and shallow, although some sinkhole ponds can be exceptionally deep when there is a direct connection with sinks or solution pipes in their bottoms. Some ponds are wooded, or may have dense mats of floating vegetation or dense stands of emergent plants.

Many ditches, sloughs, and ponds are dependent on rainfall for their water supply. As a consequence, they are subject to marked fluctuations in water levels. Ditches and sloughs may flow during periods of high runoff toward more permanent water bodies and dry out completely during periods of drought.

Many ponds also are subject to drying during drought periods. One of the major consequences of complete drying is that it tends to eliminate fishes that may have had an opportunity to invade particular water bodies during periods of high water. The presence or absence of predatory fishes influences the structure of the animal community of the site.

Like lakes many of these water bodies have been invaded by exotic plants, such as alligator weed, water-hyacinth, hydrilla, wild taro, and others which in many cases have changed not only the community's outward appearance but also its function.

20. Lakes

Nearly all of the lakes in Florida are the result of solutioning of underlying limestone; however, some such as Lake Okeechobee occupy basins that are natural depressions in the surface. Many solution-caused lakes are simple sinks that may be connected directly to underlying limestones and that never have had surface outlets. Others are part of connected wetlands and represent pooled areas in a larger wetland or riverine system.

Gilbert divided Florida lakes into sand-bottomed lakes, silt-bottomed lakes, and disappearing lakes. Most Florida lakes are fragile systems that can easily become degraded, particularly when they are exposed to urban and agricultural runoff.

Florida lakes can be circum-neutral or acidic in nature, with clear or tea-colored water. Most lakes are shallow, usually less than 3 m (10 feet) deep, and may be ringed with cypress, black gum and/or woody shrubs, or may be surrounded by open meadows of herbaceous plants. Some lakes, such as Orange Lake, have much rooted vegetation and are exceptional in having numerous floating islands of vegetation, some supporting large trees, that change positions with wind conditions.

Major river drainages of Florida:

(A) Perdido
(B) Escambia
(C) Blackwater
(D) Yellow
(E) Choctawhatchee
(F) Econfina
(G) Chipola
(H) Apalachicola
(I) Ochlockonee
(J) St. Marks/Wakulla
(K) Suwannee/Santa Fe
(L) St. Marys
(M) St. Johns
(N) Oklawaha
(O) Withlacoochee (South)
(P) Hillsborough
(Q) Kissimmee
(R) Peace
(S) Lake Okeechobee
(T) Caloosahatchee

Map of Florida split at the
Steinhatchee River (boundary of
Dixie and Taylor counties), the
boundary of Lafayette and Taylor
counties, and through Madison
County west of the N.
Withlacoochee River.

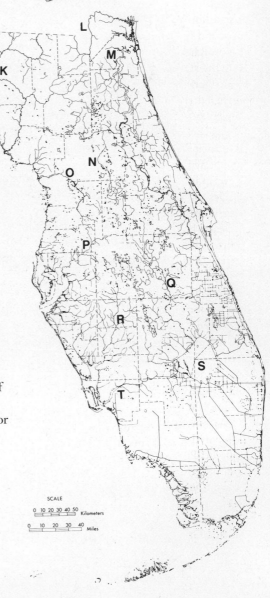

SCALE

0 10 20 30 40 50 Kilometers

0 10 20 30 40 Miles

Introduction

This volume is a revision of the 1978 edition of Volume II: Birds, a part of the Rare and Endangered Biota of Florida series prepared by the Florida Committee on Rare and Endangered Plants and Animals (FCREPA), and brings up to date the status of Florida's avifauna that are in danger of extirpation or extinction. During the 17 years since the original volume was published, much has occurred regarding the species originally listed. Many individuals, including university and agency personnel, have been investigating and generating data on many of these birds. Federal and state funds have been expended to investigate their status, behavior, and habitat requirements, and carry out conservation activities directed at endangered and threatened species. How well have these individuals and agencies done in protecting and conserving our avian species for future generations? A comparison of the current FCREPA list of 75 taxa (both species and subspecies) with the original 1978 list of 72 taxa indicates both successes and failures, along with opportunities to reverse downward trends of some species if we act appropriately. For many species, the degree of endangerment has increased.

Within the recently extinct category are the previously listed Passenger Pigeon (*Ectopistes migratorius*) and Carolina Parakeet (*Conuropsis carolinensis*), but the formerly endangered Dusky Seaside Sparrow (*Ammodramus maritimus nigrescens*) has joined these ill-fated birds. In the recently extirpated category are the previously listed Whooping Crane (*Grus americana*), Key West Quail-Dove (*Geotrygon chrysia*), and Zenaida Dove (*Zenaida aurita*). Currently a joint federal and state effort is underway to introduce a population of Whooping Cranes to Florida. As of this writing, about 30 Whooping Cranes are flying around the Kissimmee Prairie region of central Florida.

Within the endangered category, 11 species (14.7%) are currently listed compared to 10 species in 1978. The Dusky Seaside Sparrow is now extinct and the Piping Plover (*Charadrius melodus*) was elevated from a species of special concern to endangered. Whereas the Ivory-billed Woodpecker (*Campephilus principalis*) has not been recently recorded and probably is extirpated in Florida, a small population may still exist in Cuba, although no birds have been seen there in recent years. While additional populations of the Florida Grasshopper Sparrow (*A. savannarum floridanus*) recently have been located, other populations concurrently disappeared due to loss of habitat. On a positive note, Wood Storks (*Mycteria americana*) seem to be stable in north and central Florida (albeit, the south Florida colonies are still experiencing breeding failure) and increasing in numbers in Georgia and South Carolina; and Florida Snail Kites (*Rostrhamus sociabilis plumbeus*) have recolonized the upper regions of the St. Johns River, and Lakes Kissimmee, Tohopekaliga, and East Tohopekaliga. The irony is that the northern range expansion and recolonization of former range by these two species was largely due to the droughts during the early and latter 1980s that were exacerbated by the degradation and loss of wetlands in the normal breeding ranges in south Florida. Both of these birds appear to be more robust species than previously thought. Although not breeding in Florida, the Peregrine Falcon (*Falco peregrinus*) and Kirtland's Warbler (*Dendroica kirklandii*) appear to be experiencing a slow, but steady increase in numbers within their normal breeding ranges outside of the state.

In the threatened category, 13 species (17.3%) are listed, comparable with the number of species in 1978. The American Swallow-tailed Kite (*Elanoides forficatus*) is a new addition, whereas the Louisiana Seaside Sparrow (*A. m. fisheri*) has been down-listed to a species of special concern. Populations of several species in the current list appear to be stable (e.g., Crested Caracara [*Caracara plancus*], Osprey [*Pandion haliaetus*]). The number of Eastern Brown Pelicans (*Pelecanus occidentalis carolinensis*) appears to be increasing in Florida, and they have expanded their breeding range outside Florida, successfully nesting as far north as the Delmarva peninsula. In addition, the Southern Bald Eagle (*Haliaeetus leucocephalus leucocephalus*) was down-listed from endangered to threatened on the Federal list during 1995 because of recovery of the species throughout much of its range.

There are 13 species (17.3%) now in the rare category, whereas 11 species were on the 1978 list. The Black Rail ([*Lateralus jamaicensis*] elevated from status undetermined), West Indian Cave Swallow (*Hirundo fulva fulva*), and Worm-eating Warbler ([*Helmitheros vermivorus*] elevated from species of special concern) are new members in this category. Many of the species (e.g., White-tailed Kite [*Elanus leucurus*], Mangrove Cuckoo [*Coccyzus minor*], Antillean Nighthawk [*Chordeiles gundlachii*], and several of the passerines) in this category are temperate and subtropical species on the margins of their breeding range in Florida. On the basis of recent taxonomic analysis by Duncan Everid, we have deleted Stoddard's Yellow-throated Warbler (*D. dominica stoddardi*) from the rare category.

The species of special concern category currently contains 25 species with 6 subspecies (37.3%), whereas the category included 27 species and 4 subspecies in the 1978 list. New to this category are Wilson's Plover (*C. wilsonia*) and Brown Noddy (*Anous stolidus*). From the original 1978 list, the Piping Plover was elevated to endangered, the Worm-eating Warbler was changed to rare, and the Florida population of the Prairie Warbler (*D. discolor paludicola*) was changed to status undetermined. Many of the species in this category are colonial waterbirds (herons and ibises) that are dependent on freshwater wetlands or marine-estuarine birds (terns, marsh wrens, seaside sparrows) that use coastal wetland habitats. Both of these wetland-types have experienced losses in acreage in the past, but increased protection has slowed the rate of the loss.

Under status undetermined, four species (5.3%) are currently listed, whereas five species were included in the original list. This category contains species suspected of experiencing decreases in population and range, but the lack of sufficient quantitative information precluded listing them at higher levels of endangerment. The Florida Clapper Rail (*Rallus longirostris scottii*) and Mangrove Clapper Rail (*R. l. insularum*) have been deleted, but the Black Rail was elevated to the rare category in this volume. New additions are the Gull-billed Tern (*Sterna nilotica*) and Painted Bunting (*Passerina ciris*).

Overall, seven species were elevated in level of endangerment by the FCREPA Special Committee on Birds in this volume (i.e., their status of endangerment increased between 1978 and 1989 among the categories of endangered, threatened, rare, and species of special concern), two species were down-listed, and two species were deleted. As mentioned previously, the Dusky Seaside Sparrow became extinct.

At this point, we need to clarify the procedure for including or excluding a species or subspecies population on the FCREPA list. First, members of the ornithological community were encouraged to participate on the Special Committee on Birds. The initial list drawn up by this committee reflected the interests and knowledge of its members. Some controversy exists over the inclusion of peripheral populations; that is, species that are widespread and/or abundant outside of Florida, but represented in the state by a small population and/or restricted distribution. The Magnificent Frigatebird [*Fregata magnificens*], American Redstart [*Setophaga ruticilla*], and Worm-eating Warbler are examples of these species. Readers of this volume may wonder why several other peripheral species, such as the Broad-winged Hawk (*Buteo platypterus*), Mississippi Kite (*Ictinia mississippiensis*), and Swainson's Warbler (*Limnothlypis swainsonii*), or species that have nested in the state only once or twice, such as the Masked Booby (*Sula dactylatra*), Eastern Phoebe (*Sayornis phoebe*), or Northern Oriole (*Icterus galbula*) were not included in this revised volume. The answer is that we relied on the knowledge of committee members to choose which species should be listed, and we felt that one or two instances of extralimital breeding in the state did not justify listing. In the early 1980s, the Florida Game and Fresh Water Fish Commission adopted the FCREPA list of endangered, threatened, and species of special concern for the state's official list, but excluded all of the peripheral species.

Listing and categorizing a species as to its endangerment is not an exact science. Many variables must be considered, and often insufficient quantitative data exist to indicate a species' true status. Sometimes, a "better be safe than sorry" strategy is applied to listing a species, but this practice has the potential to undermine the entire listing process. Concern about the status and well-being of a major habitat type occasionally results in a general FCREPA listing that includes most members of a major taxon (e.g., colonial waterbirds such as herons and ibises in wetland habitats, and terns on beaches). Another common factor that can result in a species being listed is if its range and breeding population in Florida are discontinuous with another population outside the state. Disjunct populations or subspecies may have a very restricted range and be prone to genetic problems and catastrophic events (e.g., fires, storms, disease, etc.). Florida possesses several nonmigratory avian species that are isolated from other parts of their range, especially in south and central Florida (e.g., Short-tailed Hawk [*Buteo brachyurus*], Florida Snail Kite, Crested Caracara, Florida Burrowing Owl [*Speotyto cunicularia floridana*], Florida Sandhill Crane [*G. canadensis pratensis*], Mangrove Cuckoo, Florida Scrub-Jay [*Aphelocoma coerulescens*], and Black-whiskered Vireo [*Vireo altiloquus*]).

We admit to possible biases and oversight with this current FCREPA list. However, the FCREPA list is not set in concrete, unlike state and federal lists that must meet more rigid criteria and procedures that result in a drawn out listing procedure. This volume is meant to be dynamic and challenging. We need reliable information on population trends for most species—both those listed and those that perhaps should be listed. We welcome suggestions and data concerning the status of any bird species in Florida. These can be presented to the scientific and conservation community by publication in journals, or sent directly to the chair of the FCREPA Special Committee on Birds, to any of the authors of individual accounts, or the Nongame Wildlife Bureau of the Florida Game and Fresh Water Fish Commission in Tallahassee.

Florida's expanding human population has caused many avian species to decline in numbers and range. From 1980 to 1990 Florida's population increased by 37.8%, the third highest in the United States. A common theme expressed by the authors of most of the species' accounts in this volume is that the habitat used by these birds is being lost, degraded, or fragmented to an extent that it is becoming less than optimal. Other suspected causes of population declines are chemical contamination and human disturbance. Many of the endangered or threatened species have very specific habitat requirements that make these birds subject to extirpation. Florida Snail Kites feed almost exclusively on the freshwater apple snail (*Pomacea paludosa*); access to the snail requires shallow, clear water with just enough emergent vegetation to allow the snail to be accessible near the surface of the water. Red-cockaded Woodpeckers (*Picoides borealis*) require open, frequently burned, mature pine forests containing some trees infected with a fungus disease called heart rot that softens the interior wood so that they can excavate their nest cavities. Wood Storks are generalists when it comes to the species of prey they consume, but specialize in feeding on concentrated prey during natural water level drawdowns of freshwater sites. Florida Grasshopper Sparrows inhabit prairie grasslands that are frequently burned. Snowy Plovers (*C. alexandrinus*) require expansive open areas above sandy beaches for breeding and Snowy and Piping plovers use exposed tidal sand flats for foraging. About 130 miles of Florida coastline have been converted to seawall, and much of the remaining coastal and marine-estuarine habitats are impacted by other human activities. Many avian species (e.g., shorebirds and terns) are directly dependent on these environs as breeding or foraging sites. Several studies of neotropical migrants have shown some species require a relatively large amount of undisturbed forest in order to support minimum-sized breeding populations. Breeding Bird Survey data for the 1978–1987 period indicate that 75% of the forest-inhabiting neotropical migrants exhibited negative population trends in North America. Florida is a stop-over for many of these neotropical migrants. Loss of large tracts of forested habitat may result in lower survivorship during migration to and from the tropics. During 1936–1987, 1.57 million hectares (a reduction of 56%) of marshland in Florida were drained and converted to agriculture and other development. From 1970 to 1987, about 17% of the forested wetlands were lost. Waterbirds have experienced both a loss of quality and amount of wetlands in Florida. At a time when tourism is being touted as a "green" industry important to Florida for revenue, some people are beginning to ask at what additional costs do these visitors impact our native wildlife and other natural resources? Tourism requires roads and development, but these actions result in habitat loss and degradation. Ecotourism needs to be developed congruently with protection of Florida's natural resources.

All resident and migratory native species of birds are protected by federal and state wildlife laws against direct persecution and harassment. However, it is the indirect factors, such as loss of habitat and environmental contaminants, that now impact our avian natural resources. The authors of each species account have attempted to recommend further conservation measures and research that are needed to assist these species. Because many of these birds inhabit federal or state managed lands, a primary concern is the prevention of further habitat degradation to the land and water quality that comes from concurrent activities on these public lands or on adjacent privately held lands (e.g., see Great White Heron [*Ardea herodias occidentalis*], Florida Snail Kite, Snowy and Piping plovers, Red-cockaded Woodpecker). Additional land acquisition is a common recommendation, especially where important breeding and roosting aggregations occur or where small, sedentary populations of birds (e.g., American Swallow-tailed Kite, Florida Burrowing Owl, Red-cockaded Woodpecker, Florida Scrub-Jay) exist. The problem of conflicts over private land use and management often causes problems for some species (e.g., Red-cockaded Woodpecker, Florida Grasshopper Sparrow). Several of the shorebirds and terns are subject to human disturbance during recreational activities occurring along beach, shoreline, and marine-estuarine environs. Some species may be more susceptible to pesticides and other pollutants than previously thought (e.g., birds of prey and scavengers to pesticides, waterbirds to mercury contamination in south Florida, shorebirds to oil pollution along the coasts). Since Florida possesses many insular species (e.g., Florida Scrub-Jay, Florida Burrowing Owl, Short-tailed Hawk, Florida Snail Kite, Florida Sandhill Crane, Crested Caracara), these birds may experience genetic problems as their numbers decrease and ranges become more fragmented. It may be time to begin establishing a genetic databank, using nonlethal means, to characterize these species and their populations for future comparisons. As a last point, most authors indicate the need for further public education regarding the conservation of endangered and threatened species in Florida. This would include pointing out the effects of human disturbance on breeding and foraging birds, the biological need and value of parks, refuges, and preserves with low impact human activities, and the ultimate benefit of recycling and resource conservation (e.g., reduced freshwater consumption would stabilize some freshwater resources and habitats, thereby benefiting waterbirds; reduced energy consumption would reduce air emissions and pollution, the need for additional gas and electrical lines, and offshore drilling; recycling would greatly extend the life of landfills, reduce the resultant ground water contamination and exposure of contaminated materials to birds that frequent these sites).

Biological diversity is higher in Florida than in all but three other continental states. The reason for this phenomenon is that the Florida peninsula extends from temperate to subtropical climatic zones with a warm and humid climate. Most other land masses found at Florida's latitude are xeric-types or deserts. Florida possesses the largest reservoir of several avian species in the continental U.S. (e.g., Eastern Brown Pelican, Magnificent Frigatebird, Great White Heron, Wood Stork, Florida Snail Kite, American Swallow-tailed Kite, Sooty Tern [*S. fuscata*], Brown Noddy, Florida Sandhill Crane, White-crowned Pigeon [*Columba leucocephala*], Antillean Nighthawk, Mangrove Cuckoo, Florida Scrub-Jay, Black-whiskered Vireo, Cuban Yellow Warbler [*D. petechia gundlachi*], Cape Sable Seaside Sparrow [*A. m. mirabilus*], and several other subspecies of the seaside sparrows).

The ebbs and flows of Florida's avian populations are felt far beyond the boundaries of our state. The demise of the south Florida wetlands and associated colonial waterbird populations may have resulted in the recolonization of Georgia and South Carolina by Wood Storks during the 1980s. An increase in the resident population of Eastern Brown Pelicans in Florida may be responsible for their expansion as a breeding species to the panhandle of Florida and successful nesting up the Atlantic coast to Maryland and attempted breeding as far north as New Jersey. Furthermore, individuals of several species of birds from Florida have been used to recolonize or augment the populations of other states in the southeast United States. Nestling Eastern Brown Pelicans were sent to Louisiana in the early 1970s, eggs of American Swallow-tailed Kites were sent to Kansas in the early 1980s, young from incubator-hatched eggs of Bald Eagles were sent to several southeastern states in the mid-1980s, and most recently, Florida Sandhill Cranes were sent to Georgia during 1993–1995 to re-establish a nonmigratory population.

Listing a species at the federal level now costs about $60,000 per species. But most federal and state funds for endangered and threatened species research and conservation go to the so called "glamour" avian species: examples are the Bald Eagle, Spotted Owl (*Strix occidentalis*), California Condor (*Gymnogyps californianus*), and Whooping Crane. These species garner much public attention, whereas the lesser known or less showy species get little attention (i.e., funding, habitat acquisition, research, etc.). According to the latest U.S. Fish and Wildlife report of expenditures in fiscal year 1991, only seven species (1.1% of the endangered and threatened species) accounted for 51.5% of all funding, and the number of species receiving the rest of each year's reported expenditures has declined in each of the previous years. Thus, $24.7 million were spent on the Bald Eagle for research and conservation activities during 1991, but little was expended on many of the other endangered or threatened species. Florida needs to conserve its many avian species and habitats for four major reasons: 1) south Florida is host to several neotropical birds that are unique to the continental United States (e.g., Magnificent Frigatebird, Florida Snail Kite, White-crowned Pigeon, Antillean Nighthawk, Mangrove Cuckoo, Black-whiskered Vireo); Florida also possesses the bulk of the U.S. population of several species (e.g., Wood Stork, American Swallow-tailed Kite, Eastern Brown Pelican), or disjunct populations (e.g., Reddish Egret [*Egretta rufescens*], Roseate Spoonbill [*Ajaia ajaja*], Florida Snail Kite, Crested Caracara, Florida Burrowing Owl, Florida Sandhill Crane, Florida Scrub-Jay, Florida Prairie Warbler); 2) Florida is a migration corridor for neotropical migrants, especially among the Atlantic coastal and eastern continental species, on their way to and from the wintering grounds; 3) Florida serves as an important terminus for overwintering migrants; and, 4) by virtue of its geographic position, many species reach their southern (e.g., Mississippi Kite, American Redstart) or northern (e.g., Florida Snail Kite, Mangrove Cuckoo, Black-whiskered Vireo) breeding limit in Florida.

In the original 1978 volume, each species account contained nine sections and a map of the species' range. The text was rather abbreviated regarding the biology and habitat requirements of each species. In this current volume, there are 13 sections, each with a greatly expanded narration, along with a map of the species' entire range. Sections discussing the taxonomy and description of a species generally are brief; exceptions occur with color morphs, endemic subspecies, or subpopulations that have unique classification or special interest to Florida. Regarding taxonomy, the use of trinomials for common and scientific names is used only for those subspecies or populations whose range is limited or mostly limited to Florida. Of particular value are sections that describe the population size and trend, distribution and history of distribution, habitat requirements and trend, causes of threat, and conservation measures proposed for the species.

Who should benefit from using this expanded avian volume in the FCREPA series? The text should be a quick reference to both biologists and non-technical persons for general and specific information on the taxonomy, description, breeding biology, demographics, and habitat requirements for each species. Further, the literature cited section should be an additional source of technical information. Public educators and grade school children should be able to use this text as a valuable source of information for class work on rare and endangered species in Florida. City, county, and state planners, as well as environmental consultants, should benefit from the range maps and the sections describing the habitat requirements, vulnerability of the species and habitat, causes of threat, responses to habitat modification, and conservation measures proposed. And finally, researchers should benefit from knowing the gaps in our understanding of these species as pointed out by the authors in the sections on habitat requirements, demographics, key behaviors, and conservation measures proposed.

It will become apparent as you read over individual species accounts that we lack a significant amount of data and information for many of these species in Florida. Many authors propose research to identify important migratory and dispersal corridors, breeding range and roosting sites, the genetic relationships of the insular populations and endemic subspecies in Florida to other members of their taxon outside the state, detail population and range data, specify habitat requirements, and add demographic data for many species of birds in this volume. Many species are too rare in Florida to require extensive studies and expenditures of endangered species funds (e.g., Ivory-billed Woodpecker, Bachman's Warbler [*Vermivora bachmanii*], Kirtland's Warbler). Some endangered or threatened species such as the Wood Stork in north and central Florida, Florida Snail Kite, and Eastern Brown Pelican are stable or increasing in numbers in Florida and elsewhere. However, with the exception of several species of colonial waterbirds and the Bald Eagle, many of the authors of these accounts point out that there is little reliable information on the current status of many of the other listed species. These authors recommend well organized federal and state supported programs to obtain population data and habitat requirements for these species in Florida. Further, long term, accurate population data for all species are needed for trend analyses, as well as determining the status of their habitats and developing viable management programs in Florida. Some information is available for individual species. Avian population databases include the Nongame Wildlife Program's Breeding Bird Surveys and Colonial Waterbird Surveys, National Audubon Society's Christmas Bird Counts, and Florida Audubon Society's Breeding Bird Atlas Project. The Nongame Wildlife Program's *Closing the Gaps in Florida's Wildlife Habitat Conservation System* provides a baseline for wildlife habitat evaluation and makes recommendations to meet minimum conservation goals for some declining bird species and animal communities. In addition, recent publication of *The Birdlife of Florida* by Stevenson and Anderson and *Florida Bird Species—an Annotated List* by Robertson and Woolfenden serve as excellent compilations of the historic and current status of birds in Florida.

One of the foundations of science and conservation biology is the principle of doing research and sharing this information with other scientists through communication, especially the process of writing. This volume is the result of the contributions of many individuals who accepted the challenge to search the published literature, often including their own unpublished data, and write these species accounts so that individuals and agencies of Florida will be able to better manage and conserve our avian resources. We thank all the authors, especially those individuals who agreed to write more than one species account and turned in their first drafts and revised manuscripts within the appropriate time requested. F. James, B. Anderson, and an anonymous reviewer made many important suggestions that improved the volume. We also thank University Press of Florida for their assistance in producing this volume, and the Florida Game and Fresh Water Fish Commission, Florida Audubon Society, and Florida Department of Environmental Protection for their support of our involvement. We also acknowledge Hallie Smith for preparing the maps that illustrate the distributions of each species.

James A. Rodgers, Jr.
Herbert W. Kale II
Henry T. Smith

Designations of Status

The following are the Florida bird species in this volume according to the FCREPA and subsequent actions of the U.S. Fish and Wildlife Service (Federal) and the 1994 list of the Florida Game and Fresh Water Fish Commission (State). Also included are those species that appeared in the previous 1978 FCREPA list.

Current FCREPA status Species	Federal	State	1978 FCREPA
Recently Extinct			
Passenger Pigeon (*Ectopistes migratorius*)			RX
Carolina Parakeet (*Conuropsis carolinensis*)			RX
Dusky Seaside Sparrow (*Ammodramus maritimus nigrescens*)	RX	RX	E
Recently Extirpated			
Whooping Crane (*Grus americana*)	EN	SSC	RE
Key West Quail-Dove (*Geotrygon chrysia*)			RE
Zenaida Dove (*Zenaida aurita*)			RE
Endangered			
Wood Stork (*Mycteria americana*)	E	E	E
Florida Snail Kite (*Rostrhamus sociabilis plumbeus*)	E	E	E

Abbreviations for designated status: E, endangered; T, threatened; R, rare; SSC, species of special concern; RE, recently extinct; RX, recently extirpated; RX, recently extinct; SU, status undetermined; NL, not listed; C2, candidate for listing but not enough information exists to justify listing; and EN, experimental nonessential population.

Current FCREPA status

Species	Federal	State	1978 FCREPA
Peregrine Falcon (*Falco peregrinus*)	E	E	E
Piping Plover (*Charadrius melodus*)	T	T	SSC
Cuban Snowy Plover (*Charadrius alexandrinus tenuirostris*)	C2	T	E
Red-cockaded Woodpecker (*Picoides borealis*)	E	T	E
Ivory-billed Woodpecker (*Campephilus principalis*)	E	E	E
Kirtland's Warbler (*Dendroica kirtlandii*)	E	E	E
Bachman's Warbler (*Vermivora bachmanii*)	E	E	E
Florida Grasshopper Sparrow (*Ammodramus savannarum floridanus*)	E	E	E
Cape Sable Seaside Sparrow (*Ammodramus maritimus mirabilis*)	E	E	E
Threatened			
Eastern Brown Pelican (*Pelecanus occidentalis carolinensis*)		SSC	T
Magnificent Frigatebird (*Fregata magnificens*)			T
Osprey (*Pandion haliaetus*)		SSC	T
Southern Bald Eagle (*Haliaeetus leucocephalus leucocephalus*)	E	T	T
American Swallow-tailed Kite (*Elanoides forficatus*)			NL
Crested Caracara (*Caracara plancus*)	T	T	T
Southeastern American Kestrel (*Falco sparverius paulus*)	C2	T	T
Florida Sandhill Crane (*Grus canadensis pratensis*)		T	T
American Oystercatcher (*Haematopus palliatus*)		SSC	T

Abbreviations for designated status: E, endangered; T, threatened; R, rare; SSC, species of special concern; RE, recently extirpated; RX, recently extinct; SU, status undetermined; NL, not listed; C2, candidate for listing but not enough information exists to justify listing; and EN, experimental nonessential population.

Current FCREPA status Species	Federal	State	1978 FCREPA
Least Tern (*Sterna antillarum*)		T	T
Roseate Tern (*Sterna dougallii*)	T	T	T
White-crowned Pigeon (*Columba leucocephala*)	T	T	T
Florida Scrub-Jay (*Aphelocoma coerulescens*)	T	T	T
Rare			
Reddish Egret (*Egretta rufescens*)	C2	SSC	R
Roseate Spoonbill (*Ajaia ajaja*)		SSC	R
White-tailed Kite (*Elanus leucurus*)			R
Short-tailed Hawk (*Buteo brachyurus*)			SU
Black Rail (*Laterallus jamaicensis*)			R
Mangrove Cuckoo (*Coccyzus minor*)			R
Antillean Nighthawk (*Chordeiles gundlachii*)			NL
West Indian Cave Swallow (*Hirundo fulva fulva*)			R
Black-whiskered Vireo (*Vireo altiloquus*)			R
Worm-eating Warbler (*Helmitheros vermivorus*)			SSC
Louisiana Waterthrush (*Seiurus motacilla*)			R
American Redstart (*Setophaga ruticilla*)			R
Cuban Yellow Warbler (*Dendroica petechia gundlachi*)			R

Abbreviations for designated status: E, endangered; T, threatened; R, rare; SSC, species of special concern; RE, recently extinct; RX, recently extirpated; NL, not listed; SU, status undetermined; C2, candidate for listing but not enough information exists to justify listing; and EN, experimental nonessential population.

Current FCREPA status

Species	Federal	State	1978 FCREPA
Species of Special Concern			
Least Bittern (*Ixobrychus exilis*)			SSC
Great White Heron (*Ardea herodius occidentalis*)			SSC
Great Egret (*Casmerodius albus*)			SSC
Little Blue Heron (*Egretta caerulea*)		SSC	SSC
Snowy Egret (*Egretta thula*)		SSC	SSC
Tricolored Heron (*Egretta tricolor*)		SSC	SSC
Black-crowned Night-Heron (*Nycticorax nycticorax*)			SSC
Yellow-crowned Night-Heron (*Nyctanassa violacea*)			SSC
Glossy Ibis (*Plegadis falcinellus*)			SSC
White Ibis (*Eudocimus albus*)		SSC	SSC
Cooper's Hawk (*Accipiter cooperii*)			SSC
Limpkin (*Aramus guarauna*)		SSC	SSC
Wilson's Plover (*Charadrius wilsonia*)			NL
American Avocet (*Recurvirostra americana*)			SSC
Sooty Tern (*Sterna fuscata*)			SSC
Royal Tern (*Sterna maxima*)			SSC
Sandwich Tern (*Sterna sandvicensis*)			SSC
Caspian Tern (*Sterna caspia*)			SSC
Brown Noddy (*Anous stolidus*)			SSC

Abbreviations for designated status: E, endangered; T, threatened; R, rare; SSC, species of special concern; RE, recently extirpated; RX, recently extinct; SU, status undetermined; NL, not listed; C2, candidate for listing but not enough information exists to justify listing; and EN, experimental nonessential population.

Current FCREPA status

Species	Federal	State	1978 FCREPA
Black Skimmer (*Rynchops niger*)		SSC	SSC
Florida Burrowing Owl (*Speotyto cunicularia floridana*)		SSC	SSC
Hairy Woodpecker (*Picoides villosus*)			SSC
White-breasted Nuthatch (*Sitta carolinensis*)			SSC
Worthington's Marsh Wren (*Cistothorus palustris griseus*)		SSC	SSC
Marian's Marsh Wren (*Cistothorus palustris marianae*)		SSC	SSC
Scott's Seaside Sparrow (*Ammodramus maritimus peninsulae*)		SSC	SSC
Louisiana Seaside Sparrow (*Ammodramus maritimus fisheri*)			T
Macgillivray's Seaside Sparrow (*Ammodramus maritimus macgillivraii*)	C2		SU
Status Undetermined			
Merlin (*Falco columbarius*)			SU
Gull-billed Tern (*Sterna nilotica*)			NL
Florida Prairie Warbler (*Dendroica discolor paludicola*)			SSC
Painted Bunting (*Passerina ciris*)			NL

Abbreviations for designated status: E, endangered; T, threatened; R, rare; SSC, species of special concern; RE, recently extirpated; RX, recently extinct; SU, status undetermined; NL, not listed; C2, candidate for listing but not enough information exists to justify listing; and EN, experimental nonessential population.

Passenger Pigeon
Ectopistes migratorius
FAMILY COLUMBIDAE
Order Columbiformes

The Passenger Pigeon (*Ectopistes migratorius*) was originally described as *Columbia migratoria* in 1766. It probably evolved from *Zenaida* species origins and occupied an ecological niche similar to the Band-tailed Pigeon (*C. fasciata*) of western North America (Murton and Westwood 1977).

The male Passenger Pigeon was about 43 cm (17 in.) in length and with a wingspan of 48–50 cm. The plumage was slate-blue on the head, olivaceous-gray on the back and wings; the back and sides of the neck had golden and violet iridescence, and the wing coverts had blackish spots; the throat was light purplish-chestnut fading to white on the lower belly; the tail was mostly bluish-gray with the two central rectices blackish; soft-part colors included a black bill, red toes and bare facial skin, and orange iris. Females were similar to males, but the throat and chest were brownish-gray.

The Passenger Pigeon was probably one of the most numerous and social species in North America. Estimates of migratory flocks, many miles long, approximately a mile wide, and numbering more than 2.2 billion birds, were considered conservative during the spring and autumn of 1832 (Bent 1932). More than 100 nests in a single tree were common in colonies that were distributed over many square miles (Bent 1932). However, by the late 1800s the numbers and range of the species had become greatly reduced. Breeding habitat destruction and fragmentation, along with intense human pressures for food and sport, resulted in a decrease in population size. Social facilitation in food location was probably important for the species and the remaining birds were unable to locate a sufficient mast crop to sustain their population (Bucher 1992). The last individual Passenger Pigeon, a female named Martha in the Cincinnati Zoo, died in September 1914 (Bent 1932).

1

The Passenger Pigeon originally bred from central Montana, east-central Saskatchewan, southern Manitoba, Minnesota, Wisconsin, Michigan, Ontario, southern Quebec, New Brunswick and Nova Scotia south to eastern Kansas, Oklahoma, Mississippi, and Georgia. Its main winter distribution was from Arkansas, southern Missouri, Tennessee, and North Carolina south to Texas, the Gulf coast, and northern Florida (AOU 1983). The pigeon was a common winter visitor in northern Florida where a flock of several thousand birds was reported along the Econofina River in 1907 (Sprunt 1954).

Passenger Pigeon breeding habitat was limited to the eastern deciduous forests of the United States and Canada characterized by mast-producing trees, where they preferred beechnut (*Fagus grandifolia*), acorn (*Quercus* spp.), and chestnut (*Castanea dentata*) food sources (Bucher 1992). They exploited large areas where very large mast production occurred irregularly among years. The large-scale deforestation and fragmentation of mast-producing species resulted in large decreases in Passenger Pigeon reproduction. The viability of colonies became unstable because of limited food supply within their daily search range.

Nests of Passenger Pigeons were small structures made of twigs at heights of "10 to 50 feet or more" (Bent 1932). Clutch size was usually a single, white egg. Passenger Pigeons frequently produced multiple broods (up to 4) in a single year when the mast crop was good, but often the entire colony moved in mass to take advantage of the mast resource in another region.

Whereas, direct human pressures certainly contributed to accelerated population declines early in the 1800s, the loss of critical mast-producing habitat together with reduced social facilitation at low population densities may have been enough to cause extinction despite what appeared to be considerable remaining forest and numerous pigeons. The Passenger Pigeon was a "nomadic specialist" that exhibited a large home range where social facilitation in foraging depended upon a large viable population (Bucher 1992). Conservation biologists should note this phenomenon and its possible management implications with extant species. Other species of birds that possess this type of social behavior and food-finding strategy (e.g., colonial waterbirds) may face similar irreversible population decreases and bottlenecks that may not be detected until it is too late to manage the species.

LITERATURE CITED

AOU. 1983. Checklist of North American birds. 6th edition. American Ornithologists' Union. Allen Press, Lawrence, Kansas.

Bent, A. C. 1932. Life histories of North American gallinaceous birds. Smithsonian Inst. Press, U.S. Natl. Mus. Bull. no. 162.

Bucher, E. H. 1992. The causes of extinction of the Passenger Pigeon. Pp. 1–32 *in* Current ornithology (D. M. Power, ed.). Plenum Press, New York.

Murton, R. K., and N. J. Westwood. 1977. Avian breeding cycles. Clarendon Press, Oxford, U.K.

Sprunt, A., Jr. 1954. Florida bird life. Coward-McCann, Inc., New York.

PREPARED BY: James A. Rodgers, Jr., Florida Game and Fresh Water Fish Commission, Wildlife Research Laboratory, Gainesville, FL 32601.

Carolina Parakeet
Conuropsis carolinensis

FAMILY PSITTACIDAE

Order Psittaciformes

The Carolina Parakeet (*Conuropsis carolinensis*) was originally described as *Psittacus carolinensis* in 1758 (AOU 1983). Some authors have merged this species into the genus *Aratinga*.

Carolina Parakeets were a medium-sized parrot about 30 cm (12 in.) in length. The overall plumage of the back, tail, wings, and belly was green; the forehead, lores, and upper check were orange; the remainder of the head and upper neck was yellow; the wing coverts were tinged with greenish-yellow, and the webs of the primaries, bend of the wing, and thighs were yellow. The bill was horn-colored, iris was brown, and feet were flesh-brown (Forshaw 1977).

The only indigenous psittacine in eastern North America, the Carolina Parakeet once was a common breeding bird throughout much of the eastern United States, including Florida. They were reported occasionally in flocks of 200–300 birds. The decline of these parakeets went mostly undocumented, but their numbers had been greatly reduced by the end of the 1800s. Though there were questionable sightings of the species in the Santee Swamp of South Carolina as late as 1936 (AOU 1983), Florida appears to have been the last stronghold for the parakeet with valid sightings until the early 1920s (Sprunt 1954). The last known specimen in captivity died in the Cincinnati Zoo in February 1918 (Laycock 1969 *in* Forshaw 1977).

Originally Carolina Parakeets ranged from eastern Nebraska, Iowa, southeastern Wisconsin, southern Michigan, Ohio, Pennsylvania, and central New York south to southern Oklahoma, and the Gulf states from Louisiana to Florida (AOU 1983). The species was common throughout Florida, except in the Keys.

Carolina Parakeets preferred heavily forested riparian habitats and expansive cypress or bottomland swamps (Forshaw 1977), but they flew to adjacent upland sites to feed. They fed on a variety of fruits, berries, nuts, cocklebur,

seeds, and probably leaf buds (Forshaw 1977). Unfortunately, because they depredated cultivated fruits, nuts, and grains, these birds were regularly shot in large numbers by farmers. There are several accounts of Carolina Parakeets being shot in orange groves in Florida (Sprunt 1954).

Carolina Parakeets were gregarious birds and probably bred in small colonies. Nests were usually in tree cavities, and the usual clutch size was 2–3 white eggs (Sprunt 1954). Noisy flocks often gave "kee-kee-kee" calls as they flew to and from roost sites. They apparently would breed in captivity (Sprunt 1954), which was a missed opportunity for captive rearing of the species. Little else is known about the behavior and ecology of the species.

As with the Passenger Pigeon (*Ectopistes migratorius*), the Carolina Parakeet was a victim of both habitat destruction and human persecution as agricultural pests. Their highly social behavior often led to the demise of the entire flock because the parakeets would repeatedly return to an orchard site despite several birds having been previously shot. As their extreme rarity became evident, collectors and trappers sought out the remaining flocks in Florida (Forshaw 1977). Carolina Parakeets may have been similar to the Passenger Pigeon in that a population bottleneck could not be reversed once the large flocks of parakeets were reduced to below a certain threshold.

LITERATURE CITED:

AOU. 1983. Checklist of North American birds. 6th edition. American Ornithologists' Union. Allen Press, Inc., Lawrence, Kansas.

Forshaw, J. M. 1977. Parrots of the world. T.F.H. Publ., Inc., Neptune, New Jersey.

Sprunt, A., Jr. 1954. Florida bird life. Coward-McCann, Inc., New York.

PREPARED BY: James A. Rodgers, Jr., Florida Game and Fresh Water Fish Commission, Wildlife Research Laboratory, 4005 South Main Street, Gainesville, FL 32601.

Dusky Seaside Sparrow
Ammodramus maritimus nigrescens

FAMILY EMBERIZIDAE

Order Passeriformes

Also known as the Black-and-white Shore Finch, Merritt Island Sparrow, or Dusky Sparrow, the Dusky Seaside Sparrow (*Ammodramus maritimus nigrescens*) was first discovered at Salt Lake, a few miles west of Titusville by Charles J. Maynard in 1872 (Trost 1968), and was described as a variety or subspecies of the Seaside Sparrow by Ridgway (1873). Because of its highly distinctive blackish plumage, when compared with all other Seaside Sparrow races, it was listed by the American Ornithologists' Union as a separate species (*Ammospiza nigrescens*) until 1973 when it was relegated again to subspecific status (Eisenmann 1973). In the sixth edition of the *Check-list of North American Birds,* all the Seaside Sparrows were transferred to the genus *Ammodramus* (AOU 1983).

The Dusky Seaside Sparrow is about the size of the House Sparrow (*Passer domesticus*), measuring 13–15 cm (5 1/2–6 in.) in total length. In many respects it is similar to all other Seaside Sparrows but much darker, with a distinctive black-and-white streaked pattern on the underparts. In adults the breast and underparts are heavily streaked with black, and at a distance the bird appears entirely black. A yellow stripe is prominent on the lores and bend of the wing. Both sexes are similar in size and coloration. Immatures are lighter in color (i.e., grayish-brown), with narrower streaking on the breast. By October or November they are almost indistinguishable from adults. The Dusky's flight was normally short and low, just above the vegetation, except when it would occasionally soar 6–9 meters (20–30 ft.) above the marsh during courtship singing.

The Dusky Seaside Sparrow occurred only in Brevard County, Florida, in the St. Johns River flood plain (eastside only) between State Road 46 on the north and State Road 520 on the south, and in the Merritt Island salt marshes east of Titusville (Sharp 1968a, USFWS 1980). In the St. Johns, the Dusky inhabited the bunch cordgrass (*Spartina bakeri*) marshes and wet savannas

Dusky Seaside Sparrow,
Ammodramus maritimus nigrescens.
(Photo by Paul W. Sykes, Jr.)

mainly between 3–5 meters (10–12 ft.) above mean sea level (Sharp 1969). Occasionally, widely scattered cabbage palms (*Sabal palmetto*), either individual trees or clusters of several trees, dotted the landscape. Because Duskies preferred an unbroken horizon, the presence of too many trees or shrubs precluded occupation of otherwise suitable habitat. Small ponds, salt pans (pannes—various-sized patches of highly saline soil barren of vegetation or inhabited by low-growing halophytic species) occur throughout the marsh. On Merritt Island, the Duskies occupied salt marshes dominated by cordgrass, salt grass (*Distichlis spicata*), blackrush (*Juncus roemerianus*), and saltwort (*Batis maritima*).

Dusky Seaside Sparrows had small home ranges and appeared to occupy the same general area year round, except where habitat had recently burned. A year or two after a fire, the cordgrass again became habitable and remained so for several years until vegetation became too dense for easy ground foraging, at which time the birds would move into more recently burned habitat (Sharp 1968a, Baker 1973, Holder et al. 1980). Territories were from 0.2 to 1.0 ha (0.5 to 2+ ac.) in size. Nesting occurred from late March through August with peaks in early May and late June, probably representing two broods. Nests were constructed of grass about 20–38 cm (8–15 in.) above the ground in clumps of cordgrass, or occasionally, in groundsel (*Baccharis angustifolia*).

On Merritt Island nests were occasionally built in saltwort (Kale 1983). The usual clutch size was 3–4 white eggs, spotted with dark reddish-brown markings. Duskies were mainly ground feeders. The limited information on food habits indicated that they ate chiefly invertebrates such as spiders, grasshoppers, crickets, beetles, lepidoptera larvae, and snails, but also took seeds and other plant items (Trost 1968). Birds were difficult to observe in fall and winter, but in spring and summer the very prominent males sang from the tops of the marsh grass and scattered shrubs. The song varied but was similar to that of other Seasides—a short buzzing trill or gasp uttered from grass tops or low shrubs.

Loss of essential habitat on Merritt Island and in the St. Johns River marshes caused the extinction of the Dusky Seaside Sparrow (Sharp 1968b, Sykes 1980). Several factors, all the result of human activities, adversely impacted the Dusky population and its habitat. In the 1940s, the marshes on Merritt Island were sprayed with insecticides (chiefly DDT) to control mosquitoes. Nicholson estimated a 70% reduction in the Dusky population by 1957 (Trost 1968), which he attributed to pesticide use reducing the insect prey base. Because mosquitoes can develop resistance to DDT, the Florida Board of Health adopted a policy to fund only nonchemical means of control, such as ditching and impounding of marshes. Between the mid-1950s and late 1960s, all of the coastal marshes of Brevard County were diked and impounded. On Merritt Island, this altered or eliminated most of the Dusky's breeding habitat, and the population rapidly declined. In 1966, the U.S. Fish & Wildlife Service declared the Dusky Seaside Sparrow endangered (Committee on Rare and Endangered Wildlife Species 1966). By 1968, Sharp (1968a, b, 1970) found only 30 or so pairs of Duskies remained on Merritt Island. A limited program of marsh management on Merritt Island National Wildlife Refuge in the 1970s restored about 200 ha (500 ac.) of Dusky habitat, but by 1977 only 1–3 pairs of Duskies remained and these were gone by 1978 (Sykes 1980). Photographs of marshes on Merritt Island in Sykes (*op. cit.*) illustrate the devastating impacts of impounding on the Dusky habitat.

Sharp's 1968 survey (Sharp 1970), which was the first comprehensive survey ever made on the Dusky, found 372 singing males, or an estimated 894 pairs, in the St. Johns River marshes west of Titusville. The first human impacts on this habitat probably began in the early years of this century when shallow ditches were dug to drain the marshes for agriculture. High soil salinities restricted agricultural use to pasturage. Cattle ranching is not necessarily incompatible with the existence of the Dusky, except where drainage-ditch banks enable woody vegetation to intrude into the grass marsh habitat or where ranchers too frequently burn extensive acreages of habitat.

Beginning in the late 1960s, construction of the Beeline Expressway connecting Orlando to Cocoa and Titusville, and of the Hacienda Road north of

State Road 50 destroyed or altered vast areas of Dusky habitat. In 1969, General Development Corporation dug a deep canal through Dusky habitat west of its Port St. Johns residential development to drain the area. Even though this canal was on lands subsequently purchased for the St. Johns National Wildlife Refuge, no effort was ever undertaken to restore the site. Likewise, in the segment of the refuge located north of State Road 50, no efforts, or only very belated ones, were made to stop excessive drainage by deep roadside canals.

Because ranchers often burn their lands every winter to improve pasturage for cattle, one of the first recommendations of the Dusky Seaside Sparrow Advisory Committee, which became the Recovery Team in 1975, was to construct fire lanes around the St. Johns National Wildlife Refuge to prevent entry of wildfires from outside the refuge. Failure of the U.S. Fish & Wildlife Service to act promptly on this advice resulted in the loss of large portions of Dusky habitat in the mid-1970s. In 1972, 110 male Duskies were present on the refuge. After two winter wildfires, this number dropped to 54 males in 1973 (Baker 1973). After several more wildfires, only nine singing males remained in the refuge by 1978. An additional 14 were found on private lands (Baker 1978, USFWS 1980). In the fall of 1979, three of these birds were captured for safekeeping and study.

After intensive surveys throughout the St. Johns marshes revealed only four singing males (Delany et al. 1981), a decision was made in 1980 to bring them all into captivity and begin a breeding program with female Seaside Sparrows of the dark brown-plumaged population from Florida's Gulf coast, Scott's Seaside Sparrow (*A. m. peninsulae*). One of these females had already been mated with one of the previously captured Duskies and produced three 50% Dusky/Scott progeny (Post and Antonio 1981). In July 1980, three of the four surviving wild males (the fourth eluded capture) were brought into captivity.

After a 2-year delay, caused by failure of the U.S. Fish & Wildlife Service to grant its approval, a breeding project was initiated jointly by Santa Fe Community College Teaching Zoo (in 1982) and Walt Disney World's Discovery Island Zoological Park (in 1983–89), codirected by Florida Audubon Society. Through the use of back-crossing, several 75% and 87.5% Duskies were produced that closely resembled the pure Dusky males. Unfortunately, problems associated with the advanced age of the males, and their subsequent deaths between 1982 and 1987, terminated the project. The last surviving male Dusky Seaside Sparrow died on 16 June 1987. On 11 January 1991, the U.S. Fish & Wildlife Service officially removed the subspecies from the federal endangered species list (USFWS 1990). An extensive book-length review of the Dusky Seaside Sparrow's loosing battle for survival was written by Walters (1992), and a chapter on this subspecies in Alvarez (1993) is worth reading.

When the first editions of Florida's Rare and Endangered Biota Series were published, we still had hope that the Dusky Seaside Sparrow could be saved (Baker and Kale 1978). This present account has been critical of the U.S. Fish & Wildlife Service for failing to implement, in a timely manner, recommendations made by the Dusky Seaside Sparrow Advisory Committee, the Recovery Team, and other Seaside Sparrow experts. But, blame for the loss of this unique bird falls on many shoulders—perhaps on all of us (Kale 1983). The National Aeronautics and Space Administration and the Kennedy Space Center on Merritt Island and the City of Titusville, located directly across the Indian River Lagoon from the Dusky marshes, demanded control of the mosquitoes in these marshes. The burgeoning human population of central Florida, from the Space Center west to Orlando and Walt Disney World, demanded connecting expressways traversing the St. Johns River marshes and housing developments that required drainage. Ranchers in the St. Johns valley desired hot winter fires that burned vast acreages of dry marsh grass. In 1973, the Dusky Seaside Sparrow was relegated to a subspecies, a taxonomic decision based on sound biological data, but one with disastrous ramifications for the Dusky. Suddenly, a vast growing constituency of birdwatchers with an interest and urgency to see and save the bird vanished. On the governmental level, understandably, a smaller slice of the endangered species money pie was available for research, management, and recovery. Even when it was relatively abundant, few citizens of Brevard County ever saw this diminutive bird. To them, the Dusky was just another little brown sparrow.

LITERATURE CITED:

Alvarez, K. 1993. Twilight of the panther. Biology, bureaucracy and failure in an endangered species program. Myakka River Publ. Sarasota, Florida. 501 pp.

AOU. 1983. Check-list of North American birds. 6th edition. Amer. Ornithol. Union, Allen Press, Lawrence, Kansas.

Baker, J. L. 1973. Preliminary studies of the Dusky Seaside Sparrow on the St. Johns National Wildlife Refuge. Proc. S.E. Assoc. Game & Fish Comm. 27:207–214.

Baker, J. L. 1978. Status of the Dusky Seaside Sparrow. Georgia Dept. Nat. Res. Tech. Bull. Pp 94–99.

Baker, J. L., and H. W. Kale II. 1978. Dusky Seaside Sparrow. Pp. 16–19 *in* Rare and endangered biota of Florida. Vol. 2: birds (H. W. Kale II, ed.). Univ. Presses of Florida, Gainesville, Florida.

Delany, M. F., W. P. Leenhouts, B. Sauselein, and H. W. Kale, II. 1981. The 1980 Dusky Seaside Sparrow survey. Fla. Field Nat. 9:64–67.

Eisenmann, E. (Chair). 1973. Thirty-second supplement to the A.O.U. check-list of North American birds. Auk 90:411–419.

Holder, G. L., M. K. Johnson, and J. L. Baker. 1980. Cattle grazing and management of Dusky Seaside Sparrow habitat. Wildl. Soc. Bull. 8:105–109.

Kale, H. W., II. 1983. A status report on the Dusky Seaside Sparrow. Bird Conser. I:128–132.

Kale, H. W., II. 1983. Distribution, habitat, and status of breeding Seaside Sparrows in Florida. Pp 41–48 in The Seaside Sparrow, its biology and management (T.L. Quay, J. B. Funderberg, D. S. Lee, E. F. Potter, and C. S. Robbins, eds.). North Carolina State Mus. Raleigh, North Carolina.

Post, W., and F. Antonio. 1981. Breeding and rearing of Seaside Sparrows, *Ammospiza maritima* in captivity. Internatl. Zoo. Yearbook 21:123–128.

Ridgway, R. 1873. On some new forms of American birds. Bull. Essex Inst. 5:197–201.

Sharp, B. 1968a. Numbers, distribution, and management of the Dusky Seaside Sparrow. M.S. Thesis. Univ. of Wisconsin, Madison, Wisconsin.

Sharp, B. 1968b. Conservation of the Dusky Seaside Sparrow on Merritt Island, Florida. Biol. Conserv. 1:175–176.

Sharp, B. 1979. Let's save the Dusky Seaside Sparrow. Fla. Nat. 42:68–70.

Sharp, B. 1970. A population estimate of the Dusky Seaside Sparrow. Wilson Bull. 82:158–166.

Sykes, P. W. Jr. 1980. Decline and disappearance of the Dusky Seaside Sparrow from Merritt Island, Florida. Amer. Birds 34:728–737.

Trost, C. H. 1968. Dusky Seaside Sparrow. Pp. 849–859 in Life Histories of North American cardinals, grosbeaks, buntings, towhees, finches, sparrows, and allies (O. L. Austin, Jr., ed.). U.S. Natl. Mus. Bull. 237, Part 2.

USFWS. 1979. Dusky Seaside Sparrow recovery plan. U.S. Fish and Wildlife Service, Washington, D.C.

USFWS. 1980. Selected vertebrate endangered species of the seacoast of the United States—The Dusky Seaside Sparrow. Biol. Ser. Prog. FWS/OBS-80/01.25. Washington, D.C.

USFWS. 1990. Endangered and threatened wildlife and plants. Final rule to delist the Dusky Seaside Sparrow and remove its critical habitat designation. Fed. Reg. 55(239):51112–51114, 12 December 1990.

Walters, M. J. 1992. A shadow and a song. The struggle to save an endangered species. Chelsea Green Publ. Co., Post Mills, Vermont. 238 pp.

PREPARED BY: Herbert W. Kale II, Florida Audubon Society, 460 Highway 435, Suite 200, Casselberry, FL 32707.

Whooping Crane

Grus americana

FAMILY GRUIDAE

Order Gruiformes

No endangered species has had greater attention focused on its plight than the Whooping Crane (*Grus americana*). From a population low in 1942 of 22 individuals, the population slowly increased to 267 by the spring of 1995. At that time the wild population, which migrates from Wood Buffalo National Park in the Northwest Territories of Canada to the Aransas National Wildlife Refuge (NWR) on the Texas Coast, consisted of 133 birds. An additional 100 birds were in captive-breeding facilities in Maryland, Wisconsin, and Alberta and 34 in experimentally introduced populations.

Whooping Cranes have occurred in the southeast United States within historic times as evidenced by specimens taken in South Carolina (Waccamaw River in 1850; Sprunt and Chamberlain 1949) and Georgia (near Macon 12 Nov. 1885, St. Simons Island, and another unspecified location; Burleigh 1958). There also are sight records from Georgia (Altamaha River and the mouth of the Savannah River; Burleigh 1958), Mississippi (Bay St. Louis 15 April 1902), and several locations in Alabama (Cypress Slough of the Warrier River before 1890, Prattville in 1899, and wintering records for Dauphin Island; Imhof 1962). The two populations, one migratory one nonmigratory, which occurred in Louisiana until the late 1940s, have been well documented (Allen 1952; Lowery 1974).

Records of Whooping Cranes in Florida are not as definitive as those for other southeastern states. There are Pleistocene fossil records from several locations (Wetmore 1931, McCoy 1963, Olson 1972). The earliest allusions to Whooping Cranes in Florida by Audubon and others are suspect because there was, and still is, a tendency to refer to the Sandhill Crane (*G. canadensis*) as a "Whooping Crane." F. Beverly, writing in the late nineteenth century (Hallock 1875), states, "it is a fact beyond doubt that the whooping crane (*Grus americanus* [sic]) is a resident of Florida. There has been seen for many years upon alligator flats, about twenty miles from Ft. Capron, Indian River, a

13

Whooping Crane, *Grus americana.*
(Photo by Stephen A. Nesbitt)

large white bird as tall as a man, which the native Floridians call a stork." He
goes on to state that young taken "from a nest" and raised for 6 months were
"white from the first" but says "they agreed exactly with the description of
whooping cranes." He emphasized the large size and loud voice of these
cranes, adding some credence to the account. But references to white-plumaged young taken from a nest are characteristics that are similar to the Wood
Stork (*Mycteria americana*), a species which Beverly does not mention among
the species that possibly could be confused with the crane. Maynard (1881)
quoted a Captain Dummett as assuring him that the white Whooping Crane
occurred on the prairies east of the Kissimmee River and Lake Okeechobee, a
report later confirmed by others but never by Maynard himself. O. E. Baynard,
a respected field naturalist active in Florida during the early twentieth century,
stated that the last flock (14) of Whooping Cranes he saw in Florida was in
1911 near Micanopy, southern Alachua County (Harmon 1954). There also is
an account of two Whooping Cranes reported east of the Kissimmee River on
19 January 1936 (Shaffer 1940).

A Whooping Crane was reportedly shot by B. O. Crichlow (a taxidermist
and naturalist) near St. Marks Pond north of St. Augustine, St. Johns County,
in 1927 or 1928 (Hallman 1965). A photograph, unmistakably a Whooping

Crane, was included with the published account (Hallman 1965), but no specific date of collection could be given. The specimen, never deposited in a public collection, was eventually destroyed in a fire. Indirect contact with Crichlow's son, who was the source for the Hallman account, did not clarify the year or season when the bird was shot, but he did remember seeing the fresh, unmounted specimen (N. F. Eichholz, pers. comm.), adding another level of confidence to the record. Otherwise there could be no assurance that the bird in Crichlow's collection did not come from elsewhere and the "Whooper" he reported shooting in 1927 or 1928 was a colloquial reference to a Sandhill Crane.

There seems to be little doubt that the Whooping Crane occurred in Florida during recent times. There is no disputing their regular occurrence elsewhere in the southeastern United States; and until quite recently there was a nonmigratory population in southwestern Louisiana. Although it is less well known, there also was a nonmigratory population of Sandhill Cranes in Louisiana (Lowrey 1974).

A crucial step to removing the Whooping Crane from endangered species status is the establishment of two additional self-sustaining populations, both of which should be distinct from the remaining wild population (USFWS 1986). In 1984, the Whooping Crane recovery team supported studies in the eastern United States to identify the most appropriate site for another population of Whooping Cranes. The sites considered were: Seney NWR in upper Michigan—a population that would be migratory and would most likely winter in Florida (as do the Sandhill Cranes from that area); Okefenokee NWR in the Okefenokee Swamp in southeastern Georgia—a population that would be nonmigratory; and three areas in Florida (Kissimmee Prairie, Myakka River State Park, and Cecil Webb Wildlife Management Area)—also to be a nonmigratory population. Because migration is a source of significant annual mortality in the Wood Buffalo–Aransas population and there was no proven technique for establishing a self-sustaining migratory population, the decision was made in 1989 that an attempt should be made to establish a nonmigratory population of Whooping Cranes east of the Mississippi River and that the effort be made in Florida.

The first release of Whooping Cranes in Florida occurred in February 1993. Fourteen young cranes of the year, reared in captivity but isolated from human contact at the USFWS Patuxent Wildlife Research Center and at the International Crane Foundation, were soft-released on the Kissimmee Prairie on the Three Lakes Wildlife Management Area. Soft-release or gentle-release involves the slow transition of the birds from a large (0.5–0.75 ha) open-topped enclosure to free-ranging life. Between December 1993 and April 1995, an additional 38 birds were released. In September 1995 there were 24 birds surviving from these first releases.

If results from these initial releases do not reveal unseen biological or sociological problems, annual releases of ≥20 birds a year will follow, beginning in perhaps 1996, and continue for ≥10 years. The goal is to have a self-sustaining population of at least 25 breeding pairs of Whooping Cranes by the year 2020.

LITERATURE CITED:

Allen, R. P. 1952. The Whooping Crane. Res. Rept. No. 2, Natl. Audubon Soc., New York.

Burleigh, T. D. 1958. Georgia birds. Univ. of Oklahoma Press, Norman, Oklahoma.

Hallman, R. C. 1965. Record of Whooping Crane killed in St. Johns County, Florida. Fla. Nat. 38:23.

Hallock, C. 1875. Camp life in Florida. Smith and McDougal Inc., New York.

Harmon, W. Z. 1954. Notes on cranes. Fla. Nat. 27:22.

Imhof, T. A. 1962. Alabama birds. Univ. of Alabama Press, Tuscaloosa, Alabama.

Lowery, G. H., Jr. 1974. Louisiana birds. Louisiana State Univ. Press, Baton Rouge, Louisiana.

Maynard, C. J. 1881. The birds of eastern North America. C. J. Maynard and Co., Newtonville, Massachusetts.

McCoy, J. J. 1963. The fossil avifauna of Ichetucknee River, Florida. Auk 80:335–351.

Olson, S. L. 1972. A Whooping Crane from the pleistocene of north Florida. Condor 74:341.

Shaffer, C. 1940. Whooping Crane, *Grus americana*. Redstart 7:65.

Sprunt, A., Jr., and E. B. Chamberlain. 1949. South Carolina bird life. Univ. of South Carolina Press, Columbia, South Carolina.

USFWS. 1986. Whooping Crane recovery plan. U.S. Fish and Wildlife Service, Albuquerque, New Mexico.

Wetmore, A. 1931. The avifauna of the pleistocene in Florida. Smithsonian Misc. Coll. 85:1–41.

PREPARED BY: Stephen A. Nesbitt, Florida Game and Fresh Water Fish Commission, Wildlife Research Laboratory, 4005 South Main Street, Gainesville, FL 32601.

Key West Quail-Dove

Geotrygon chrysia

FAMILY COLUMBIDAE

Order Columbiformes

TAXONOMY: The Key West Quail-Dove (*Geotrygon chrysia*), like other American quail-doves, is similar in general appearance and color pattern to the Old World quail-doves (*Gallicolumba*); however, the resemblance is more likely due to convergence than to phylogenetic affinity (Goodwin 1970). *G. chrysia* forms a superspecies with the Bridled Quail-Dove (*G. mystacea*) (Goodwin 1970) although some consider them conspecific (AOU 1983). Both appear closely related to the Violaceous Quail-Dove (*G. violacea*), which may form a link between quail-doves and doves of the genus *Leptotila*.

DESCRIPTION: The Key West Quail-Dove is a plump, terrestrial pigeon with iridescent brown upperparts suffused with green and purple on the crown, hindneck, mantle, wing coverts, and rump. Its underparts are white, shading to pale vineaceous on the breast and sides of the throat. The forehead is rich rufous offset by a broad, white facial stripe extending from the lower mandible beneath the eye. The throat is of the same color, but beneath the white facial stripe is a small rufous facial stripe. Unfeathered parts are pinkish-red and the bill is buff. Little size dimorphism exists between the sexes, but females are slightly duller with less iridescence. Juveniles have little or no iridescence and most feathers have a broad rusty fringe. Measurements of a single male were as follows: 297 mm, total length; 21.2 mm, bill length; 29.7 mm, tarsus length; 8.5 mm, middle toe length; and 85.0 g, total weight (Audubon 1840).

POPULATION SIZE AND TRENDS: Audubon (1840) found Key West Quail-Doves resident and breeding during the summer in and around Key West. On 20 May 1832 he described a nest, stating that it contained "two pure white eggs, about the size of those of the White-headed Pigeon."

Key West Quail-Dove, *Geotrygon chrysia*. (Photo by Lee F. Snyder)

However, Key West Quail-Doves lay buff-colored eggs, but Audubon's additional extensive notes on these birds during their nesting season suggest that breeding was common. It seems unlikely that Key West Quail-Dove breeding was confined to Key West, given the extensive amounts of suitable habitat throughout the Florida Keys at that time. Audubon believed quail-doves migrated to the West Indies during October, but populations during July were large enough to "enable sportsmen to shoot as many as a score in a day." No breeding records of Key West Quail-Doves in Florida have occurred since this time. Maynard (1881 in Robertson 1978) failed to find any quail-doves in an extensive search of the lower Keys during 1870. He was told that quail-doves disappeared because of deforestation. A specimen in the Milwaukee Public Museum was collected on Duck Key, about 100 km northeast of Key West in 1889. A set of eggs attributed to this specimen were larger than measurements given by Bent (1932) but within the range of those for the White-crowned Pigeon (*Columba leucocephala*) (Stevenson and Anderson 1994). An egg, collected at Key West in 1905 and currently in the Florida Museum of Natural History, is the appropriate size but in shape and color more closely resembles eggs of the Ruddy Quail-Dove (*G. montana*) (Sorrie 1979). After many years of collecting near Key West, J. W. Atkins obtained only three specimens, all of which had been collected during the fall (Scott 1890; Brewster 1898). More recently the Key West Quail-Dove has been a sporadic straggler (approximately 12 reports) to the Keys and southern mainland (Robertson and Woolfenden 1992). Although several sightings since the 1960s have occurred during the breeding season (Nelson 1966; Sorrie 1979; Kale 1987; Stevenson and Anderson 1994; Langridge 1992), all have been of individual birds and none made territorial calls or otherwise behaved in a

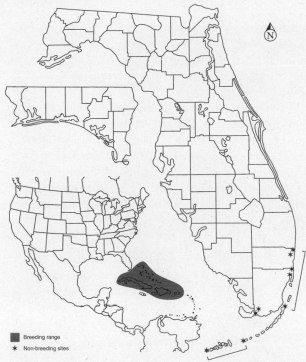

Distribution map of the Key West Quail-Dove, *Geotrygon chrysia*.

Breeding range
✳ Non-breeding sites

manner indicative of breeding. Of all records since Audubon, Sorrie (1979) suggested two might have been due to severe weather or escaped cage birds. Most of the other records are consistent with late summer or fall post-breeding dispersal from Cuba or the Bahamas (Stevenson and Anderson 1994; Pranty 1995). Sorrie also raised the possibility that a remnant, resident breeding population may still exist, not only in the remaining hardwood hammocks of the Keys, but in the scattered hammocks dotting the sawgrass prairies of the southwestern coast. Over the last 5 years, the Florida Breeding Bird Atlas has conducted many breeding season surveys throughout the Florida Keys without recording a quail-dove. Although coverage of isolated hammocks along the coast was very light, the possibility of isolated quail-dove breeding seems remote.

Little is known about population trends of Key West Quail-Doves in the West Indies, although the general feeling is that they may be declining.

DISTRIBUTION AND HISTORY OF DISTRIBUTION: The Key West Quail-Dove ranges throughout the Bahamas and much of the Greater Antilles, excluding Jamaica. Bond (1960) reported it in Cuba, Isle of Pines, Hispaniola, southern Puerto Rico, and perhaps Mona Island, although Raffaele (1989) makes no mention of its occurrence at the latter location. The Key West Quail-Dove is not known from the Virgin Islands (Raffaele 1989). Its historic range probably extended northward to the Florida Keys.

Barbour (1923, 1943) expressed concern that widespread deforestation throughout the range of the Key West Quail-Dove would ultimately lead to its extirpation. Goodwin (1970) reported the quail-dove rare in most parts of its range. Though rare in much of Cuba, it is more common on the eastern portion of the island and very common in parts of Isle of Pines (Garrido and Montana 1975). However, quail-doves were rare in 1916 on Isle of Pines (Todd 1916). J. F. Clements (in Sorrie 1979) reported that quail-doves and other game birds in Cuba have probably undergone population increases because of strict gun-control policies. The recent increase in Florida sightings (eight from 1965 to 1991 versus three from 1832 to 1965) may reflect increases in Cuban populations. Cuba is less than 100 km from southern Florida and should certainly be considered a possible source of dispersing birds (Sorrie 1979).

HABITAT REQUIREMENTS AND HABITAT TRENDS: Key West Quail-Doves have been reported from a range of habitats, most frequently arid lowland forests and scrub, often in densely wooded areas, including dense, disturbed coppice and overgrown orchards (Bond 1960; Goodwin 1970; Brudnell-Bruce 1975; Sorrie 1979). In Cuba, it occurs in upland woods in the limestone hills of Pinar del Rio and on wooded islands within the Zapata Swamp (Barbour 1923). In Hispañiola, Wetmore and Swales (1931 in Sorrie 1979) reported it in "areas with considerable rainfall" up to 500 meters in elevation.

Extensive deforestation has occurred and continues to occur throughout much of the Key West Quail-Dove's range (Johnson 1988). Although the Key West Quail-Dove appears to have disappeared before large-scale human impacts occurred throughout the Florida Keys, deforestation and over-hunting may have contributed to its extirpation in the mid-1800s (Howell 1932).

VULNERABILITY OF SPECIES AND HABITAT: Increasing human populations and subsequently increased pressure from development and hunting in many regions of the Caribbean are detrimental to remaining Key West Quail-Dove populations and their habitats. Hardwood hammocks in the Florida Keys have been extensively developed, resulting in the decline of many plant and animal species (Wood 1990). Relatively dry, lowland forests are well suited for human development. Presumably habitat loss would similarly affect quail-dove populations. Quail-doves also are hunted throughout most of their range. Other than the Ruddy Quail-Dove, few life-history data are available for species of this genus. Setting appropriate harvest limits may be difficult given the paucity of reproductive data.

CAUSES OF THREAT: Increasing human populations resulting in habitat conversion and intense hunting pressure pose the greatest threat to extant populations of Key West Quail-Doves. Introduction of mongooses on many Caribbean islands may also negatively influence quail-doves.

RESPONSES TO HABITAT MODIFICATION: Overhunting and habitat loss may have contributed to the extirpation of Key West Quail-Doves from the Florida Keys (Howell 1932), whereas reduced hunting pressure in Cuba may have led to population increases. Both examples suggest a direct relationship between hunting and development pressure and the status of quail-dove populations in the Caribbean basin.

DEMOGRAPHIC CONSIDERATIONS: Key West Quail-Doves lay 2-egg clutches and, presumably, like others columbids are capable of rearing multiple broods during the breeding season. In Cuba, the breeding season lasts from February through July (Barbour 1923). Little is known about the incubation or nestling periods for Key West Quail-Doves, but their closely-related congener, the Ruddy Quail-Dove, has an incubation period of 11 days and nestlings fledge as soon as 10 days of age (Skutch 1949). Because adults may renest within 3–4 weeks of fledging their first brood, it seems probable that Key West Quail-Doves could rear 3–4 broods during a single breeding season.

KEY BEHAVIORS: Little is known about the behavior of the Key West Quail-Dove or other members of this genus. Aptly named, most of these birds are ground feeders, as are quail, foraging on the forest floor for fallen fruit, seeds, and insects (Goodwin 1970). Although preferring the cover of trees or shrubs, the birds often forage where the forest floor is relatively open, such as in clearings or small lanes. The quail-dove residing at Snake Bight Road in Everglades National Park in 1987 foraged on the edge of a small tramway in an area of scrubby hardwood hammock.

The nest is loosely constructed of small twigs in a small tree or shrub, usually near and sometimes on the ground. The birds appear to be territorial, the call having been described as a "loud, resonant and protracted booming" vocalization (Goodwin 1970).

Although Audubon (1840) believed quail-doves to be migratory, they appear nonmigratory within their current range (Pough 1951). However, their extensive range and lack of phenotypic variation throughout it suggests interisland movement is common, as does the persistent occurrence of stragglers in Florida.

CONSERVATION MEASURES TAKEN: The Key West Quail-Dove is not listed at the federal or state level, nor does it appear to be listed in any of the Caribbean countries within its range (Collar and Andrews 1988).

CONSERVATION MEASURES PROPOSED: The Key West Quail-Dove has been extirpated from Florida as a breeding species since the end of the nineteenth century. Although it seems likely it once bred throughout the Florida Keys (Robertson 1978), the exact cause of its extirpation seems unclear. Considered rare or uncommon over most of its range, no historical data exist to document population declines, except anecdotal references, such as its loss in the Florida Keys. Population surveys and regulation of both habitat conversion and hunting may prevent further declines throughout its existing range.

Reintroduction may be appropriate in areas where suitable habitat exists. Second-growth hammock over much of the Florida Keys is similar to Key West Quail-Dove habitats in the Bahamas. The historical columbid community of the Keys included Key West Quail-Doves. Extant Florida Key columbids occur sympatrically with quail-doves in other areas of their range. The reintroduction of Key West Quail Doves in the Florida Keys would refill an available niche once occupied by this species and establish a population in an area where habitat loss and hunting may be carefully regulated.

ACKNOWLEDGMENTS: William B. Robertson, Jr., who wrote the original account of Key West Quail-Doves for this volume, generously shared his observation of Key West Quail-Doves in the West Indies. Both he and Fred Lohrer gave valuable comments on an earlier draft of this manuscript.

LITERATURE CITED:

AOU. 1983. Check-list of North American birds. American Ornithologists' Union, Baltimore, Maryland. 691 pp.

Audubon, J. J. 1840–1844. The birds of America. 7 vols. Reprinted by Dover Publ., Inc., New York.

Barbour, T. 1923. The birds of Cuba. Memoirs Nuttall Ornithol. Club no. 6. Nuttall Ornithol. Club, Cambridge, Massachusetts. 141 pp.

Barbour. T. 1943. Cuban ornithology. Memoirs Nuttall Ornithol. Club no. 9, Nuttall Ornithol. Club, Cambridge, Massachusetts. 144 pp.

Bent, A. C. 1932. Life histories of North American gallinaceous birds. Bull. Mus. Nat. Hist. no. 168. Smithsonian Inst., Washington, D.C.

Bond, J. 1960. Birds of the West Indies. Houghton Mifflin Co., Boston, Massachusetts. 256 pp.

Brewster, W. 1898. *Geotrygon chrysia* again at Key West. Auk 15:185.

Brudnell-Bruce, P. G. C. 1975. The birds of New Providence and the Bahama Islands. Collins, St. James Place, London. 142 pp.

Collar, N. J., and P. Andrew. 1988. Birds to watch—the ICBP world's checklist of threatened birds. ICBP Tech. Publ. no. 8. Smithsonian Inst. Press, Washington, D.C. 303 pp.

Garrido, O. H., and F. G. Montana. 1975. Catalogo de las Aves de Cuba. Acedemia de Ciencias de Cuba, La Habana, Cuba.

Goodwin, D. 1970. Pigeons and doves of the world, 2nd ed. Brit. Mus. Nat. Hist., London. 446 pp.

Howell, A. H. 1932. Florida bird life. Coward-McCann, Inc., New York. 579 pp.

Johnson, T. H. 1988. Biodiversity and conservation in the Caribbean: profiles of selected islands. ICBP Monog. no. 1. Cambridge, United Kingdom. 144 pp.

Kale, H. W. 1987. Florida birds: rarities. Fla. Nat. 60(2):16.

Langridge, H. P. 1992. The spring report: Florida region. Amer. Birds 46: 412–15.

Nelson, M. G. 1966. Key West Quail-Dove (*Geotrygon chrysia*) at Lake Worth. Fla. Nat. 39:154.

Pough, R. H. 1951. Audubon water bird guide. Doubleday, Inc. Garden City, New York. 352 pp.

Pranty, B. 1995. Florida Ornithological Society field observations committee fall report: August–November 1994. Fla. Field Nat. 23:44–56.

Raffaele, H. A. 1989. A guide to the birds of Puerto Rico and the Virgin Islands. Princeton Univ. Press, Princeton, New Jersey. 254 pp.

Robertson, W. B., Jr. 1978. Key West Quail-Dove. Pp. 119 in Rare and endangered biota of Florida, Vol. 2, birds. (H. W. Kale, II, ed.). Univ. Presses Fla., Gainesville, Florida. 121 pp.

Robertson, W. B., Jr., and G. E. Woolfenden. 1992. Florida bird species: an annotated list. Fla. Ornithol. Soc. Spec. Publ. no. 6. Gainesville, Florida.

Scott, W. E. D. 1890. The Key West Quail-Dove (*Geotrygon martinica*) at Key West. Auk 7:90.

Skutch, A. F. 1949. Life history of the Ruddy Quail-Dove. Condor 51:3–19.

Sorrie, B. A. 1979. A history of the Key West Quail-Dove in the United States. Amer. Birds 33:728–731.

Stevenson, H. M., and B. H. Anderson. 1994. Birdlife of Florida. Univ. Press of Fla., Gainesville, Florida.

Todd, W. E. C. 1916. The birds of the Isle of Pines. Ann. Carnegie Mus. 10:146–296.

Wood, D. A. 1990. Official lists of endangered and potentially endangered fauna and flora in Florida. Fla. Game and Freshwater Fish Comm., Talla-hassee, Florida.

PREPARED BY: Reed Bowman, Archbold Biological Station, P.O. Box 2057, Lake Placid, FL 33862.

Zenaida Dove
Zenaida aurita

FAMILY COLUMBIDAE

Order Columbiformes

TAXONOMY: Though doves of the genus *Zenaida* bear superficial resemblance to the Old World Turtle-Doves (*Streptopelia*), this resemblance is almost certainly due to convergence. Their closest relatives appear to be the American ground-doves and the American quail-doves (Goodwin 1970). The Zenaida Dove (*Z. aurita*) may form a link between the Galapagos Dove (*Z. galapagoensis*), a stout-bodied, highly terrestrial dove, and the superspecies group of Mourning Dove (*Z. macroura*) and Eared Dove (*Z. auriculata*) (Goodwin 1970). The Zenaida Dove forms three distinct subspecies: the nominate race, *Z. a. aurita,* is found in the Lesser Antilles and forms an intergrade with *Z. a. zenaida* in the northern portion of its range. The latter subspecies inhabits the Greater Antilles, Cuba, Jamaica, and the Bahamas. A third subspecies, *Z. a. salvadorii,* is restricted to the eastern coast of the Yucatan Peninsula (Goodwin 1970).

DESCRIPTION: The Zenaida Dove is slightly larger than the Mourning Dove but with longer legs and a shorter tail. It differs from other members of the genus *Zenaida* in having 12 rectrices instead of 14 (Goodwin 1970). Slight plumage variation exists among the subspecies; the following description is for the Greater Antilles race *Z. a. zenaida*, presumably the subspecies that once occurred in Florida. The upperparts are warm reddish-brown with iridescent pink and purple on the sides of the neck. Two dark iridescent facial stripes extend behind and below the eye. The breast is a dark mauve-vinaceous extending onto the belly and under tail coverts where it intermixes with bluish-gray. The Zenaida Dove is easily distinguished from the Mourning Dove by white on the trailing edge of secondaries and a shorter, rounder, gray-tipped tail. Zenaida Doves lack the white wing patches and broadly white-tipped tail of the White-winged Dove (*Z. asiatica*). The bill is black and the legs and feet are dull red. The female is paler and slightly less red than the male. Males are significantly larger than females. Average measurements of 27 males and 20 females are, respectively, 163.2 and 132.6 g in weight, 9.5 and 8.6 mm in culmen length, 23.6 and 22.3 mm in tarsus length, and 103.5 and 100.8 mm in 10th primary length (Wiley 1991). Juvenile plumage is much like the females but iridescence on the neck is absent and the back and wing feathers have a rufous-buff fringe.

POPULATION SIZE AND TRENDS: Audubon (1840) asserted that Zenaida Doves nested on the islands near Indian Key, in the middle of the Florida Keys, and on a small islet between Key West and the Dry Tortugas. Though not as common as the White-crowned Pigeon (*Columba leucocephala*), Zenaida Doves were abundant at these sites. Audubon believed they were migratory, arriving in the Keys by mid-April and departing in October, similar to the migratory patterns of White-crowned Pigeons (Bancroft et al. 1990). The subspecies *Z. a. zenaida* was described by Bonaparte in 1825 from a specimen collected by T. R. Peale "from the southern part of Florida," presumably from the Keys. The doves appear to have been extirpated from the Keys sometime during the 1860s. Ornithologists working there at that time failed to find nesting doves (Robertson 1978). With the exception of Key West, the Keys were relatively sparsely inhabited, thus the loss of this bird predated significant habitat disturbance. Since the breeding population appears to have been small and local, it may have been extremely susceptible to human predation and loss due to storms (Robertson 1978). Since then the Zenaida Dove has been only a rare and sporadic visitor to southern Florida (Robertson and Woolfenden 1992). Since 1900 about nine reliable sight records exist. Of these, six are from the Florida Keys, two from the southern mainland, and one from central Florida (Langridge et al. 1982; Loftin et al. 1991). Several other reports exist from both the Keys and central Florida, but many are of questionable accuracy (Langridge et al. 1982).

Most recent sightings have occurred during the fall or winter, suggesting that post-breeding dispersal from the West Indies may account for most Zenaida Doves arriving in Florida. Bent (1932) believed he observed Zenaida Doves on Indian Key in April 1903; however, he was unsure of his identification. Two Zenaida Doves were reported during the summer of 1988 from northern Key Largo and from Key West. Because the sightings did not overlap in time, they may represent the same individual (Stevenson 1988).

The Zenaida Dove is common throughout most of its range. Nellis et al. (1984) estimated a breeding season population of over 14,000 birds on St. Croix, U.S. Virgin Islands. In many places it is one of only a few native species that have increased in number and range as a result of human agricultural practices in the West Indies (Wiley 1985).

DISTRIBUTION AND HISTORY OF DISTRIBUTION: The Zenaida Dove ranges throughout most of the West Indies. It also is found on the eastern

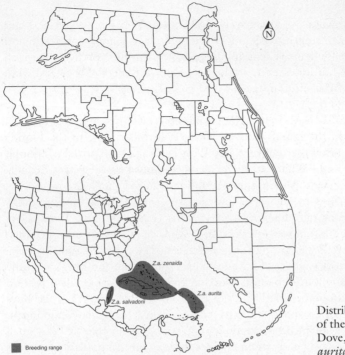

Distribution map
of the Zenaida
Dove, *Zenaida
aurita.*

Yucatan coast and adjacent islands and formerly bred in the Florida Keys.
However, it is absent from Trinidad and Tobago, Swan Islands, Old Providence, and St. Andrew (AOU 1983).

HABITAT REQUIREMENTS AND HABITAT TRENDS: The Zenaida
Dove uses a wide variety of habitats. In Puerto Rico it is characteristic of lower
slopes and the coastal plain. It is found in savannas, mangrove swamps, open
woodlands and second growth forests, and in and around cultivated fields
(Wiley 1991). Raffaele (1989) noted that the grounds of hotels and universi-
ties and public beaches were all ideal localities for this dove. However,
Barbour's (1923) statement that Zenaida Doves in Cuba shun human habita-
tions suggests that during recent years they may have habituated to human
encroachment. It is rarely found in deep forest (Barbour 1923; Raffaele
1989).

VULNERABILITY OF SPECIES AND HABITAT: As islands throughout
the Caribbean become increasingly developed, a shift from an agrarian-based
society to one founded on light industry and business has occurred, especially
on larger islands such as Puerto Rico (Wiley 1985). Half of Puerto Rico's
890,340 ha is abandoned agricultural land and much of this has reverted to

second-growth forest. These land-use patterns have probably increased the amount of habitat available to Zenaida Doves. Zenaida Doves remain one of the few columbids legally hunted in the Caribbean. Until recently hunting seasons and bag limits have been based on inadequate knowledge of the species' biology. Recent population estimates and breeding biology studies of Zenaida Doves in the U.S. Virgin Islands and Puerto Rico (Nellis et al. 1984; Wiley 1991) may provide a biological basis for sound management decisions.

CAUSES OF THREAT: Although Zenaida Dove populations are increasing, several factors exist that could have detrimental effects on local populations. Inappropriate hunting seasons or bag limits could dramatically reduce local breeding populations. Raffaele (1989) stated that where hunting was re-stricted this dove became both tame and abundant. Zenaida Doves commonly nest on the ground on islands free from introduced terrestrial predators (rats, mongooses, cats, and dogs) (Burger et al. 1989; Wiley 1991). Where terres-trial predators occur, doves commonly nest in low shrubs and trees. The increased spread of exotic predators could severely impact those doves in habitats that are currently predator-free.

RESPONSES TO HABITAT MODIFICATION: In many parts of the Carib-bean, changes in land-use patterns, primarily away from agrarian uses, have benefited Zenaida Dove populations. In Puerto Rico, the recent decline (since the 1960s) in the sugar-cane industry also has benefited Zenaida Doves (Wiley 1985). Despite improvements in game management, hunting season and bag limits are often determined in the absence of baseline studies on reproductive and population ecology. Management decisions may be made on data from closely related species (such as basing Zenaida Dove management on Mourn-ing Dove natural history) or on the same species but from other regions (Wiley 1985). Poorly managed hunting can have dramatic effects on species, even though adequate habitat is available.

DEMOGRAPHIC CHARACTERISTICS: In Puerto Rico, Zenaida Doves may nest at any time of year (Wiley 1991), but peak breeding activity occurs from March through July. Nellis et al. (1984) reported a peak breeding period of May to August in the U.S. Virgin Islands, but also found eggs throughout the year. Barbour (1923) reported that Zenaida Doves in Cuba nested from April to July. Zenaida Doves lay 2-egg clutches and may raise up to four broods per year; most successful pairs (69%) produced at least two broods per year in Puerto Rico (Wiley 1991). Zenaida Doves also rapidly recycle follow-ing a failed nesting attempt, averaging less than 14 days (Wiley 1991). However, nest success is relatively high for columbids, ranging from 40–60% at various sites in Puerto Rico. Nellis et al. (1984) reported lower reproductive

success in the Virgin Islands, ranging from 18–31%. They found great variation in success in different habitat types, suggesting that nests in preferred
habitats were not the most successful. Nests in cracks and small holes in rocks
were the most successful; however birds only nested in such sites in areas that
were relatively free of terrestrial predators. In Puerto Rico, nests in mixed
agriculture/urban areas were more successful than those in dry lowland
forests, even though fewer mammalian and avian predators occur in this area
and the incidence of warble fly parasitism is lower (Wiley 1991). Clearly,
however, Zenaida Doves seem to breed successfully in human-impacted environments.

KEY BEHAVIORS: Many of the behaviors of the Zenaida Dove are typical of
other columbids, especially doves of the genus *Zenaida*. They are largely
generalist seed and fruit eaters. In Puerto Rico, Wiley (1991) recorded 77
plant species in the dove's diet. Wetmore (1927) reported that Zenaida Doves
fed heavily on waste grains. It normally forages on the ground, especially in
cultivated regions.

Typical of columbids, its nests are loosely constructed of twigs and normally placed 2–5 m above ground. Wiley (1991) suggested that tree species
was not as important in nest site selection as was horizontal support for the
nest. In Puerto Rican woodlands, doves often built their nests in bromeliads,
close to the tree trunk. Though not normally gregarious nesters, Danforth
(1935) described large colonies of "thousands" of birds on Little Saba Cay.
Breeding aggregations also have been reported on cays of the Virgin Islands
(Robertson 1962).

Zenaida Doves have two common calls. The advertisement call, often
described as a musical "coo-oo coo-oo coo-oo," similar to that of the Mourning Dove, is often given in assertive or sexual contexts. The nest call is used
near the nest, often during nest exchanges during the incubation and nestling
periods.

Nellis et al. (1984) noted seasonal population fluctuations in the Virgin
Islands, suggesting that part of the population was resident and part migratory, arriving in March and April and departing in late July and August. These
migratory birds likely bred in the Virgin Islands, since peak population counts
coincide with maximum breeding activity. Certainly much interisland movement exists in Zenaida Doves.

CONSERVATION MEASURES TAKEN: Recent studies (Nellis et al. 1984;
Wiley 1991) of the reproductive and population ecology of Zenaida Doves
have resulted in management recommendations for the establishment of
appropriate hunting seasons and bag limits.

CONSERVATION MEASURES PROPOSED: Management recommendations have been proposed recently for Zenaida Doves in Puerto Rico (Wiley 1991). Monitoring of regional populations should include information on breeding chronology, nesting success, and productivity. Hunting seasons should be set to exclude the period of greatest breeding activity and bag limits should reflect the harvest rates populations can sustain above the normal mortality rates. Both hunting season and bag limits should also reflect regional differences in Zenaida Dove population biology. Interisland movement seems common, yet few data exist on metapopulation dynamics. Cooperative research between neighboring islands (Puerto Rico, Dominican Republic, U.S. Virgin Islands, etc.) might dramatically improve our present state of knowledge.

Breeding Zenaida Doves appear to have been extirpated from Florida prior to extensive habitat changes or persecution by man. Though the historic columbid community of the Florida Keys included Zenaida and Mourning doves, among others, the recent inclusion of exotic species such as White-winged Dove (*Z. asiatica*), Eurasian Collared-Dove (*S. decaocto*) and Rock Dove (*C. livia*) may have filled the niche once occupied by Zenaida Doves. It seems improbable that the native columbid community might be restored, even with intensive management. Since Zenaida Dove populations appear stable or growing elsewhere in their range, reintroduction into the Florida Keys seems unwarranted at this time.

ACKNOWLEDGMENTS: William B. Robertson, Jr. and Fred Lohrer shared ideas and provided comments on an earlier draft of this manuscript.

LITERATURE CITED:

AOU. 1983. Check-list of North American birds. American Ornithologists' Union, Washington, DC. 691 pp.

Audubon, J. J. 1840. The birds of America. 7 vols. Reprinted by Dover Publ., Inc., New York.

Bancroft, G. T., R. Bowman, R. J. Sawicki, and A. M. Strong. 1990. Relationship between the reproductive ecology of the White-crowned Pigeon and the fruiting phenology of tropical hardwood hammock trees. Fla. Game and Fresh Water Fish Comm., Nongame Wildl. Prog. Tech. Rept., Tallahassee, Florida.

Barbour, T. 1923. The birds of Cuba. Memoirs Nuttall Ornithol. Club no. 6. Nuttall, Massachusetts. 141 pp.

Bent, A. C. 1932. Life histories of North American gallinaceous birds. Bull. Mus. Nat. Hist. no. 162. Smithsonian Inst. Press, Washington, DC.

Burger, J., M. Gochfeld, D. J. Gochfeld, and J. E. Saliva. 1989. Nest site selection in Zenaida Doves (*Zenaida aurita*) in Puerto Rico. Biotropica 21:244–249.

Danforth, S. T. 1935. Supplementary account of the birds of the Virgin Islands, including Culebra and adjacent isles pertaining to Puerto Rico, with notes on their food habits. Jour. Agric. Univ. Puerto Rico 19:439–472.

Goodwin, D. 1970. Pigeons and doves of the world, 2nd ed. Brit. Mus. Nat. Hist., London. 446 pp.

Langridge, H. P., P. W. Sykes, Jr., A. Y. Ayres, G. S. Hunter, and P. S. Weinrich. 1982. Zenaida Dove sighting in Palm Beach County, Florida. Fla. Field Nat. 10:56–59.

Loftin, R. W., G. E. Woolfenden, and J. A. Woolfenden. 1991. Florida bird records in American Birds and Audubon Field Notes 1947–1989. Fla. Ornithol. Soc. Spec. Publ. no. 4. Gainesville, Florida. 99 pp.

Nellis, D. W., R. A. Dewey, M. A. Hewitt, S. Imsand, R. Philobosian, and J. A. Yntema. 1984. Population status of Zenaida Doves and other columbids in the Virgin islands. Jour. Wildl. Manage. 48:889–894.

Raffaele, H. A. 1989. A guide to the birds of Puerto Rico and the Virgin Islands. Princeton Univ. Press, Princeton, New Jersey. 254 pp.

Robertson, W. B., Jr. 1962. Observations on the birds of St. John, Virgin Islands. Auk 79:44–76.

Robertson, W. B., Jr. 1978. Zenaida Dove. Pp. 120 in Rare and endangered biota of Florida, Birds, vol. 2, (H. W. Kale, II, ed.). Univ. Presses Fla., Gainesville, Florida. 121 pp.

Robertson, W. B., Jr., and G. E. Woolfenden. 1992. Florida bird species: an annotated list. Fla. Ornithol. Soc. Spec. Publ. no. 6, Gainesville, Florida.

Stevenson, H. M. 1988. Florida region. Amer. Birds 42:1280.

Wetmore, A. 1927. The birds of Puerto Rico and the Virgin Islands. New York Acad. Sci., Sci. Surv. Puerto Rico and Virgin Islands 9(3):245–406.

Wiley, J. W. 1985. Bird conservation in the United States Caribbean. Bird Conserv. 2:107–159.

Wiley, J. W. 1991. Ecology and behavior of the Zenaida Dove. Ornithol. Neotropical 2:49–75.

PREPARED BY: Reed Bowman, Archbold Biological Station, P.O. Box 2057, Lake Placid, FL 33862.

Wood Stork

Mycteria americana

FAMILY CICONIIDAE

Order Ciconiiformes

TAXONOMY: The most recent taxonomic treatment of the Class Aves, based on DNA characteristics, joins the New World vultures in the Subfamily Cathartinae with the storks in the Subfamily Ciconiinae into the Family Ciconiidae (Sibley et al. 1988). Of the 17 species of storks worldwide, the American Wood Stork (*Mycteria americana*) is the only New World representative of the tribe Mycteriini, which includes four species of "wood storks" (*Mycteria*), and two species of openbill storks (*Anastomus*). As adults, the wood storks have unfeathered heads and necks, relatively heavy, decurved bills, and show varying amounts of pink, yellow, or salmon-colored feathers during the breeding season. They are highly colonial in their nesting and foraging behaviors and occur widely in tropical and hot temperate regions. The American Wood Stork is a monotypic species throughout its extensive range between the southeastern United States and northern Argentina (Palmer 1962; Ogden 1984).

DESCRIPTION: The Wood Stork is a large, long-legged wading bird, with a head to tail length of 85–115 cm (35–45 in.) and a wingspread of 150–165 cm (60–65 in.). The plumage is white, except for iridescent black primary and secondary wing feathers and a short black tail. Storks soar with necks and legs extended. On adults, the rough scaly skin of the head and neck is unfeathered and dark grayish in color, the legs are dark, and the feet are flesh-colored. The bill color is blackish.

During courtship and the early nesting season, adults have pale salmon coloring under the wings, fluffy, white undertail coverts that are longer than the tail, and toes that brighten to a vivid pink. Immature storks, up to the age of about 3 years, differ from adults in having a yellowish or straw-colored bill and varying amounts of dusky feathering on the head and neck.

Wood Stork,
*Mycteria
americana.*
(Photo by James A.
Rodgers, Jr.)

POPULATION SIZE AND TREND: The Wood Stork continues to be a common species in large, undrained wetlands throughout the region between coastal Mexico and northern Argentina (Blake 1977). Historically, the largest Wood Stork nesting colonies in the United States, collectively containing between 5,000 and 15,000 pairs annually as recently as the 1930s, were located in the Corkscrew Swamp, Okaloacoochee Slough, and southern Everglades regions of south Florida (Ogden 1977; Kushlan and Frohring 1986). This historical population almost certainly did not include single colonies as large as 15,000–20,000 pairs as was suggested by Allen (Palmer 1962). Storks also were known to have once nested in 50 or more smaller colonies that were scattered throughout most of the remainder of the state. Information on the years of active use and numbers of storks in each of these colonies was only partially preserved for a few of these sites. While most sites contained much fewer than 500 pairs, the total number of sites active in any single year is not known. Thus, before 1940, the statewide nesting population was perhaps in the range of 15,000–25,000 pairs.

The first statewide aerial search for stork colonies conducted during 1958–1960 was prompted by a concern that a declining Florida population had been further stressed by a period of drought years during the mid-1950s. This census revealed 7,657 nesting pairs in 1959 and 10,060 pairs in 1960 at 17 colonies statewide; about 80–88% were in the six south Florida sites (Ogden and Nesbitt 1979). Annual, aerial censuses of stork colonies throughout Florida between 1976 and 1986 showed a progressive decline from 5,254 pairs in 1976 to 3,045 pairs in 1982 (with the exception of 2,520 pairs in high

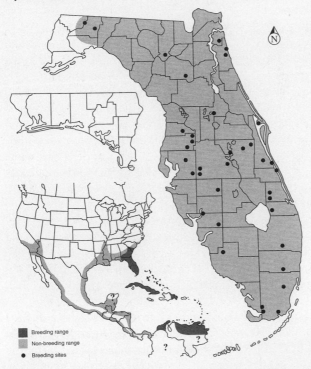

Breeding range
Non-breeding range
Breeding sites

Distribution map of
the Wood Stork,
Mycteria americana.

water year 1978, when no storks nested in south Florida), followed by an increase of between 4,597 and 5,551 pairs during 1983–1986 (Ogden et al. 1987). The number of colonies detected annually ranged between 15 (1978) and 28 (1986), and the percentage of pairs nesting in south Florida colonies declined from 68% (1976) to 13% (1986). No complete aerial census of all known stork colonies in Florida was conducted again until May 1991, when a disturbingly low total of 2,467 nesting pairs were found at 25 sites following 2–3 years of statewide drought (W. Hoffman and A. Sprunt, pers. comm.). One year later, and following a summer and fall of above average rain, over 2,300 pairs nested in south Florida alone. Statewide surveys in 1993, 1994, and 1995, produced estimates of 4,402 (29 colonies), 3,588 (26 colonies), and 5,523 (33 colonies), respectively, in Florida.

   Although storks were reported to have nested historically in the coastal plain regions of all states between South Carolina and Texas, those colonies outside Florida apparently were small in size and were active only irregularly. More recently, storks began to nest annually in Georgia beginning in 1976 and in South Carolina in 1981. The numbers of storks nesting in these two states has increased rapidly to a recent peak of 1,661 pairs at 11 colonies in Georgia (M. Harris, pers. comm.) and 806 pairs at 3 colonies in South Carolina (T. Murphy, pers. comm.) during 1993.

DISTRIBUTION AND HISTORY OF DISTRIBUTION: The northern limit of nesting by Wood Storks is in the coastal plain of South Carolina and Georgia (recent nesting in Alabama is suspected), throughout most of Florida (AOU 1983), and in the coastal regions of Mexico as far north as Guerrero on the Pacific coast and Tabasco on the Gulf of Mexico (Knoder et al. 1980; Sprunt and Knoder 1980). Wood Storks also nest in Cuba and the Dominican Republic and in lower subtropical and tropical zones throughout Central and South America as far south as eastern Peru, Bolivia, and northern Argentina (AOU 1983). Especially large breeding populations occur in the Usumacinta Delta in southeastern Mexico (Ogden et al. 1989), in the llanos region of Venezuela (B. T. Thomas, pers. comm.), and the Pantanal wetlands in Brazil (Mittermeier et al. 1989).

Prior to the 1970s, a majority of Wood Storks in the U.S. population nested in colonies located south of Lake Okeechobee, and in most years (at least during the 1900s) the entire population nested in Florida. Since the late 1970s, a majority of storks have nested in central and northern Florida and as far west as Leon County. An increasing number also have nested in colonies located in southern Georgia and coastal South Carolina.

Tagged, juvenile storks from colonies in central and southern Florida dispersed during the summer-fall, post-fledgling period throughout the Florida peninsula, into southern Georgia, coastal South Carolina as far as Charleston County, and as far west as central Alabama and east-central Mississippi (Ogden, unpubl. data). Adult and juvenile storks that were marked in an east-central Georgia colony during the spring or summer were found, in winter, as far south as the central Everglades (Coulter 1987). Although relatively small numbers of storks still nest in south Florida, the Everglades wetlands continue to be important feeding habitat for large numbers during winter-spring dry seasons (Bancroft et al. 1992).

Although colony sites for the U.S. population are widely disjunct from the known nesting colonies in southern Mexico, post-nesting dispersal of birds from these separate nesting areas may result in overlap. Storks from Mexico disperse annually as far north as southern California, southern Texas, and Louisiana, during the tropical rainy season between June and October (Palmer 1962). Storks that once dispersed as far north along the Mississippi River as southeastern Missouri (Palmer 1962) could have included birds from both populations.

HABITAT REQUIREMENTS AND HABITAT TRENDS: Wood Storks nest in colonies located in woody vegetation over standing water or on islands surrounded by relatively broad expanses of open water (Nesbitt et al. 1982). Most natural colony sites in Florida have been in cypress (*Taxodium* sp.) or mangrove (often *Rhizophora mangle*), although colonies also have been located in southern willow (*Salix caroliniana*), pond apple (*Annona glabra*), and in mixed associations of swamp hardwoods (e.g., *Magnolia, Nyssa*) (Rodgers et al. 1988; Ogden 1991). Primarily since the 1970s, storks also have nested at sites where water has been artificially impounded by roads or levees or where islands have been created by dredge activities (Ogden 1991). Nests in these altered or artificially created colony sites may be in the same species of trees as in the natural sites, but also have been in dead or dying upland trees (e.g., *Pinus, Quercus*), in exotic species such as Australian pine (*Casuarina* sp.) and Brazilian pepper (*Schinus terebinthefolius*), or even in low thickets of cactus (*Opuntia* sp.) on islands. The use of altered or artificial colony sites suggests that, in some regions or in years of low rainfall, storks have been unable to locate natural nesting habitat that is adequately flooded during the nesting season. Use of altered or artificial habitats as stork nesting habitat in central and north Florida has increased from approximately 10% of all nesting pairs in 1959–1960 to 60–82% between 1976 and 1986.

Storks feed primarily in water between 5 and 40 cm (2–15 in.) deep, where the water is relatively calm and uncluttered by aquatic vegetation (Kahl 1964; Coulter 1987). Almost any shallow wetland depression where fish tend to become concentrated, either through local reproduction by fishes or as a consequence of area drying, may be good feeding habitat. These sites include drying marshes, shallow roadside or agricultural ditches, narrow tidal creeks and pools, and depressions in cypress heads or swamp sloughs. However, all such sites must have sufficiently long annual hydroperiods or adequately strong hydrological connections with more permanent water to produce or make available necessary densities of fishes as prey for storks.

Differences among years in patterns and amounts of rainfall result in differences among years in where and when storks feed. Colony sites that are successful over time will be those that have a large number of potential feeding sites, including relatively shallow and deep sites that may only be suitable in years of rainfall extremes (Coulter 1987).

The increase in both number and percentage of the population nesting in central and northern Florida since the 1970s has been characterized by a regional increase in the number of colonies active each year, rather than by an increase in the size of existing colonies (Ogden et al. 1987). Presumably limitations in the total area of wetland foraging habitat within flight range of each site may limit colony size in this region. By contrast, the south Florida region, where much more expansive wetlands once occurred, was formerly characterized by a relatively small number of much larger colonies being active each year.

VULNERABILITY OF SPECIES AND HABITAT: Wood Storks are relatively long-lived birds and are highly mobile within their range, thus the threat of a rapid population decline is low. A lack of genetic differentiation among colonies strongly suggests that the storks nesting in Florida represent a single population (Stangel et al. 1990). Changes in population size and distribution over the past several decades primarily have been caused by regional changes in the quality and quantity of wetland foraging habitat. Smaller wetlands, and those with relatively shorter annual hydroperiods, have been especially suscep- tible to conversion to other land uses. The feeding habits and/or the physiol- ogy of Wood Storks potentially enhance the ability of this species to accumu- late organochlorine contaminants from the environment (Ohlendorf et al. 1978; Fleming et al. 1984).

CAUSES OF THREAT: In south Florida, Wood Stork colonies that tradi- tionally formed during November–December in most years now form during January–March. This change in timing has correlated with a sharp decline in the number of pairs in colonies and with increased rates of nesting failures when nestlings do not fledge before the initiation of summer rains in May– June (Ogden, unpubl. data). The changes in timing of colony formation, primarily occurring in the Everglades and Big Cypress regions, apparently are due to the loss or degradation of substantial areas of early dry season foraging habitat in relatively higher elevation marshes and in the mainland estuaries.

Throughout the peninsula, but especially in central and northern Florida, many traditional colony sites have been either abandoned or are used only in wetter years, due to the lowering of surface-water levels that has occurred in all regions. Storks generally will not initiate nesting in swamps that are dry. Although no contaminant problem has been identified in the Florida popula- tion, elevated levels of organochlorine pesticides, PCBs, and mercury have been detected in small samples of storks (Ohlendorf et al. 1978; Fleming et al. 1984; Facemire and Chlebowski 1991).

RESPONSES TO HABITAT MODIFICATION: The readiness with which Wood Storks will use water impoundments or other human-altered sites for nesting suggests that colony sites could be intentionally created and main- tained through long-term site management plans. Large numbers of storks will feed in shallow water impoundments or flooded agricultural fields, created intentionally for storks (Coulter 1987) or for soil oxidation and nematode control (Sykes and Hunter 1978).

DEMOGRAPHIC CHARACTERISTICS: Wood Stork nesting colonies usu- ally form between late November and early March in south Florida (now rarely before January) and during February–March in central and northern Florida. In years when regional water conditions are excessively wet or dry, the total regional number of nesting Wood Storks may be depressed compared to other years, suggesting that not all adult birds attempt to nest in these years (Ogden et al. 1980). The entire reproductive process requires between 110 and 150 days, including a prenesting courtship period at the nest site and a prolonged period of post-flight dependency by chicks returning to the nest to be fed (Kahl 1964). Clutch size ranges between 1–6 eggs, with 3 eggs being by far the most common clutch size in colonies studied during the 1970s and 1980s (J. Ogden, unpubl. data; J. Rodgers, pers. comm.). A relatively high percentage of nests may have clutches larger than 3 eggs in some years and locations, apparently when and where food resources are relatively greater. For example, 4 eggs was the most common clutch size in 250 examined nests at Alligator Lake, Monroe County, in 1933 (Howell, in litt.). The average number of young fledged per active nest often ranges between 0.5 and 1.0 in colonies that have been severely stressed by food limitations and between 2.0 and 2.9 in the most successful colonies (Kahl 1964; Ogden, unpubl. data). The percentage of successful nests in colonies varies considerably between locations and years, with many or most nests failing when storms, predators, or inadequate food resources impact sites (Coulter 1987; Rodgers 1987; Rodgers et al. 1987). When many or all nests in south Florida colonies fail early in the nesting season, a second nesting effort may occur some weeks later. It is not known if the adults in the second nesting are the same storks that failed earlier. A small sample of marked, known-aged storks (<10) in Florida still showed immature plumage characteristics at age 3 and were in adult plumage and nesting at age 4 years (Ogden, unpubl. data). Mortality rates for fledged storks are not known.

KEY BEHAVIORS: Wood Storks feed almost entirely on small fishes between 2.0 and 25.0 cm in length (Kahl 1964; Ogden et al. 1976; Coulter 1987). Means of fish lengths from samples collected from nestling storks in several colonies ranged between 5.0 and 10.0 cm. Fish densities at stork feeding sites have been reported at 15 to 141 fish/m^2.

A study in Everglades National Park showed that feeding storks selected certain species and sizes of fish in numbers proportionally greater than their relative abundance at the feeding sites (Ogden et al. 1976). Relatively abundant mosquitofish (*Gambusia affinis*) were greatly underrepresented in the stork diet; whereas, the relatively common flagfish (*Jordanella floridae*), sailfin mollies (*Poecilia latipinna*), marsh killifish (*Fundulus confluentus*) and the relatively scarce sunfish (*Lepomis* sp.) were captured selectively. Storks in the Everglades study also captured the larger fishes. The mean length of fishes consumed was significantly larger (4.5 cm) than the mean length of fishes available (2.5 cm). Other prey reported have included frogs, crayfish, crabs, and snakes.

Wood Storks are tactile feeders in that they capture prey by feeling in

shallow water with a partially open bill (Kahl and Peacock 1963; Kahl 1964).
A foraging bird occasionally stirs underwater vegetation with its feet, apparently to startle potential prey into movement, and snaps the bill shut on any
prey item that comes in contact with the mandibles. Locating prey tactilely
allows storks to make captures in turbid water or dense vegetation, but for
such a technique to be effective requires a relatively high density of prey
animals.

Storks often fly relatively great distances between roosts or colonies and
feeding sites, compared with distances flown by other wading birds. Storks
nesting in southern Florida colonies routinely flew 10–40 km to feeding areas
and as far as 95–130 km when closer wetlands became dry (Ogden et al.
1978; Browder 1984). The longer distance flights require overnight roosting
at or near the foraging grounds, and result in a single, mid-day feeding trip to
the colony by each adult; such a pattern may only be possible when chicks are
large enough to not require brooding and both adults can participate in
foraging. Storks nesting at several central Florida colonies flew 5–35 km to
foraging grounds (J.Ogden; K. Scott Clark, pers comm.). Recent studies in
coastal Georgia have shown that storks commonly forage at night when tides
are dropping or at low levels (A. L. Bryan, pers. comm.).

Wood Storks perform elaborate pair formation displays in the nesting
colonies (Kahl 1971, 1972). Male birds establish themselves at potential nest
sites and employ a ritualized Display Preening behavior as a female bird approaches. Females respond with a spread-winged Balancing Posture and bill
Gaping. Actual copulation is accompanied by loud bill clattering by the male.
Mated pairs perform a greeting that includes an exaggerated, mutual Up-
Down head movement and hissing calls.

Both adults in a pair participate in incubation and feeding the nestlings.
Incubation begins with the first egg laid and lasts about 30 days for each egg
(Kahl 1964). After hatching, one adult remains at the nest to brood the young
for the first 3–4 weeks of the nestling period. A pair of adults will usually
deliver food to a nest from 3 to 12 times daily, although fewer feedings occur
when food is scarce or adults are traveling great distances to find it. An
incoming adult will often bring enough food so that it can regurgitate several
separate feedings into the nest over a period of 1 hour or more; this pattern is
especially characteristic at nests with small young.

CONSERVATION MEASURES TAKEN: The population of Wood Storks
that nests in Florida, Georgia, South Carolina, and perhaps in Alabama was
listed as Endangered by the U.S. Fish and Wildlife Service in February, 1984.
The *Official Lists of Endangered and Potentially Endangered Fauna and Flora
in Florida* dated 1 July 1988 includes the Wood Stork, listed as "endangered"
by the Florida Game and Fresh Water Fish Commission. Many nesting colony

sites throughout Florida receive protection, either on public lands or through isolation on private lands. The Fish and Wildlife Service has an approved Wood Stork Recovery Plan (USFWS 1986) and has more recently prepared *Habitat Management Guidelines for the Wood Stork in the Southeast Region* (Ogden, nd.).

CONSERVATION MEASURES PROPOSED: Systematic, aerial censuses of Wood Stork nesting colony sites, combined with ground visits, may be the most efficient and accurate method for tracking population trends and identifying the factors that regulate nesting success in Florida. A schedule of regular aerial and ground censuses should be established and maintained. The future of the Wood Stork population will depend on identification and protection of the important stork feeding habitat statewide. Proposed restoration plans for the Everglades region, including Everglades National Park, if implemented could substantially benefit the south Florida colonies. Water management practices at colony sites could enhance the suitability of existing sites for nesting and create new colony sites.

ACKNOWLEDGMENTS: This account contains unpublished data contributed by John C. Ogden. Much of my understanding of Wood Stork biology and ecology has come from numerous discussions with Joan A. Browder, E. Scott Clark, Malcolm C. Coulter, William B. Robertson, and James A. Rodgers. Earlier drafts of this account were improved by suggestions provided by James A. Rodgers. My time on this project was supported by the South Florida Natural Resources Center, Everglades National Park.

LITERATURE CITED:

AOU. 1983. Check-list of North American birds. Sixth edition. American Ornithologists' Union, Washington, D.C.

Bancroft, G. T., W. Hoffman, R. J. Sawicki, and J. C. Ogden. 1992. The importance of the water conservation areas in the Everglades to the endangered Wood Stork (*Mycteria americana*). Conser. Biol. 6:322–97.

Blake, E. R. 1977. Manual of neotropical birds. Vol. 1. Univ. Chicago Press, Chicago, Illinois.

Browder, J. A. 1984. Wood Stork feeding areas in southwest Florida. Fla. Field Nat. 12:81–96.

Coulter, M. C. 1987. Wood Storks of the Birdsville colony and the swamps of the Savannah River plant. 1986 annual report. SREL-31-UC-66e. Savannah River Ecol. Lab., Aiken, South Carolina. 237 pp.

Facemire, C. F., and L. Chlebowski. 1991. Mercury contamination in a Wood Stork (*Mycteria americana*) from west-central Florida. Publ. no. VBFO-91-CO3, U.S. Fish and Wildlife Service, Vero Beach, Florida.

Fleming, W. F., J. A. Rodgers, Jr., and C. J. Stafford. 1984. Contaminants in Wood Stork eggs and their effects on reproduction, Florida, 1982. Colon. Waterbirds 7:88–93.

Kahl, M. P., Jr. 1964. Food ecology of the Wood Stork (*Mycteria americana*) in Florida. Ecol. Monogr. 34:97–117.

Kahl, M. P. 1971. Social behavior and taxonomic relationships of the storks. Living Bird 10:151–170.

Kahl, M. P. 1972. Comparative ethology of the Ciconiidae. Part 3. The Wood-Storks (genera *Mycteria* and *Ibis*). Ibis 114:15–29.

Kahl, M. P., and L. J. Peacock. 1963. The bill-snap reflex: a feeding mechanism in the American Wood Stork. Nature 199:505–506.

Knoder, C. E., P. D. Plaza, and A. Sprunt, IV. 1980. Status and distribution of the Jabiru stork and other water birds in western Mexico. Pp. 58–127 in The birds of Mexico. Their ecology and conservation (P. P. Schaeffer and S. M. Ehlers, eds.). Proc. Natl. Aud. Soc. Symp. Tiburon, California.

Kushlan, J. A., and P. Frohring. 1986. The history of the southern Florida Wood Stork population. Wilson Bull. 98:368–386.

Mittermeier, R. A., I. G. Camara, M. T. J. Padua, and J. Blanck. 1989. Conservation in the Pantanal region of Brazil: Introduction, threats, and priorities for action. Unpubl. ms. 39 pp.

Nesbitt, S. A., J. C. Ogden, H. W. Kale, II, B. W. Patty, and L. A. Rowse. 1982. Florida atlas of breeding sites for herons and their allies: 1976–78. FWS/OBS-81/49. U.S. Fish and Wildlife Service, Washington, D.C.

Ogden, J. C. Undated. Habitat management guidelines for the Wood Stork in the Southeastern Region. U.S. Fish and Wildlife Service, Southeast Region, Atlanta, Georgia. 9 pp.

Ogden, J. C. 1977. Recent population trends of colonial wading birds on the Atlantic and Gulf coastal plains. Pp. 137–153 in Wading birds (A. Sprunt, IV, J. C. Ogden, and S. Winkler, eds.). Nat. Aud. Soc. Res. Rept. no. 7. New York, New York.

Ogden, J. C. 1984. Stork. Pp. 563–565 in A dictionary of birds (B. Campbell and E. Lack, eds.). Buteo books, Vermillion, South Dakota.

Ogden, J. C. 1991. Nesting by Wood Storks in natural, altered, and artificial wetlands in central and northern Florida. Colon. Waterbirds 14:39–45.

Ogden, J. C., and S. A. Nesbitt. 1979. Recent Wood Stork population trends in the United States. Wilson Bull. 91:512–523.

Ogden, J. C., C. E. Knoder, and A. Sprunt, IV. 1989. Colonial wading bird populations in the Usumacinta delta, Mexico. Ecologia y conservacion del Delta de los rios Usumacinta y Grijalva (Memorias). INIREB, Division Regional. Tabasco, Mexico. Pp. 595–605.

Ogden, J. C., J. A. Kushlan, and J. T. Tilmant. 1976. Prey selectivity of the Wood Stork. Condor 78:324–330.

Ogden, J. C., J. A. Kushlan, and J. T. Tilmant. 1978. The food habits and nesting success of Wood Storks in Everglades National Park 1974. Natl. Park Serv. Res. Rept. no. 16. Washington, D.C.

Ogden, J. C., H. W. Kale, II, and S. A. Nesbitt. 1980. The influence of annual variation in rainfall and water levels on nesting by Florida populations of wading birds. Trans. Linn. Soc. N.Y. 9:115–126.

Ogden, J. C., D. A. McCrimmon, Jr., G. T. Bancroft, and B. W. Patty. 1987. Breeding populations of the Wood Stork *Mycteria americana* in the southeastern United States. Condor 89:752–759.

Ohlendorf, H. M., E. E. Klaas, and T. E. Kaiser. 1978. Organochlorine residues and eggshell thinning in Wood Storks and Anhingas. Wilson Bull. 90:608–618.

Palmer, R. S. (Ed.) 1962. Handbook of North American birds. Vol. 1, Loons through Flamingos. Yale Univ. Press, New Haven, Connecticut.

Rodgers, J. A., Jr. 1987. On the antipredator advantages of coloniality: a word of caution. Wilson Bull. 99:269–271.

Rodgers, J. A., A. S. Wenner, and S. T. Schwikert. 1987. Population dynamics of Wood Storks in north and central Florida, USA. Colon. Waterbirds 10:151–156.

Rodgers, J. A., Jr., A. S. Wenner, and S. T. Schwikert. 1988. The use and function of green nest material by Wood Storks. Wilson Bull. 100:411–423.

Sibley, C. G., J. E. Ahlquist, and B. L. Monroe, Jr. 1988. A classification of the living birds of the world based on DNA-DNA hybridization studies. Auk 105:409–423.

Sprunt, A., IV, and C. E. Knoder. 1980. Populations of wading birds and other colonial nesting species on the Gulf and Caribbean coasts of Mexico. Pp. 3–16 in The birds of Mexico. Their ecology and conservation (P. P. Schaeffer and S. M. Ehlers, eds.). Proc. Nat. Aud. Soc. Symp. Tiburon, California.

Stangel, P. W., J. A. Rodgers, Jr., and A. L. Bryan. 1990. Genetic variation and population structure of the Florida Wood Stork. Auk 107:614–619.

Sykes, P. W., and G. S. Hunter. 1978. Bird use of flooded agricultural fields during summer and early fall and some recommendations for management. Fla. Field Nat. 6:36–43.

PREPARED BY: John C. Ogden, National Park Service, Everglades National Park, 40001 State Road 9336, Homestead, FL 33034-6733.

Florida Snail Kite

Rostrhamus sociabilis plumbeus

FAMILY ACCIPITRIDAE

Order Falconiformes

TAXONOMY: Formally called the Everglade Kite, Amadon (1975) recognized three subspecies of the Snail Kite, of which *Rostrhamus sociabilis plumbeus* Ridgway occurs in Florida and Cuba, including the Isle of Pines (Isla de la Juventud). However, Brown and Amadon (1976) stated that the subspecies of *R. sociabilis* are "doubtfully distinct." Florida birds are intermediate in measurements between the other two subspecies, but little color or pattern variation is evident among the subspecies (Beissinger 1988).

DESCRIPTION: The Snail Kite is a medium-sized raptor with an overall length of about 43–45 cm and a wingspan of about 112–118 cm. Females are slightly larger than males in weight (Beissinger 1988) and body measurements (Friedmann 1950), but these variables cannot be used to distinguish the sexes in the field. However, the definitive adult plumage is strongly sexually dimorphic. The adult male's entire head, back, wings, breast, abdomen, sides, flanks, and thighs are a uniform slate or blackish-slate color becoming nearly black on the remiges and rectrices, with a faint brownish-gray tone on the upper wing coverts; the upper and under tail coverts and base of the tail are whitish; the tips of the rectrices are whitish with a broad subterminal band of grayish drab; the lores, external rim of eyelids, cere, gape, and mandibular rami are yellow (nonbreeding) to scarlet; the iris is brownish-red to ruby; the tarsus and toes are yellow-orange (nonbreeding) to scarlet-orange; the talons and most of the bill are black. The adult female's top of head, back, wings, and tail are buffy-brown becoming streaked with brown or light buff on the sides of the head, throat, breast and abdomen; a prominent eye-stripe and the cheek are light buff; the upper wing coverts, scapulars, and secondaries are tipped with a cinnamon-buff; the upper and middle tail coverts are white; the soft-part colors are as in males.

Subadult males and females are similar in appearance to the adult female.

Florida Snail Kite, *Rostrhamus socia- bilis plumbeus.* (Photo by Betty Wargo)

Juveniles of both sexes are similar to adult nonbreeding females, except that the upper parts are streaked with brown on cinnamon-brown, whereas the under parts are more tawny.

POPULATION SIZE AND TREND: Several authors (Nicholson 1926; Howell 1932; Bent 1937) indicated that the Snail Kite was numerous in central and south Florida marshes during the early 1900s, with scattered flocks of over 100 kites. Sprunt (1945) believed there were only 50–100 kites left by the early 1940s, with a steady decline at Lake Okeechobee and disappearance from the headwaters of the St. Johns River. Stieglitz and Thompson (1967) could find only 21 kites in 1966, but this was an incomplete census, as were the accounts above cited. The first systematic surveys were initiated by Paul Sykes in the late 1960s. The population reached the lowest count in 1972 (65 kites) and peaked in 1980 at 651 kites (Sykes 1983). After a precipitous decrease associated with a drought in 1981, kites rebounded to peak at 668 birds in 1984 (Rodgers et al. 1988). Thereafter, the population has exhibited fluctuating numbers among years through 1993 (range 300–600 kites). Much interyear variation occurs in the population counts for individual wetlands and is often associated with low water levels and droughts causing dispersal from these wetlands. During the last mid-winter statewide census in 1994, 996 kites were counted, of which 470 (47.2%) were sited in Water Conservation Area 3 (R. Bennetts, pers. comm.).

DISTRIBUTION AND HISTORY OF DISTRIBUTION: The Snail Kite occurs widely in tropical Central and South America and Cuba. The original range (both breeding and nonbreeding) in Florida consisted of the headwaters of the St. Johns River northward to the Oklawaha drainage (including Alachua

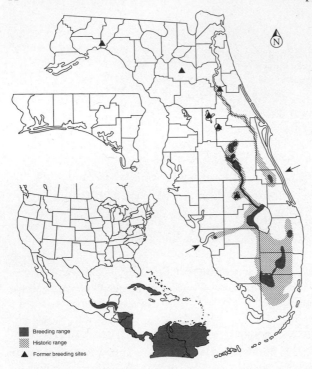

Distribution map of the Florida Snail Kite, *Rostrhamus sociabilis plumbeus.*

■ Breeding range
▨ Historic range
▲ Former breeding sites

Lake [Paynes Prairie] and Orange Lake), the Kissimmee River basin (including Lake Kissimmee), southward through Lake Okeechobee, the Everglades, and near Florida Bay (Sykes 1984). Miscellaneous sightings and egg-sets are recorded from central Florida lakes and marshes, and a small region in Wakulla and Jefferson counties in the panhandle (Howell 1932; Sykes 1984).

By the late 1960s, Sykes (1984) found Snail Kites mostly at Lake Okeechobee, Conservation Area 1 (CA1, Loxahatchee NWR), Conservation Area 2A (CA2A), Conservation Area 2B (CA2B), and the southern half of Conservation Area 3A (CA3A). By the late 1970s, the Snail Kite had become restricted to the marshes on the west side of Lake Okeechobee and the southeastern region of CA3A (Sykes 1984).

During the 1980s, kites expanded their nesting range to recolonize Lake Kissimmee, Lake Tohopekaliga, East Lake Tohopekaliga, the upper St. Johns River marshes in Indian River County, and several smaller wetlands in Hendry and Okeechobee Counties (Takekawa and Beissinger 1989; Rodgers, unpubl. data). Range expansion and dispersal by Snail Kites into central Florida wetlands often was associated with droughts and low water levels in south Florida, especially in the Everglades and at Lake Okeechobee (Beissinger and Takekawa 1983; Rodgers et al. 1988; Takekawa and Beissinger 1989). The 1990 midwinter census resulted in 418 kites counted (Rodgers, unpubl. data); however, because of droughts during 1988–1990, 71.8% of the kites were in a few central Florida wetlands (i.e., East Lake Tohopekaliga, Lake Tohopekaliga, Lake Kissimmee, St. Johns River marshes, and miscellaneous sites) that have not been designated as critical Snail Kite habitat (USFWS 1986). By 1992, water levels had returned to near normal conditions and kites had returned to breed in large numbers at Lake Okeechobee, CA2B, and CA3A.

R. s. plumbeus is restricted to certain freshwater wetlands in central and southern Florida and Cuba. Movement between Florida and Cuba is unknown, but it is doubtful given the lack of foraging habitat in extreme south Florida (i.e., southern Everglades National Park, Florida Bay, and the Keys), short-distance nomadic dispersal in Florida as opposed to migration, and the relatively large expanse of open water separating Florida and Cuba. The lack of suitable foraging habitat providing access to the apple snail (*Pomacea paludosa*) precludes significant northern recolonization.

HABITAT REQUIREMENTS AND HABITAT TREND: Though the Florida Snail Kite occasionally takes other food items (Sykes and Kale 1974; Beissinger 1988, 1990), it preys almost exclusively on freshwater apple snails (Snyder and Snyder 1969). Kites capture snails by aerial hunting over foraging habitat that consists of relatively shallow (30–90 cm), clear, and calm water (Sykes 1987a). Furthermore, ideal foraging habitat must have relatively open water with a low density of emergent vegetation (e.g. *Eleocharis* spp., maidencane [*Panicum hemitomon*], etc.), allowing kites to see and capture snails as they move along the stems feeding or rising to the surface to breath or lay eggs. This open slough habitat must be inundated throughout the year with infrequent dry-downs to sustain snails. The foraging habitat requires 2–5 years of recovery in order for kite numbers and nests to return to average or predrought numbers if the wetland dries up (Rodgers et al. 1988, unpubl. data; Takekawa and Beissinger 1989). Though the apple snail occurs throughout north Florida, parts of Georgia, and Alabama, the lack of suitable foraging habitat providing access to the snail will prevent significant northern recolonization.

Snail Kites in Florida nest in a variety of woody vegetation, including melaleuca (*Melaleuca quinquenervia*), cypress (*Taxodium distichum*), pond apple (*Annona glabra*), cocoplum (*Chrysobalanus icaco*), southern willow (*Salix caroliniana*), wax myrtle (*Myrica cerifera*), and buttonbush (*Cephalanthus occidentalis*), as well as nonwoody substrates, such as cattail (*Typha* spp.), giant bulrush (*Scirpus validus*), sawgrass (*Cladium jamaicense*), and reed grass (*Phragmites australis*) (Sykes 1987b; Rodgers, unpubl. data). Nest collapse is rare in woody vegetation but common in nonwoody vegetation, especially on lake margins and early in the season. Kites appear to prefer woody vegetation when water levels are adequate to inundate the site but are forced to nest in nonwoody plants (especially at lake sites) during low water levels. Kites will abandon nests if the site loses standing water.

Much of the original Snail Kite habitat has been impacted by marsh drainage (Everglades agricultural area south of Lake Okeechobee), artificial water schedules and altered water levels (Lake Okeechobee), dredging (Kissimmee River), and impounding (Everglades water conservation areas). Demands on these wetlands for recreational use and water resources (both drinking and agricultural irrigation) further reduce the area of suitable foraging habitat.

VULNERABILITY OF SPECIES AND HABITAT: The Florida Snail Kite is vulnerable to a variety of proximate and ultimate biological and environmental factors. Direct human persecution of adults and nests appears rare. Predation of both adults and nest contents occurs, but is of low frequency (Snyder et al. 1989; Rodgers, unpubl. data; however, see Sykes 1987c). Pesticides (Sykes 1985) and parasites/diseases (Sykes and Forrester 1983; Snyder et al. 1984; Forrester, unpub. data) likewise probably have little impact on survivorship. Despite fluctuating population numbers and a fragmented habitat in Florida, Snail Kites still exhibit average avian genetic variability (Stangel and Rodgers, unpubl. data). Major reproductive failure is associated with brood reduction, nest abandonment, and nest collapse (Snyder et al. 1989; Rodgers, unpubl. data). All three factors increase in frequency during drought or low water periods. Major de-watering events (East Lake Tohopekaliga 1990, Lake Tohopekaliga 1986, St. Johns River marshes 1990) have caused significant reproductive failure and nesting abandonment. Droughts reduce the amount of inundated marsh (foraging area and access to snails) and force kites to nest in nonwoody vegetation that increases the frequency of nest collapse due to wind and wave action. Furthermore, since nonwoody substrates at lake sites are often at marsh edges, negative interaction with human activities (especially airboats) may contribute to some nest failure. Nesting in nonwoody vegetation at several Florida lakes (e.g., Lakes Okeechobee and Kissimmee) has resulted in nest collapse following herbicide applications.

CAUSES OF THREAT: Originally, Snail Kite foraging and nesting habitat extended northward into the Florida panhandle and included riparian sites (e.g. Wakulla, St. Johns, Oklawaha, and Kissimmee Rivers). However, foraging habitat is currently limited to several central and southern Florida lakes and marshes where water levels (and hence area of marsh inundated) are manipulated with a system of manmade canals and water control structures. Furthermore, the Everglades habitat has been reduced to half the original area, impounded, and water levels artificially regulated.

The introduction of non-native aquatic vegetation (e.g., water hyacinth [*Eichhornia crassipes*], water lettuce [*Pistia stratiotes*], torpedo grass [*Panicum repens*], and hydrilla [*Hydrilla verticillata*]) decreases the amount of foraging area and reduces access to snails in many wetlands (i.e., Lake Okeechobee, Lake Kissimmee, Lake Tohopekaliga). Finally, the drainage and back-pumping of nutrient-laden water from agricultural and dairy sources into several wetlands (e.g., Lakes Okeechobee and Kissimmee, CA1, CA2A, CA3A) has contributed to nutrification, organic detritus build-up, and die-offs of snails. Nutrification further accelerates aquatic plant growth and necessitates continued herbiciding programs to control non-native vegetation.

RESPONSES TO HABITAT MODIFICATION: Habitat modifications have both benefited and adversely affected Snail Kites in Florida. Though pre-1960s data are limited, it appears that kites benefited from the impounding of CA3A. This benefit is illustrated by their increased use of the area and increased population numbers. Similar impounding of marshes and historic wetlands in the Upper St. Johns River basin by the St. Johns Water Management District has recreated favorable kite habitat in Indian River County in the 1990s. However, most habitat modifications have had negative impacts on Snail Kites. Altered water levels and high nutrient-laden waters probably produced habitat changes and caused the abandonment of CA1 and CA2A. Lower water levels at Lakes Okeechobee and Kissimmee have reduced the littoral zone for foraging and forced kites to nest in unstable, nonwoody vegetation. Altered water schedules and levels resulting in snail reduction or alteration of foraging habitat have caused kites to abandon the East Everglades, CA3B and Everglades National Park. Prolonged droughts have forced kites to disperse from fragmented wetlands to other refugia (Takekawa and Beissinger 1989; Rodgers, unpubl. data). These wetlands require several years of normal rainfall and water levels before the snail population will support pre-drought nesting and numbers of kites.

Snail Kites will continue to use a nest that has been placed in an artificial basket or support because it was in danger of collapse. However, kites show no indication of reusing the artificial substrate the next breeding season.

DEMOGRAPHIC CHARACTERISTICS: Banded, known-age Snail Kites have bred as yearlings, but most kites probably breed at 2 years of age (Beissinger 1988; Snyder et al. 1989). Modal clutch size is 3 eggs (65–76% of clutches in central and south Florida), with minor interyear and intersite variation (Sykes 1987c; Snyder et al. 1989; Rodgers, unpubl. data). Fledging success is highly variable among sites and years, ranging from 0.1 to 0.48 fledgling per egg. Most nest failures occur during the egg-laying to hatching period, with a second greatest amount of mortality associated with brood reduction before the nestlings are 2 weeks of age. Thereafter, brood reduction is generally much lower. Clutch sizes are similar throughout the nesting season, but earlier nesting kites exhibit higher fledging rates than birds nesting later in the season (Rodgers, unpubl. data). Exceptions occur during droughts and lower water levels when nest failure is high throughout the season and nests and nestlings can be abandoned up to the age of fledging. Also, during droughts many kites probably do not attempt breeding. Kite egg-sets have been observed in all months of the year in Florida (Sykes 1987c), but in general, kites breed from December to June in southern Florida and from February to August in central Florida. Life span is not known, but kites probably live for 12–15 years (Beissinger 1988).

KEY BEHAVIORS: The Snail Kite forages by flying over a marsh in slow, flapping flight with short glides, the wings held flat to slightly dihedral as in the Osprey (*Pandion haliaetus*). Important vocalizations include a harsh, cackling "ka-ka-ka-ka-ka-ka" call uttered aggressively toward intruders near nests and a soft, rasping "ker-wuck ker-wuck" call given while perched or flying into an evening roost.

Primary courtship displays are performed mostly by male Snail Kites. A Sky-dance consists of the male repeatedly flying upward, then closing its wings and descending steeply before the wings are opened again and the kite rises. This display is directed toward a potential or established mate, and occasionally towards a male as an agonistic display. Deep-wingbeats consist of exaggerated downward strokes of the wings as the kite flies up at a steep angle. This display is often performed in the same contexts as the Sky-dance, but is typical of both sexes flying up from the territory or nest.

Male Snail Kites typically establish a territory and commence nest building and courtship displays. The nest may reach a nearly complete stage of construction before the male successfully pairs or abandons the territory without pairing. Once a mate is secured, the male brings material to the nest and the female finishes the construction. The male also feeds the female during the nest building and egg-laying periods (Beissinger 1987).

Nests are bulky structures made of dead twigs. The upper surface is slightly to deeply concave, usually finished with some fresh green vegetation. Eggs are laid at intervals of about two days (Beissinger 1988). Incubation by both sexes begins with the first egg laid. Age of first flight is about 6 weeks of age, but parents will feed fledglings until 9–10 weeks old. Snail Kites maintain sequential monogamy or "ambisexual mate desertion" (Beissinger 1986; Beissinger and Snyder 1987). If snails are plentiful and time permits, one parent deserts its mate and nest when the nestlings are 3–6 weeks old and initiates a new nesting cycle while its former mate raises the first brood alone.

Florida Snail Kites will nest solitarily or in loose colonies, sometimes in association with other species of water birds. Infrequently, nonbreeding kites may associate with a breeding pair and assist in nest defense. During the nonbreeding season, kites become gregarious and form communal roosts, often very large (2–247 birds). Roosts tend to be used for many consecutive years, if water levels and snail populations are stable.

CONSERVATION MEASURES TAKEN: The Florida Snail Kite is listed as endangered by the U.S. Fish & Wildlife Service (USFWS 1976) and by the Florida Game & Fresh Water Fish Commission (FGFWFC 1991). A Snail Kite Recovery Plan has been prepared and adopted (USFWS 1986).

Beginning in the late 1960s, annual mid-winter surveys have been conducted that have revealed changes in the population and wetlands used. Studies of Snail Kite reproductive success and breeding ecology have been conducted during the last two decades, providing an excellent database for conservation and management decisions and plans.

Various private and public groups and agencies have cooperated to reduce negative impacts on the Snail Kite in Florida. The National Audubon Society has placed nests that were in danger of collapse in nest baskets along the northwestern shoreline of Lake Okeechobee (Sykes and Chandler 1974). Similar nest supports have been used by the FGFWFC on East Lake Tohopekaliga and Lake Tohopekaliga. A cooperative effort among the DEP, FGFWFC and SFWMD has reduced herbicide-related nest collapse in cattail and giant bulrush substrate at Lake Okeechobee, Lake Kissimmee, and Lake Tohopekaliga.

CONSERVATION MEASURES PROPOSED: Continued mid-winter Snail Kite surveys would allow monitoring of the population's status and range in Florida. This is especially important during drought periods and if lake drawdowns are recommended as part of fisheries and littoral zone management of central and south Florida wetlands important to Snail Kites. The identification of refugia during droughts and new nesting locations will enable efforts for the continued availability of these important sites for future drought events (Takekawa and Beissinger 1989). Cooperative agreements and annual management are required to avoid future negative impacts of herbiciding nonnative aquatic vegetation where Snail Kites nest, especially at central Florida sites such as Lakes Okeechobee, Kissimmee, and Tohopekaliga.

Well-planned prescribed burning and water level management schedules need to be developed for several wetlands in order to encourage and maintain woody vegetation used for nesting by Snail Kites and to insure that these substrates are appropriately inundated during the breeding season. For example, maintaining Lake Okeechobee at 4.25 m (14.0 ft.) msl. would inundate much woody vegetation and maintain about 90% of the littoral zone kites use for foraging. Draw-downs of lakes in central Florida coincidental with low water level conditions at Lake Okeechobee and the Everglades water conservation areas should be avoided in order to provide alternative nesting areas during droughts. Otherwise kites would be precluded from nesting throughout most, if not all, of their Florida range.

ACKNOWLEDGMENTS: I thank S. Nesbitt and D. Wood for reviewing this manuscript. This report is a contribution from the Wildlife Research Laboratory, Florida Game and Fresh Water Fish Commission, Gainesville, Florida.

LITERATURE CITED:

Amadon, D. 1975. Variation in the Everglade Kite. Auk 92:380–382.

Beissinger, S. R. 1986. Demography, environmental uncertainty, and the evolution of mate desertion in the Snail Kite. Ecology 67:1445–1459.

Beissinger, S. R. 1988. Pp. 148–165 in Handbook of North American birds, volume 4 (Palmer, R. S., ed.). Yale Univ. Press, New Haven, Connecticut.

Beissinger, S. R. 1990. Alternative food of a diet specialist, the Snail Kite. Auk 107:327–333.

Beissinger, S. R., and J. E. Takekawa. 1983. Habitat use and dispersal by Snail Kites in Florida during drought conditions. Fla. Field Nat. 11:89–106.

Beissinger, S. R., and N. R. Snyder. 1987. Mate desertion in the Snail Kite. Anim. Behav. 35:477–487.

Bent, A. C. 1937. Life histories of North American birds of prey. U.S. Natl. Mus. Bull., no. 167. Washington, D.C.

Brown, L. H., and D. Amadon. 1976. Eagles, hawks, and falcons of the world. McGraw-Hill Book Co., New York.

FGFWFC. 1991. Official lists of endangered and potentially endangered fauna and flora in Florida. Florida Game & Fresh Water Fish Commission, Tallahassee, Florida.

Friedmann, H. 1950. The birds of North and Middle America. U.S. Natl. Mus. Publ. 50, part XI. Washington, D.C.

Howell, A. H. 1932. Florida bird life. Coward-McCann, Inc., New York.

Nicholson, D. J. 1926. Nesting habits of the Everglade Kite in Florida. Auk 43:62–67.

Rodgers, J. A., S. T. Schwikert, and A. S. Wenner. 1988. Status of the Snail Kite in Florida: 1981–1985. Amer. Birds 42:30–35.

Snyder, N. F. R., and H. A. Snyder. 1969. A comparative study of mollusc predation by Limpkins, Everglade Kites, and Boat-tailed Grackles. Living Bird 8:177–223.

Snyder, N. F. R., J. C. Odgen, J. D. Bittner, and G. A. Grau. 1984. Larval dermestid beetles feeding on nestling Snail Kites, Wood Storks, and Great Blue Herons. Condor 86:170–174.

Snyder, N. R. R., S. R. Beissinger, and R. Chandler. 1989. Reproduction and demography of the Florida Everglade (Snail) Kite. Condor 91:300–316.

Sprunt, A. 1945. The phantom of the marshes. Audubon Mag. 47:15–22.

Stieglitz, W. O., and R. L. Thompson. 1967. Status and life history of the Everglade Kite in the United States. Spec. Sci. Rept.—Wildl. no. 109, U.S.D.I., Bur. Sport. Fish. & Wildl., Washington, D.C.

Sykes, P. W., Jr. 1983. Recent population trends of the Everglade Snail Kite in Florida and its relationship to water levels. Jour. Field Ornith. 54:237–246.

Sykes, P. W., Jr. 1984. The range of the Everglade Snail Kite and its history in Florida. Bull. Fla. State Mus., Biol. Sci. 29:211–264.

Sykes, P. W., Jr. 1985. Pesticide concentrations in Snail Kite eggs and nestlings in Florida. Condor 87:438.

Sykes, P. W., Jr. 1987a. The feeding habits of the Snail Kite in Florida, USA. Colon. Waterbirds 10:84–92.

Sykes, P. W., Jr. 1987b. Snail Kite nesting ecology in Florida. Fla. Field Nat. 15:57–84.

Sykes, P. W., Jr. 1987c. Some aspects of the breeding biology of the Snail Kite in Florida. Jour. Field Ornith. 58:171–189.

Sykes, P. W., Jr., and H. W. Kale, II. 1974. Everglades Kite feed on non-snail prey. Auk 91:818–820.

Sykes, P. W., Jr., and D. J. Forrester. 1983. Parasites of the Snail Kite in Florida and summary of those reported for the species. Fla. Field Nat. 11:111–116.

Sykes, P. W., Jr., and R. Chandler. 1974. Use of artificial nest structures by Everglade Kites. Wilson Bull. 86:282–284.

Takekawa, J. E., and S. R. Beissinger. 1989. Cyclic drought, dispersal, and the conservation of the Snail Kite in Florida: lessons in critical habitat. Conserv. Biol. 3:302–311.

USFWS. 1976. Federal register 32:4001.

USFWS. 1986. Everglade Snail Kite (*Rostrahamus sociabilis plumbeus* Ridgway) revised recovery plan. U.S. Fish & Wildlife Service, Atlanta, Georgia.

PREPARED BY: James A. Rodgers, Jr., Florida Game & Fresh Water Fish Commission, Wildlife Research Laboratory, 4005 South Main Street, Gainesville, FL 32601.

Peregrine Falcon

Falco peregrinus

FAMILY FALCONIDAE

Order Falconiformes

TAXONOMY: Currently, 19 subspecies of Peregrine Falcon (*Falco peregrinus*) are recognized (Palmer and White 1988; White and Boyce 1988). Morizot's (1988) analysis of genetic variability among Peregrine subspecies revealed that the common alleles at most loci occur worldwide, suggesting a recent evolutionary origin or extensive mixing among wild populations in the recent past. Morphologic features appear strongly related to geography and divide the subspecies into two broad groups: northern subspecies, including the North American forms; and a southern, more tropical set of subspecies (White and Boyce 1988). White (1968) and White and Boyce (1988) described the morphology of the three North American races: *F. p. pealei* (restricted to northern Pacific coastal islands and the Aleutians), *F. p. tundrius* (breeding north of the treeline), and *F. p. anatum* (breeding mainly south of the treeline).

Since the mid-1970s, captive-reared falcons have been released into parts of the former range of *F. p. anatum*, which was nearly extirpated by the 1960s as a result of organochlorine contamination. These birds are the progeny of northern and western *F. p. anatum* parents (released in Canada; Fyfe 1988), and various hybrids of seven subspecies native to North America, South America, Europe, Asia, and Australia (released in the United States; Barclay and Cade 1983).

Migrant and wintering Peregrine Falcons observed in Florida include *F. p. anatum*, *F. p. tundrius* (Ward et al. 1988), and various hybrids of native and introduced subspecies.

DESCRIPTION: Peregrine Falcons are large and powerfully built birds of prey with long, pointed wings typical of falcons. The wingtips of a perched adult extend to the tip of the tail; the wings of juveniles are slightly shorter. Total length is 35–50 cm, and wingspan about 1 m. Weights average about 0.60 kg for males and 0.85 kg for females (Brown and Amadon 1968; Clark

Peregrine Falcon,
Falco peregrinus.
(Photo by Brian A.
Millsap)

and Wheeler 1987; Palmer and White 1988). The sexes are nearly identical in plumage. Plumage characteristics and size vary sufficiently within each sex to preclude reliable sexing in the field.

There is considerable variation in plumage among the 19 subspecies (Palmer and White 1988; White and Boyce 1988). The following features generally describe peregrines observed in Florida. In flight, the undersides of the wings and the medium-length tail are dark. Adults are white to rufous below with dark spots or barring; juveniles are more heavily streaked. The head appears darkly hooded, with a prominent moustachial stripe. Adults have slate-gray backs, whereas juveniles are more brownish with light feather margins. The cere, eye ring, legs, and feet are yellow to yellow-orange, the talons are black, and the irides are very dark brown.

POPULATION SIZE AND TREND: Historically, Peregrine Falcon populations in North America rarely approached the densities found in other parts of the world (Ratcliffe 1980; Kiff 1988). Kiff (1988) reviewed published population estimates and concluded that the continent once supported 7,000 to 10,000 nesting territories, with about 80–90% occupancy in a given year. The eastern United States and maritime Canada probably accounted for only about 400 territories (Kiff 1988). The dramatic decline that began in the 1940s with

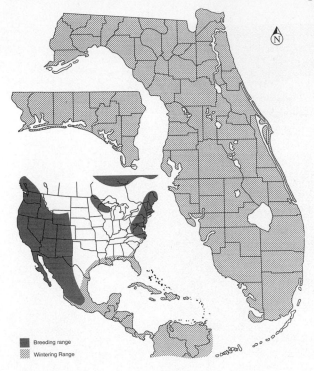

Distribution map of
the Peregrine Falcon,
Falco peregrinus.

the introduction of organochlorine pesticides continued until the mid-1970s.
By 1965, the species was extirpated east of the Mississippi south of the boreal
forest (Ratcliffe 1980; Evans 1982; Kiff 1988; Risebrough and Peakall 1988).
At the population's lowest point in 1975, only 324 active nest sites were
confirmed in North America (Fyfe et al. 1976).

A survey in 1980 indicated that the North American population had at least
stabilized (C. M. White and R. Fyfe, unpubl. ms., cited in Kiff 1988). By
1985, the species clearly was recovering where it still occurred (Kiff 1988).
Analysis of Audubon Society Christmas Bird Counts (CBCs) conducted in
Florida revealed a significant increase in the number of Peregrine Falcons over
the period from 1970 to 1988 (raw data published in *American Birds,* vols.
25–43, 1971–1989).

DISTRIBUTION AND HISTORY OF DISTRIBUTION: Peregrine Falcons
occur on all continents except Antarctica (Brown and Amadon 1968; Palmer
and White 1988). In North America, *F. p. pealei* breeds on the Queen Charlotte Islands, north along Canada's Pacific coast, and throughout the Aleutians; it winters in the southern portion of this range and slightly inland (Evans
1982). *F. p. tundrius* breeds north of the treeline in Alaska, Canada, and
Greenland and winters from the southern United States south to Chile and

Argentina (White 1968; Evans 1982; Palmer and White 1988). *F. p. anatum* formerly bred in northern Mexico, eastern and western Canada north to the treeline, and over most of the United States. Nesting has been reported for all states except Ohio and Florida (Snyder 1978). Since the 1960s, *F. p. anatum's* breeding range has been limited to scattered areas of the western United States and Mexico, Alaska, and northern Canada (Evans 1982; Palmer and White 1988). Northern populations of *F. p. anatum* tend to winter in the southern United States and south to Central America, while southern birds are mainly resident. The extirpated eastern population of *F. p. anatum* wintered along the Atlantic coast (Evans 1982).

Peregrines have been observed throughout Florida during the winter, but are encountered most often near the coasts. For the 22 CBC locations in Florida that were censused each year between 1970 and 1988, inland locations (all peninsular) had Peregrine counts significantly lower than expected by chance.

HABITAT REQUIREMENTS AND HABITAT TRENDS: Although migrant and wintering Peregrine Falcons may occur anywhere in Florida, they rely mainly on open terrain that permits the detection and pursuit of avian prey, which must be abundant and consistently available. Typical habitats include coastal and barrier island shorelines, lake and river margins, prairies, coastal ponds, sloughs, and marshes, and urban areas with adequate prey (Snyder 1978; Evans 1982; Palmer and White 1988).

Sherrod's (1978) summary of nine Peregrine studies indicated that birds comprised 70–100% of the diet. Waterfowl and shorebirds are particularly important prey (Howell 1932; Sprunt 1954; Sherrod 1978). The Peregrine's choice of habitats obviously is related to its prey preferences and foraging methods.

Wetlands in Florida were reduced from about 7,000,000 ha in 1954 to only 1,500,000 ha by 1982 (Mitsch and Gosselink 1986). The development of coastal wetlands, where Peregrines most frequently occur, accounts for much of this habitat loss.

VULNERABILITY OF SPECIES AND HABITAT: The Peregrine Falcon's small numbers, strong site fidelity, and limited distribution in Florida make the species particularly sensitive to changes in habitat. The loss or degradation of wetlands, particularly along the coast, probably reduces the availability of prey.

CAUSES OF THREAT: At present, infrequent direct persecution (shooting, capture) probably has a negligible effect on Peregrine Falcon populations. Migratory birds that accumulate DDT and other organochlorine pesticides in Latin America (Henny et al. 1982; Gilroy and Barclay 1988) are eaten by

Peregrines mainly during the breeding season and migration. Peregrines wintering in Florida feed on species that winter and breed from Florida northward; however, residual DDE in the southeast, resulting from heavy applications of DDT prior to the 1970s, still contaminates top-level predators such as Peregrine Falcons (Beyer and Gish 1980; R. Risebrough, pers. comm.). Currently approved compounds, such as Dicofol, may be a significant source of DDE (Hunt et al. 1986).

The destruction of habitat poses the greatest threat to Peregrine Falcons in Florida. Coastal wetlands, particularly important to the species, suffer the highest rates of development and urbanization. More than 10,500 ha of Florida's wetlands are destroyed each year (Hefner 1990).

RESPONSES TO HABITAT MODIFICATION: Peregrine Falcons exhibit their most notable response to altered habitat during the breeding season, when they nest on buildings, bridges, towers, and other structures in urban and coastal areas with abundant prey. Use of urban sites outside the breeding season has been well documented (Howell 1932; Sprunt 1954; Ratcliffe 1980).

The lack of systematic monitoring of winter populations precludes an analysis of the Peregrine's response to habitat modifications in Florida.

DEMOGRAPHIC CHARACTERISTICS: Most Peregrine Falcons begin breeding at 2 or 3 years of age (Evans 1982; Palmer and White 1988). The clutch usually consists of 3 or 4 eggs (Ratcliffe 1980; Evans 1982). Productivity in healthy populations probably averages between one and two fledged young per egg-laying pair (Brown and Amadon 1968; Ratcliffe 1980). First-year mortality is estimated to be 50–70% (Enderson 1969; Ratcliffe 1980; Palmer and White 1988). The maximum age reported for a wild bird was about 20 years (Enderson 1969), though most adults probably live less than five years after reaching sexual maturity (Brown and Amadon 1968; Ratcliffe 1980; Palmer and White 1988).

KEY BEHAVIORS: Peregrines Falcons arrive in Florida in September and October, typically following the passage of a cold front (Snyder 1978). Wintering birds, which may establish well-defined ranges, begin their northward migration in March (Snyder 1978; Palmer and White 1988). Most wintering and migrating Peregrines have departed the state by late May.

The wingbeat is fairly shallow but rapid and strong; flight is fast, agile, and appears effortless. The Peregrine's hunting style is characterized by inspiring displays of speed, power, and agility. They begin their pursuit of a bird from the air or, perhaps more frequently and successfully, from a perch with a good view of the surrounding terrain (Evans 1982; Palmer and White 1988). The prey may be forced toward the ground or water by repeated dives, struck from the air, or simply grasped in mid-flight (Brown and Amadon 1968; Evans 1982; Palmer and White 1988). This falcon is legendary among raptors for its astonishing ability to seize and subdue a variety of birds that are themselves distinguished as fast, powerful flyers.

CONSERVATION MEASURES TAKEN: *F. p. tundrius* and *F. p. anatum* were listed as endangered by the United States Fish and Wildlife Service (USFWS) in 1970 (Kiff 1988). Captive breeding programs were begun in the late 1960s (Cade 1988) to supply birds for reintroduction into the former range of *F. p. anatum*. Release of captive-reared birds began in 1975 (Barclay 1988), following bans on the use of DDT in the United States and Canada. In 1978, the USFWS moved to permit further reintroductions by granting an unprecedented exception to its policy prohibiting release of non-native stock into the former range of an endangered species (Cade and Dague 1978). By 1985, over 750 Peregrines had been released in the eastern United States (Barclay 1988). By 1988, 61 pairs were known to be breeding in the eastern United States and Canada (Kiff 1988). The relative numbers of wild and captive-reared birds among these breeding pairs can not be determined from published information.

Since the 1960s, some relatively undisturbed areas along the middle and southern Atlantic coasts that apparently serve as staging areas for migrant Peregrines (Palmer and White 1988) have been granted various forms of protection (e.g., National Wildlife Refuges, National Seashores).

Presently, *F. p. anatum* is listed as endangered by the USFWS (FGFWFC 1990). *F. p. tundrius* is listed as threatened by the USFWS and endangered by the Florida Game and Fresh Water Fish Commission (FGFWFC 1990). Although reintroduced birds have no listing status, they are protected under the similarity-of-appearance conditions of the Endangered Species Act.

CONSERVATION MEASURES PROPOSED: The present listing status of the Peregrine Falcon should be maintained. Reintroduction efforts should be phased out, with the lowest priorities given to unnatural sites and areas with no record of former breeding.

A long-term program to monitor the numbers of Peregrines wintering in Florida should be established. Prey preferences should be studied, and densities and contaminant levels of prey species in areas consistently used by migrant and wintering Peregrines should be monitored. The threat of organochlorine contamination would be diminished by restricting the export of domestically banned substances by U. S. manufacturers.

ACKNOWLEDGMENTS: James A. Rodgers provided a thoughtful review of an earlier draft.

LITERATURE CITED:

Barclay, J. H. 1988. Peregrine restoration in the eastern United States. Pp. 549–558 in Peregrine Falcon populations (T. J. Cade, J. H. Enderson, C. G. Thelander, and C. M. White, eds.). The Peregrine Fund, Inc., Boise, Idaho. 949 pp.

Barclay, J. H., and T. J. Cade. 1983. Restoration of the Peregrine Falcon in the eastern United States. Bird Conservation 1:3–37.

Beyer, W. N., and C. D. Gish. 1980. Persistence in earth worms and potential hazards to birds of soil applied DDT, dieldrin, and heptachlor. Jour. Appl. Ecol. 17:295.

Brown, L., and D. Amadon. 1968. Eagles, hawks and falcons of the world, vol. 1. Country Life Books, London. 414 pp.

Cade, T. J. 1988. The breeding of Peregrines and other falcons in captivity: an historical perspective. Pp. 539–548 in Peregrine Falcon populations (T. J. Cade, J. H. Enderson, C. G. Thelander, and C. M. White, eds.). The Peregrine Fund, Inc., Boise, Idaho. 949 pp.

Cade, T. J., and P. R. Dague. 1978. Peregrine politics. P. 6 in The Peregrine Fund Newsletter, no. 6 (T. J. Cade and P. R. Dague, eds.). Cornell Univ. Lab. Ornith., Ithaca, New York. 12 pp.

Clark, W. S., and B. K. Wheeler. 1987. A field guide to the hawks of North America. Houghton Mifflin, Boston, Massachusetts. 198 pp.

Enderson, J. H. 1969. Coastal migration data as population indices for the Peregrine Falcon. Pp. 275–278 in Peregrine Falcon Populations: their biology and decline (J. J. Hickey, ed.). Univ. Wisconsin Press, Madison, Wisconsin. 596 pp.

Evans, D. L. 1982. Status reports on twelve raptors. Spec. Sci. Rept., Wildl., no. 238. U.S. Fish and Wildlife Service, Washington, D.C. 68 pp.

FGFWFC. 1990. Official lists of endangered and potentially endangered fauna and flora in Florida. Fla. Game and Fresh Water Fish Comm., Tallahassee, Florida. 3 pp.

Fyfe, R. W. 1988. The Canadian Peregrine Falcon recovery program. Pp. 599–610 in Peregrine Falcon populations (T. J. Cade, J. H. Enderson, C. G. Thelander, and C. M. White, eds.). The Peregrine Fund, Inc., Boise, Idaho. 949 pp.

Fyfe, R. W., S. A. Temple, and T. J. Cade. 1976. The 1975 North American Peregrine Falcon survey. Can. Field Nat. 90:228–273.

Gilroy, M. J., and J. H. Barclay. 1988. DDE residues and eggshell characteristics of reestablished Peregrines in the eastern United States. Pp. 403–412 in Peregrine Falcon populations (T. J. Cade, J. H. Enderson, C. G. Thelander, and C. M. White, eds.). The Peregrine Fund, Inc., Boise, Idaho. 949 pp.

Hefner, J. 1990. Florida's wetlands fact sheet. National Wetlands Inventory, U.S. Fish and Wildlife Service, Atlanta, Georgia. 5 pp.

Henny, C. J., F. P. Ward, K. E. Riddle, and R. M. Prouty. 1982. Migratory Peregrine Falcons, *Falco peregrinus,* accumulate pesticides in Latin America during winter. Can. Field Nat. 96:333–338.

Howell, A. H. 1932. Florida bird life. Cowan-McCann, Inc., New York. 579 pp.

Hunt, W. G., B. S. Johnson, C. G. Thelander, B. J. Walton, R. W. Risebrough, W. M. Jarman, A. M. Springer, J. G. Monk, and W. Walker. 1986. Environmental levels of p,p,' DDE indicate multiple sources. Environ. Toxicol. Chem. 5:21–27.

Kiff, L. F. 1988. Changes in the status of the Peregrine in North America. Pp. 123–140 in Peregrine Falcon populations (T. J. Cade, J. H. Enderson, C. G. Thelander, and C. M. White, eds.). The Peregrine Fund, Inc., Boise, Idaho. 949 pp.

Mitsch, W. J., and J. G. Gosselink. 1986. Wetlands. Van Nostrand Reinhold, New York. 539 pp.

Morizot, D. C. 1988. Biochemical genetic variability in Peregrine Falcon populations. Pp. 773–778 in Peregrine Falcon populations (T. J. Cade, J. H. Enderson, C. G. Thelander, and C. M. White, eds.). The Peregrine Fund, Inc., Boise, Idaho. 949 pp.

Palmer, R. S., and C. M. White. 1988. Peregrine Falcon. Pp. 324–380 in Handbook of North American birds, vol. 5, diurnal raptors, part 2 (R. S. Palmer, ed.). Yale Univ. Press, New Haven, Connecticut. 465 pp.

Ratcliffe, D. 1980. The Peregrine Falcon. Buteo Books, Vermillion, South Dakota. 416 pp.

Risebrough, R. W., and D. B. Peakall. 1988. Commentary: the relative importance of the several organochlorines in the decline of Peregrine Falcon populations. Pp. 449–462 in Peregrine Falcon populations (T. J. Cade, J. H. Enderson, C. G. Thelander, and C. M. White, eds.). The Peregrine Fund, Inc., Boise, Idaho. 949 pp.

Sherrod, S. K. 1978. Diets of North American Falconiformes. Raptor Res. 12:49–121.

Snyder, H. 1978. Peregrine Falcon. Pp. 7–8 in Rare and endangered biota of Florida, vol. 2, birds (H. W. Kale, II, ed.). Univ. Presses of Florida, Gainesville, Florida. 121 pp.

Sprunt, A., Jr. 1954. Florida bird life. Cowan-McCann, Inc., New York. 527 pp.

Ward, F. P., K. Titus, W. S. Seegar, M. A. Yates, and M. R. Fuller. 1988. Autumn migrations of Peregrine Falcons at Assateague Island, Maryland/Virginia, 1970–1984. Pp. 485–496 in Peregrine Falcon populations (T. J.

Cade, J. H. Enderson, C. G. Thelander, and C. M. White, eds.). The Peregrine Fund, Inc., Boise, Idaho. 949 pp.

White, C. M. 1968. Biosystematics of the North American Peregrine Falcons. Ph.D. dissertation, Univ. of Utah, Salt Lake City, Utah.

White, C. M., and D. A. Boyce, Jr. 1988. An overview of Peregrine Falcon subspecies. Pp. 789–812 in Peregrine Falcon populations (T. J. Cade, J. H. Enderson, C. G. Thelander, and C. M. White, eds.). The Peregrine Fund, Inc., Boise, Idaho. 949 pp.

PREPARED BY: Kenneth D. Meyer and John A. Smallwood, Department of Wildlife Ecology Conservation, 118 Newins-Ziegler Hall, University of Florida, Gainesville, FL 32611 (Current address of KDM: National Park Service, Big Cypress National Preserve, Box 110, Ochopee, FL 33943; JAS: Department of Biology, Montclair State University, Upper Monclair, NJ 07043).

Piping Plover

Charadrius melodus

FAMILY CHARADRIIDAE

Order Charadriiformes

TAXONOMY: The Piping Plover (*Charadrius melodus*), originally considered a race of the Ringed Plover (*C. hiaticula*), was first described as a separate species *Aegialitis meloda* by Ord in 1824. The American Ornithologists' Union (AOU 1931) checklist of 1931 returned the binomial to the present *C. melodus*. The AOU has fluctuated between accepting and rejecting the designation of two subspecies; *C. m. melodus* (coastal population) and *C. m. circumcinctus* (interior population). Moser (1942) argued for subspecies designation based on breast band patterns and geographic distribution. However, Wilcox (1959) reputed this breast band distinction finding a variety of patterns in plovers breeding on Long Island, New York. Additionally, Haig and Oring (1988a) conducted electrophoretic analyses and did not find significant genetic differences between populations sampled in Saskatchewan, Manitoba, Minnesota, and New Brunswick. The subspecies designation is currently maintained by the AOU (1957, 1983), but is under review for the next edition. Additional morphological analyses and more sophisticated genetic techniques may be needed to resolve this issue (Haig 1990).

DESCRIPTION: The Piping Plover is a small migratory shorebird about 17–18 cm (7 in.) long with a wingspread of about 38 cm (15 in.) (Johnsgard 1981) and weighing 46–64 g (average of 55 g).

Breeding birds are characterized by a single black breast and forehead band and an orange bill tipped with black (Hayman et al. 1986). There are subtle morphological differences between the sexes; males are generally brighter overall with a more complete breast band and prominent white eye-line. Like other shorebird species, Piping Plovers appear drab in winter plumage. Although the legs remain orange, the black on the forehead and breast band fade to lateral gray patches. Adults and juveniles are similar in appearance on the wintering grounds, with the juveniles acquiring their adult plumage the spring

Piping Plover,
*Charadrius
melodus.* (Photo
by John Sidle)

after they fledge (Prater et al. 1977). General features that separate the Piping
Plover from the other five North American belted plovers include: sandy-
colored upperparts, white undersides, bright orange legs, and a white patch
across the upper-tail coverts contrasting with the back color (Haig 1990). In
Florida, wintering Piping Plovers can be confused with the Semipalmated
Plover (*C. semipalmatus*) and the Snowy Plover (*C. alexandrinus*). Semipalmated Plovers are darker overall in plumage with no color contrast between
the back and upper-tail coverts, whereas Snowy Plovers are lighter with thinner bills and black legs.

POPULATION SIZE AND TREND: Historical population estimates of Piping Plovers consist primarily of sporadic anecdotal reports; however, there is
evidence that the species experienced a serious decline in numbers across its
breeding range (Cairns and MacLaren 1980; Haig and Oring 1985; Haig and
Oring 1987). During the Market Hunting Era of the early 1900s, the Piping
Plover was shot like many other shorebird species to near extinction for the
millinery trade. The passage of the Migratory Bird Treaty Act of 1918 allowed
for partial recovery of the population (Bent 1929; Wilcox 1939; Griscom and
Snyder 1955). After the 1940s, increased human development and recreation
on the Atlantic Coast contributed to another downward spiral (Tate 1981;
USFWS 1985). This population trend in the Piping Plover prompted national
attention as increased disturbance and vulnerability warranted inclusion in the
National Audubon Society's 1973 "Blue List" of threatened species (Arbib
1974; Tate 1981). The Canadian Committee on the Status of Endangered

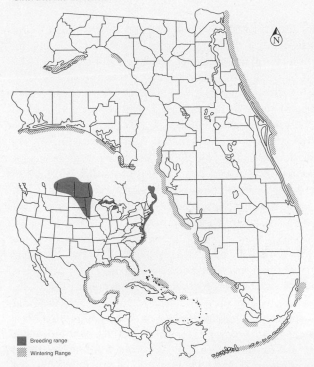

Distribution map of
the Piping Plover,
Charadrius melodus.

Breeding range

Wintering Range

Wildlife declared it as a threatened species in 1978, then elevated it to endangered status by 1985 (Haig 1987). By January 1986, the U.S. Fish and Wildlife Service listed the species as endangered in the Great Lakes region and threatened throughout the remainder of its range (USFWS 1985).

Present North American population estimates reflecting the 1994 breeding season are as follows: 1,250–1,255 breeding pairs in the Great Plains, 19 pairs in the Great Lakes, and 1,150 pairs on the Atlantic Coast. An intensive rangewide survey was conducted across the species' range as part of the 1991 International Piping Plover Census. Population estimates for the 1991 census were as follows: 1,485 breeding pairs in the Great Plains, 17 pairs in the Great Lakes, and 938 pairs on the Atlantic coast. The increased survey effort and coverage during the 1991 census make a comparison with previous years difficult. However, a 4-year trend from 1987–1990 indicates the species has declined 16–20% in the Great Plains, stabilized in the Great Lakes, and increased about 2.0–3.5% on the Atlantic Coast (USFWS 1991). Prolonged drought and inappropriate water regulation policies are believed partially responsible for the decline in the prairie states, whereas intensive monitoring and management may have contributed to the increase in the Great Lakes and Atlantic Coast breeding populations. Little information is available on population trends for wintering areas. Raithel (1985) summarized 14 years of National Audubon Society Christmas Bird Count data (1969–1982) and found evidence of declines at several sites. Haig and Oring (1985) and Nicholls and Baldassarre (1990a) conducted the first on-site assessments of winter populations and found about 25 and 43%, respectively, of the known breeding population. In the latter survey, a total of 375 plovers were observed in Florida; 24 on the Atlantic and 351 on the Gulf coasts. It is impossible to quantify an increase or decrease in plover numbers in Florida because there are no prior population estimates. However, the numbers of nonbreeding Piping Plovers recorded in a single year in Florida CBCs is less than 100 over the last 10 years. The 1991 International Census contributed substantial information on wintering plovers and a total of 582 plovers were sighted in Florida; 71 on the Atlantic and 511 on the Gulf coasts. This census represented the most comprehensive effort to date to locate wintering birds.

DISTRIBUTION AND HISTORY OF DISTRIBUTION: The historical breeding range for the Piping Plover included: the northern Great Plains, from Saskatchewan to Ontario and south to Nebraska; the Great Lakes Region; and the Atlantic Coast from maritime Canada to North Carolina (Haig and Oring 1985). The species still maintains this regional breeding distribution, but is locally absent from many former nesting beaches (Cairns and MacLaren 1980; Raithel 1984). Indeed, the species has been nearly extirpated from the Great Lakes, with nesting restricted to the Lake Superior and Lake Michigan shorelines in Michigan (Haig and Oring 1985).

Historical records documenting the winter distribution of Piping Plovers are scarce. National Audubon Society Christmas Bird Count data provide a crude delineation of plover winter distribution allowing areas of concentration to be identified (Raithel 1985). Even with recent winter surveys, only 10–15% of breeding plovers can be accounted for during the winter (Haig and Oring 1985; Nicholls and Baldassarre 1990a) on the Atlantic Coast. A large percentage (about 60–80%) of the interior breeding population can be accounted for during the winter along the U.S. Gulf coast. Winter distribution on the Atlantic Coast is uneven with birds found in small groups (average of 6) from North Carolina to Florida. On the Gulf Coast, plovers seem to occur in larger groups (average of 20) from Florida to Texas. A few anecdotal accounts mention that Piping Plovers winter sporadically in the Caribbean (Wetmore and Swales 1931; Bond 1947; Maurice 1953; Raffaele 1983; Haig and Oring 1985). The paucity of wintering birds on the Atlantic Coast highlights the need for information on migratory routes and for more extensive surveys in the Caribbean. Numerous museum records and CBCs indicate that Piping Plovers regularly overwintered in the following counties in Florida: Bay, Brevard, Broward, Collier, Dade, Duval, Escambia, Franklin, Gulf, Hillsborough, Indian River, Lee, Monroe, Nassau, Palm Beach, Pinellas, St. Johns, St. Lucie,

Sarasota, Volusia, and Wakulla. Plovers are believed to no longer winter in Broward, Indian River, Nassau and Palm Beach counties (USFWS 1988, 1995) and are rare in Brevard, Dade, Hillsborough, Sarasota, Volusia, and Wakulla Counties (Nicholls 1989; USFWS 1995). Presently, Piping Plovers utilize northeastern beaches from Jacksonville to Fort Pierce (except Indian River Co.), and mudflats around the Miami area. On the Gulf Coast, plovers are reliably found scattered along panhandle beaches from Perdido Key (Escambia County) to Dog Island (Franklin County), and from the Tampa/ St. Petersburg area (Pinellas County) to Marco Island (Collier County). A small population overwinters in the Keys (Nicholls 1989).

HABITAT REQUIREMENTS AND HABITAT TREND: The Piping Plover nests on sandy beaches along the Atlantic Coast and Great Lakes, and on river sandbars and shallow alkali wetlands throughout the Great Plains region (USFWS 1985). Piping Plovers are primarily associated with barrier beach systems during the wintering period. Haig and Oring (1985) found plovers on sandy beaches adjacent to inlets on their winter survey of the Gulf of Mexico. Similarly, Nicholls and Baldassarre (1990b) observed plovers on accreting ends of barrier islands and spits, at coastal inlets, and on low-lying barrier islands with overwash intertidal flats. In this study, comparisons along 36 Atlantic Coast and 75 Gulf Coast wintering sites indicated that foraging activity was most associated with sandflats (27%), mudflats (25%), sandy-mudflats (32%), and occasionally lower beach or foreshore (10%) and dredge spoil (6%). Roosting birds were primarily observed along the upper beach or berm area adjacent to intertidal feeding areas. However, more roosting sites need to be located and characterized to determine specific features because few roosting birds were found (Nicholls and Baldassarre 1990b). Nicholls and Baldassare (1990b) noted that sites with the highest concentrations of plovers such as Honeymoon Island State Recreation Area and Fort Desoto County Park (Pinellas County) consist of complex systems with expansive sand/mudflats in close proximity. These diverse coastal systems may concentrate plovers because of the juxtaposition of foraging and roosting areas. Winter habitat loss is difficult to document, but historical data suggests that degradation has occurred along portions of the Atlantic and Gulf coasts (Baldassarre 1986; Dyer et al. 1988; USFWS 1988, 1994, 1995). For example, on the Atlantic Coast of Florida, plovers were considered abundant from July to August (Bent 1929; Stevenson 1960), but now only number from 20–30 birds, excluding the Keys (Nicholls 1989).

VULNERABILITY OF SPECIES AND HABITAT: Piping Plovers utilize ephemeral wetland habitats throughout their annual cycle. These transitory habitats are created and maintained by natural processes such as inlet movements and breakthroughs, storm overwashes, and sandbar formation and scouring. Man has increasingly tried to control these natural processes by stabilizing inlets and shorelines and building extensive dune systems. Purportedly, this has caused both direct and indirect losses of nesting and overwintering habitat (USFWS 1985, 1988, 1994, 1995). In Florida, numerous manmade structures such as seawalls, jetties, and groins are present, which may have reduced wintering plover habitat by eliminating foraging and roosting areas (USDI 1985). Also, increased recreational activities in Florida may have contributed to habitat loss. It is anticipated that several important wintering sites in Florida may be eliminated or functionally altered in the near future due to human development and recreational pressure (Nicholls 1989).

CAUSES OF THREAT: Loss of sandy beaches and other littoral habitats due to recreational and commercial developments and inlet/dune stabilization on the Great Lakes, Atlantic Coast, and Gulf of Mexico are partially responsible for the decline of the Piping Plover (Bent 1929; Flemming 1984; Haig and Oring 1985; USFWS 1985, 1994, 1995). Recently, an increased human population along the Atlantic Coast has created numerous pressures on breeding birds. Factors associated with this growth such as off-road vehicle and pedestrian traffic, unleashed pets, and an unnatural proliferation of predators have curtailed productivity (Cairns 1977; Erwin 1979; Drury and Kadlec 1984; Flemming 1984; Burger 1987; MacIvor et al. 1985; Hoopes et al. 1990).

Threats to wintering birds are still relatively unknown. During their winter surveys, Nicholls and Baldassarre (1990a) noted a variety of manmade disturbance factors along the Atlantic and Gulf coasts that may affect Piping Plover survival and utilization of wintering habitat. These included recreational traffic, inlet or shoreline stabilization features, dredging of inlets, beach maintenance and restoration, and even pollution (i.e., oil spills). Although Nicholls and Baldassarre (1990a) implied these factors may disrupt foraging or roosting birds, the exact degree and mechanism still needs to be determined.

RESPONSES TO HABITAT MODIFICATION: Piping Plovers have been observed foraging on dredge spoil during the wintering period on both the Atlantic and Gulf coasts (Nicholls 1989; R. Martin, pers. comm.; T. Eubanks, pers. comm.). Although there is no specific published information available, wintering Piping Plovers are probably adversely affected by manmade alterations in the amount and quality of feeding and roosting habitat.

DEMOGRAPHIC CHARACTERISTICS: Piping Plovers arrive on their breeding grounds from late March to early May and set up nesting territories. Generally, 3–4 eggs are laid in a shallow depression often near a clump of vegetation or large bits of debris. Incubation lasts for about 27–30 days and is shared by both parents (Haig 1987). The precocial chicks leave the nest immediately after hatching, but remain with the parents on the nesting territory until fledging at 28–35 days (Whyte 1985; Haig 1987). Piping Plovers will renest if their initial clutch is lost, but rarely raise more than one brood per year. Average productivity is difficult to gauge since it is dependent on numerous factors and varies greatly from site to site. Plovers will breed the first spring after hatching with most birds breeding each year (Wilcox 1959; Haig 1987). Mortality during migration and the first winter is largely unknown but is believed to be quite high. Minimum average life span is 3–5 years, with some birds known to have lived up to 14 years (Wilcox 1962).

KEY BEHAVIORS: A growing volume of literature addresses breeding biology and behavior (Wilcox 1959; Cairns 1982; Whyte 1985; Haig 1987; USFWS 1994, 1995), yet little is known about wintering Piping Plovers. Johnson and Baldassarre (1988) conducted a time budget study on a wintering population in Mobile Bay, Alabama, and found that plovers spend 76% of their time foraging, 19% roosting, and 5% in alert, agonistic, and territorial behaviors. Johnson and Baldassarre (1988) suggested that plovers may need to maintain a high foraging effort during winter because of high energy requirements associated with winter conditions. The Piping Plover forages in the Stop-run-peck style characteristic of plovers (Pienkowski 1982; Johnson and Baldassarre 1988). They also will Foot-tap, trembling the foot on the substrate, which may stimulate movement of invertebrates to the surface (Evans 1976; Pienkowski 1983). Little is known about the species' diet. Fecal samples collected and analyzed from birds wintering along the Gulf of Mexico Coast indicated the presence of the following invertebrate phyla: Mollusca, Annelida, Arthropoda, Crustacea, and Nematoda (Nicholls 1989).

Piping Plovers make local movements during the wintering period depending on tidal and weather conditions (Zivojnovich and Baldassarre 1987). Plovers may concentrate when or where feeding conditions are optimal (i.e., receding tide). Roosting or loafing is believed to occur during high tides when intertidal flats are submerged. Roosting behavior involves either standing on one leg with the bill tucked into back plumage or sitting huddled in the sand. During both feeding and roosting, Piping Plovers tend to occur in mixed flocks of shorebirds, often keeping together within these groups (Nicholls and Baldassarre 1990b). Intra- and interspecific interactions are poorly understood but may involve agonistic and territorial displays similar to those observed on the breeding areas (Johnson 1987).

Little is known about specific migration routes or sites. However, from winter sightings of birds banded on the breeding grounds, plovers from interior breeding sites generally overwinter on the Gulf of Mexico Coast, while the Atlantic Coast birds move further down the Atlantic coast to winter (Haig and

Oring 1988b). Winter site fidelity is believed to be relatively high (Johnson and Baldassarre 1988; Fussell 1990; T. Eubanks, pers. comm.; T. Below, pers. comm.).

CONSERVATION MEASURES TAKEN: During the past decade there has been an explosion of interest in the Piping Plover at the state and federal levels as well as among private conservation groups. Following the species' official listing, inland and Atlantic coast Recovery Teams were appointed in both the United States and Canada. These recovery teams formulated long-term management plans for the species' recovery and have cooperated in implementing recovery tasks. Local conservation efforts have focused primarily on breeding birds and have included a variety of intensive and often innovative management activities, including nest monitoring, roping off nesting or feeding areas, restricting pedestrian and off-road vehicle traffic near nesting areas, construction of predator exclosures around nest sites, trapping and removing avian and mammalian predators, creation of artificial nesting habitat, and public education.

To date, efforts to protect wintering plovers and their habitat have been minimal. However, the U.S. Fish and Wildlife Service has conducted several biological consultations regarding potential impacts of Federally authorized projects on wintering Piping Plovers to ensure that these actions do not jeopardize the continued existence of the species. Data collected from the 1991 International Census will greatly enhance efforts by state and federal biologists to protect plover wintering habitat. Recent recovery team designations of representatives from wintering areas also should be a positive step toward addressing winter recovery needs. The U.S. Fish and Wildlife Service is reviewing the potential acquisition of Ohio Key, an important wintering area in the Florida Keys.

CONSERVATION MEASURES PROPOSED: Intensive monitoring and management of Piping Plover breeding sites is anticipated to continue. The recovery teams realize that a comprehensive management program also must incorporate strategies to understand and protect wintering birds and have outlined specific conservation needs in their respective recovery plans (USFWS 1994, 1995). Survey and monitoring efforts are preliminary goals. Despite extensive coverage during the International Census, knowledge of winter distribution is not complete. The International Census hopefully will be repeated every 5 years (the next census is scheduled for 1996), which should further elucidate winter distribution and relative site importance. Coordinated annual censuses of select wintering sites are needed to help monitor population status and trends. Winter ecology research should focus on determining winter habitat characteristics, interspecific associations, prey preferences and diet, local movements, and potential disturbance factors. Protection of preferred feeding and roosting areas from development or other human disturbance may be warranted (Johnson and Baldassare 1988; Fussell 1990; Nicholls and Baldassarre 1990a). Considering the fact that Piping Plovers spend up to 7–8 months of their annual cycle on wintering areas underscores the importance in addressing conservation priorities for nonbreeding birds (Haig and Oring 1985).

ACKNOWLEDGMENTS: I sincerely thank Dr. Guy A. Baldassarre for his assistance and support during my research on this species and David P. Flemming for providing the opportunity to be involved in Piping Plover recovery. I am grateful to William C. Hunter and Andrew C. Eller, Jr. for reviewing and providing comments on this manuscript.

LITERATURE CITED:

AOU. 1931. Checklist of North American birds. Fourth ed. American Ornithologists' Union, Washington, D.C.

AOU. 1957. Checklist of North American birds. Fifth ed. American Ornithologists' Union, Washington, D.C.

AOU. 1983. Checklist of North American birds. Sixth ed. American Ornithologists' Union, Lawrence, Kansas.

Arbib, R. 1974. The Blue List for 1975. Amer. Birds 29:1067–1077.

Baldassarre, G. A. 1986. Pp. 90–91 in Vertebrate animals of special concern in Alabama (Robert Mount, ed.). Alabama Agric. Exper. Station, Auburn, Alabama.

Bent, A. C. 1929. Life histories of North American shorebirds. U.S. Natl. Mus. Bulletin 146:236–246.

Bond, J. 1947. Field guide to birds of West Indies. MacMillan Co., N. Y. 77 pp.

Burger, J. 1987. Physical and social determinants of nest site selection in Piping Plovers in New Jersey. Condor 89:881–818.

Cairns, W. E. 1977. Breeding biology and behavior of the piping plover *Charadrius melodus* in southern Nova Scotia. M.Sc. thesis. Dalhousie Univ., Halifax, Nova Scotia. 155 pp.

Cairns, W. E. 1982. Biology and behavior of breeding Piping Plovers. Wilson Bull. 94:531–545.

Cairns, W. E., and I. A. MacLaren. 1980. Status of the Piping Plover on the east coast of North America. Amer. Birds 34:206–208.

Drury, W. H., and J. A. Kadlec. 1974. The current status of the Herring Gull population in the northeastern United States. Bird Banding 45:297–306.

Dyer, R. W., A. Hecht, C. Raithel, K. Terwilliger, and S. Melvin. 1987. Atlantic Coast piping plover recovery plan. U.S. Fish and Wildl. Serv. Region 5. Newton Corner, Massachusetts. 74 pp.

Erwin, R. M. 1979. Historical breeding records of colonial seabirds, 1900–1977, Cape Elizabeth Maine to Virginia. Supplement to final report prepared for U.S. Fish and Wildlife Service, Coastal Ecosystems Project, Washington, D.C.

Evans, P. R. 1976. Energy balance and optimal foraging strategies in shorebirds: some implications for their distributions and movements in the nonbreeding season. Ardea 64:117–139.

Flemming, S. 1984. The status and responses of piping plovers to recreational activity in Nova Scotia. B.S. honors thesis, Acadia University, Wolfville, Nova Scotia.

Fussell, J. 1990. Census of wintering piping plovers on the North Carolina Coast. Final proj. rept. submitted to North Carolina Wildl. Res. Comm., Raleigh, North Carolina. 58 pp.

Griscom, L., and D. E. Synder. 1955. The birds of Massachusetts. Peabody Museum, Salem, Massachusetts. 88 pp.

Haig, S. M. 1987. Population biology, and life history patterns of the Piping Plover. Ph.D. dissertation. Univ. of North Dakota, Grand Forks, North Dakota.

Haig, S. M. In press. The Piping Plover. American Ornithologists' Union avian species biography series. 63 pp.

Haig, S. M., and L. W. Oring. 1985. The distribution and status of the Piping Plover throughout the annual cycle. Jour. Field Ornith. 56:334–345.

Haig, S. M., and L. W. Oring. 1987. The Piping Plover. Pp. 509–518 in Audubon Wildlife Report (Roger L. Di Silvestro, ed.). National Audubon Society, Academic Press, N.Y.

Haig, S. M., and L. W. Oring. 1988a. Genetic differentiation of Piping Plovers across North America. Auk 105:260–267.

Haig, S. M., and L. W. Oring. 1988b. Distribution and dispersal in the Piping Plover. Auk 105:630–638.

Hayman, P., J. Marchant, and T. Prater. 1986. Shorebirds: an identification guide. Houghton Mifflin Co. Boston, Massachusetts. 412 pp.

Hoopes, E. M., C. R. Griffin, and S. M. Melvin. 1990. Relationships between human recreation on Piping Plover foraging ecology and chick survival. Progress report submitted to U.S. Fish and Wildl. Serv.. Amherst, Massachusetts. 21 pp.

Johnsgard, P. A. 1981. The plovers, sandpipers, and snipes of the world. Univ. of Nebraska press. Lincoln, Nebraska. 493 pp.

Johnson, C. M. 1987. Aspects of the winter ecology of the piping plover in coastal Alabama. M.S. thesis. Auburn University, Auburn, Alabama. 39 pp.

Johnson, C. M., and G. A. Baldassarre. 1988. Aspects of the wintering ecology of Piping Plovers in coastal Alabama. Wilson Bull. 100:14–233.

MacIvor, L. M., C. R. Griffin, and S. M. Melvin. 1985. Management, habitat selection, and population dynamics of piping plovers on Outer Cape Cod, Massachusetts. Unpubl. rept. Univ. of Mass., Amherst, Massachusetts.

Maurice, C. 1953. Birds of Bimini. Auk 70:38–48.

Moser, R. A. 1942. Should the belted Piping Plover be recognized as a valid race? Nebraska Bird Rev. 10:31–37.

Nicholls, J. L. 1989. Distribution and other ecological aspects of Piping Plovers wintering along the Atlantic and Gulf Coasts. M.S. thesis, Auburn University, Auburn, Alabama. 164 pp.

Nicholls, J. L., and G. A. Baldassarre. 1990a. Winter distribution of Piping Plovers along the Atlantic and Gulf Coasts of the United States. Wilson Bull. 102:400–412.

Nicholls, J. L., and G. A. Baldassarre. 1990b. Habitat associations of Piping Plovers wintering in the United States. Wilson Bull. 102:581–590.

Pienkowski, M. W. 1981. How foraging plovers cope with environmental effects on invertebrate behavior and availability. Pp. 179–182 in Feeding and survival strategies of estuarine organisms (N. V. Jones and W. J. Wolff, eds.). Plenum Press, N.Y.

Pienkowski, M. W. 1982. Surface activity of some intertidal invertebrates in relation to temperature and the foraging behavior of their shorebird predators. Marine Ecol. 11:141–150.

Pienkowski, M. W. 1983. Changes in the foraging patterns of plovers in relation to environmental factors. Anim. Behav. 31:244–264.

Prater, A. J., J. H. Marchant, and J. Vuorinen. 1977. Guide to the identification and ageing of Holarctic waders. British Trust for Ornithology. Guide no. 17. Maund and Irvine Ltd. Beech Grove, Tring, Herts.

Raffaele, J. 1983. A guide to the birds of Puerto Rico and the Virgin Islands. Fondo Interamericano, Rio Piedras, Puerto Rico. 249 pp.

Raithel, C. 1984. The Piping plover in Rhode Island. Unpubl. ms. 16 pp.

Raithel, C. 1985. An analysis of piping plover winter population trends using Christmas Bird Count data. Unpubl. ms. 20 pp.

Stevenson, H. 1960. A key to Florida birds. Peninsula Publ. Co., Tallahassee, Florida. 158 pp.

Tate, J. 1981. The blue list for 1981. Amer. Birds 35:3–10.

USDI. 1985. Coastal barrier resources system. Draft report to Congress. Washington, D.C. 466 pp.

USFWS. 1985. Determination of endangered and threatened status for the Piping Plover. Fed. Reg. 50(238):50720–50734.

USFWS. 1988. Great Lakes and Northern Great Plains Piping Plover Recovery Plan. U.S. Fish and Wildl. Serv., Twin Cities, Minnesota. 160 pp.

USFWS. 1991. Summary of the U.S. Atlantic Coast Piping Plover. Northeast Region, Newton Corner, Massachusetts 70 pp.

USFWS. 1994. Recovery plan for Piping Plovers breeding on the Great Lakes and northern Great Plains of the United States. Technical/Agency draft. U.S. Fish and Wildl. Serv., Twin Cities, Minnesota.

USFWS. 1995. Piping Plover, Atlantic coast population. Revised recovery plan. Technical/Agency draft. U.S. Fish and Wildl. Serv., Hadley, Massachusetts.

Wetmore, A., and B. H. Swales. 1931. Birds of Haiti and the Dominican Republic. Bull. U.S. Nat. Museum 155. Smithsonian Institution Press. Washington, D.C. 483 pp.

Whyte, A. J. 1985. Breeding ecology of the piping plover in central Saskatchewan. M.S. thesis, Univ. of Saskatchewan. Saskatoon, Saskatchewan.

Wilcox, L. 1939. Notes on the life history of the Piping Plover. Birds of Long Island 1:343.

Wilcox, L. 1959. A twenty year banding study of the Piping Plover. Auk 76:129–152.

Wilcox, L. 1962. Oldest known shorebird in North America. East. Bird Band. Assoc. :45–46.

Zivojnovich, M., and G. A. Baldassarre. 1987. Habitat selection, movements, and numbers of piping plovers wintering in coastal Alabama. Final rept. to Alabama Dep. Conser. Nat. Res. Auburn, Alabama. 16 pp.

PREPARED BY: Janice L. Nicholls, U.S. Fish and Wildlife Service, Asheville Field Office, 160 Zillicoa Street, Asheville, NC 28801.

Cuban Snowy Plover

Charadrius alexandrinus tenuirostris

FAMILY CHARADRIIDAE

Order Charadriiformes

TAXONOMY: The Snowy Plover (*Charadrius alexandrinus*) is widely distributed and several subspecies are recognized (AOU 1957; Johnsgard 1981). Two subspecies occur in North America. *C. a. nivosus* occurs west of the Rocky Mountains; *C. a. tenuirostris,* the Cuban Snowy Plover, occurs east of the Rocky Mountains and is the form found in Florida. Recent reviews have considered all Snowy Plovers in North America as *C. a. nivosus* (Hayman et al. 1986; Sibley and Monroe 1990).

DESCRIPTION: Snowy Plovers are about 17 cm long with a wingspan of 30 cm. The plumage is pale gray or brown above and pure white below. The bill and legs are dark. Breeding males show a black band on the forehead, a black ear patch, and a black shoulder patch or partial collar. On breeding females these markings are lighter and less prominent. In winter, the dark markings on the head and shoulders become brownish and indistinct, and both sexes appear similar. The winter plumage of juveniles is like that of adults, except many of the feathers have a buffy tip.

POPULATION SIZE AND TREND: Several surveys have been conducted to estimate the abundance of Snowy Plovers in western North America (Page et al. 1991), but similar quantitative data are lacking for the eastern subspecies (Page et al. 1995). Boyd (1981a) found 129 Snowy Plover nests at five sites in Kansas and Oklahoma, and as many as 1,000 breeding pairs occur throughout the Great Plains (Page et al. 1995). Fewer than 300 pairs are thought to breed along the Gulf Coast (Page et al. 1995).

Woolfenden (1978) speculated that fewer than 100 breeding pairs of Snowy Plovers remained in Florida. Chase and Gore (1989) surveyed the eastern Gulf coast and found at least 167 pairs bred in Florida in 1989. Their survey was most complete in northwest Florida where they found 145 (87%) of the

Cuban Snowy Plover, *Charadrius alexandrinus tenuirostris*. (Photo copyright by Allan D. Cruickshank, courtesy of Florida Audubon Society)

Snowy Plover nests. Subsequent surveys suggest a more accurate estimate for Florida is between 170–200 breeding pairs of Snowy Plovers, including about 30 pairs (15–18%) in south Florida (C. A. Chase, pers. comm.). The coasts of Alabama and Mississippi, including offshore islands, probably support an additional 30 breeding pairs (Chase and Gore 1989).

Given the absence of earlier estimates of population size, it is impossible to quantitatively identify any trends in Snowy Plover populations. Nevertheless, the increasing human population in Florida has clearly caused substantial losses of open beaches over the past few decades, particularly in south Florida. This undoubtedly has resulted in marked declines in available nesting habitat and, consequently, in the number of breeding Snowy Plovers.

DISTRIBUTION AND HISTORY OF DISTRIBUTION: The Snowy Plover occurs along sandy coastlines and sparsely vegetated interior plains throughout the world (Johnsgard 1981). Breeding distribution includes suitable coastal and interior habitats across the Eurasian continent from Sweden and Siberia south to China, India, and the Mediterranean Sea; along coastal North Africa and the Red Sea; along the western coast of South America; and throughout most of the Bahamas, Antilles, and coastal Venezuela (AOU 1983). In North America, the western subspecies, *C. a. nivosus,* occurs along the Pacific Coast from Washington south to Baja California and is locally common in inland desert regions from Washington south to Arizona (Page et al. 1991). *C. a. tenuirostris,* the subspecies found in Florida, breeds along the coast of the Gulf of Mexico from Mexico and Texas to Florida and throughout the Caribbean (AOU 1983). The eastern subspecies also breeds locally on interior plains from Kansas and Colorado south to New Mexico and north-central Texas. Snowy Plovers are present throughout the year on the Gulf coast.

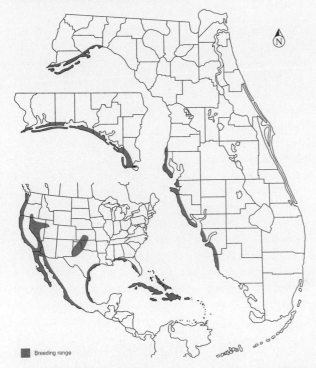

Breeding range

Distribution map of the Cuban Snowy Plover, *Charadrius alexandrinus tenuirostris.*

Snowy Plovers occur along the west coast of Florida wherever there are dry, sandy beaches. The species is most abundant in northwest Florida from Franklin County west to Escambia County (Chase and Gore 1989; Kale et al. 1992). In south Florida, Snowy Plovers occur primarily from Pinellas County south to Marco Island in Collier County. Due to the scarcity of undeveloped beach habitat, nesting pairs in south Florida are much fewer in number and more sporadically distributed than along the northwest coast. Small numbers of Snowy Plovers formerly nested in the Florida Keys and individuals are occasionally seen along the Atlantic coast in winter.

HABITAT REQUIREMENTS AND HABITAT TREND: Snowy Plovers primarily inhabit the open, dry stretches of sandy beach above the mean high tideline in Florida (Woolfenden 1978; Chase and Gore 1989). The birds roost, nest, and forage in this habitat, but they also frequently forage on tidal sand flats along adjacent beaches and tidal creeks (Bent 1929; Woolfenden 1978).

Snowy Plovers nest in shallow depressions that they hollow out in the sand and line with shells or small pebbles (Bent 1929). Typically a nest is located on an open expanse of sand, but near a bit of debris or vegetation that may help conceal or shield the nest (Page et al. 1985). Chase and Gore (1989) found all

Snowy Plover nests (n = 85) in northwest Florida were within 1 m of vegetation or debris, 85% were on small (5–10 cm) rises in the beach, and 80% had an unobscured view of the shoreline. Early nests often were found seaward of the front dunes, but nests initiated later in the summer were typically located in open areas within or behind breaks in the line of dunes. Only 7% of nests were found greater than 10 m from vegetation, and the mean distance from the nests to the recent high tide mark was 62 m.

The beach habitat used by Snowy Plovers also is prized by humans for recreational and residential use. Consequently, most privately owned beach habitat in Florida has been developed for human use and is no longer suitable for Snowy Plovers or is only marginally suitable. The declining trend in available Snowy Plover habitat in Florida, resulting from development of beach and dune habitat, has probably now stabilized because nearly all remaining habitat is on publicly owned land. Similar problems affect Snowy Plover habitat along the Gulf coast from Alabama to Texas and Mexico. Populations in the central United States inhabit primarily salt flats and river sandbars (Boyd 1981a, 1981b). These habitats are subject to natural and human-caused flooding and revegetation can quickly make cleared sites unsuitable for nesting (Boyd 1981a, 1981b).

VULNERABILITY OF SPECIES AND HABITAT: Snowy Plovers nest on open ground and depend on camouflaged eggs and distracting behavior by adults to deter predators. If predators are abundant, or if frequent disturbance by humans keeps birds off their nests, losses to predators are likely to be high. Eggs and chicks also are directly vulnerable to human footsteps, vehicles, and unrestrained pets. Although the birds nest above the mean high tide line, nests are easily flooded by storm-driven high tides. The Snowy Plover's beachfront nesting habitat is highly vulnerable to erosion, but the same forces also deposit sand and create new nesting habitat. A more permanent and important loss occurs when beach and dune habitat used by Snowy Plovers is usurped and developed for use by humans.

CAUSES OF THREAT: Snowy Plover populations are threatened by loss of habitat and reduced productivity. Most of the suitable nesting habitat for Snowy Plovers in Florida has either been intensely developed for human use or is in public ownership (Chase and Gore 1989). Consequently, direct loss of suitable nesting habitat, although important, has become a less common threat over much of the Snowy Plover's range in Florida. Walton County probably contains the greatest amount of privately owned, undeveloped beachfront property in Florida, and that land is rapidly being developed.

A more serious threat is posed by recreational activity on the beach. Snowy Plovers move quickly away from their nest when humans, pets, or vehicles pass along the beach. Although this behavior is effective in distracting intruders away from the nest, it causes the birds to expend time and energy needed to tend eggs and feed chicks. More importantly, when the adults are off the nest the eggs and chicks are exposed to sun, wind and predators. This becomes a serious threat if the disturbance is frequent and the birds are flushed from the nest many times a day. In addition to this indirect disturbance, people can easily step or drive on the cryptically colored eggs and chicks, or their cats and dogs may prey on the young birds. Snowy Plovers are unable to fledge young on beaches where these human-caused disturbances are frequent. Therefore, development of coastal property remains a major threat because construction along the coast usually leads to increased human activity on the beach, even if the front dune habitat is not displaced.

RESPONSES TO HABITAT MODIFICATION: The coastal shoreline is very dynamic and any location is subject to drastic physical changes due to the gradual and catastrophic forces of wind and water. Consequently, Snowy Plovers are well adapted to a changing environment. They sometimes nest on dredged-material islands, particularly after some vegetation has become established. Unlike Least Terns (*Sterna antillarum*) and other beach-nesting species that have adapted to various human-formed habitats, Snowy Plovers seldom nest on construction sites, gravel-covered roofs, roadsides, and other artificial habitats. Because Snowy Plovers both nest and forage on the dunes and sand flats, they may be unable to exploit the barren artificial sites as do the terns that fly away to forage over water.

DEMOGRAPHIC CHARACTERISTICS: Though Snowy Plovers begin nesting in northwest Florida about the last week of March, birds may form pair bonds and defend territories as early as January (Chase and Gore 1989). Birds often pair with a mate from the previous season, although this is apparently not usual in the western United States (Warriner et al. 1986).

A 3-egg clutch is typical (range = 2–4) and incubation lasts about 25–27 days (Boyd 1972; Warriner et al. 1986; Chase and Gore 1989). Both sexes incubate the eggs, but during the day females are on the nest most often (Boyd 1972; Warriner et al. 1986). Chicks are fledged 29–30 days after hatching. Both parents initially care for chicks, but one parent may leave before the young are fledged (Warriner et al. 1986; Chase and Gore 1989). Before midsummer, Snowy Plovers are likely to renest following failure of their initial nest. Some birds produce two broods in one year (Warriner et al. 1986; Chase and Gore 1989).

KEY BEHAVIORS: Snowy Plovers often nest on the same territory they used in previous years. Males establish new territories, but once birds are paired both sexes defend the territory by posturing, chasing, and fighting with neigh-bors (Johnsgard 1981; Warriner et al. 1986). Just prior to copulation the male makes one or more shallow scrapes in the sand and the female typically sits in one of the scrapes during copulation (Boyd 1972; Warriner et al. 1986).

Because Snowy Plovers nest in simple depressions in open expanses of sand, nesting birds are wary of intruders. It is not unusual for an incubating adult to leave the nest when a human or other intruder approaches within 100 m. The bird then moves away just ahead of the intruder, drawing them from the nest. If the intruder continues toward the nest, the parent may feign a broken wing to create a distraction. Where nesting habitat is scarce and beaches are crowded with people, Snowy Plovers may become somewhat habituated to disturbance by humans.

The precocial chicks leave the nest after a few days, but they stay near the cover of vegetation and the watchful care of an adult bird. After fledging, juvenile Snowy Plovers typically move from their natal site and join with other juveniles in loosely formed groups. Most juveniles from the northwest coast of Florida move to the southwest coast for the winter and some stay to breed in south Florida the following year (C. A. Chase, pers. comm.). Post-breeding adults tend to winter in the region where they nested (C. A. Chase, pers. comm.).

Snowy Plovers feed on a variety of invertebrates (Johnsgard 1981). In coastal habitats, they scurry along the tide's edge and probe for small crusta-ceans, mollusks, and annelid worms. Snowy Plovers have a habit of rapidly patting the ground with one foot in order to stimulate movement of prey burrowed in the sand. On the higher beach and among the dunes, the birds feed primarily on adult and larval insects, especially flies and beetles.

Snowy Plovers are quiet birds. However, they do utter a variety of soft calls, mostly during territorial defense, prior to copulation, in response to intruders, or when searching for lost chicks (Bent 1929; Johnsgard 1981; Warriner 1986).

CONSERVATION MEASURES TAKEN: The Snowy Plover is listed as a threatened species by the FGFWFC (Wood 1992) and harming the birds, eggs, or nests is prohibited. The federal Migratory Bird Treaty Act also pro-hibits such activities. Many colonies of seabirds in Florida are fenced or posted during the breeding season to keep people from disturbing the nesting birds. Because Snowy Plovers sometimes nest on the periphery of seabird colonies, they also benefit from this protection. Some of the most important seabird colonies are designated as Critical Wildlife Areas by the FGFWFC and these sites, and any associated Snowy Plover nests, receive increased protection against human intruders.

A report discussing the distribution, biology, and conservation needs of the Snowy Plover (Chase and Gore 1989) was provided to managers of public lands within the species' nesting range in Florida. Most stretches of public beach are closed to vehicles and pets, partly to protect nesting birds such as the Snowy Plover. Impacts to nesting Snowy Plovers are routinely considered in management and activity plans on public lands. Persons who conduct daily surveys for sea turtle nests in northwest Florida are specifically informed about nesting Snowy Plovers and warned of the danger of survey vehicles crushing nests.

CONSERVATION MEASURES PROPOSED: Wherever predation or human disturbance is a serious detriment to Snowy Plovers, steps should be taken to minimize these problems. Educating the public about the birds and the need to protect them would be most helpful. Fences, predator exclosures, and predator reduction may need to be applied more vigorously and consistently at some locations. Acquisition or restoration of beach dune habitat may be an effective means of enhancing Snowy Plover populations, particularly in southwest Florida where undisturbed nesting beaches are scarce. Periodic surveys of nesting Snowy Plovers would be useful in tracking trends in the number of nesting pairs in Florida. Ideally, such surveys would be conducted in concert with surveys of other beach-nesting species.

Predation can greatly influence the productivity of ground-nesting species such as the Snowy Plover (Page et al. 1983, 1985). Several techniques have been used to exclude predators from Piping Plover (*Charadrius melodus*) nests (Deblinger et al. 1992). These and related methods should be employed where predation is suspected to be a problem. Direct control of predators also may be required in some situations.

ACKNOWLEDGMENTS: I thank C. A. Chase for insights into the current status and breeding biology of the Snowy Plover in Florida. J. L. Morris assisted with a review of the literature, and J. A. Rodgers provided editorial comments that improved the manuscript.

LITERATURE CITED

AOU. 1957. Check-list of North American birds. 5th ed. Amer. Ornithol. Union, Lancaster, Pennsylvania.

Bent, A. C. 1929. Life histories of North American shore birds, part II. U.S. Natl. Mus. Bull. no. 146. Smithsonian Inst., Washington, D.C.

Boyd, R. L. 1972. Breeding biology of the Snowy Plover at Cheyenne Bottoms Waterfowl Management Area, Barton County, Kansas. M.S. thesis, Kansas State Teacher's College, Emporia, Kansas.

Boyd, R. L. 1981a. Population ecology of Snowy Plover and Least Tern in Kansas and Oklahoma. Unpubl. rept., Kansas Fish and Game Comm., Pratt, Kansas. 33 pp.

Boyd, R. L. 1981b. Distribution and abundance of Snowy Plovers in Kansas and northern Oklahoma. Kansas Ornith. Soc. Bull. 3:25–28.

Chase, C. A., and J. A. Gore. 1989. Snowy Plover breeding distribution. Unpubl. final rept., Fla. Game and Fresh Water Fish Comm., Tallahassee, Florida. 23 pp.

Deblinger, R. D., J. J. Vaske, and D. W. Rimmer. 1992. An evaluation of different predator exclosures used to protect Atlantic coast Piping Plover nests. Wildl. Soc. Bull. 20:274–279.

Hayman, P., J. Jarchant, and T. Prater. 1986. Shorebirds: An identification guide. Houghton Mifflin Co., Boston, Massachusetts.

Johnsgard, P. A. 1981. The plovers, sandpipers, and snipes of the world. Univ. of Nebraska Press, Lincoln, Nebraska.

Kale, H. W., II, B. M. Stith, and C. W. Biggs. 1992. Atlas of breeding birds of Florida. Draft ms. submitted to the Fla. Game and Fresh Water Fish Comm., Tallahassee, Florida.

Page, G. W., L. E. Stenzel, D. W. Winkler, and C. W. Swarth. 1983. Spacing out at Mono Lake: breeding success, nest density, and predation in the Snowy Plover. Auk 100:13–24.

Page, G. W., L. E. Stenzel, and C. A. Ribic. 1985. Nest site selection and clutch predation in the Snowy Plover. Auk 102:347–353.

Page, G. W., L. E. Stenzel, and W. D. Shuford. 1991. Distribution and abundance of the Snowy Plover on its western North American breeding grounds. Jour. Field Ornith. 62:245–255.

Page, G. W., J. S. Warriner, J. C. Warriner, and P. W. C. Paton. 1995. Snowy Plover (*Charadrius alexandrinus*). In *The birds of North America* no. 154 (A. Poole and F. Gill, eds.). Amer. Ornithol. Union and Philadelphia Acad. Sci., Philadelphia, Pennsylvania.

Sibley, C. G., and B. L. Monroe, Jr. 1990. Distribution and taxonomy of birds of the world. Yale Univ. Press, London, England.

Warriner, J. S., J. C. Warriner, G. W. Page, and L. E. Stenzel. 1986. Mating system and reproductive success of a small population of polygamous Snowy Plovers. Wilson Bull. 98:15–37.

Wood, D. A. 1992. Official lists of endangered and potentially endangered fauna and flora in Florida. Fla. Game and Fresh Water Fish Comm., Tallahassee, Florida.

Woolfenden, G. E. 1978. Snowy Plover. Pp. 8–10 in Rare and endangered biota of Florida, vol. II birds (H. W. Kale, II, ed.). Univ. Presses of Fla., Gainesville, Florida.

PREPARED BY: Jeffery A. Gore, Florida Game and Fresh Water Fish Commission, 3911 Highway 2321, Panama City, FL 32409.

Red-cockaded Woodpecker

Picoides borealis

FAMILY PICIDAE

Order Piciformes

TAXONOMY: The Red-cockaded Woodpecker (*Picoides borealis*) was first described as *Picus borealis* in 1807 by Vieillot based on a sketch and written description of the species, both of which were partially in error (Jackson 1971). Furthermore, no type specimen is extant (Mengel and Jackson 1977). Wilson (1877) provided a more accurate and complete description of the species and gave it the currently recognized common name, Red-cockaded Woodpecker (Jackson 1971). Following a series of generic name changes, the species was placed in the genus *Picoides* by Mayr and Short (1970). Wetmore (1941) separated the Red-cockaded Woodpecker into two subspecies, but the species is now considered to be monomorphic (Short 1982).

DESCRIPTION: The Red-cockaded Woodpecker is a diminutive species, about 18–20 cm in length, with a wingspan between 35 and 38 cm. Adults weigh about 45 g, with males being slightly heavier than females (Porter 1984). The species is distinguished from other Florida woodpeckers by its black cap and nape, large white cheek patch, and black-and-white barred back and wings. The throat and belly are white, the flanks are flecked with black, and the white outer tail feathers are barred with black. The adult male has a small patch, or "cockade," of red feathers on each side of the head; in contrast, the adult female has no red feathers on the head. Because the male's cockade is rarely visible, adult males and females are difficult to distinguish in the field. However, juvenile males are readily identified by a red patch of feathers on the crown, which also is absent in juvenile females. The crown patch on juvenile males is retained through the post-fledging period but is lost during the first molt in the fall.

POPULATION SIZE AND TREND: Two units of measure have been used to estimate the abundance of Red-cockaded Woodpeckers: the number of

Red-cockaded Woodpecker,
Picoides borealis. (Photo by Barry Mansell)

cavity-tree clusters (i.e., colonies) and the number of birds. Estimates of cavity-tree clusters usually are based on field surveys, whereas bird numbers typically are derived from the number of clusters, using an average of two or three birds per cluster (Jackson 1971, 1978; Wood and Wenner 1983). In Florida, the average number of birds per cluster ranges between 2.5 and 3.1 (Hovis 1982; DeLotelle et al. 1983).

Jackson (1971) provided a preliminary, rangewide population estimate of 2,939 birds; this estimate, based on limited data, was considered conservative. Jackson (1971) speculated that the population could be two to three-fold greater, but doubted that it exceeded 10,000 birds. Later, Jackson (1978) revised his estimate to 1,500–3,500 active and inactive clusters and 4,500–10,000 birds on the basis of a more complete survey. If a cluster is inhabited by Red-cockaded Woodpeckers, it is considered "active"; uninhabited clusters are regarded as "abandoned" or "inactive."

The most extensive, rangewide population surveys for Red-cockaded Woodpeckers have been conducted on federal lands. In the late 1970s, there were an estimated 2,904 active and inactive clusters on federal lands in the southeastern United States (Jackson 1978). A resurvey of these properties during 1980–82 yielded an estimate of 2,677 active clusters (Lennartz et al. 1983a). About

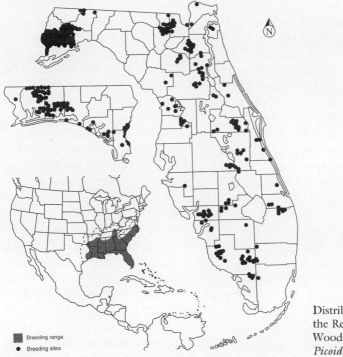

Distribution map of
the Red-cockaded
Woodpecker,
Picoides borealis.

2,115 (79%) of the active clusters on federal lands occurred in national forests (Lennartz et al. 1983a; Costa and Escano 1989).

Three estimates of Red-cockaded Woodpecker abundance are available for Florida. Baker et al. (1980) estimated the statewide population at 943 active and inactive clusters and 2,646 birds between 1969 and 1978; Wood and Wenner (1983) estimated the population at 1,139 active clusters and 2,262–3,431 birds in 1983; and Cox et al. (1995) estimated the population at 1,146 active clusters in 1992. The comparative increase in the number of clusters reported between the first estimate and those of 1983 and 1992 reflected a greater thoroughness of the later surveys rather than an actual increase in population abundance (Wood and Wenner 1983; Cox et al. 1995). The Red-cockaded Woodpecker population on the Apalachicola National Forest in northwestern Florida, which was estimated at 590 active clusters in 1992 (Cox et al. 1995), has been the largest single population in Florida and the species' entire range for the past 25 years. The second largest population in Florida, with an estimated 208 active clusters in 1992 (Cox et al. 1995), occurs at Eglin Air Force Base, which also is located in northwestern Florida.

Few Red-cockaded Woodpecker populations are considered to be secure. Most populations are small (<50 active clusters) and geographically isolated;

only three populations with >250 active clusters were reported in the early
1980s (Lennartz et al. 1983a). Local declines have occurred throughout the
species' range (Carter et al. 1983; Ortego and Lay 1988; Conner and Rudolph
1989; Costa and Escano 1989), and the species has been extirpated in several
areas (Baker 1983; Lennartz and Henry 1985; Costa and Escano 1989). Only
one case of an expanding population has been reported; Hooper et al. (1991)
documented a 10% net increase in the population on the Francis Marion
National Forest in South Carolina between 1980–81 and 1987–88. This increase was attributed to an abundance of high quality habitat and a favorable
forest management regime. Ironically, the Francis Marion population was
reduced by >60% by Hurricane Hugo in September 1989 (Hooper et al.
1990).

DISTRIBUTION AND HISTORY OF DISTRIBUTION: The Red-cockaded
Woodpecker is a nonmigratory, year-round resident of mature pine forests in
the southeastern United States. Historically, the species was more numerous
and contiguously distributed than it is today. In the early 1800s, according to
Audubon (1967), Red-cockaded Woodpeckers were "found abundantly from
Texas to New Jersey, and inland as far as Tennessee" and were "nowhere more
numerous" than in the pinelands of Florida, Georgia, and South Carolina.
The species currently occurs in all coastal states from eastern Texas to southern
Virginia and inland to southeastern Oklahoma, southern Arkansas, eastern
Tennessee, and southeastern Kentucky (Lennartz and Henry 1985). Despite
this widespread distribution, the population is extremely fragmented with the
largest concentrations occurring in the Coastal Plain forests of the southern
United States and in the Carolina Sandhills (Lennartz et al. 1983a).

Red-cockaded Woodpeckers are more abundant on public than private
lands (Jackson 1978). Although there is a substantial amount of potential
habitat in private ownership, most private forests are too small and fragmented
to support large populations of Red-cockaded Woodpeckers (Lennartz and
Henry 1985). Furthermore, private forests usually are managed on relatively
short-term stand rotations for maximum timber production, a practice that is
incompatible with sustaining large or stable populations of Red-cockaded
Woodpeckers (Jackson 1978; Lennartz et al. 1983a). Federal lands support
more Red-cockaded Woodpeckers than state or municipal lands (Jackson 1978),
and on federal lands the largest populations occur in national forests (Lennartz
et al. 1983a). As of 1986, the species was found in 21 national forests in the
southeastern United States (Costa and Escano 1989). However, the population was fragmented and unevenly distributed, with >70% of the active clusters
occurring in four national forests (Apalachicola, Francis Marion, Kisatchie,
and Talladega) in four different states (Florida, South Carolina, Louisiana, and
Alabama, respectively).

The distribution of the Red-cockaded Woodpecker in Florida also is widespread but fragmented, with local concentrations occurring on federal and state lands (Baker et al. 1980; Wood and Wenner 1983; Cox et al. 1995), where the most extensive tracts of mature pine remain. Historically, Red-cockaded Woodpeckers ranged as far south as Florida City and Royal Palm Hammock in Dade County (Howell 1921), but probably did not occur in the Florida Keys (Murphey 1964; Patterson and Robertson 1981). The current southernmost range of the species terminates in the Big Cypress National Preserve in Collier and Monroe counties (Patterson and Robertson 1981; Cox et al. 1995).

HABITAT REQUIREMENTS AND HABITAT TREND: The distribution of the Red-cockaded Woodpecker is related closely to the occurrence of fire. Throughout Florida and the northern Gulf coast states, weather patterns associated with the Gulf of Mexico result in a frequency of electrical storms matched nowhere else in North America (Jackson et al. 1986). Average annual thunderstorm frequency ranges from 90 days in central Florida to 60 days in the more northern portions of the southeastern United States. Prior to human intervention, lightning-caused fires occurred annually in peninsular Florida and at 3–5 year intervals elsewhere in the coastal plain (Komarek 1974). This fire-dominated community was the primary selective force in the formation of the southern pine ecosystem with which the Red-cockaded Woodpecker is so intricately associated. Under this fire regime, the southern pines evolved adaptations for fire resistance—their bark and needles form insulating layers that protect the growing tissues from fire (Jackson 1987). In turn, the Red-cockaded Woodpecker adapted to this fire-climax ecosystem by excavating cavities in fire-tolerant living pines.

Red-cockaded Woodpeckers require old-growth, living pines for nesting and roosting. Although longleaf pine (*Pinus palustris*) is preferred when available (Hopkins and Lynn 1971; Lennartz et al. 1983a; Hovis and Labisky 1985), cavities also are constructed in loblolly (*P. taeda*), shortleaf (*P. echinata*), pond (*P. serotina*), slash (*P. elliottii*), pitch (*P. rigida*), and Virginia (*P. virginiana*) pines. Regardless of species, Red-cockaded Woodpeckers preferentially select old-age pines for cavity excavation (Hovis and Labisky 1985; Conner and O'Halloran 1987; DeLotelle and Epting 1988; Rudolph and Conner 1991). Average cavity-tree ages range between 63 and 130 years for longleaf pine and between 62 and 149 years for all other pine species (Hopkins and Lynn 1971; Jackson et al. 1979b; Wood 1983; Rudolph and Conner 1991). Cavity trees have thinner sapwood and greater heartwood diameter than other mature pines (Conner et al. 1994) and typically are infected with *Phellinus pini*, a fungus that decays the heartwood and facilitates cavity excavation (Jackson 1977b; Conner and Locke 1982; Conner and O'Halloran

1987; Hooper 1988; Conner et al. 1994). Cavity excavation usually requires from one to several years, but once a cavity is completed it often is used for many years (Jackson et al. 1979b). Red-cockaded Woodpeckers always construct their cavities in live pines; however, after a cavity tree dies the birds may continue to use it for several years (Hooper 1982). The number of cavities per tree typically ranges between one and two (Hopkins and Lynn 1971; Shapiro 1983; Hovis and Labisky 1985).

Most active clusters occur in open, mature pine stands with sparse midstory vegetation. Rangewide, overstory basal areas and stem densities within active clusters are consistently <18 m²/ha and <300 stems/ha, respectively (Thompson and Baker 1971; Locke et al. 1983; Shapiro 1983; Hovis and Labisky 1985). Midstory basal area and stem density are typically <5.0 m²/ha and <400 stems/ha, respectively (Van Balen and Doerr 1978; Locke et al. 1983; Hovis and Labisky 1985). Although most biologists agree that Red-cockaded Woodpeckers cannot tolerate a well-developed hardwood midstory, Conner and Rudolph (1989) were the first to statistically correlate hardwood encroachment with cluster abandonment.

Red-cockaded Woodpeckers feed primarily on arthropods (Beal 1911; Ligon 1970; Baker 1971), which they locate by scaling the bark from trees. Fruits and mast also may be eaten but comprise a minor portion of the diet. Throughout their range, Red-cockaded Woodpeckers prefer to forage in pine-dominated habitats, and within these habitats, large (>20 cm dbh) living pines are the preferred foraging substrate (Ramey 1980; Hooper and Lennartz 1981; DeLotelle et al. 1983; Porter and Labisky 1986). However, home range size is variable and apparently is related to the amount and quality of available habitat. In general, home ranges tend to be larger in habitats with poorly stocked pine stands and a paucity of larger trees. In central and southern Florida, where the habitat is considered to be relatively poor (<7m²/ha pine basal area), home range size averages about 150 ha (Nesbitt et al. 1983b; DeLotelle et al. 1987). In coastal South Carolina, where the habitat is better (pine basal area averages 11.8m²/ha), home range size averages 86.9 ha (Hooper et al. 1982). Habitat in northern Florida appears to be intermediate between the two extremes. Porter and Labisky (1986) reported a mean home range size of 129 ha for a population on the Apalachicola National Forest and the birds preferred to forage in pine stands with a mean basal area of 16.1 m²/ha.

Red-cockaded Woodpecker habitat, particularly nesting and roosting habitat, has declined throughout the species' range. Lennartz et al. (1983b) estimated that only 2.5% of the commercial pine acreage in the southeastern United States was suitable as nesting and roosting habitat. Between 1953 and 1977, the amount of old-growth pine in the southeastern United States declined by 13%; the loss was most severe in the longleaf and slash pine forest-type where a 25% decline occurred over the 25-year period. In Florida, the acreage of longleaf pine declined by 83% in the 30 years between 1950 and 1980 (Bechtold and Knight 1982). However, the reduction in old-growth pine forests has been most rapid on private lands where there are no legal requirements or incentives to perpetuate the habitat for this endangered species (Lennartz 1988).

VULNERABILITY OF SPECIES AND HABITAT: The specialized nesting and roosting requirements of the Red-cockaded Woodpecker render the species highly vulnerable to habitat loss. Protecting existing active clusters and cavity trees will provide for the immediate survival of the species. However, future survivorship of the Red-cockaded Woodpecker is dependent on the continual availability of old-growth pine forests on a long-term basis (Hovis and Labisky 1985; Lennartz and Henry 1985).

CAUSES OF THREAT: Loss of nesting and roosting habitat, due to current trends in commercial forestry practices, constitutes the primary threat to the Red-cockaded Woodpecker. Silvicultural techniques that maximize timber production, such as short-term stand rotations and clearcutting, are incompatible with sustaining large or stable populations of Red-cockaded Woodpeckers because they reduce the amount of old-growth forest available to the birds. Forest removal also reduces the amount of available foraging habitat, which results in population isolation due to habitat fragmentation (Conner and Rudolph 1991).

Natural causes of cavity-tree mortality include bark beetles, wind, fire, and lightning (Conner et al. 1991). In addition, cavity trees may be abandoned due to hardwood encroachment (Conner and Rudolph 1989) or competition with other cavity-dwelling species (Harlow and Lennartz 1983). Cavity trees and birds also can be destroyed during hurricanes or other catastrophic events (Engstrom and Evans 1990; Hooper et al. 1990).

RESPONSES TO HABITAT MODIFICATION: Most Red-cockaded Woodpecker populations respond well to habitat modifications that maintain or create the open, mature pine forests that are preferred by the species. Accordingly, recommendations for enhancing both current and potential nesting and roosting habitat include prescribed fire and/or periodic thinning to control hardwood vegetation. The species also responds favorably to the creation of artificial cavities within suitable habitat. Copeyon et al. (1991) found that Red-cockaded Woodpeckers would use artificially created cavities for both nesting and roosting, even when natural cavities were available. In fact, they were able to increase the number of woodpecker territories on their North

Carolina study area by provisioning both vacant habitats and abandoned clusters with artificial cavities. These findings suggest that availability of cavity trees may be the greatest limiting factor for Red-cockaded Woodpecker populations (Walters 1991).

Although most biologists agree that Red-cockaded Woodpecker populations are negatively affected by habitat fragmentation, few quantitative studies have been conducted. Wood et al. (1985) measured the effects of clearcutting within Red-cockaded Woodpecker territories in South Carolina and found no relationship between the amount of cutting and subsequent territory size or nestling survival. In contrast, Conner and Rudolph (1991) found that small, isolated populations of woodpeckers in eastern Texas were more vulnerable to forest removal than larger, more abundant populations. As forest removal and fragmentation increased within either 400 or 800 m of clusters in small populations, both woodpecker group size and the number of active clusters decreased. In larger populations, cluster abandonment was significantly associated with habitat loss within 800 m of clusters, but there was no relationship between woodpecker group size and forest removal. Accordingly, Conner and Rudolph (1991) concluded that dispersal and foraging sufficiency problems associated with forest removal negatively impacted woodpecker populations by reducing group size, but they were unable to determine which problem had the greater effect. Similarly, Rudolph and Conner (1994) examined the effects of habitat fragmentation on a large population in eastern Texas and found a positive correlation between the amount of forest area >60 years old and the number of active clusters, number of woodpeckers, and number of woodpeckers per cluster. It is important to note that the South Carolina and Texas studies were relatively short in duration (1.5–2 years). Clearly, more long-term research is needed before we can fully understand the effects of forest fragmentation and habitat loss on Red-cockaded Woodpecker populations.

DEMOGRAPHIC CHARACTERISTICS: Red-cockaded Woodpeckers are monogamous (Lennartz et al. 1987) and nest from late April through mid-July. A clutch of 2–4 eggs is usually laid in the roost cavity of the breeding male (Ligon 1970). The incubation period is about 10 days, and the nestlings fledge 26–29 days after hatching (Ligon 1970). Incubation may begin before the clutch is complete and brood reduction is common (Ligon 1970; Lennartz et al. 1987; LaBranche and Walters 1994). Fledging success consistently ranges between one and two young per nest, and groups with helpers typically fledge more young than unassisted pairs (Lennartz et al. 1987; Walters 1990; Neal et al. 1993). Nest predators include tree-climbing snakes and flying squirrels (*Glaucomys volans*) (Lennartz and Heckel 1987). Until recently, no more than one nest per group had been reported during a single nesting season (Jackson

1977a). In 1991 LaBranche et al. (1994) observed double brooding in three separate populations in the Carolinas, albeit the phenomenon was rare (7 of 241 nesting groups). Double brooding also has been observed at Eglin Air Force Base in northwest Florida (Schillaci and Smith 1994).

Fledgling dispersal patterns vary considerably between the sexes. Most females typically disperse within 1 year after fledging to search for a breeding vacancy. Some fledgling males also disperse, whereas others remain on their natal territory as helpers until a breeding opportunity arises in the immediate vicinity (Walters et al. 1988). Findings from North Carolina suggest that mortality is greater for fledgling females (68%) than males (57%) during the first year (Walters et al. 1988). Dispersing females that survive typically attain breeding status in another territory or become floaters that are not definitively associated with a particular group of birds or cluster of cavity trees. Dispersing males also may become breeders or floaters, or they may establish and defend a territory, but remain solitary (Walters et al. 1988). Although both sexes are capable of breeding at 1 year, reproductive success improves with increased age (Walters 1990).

KEY BEHAVIORS: Red-cockaded Woodpeckers are unique among North American woodpeckers because they excavate their cavities in the trunks of living pine trees. They also have a peculiar habit of drilling small holes, called "resin wells," in their cavity trees (Jackson 1977a). These holes, which are typically concentrated around the cavity entrance, penetrate the cambium and cause the resin to flow and accumulate on the trunk of the tree. The condition of the resin wells and accumulated pine gum are indicative of the status of a cavity tree. In general, cavity trees with reddish resin wells and clear, sticky gum are considered active, whereas cavity trees with grayish resin wells and white, dry gum are usually inactive (Jackson 1977a). The gum accumulated on a cavity tree may serve as a deterrent to egg and nestling predators, such as tree-climbing snakes (Rudolph et al. 1990).

Cavity trees tend to be aggregated into geographic areas known as "clusters" (Walters 1990) or "colonies" (Jackson and Thompson 1971). The number of cavity trees per cluster ranges between 1 and 29 (Jackson 1977a) but is usually <15 trees. Although the individual cavity trees in a cluster may be >1 km apart (Jackson 1977a), most are within 460 m of each other (Harlow et al. 1983). Within a typical active cluster, some cavities are under construction (i.e., "starts"), some are completed and in use (i.e., "active"), and others have been abandoned or usurped by other cavity-dwelling species (i.e., "inactive") (Lennartz and Henry 1985).

The Red-cockaded Woodpecker is a cooperative breeder that lives in social units known as "groups" (Walters 1990) or "clans" (Jackson and Thompson

1971). A typical group consists of a breeding pair and several additional nonbreeders, which are referred to as "helpers" because they assist with the incubation, brooding, and feeding of the young of the breeding pair (Lennartz and Harlow 1979). Helpers are usually the male offspring of at least one of the breeders, but not all groups include helpers (Walters 1990). Each group member typically roosts alone in its own cavity within a cluster. However, if the number of available cavities is insufficient, some birds may roost in branch forks, scars on the trunks of pines, or cavities in adjacent clusters (Hooper and Lennartz 1983).

Ligon (1970) described 13 distinct vocalizations of the Red-cockaded Woodpecker. Adults give the "szrek" or "shrit" call when they are mildly excited or disturbed, whereas the "she-u" and "wic-a wic-a" calls are indicative of agitation, as when an intruding Red-cockaded Woodpecker enters a group's territory. When highly agitated, Red-cockaded Woodpeckers also exhibit an open-wing display and often fly in a corkscrew-like pattern (Ligon 1970).

CONSERVATION MEASURES TAKEN: The Red-cockaded Woodpecker was first protected under the Migratory Bird Treaty Act of 1918. The species was federally listed as endangered in 1970 under authority of the Endangered Species Preservation Act of 1969, which was replaced by the existing Endangered Species Act of 1973. Four factors contributed to the listing of the Red-cockaded Woodpecker as endangered (U.S. Forest Service 1985): (1) the exploitative logging of mature pine forests throughout the southeastern United States in the early 1900s, (2) the practice of managing replanted pine forests under short harvest-rotation systems, (3) the specialized habitat requirements of the species, and (4) the fragmentation and degradation of the remaining pine forests by the expanding human population. The species was first afforded legal protection by the State of Florida in 1974, when it was listed as threatened. That status was changed to endangered in 1975, and then subsequently back to the current threatened status in 1979.

The first U.S. Recovery Plan for the Red-cockaded Woodpecker (Jackson et al. 1979a) represented the "state of the art," but suffered from a paucity of available biological data. Increased interest in the species stimulated additional research, which subsequently led to preparation of the second, and current, Recovery Plan (Lennartz and Henry 1985). This plan was approved despite concerns of the scientific community that recommended recovery strategies were minimal because they were derived principally from Red-cockaded Woodpecker populations in prime habitat (Ligon et al. 1986; Porter and Labisky 1986). Subsequently, the *Wildlife Habitat Management Handbook of the U.S. Forest Service* (1985) was updated to incorporate recovery actions set forth in the revised Recovery Plan.

Management guidelines outlined in the revised handbook, applicable only on national forest lands, establish a 60-meter buffer zone around each cavity tree within which logging can be undertaken only to preserve or enhance the habitat. No timber-harvest rotations are to be set for stands with clusters. Clusters should be burned at 1–5 year intervals to control hardwood encroachment, and when necessary, timber stands within clusters may be thinned to maintain a basal area of 12–18 m^2/ha or to remove any crowns or stems that threaten to block cavity entrances. A replacement stand must be established for each active cluster for the purpose of providing replacement nesting habitat. Replacement stands of pine, longleaf pine if available, should be >4 ha in size, >60 years in age, and located between 400 and 1,200 m from active clusters or other replacement stands. The revised guidelines also establish a Red-cockaded Woodpecker population goal, expressed as the number of active clusters, for each national forest within the range of the species. These goals are based on the amount of suitable habitat, the number of existing clusters, and the feasibility of meeting the goal given other resource obligations or constraints. In national forests, where the existing population is below the defined goal, recruitment stands (same specifications as replacement stands) are to be established in suitable habitat to provide for population expansion (new clusters). To provide adequate foraging habitat, 50.6 ha of well-stocked (13.8–20.7 m^2/ha) pine and pine-hardwood stands (>50% basal area in pine) that are >30 years in age (40% >60 years) with 59.3 pines/ha >25.4 cm dbh must be connected to and located within 800 m of each active cluster or replacement or recruitment stand. The option exists to provide an expanded foraging area in younger or sparsely stocked forests.

Despite revisions to the *Handbook,* a survey conducted in 1986 indicated a decline in the number of active clusters for most national forests with <250 active clusters (Costa and Escano 1989). Population declines were alarmingly precipitous in the Angelina, Davy Crockett, and Sabine National Forests in Texas in the late 1980s (Conner and Rudolph 1989). The Texas situation precipitated a legal action filed by the Sierra Club, The Wilderness Society, and the Texas Committee on Natural Resources (nonprofit organizations) against the U.S. Forest Service. On 17 June 1988, District Judge Robert M. Parker, Eastern District Court of Texas, issued a precedent-setting injunction that greatly increased habitat protection for the Red-cockaded Woodpecker in the national forests in Texas. Judge Parker ruled that the U.S. Forest Service had failed to fully implement the *Wildlife Habitat Management Handbook* as it relates to Red-cockaded Woodpecker habitat preservation or improvement. Consequently, he found the U.S. Forest Service in violation of Section 7 (jeopardy) and Section 9 (taking) of the Endangered Species Act. Although the U.S. Forest Service sought modifications to the injunction, Judge Parker's ruling on 20 October 1988 retained the substance of the recovery actions imposed in the initial ruling. These court-ordered management guidelines dictated a strengthening of the actions set forth in the *Wildlife Habitat Management Handbook*. Management is to be focused on active clusters, and the removal of hardwood midstory vegetation in clusters is to be pursued aggressively. A program of prescribed burning of clusters is to be conducted every 2 years on longleaf pine sites and every 3–4 years on loblolly pine sites. Logging roads and other off-pavement roads are to be eliminated within cluster sites, stands within 1,200 m of all active clusters are to be thinned to 13.8 m^2/ha basal area, and all clearcutting within 1,200 m of active clusters is prohibited, being replaced by selective cutting (i.e., old growth trees excluded) on minimum rotations of 70–80 years. Furthermore, the size of foraging areas should be increased to satisfy the requirements of the species on a habitat-by-habitat basis, and not be restricted to the 50.6 ha recommended in the *Handbook*.

Following Judge Parker's ruling, conservation groups filed notices of intent to sue the U.S. Forest Service for violating the Endangered Species Act on all national forests with Red-cockaded Woodpecker populations. They charged that the U.S. Forest Service had failed to take actions to provide adequate habitat for the species. Based on data collected by the U.S. Forest Service (Costa and Escano 1989), which showed population declines in most national forests in the southeastern United States, the Forest Service ultimately adopted habitat management actions similar to those imposed in Texas for all national forests with Red-cockaded Woodpecker populations. Management of the species on national forests outside of Texas currently is governed by the working document, "Interim Standards and Guidelines for the Protection and Management of RCW Habitat Within 3/4 Mile of Colony Sites" (U.S. Forest Service 1990, 1991). These "interim standards and guidelines" are designed to protect Red-cockaded Woodpeckers and their habitat on national forests until a new long-range management strategy is adopted and implemented in compliance with the National Environmental Policy Act and the Endangered Species Act. In brief, the interim guidelines prohibit clearcutting within 400 m of clusters, except to convert off-site species back to longleaf pine, and recommend using shelterwood and seed-tree methods to regenerate stands between 400 and 1,200 m of clusters.

In June 1995, the U.S. Forest Service issued its Record of Decision and Final Environmental Impact Statement (FEIS) for the management of Red-cockaded Woodpeckers in the southern national forests (U.S. Forest Service 1995). The FEIS will be implemented within 1–3 years. Immediate habitat protection beyond the "interim standards and guidelines" will be accomplished by establishing tentative habitat management areas (HMA) and population objectives for each national forest where the species occurs. Within each tentative HMA, silvicultural practices will be limited to thinning, irregular shelterwood, single tree, or group selection methods. Clearcutting will not be allowed except to restore off-site pines to longleaf or other desirable species. The *Wildlife Habitat Management Handbook*, which will be revised in accordance with FEIS, will establish criteria for delineating final HMAs, determine population objectives to ensure demographic stability, and establish management intensity levels for each HMA based on the risk of extirpation to the resident woodpecker population. Pursuant to the revised *Handbook*, the Forest Service Plan for each national forest where the species occurs will be amended or revised.

In addition to the legal aspects of Red-cockaded Woodpecker conservation, several important management techniques have been developed in recent years. For example, restrictor plates have been used to protect Red-cockaded Woodpecker cavities in areas where interspecific competition for cavities exists (Carter et al. 1989). The plates, which are positioned around the entrance to a cavity, are designed to prevent entrance into or enlargement of the cavity by other cavity-dwelling species such as Pileated Woodpeckers (*Dryocopus pileatus*) or Red-bellied Woodpeckers (*Melanerpes carolinus*). Another new management technique involves the creation of artificial cavities, either by drilling a hole (Copeyon 1990; Taylor and Hooper 1991) or inserting a prefabricated cavity (Allen 1991) in the trunk of a living pine. These methods were used to stabilize the Red-cockaded Woodpecker population on the Francis Marion National Forest in the aftermath of Hurricane Hugo (Hooper et al. 1990).

Other current research has focused on relocation as a management tool. Initial efforts to relocate Red-cockaded Woodpeckers primarily were for mitigative purposes and met with limited success (Odom et al. 1982; Jackson et al. 1983; Nesbitt et al. 1983a; Odom 1983). More recent relocation efforts, termed augmentation, have focused on relocating yearling females from relatively large Red-cockaded Woodpecker populations to smaller populations with an abundance of solitary males (DeFazio et al. 1987). Yearling females are preferred for relocation because they generally disperse from their natal territory and, therefore already experience a high rate of mortality (Walters et al. 1988). Preliminary results are encouraging and suggest that this tool may become important for augmenting small or declining populations of Red-cockaded Woodpeckers (Costa and Escano 1989). However, relocation and augmentation are "stop-gap" measures that should not become substitutes for providing suitable habitat for this endangered species.

CONSERVATION MEASURES PROPOSED: Despite protected legal status and accelerated habitat management, the population abundance of Red-cockaded Woodpeckers has continued to decline throughout much of its range, principally as a result of habitat deterioration (Conner and Rudolph 1989; Costa and Escano 1989; James 1991). Although the genetic variability across populations appears "normal," heterozygosity is significantly, albeit weakly, related to population size (Stangel et al. 1992). Further, the best estimate of minimum viable population size is 509 breeding pairs (Reed et al. 1988), which means the population of Red-cockaded Woodpeckers on the Apalachicola National Forest in Florida is the only genetically viable population in existence. This body of knowledge suggests the need to place special emphasis on the management of selected populations of Red-cockaded Woodpeckers on public lands for the focused purpose of recovering them to self-sustaining levels—genetically, demographically, and environmentally. Candidate populations for consideration would include the Apalachicola National Forest and Eglin Air Force Base in Florida, Kisatchie National Forest in Louisiana, Talladega National Forest in Alabama, and Fort Bragg Military Reservation in North Carolina.

The Red-cockaded Woodpecker is limited by the quantity, fragmentation, and quality of old-growth pine available for both nesting and foraging in the southeastern United States. Thus, immediate management should focus on improvement of habitat quality—incorporating prescribed fire and mechanical control to reduce hardwood midstory encroachment. Measures also should be taken to prevent further fragmentation of suitable habitat by creating corridors of old-growth pine between population centers. The finding that cavity availability may limit expansion in some populations (Walters 1991) offers promise for the accelerated use of artificial cavities to enhance population growth, particularly in recruitment stands and in young or sparsely stocked forests. The practice of augmentation, or the relocating of "surplus" juvenile females from donor populations into the territories of solitary males in declining populations, should be pursued if the strategy is proven successful and feasible. However, the ultimate recovery of the Red-cockaded Woodpecker to a self-sustaining level will require a long-term and comprehensive recovery strategy that is based on a conservation philosophy that is embraced by both the public and land-management agencies.

The pulse of new knowledge on Red-cockaded Woodpeckers in recent years, especially as related to demographics and sociobiology, begets the need for adoption of a new U.S. Recovery Plan. Critical to the development and success of this new plan is the philosophy that management prescriptions must exceed the minimum requirements of the species. Also, the management of Red-cockaded Woodpeckers on private lands essentially has been a neglected component in efforts to recover the species. Small populations are reservoirs of unique gene combinations (Stangel et al. 1992), a fact that necessitates the careful surveying and monitoring of the species on private lands. Accordingly, a final recommendation is that those states characterized by reservoir populations on state and private lands develop individual recovery plans that are in concert with management standards implemented on federal lands.

ACKNOWLEDGMENTS: We thank R. Costa, T. E. O'Meara, D. J. White, and D. A. Wood for reviewing an earlier draft of the manuscript. The distribution map for Florida was provided by J. Cox.

LITERATURE CITED:

Allen, D. H. 1991. An insert technique for constructing artificial Red-cockaded Woodpecker cavities. Gen. Tech. Rept. SE-73. U.S. Dept. Agric., For. Serv., Southeastern For. Exper. Stat., Asheville, North Carolina.

Audubon, J. J. 1967. The birds of America. Vol. 4. Dover Publications, Inc., New York.

Baker, W. W. 1971. Observations on the food habits of the Red-cockaded Woodpecker. Pages 100–107 in The ecology and management of the Red-cockaded Woodpecker (R. L. Thompson, Ed.) Bur. Sport Fish. Wildl., U.S. Dept. Int., and Tall Timbers Res. Stat., Tallahassee, Florida.

Baker, W. W. 1983. Decline and extirpation of a population of Red-cockaded Woodpeckers in northwest Florida. Pages 44–45 in Red-cockaded Woodpecker symposium II proceedings (D. A. Wood, ed.). Fla. Game and Fresh Water Fish Comm., Tallahassee, Florida.

Baker, W. W., R. L. Thompson, and R. T. Engstrom. 1980. The distribution and status of Red-cockaded Woodpecker colonies in Florida: 1969–1978. Fla. Field Nat. 8:41–45.

Beal, F. E. L. 1911. Food of the woodpeckers of the United States. U.S. Dept. Agric. Biol. Surv. Bull. 37.

Bechtold, W. A., and H. A. Knight. 1982. Florida's forests. Resour. Bull. SE-62. U.S. Dept. Agric., For. Serv., Southeastern For. Exper. Stat., Asheville, North Carolina.

Carter, J. H., III, R. T. Stamps, and P. D. Doerr. 1983. Status of the Red-cockaded Woodpecker in the North Carolina Sandhills. Pages 24–29 in Red-cockaded Woodpecker symposium II proceedings (D. A. Wood, ed.). Fla. Game and Fresh Water Fish Comm., Tallahassee, Florida.

Carter, J. H., III, J. R. Walters, S. H. Everhart, and P. D. Doerr. 1989. Restrictors for Red-cockaded Woodpecker cavities. Wildl. Soc. Bull. 17:68–72.

Conner, R. N., and B. A. Locke. 1982. Fungi and Red-cockaded Woodpecker cavity trees. Wilson Bull. 94:64–70.

Conner, R. N., and K. A. O'Halloran. 1987. Cavity-tree selection by Red-cockaded Woodpeckers as related to growth dynamics of southern pines. Wilson Bull. 99:398–412.

Conner, R. N., and D. C. Rudolph. 1989. Red-cockaded Woodpecker colony status and trends on the Angelina, Davy Crockett, and Sabine national forests. Res. Pap. SO-250. U.S. Dept. Agric., For. Serv., Southern For. Exper. Stat., New Orleans, Louisiana.

Conner, R. N., and D. C. Rudolph. 1991. Forest habitat loss, fragmentation, and Red-cockaded Woodpecker populations. Wilson Bull. 103:446–457.

Conner, R. N., D. C. Rudolph, D. L. Kulhavy, and A. E. Snow. 1991. Causes of mortality of Red-cockaded Woodpecker cavity trees. Jour. Wildl. Manage. 55:531–537.

Conner, R. N., D. C. Rudolph, D. Saenz, and R. R. Schaefer. 1994. Heartwood, sapwood, and fungal decay associated with Red-cockaded Woodpecker cavity trees. Jour. Wildl. Manage. 58:728–734.

Copeyon, C. K. 1990. A technique for constructing cavities for the Red-cockaded Woodpecker. Wildl. Soc. Bull. 18:303–311.

Copeyon, C. K., J. R. Walters, and J. H. Carter III. 1991. Induction of Red-cockaded Woodpecker group formation by artificial cavity construction. Jour. Wildl. Manage. 55:549–556.

Costa, R., and R. E. F. Escano. 1989. Red-cockaded Woodpecker: status and management in the Southern Region in 1986. Tech. Publ. R8-TP 12. U.S. Dept. Agric., For. Serv., Atlanta, Georgia.

Cox, J., W. W. Baker, and D. Wood. 1995. Status, distribution, and conservation of the Red-cockaded Woodpecker in Florida: a 1992 update. Pages 457–464 in Red-cockaded Woodpecker: recovery, ecology, and management (D. L. Kulhavey, R. G. Hooper, and R. Costa, eds.). Center for Applied Studies in Forests, College of Forestry, Stephen F. Austin State Univ., Nacogdoches, Texas.

DeFazio, J. T., Jr., M. A. Hunnicutt, M. R. Lennartz, G. L. Chapman, and J. A. Jackson. 1987. Red-cockaded Woodpecker translocation experiments in South Carolina. Proc. Ann. Conf. S.E. Assoc. Fish Wildl. Agencies 41:311–317.

DeLotelle, R. S., and R. J. Epting. 1988. Selection of old trees for cavity excavation by Red-cockaded Woodpeckers. Wildl. Soc. Bull. 16:48–52.

DeLotelle, R. S., J. R. Newman, and A. E. Jerauld. 1983. Habitat use by Red-cockaded Woodpeckers in central Florida. Pages 59–67 in Red-cockaded Woodpecker symposium II proceedings (D. A. Wood, ed.). Fla. Game and Fresh Water Fish Comm., Tallahassee, Florida.

DeLotelle, R. S., R. J. Epting, and J. R. Newman. 1987. Habitat use and territory characteristics of Red-cockaded Woodpeckers in central Florida. Wilson Bull. 99:202–217.

Engstrom, R. T., and G. W. Evans. 1990. Hurricane damage to Red-cockaded Woodpecker (*Picoides borealis*) cavity trees. Auk 107:608–610.

Harlow, R. F., and M. R. Lennartz. 1983. Interspecific competition for Red-cockaded Woodpecker cavities during the nesting season in South Carolina. Pages 41–43 in Red-cockaded Woodpecker symposium II proceedings (D. A. Wood, ed.). Fla. Game and Fresh Water Fish Comm., Tallahassee, Florida.

Harlow, R. F., R. G. Hooper, and M. R. Lennartz. 1983. Estimating numbers of Red-cockaded Woodpecker colonies. Wildl. Soc. Bull. 11:360–363.

Hooper, R. G. 1982. Use of dead cavity trees by Red-cockaded Woodpeckers. Wildl. Soc. Bull. 10:163–164.

Hooper, R. G. 1988. Longleaf pines used for cavities by Red-cockaded Woodpeckers. Jour. Wildl. Manage. 52:392–398.

Hooper, R. G., and M. R. Lennartz. 1981. Foraging behavior of the Red-cockaded Woodpecker in South Carolina. Auk 98:321–334.

Hooper, R. G., and M. R. Lennartz. 1983. Roosting behavior of Red-cockaded Woodpecker clans with insufficient cavities. Jour. Field Ornithol. 54:72–76.

Hooper, R. G., L. J. Niles, R. F. Harlow, and G. W. Wood. 1982. Home ranges of Red-cockaded Woodpeckers in coastal South Carolina. Auk 99:675–682.

Hooper, R. G., J. C. Watson, and R. E. F. Escano. 1990. Hurricane Hugo's initial effects on Red-cockaded Woodpeckers in the Francis Marion National Forest. Trans. North Amer. Wildl. and Nat. Resour. Conf. 55:220–224.

Hooper, R. G., D. L. Krusac, and D. L. Carlson. 1991. An increase in a population of Red-cockaded Woodpeckers. Wildl. Soc. Bull. 19:277–286.

Hopkins, M. L., and T. E. Lynn, Jr. 1971. Some characteristics of Red-cockaded Woodpecker cavity trees and management implications in South Carolina. Pages 140–169 in The ecology and management of the Red-cockaded Woodpecker (R. L. Thompson, ed.). Bur. Sport Fish. Wildl., U.S. Dept. Int., and Tall Timbers Res. Stat., Tallahassee, Florida.

Hovis, J. A. 1982. Population biology and vegetative requirements of the Red-cockaded Woodpecker (*Picoides borealis*) in Apalachicola National Forest, Florida. M.S. thesis, Univ. Florida, Gainesville, Florida.

Hovis, J. A., and R. F. Labisky. 1985. Vegetative associations of Red-cockaded Woodpecker colonies in Florida. Wildl. Soc. Bull. 13:307–314.

Howell, A. H. 1921. A list of the birds of Royal Palm Hammock, Florida. Auk 38:250–263.

Jackson, J. A. 1971. The evolution, taxonomy, distribution, past populations and current status of the Red-cockaded Woodpecker. Pages 4–29 in The ecology and management of the Red-cockaded Woodpecker (R. L. Thompson, ed.). Bur. Sport Fish. Wildl., U.S. Dept. Int., and Tall Timbers Res. Stat., Tallahassee, Florida.

Jackson, J. A. 1977a. Determination of the status of Red-cockaded Woodpecker colonies. Jour. Wildl. Manage. 41:448–452.

Jackson, J. A. 1977b. Red-cockaded Woodpeckers and pine red heart disease. Auk 94:160–163.

Jackson, J. A. 1978. Analysis of the distribution and population status of the Red-cockaded Woodpecker. Pages 101–111 in Proceedings of the rare and endangered wildlife symposium (R. R. Odom and L. Landers, eds.). Tech. Bull. WL4, Ga. Dept. Nat. Resour., Athens, Georgia.

Jackson, J. A. 1987. The Red-cockaded Woodpecker. Pages 478–493 in Audubon wildlife report 1987 (R. L. Di Silvestro, W. J. Chandler, K. Barton, and L. Labate, eds.). Academic Press, Orlando, Florida.

Jackson, J. A., and R. L. Thompson. 1971. A glossary of terms used in association with the Red-cockaded Woodpecker. Pages 187–188 in The ecology and management of the Red-cockaded Woodpecker (R. L. Thompson, ed.). Bur. Sport Fish. Wildl., U.S. Dept. Int., and Tall Timbers Res. Stat., Tallahassee, Florida.

Jackson, J. A., W. W. Baker, V. Carter, T. Cherry, and M. L. Hopkins. 1979a. Recovery plan for the Red-cockaded Woodpecker. U.S. Fish and Wildl. Serv., Atlanta, Georgia.

Jackson, J. A., M. R. Lennartz, and R. G. Hooper. 1979b. Tree age and cavity initiation by Red-cockaded Woodpeckers. Jour. For. 77:102–103.

Jackson, J. A., B. J. Schardien, and P. R. Miller. 1983. Moving Red-cockaded Woodpecker colonies: relocation or phased destruction? Wildl. Soc. Bull. 11:59–62.

Jackson, J. A., R. N. Conner, and B. J. S. Jackson. 1986. The effects of wilderness on the endangered Red-cockaded Woodpecker. Pages 71–78 in Wilderness and natural areas in the eastern United States: a management challenge (D. L. Kulhavy and R. N. Conner, eds.). Ctr. Applied Studies, School For., Stephen F. Austin State Univ., Nacogdoches, Texas.

James, F. C. 1991. Signs of trouble in the largest remaining population of Red-cockaded Woodpeckers. Auk 108:419–423.

Komarek, E. V. 1974. Effects of fire on temperate forests and related ecosystems: southeastern United States. Pages 251–277 in Fire and ecosystems (T. T. Kozlowski and C. E. Ahlgren, eds.). Academic Press, New York.

LaBranche, M. S., and J. R. Walters. 1994. Patterns of mortality in nests of Red-cockaded Woodpeckers in the sandhills of southcentral North Carolina. Wilson Bull. 106:258–271.

LaBranche, M. S., J. R. Walters, and K. S. Laves. 1994. Double brooding in Red-cockaded Woodpeckers. Wilson Bull. 106:403–408.

Lennartz, M. R. 1988. The Red-cockaded Woodpecker: old-growth species in a second-growth landscape. Nat. Areas Jour. 8:160–165.

Lennartz, M. R., and R. F. Harlow. 1979. The role of parent and helper Red-cockaded Woodpeckers at the nest. Wilson Bull. 91:331–335.

Lennartz, M. R., and V. G. Henry. 1985. Endangered species recovery plan:

Red-cockaded Woodpecker (*Picoides borealis*). U.S. Fish and Wildl. Serv., Atlanta, Georgia.

Lennartz, M. R., and D. G. Heckel. 1987. Population dynamics of a Red-cockaded Woodpecker population in Georgia Piedmont loblolly pine habitat. Pages 48–55 in Proceedings of the third southeastern nongame and endangered wildlife symposium (R. R. Odom, K. A. Riddleberger, and J. C. Ozier, eds.). Ga. Dept. Nat. Resour., Athens, Georgia.

Lennartz, M. R., P. H. Geissler, R. F. Harlow, R. C. Long, K. M. Chitwood, and J. A. Jackson. 1983a. Status of the Red-cockaded Woodpecker on federal lands in the South. Pages 7–12 in Red-cockaded Woodpecker symposium II proceedings (D. A. Wood, ed.). Fla. Game and Fresh Water Fish Comm., Tallahassee, Florida.

Lennartz, M. R., H. A. Knight, J. P. McClure, and V. A. Rudis. 1983b. Status of Red-cockaded Woodpecker nesting habitat in the South. Pages 13–19 in Red-cockaded Woodpecker symposium II proceedings (D. A. Wood, ed.). Fla. Game and Fresh Water Fish Comm., Tallahassee, Florida.

Lennartz, M. R., R. G. Hooper, and R. F. Harlow. 1987. Sociality and cooperative breeding of Red-cockaded Woodpeckers, *Picoides borealis*. Behav. Ecol. Sociobiol. 20:77–88.

Ligon, J. D. 1970. Behavior and breeding biology of the Red-cockaded Woodpecker. Auk 87:255–278.

Ligon, J. D., P. B. Stacey, R. N. Conner, C. E. Bock, and C. S. Adkisson. 1986. Report of the American Ornithologists' Union Committee for the conservation of the Red-cockaded Woodpecker. Auk 103:848–855.

Locke, B. A., R. N. Conner, and J. C. Kroll. 1983. Factors influencing colony site selection by Red-cockaded Woodpeckers. Pages 46–50 in Red-cockaded Woodpecker symposium II proceedings (D. A. Wood, ed.). Fla. Game and Fresh Water Fish Comm., Tallahassee, Florida.

Mayr, E., and L. L. Short. 1970. Species taxa of North American birds: a contribution to comparative systematics. Publ. Nuttall Ornithol. Club 9:1–127.

Mengel, R. M., and J. A. Jackson. 1977. Geographic variation of the Red-cockaded Woodpecker. Condor 79:349–355.

Murphey, E. E. 1964. Red-cockaded Woodpecker. Pages 72–79 in Life histories of North American woodpeckers (A. C. Bent, ed.). Dover Publ., Inc., New York.

Neal, J. C., D. A. James, W. G. Montague, and J. E. Johnson. 1993. Effects of weather and helpers on survival of nestling Red-cockaded Woodpeckers. Wilson Bull. 105:666–673.

Nesbitt, S. A., B. A. Harris, A. E. Jerauld, P. J. Skoog, C. B. Brownsmith, and G. L. Evink. 1983a. Response of a male Red-cockaded Woodpecker to drastic habitat alteration. Pages 101–104 in Red-cockaded Woodpecker symposium II proceedings (D. A. Wood, ed.). Fla. Game and Fresh Water Fish Comm., Tallahassee, Florida.

Nesbitt, S. A., A. E. Jerauld, and B. A. Harris. 1983b. Red-cockaded Woodpecker summer range sizes in southwest Florida. Pages 68–71 in Red-cockaded Woodpecker symposium II proceedings (D. A. Wood, ed.). Fla. Game and Fresh Water Fish Comm., Tallahassee, Florida.

Odom, R. R. 1983. Georgia's Red-cockaded Woodpecker relocation experiment: a 1983 update. Pages 106–108 in Red-cockaded Woodpecker symposium II proceedings (D. A. Wood, ed.). Fla. Game and Fresh Water Fish Comm., Tallahassee, Florida.

Odom, R. R., J. Rappole, J. Evans, D. Charbonneau, and D. Palmer. 1982. Red-cockaded Woodpecker relocation experiment in coastal Georgia. Wildl. Soc. Bull. 10:197–203.

Ortego, B., and D. Lay. 1988. Status of Red-cockaded Woodpecker colonies on private land in East Texas. Wildl. Soc. Bull. 16:403–405.

Patterson, G. A., and W. B. Robertson, Jr. 1981. Distribution and habitat of the Red-cockaded Woodpecker in Big Cypress National Preserve. Rept. T-613. Natl. Park Serv., South Fla. Res. Ctr., Homestead, Florida.

Porter, M. L. 1984. Home range size and foraging habitat requirements of the Red-cockaded Woodpecker (*Picoides borealis*) in pine habitats of north Florida. M.S. thesis, Univ. Florida, Gainesville, Florida.

Porter, M. L., and R. F. Labisky. 1986. Home range and foraging habitat of Red-cockaded Woodpeckers in northern Florida. Jour. Wildl. Manage. 50:239–247.

Ramey, P. 1980. Seasonal, sexual, and geographical variation in the foraging ecology of Red-cockaded Woodpeckers (*Picoides borealis*). M.S. thesis, Mississippi State Univ., Mississippi State, Mississippi.

Reed, J. M., P. D. Doerr, and J. R. Walters. 1988. Minimum viable population size of the Red-cockaded Woodpecker. Jour. Wildl. Manage. 52:385–391.

Rudolph, D. C., and R. N. Conner. 1991. Cavity tree selection by Red-cockaded Woodpeckers in relation to tree age. Wilson Bull. 103:458–467.

Rudolph, D. C., and R. N. Conner. 1994. Forest fragmentation and Red-cockaded Woodpecker population: an analysis at intermediate scale. Jour. Field Ornithol. 65:365–375.

Rudolph, D. C., H. Kyle, and R. N. Conner. 1990. Red-cockaded Woodpeckers vs rat snakes: the effectiveness of the resin barrier. Wilson Bull. 102:14–22.

Schillaci, J. M., and R. J. Smith. 1994. Red-cockaded Woodpeckers in northwestern Florida produce a second clutch. Fla. Field Nat. 22:112–113.

Shapiro, A. E. 1983. Characteristics of Red-cockaded Woodpecker cavity trees and colony areas in southern Florida. Fla. Sci. 46:89–95.

Short, L. L. 1982. Woodpeckers of the world. Del. Mus. Nat. Hist., Monogr. Ser. 4, Greenville, Delaware.

Stangel, P. W., M. R. Lennartz, and M. H. Smith. 1992. Genetic variation and population structure of Red-cockaded Woodpeckers. Conserv. Biol. 6:283–292.

Taylor, W. E., and R. G. Hooper. 1991. A modification of Copeyon's drilling technique for making artificial Red-cockaded Woodpecker cavities. Gen. Tech. Rept. SE-72. U.S. Dept. Agric., For. Serv., Southeastern For. Exper. Stat., Asheville, North Carolina.

Thompson, R. L., and W. W. Baker. 1971. A survey of Red-cockaded Woodpecker habitat requirements. Pages 170–186 in The ecology and management of the Red-cockaded Woodpecker (R. L. Thompson, ed.). Bur. Sport Fish. Wildl., U.S. Dept. Int., and Tall Timbers Res. Stat., Tallahassee, Florida.

U.S. Forest Service. 1985. Wildlife habitat management handbook. Ch. 400—Management by wildlife species: 420—Red-cockaded Woodpecker. U.S. Dept. Agric., For. Serv., Atlanta, Georgia.

U.S. Forest Service. 1990. Decision notice: finding of no significant impact and environmental assessment—interim standards and guidelines for the protection and management of RCW habitat within 3/4 mile of colony sites. U.S. Dept. Agric., For. Serv., Atlanta, Georgia.

U.S. Forest Service. 1991. Decision notice: finding of no significant impact and supplement to the environmental assessment interim standards and guidelines for protection and management of RCW habitat within 3/4 mile of colony sites (as it pertains to the Apalachicola and Kisatchie national forests). U.S. Dept. Agric., For. Serv., Atlanta, Georgia.

U.S. Forest Service. 1995. Record of decision: final environmental impact for the Red-cockaded Woodpecker and its habitat in national forests in the southern region. Manage. Bull. R8-MB 73. U.S. Dept. Agric., For. Serv., Atlanta, Georgia.

Van Balen, J. B., and P. D. Doerr. 1978. The relationship of understory vegetation to Red-cockaded Woodpecker activity. Proc. Annu. Conf. S.E. Assoc. Fish Wildl. Agencies 32:82–92.

Walters, J. R. 1990. Red-cockaded Woodpeckers: a "primitive" cooperative breeder. Pages 69–101 in Cooperative breeding in birds (P. B. Stacey and W. D. Koenig, eds.). Cambridge Univ. Press, Cambridge, England.

Walters, J. R. 1991. Application of ecological principles to the management of endangered species: the case of the Red-cockaded Woodpecker. Annu. Rev. Ecol. Syst. 22:505–523.

Walters, J. R., P. D. Doerr, and J. H. Carter III. 1988. The cooperative breeding system of the Red-cockaded Woodpecker. Ethology 78:275–305.

Wetmore, A. 1941. Notes on the birds of North Carolina. Proc. U.S. Natl. Mus. 90:483–499.

Wilson, A. 1877. American ornithology. Vol. 1. J. W. Bouton, New York.

Wood, D. A. 1983. Foraging and colony habitat characteristics of the Red-cockaded Woodpecker in Oklahoma. Pages 51–58 in Red-cockaded Woodpecker symposium II proceedings (D. A. Wood, ed.). Fla. Game and Fresh Water Fish Comm., Tallahassee, Florida.

Wood, D. A., and A. S. Wenner. 1983. Status of the Red-cockaded Woodpecker in Florida: 1983 update. Pages 89–91 in Red-cockaded Woodpecker symposium II proceedings (D. A. Wood, ed.). Fla. Game and Fresh Water Fish Comm., Tallahassee, Florida.

Wood, G. W., L. J. Niles, R. M. Hendrick, J. R. Davis, and T. L. Grimes. 1985. Compatibility of even-aged timber management and Red-cockaded Woodpecker conservation. Wildl. Soc. Bull. 13:5–17.

PREPARED BY: Julie A. Hovis, Florida Game and Fresh Water Fish Commission, 1239 S.W. 10th Street, Ocala, FL 34474; and Ronald F. Labisky, Department of Wildlife and Conservation, P.O. Box 110430, University of Florida, Gainesville, FL 32611.

Ivory-billed Woodpecker

Campephilus principalis

FAMILY PICIDAE

Order Piciformes

TAXONOMY: The Ivory-billed Woodpecker (*Campephilus principalis*) is the northernmost of 11 species recognized in the Neotropical genus *Campephilus* and is most closely related to the Imperial Woodpecker (*C. imperialis*) of the mountains of western Mexico. Short (1982) suggests that the two could be conspecific. Two races are generally recognized, *C. p. principalis* of the United States and *C. p. bairdi* of Cuba.

DESCRIPTION: The Ivory-billed Woodpecker is the largest Woodpecker in the United States and perhaps the third largest in the world. Its wing length has been reported (Short 1982) to range from 237–264 mm, varying geographically more than between the sexes, and the only weight reported was about 1 pound (448 g). Generally a black bird, the most distinctive markings are the extensive white on secondaries and inner primaries, showing a white trailing edge on birds in flight and an extensive shield of white on the wings folded over the back when the bird is perched. A white stripe extends up the neck to the bill. Males have a black forehead and red crest, whereas, females lack red on the head. The crest is quite pointed and often curves forward in both sexes, but especially in the female. The iris is yellow in adults and more brown in juveniles. The ivory-colored bill is the character that gave the bird its name, but this alone should not be used to identify the species.

POPULATION SIZE AND TREND: Ivory-billed Woodpeckers were described as common by some early naturalists in the southeast United States. By the late 1800s they were considered enroute to extinction, although Maynard (1881) still considered them "common" and "quite numerous" in the "Gulf Hummock of Florida." Most specimens of Ivory-billed Woodpeckers were collected between 1880 and 1910, an era of rapid expansion of railroads in the Southeast. These brought in the collectors and took out wood and other

products, thus depleting both the Ivory-billed Woodpecker population and its habitat.

Ivory-billed Woodpeckers continue to be reported (although unsubstantiated) from many of the more southern areas of the species' former range, but most, if not all, such reports are likely cases of misidentification. The only recent records that are considered reliable are those in the late 1980s from the mountains of eastern Cuba. No birds are known to exist in North America today, and the population in Cuba may include fewer than a dozen birds.

There are no known Ivory-billed Woodpeckers remaining in Florida, yet undocumented reports come in each year. Most can easily be dismissed as sightings of Pileated Woodpeckers (*Dryocopus pileatus*), which have a crest and are of similar size, or even of Red-headed Woodpeckers (*Melanerpes erythrocephalus*), which have white on the folded wings in much the same way as the Ivory-billed and often have a whitish appearing bill. However, a tantalizing few reports simply cannot be ruled out as having truly not been of an Ivory-billed Woodpecker. Recent such reports (1990–1991) have been winter sightings from the Fakahatchee Strand and from the lower Chipola/Appalachicola swamp areas.

DISTRIBUTION AND HISTORY OF DISTRIBUTION: Two centuries ago, the Ivory-billed Woodpecker was known from throughout the southeast

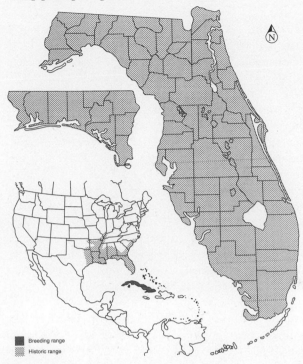

Distribution map of
the Ivory-billed
Woodpecker,
*Campephilus
principalis.*

Breeding range
Historic range

as far west as eastern Texas and southeastern Oklahoma and as far north as
southern Illinois and southern North Carolina. By far the greatest written
record and the greatest number of Ivory-billed Woodpecker specimens are
from Florida. This is undoubtedly due, in part, to the accessibility of Florida to
the "northeastern establishment ornithologists" of the late 1800s and early
1900s, for they are the ones who established the records. They also are the
ones who established the market for Ivory-billed Woodpecker specimens that
several Floridians took advantage of.

Ivory-billed Woodpeckers are known from the panhandle to the Everglades
and from Merritt Island on the east coast to Cedar Key on the west coast.
Areas figuring prominently in our knowledge of the distribution of Ivory-
billed Woodpeckers in Florida include: (1) the Chipola/Appalachicola river
swamps (Eastman 1958), (2) the lower Suwannee River and adjacent California Swamp of the "Big Bend" area (several specimens; Austin 1967), (3) the
Big Cypress Swamp of south central and southwest Florida, (4) numerous
areas in central Florida, including swamp forests associated with the Oklawaha,
Wekiva, Withlacoochee, St. Johns, Indian, and Crystal Rivers.

There are many specimens of Ivory-billed Woodpeckers from Florida, the
largest number of which, about 40, are at the Museum of Comparative Zoology, Harvard University. Hahn (1963) tallies most known specimens, and I
have located a few others in small collections. However, many of the speci-

mens lack sufficient data to identify even the county of origin. Those counties from which specimens are known to have come include: Baker, Brevard, Citrus, Dade, De Soto, Hernando, Hillsborough, Jackson, Jefferson, Lafayette, Lake, Lee, Levy, Manatee, Orange, Osceola, Polk, Taylor, and Volusia. Additional likely counties of origin for specimens are based on named localities and include: Charlotte, Clay, Marion, Putnam, Seminole, Sumter, and Wakulla.

Specific Florida localities for Ivory-bills that are not mentioned in Tanner (1942) include: (1) the entrance to Vista Creek on the Suwannee River (sight record by Frank M. Chapman in 1890; Austin 1967:111), (2) west of the Suwannee at Fort Fannin (sight record, 1891; Austin 1967:127), (3) Paradise Key (record states that it is known from ". . .this region," but a precise locality is not mentioned; Safford 1919), and (4) Tortugas (Bartsch 1919). The last record seems to be in error. Howell (1932:313) notes that it "is apparently based on an error of a copyist; the original entry in the museum catalog is without locality." I wonder if the specimen in question might not have been from Long Key in the middle of the Everglades, since there also is a Long Key in the Tortugas and an original mention of "Long Key" might have been misinterpreted.

There have been many recent reports and searches for Ivory-billed Woodpeckers in Florida. Ivory-bills were reported in the Chipola River Swamp in 1950 by Whitney Eastman (1958) and also apparently from there by Crompton (1950). Dennis (1979) believed that the last evidence of Ivory-bills in the Chipola Swamp was his hearing a bird there in April 1951. Samuel Grimes reported seeing an Ivory-bill in July 1952 about 20 miles south of Tallahassee (James Tanner, pers. comm.). John K. Terres (1986, 1987), former editor of *Audubon Magazine,* reported seeing two Ivory-bills on 9 April 1955, south of Homosassa Springs. William L. Rhein reported seeing a female Ivory-bill near Perry, about one mile east of the Aucilla River, in 1959 (James Tanner, pers. comm.). In August 1966, Bedford P. Brown, Jr. and Jeffrey R. Sanders, Chicago birdwatchers, watched two Ivory-billed Woodpeckers as they fed on beetle-infested pines near Eglin Air Force Base. John Dennis searched the area and did not find the birds, but believed the sighting was valid (Dennis 1979). Between 1967 and 1969, Agey and Heinzman (1971) spent 41 days in an area of Highlands and Polk Counties northwest of Lake Okeechobee, where they reported having seen or heard an Ivory-bill on 11 occasions. The only tangible proof of their observations was the innermost secondary of an Ivory-bill (plus some body feathers that might have been from an Ivory-bill) found near a cavity that had broken open when the cavity tree fell. The identity of the secondary was confirmed by Alexander Wetmore of the Smithsonian. Dennis G. Garratt (1985) described seeing a male Ivory-bill along the Loxahatchee River within Jonathan Dickinson State Park on 30 April 1985, and his description of plumage and call note are more suggestive of the Ivory-billed than of the Pileated Woodpecker. James Tanner (pers. comm.) made numerous trips to Florida in search of Ivory-billed Woodpeckers between 1950 and 1978, checking out many of the above sightings, but also searching what he considered potential habitat for the birds. Areas visited included: the Appalachicola-Chipola swamps (1950), Wakulla River (1960–1978), Aucilla River (1962), Altamaha River (1965), lower Suwannee River (1973), Wacissa River (1975), St. Marks (1960–1978), Lake Okeechobee (date unknown), and Everglades (date unknown). He found no evidence suggesting the presence of Ivory-billed Woodpeckers.

Between 1987 and 1992, I searched for Ivory-billed Woodpeckers in what I considered to be the most promising remaining habitats. These included swamps associated with the Chipola and Apalachicola rivers, the Wekiva River, Fort Drum Swamp, and the lower Suwannee River. In the 1970s and early 1980s, I also visited the Big Cypress Preserve and areas of the Florida Everglades with Ivory-billed Woodpeckers in mind, but not specifically searching for them. None of my efforts has yielded evidence that Ivory-billed Woodpeckers continue to exist in Florida. The Ivory-billed Woodpecker is probably extirpated in North America, but if the Ivory-bill continues to exist here, Florida remains one of the areas of highest probable occurrence. A few birds remain in the mountains of eastern Cuba (Short and Horne 1986; Jackson, pers. observ. in 1988), but their continued survival there is tenuous in spite of Cuban efforts to protect them. Searches by Cuban and Dutch ornithologists since 1988 have resulted in neither further sightings nor fresh signs of feeding activities of the species (Lammertink and Estrada 1995).

HABITAT REQUIREMENTS AND HABITAT TREND: Tanner (1942) provides an excellent review of the habitats used by Ivory-billed Woodpeckers, coming to the conclusion that "all Ivory-bill records have been located in or very near swamps or Florida hammocks." However, Tanner did most of his work with the species in the bottomland forests along the Tensas River in Louisiana, and his intensive studies there have influenced what we commonly think of as "Ivory-bill habitat." Early records suggest that the Ivory-billed Woodpecker in both the United States and Cuba was a bird of extensive old growth forest, perhaps favoring the ecotone between bottomland and upland. In North America the species retreated to the swamps as upland habitats were disturbed by man; in Cuba the sole remaining birds have retreated to montane pines.

The Ivory-bill habitat of north Florida belongs in the "river bottom" category, but in southern areas of the panhandle and in peninsular Florida, the limestone topography and sandy soils have generated a forest mosaic that is substantially different. In these areas, bald cypress (*Taxodium distichum*) was a dominant component of Ivory-bill habitat. Other species associated with the

Ivory-bill habitats of Florida include black gum (*Nyssa sylvatica*), red maple (*Acer rubrum*), red bay (*Persea borbonia*), sweet bay (*Magnolia virginiana*), laurel oak (*Quercus laurifolia*), American elm (*Ulmus americana*), and cabbage palmetto (*Sabal palmetto*). Longleaf (*Pinus palustris*) and slash (*P. elliottii*) pines also must be included as Ivory-bill habitat, for the birds are well known to have fed on beetles from recently dead pines and several Florida nests of Ivory-bills were recorded from pines. One of the most important components of Ivory-billed Woodpecker habitat throughout the species range is the extent of available undisturbed area. A second quality of Ivory-bill habitat is the size of the trees. Large old trees are needed for cavity excavation. A third quality needed is the presence of a continuing supply of large, recently dead trees on which to forage for the larvae of large wood-boring beetles that seem to form the core of their diet. Other foods include other arthropods and a variety of fruits.

Maynard (1881) noted that the Ivory-bill was common in only one section of Florida, "the Gulf Hummock," where the birds were "quite numerous." Eight years later, Frank M. Chapman, referring to a trip down the last 100 km of the Suwannee River into the same region, commented that "We go through the best Ivory-bill region in the state. . ." Tanner (1942) estimated that in the virgin forests of this region, specifically in the California and Wacissa Swamps, the density of Ivory-bills was about one pair per 10 and 6.25 square miles, respectively. In lesser quality habitat, we can assume the area needed per pair would be greater.

The trend in Ivory-billed Woodpecker habitat has been a continuous decline since the arrival of Europeans, with acceleration of the decline in the last decades of the 1800s and first decades of the 1900s. Further accelerated decline can be linked to cutting during World War II and the commercial use of the chainsaw in the late 1940s. A human population explosion in Florida since the 1950s has resulted in further losses. Today there are few areas that are not regularly visited by man. On the positive side, large tracts have been set aside in parks, national forests, wildlife refuges, and other protected areas. Given time and proper management, we could once again have adequate habitat to support Ivory-billed Woodpeckers, if only we had the birds to occupy it.

VULNERABILITY OF SPECIES AND HABITAT: The Ivory-billed Woodpecker shuns humans and requires very large areas of undisturbed forest. With continuing human population growth, accompanying clearing of forest lands, and recreational use of remaining areas, any remaining birds are extremely vulnerable. If the species survives in North America, it may be functionally extinct as a result of habitat and population fragmentation.

CAUSES OF THREAT: Hahn (1963) lists over 400 specimens of Ivory-billed Woodpeckers in museum collections. I have documented an additional 20+ specimens. Of the total, the largest number were collected in Florida. Maynard (1881) noted ". . .they have not only been persistently hunted by collectors, but many have met their fate at the hands of tourists!" These woodpeckers also were considered good to eat. Clearly overhunting was a major problem. Whereas direct killing of birds was important and may still be (they are a big target), the other major threat of the past century has been habitat destruction.

RESPONSES TO HABITAT MODIFICATION: Loss of old growth forest eliminates both foraging habitat and nesting sites of Ivory-billed Woodpeckers. In addition, the birds seem very sensitive to human activity (Jackson, pers. observ. in Cuba). On the other hand, Dennis (1948) published a photograph of an Ivory-billed Woodpecker at its nest in a dead stub in a clearcut area in Cuba. The birds are capable of showing some tenacity, and this offers a little hope.

DEMOGRAPHIC CHARACTERISTICS: As with all woodpeckers, the eggs of Ivory-bills are glossy white. Thirteen Ivory-bill eggs measured by Bendire (1895) averaged 34.87x25.22 mm. Clutch sizes recorded vary from 1–5 eggs (average 2.9). No quantitative data are available for incubation period (probably about 18–20 days), hatching success, nestling period (probably 5–6 weeks based on data in Tanner 1942), or fledging success. Egg dates range from February to May, with chicks found in early February indicating January laying (Tanner 1942). Based on their size and our knowledge of other woodpecker species, it seems likely that Ivory-billed Woodpeckers could live twenty years or more.

KEY BEHAVIORS: Three behaviors that are most useful in identifying Ivory-billed Woodpeckers are its calls, a double-rap it gives with its beak against a tree, and its habit of scaling bark from the trees on which it forages. The calls of Ivory-billed Woodpeckers were recorded in 1935 by Peter Paul Kellogg and Arthur Allen and are available on the records prepared by Kellogg et al. (1971) and Reynard and Garrido (1988). The call consists of a single or double "kent" note, likened to the sound of a child's toy horn. One can imitate the very distinctive sound with a clarinet mouthpiece. I heard Ivory-bills give these calls on eight different days in March 1988 in Cuba, and could distinguish no difference from those recorded in North America. The double-rap is a distinctive behavior of other *Campephilus* woodpeckers and is described by Short (1982); a brief sequence described as the "double-knock" sounds of an Ivory-billed Woodpecker recorded by Reynard in the Big Thicket of Texas in 1969 is available on the record by Reynard and Garrido (1988).

Like most other woodpeckers, Ivory-bills roost solitarily in excavated or natural cavities each night. Both sexes excavate cavities and incubate eggs and care for nestlings and fledglings; the male incubates and broods at night. Family groups remain together for at least a few months (Tanner 1942). Tanner (1942) found that Ivory-bills usually travel in pairs. Flight of the Ivory-billed Woodpecker has been described as level, like that of a crow (*Corvus*), thus different from the undulating flight of most woodpeckers. However, other authors have mentioned an undulating flight. Tanner (1942) observed both patterns, although usually a direct, nonundulating flight. To reach the large beetle larvae on which they feed, Ivory-bills use their chisel-like beak to knock large slabs of bark from trees on which they forage. This extensive scaling can be a good indicator of the presence of Ivory-billed Woodpeckers in an area. Scaling that Reynard (1988), L. L. Short (pers. comm.), and Jackson (pers. observ.) observed in Cuba was distinctive and indistinguishable from that described by Tanner (1942).

CONSERVATION MEASURES TAKEN: Little has been done to protect Ivory-billed Woodpeckers except to urge protection. The cry for protection came early. Maynard (1881) wrote eloquently: ". . .the last stronghold of the Ivory-billed Woodpecker is in the Gulf Hummock but how long they will remain unmolested in this fastness, is a problem which the settlement of that portion of the country will solve before many years have passed. Then, unless they be protected by stringent laws, they will disappear from the surface of the globe."

Following Crompton's (1950) report of Ivory-bills in the Chipola River Swamp, John Baker (1950), president of the National Audubon Society, reported that through the combined efforts of the National Audubon Society, the Florida Game and Fresh Water Fish Commission, local land owners, St. Joe Paper Company, and the Neal Lumber and Manufacturing Company, a Chipola River Wildlife Sanctuary was established to protect the birds. I have found no further mention of this sanctuary in the Ivory-bill literature.

Perhaps it is the seeming futility of the effort, but neither the Federal nor the Florida government had made a major effort to search for this bird until 1986. In 1986, the U.S. Fish and Wildlife Service (USFWS) appointed an Ivory-billed Woodpecker Advisory Committee to examine the status of the species in North America. This committee included woodpecker specialists James Tanner (now deceased), Lester L. Short, and myself. The USFWS funded my efforts to search promising areas of the southeast United States for any evidence of the species' continued existence in 1987–1989. This effort may have been too little, too late.

CONSERVATION MEASURES PROPOSED: If no conclusive evidence of the existence of Ivory-billed Woodpeckers in the United States is produced, the U.S. Fish and Wildlife Service plans to initiate action to declare the *C. p. principalis* population officially extinct. Certainly the remaining population in Cuba should be intensively studied and protected, and the Cuban government has indicated its intent to do both. I have had discussions with both Cuban and U.S. officials about the feasibility of reintroducing birds to the U.S. from Cuba if the Cuban population reaches a stable level. Both sides have unofficially expressed interest in such a move. The sad truths are that the birds in Cuba also are at the brink of extinction, that in spite of sightings by competent ornithologists neither photographs nor sound recordings document the recent occurrence of the Cuban birds, and political barriers at present might be insurmountable.

ACKNOWLEDGMENTS: I thank my wife Bette who has assisted me in the field under the most adverse conditions and has been my best editor. My field work in search of Ivory-billed Woodpeckers in the U.S. was generously supported by the USFWS. My work in the Ivory-bill habitat of Cuba was supported by the National Geographic Society with the cooperation of the Cuban Academy of Sciences and the Cuban National Museum. I acknowledge very valuable discussions and correspondence with James Tanner, Lester Short, and John Dennis, and many others. Curators at numerous museums were most helpful in providing access to specimens.

LITERATURE CITED:

Agey, H. N., and G. M. Heinzmann. 1971. The Ivory-billed Woodpecker found in central Florida. Fla. Nat. 44:46–47, 64.

Austin, E. S. (ed.). 1967. Frank M. Chapman in Florida: his journals and letters. Univ. Florida Press, Gainesville, Florida.

Baker, J. H. 1950. News of wildlife and conservation. Audubon Mag. 46:54–59.

Bartsch, P. 1919. The bird rookeries of the Tortugas. Annu. Rept. Smithson. Inst., 1917:469–500.

Bendire, C. 1895. Life histories of North American birds, from the parrots to the grackles. Spec. Bull. U.S. Natl. Mus. 3.

Crompton, D. H. 1950. My search for the Ivory-billed Woodpecker in Florida. Massachusetts Audubon Soc. Bull. 34(6):235–237.

Dennis, J. V. 1948. Last remnant of Ivory-billed Woodpeckers in Cuba. Auk 65:497–507.

Dennis, J. V. 1979. The Ivory-billed Woodpecker (*Campephilus principalis*). Avicult. Mag. 85:75–84.

Eastman, W. 1958. Ten year search for the Ivory-billed Woodpecker. Atl. Nat. 13:216–228.

Garratt, D. G. 1985. Possible sighting of an Ivory-billed Woodpecker (*Campephilus principalis*) in Jonathan Dickinson State Park South Central Florida. Unpubl. ms.

Hahn, P. 1963. Where is that vanished bird. Royal Ontario Mus., Univ. Toronto Press, Toronto, Ontario.

Howell, A. H. 1932. Florida bird life. Fla. Dept. of Game and Fresh Water Fish, Tallahassee, Florida.

Kellogg, P. P., A. A. Allen, and R. T. Peterson. 1971. A field guide to bird songs. Houghton Mifflin Publ. Co., Boston, Massachusetts.

Lammertink, J. M., and A. R. Estrada. 1995. Status of the Ivory-billed Woodpecker *Campephilus principalis* in Cuba: almost certainly extinct. Bird Conserv. Internat. 5:53–59.

Maynard, C. J. 1881. The birds of eastern North America. C. J. Maynard & Co., Newtonville, Massachusetts.

Reynard, G. B. 1988. The Ivory-billed Woodpecker in Cuba. Pp. 8–10 in Proc. third southeastern nongame and endangered wildlife symposium (R. R. Odom, K. A. Riddleberger, and J. C. Ozier, eds.). Athens, Georgia.

Reynard, G. B., and O. H. Garrido. 1988. Bird songs in Cuba. Cornell Lab. Ornithol., Ithaca, New York.

Safford, W. E. 1919. Natural history of Paradise Key and the nearby Everglades of Florida. Annu. Rept. Smithson. Inst., 1917:377–434.

Short, L. L. 1982. Woodpeckers of the world. Delaware Mus. Nat. Hist. Monogr. Ser. no. 4.

Short, L. L., and J. F. M. Horne. 1986. The Ivory-bill still lives. Nat. Hist. 95(7):26–28.

Tanner, J. T. 1942. The Ivory-billed Woodpecker. Res. Rept. no. 1, Natl. Audubon Soc., New York.

Terres, J. K. 1986. [Article on Ivory-billed Woodpeckers.] Linnean Soc. New York Newsletter, December.

Terres, J. K. 1987. [Correction of locality for Ivory-billed Woodpecker sighting described in December 1986 article.] Unpubl. ms. at the Cornell Lab. Ornithol., Ithaca, New York.

PREPARED BY: Jerome A. Jackson, Department of Biological Sciences, Mississippi State University, Mississippi State, MS 39762.

Kirtland's Warbler

Dendroica kirtlandii

FAMILY EMBERIZIDAE

Order Passeriformes

TAXONOMY: Kirtland's Warbler (*Dendroica kirtlandii*) was originally described by Spencer F. Baird as *Sylvicola kirtlandii* from a specimen secured near Cleveland, Ohio, in 1851 and named in honor of Jared P. Kirtland, a well-known naturalist of that time (Baird 1852; Mayfield 1960). This monotypic species is now placed in the genus *Dendroica* (AOU 1983).

DESCRIPTION: The Kirtland's Warbler is the largest member of the genus *Dendroica* at 12.3–16.5 g (mean = 13.8 g), 149–153 mm in length, and with a wing chord of 64–75 mm (Mayfield 1960; Walkinshaw 1983; Sykes and Kepler, unpubl. data). The plumage is sexually dimorphic. The adult male in alternate plumage is blue-gray above with black streaks on the back, black lores and forehead, a white eye-ring split anteriorly and posteriorly, bright yellow underparts with black streaking along the sides, flanks, and, in some individuals, across the breast, and two narrow, whitish wing bars. The bill, legs, and feet are black. The tail is blue-gray with white spots at the distal end of the outer two rectrices. The adult female in alternate plumage is duller, more subdued in color than the male and without the black lores and forehead. The basic plumage of both sexes in the fall is duller, showing much brown on the upperparts; the males and females become difficult to separate in the field and closely resemble immatures. This species frequently pumps its tail.

POPULATION SIZE AND TREND: The first organized effort to measure the population of the Kirtland's Warbler was in 1951: 432 singing males were located (Mayfield 1953). In 1961, 502 males were counted (Mayfield 1962), but in 1971 only 201 males were reported (Mayfield 1972a). Because of the population drop between 1961 and 1971, it was decided to monitor the population annually (Mayfield 1972a).

113

Kirtland's Warbler, *Dendroica kirtlandii*. (Photo by Paul W. Sykes, Jr.)

Since 1971, the population has been monitored during a ten-day period in mid-June of each year at all known and potential breeding sites. From 1971 through 1989, the singing male count averaged 206 birds and ranged from 167 to 242 (Weinrich 1991). It is generally assumed that the sex ratio is about equal, but recent findings suggest more males than females (Bocetti 1994; Sykes and Kepler, unpubl. data). The population began to increase in 1990 with 265 singing males (Weinrich 1991); this trend continued with 633 males in 1994 and 766 in 1995 (Weinrich 1994, pers. comm.). This increase in the population is believed to be the direct result of the Mack Lake wildfire that occurred in May 1980.

DISTRIBUTION AND HISTORY OF DISTRIBUTION: The Kirtland's Warbler currently breeds in 12 counties of upper (2) and lower (10) Michigan and winters throughout the Bahama Archipelago (Mayfield 1960; Walkinshaw 1983; Sykes 1989; J. Weinrich 1994, pers. comm.). Migration of this species is poorly known (Mayfield 1960; Clench 1973; Walkinshaw 1983). In Florida, the species is an extremely rare irregular transient during 12 April–1 May (Palm Beach County, 3 reports; Alachua County, 2; Duval County, 1) and 9 September–26 November (Dade County, 2 reports, and 1 sighting each for Escambia, Collier, Martin, Palm Beach, St. Lucie, St. Johns, and Wakulla Coun-

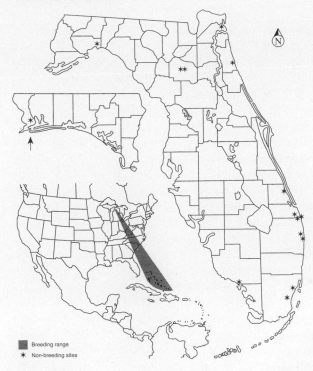

Distribution map
of the Kirtland's
Warbler, *Dendroica
kirtlandii.*

■ Breeding range
✳ Non-breeding sites

ties) throughout the state, except for the Florida Keys, with a least 15 reports: 6 in spring and 9 in fall, however several one-person sightings may be questionable (Sprunt 1954, 1963; Clench 1973; Langridge and Hunter 1984; Robertson and Woolfenden 1992). Because of its extremely small population, solitary behavior on migration, and skulking nature, migrant Kirtland's Warblers may frequent the state more often and in greater numbers than evidence indicates. The historic breeding range of the warbler included 12 counties in northern lower Michigan, which ranks it among the most limited of continental North American nesting species (Mayfield 1960).

Published Florida reports are as follows (starting west end of panhandle and listed north to south in the peninsula): (1) Near Pensacola, Escambia, 26 Nov. 1953, sight record by (SRB) Francis M. Weston (Sprunt 1954); (2) East Goose Creek [now within St. Marks Natl. Wildl. Refuge], Wakulla, 9 Sept. 1919, SRB Ludlow Griscom and John T. Nichols (Mayfield 1960); (3) several kilometers west of Black Hammock Island about midway between New Berlin Road and Pumpkin Hill Creek, Duval, 1 May 1932, specimen of female collected by Samuel A. Grimes but material lost (Mason 1960; Langridge and Hunter 1984; C. Wesley Biggs, pers. comm.); (4) near Salt Run, Anastasia Island, St. Johns, 13 Oct. 1935, specimen collected by Roy C. Hallman (location of specimen unknown) (Mason 1960; Sprunt 1963); (5) Gainesville,

Alachua, 26 April 1934, SRB Robert C. McClanahan (McClanahan 1935);
(6) Gainesville, Alachua, 12 April 1970, SRB James Horner and Robert Wallace
(Wallace 1971); (7) vicinity of Fort Pierce, St. Lucie, 1 Nov. 1918, SRB Hugo
H. Schroder (Schroder 1923); (8) Jonathan Dickinson State Park, Martin,
27 Oct. 1978, SRB Lorne K. Malo (Edscorn 1979); (9) West Jupiter/Jupiter
Inlet, Palm Beach, 19 April 1897, SRB Charles B. Cory (Cory 1898); (10) West
Jupiter/Jupiter Inlet, Palm Beach, 27 April 1897, male (FMNH 20515),
collected by Charles B. Cory (specimen label and computer at Field Mus. Nat.
Hist., Chicago, list year as 1896, but note in Auk by Cory is 1897) (Cory
1898); (11) West Palm Beach, Palm Beach, 2 and 3 Nov. 1961, SRB Veronica
I. Carmen (Stevenson 1962); (12) Hypoluxo Island, Lantana, Palm Beach,
29 April 1982, SRB Howard P. Langridge and Gloria S. Hunter (Langridge
and Hunter 1984); (13) Chokoloskee, Collier, 11 Oct. 1915, SRB J. B. Ellis
(Ellis 1915); (14) Miami, Dade, 21 Sept. 1958, SRB Richard L. Cunningham
and Art Schaffner (Stevenson 1959); and (15) Princeton, Dade, 25 Oct. 1915,
SRB Mrs. Hiram Byrd (Howell 1932).

HABITAT REQUIREMENTS AND HABITAT TREND: The habitat of the
Kirtland's Warbler on its breeding grounds is restricted to young Christmas
tree-sized jack pines (*Pinus banksiana*); the best habitat results from wildfires.
The birds generally occupy stands 6–8 years after establishment and use them
until they reach 20–22 years of age, when they become more mature forest-
like in structure (Mayfield 1960; Walkinshaw 1983; Probst 1986, 1988; Kepler
et al., in press). Stands must be at least 34 ha, but the species prefers 83+ ha
stands. The open landscape is essential to attracting warblers. Northern pin
oaks (*Quercus ellipsoidalis*) are commonly interspersed with the jack pines as a
key component of the community. Such a community also has numerous
small open areas of various sizes and shapes. Wildfires produce the optimum
pattern of densely stocked jack pine with a mosaic distribution of openings.
The ground cover is mostly blueberry (*Vaccinium angustifolium, V.
myrtilloides*), bearberry (*Arctostaphylos uva-ursi*), sweet-fern (*Comptonia
peregrina*), sedge (*Carex pennsylvanica*), some grasses, bracken fern (*Pteridium
aquilinum*), and other associated species on sandy, well-drained soils of low
nutrient content (Mayfield 1960; Smith 1979; Walkinshaw 1983; Zou et al.
1992). Because the well-hidden nests always are placed on the ground, it is
essential that the soil be porous and well-drained to prevent flooding during
rains, and that adequate low cover be present to hide and shade them. The
lower branches of young jack pine also are important for nest cover. On the
wintering grounds the warbler appears to favor low, second-growth coppice
and low, broad-leaved scrub 1–4 m in height (Mayfield 1960, 1972b;
Radabaugh 1974; Sykes 1989).

For socioeconomic reasons and because of adherence to anti-fire sentiment by most land managers, wildfires in the breeding range of the Kirtland's Warbler have been actively suppressed in the last few decades. Such policies have been detrimental to the creation of enough quality habitat for the warbler (Kepler et al., in press). This was evident in the case of the 1980 Mack Lake fire, which started as a prescribed burn and became a wildfire when weather conditions changed (Simard et al. 1983). In 1994, this one burn site (9,646 ha) had about 50% of the entire Kirkland's Warbler breeding population (Weinrich 1994). In lieu of wildfires and hot prescribed burns (crown fires), jack pines are planted to create warbler habitat (Radtke and Byelich 1963; Byelich et al. 1985; Probst 1988). In the past few years about 20–25% of the warblers have nested in these plantations, while 75–80% have used wildfire-created habitat (Weinrich 1988, 1989, 1990a,b, 1991), but in 1994 this shifted to about 50:50 and in 1995 to 57:43 (Weinrich 1994, pers. comm.). With the warbler population on the increase, the question arises as to whether there will be enough quality habitat to sustain the population at this level. Because of funding shortages or logistic problems, the amount of area planted to jack pine has often fallen short of recommended goals (Byelich et al. 1985; minutes of Kirtland's Warbler Recovery Team meetings 1986–1994).

VULNERABILITY OF SPECIES AND HABITAT: Like many other endangered species, the Kirtland's Warbler has been affected by land uses that prohibit optimum management (i.e., widescale burning). Private inholdings with permanent homes, recreational cabins, and other human activities scattered through most warbler habitat prevent using fire in a manner (hot ground and crown fires) that produces the best habitat. However, in recent years occasional large wildfires that were not controllable have created high-quality habitat. In addition, habitat is being created by planting jack pine plantations. Habitat on the wintering grounds and in migration do not appear to be a problem as the limiting factor is on the breeding area (Sykes 1989; Sykes and Kepler, in prep.).

Brood parasitism by the Brown-headed Cowbird (*Molothrus ater*) is an ongoing problem in breeding habitat of the Kirtland's Warbler and has been widely studied (Mayfield 1960, 1961, 1977, 1978; Radtke and Byelich 1963; Walkinshaw 1983). Management procedures in place since 1972 have proven to be highly successful in relieving the situation (Shake and Mattsson 1975; Kelly and DeCapita 1982; Walkinshaw 1983; DeCapita 1991). Most biologists that have worked with the Kirtland's Warbler believe the species would now be extinct if a cowbird control program (i.e., trapping and eliminating cowbirds) had not been implemented (Kepler et al., in press; pers. observ.). Such a direct control program must be continued until an alternative method of control is developed.

CAUSES OF THREATS: In addition to problems with habitat and Brown-headed Cowbirds, there are local demands to eliminate controlled burning and clearcutting and increasing pressure for recreational use of the breeding areas when Kirtland's Warblers are still present (i.e., off-road vehicle use, blueberry picking, hiking, firewood gathering, training and conditioning of dogs for hunting, and early fall rabbit hunting starting in mid-September before all warblers have migrated south). More permanent homes and week-end vacation cabins are being built, bringing with them free-roaming house cats. There is pressure to replace jack pine with more economically valuable tree species, develop oil and natural gas, and build new utility corridors (i.e., power lines, oil pipe lines, and roads). Potential funding shortfalls for Kirtland's Warbler management are always a concern.

RESPONSES TO HABITAT MODIFICATION: The Kirtland's Warbler occupies only the early stages of seral succession in jack pine stands, so modification by fire, clearcutting with natural regeneration, or planting to re-establish this condition are essential to continued survival. On the Bahama wintering grounds, the natural shrubby structure of many of the native upland plant communities, slash-and-burn agriculture with subsequent abandonment after several years and regrowth, provide abundant habitat for the warbler (Sykes and Clench, in prep.).

DEMOGRAPHIC CHARACTERISTICS: Kirtland's Warblers breed in their second year and tend to nest in loose colonies with territories 4.1–8.5 ha in size (Mayfield 1960; Walkinshaw 1983). Most males are monogamous, but a few are polygynous (Mayfield 1960; Walkinshaw 1983; Probst and Hayes 1987; Bocetti 1995). Two broods may be raised per year. The nest, an open cup composed mostly of dried plant material (Southern 1961), is built by the female. The nest is placed on the ground, well concealed under low vegetation, and often near or under a jack pine or northern pin oak. The eggs are light colored with small brownish spots. They are laid in early morning, one a day until the 3–5 egg clutch is completed, and incubated by the female. The incubation period is 13–16 days. Eggs are laid from late May to mid-July. The nestling period is generally nine days; both parents feed the young. Both parents continue to feed the fledglings up to 44 days after they leave the nest (Mayfield 1960; Walkinshaw 1983).

For 208 nests, the hatching success was 82% (n = 171 nests) and fledging success was 68% (n = 142 nests) (Walkinshaw 1983). The fledging rate per pair is 3.3 per year with cowbird control and 0.8 without cowbird control (Mayfield 1960; Walkinshaw 1983). Annual survival rates for adults returning to the breeding grounds in the spring are quite good (Kepler, Sykes, Probst, Bocetti, and Bart, unpubl. data). Life expectancy of males surviving their first winter is 4.0 ± 1.9 years (Walkinshaw 1983). Two banded warblers lived to be 9 years old (Mayfield 1960; Walkinshaw 1983), and recently a third bird was determined to be 10 years old (Probst and Sykes, unpubl. data).

KEY BEHAVIORS: The Kirtland's Warbler is habitat specific, preferring low stature communities; young, dense jack pine with northern pin oak for breeding and dense, low coppice and scrub for wintering. It is known to nest only in Michigan (Mayfield 1960; Walkinshaw 1983; Byelich et al. 1985). It returns to its Michigan breeding areas about 12 May (±5 days), and males immediately set up territories that they vigorously defend (Mayfield 1960; M. E. DeCapita and M. E. Petrucha, pers. comm.). About 20% of the males establish two territories simultaneously, although only 15% of the males attract two females at the same time (Bocetti 1994). The warblers remain on the breeding grounds through most of September (Sykes et al. 1989), with the latest reports on 1 and 6 October (Sykes and Munson 1989; Sykes, unpubl. data). The immature warblers leave earlier than the adults (Sykes et al. 1989). The males are site tenacious on both the breeding and wintering grounds (Mayfield 1960; Walkinshaw 1983; Sykes 1989). Only the male sings from May into July. The song is often given from an elevated perch and can be heard at a distance of up to 0.4 km under calm conditions (Mayfield 1953, 1960, 1962). The song is loud, with three or four low, staccato notes followed by rapid, ringing notes on a higher pitch, and ends abruptly (three sets of couplets; typical song is six notes). There are several variations of the song. The "chip" note is loud and strong, similar to that of the Ovenbird (*Seiurus aurocapillus*).

Foraging generally takes place on the ground and in vegetation up to 4 m high and ranges to over 10 m in scattered taller trees. Foraging methods employed are mainly gleaning, probing and hover-gleaning (Sykes 1989, unpubl. data). On the breeding grounds the diet consists mainly of adult and immature arthropods with some small fruits taken (Mayfield 1960; Sykes and Kepler, unpubl. data), and on the wintering grounds the diet is reversed, being primarily small fruits with some arthropods consumed (Sykes 1989). Caterpillars (generally those species without many bristles) comprise a high percent of the food fed to the young (Mayfield 1960; Bocetti, Kepler, and Sykes, pers. observ.).

CONSERVATION MEASURES TAKEN: Both federal and state laws protect the Kirtland's Warbler as a neotropical migrant songbird and as an endangered species. An Endangered Species Recovery Plan, in place since 1976 (revised in 1985), spells out steps needed to ensure the warbler's recovery. Most management and research listed in the recovery plan have been underway since the plan was completed (Byelich et al. 1985). The species has been censused by a singing male count since 1951, and annually since 1971, to monitor the population (Mayfield 1953, 1962, 1972a; Weinrich 1991, 1994). Designated areas of Michigan's State Forests and Huron National Forest (Mayfield 1963), about 51,600 ha, are managed for the warbler, and public access and activities within these areas are restricted. All designated warbler areas are posted and closed to entry from 1 May–15 August, with several key areas closed through 10 September, in an effort to eliminate disturbance during nesting activities and until the young are independent (Byelich et al. 1985; minutes of Kirtland's Warbler Recovery Team meetings 1987, 1988, 1989). A cowbird control program has been in place since 1972 (Shake and Mattsson 1975; Kelly and DeCapita 1982; DeCapita 1991).

CONSERVATION MEASURES PROPOSED: Continue annual singing male Kirtland's Warbler census to monitor results of management activities, as well as continue research efforts to provide data needed for effective management. Annual cowbird control should be continued on a permanent basis. Management for the warbler should include a prescribed burning schedule to insure that some high quality habitat is always available on a continuing basis. This is in addition to the various treatments used in creating jack pine plantations for use by this endangered species. Revisions to the recovery plan should be undertaken as required.

Research on the Kirtland's Warbler in progress or proposed includes: color marking individuals to determine movements, dispersals, over-winter survival, productivity, etc.; landscape scale of population response to habitat availability; within season movements of warblers as related to habitat quality; changing pattern of warbler occupancy related to ecosystem types and their physiography, soil, microclimate, and vegetation; landscape ecosystems of former and current areas where the species has developed successful populations; population modeling; aging of individual birds in the field by plumage scoring; determine best treatment methods to create cost-effective habitat regeneration; and examine foraging ecology on the breeding grounds.

ACKNOWLEDGMENTS: I thank C. I. Bocetti, C. B. Kepler, and H. F. Mayfield for review of the manuscript and B. J. Fancher for typing.

LITERATURE CITED:

AOU. 1983. Check-list of North American birds. American Ornithologists' Union, Allen Press, Inc., Lawrence, Kansas.

Baird, S. F. 1852. Description of a new species of *Sylvicola*. Ann. Lyc. Nat. Hist. New York 5:217–218.

Bocetti, C. I. 1994. Density, demography, and mating systems in managed and natural habitats. Ph.D dissertation. Ohio State Univ., Columbus, Ohio.

Byelich, J., M. E. DeCapita, G. W. Irvine, R. E. Radtke, N. I. Johnson, W. R. Jones, H. Mayfield, and W. J. Mahalak. 1985. Kirtland's Warbler recovery plan. U.S. Fish & Wildl. Serv., Twin Cities, Minnesota. 78 pp.

Clench, M. H. 1973. The fall migration route of Kirtland's Warbler. Wilson Bull. 85:417–428.

Cory, C. B. 1898. Kirtland's Warbler in Florida. Auk 15:331.

DeCapita, M. E. 1991. Control of Brown-headed Cowbirds on Kirtland's Warbler nesting areas in northern Michigan. Unpubl. Rept., U.S. Fish & Wildl. Serv., East Lansing, Michigan. 9 pp.

Edscorn, J. B. 1979. Florida region. Aud. Field Notes 33:169–171.

Ellis, J. B. 1915. Migratory notes taken fall 1915 by J. B. Ellis, Chokoloskee, Florida. Oologist 32:207,209.

Howell, J. C. 1932. Florida bird life. Florida Dept. Game and Fresh Water Fish, Tallahassee, Florida. 579 pp.

Kelly, S. T., and M. E. DeCapita. 1982. Cowbird control and its effect on Kirtland's Warbler reproductive success. Wilson Bull. 94:363–365.

Kepler, C. B., G. W. Irvine, M. E. DeCapita, and J. Weinrich. 1996. The conservation and management of the Kirtland's Warbler, *Dendroica Kirtlandii*. Bird Conservation International 6.

Langridge, H. P., and G. Hunter. 1984. Kirtland's Warbler sighting in Palm Beach County, Florida. Fla. Field Nat. 12:9–10.

Mason, C. R. 1960. Heretofore unpublished records of the Kirtland's Warbler. Florida Nat. 33:226.

Mayfield, H. F. 1953. A census of the Kirtland's Warbler. Auk 70:17–20.

Mayfield, H. F. 1960. The Kirtland's Warbler. Bull. 40, Cranbrook Inst. Sci., Bloomfield Hills, Michigan. 242 pp.

Mayfield, H. F. 1961. Cowbird parasitism and the population of the Kirtland's Warbler. Evolution 15:174–179.

Mayfield, H. F. 1962. 1961 Decennial census of the Kirtland's Warbler. Auk 79:173–182.

Mayfield, H. F. 1963. Establishment of preserves for the Kirtland's Warbler in the state and national forests of Michigan. Wilson Bull. 75:216–220.

Mayfield, H. F. 1972a. Third decennial census of the Kirtland's Warbler. Auk 89:263–268.

Mayfield, H. F. 1972b. Winter habitat of Kirtland's Warbler. Wilson Bull. 84:347–349.

Mayfield, H. F. 1977. Brown-headed Cowbird: agent of extermination? Amer. Birds 31:107–113.

Mayfield, H. F. 1978. Brood parasitism—reducing interactions between Kirtland's Warbler and Brown-headed Cowbirds. Pp. 85–91 in Endangered birds—management techniques for preserving threatened species (S. A. Temple, ed.). Univ. Wisconsin Press, Madison, Wisconsin. 466 pp.

McClanahan, R. C. 1935. Fifty years after. Florida Nat. (8)53–59.

Probst, J. R. 1986. A review of factors limiting the Kirtland's Warbler on its breeding grounds. Amer. Midl. Nat. 116:87–100.

Probst, J. R. 1988. Kirtland's Warbler breeding biology and habitat management. Pp. 28–35 in Integrating forest management for wildlife and fish (J. W. Hoekstra and J. Capp, comp.). U.S. Dept. Agric. Gen. Tech. Rept. NC-122.

Probst, J. R., and J. P. Hayes. 1987. Pairing success of Kirtland's Warblers in marginal versus suitable habitat. Auk 104:234–241.

Radabaugh, B. E. 1974. Kirtland's Warbler and its Bahama wintering grounds. Wilson Bull. 86:374–383.

Radtke, R., and J. Byelich. 1963. Kirtland's Warbler management. Wilson Bull. 75:208–215.

Robertson, W. B., Jr., and G. E. Woolfenden. 1992. Florida bird species: an annotated list. Fla. Ornith. Soc. Spec. Publ. no. 6.

Schroder, H. H. 1923. Notes from Fort Pierce, Florida. Bird Lore 25:122–123.

Shake, W. F., and J. P. Mattsson. 1975. Three years of cowbird control: an effort to save the Kirtland's Warbler. Jack-Pine Warbler 53:48–53.

Simard, A. J., D. A. Haines, R. W. Blank, and J. S. Frost. 1983. The Mack Lake fire. U.S Dept. Agric. Tech. Rept. NC-83.

Smith, E. 1979. Analysis of Kirtland's Warbler breeding habitat in Ogemaw and Roscommon Counties, Michigan. M.S. thesis, Michigan State University. East Lansing, Michigan. 36 pp.

Southern, W. E. 1961. A botanical analysis of Kirtland's Warbler nests. Wilson Bull. 73:148–154.

Sprunt, A., Jr. 1954. Florida bird life. Coward-McCann, Inc., New York, New York. 527 pp.

Sprunt, A., Jr. 1963. Addendum to Florida bird life. Privately published. 24 pp.

Stevenson, H. M. 1959. Florida region. Aud. Field Notes 13:21–25.

Stevenson, H. M. 1962. Florida region. Aud. Field Notes 16:21–25.

Sykes, P. W., Jr. 1989. Kirtland's Warblers on their winter grounds in the Bahama Archipelago—a preliminary report. P. 28 in At the crossroads—extinction or survival? (K. R. Ennis, ed.). Proc. Kirtland's Warbler Symp., U.S. Forest Serv., Cadillac, Michigan. 97 pp.

Sykes, P. W., Jr., and D. J. Munson. 1989. Late record of Kirtland's Warbler on the breeding grounds. Jack-Pine Warbler 67:101.

Sykes, P. W., Jr., C. B. Kepler, D. A. Jett, and M. E. DeCapita. 1989. Kirtland's Warblers on the nesting grounds during the post-breeding period. Wilson Bull. 101:545–558.

Walkinshaw, L. H. 1983. Kirtland's Warbler: the natural history of an endangered species. Bull. 58, Cranbrook Inst. Sci., Bloomfield Hills, Michigan. 207 pp.

Wallace, R. 1971. Interesting sightings at St. Marks Wildlife Refuge and elsewhere. Florida Nat. 44:63.

Weinrich, J. 1988. Status of the Kirtland's Warbler, 1987. Jack-Pine Warbler 66:154–158.

Weinrich, J. 1989. Status of the Kirtland's Warbler, 1988. Jack-Pine Warbler 67:69–72.

Weinrich, J. 1990a. Status of the Kirtland's Warbler, 1989. Michigan Dept. Nat. Res., Wildl. Div. Rept. no. 3116. 10 pp.

Weinrich, J. 1990b. Status of the Kirtland's Warbler, 1990. Michigan Dept. Nat. Res., Wildl. Div. Rept. no. 3133. 10 pp.

Weinrich, J. 1991. Status of the Kirtland's Warbler, 1991. Michigan Dept. Nat. Res., Wildl. Div. Rept. no. 3150. 10 pp.

Weinrich, J. 1994. The Kirtland's Warbler in 1994. Michigan Dept. Nat. Res., Wildl. Div. Rept. no. 3222. 13 pp.

Zou, X., C. Theiss, and B. V. Barnes. 1992. Pattern of Kirtland's Warbler occurrence in relation to landscape structure in its summer habitat northern lower Michigan. Landscape Ecol. 6:221–231.

PREPARED BY: Paul W. Sykes, Jr., National Biological Service, Athens Research Station, Warnell School of Forest Resources, University of Georgia, Athens, GA 30602-2152.

Bachman's Warbler

Vermivora bachmanii

FAMILY EMBERIZIDAE

Order Passeriformes

TAXONOMY: Bachman's Warbler (*Vermivora bachmanii*) is a monotypic species thought to be closely related to the Blue-winged Warbler (*V. pinus*) and Golden-winged Warbler (*V. chrysoptera*).

DESCRIPTION: One of the smallest passerines, Bachman's Warbler has a total length of 10–11 cm (4–4.5 in.). In the adult male plumage the forehead, sides of head, and underparts are mostly yellow, interrupted by a large black patch on the throat and breast; the anal region and undertail coverts are white; the crown is blackish, fading to gray on the nape; the back is green; and the wings and tail are dusky, the latter with white patches laterally. Adult female and immature male plumages differ from adult male in the usual absence of black on the crown and underparts, the smaller white patches on the tail, and paler yellow ventral regions (sometimes virtually lacking the yellow underneath; Stevenson 1938).

POPULATION SIZE AND TREND: Though the range of Bachman's Warbler encompassed scattered parts of the lowlands deciduous forests of much of the southeast United States, it may have been rare in much of its range (Morse 1989). However, according to all objective data, the warbler decreased dramatically from about 1900 to the 1950s. There are two accepted nonbreeding Florida records since 1950; the last sighting was a single warbler observed and photographed near Melbourne by R. Barber in 1977. If not extinct, Bachman's Warbler is on the verge of extinction (Stevenson 1972).

DISTRIBUTION AND HISTORY OF DISTRIBUTION: Bachman's Warbler formally bred locally from northeastern Arkansas, southeastern Missouri, and south-central Kentucky southeastward to west-central and central Alabama and southeastern South Carolina; perhaps also westward to Louisiana and northward to eastern North Carolina and Virginia. This warbler is known to have wintered only in Cuba, Isle of Pines, and Florida (one winter record).

Bachman's Warbler has appeared in migration as early as 17 July in Florida (Howell 1932). Strangely, most of the fall migration records (July–September) have come from Key West. Spring migration also is very early; the earliest records in Florida are in late February, and a few known migrants were sighted later than early April.

HABITAT REQUIREMENTS AND HABITAT TREND: In the breeding season, Bachman's Warbler is found in bottomland hardwood swamps with large openings to permit the growth of blackberry (*Rubus* sp.) bushes and other understory second-growth plants, with some standing water throughout the year. Most nests were found in low, wet, deciduous forested areas, but inundated for relatively short periods (Hooper and Hamel 1977). Remsen (1984) suggested the warbler was a cane (*Arundinaria gigantea*) specialist, once a dominant feature of southern lowlands, which either was cleared or exhibited periodic mass die-offs following flowering. However, cane may be only incidental to the warbler's choice of breeding habitat (Morton 1989). Migrants in Florida have been reported from a variety of woodlands, usually in lowlands, and have ranged higher in the trees than the species usually occurs on the breeding grounds. It is unclear how much this species is a microhabitat specialist as Kirtland's Warbler (*Dendroica kirtlandii*).

VULNERABILITY OF SPECIES AND HABITAT: As with any small migrant, Bachman's Warbler is subject to mortality due to inclement weather while migrating. Just prior to the turn of the century individual warblers were reported as casualties at the Sombrero Key lighthouse, although none have been reported at lighted structures this century. Large numbers of Bachman's Warblers were taken by early collectors and Brewster and Chapman (Howell 1932) considered this migrant to be more numerous than the Red-eyed Vireo (*Vireo olivaceus*) along the Suwannee River in the early spring of 1890. Although the species would be in Florida for only brief periods and distributed throughout the state during migration, the few individual warblers would be especially vulnerable to changes in the availability of bottomland hardwood habitats.

CAUSES OF THREAT: It is not known what caused the rapid decline of Bachman's Warbler throughout its range, though the warbler does not appear to have been pushed largely to its present condition by human intervention (Morse 1989). Limitations on the wintering grounds have been suggested responsible for the decline of many neotropical migrants (Keast and Morton 1980). With the winter range restricted to western Cuba and Isle of Pines, the warbler's winter resources may have been decimated rather than on the breeding grounds due to extensive conversion of land on these islands to agriculture, especially sugar cane. The most immediate problem facing the warbler is on its breeding grounds north of Florida where there are so few individuals

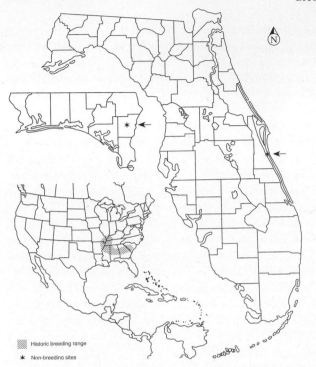

Distribution map of
the Bachman's
Warbler, *Vermivora
bachmanii.*

Historic breeding range

★ Non-breeding sites

over such a vast geographic area that individual birds are unlikely to find mates
and breed. Possible hazards in Florida during migration may be lack of suitable foraging habitat and collisions with lighted structures.

RESPONSES TO HABITAT MODIFICATION: Though poorly known because Bachman's Warbler has been so rare throughout this century, there is
evidence that this warbler requires large stands of mature forested swamps.

DEMOGRAPHIC CHARACTERISTICS: Bachman's Warbler is known to
have nested in the undergrowth of bottomland hardwood swamps within a
meter of the ground. The few nests located were small (height 8.9 cm, 3.5 in.;
width 10 cm, 4 in.) and made of small twigs and lined with leaves, grasses, and
mosses (Bent 1953). The species generally lays 3–5 (usually 3) glossy white
eggs from March to June (Terres 1980). Nothing is known regarding other
aspects of its reproductive success or mortality factors.

KEY BEHAVIORS: According to Brewster (1891), Bachman's Warbler often
feeds while hanging upside-down, like a chickadee, or by poking its bill in
clusters of dead leaves as does the Worm-eating Warbler (*Helmitheros
vermivorus*). Their movements are slow and deliberate; the warbler is a gleaner

as is the case with some other members of the genus (Bent 1953, Morse 1989). Stomach contents yielded the remains of caterpillars and ants (Bent 1953).

The only songs H. Stevenson has heard bore a strong resemblance to that of the Worm-eating Warbler, but other observers have reported songs with longer intervals between notes and described as a hissing "zee-e-eep" (Bent 1953). Displaying males are said to call from numerous perches and singing stations, often in the tree canopy.

CONSERVATION MEASURES TAKEN: Bachman's Warbler is protected by federal and state wildlife regulations, including collecting for scientific purposes.

CONSERVATION MEASURES PROPOSED: Because Florida is south of the breeding range and north of the winter range of Bachman's Warbler, there is little that can be done in the state to ensure the survival of the remnant population that migrates through Florida. However, identifying important stop-over habitats in Florida might reduce the hazards to migrant warblers.

LITERATURE CITED:

Bent, A. C. 1953. Life histories of North American wood warblers. U.S. Natl. Mus. Bull. no. 203. Smithsonian Inst., Washington, D.C.

Brewster, W. 1891. Notes on Bachman' Warbler (*Helminthophila bachmani*). Auk 8:149–157.

Hooper, R. G., and P. B. Hamel. 1977. Nesting habitat of Bachman's Warbler—a review. Wilson Bull. 89:373–379.

Howell, A. H. 1932. Florida bird life. Coward-McCann, Inc., New York.

Keast, A., and E. S. Morton (Eds.). 1980. Neartic avian migrants in the neotropics: ecology, behavior, distribution, and conservation. Smithsonian Inst. Press, Washington, D.C.

Morse, D. H. 1989. American warblers—an ecological and behavioral perspective. Harvard Univ. Press, Cambridge, Massachusetts. 406 pp.

Stevenson, H. M. 1938. Bachman's Warbler in Alabama. Wilson Bull. 50:36–41.

Stevenson, H. M. 1972. A recent history of Bachman's Warbler. Wilson Bull. 84:344–347.

Terres, J. K. 1980. The Audubon Society encyclopedia of North American birds. Alfred A. Knopf, New York.

PREPARED BY: Bruce H. Anderson, 2917 Scarlet Road, Winter Park, FL 32792; and Henry M. Stevenson, Tall Timbers Research Station, Route 1, Box 678, Tallahassee, FL 32312 (Deceased).

Florida Grasshopper Sparrow

Ammodramus savannarum floridanus

FAMILY EMBERIZIDAE

Order Passeriformes

TAXONOMY: The Florida Grasshopper Sparrow (*Ammodramus savannarum floridanus*) was first described by Mearns (1902) from one male and two females collected in 1901 in south Osceola County, Florida. It is one of 12 recognized subspecies (Paynter and Storer 1970; Wetmore et al. 1984). The Florida race is geographically isolated during the breeding season and distinctly marked. Compared to the eastern race (*A. s. pratensis*), the Florida Grasshopper Sparrow is smaller (however the bill and tarsi are longer), dorsally darker, and ventrally paler (Mearns 1902; Smith 1968; M. Delany, pers. observ.). The Florida form has been universally accepted as a valid subspecies (AOU 1910, 1931, 1957; Hellmayr 1938, Paynter and Storer 1970).

DESCRIPTION: Adult Florida Grasshopper Sparrows are flat-headed, short-tailed sparrows about 13 cm in total length. The bill is thick at the base. The wing chord of 25 adult males averaged 60.7 mm (SE = 0.25) and mean weight was 17.2 g (SE = 0.21). Measurements of both wing length and body weight appear to be a reliable indicator of sex (Delany et al. 1994). No sexual chromatic differences have been reported. Dorsally they are mostly black and gray with a pale median stripe at the top of the head, and streaked with brown on the nape and upper back. The stripe over the eye is pale gray to ochraceous. Ventrally adults are whitish and unstreaked with some buff on the throat and breast. The bend of the wing is yellow and the feet are pinkish. The upper breast is streaked in the juvenile plumage. Because of their small size, drab appearance, and cryptic habits, Grasshopper Sparrows are usually heard before they are seen.

POPULATION SIZE AND TREND: Early reports (Howell 1932; Nicholson 1936; Schroeder 1956) provide few documented records of Florida Grasshopper Sparrow abundance but imply a relatively large, widespread population

Florida Grasshopper
Sparrow, *Ammodramus
savannarum floridanus.*
(Photo by D. Bob
Progulske, Jr.)

occurring in scattered "colonies." According to Nicholson (Smith 1968), colonies ranged from 3–12 breeding pairs. Howell (1932) found a colony of "perhaps 30 individuals." Information from Florida Grasshopper Sparrow egg data slips in museum collections evince a minimum of 19 breeding pairs at one location in 1933 (McNair 1986). More recent searches (Stevenson 1968, 1978; Ogden 1971) failed to locate Grasshopper Sparrows or found only isolated pairs or individuals at former colonies. Surveys between 1980–1982 (Delany et al. 1985) and during 1984 (Delany and Cox 1985) located 182 Florida Grasshopper Sparrows at nine sites. The sparrow was found at only two former locations. Searches of 6 other former locations and 11 areas of potential habitat within the bird's range failed to locate Grasshopper Sparrows. Based on singing male surveys from 1989–1993, 212 male Florida Grasshopper Sparrows are now known from seven breeding aggregations (FGFWFC, unpubl. data; Walsh et al. 1995). Assuming an equal sex ratio, the 424 adults would represent a minimum estimate of the total population size. Other colonies and outlying sparrows at known locations probably exist. Although *floridanus* may never have been abundant, recent surveys (Delany and Linda 1994) suggest a continued decline at some locations.

DISTRIBUTION AND HISTORY OF DISTRIBUTION: Grasshopper Sparrows breed throughout most of the continental United States with additional populations locally distributed from southern Mexico to Ecuador and the West Indies. The eastern race is migratory and overwinters in Florida. The Florida Grasshopper Sparrow is presumably nonmigratory (Stevenson 1978, but see Bailey 1925) and limited to the prairie region of southcentral Florida,

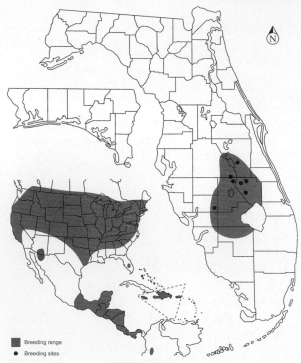

Distribution map of the Florida Grasshopper Sparrow, *Ammodramus savannarum floridanus.*

Breeding range

Breeding sites

isolated from *pratensis* by over 500 km. Its scattered distribution extends from a northern limit 32 km southwest of St. Cloud (Osceola County) to Okeechobee (Okeechobee County) (Nicholson 1936) and indefinite locations southeast of Immokalee and south of Lake Hicpochee (Hendry County) (Howell 1932). The type locality is 11.3 km east of Alligator Bluff on the Kissimmee Prairie, 16 km south of Lake Kissimmee (Osceola County) (Mearns 1902). Most references are to a population(s) 8.0–15.5 km west and southwest of Kenansville (Osceola County) (Howell 1932; Nicholson 1936; Sutton 1946; Schroeder 1956; Stevenson 1978; McNair 1986). Other Florida Grasshopper Sparrows were located 24 km northwest of Basinger (Howell 1932), 14.5–24 km south of Fort Drum (Mason 1932), 1.6 km south of Brighton (Stevenson 1978) (Okeechobee County); an unspecified location west of Lake Okeechobee (Ogden 1971) (Glades County); 1.6 km south of Fort Basinger (Highlands County) (K. C. Parks, pers. comm.); and near the Everglades National Park (Dade County) (Stevenson 1968). Attempts to determine the current distribution of *floridanus* (Delany et al. 1985; Delany and Cox 1986; FGFWFC, unpubl. data) found Grasshopper Sparrows at only two previously recorded sites: 24 km northwest of Basinger and four locations southwest of Kenansville. Florida Grasshopper Sparrows were found at previously unknown sites 11 and

16 km west of Palmdale (Glades County), 22 and 29 km east of Avon Park (Highlands and Polk Counties), 11.0 km southeast and 13.5 km and 20.2 km northeast of Basinger, and 24 km southeast of Arcadia (De Soto County). However, six of nine sites identified by Delany and Cox (1986) have since been abandoned (Delany and Linda 1994). Because movement patterns of Florida Grasshopper Sparrows are not well known, it is difficult to determine what constitutes a discrete site. Despite the location of several new breeding sites, there appears to be an overall contraction of range for *floridanus*.

HABITAT REQUIREMENTS AND HABITAT TREND: Grasshopper Sparrows are grassland birds that require open areas (bare ground) for foraging but enough vegetation for nesting sites (Whitmore 1979). Florida Grasshopper Sparrows occupy large (>50 ha), treeless, relatively poorly drained sites that have burned frequently. A minimum viable population of 50 breeding pairs may require 240–1,348 ha of prairie habitat (Delany et al. 1995). Saw palmetto (*Serenoa repens*) is a dominant plant in the dry prairie plant community and occurred in 34% of 320 m² plots located on 32 sparrow territories. Other common plants included dwarf oak (*Quercus minima*), St. Johns wort (*Hypericum* spp.), pineland three awn (*Aristida stricta*), and bluestems (*Andropogon* spp.) (Delany et al. 1985). Suitable habitat ranged from thick (34% shrub cover), low (57 cm) palmetto scrub to grass pastures with a sparse (<10% shrub cover) or patchy cover of shrubs and saw palmetto. Compared to other Grasshopper Sparrows, habitat used by *floridanus* is characterized by higher values for mean shrub cover (19.2%), bare ground (21.9%), and lower values for mean vegetation height (27.8 cm), and mean litter cover (14.4%). The proportion of grass cover (25.5%) is similar to that reported for other subspecies (Delany et al. 1985). Although the original habitat of *floridanus* may have been "the stunted growth of saw palmetto and dwarf oaks. . ." of the native prairie (Howell 1932), it has adapted to and benefited from conditions induced by range management at some cattle pastures. Frequent fires maintain the vegetation in a structurally simple, early successional stage preferred by the sparrow. Because of its nesting requirements (Nicholson 1936), however, it is unlikely that the sparrow can persist in intensively managed pastures where all shrubs and clumps of grass are removed. Much of the native prairie has been converted to improved pasture (Davis 1980) or reduced by agriculture (Callahan et al. 1990). The cessation of range management activities also is detrimental. The exclusion of fire may allow vegetation to develop toward a successional stage unusable by Grasshopper Sparrows. Dense vegetation and accumulated litter may preclude effective foraging. Land-use trends at former locations indicate continued loss of habitat for *floridanus* (Delany and Cox 1986; Delany and Linda 1994).

VULNERABILITY OF SPECIES AND HABITAT: The Florida Grasshopper Sparrow is limited to a relatively small geographic area and disappearing plant community. Sedentary populations that depend on immigration for stability are jeopardized by isolation due to habitat loss. Most populations occur on private lands that are vulnerable to conversion. Range management at occupied sites may change and render them unsuitable for Grasshopper Sparrows. No critical habitat was designated (Federal Register, Vol. 51, No. 147, 1986). The cooperation of ranchers is essential to the recovery of the subspecies; however, most are not aware of the sparrow or its habitat requirements. Additional public information is needed. The Florida Grasshopper Sparrow could be delisted if 50–100 breeding pairs become established at each of 25 secure, discrete sites throughout its former range (USFWS 1988).

CAUSES OF THREAT: The principle threat to *floridanus* is habitat loss or degradation. Intensive pasture improvements eliminate foraging areas and potential nest sites. The exclusion of range management (especially prescribed burns) allows the vegetation to become too tall and dense to be usable by Grasshopper Sparrows. Habitat also is lost when prairie pastures are converted to farmland and pine plantations.

RESPONSES TO HABITAT MODIFICATION: Other Grasshopper Sparrows occur in scattered breeding aggregations and their range and abundance fluctuate in response to alterations to grasslands (Smith 1963, 1968; Cody 1985). This nonmigratory race occurring in what appears to be sedentary breeding aggregations may be slower to follow a shifting resource and be at a disadvantage. Most Florida Grasshopper Sparrows are located on pastures where ranchers conduct prescribed burns during the winter (November–January) at 2–3-year intervals. Grasshopper Sparrows will breed at locations as soon as one month post-burn (pers. observ.) and three months after roller chopping (Delany and Cox 1986). After an intervening fire, territory locations of color-marked adult males corresponded generally with locations the previous year (Delany et al. 1992). However, frequent burning seems to encourage habitat compositions associated with greater densities of sparrows (Delany and Cox 1986; Walsh et al. 1995). Cattle grazing at 1 animal/8 ha does not appear to be detrimental. Florida Grasshopper Sparrows probably cannot remain in pastures that become intensively managed, converted to pine plantations, or farmland. The abandonment of some known sites was probably a response to changes in land management (Delany and Linda 1994). Interestingly, breeding populations were found in abandoned agricultural plots that were reverting to prairie (L. E. Williams, pers. comm.; M. Delany, pers. observ.). The Florida Grasshopper Sparrow may be responsive to habitat restoration. However, additional information on colonization, habitat use, and breeding success is needed before responses can be fully assessed.

DEMOGRAPHIC CHARACTERISTICS: The female Grasshopper Sparrow incubates 3–5 eggs for 11–12 days, and broods young for 6–8 days. Two broods may occur. Eggs are white, speckled with reddish-brown, and measure 1.83 x 1.40 cm (Sprunt 1954). Florida grasshopper sparrow nests are located on the ground shielded by saw palmetto, clumps of grass (Nicholson 1936), dwarf oak, dwarf huckleberry (*Gaylussacia dumosa*), or St. Johns wort (M. Delany, pers. observ.). A nest with eggs was found as early as 2 April (Howell 1932). Nicholson (1936) found nests with eggs and nests under construction on 23 April. Using information from oology slips for 51 egg sets, McNair (1986) calculated the mean clutch size to be 3.7 eggs and estimated that dates of clutch initiation ranged from 21 March to 22 June. The annual survival rate for 48 color-marked adult males was 0.60 and mean life expectancy for adults was 1.95 years (Delany et al. 1993).

Sizes of 30 breeding territories ranged from 0.57 to 4.82 ha and averaged 1.77 ha (Delaney et al. 1995). Most (21 of 25) resighted or recaptured individuals occupied the same breeding territory during 2–4 successive years. Movements outside the previous year's territory were ≤570 m. Territories were often near or partly overlapped those of Bachman's Sparrows (*Aimophila aestivalis*). However, Bachman's Sparrows usually occupied areas of taller, more dense saw palmettos. No interspecific aggression was observed. Florida Grasshopper Sparrow breeding aggregations are comprised of 2 to (an estimated) 233 pairs and can cover several km² (Nicholson 1936; Walsh et al. 1995). The minimum distance between known, apparently discrete breeding locations is 11 km. Breeding locations may be separated by up to 48 km (Smith 1968). Little information is available on Florida Grasshopper Sparrows outside the breeding season. Two males banded during April were recaptured in January, 15 m and 120 m from their original locations. Males apparently remain on the breeding territory throughout the year.

KEY BEHAVIORS: Grasshopper Sparrows are secretive and easily overlooked during surveys. In Florida, searches for singing males should be conducted between April and July. Singing occurs throughout the day but is more frequent from sunrise to 0900 hours, and for about 15 minutes before sunset. The male's song is weak and insect-like, giving rise to the birds' common name. The song usually consists of three low-pitched introductory notes, followed by a longer, higher pitched "buzz." The "grasshopper song," sustained song, and trill vocalizations are similar to those described by Smith (1959). The species is monogamous and both sexes care for the young. Nonparental attendants have been reported (Kaspari and O'Leary 1988).

CONSERVATION MEASURES TAKEN: The Florida Grasshopper Sparrow is listed as endangered by the State of Florida (Chapter 39–27, Florida Administration code) and the U.S. Fish and Wildlife Service (Federal Register, Vol. 51, No. 147, 1986). Both listings provide protection from take. The Endangered Species Act also protects some habitat. Consultations between federal agencies have reduced or eliminated adverse impacts to Grasshopper Sparrows on the U.S. Air Force Avon Park Range (Highlands and Polk counties). Suitable habitat is maintained for Florida Grasshopper Sparrows on the Avon Park Range, Three Lakes Wildlife Management Area (Osceola County), and the Audubon Society's Kissimmee Prairie Sanctuary (Okeechobee County). During the breeding season, surveys are conducted to monitor known colonies and search for new populations (FGFWFC, Project 7514, U.S. Air Force surveys).

CONSERVATION MEASURES PROPOSED: Actions designed to benefit the subspecies are outlined in the Florida Grasshopper Sparrow Recovery Plan (USFWS 1988). These include measures to protect and enhance habitat, determine the sparrows' biological needs, increase public information, and develop a captive breeding program if populations continue to decline.

ACKNOWLEDGMENTS: H. Blackburn, R. Bowman, S. D. Coltman, P. Ebersbach, J. W. Fitzpatrick, C. Ford, D. Ford, G. Goldstein, S. A. Hedges, R. Hooten, T. Logue, K. Olsen, D. R. Progulske, Jr., Col. J. Rogers, J. A. Rodgers, Jr., H. B. Tordoff, S. Van Hook, V. Wallers, P. B. Walsh, H. Whitaker, and G. Wolfenden assisted with banding efforts. I thank the U.S. Air Force for access to the Avon Park Range. Z. Browning, N. Chandler, and J. Huffman participated in recent surveys. D. A. Darrow, R. S. DeLotelle, and D. R. Progulske, Jr. provided survey data for some locations. Special appreciation is extended to ranchers who allowed access to their properties. J. R. Brady, S. A. Nesbitt, J. A. Rodgers, Jr., H. M. Stevenson, and T. Webber reviewed earlier drafts of this manuscript. C. T. Moore and T. L. Steele assisted with its preparation.

LITERATURE CITED:
AOU. 1910. Check-list of North American birds, 3rd edition. American Ornithologists' Union, New York.
AOU. 1931. Check-list of North American birds, 4th edition. American Ornithologists' Union, Lancaster, Pennsylvania.
AOU. 1957. Check-list of North American birds, 5th edition. American Ornithologists' Union, Baltimore, Maryland.
Bailey, H. H. 1925. The birds of Florida. The Williams and Wilkins Co., Baltimore, Maryland. 146 pp.

Callahan, J. L., C. Barnett, and J. W. H. Cates. 1990. Palmetto prairie creation on phosphate-mined lands in central Florida. Restor. and Manage. Notes 8:94–95.

Cody, M. L. 1985. Habitat selection in grassland and open-country birds. Pp. 191-251 in Habitat selection in birds (M. L. Cody, ed.). Academic Press, Inc. Orlando, Florida. 558 pp.

Davis, J. H. 1980. General map of natural vegetation of Florida. Agric. Exp. Stn. Circ. S-178 Univ. Florida. Gainesville, Florida.

Delany, M. F., and J. A. Cox. 1985. Florida Grasshopper Sparrow survey. Unpubl. Rept. U.S. Fish and Wildlife Service, Jacksonville, Florida. 21 pp.

Delany, M. F., and J. A. Cox. 1986. Florida Grasshopper Sparrow breeding distribution and abundance in 1984. Fla. Field Nat. 14:100-104.

Delany, M. F., H. M. Stevenson, and R. McCracken. 1985. Distribution, abundance, and habitat of the Florida Grasshopper Sparrow. Jour. Wildl. Manage. 49:626-631.

Delany, M. F., D. R. Progulske, and S. D. Coltman. 1992. Netting and banding Florida Grasshopper Sparrows. North Amer. Bird Bander 17:45–47.

Delany, M. F., C. T. Moore, and D. R. Progulske, Jr. 1993. Survival and longevity of adult male Florida Grasshopper Sparrows. Proc. Ann. Conf. Southeast. Assoc. Fish and Wildl. Agencies 47: 336–369.

Delany, M. F., and S. B. Linda. 1994. Characteristics of occupied and abandoned Florida Grasshopper Sparrow territories. Fla. Field Nat. 22:106–109.

Delany, M. F., C. T. Moore, and D. R. Progulske, Jr. 1994. Distinguishing gender of Florida Grasshopper Sparrows using body measurements. Fla. Field Nat. 22:48–51.

Delany, M. F., C. T. Moore, and D. R. Progulske, Jr. 1995. Territory size and movements of Florida Grasshopper Sparrows. Jour. Field Ornithol. 66:305–309.

Hellmayr, C. E. 1938. Catalogue of birds of the Adjacent Islands. Part XI. Field Museum of Natural History, Zoological Series, Vol. XIII, Part XI.

Howell, A. H. 1932. Florida bird life. Coward-McCann, New York. 579 pp.

Kaspari, M., and H. O'Leary. 1988. Nonparental attendants in a north-temperate migrant. Auk 105:792–793.

Mason, C. R. 1932. Notes from correspondents. Fla. Nat. 6:15.

McNair, D. B. 1986. Clutch information for the Florida Grasshopper Sparrow from oological collections. Fla. Field Nat. 14:48-49.

Mearns, E. A. 1902. Descriptions of three new birds from the southern United States. Proc. U.S. Nat. Mus. 24:915-926.

Nicholson, W. H. 1936. Notes on the habits of the Florida Grasshopper Sparrow. Auk 53:318-319.

Ogden, J. C. 1971. Florida region. Amer. Birds 25:280-281.

Paynter, R. A., Jr., and R. W. Storer. 1970. Check-list of birds of the world. Vol. XIII. Museum of Comparative Zoology, Cambridge, Massachusetts.

Schroeder, H. H. 1956. The Florida Grasshopper Sparrow. Audubon Mag. 58:70-71, 92.

Smith, R. L. 1959. The songs of the Grasshopper Sparrow. Wilson Bull. 71:141–152.

Smith, R. L. 1963. Some ecological notes on the Grasshopper Sparrow. Wilson Bull. 75:159–165.

Smith, R. L. 1968. Grasshopper Sparrow. Pp. 725-745 in Life histories of North American cardinals, grosbeaks, buntings, towhees, finches, sparrows, and allies. Part 2 (O. L. Austin, Jr., ed.). U.S. Nat. Mus., Bull. 237, part 2. Dover Publ. Inc., New York.

Sprunt, A., Jr. 1954. Florida bird life. National Audubon Society and Coward-McCann, Inc., New York. 527 pp.

Stevenson, H. M. 1968. Florida region. Aud. Field Notes 22:599-602.

Stevenson, H. M. 1978. Endangered Florida Grasshopper Sparrow. Pages 15-16 in Rare and endangered biota of Florida, Vol. 2—birds (H. W. Kale, II, ed.). Univ. Florida Presses, Gainesville, Florida.

Sutton, G. M. 1946. A baby Florida Sandhill Crane. Auk 63:100-101.

USFWS. 1988. Recovery plan for Florida Grasshopper Sparrow. U.S. Fish and Wildlife Service, Atlanta, Georgia. 22 pp.

Walsh, P. B., D. A. Darrow, and J. G. Dyess. 1995. Habitat selection by Florida Grasshopper Sparrows in response to fire. Southeast. Assoc. Fish and Wildl. Agencies 49: in press.

Wetmore, A., R.F. Pasquier, and S.L. Olson. 1984. The birds of the republic of Panama, part 4. Smithsonian Institution Press, Washington, D.C. 670 pp.

Whitmore, R. C. 1979. Short-term changes in vegetation structure and its effects on Grasshopper Sparrows in West Virginia. Auk 96:621–625.

PREPARED BY: Michael F. Delany, Florida Game and Fresh Water Fish Commission, Wildlife Research Laboratory, 4005 South Main Street, Gainesville, FL 32601.

Endangered

Cape Sable Seaside Sparrow
Ammodramus maritimus mirabilis

FAMILY EMBERIZIDAE

Order Passeriformes

TAXONOMY: The Seaside Sparrow (*Ammodramus maritimus*) is divided into nine recognized subspecies (Funderburg and Quay 1983). Of these, the Dusky Seaside Sparrow (*A. m. nigrescens,* recently extinct) of central Florida's Atlantic coast and the Cape Sable Seaside Sparrow (*A. m. mirabilis*) of southern Florida have isolated and restricted ranges and were once considered separate species (AOU 1983). The other seven subspecies are divided between two relatively contiguous ranges from Massachusetts south to northeastern Florida and along the Gulf coast from western Florida west to southeastern Texas.

Often placed in the genus *Ammospiza* (AOU 1983), the Seaside Sparrows probably evolved from a salt-marsh dwelling Savannah Sparrow (*Passerculus sandwichensis*) ancestor (Funderburg and Quay 1983). Fluctuating sea levels and geologic events, especially the emergence of the Florida peninsula, divided the ancestral population among isolated patches of Seaside Sparrow habitat. Over time most of these patches merged and split with changing geologic conditions, thus, causing differing levels of isolation and interbreeding within the metapopulation. The Cape Sable Seaside Sparrow, located at the extreme southern tip of the Florida peninsula, is currently the most isolated of all the groups, and probably has been so for most of its existence. Its nearest neighbor is Scott's Seaside Sparrow (*A. m. peninsulae*), about 300 km north along the mangrove forest-dominated Gulf coast. If the Cape Sable Seaside Sparrow survives long enough, it may speciate away from the Seaside Sparrow complex.

DESCRIPTION: Much of the following is taken from Werner's (1978) account of the Cape Sable Seaside Sparrow. A medium-sized sparrow (14 cm long) with an olive-gray back, it is the palest of all Seaside Sparrows (Funderburg and Quay 1983). The dorsal side of the tail and wings is olive-brown. The breast and sides are light gray with dark olive-gray streaks, and the belly is

Cape Sable Seaside
Sparrow, *Ammo-
dramus maritimus
mirabilis.* (Photo
by Stuart Pimm)

unstreaked. The legs, ear patch, and bill are gray. The head is accented by
yellow lores and white lines extending along the jaw above the dark olive-gray
to black whisker stripes. Sexes are similar. Immatures are streaked with brown
on the back, have reduced streaking on the breast and sides, and are lacking
the whisker mark and yellow of the head.

POPULATION SIZE AND TREND: Oron Bass, Jr. conducted three similar,
comprehensive censuses of the Cape Sable Seaside Sparrow. The first census in
1981 produced an estimated 6,600 birds. The second survey 11 years later
(1992) had virtually the same results (6,400 birds). However, Bass' last census, conducted during the breeding season (spring) of 1993, resulted in an
estimate of 3,700 birds.

   There are two possible, though not mutually exclusive, explanations for the
low numbers of sparrows observed in 1993: 1) the 1993 breeding season was
the first after Hurricane Andrew ripped a path across the bird's entire range in
August 1992, possibly resulting in high mortality; and 2) it was a very wet
spring, with much of the sparrow's habitat covered by surface water, which
may have suppressed breeding activity (i.e., singing is the primary means of
detecting birds). Following Bass' protocol, Thomas Brooks estimated the
population of sparrows to be 2,800 birds in 1995. Nearly the entire population was found east of Shark Slough. Thus, the decline in the sparrow population from 1992 to 1995 can be mostly accounted for by the disappearance of
birds from the western half of their range.

   Certain aspects of this subspecies' biology preclude defining long-term
population trends. Its range is restricted to patches of suitable habitat somewhat isolated from each other by physiographic features (pine forest, deep

Distribution map of the Cape Sable Seaside Sparrow, *Ammodramus maritimus mirabilis.*

slough). The dynamics of hydrology, fire, vegetation structure, and hurricanes effect each of these patches independently. This complex geographical-habitat array means that in any one breeding season a variable number of patches will be either very productive for sparrows, uninhabitable, or intermediate between these two conditions. Also, when suitable habitat becomes available, abandoned patches could be recolonized. The result is a great deal of annual variation in the amount of habitat the sparrows could occupy and, consequently, variation in the number of birds. This high level of variation has probably caused occasions where the entire population numbered only a few thousand individuals in one or two patches. Whereas defining trends in the population of Cape Sable Seaside Sparrows may be artificial, there are real trends in habitat (i.e., shrub invasion) that directly affect sparrow numbers over time (see below).

DISTRIBUTION AND HISTORY OF DISTRIBUTION: The original range of this secretive subspecies of seaside sparrow probably included all suitable habitat of southern and southwestern peninsular Florida (Werner 1978). The limits of known occurrence are bounded to the south by Cape Sable (Monroe County), where it was discovered by Howell (1919), to the northwest by Ochopee (Collier County; Anderson 1942), and, to the east through Taylor

Slough and East Everglades (Dade County; Ogden 1972; Bass and Kushlan 1982).

Changes in vegetation, both natural and man-caused, have resulted in a constriction of Cape Sable Seaside Sparrow distribution. Cape Sable was populated by sparrows until a 1935 Hurricane apparently extirpated them by causing long-term changes to the vegetational composition in the coastal prairie (Werner 1983). A small population was found there in the early 1970s (Werner 1975), but none have been seen there since 1979 (Kushlan et al. 1982). The environs of Ochopee, the northernmost portion of the sparrow's range, held a few birds as late as 1979, but none have been recorded in recent years as saltwater intrusion and off-road vehicle use have drastically altered the habitat (Kushlan et al. 1982; Bass, unpubl. data). A noticeable downward trend in sparrow occurrence also has occurred in the east Everglades area—altered hydrologic conditions have allowed invasion of the prairie by hardwood species. A 1992 survey of the area showed a notable decline in sparrows compared to 1981 at those sites with shrub invasion. In 1993, no birds were found at shrub-invaded sites.

Through 1992 the distribution was composed of two large areas on either side of Shark Slough that together accounted for 87% of the estimated 1992 population. The remaining birds were found in the upper reaches of Taylor Slough and on the eastern flank of Shark Slough, north of Long Pine Key. Since 1993, birds have all but disappeared from areas west of Shark Slough possibly due to the artificial maintenance of high surface water in that area.

HABITAT REQUIREMENTS AND HABITAT TREND: Cape Sable Seaside Sparrows are found in fresh to slightly brackish interior marshes (Werner 1978). The highest densities of sparrows are found in *Muhlenbergia* prairie, although species composition is less important than the structure of the vegetation (i.e., stem density, proportion of living to dead plant material, and absence of woody vegetation apparently are important [Werner 1975]). Areas with more or less continuous hydroperiod, usually dominated by sawgrass (*Cladium jamaicensis*), are either avoided or exhibit low sparrow density. Fire is an essential element in maintaining sparrow habitat. Periodic fires inhibit invasion of hardwood species into the marsh and prevent build-up of dead plant material, either of which makes an area uninhabitable for sparrows. In Taylor Slough, Werner (1975) found sparrow numbers increasing up to 3 years after a fire, then declining until absent by the sixth year.

Sparrow habitat outside of federally owned and managed lands (Ochopee and east Everglades) has deteriorated over the last several decades. Fortunately, these areas make up a relatively small portion of the subspecies' range. Most sparrow habitat inside Everglades National Park and Big Cypress National Preserve is safe. However, an impending effort to restore a more natural water regime to Taylor Slough will increase hydroperiod and surface water depth in some sparrow habitat. To date, the consequences of this action have not been conclusively investigated.

VULNERABILITY OF SPECIES AND HABITAT: The Cape Sable Seaside Sparrow's vulnerability to extinction lies in factors that are unpredictable and, for the most part, outside of the realm of management. Given the sparrow's limited range, it is not difficult to imagine a worst-case scenario where the dynamics of fire and hydrology coincide to restrict the population to a small area that is subject to a hurricane or other natural disaster. That the sparrow has existed for a long time in its limited range suggests that it is capable of overcoming such rare catastrophic events. Aggressive control of exotic species and prudent use of fire management ensures that most Cape Sable Seaside Sparrow habitat within federally owned lands can be maintained.

RESPONSES TO HABITAT MODIFICATION: Modification of Cape Sable Seaside Sparrow habitat usually is the result of fire exclusion, repeated dry-season fires, or permanent hydroperiod extension or contraction. In each of these cases sparrows would probably disappear from the affected area. Fire exclusion or shortened hydroperiod allow for invasion of hardwood plants and overgrowth of grasses, while repeated fires or lengthened hydroperiod decrease plant species composition and diversity. Obviously, gross alteration of habitat by humans (e.g., agriculture, repeated off-road vehicle use) also would extirpate sparrows from an area.

DEMOGRAPHIC CHARACTERISTICS: To date the only data available concerning Cape Sable Seaside Sparrow demographics are from Werner's (1975, 1978) work conducted mostly in Taylor Slough. Nesting can occur from February through August with most activity during April and May. Hydroperiod dictates the length of the nesting season; however, rising surface water abruptly halts breeding activity. Clutch size is usually 3–4 eggs (mean = 3.53) and 2–3 clutches are laid each season. Incubation is probably 12 days and young fledge at 9–11 days old. Werner (1975) reported a 75% success rate for nests, 2.12 fledglings per nesting attempt, and 2.83 fledglings per successful nest. As with most small passerines, longevity probably rarely exceeds 5 years. In short, this species has remarkable reproductive capacity that allows it to persist in its spatially and temporally patchy environment.

CONSERVATION MEASURES TAKEN: Few conservation measures have been taken specifically for the Cape Sable Seaside Sparrow. Until recently, concern centered on the nearly complete lack of knowledge of this subspecies' ecology. Werner (1975) and Bass and Kushlan (1982) provided important baseline information on its life history and distribution, respectively. However, it was only with the repetition of the comprehensive census in 1992 and 1993 that this information could be applied in a meaningful way. These results are currently being analyzed in an attempt to predict the effects of proposed changes in the hydrology of the Taylor Slough basin on the sparrow (Curnutt, unpubl. data).

CONSERVATION MEASURES PROPOSED: Although the Cape Sable Seaside Sparrow is not in immanent danger of extinction, it should be kept in mind that there is a frighteningly small amount of data concerning this bird. Research efforts should include continuing the comprehensive survey annually for at least 5 consecutive years to test hypotheses concerning the dynamics of sparrow distribution and numbers, and the collection of more data on the response of sparrows to fire for the development of a realistic species-specific fire management plan. Data on sparrow response to the timing and amount of surface water should also be collected and analyzed so that an informed management decision can be made with regards to the proposed "Everglades Restoration" Projects. The current National Park Service management plan (Kushlan et al. 1982) should be reviewed and possibly revised in light of more current information and the management plan should be implemented.

ACKNOWLEDGMENTS: I thank Sonny Bass of Everglades National Park for sharing his field data on the Cape Sable Seaside Sparrow. I also thank one anonymous reviewer.

LITERATURE CITED:

AOU. 1983. Checklist of North American birds. 6th ed. Amer. Ornithol. Union, Allen Press, Lawrence, Kansas.

Anderson, W. 1942. Rediscovery of Cape Sable Sparrow in Collier County. Fla. Nat. 16:12.

Bass, O. L., Jr., and J. A. Kushlan. 1982. Status of the Cape Sable Sparrow. Report T-672, South Fla. Res. Ctr., Everglades Natl. Park. Homestead, Florida. 41 pp.

Funderberg, J. B., Jr., and T. L. Quay. 1983. Distributional evolution of the Seaside Sparrow. Pages 19–27 in The Seaside Sparrow, its biology and management (Quay, T.L., J. B. Funderburg, Jr., D. S. Lee, E. F. Potter, and C. S. Robbins, eds.). Occas. Papers of the North Carolina Biol. Surv., 1983–5. Raleigh, North Carolina.

Howell, A. H. 1919. Description of a new Seaside Sparrow from Florida. Auk 36:86–87.

Kushlan, J. A., O. L. Bass, Jr., L. L. Loope, W. B. Robertson, Jr., P. C. Rosendahl, and D. L. Taylor. 1982. Cape Sable Sparrow management plan. Report M-660, South Fla. Res. Ctr., Everglades Natl. Park. Homestead, Florida. 37 pp.

Ogden, J. C. 1972. Florida region. Amer. Birds 26:852.

Werner, H. W. 1975. The biology of the Cape Sable Sparrow. Unnumbered rept., Everglades Natl. Park. Homestead, Florida. 215 pp.

Werner, H. W. 1978. Cape Sable Seaside Sparrow. Pages 19–20 in Rare and Endangered Biota of Florida, Vol. 2: birds (H. W. Kale, II, ed.). Univ. Presses of Florida, Gainesville, Florida.

Werner, H. W. 1983. The Cape Sable Sparrow: its habitat, habits, and history. Pages 55–75 in The Seaside Sparrow, its biology and management (Quay, T.L., J. B. Funderburg, Jr., D. S. Lee, E. F. Potter, and C. S. Robbins, eds.). Occas. Papers of the North Carolina Biol. Surv., 1983–5. Raleigh, North Carolina.

PREPARED BY: John L. Curnutt, Department of Ecology and Evolutionary Biology, University of Tennessee, Knoxville, TN 37996-0810.

Eastern Brown Pelican

Pelecanus occidentalis carolinensis

FAMILY PELECANIDAE

Order Pelecaniformes

TAXONOMY: The Eastern Brown Pelican (*Pelecanus occidentalis carolinensis*) is larger and, in breeding plumage, lighter colored than the nominate (West Indies) race (*P. o. occidentalis*), and also lighter gray on the dorsal surface in nonbreeding plumage (Wetmore 1945). *P. o. carolinensis* is smaller than the Pacific coast race (*P. o. californicus*). The brown neck of *californicus* (in breeding plumage) is darker than *carolinensis* (Wetmore 1945), and the lower pouch is distinctly reddish.

The Brown Pelican is in the subgenus Leptopelicanus whereas the American White Pelican (*P. erythrorhynchos*), the only other new world pelican, is in the subgenus Cyrtopelicanus. The eastern subspecies was described from a specimen taken in Charleston Harbor, South Carolina (Gmelin 1789). The validity and ranges of all four subspecies of Brown Pelicans were elucidated by Peters (1931), Murphy (1936), and Wetmore (1945).

DESCRIPTION: An obvious and engaging member of the avifauna wherever it occurs, the Brown Pelican is a large, colonial, marine species. The eastern subspecies averages between 3 and 4 kg (Schorger 1962); 26 adults averaged 3.1 kg (males 3.3, females 2.8) (Schreiber et al. 1989). The bill is elongated to support the prominent gular pouch. The wings are long and narrow with a spread of 2 m or more. Brown Pelicans are monochromatic, males are slightly larger than females; bill length averaged 319 mm and 294 mm for 28 males and 23 females, respectively (Wetmore 1945).

Adult Brown Pelicans are truest to their name in breeding dress when the occiput, nape, and upper breast are dark brown. The iris is light sky-blue with a pink eye-ring, the forehead is deep yellow-orange, and the ventral neck is white with a prominent yellow patch. The bill is a bluish pearl-gray to pinkish-orange toward the tip, with a significant, yellowish hook (nail). Following the nesting season, the brown on the head and neck is replaced by white, the iris

144

Eastern Brown Pelican, *Pelecanus occidentalis carolinensis.* (Photo by Stephen A. Nesbitt)

changes to brown, the forehead, breast patch, upper breast, and eye ring lighten noticeably, and the bill becomes more grayish. In all seasons the back and wing coverts are silver-gray, the belly is dark brown, the legs and the totipalmate (all four toes connected by webs) feet are dark gray to black, and the pouch is dark gray-green (plumage description follows Schreiber et al. 1989). Eggs are a chalky, flat white and usually conspicuously stained and discolored. At hatching, young are naked, color is pinkish, changing within a few days to dark grayish-purple (Schreiber 1976a). During the second week, a white down coat begins appearing (Schorger 1962). When they leave the nest, juveniles are uniformly brown-tan with a white belly grading gradually darker on the breast and flanks. By the second year the worn and ragged juvenile plumage is replaced by white feathers on the head and neck and darker feathers on the sides and belly. By the beginning of the third year, the adult head pattern emerges, and by 32–36 months, most birds have acquired adult plumage (Schreiber et al. 1989).

POPULATION SIZE AND TREND: Between 1968 and 1976 the average estimated annual Florida nesting population, based on statewide aerial surveys, was 6,339 pairs of Brown Pelicans (Nesbitt et al. 1977). Schreiber (1978)

Distribution map of
the Eastern Brown
Pelican, *Pelecanus
occidentalis
carolinensis.*

Breeding range
Non-breeding range
● Breeding sites

concluded an annual population of 6,000 to 8,000 pairs represented a total
population of less than 30,000 individuals.

A noticeable increase in nesting population occurred through the 1980s.
From 1977 through 1985 the average annual Florida nesting population was
estimated at 8,012 pairs (Florida Game and Fresh Water Fish Commission,
unpubl. data). The estimated nesting population in 1989 was 12,310 pairs; in
1995 it was 9,950 pairs (Florida Game and Fresh Water Fish Commission,
unpubl. data). The 1995 nesting population was assumed to represent a total
population of between 27,100 and 43,800 individuals (Florida Game and
Fresh Water Fish Commission, unpubl. data).

DISTRIBUTION AND HISTORY OF DISTRIBUTION: The Brown Peli-
can occurs from southern British Columbia south to Cape Horn on the Pacific
coast; and from eastern Venezuela throughout the Gulf of Mexico and the
Caribbean northward to coastal Virginia and Maryland. Along both coasts in
Florida, Brown Pelicans are common; freshwater records are rare, but they
recently began breeding at a site in Lake Okeechobee (Smith and Goguen
1993). Since 1968 pelicans have nested at 49 sites (Florida Bay and the Lower
Keys, a series of various small colonies [9–17, Kushlan and Frohring 1985]
were lumped as one site) from St. Andrews Bay in Bay County southward

through the Keys to the Marquesas Keys and the Dry Tortugas (Schreiber et al. 1975a) and north along the Atlantic coast to Port Orange in Volusia County. Between 1968 and 1976 an average of 23 sites were occupied (range 17–26); from 1977 to 1981 an average of 28 sites were used (range 26–29); and from 1982 to 1994 the average was 36 (range 30–39). In 1994 the number of pairs per colony ranged from 18 to 1,125.

Historically, Eastern Brown Pelicans nested in Texas, Louisiana, Florida, South Carolina, and North Carolina. Prior to the 1980s, successful nesting had not occurred between Cedar Key (Levy County) and Louisiana. Although unsuccessful, nesting (<2 dozen pairs) was attempted in 1971 and 1972 near Port St. Joe (Gulf County). In 1982 a colony, now estimated at 150 pairs, developed near Panama City in St. Andrews Bay. Concurrent with the increases in Florida during the 1980s, the nesting range of the subspecies expanded to include Alabama, Georgia, Virginia, Maryland, Delaware, and New Jersey (Wilkinson et al. 1994).

The Louisiana population, over 40,000 individuals (Schreiber 1978) was extirpated during the late 1950s and early 1960s. To reestablish that population, 1,318 prefledged young pelicans from Florida were reintroduced in Louisiana from 1968 to 1980 (Nesbitt et al. 1978, McNease et al. 1984). The restored population has produced over 900 young per year since the early 1980s (McNease et al. 1984). Other populations in Texas and South Carolina that experienced varying degrees of decline (King et al. 1977a; Blus et al. 1979; King et al. 1985) have increased without augmentation.

The increases in the nesting population did not occur equally throughout Florida. Kushlan and Frohring (1985) identified a 40% decrease in the population nesting in south Florida (lower peninsula, Florida Bay, and the Florida Keys). They attributed the decrease to a change in food availability. Comparison of the statewide aerial survey results between 1977 and 1989 (Florida Game and Fresh Water Fish Commission, unpubl. data) show where other changes have occurred. Nesting from Tampa Bay northward along the Gulf coast increased 230%, while nesting south of Tampa Bay through the Keys (including the area of concern to Kushlan and Frohring) increased by only 62%. Nesting along the Atlantic coast from Stuart northward to include Vero Beach decreased by 20% and nesting north of Vero Beach increased by 255%. Though the Florida nesting population from 1977 to 1989 increased by 89%, a majority of this increase occurred in the northern half of the state. The decreases identified by Kushlan and Frohring (1985) may extend beyond extreme south Florida and their suggestion that "the missing bird emigrated" is perhaps born out.

Pelicans that fledged on the Atlantic coast of Florida, while they wandered extensively (primarily south), tended to remain on the Atlantic coast (Schreiber and Mock 1988). Similarly, those hatched on Florida's Gulf coast, although they moved south, remained loyal to the Gulf coast (Schreiber and Mock 1988). Although there were examples of individuals from one coast moving to the other coast, the basic affinity to coast of origin was consistent (Schreiber 1976b; Schreiber and Mock 1988). A large number of the Carolina-hatched Brown Pelicans winter in Florida, principally along the Atlantic coast from Stuart northward (Schreiber 1976b).

HABITAT REQUIREMENTS AND HABITAT TREND: Nesting sites used by Brown Pelicans in Florida have consistently been small to medium-sized islands (most <5 ha; some to 10 ha), and most have been located along the Intracoastal Waterway. Only 4 of 49 sites used for nesting were not originally vegetated with mangrove (*Avicennia germinans* and *Rhizophora mangle*). Nesting occurs from 0.5–10.7 m above the high tide line (Schreiber 1978).

In addition to nesting sites, Brown Pelicans require loafing and roosting habitats. Sand bars are "an important, non-nesting habitat used for roosting and loafing" (Schreiber and Schreiber 1982). Loafing and roosting mangrove islands often evolve into nesting sites after a period of increasing use (Schreiber and Schreiber 1982).

Feeding habitat is not well understood and should be better researched since access to prey in adequate abundance is essential for successful reproduction (Anderson et al. 1982).

Many (>75%) of the Florida nesting sites are on state or federal land (Williams et al. 1980). There is no security or protection for non-nesting habitats and undoubtedly many important sites have been lost to direct or indirect degradation through disturbance (Schreiber and Schreiber 1982) or pollution.

VULNERABILITY OF SPECIES AND HABITAT: Rachel Carson writes in *Silent Spring* of "the peril that faces birds in our modern world . . . in the wake of pesticides" (Carson 1962). In the late 1950s and early 1960s, as *Silent Spring* was being written, the Brown Pelican was disappearing from Louisiana as a consequence of environmental pesticide contamination. By some estimates the Louisiana population may have been as large as 75,000 to 85,000 individuals (Arthur 1931). Regardless of the exact number, the disappearance occurred so quickly that it was virtually undetected. Pesticides, specifically DDT and endrin, have been further implicated in reproductive failure of Eastern Brown Pelicans in South Carolina (Blus 1982) and declines in Texas (King et al. 1977a). Endrin also was responsible for a die-off of 35–40% of the restored population in Louisiana in 1975 (Nesbitt et al. 1978). Both Brown and American White pelicans were involved, but few other species were affected. This led to the conclusion that pelicans were perhaps more sensitive to chemical contamination than other species (Nesbitt et al. 1978).

Brown Pelicans from Florida were found to have residues of DDT, DDD, and DDE, dieldrin, and PCBs below critical levels (Thompson et al. 1977; Nesbitt et al. 1981).

In addition to chemical contamination, there are a number of parasites and diseases that are known to affect Eastern Brown Pelicans in Florida (Courtney and Forrester 1974; Humphrey et al. 1978) and elsewhere (King et al. 1977b). Brown Pelicans are vulnerable to oil spills and can also be affected by variations in abundance of their primary prey species. Decreases in prey base result in reduced reproductive performance (Anderson et al. 1982).

Cold weather can affect Brown Pelicans. In addition to susceptibility to hypothermia, extended periods of low temperatures (<-4°C) produce areas of frostbite on the feet and pouch. These areas can become necrotic and result in the loss of feet or significant amounts of the pouch, seriously impairing an individual's ability to survive. Freezes in the 1980s affected pelicans directly and killed mangroves from Mosquito Lagoon northward on the Atlantic coast and from John's Pass northward on the Gulf coast, eliminating substrate on a number of nesting sites (Florida Game and Fresh Water Fish Commission, unpubl. data). Nesting and loafing habitats are essential to the continuation of Brown Pelicans in Florida at the levels that have existed in the past. Disturbance during the nesting season can decrease reproductive performance (Schreiber 1979; Anderson 1988). Anderson (1988) identified a critical distance threshold estimate of <600 m for negative effects from disturbance. Use of nesting and loafing habitats has been reduced or eliminated after erosion of the island. Use also has declined following degradation of the vegetative substrate as a direct or indirect consequence of occupation by pelicans. Pelicans, when nesting, loafing, etc., tear and break the limbs and branches to such an extent that the vegetation substrate will no longer support the colony. The build-up of waste under the colony also may degrade the vegetative substrate.

A most unfortunate source of non-natural mortality comes from sport fishing equipment. Both Brown and American White pelicans in Florida and elsewhere (Johnson and Sloan 1975) have been found with imbedded hooks, cuts, and amputation caused by monofilament line. Hooks and lures usually affect only individuals but monofilament line may, over a period of time, kill many birds. After a pelican has become entangled in monofilament and returns to the colony (roosting, loafing, and nesting) area, the line becomes wrapped among the vegetation and the entangled bird soon succumbs. However, the line remains and continues to snare and kill others. As many as six pelicans have been found dead on as little as 30 m of line. Schreiber (1978) estimated that 80% of the Brown Pelicans he looked at had, at some time, been injured by fishing equipment and that 500 or more are killed annually after contact with fishing tackle.

CAUSES OF THREAT: Historically, Brown Pelican populations have been reduced as a consequence of biomagnification of pesticides through the food chain. The level of DDT and its metabolites build up until calcium metabolism is interrupted, producing thin-shelled eggs that do not survive incubation. Environmental endrin (200 times more toxic than DDT) can kill pelicans directly. Toxic chemicals enter the aquatic environment through run-off, direct spills, or as by-products of manufacturing.

Development and its associated disturbance proximate to major use areas can reduce or eliminate their value as foraging and loafing sites. Indirect effects (i.e., reduced water quality, increased turbidity, alteration of estuarine salinities) can also have adverse impacts.

At piers and marinas throughout Florida, habituated Brown Pelicans that beg or pirate bait and catch wastes often become hooked or otherwise entangled in fishing line and are often cut loose with a length of line attached.

RESPONSE TO HABITAT MODIFICATION: Subsequent to the loss of nesting, loafing, or roosting substrate, Brown Pelicans have established new sites or merged with others. Pelicans also have shifted to ground nesting or to use of an alternate substrate following the loss of mangroves due to freezes. To some extent such periodic site changes may be cyclic and a natural consequence of occupation by pelicans, effectively maintaining local populations.

In spite of the large number of apparently suitable nesting, loafing, and roosting sites along the Florida coast, only a few satisfy all the necessary characteristics. Therefore, the loss or degradation of any site could be significant to the population.

DEMOGRAPHIC CHARACTERISTICS: There is substantial annual variation in Brown Pelican clutch size, but the mean for 328 nests was 2.62 (Schreiber 1979). Seventy-one percent of all eggs laid hatched with 82% of the nests hatching ≥1 egg (Schreiber 1979). Young fledged from 65% of the nests with an average fledging rate (brood size) of 1.48 young per successful nest (Schreiber 1979). First-year mortality is high; 70% probably die from starvation (Schreiber 1978). Maximum life span exceeds 20 years, but only 2.0% live beyond 10 years (Schreiber and Mock 1988). However, significant band loss begins 12–15 years after banding (Henny 1972), so some of these results may be an artifact of band loss.

In captivity or in unusual natural situations, successful reproduction can begin early in the third year after hatching (Williams and Joanan 1974; Nesbitt et al. 1980). Under normal conditions in Florida, Brown Pelicans do not successfully reproduce until after they have acquired adult plumage at 34–36 months (Blus and Keahey 1978; Schreiber et al. 1989). Birds that do nest in immature plumage are not as successful as adults (Blus and Keahey 1978).

KEY BEHAVIORS: Brown Pelicans are the smallest and darkest of the world's pelicans (the others are mostly white). Additionally, they are the only exclusively marine species and the only pelican that plunge-dives for food. The height from which they dive is variable and correlates to the depth of potential prey. During the dive, wings are folded back, and the neck is curled with the head positioned between the shoulders (Schreiber et al. 1975b). When the bird enters the water, the lower mandible and the gular pouch function in coordination with the upper mandible as a "trap" (Schreiber et al. 1975b). If successful, excess water is drained from the pouch before the catch is swallowed. When feeding small young, adults will adjust the prey size to accommodate the young's inability to handle large fish. When feeding young, adults regurgitate stomach contents into the nest or young may feed directly from the pouch. Brown Pelicans are exclusively fish eaters. In Florida, principle prey species are menhaden (*Brevoortia spp.*) and other herring, especially Spanish sardines (*Sardinella anchovia*), Atlantic threadfins (*Polydactylus octonemus*), mullet (*Mugil* spp.), various drum (*Sciaenidae*), and pinfish (*Lagodon rhomboides*) (Fogarty et al. 1981; Schreiber 1978).

Brown Pelicans are seasonally monogamous, pair bonds persisting only through one year's reproductive effort. Each year a new pair bond is formed. The male selects and occupies a potential nest site and advertises for a female with the Head-swaying display (Schreiber 1977). A mate is secured usually in 2–4 days, then nest building commences. Nest building may additionally reinforce the pair bond. Egg-laying begins within 3 days of nest completion (Schreiber 1977). A normal clutch takes 4–6 days to complete (Schreiber 1977). Both sexes participate in incubation, brooding, and rearing the young. Incubation takes 30 days and begins with the laying of the first egg, therefore, hatching is asynchronous. Young are altricial and nidicolous, eyes open the day after hatching. The average age at fledging is 76 days (range 71–88) (Schreiber 1976a). In Florida, egg-laying generally is initiated from December through February with nesting continuing through the summer. Fall nesting also occurs in the Florida Keys and on the lower Atlantic coast (Schreiber 1980). At some sites, nesting has occurred year-round, although this may have involved different segments of the population using the same site.

CONSERVATION MEASURES TAKEN: The Brown Pelican was listed as an endangered species in the United States on 13 October 1970 (Federal Register 1970). In July 1972, partially as a result of the Brown Pelican's susceptibility to DDT biomagnification, DDT use was banned in the United States (Federal Register 1972). The use of endrin also was curtailed. On 23 September 1975, the U.S. Fish and Wildlife Service appointed the Eastern Brown Pelican Recovery Team. The team prepared an Agency Review Draft of the Recovery Plan For The Eastern Brown Pelican (Williams et al. 1980) that was approved by the Director, U.S. Fish and Wildlife Service in July of 1979. Based on levels of survival and reproductive performance, on 6 March 1985 (Federal Register 1985), the species was removed from the Federal endangered species list in Alabama, Florida, Georgia, South Carolina, North Carolina, and points northward along the Atlantic coast. The species retains endangered status throughout the remainder of its range.

CONSERVATION MEASURES PROPOSED: The Eastern Brown Pelican appears to be increasing throughout much of its range but, as was demonstrated by its disappearance in Louisiana, there is no security in population size. Brown Pelicans in Florida still remain vulnerable to chemical contamination, oil spills, and habitat degradation. Monitoring of the health of the population should continue. The susceptibility of colonial waterbirds to mortality from entanglement in monofilament line is not widely known within the sport fishing community. More could be done through education and legislation (mandatory warning on line packaging) to reduce or eliminate the loss of pelicans and other wildlife to this easily prevented problem.

Although no longer protected in Florida under the endangered species act, the security of nesting sites is protected by the Migratory Bird Treaty Act and by rules of the Florida Game and Fresh Water Fish Commission from man-caused disturbance or destruction if designated as a Critical Wildlife Area. Such protection should be afforded all known Brown Pelican nesting sites and if possible extended to include important loafing and roosting areas.

ACKNOWLEDGMENTS: This update has been founded on the work of R. W. Schreiber. Were it not for his and E. A. Schreiber's indefatigable efforts, little new would have been added to our understanding of the biology and ecology of the species. With his death on 29 March 1988, an ever urging voice for understanding and protection of the Brown Pelican and its habitat was lost.

LITERATURE CITED:

Anderson, D. W. 1988. Dose-response relationship between human disturbance and Brown Pelican breeding success. Wildl. Soc. Bull. 16:339–345.

Anderson, D. W., F. Gress, and K. F. Mais. 1982. Brown Pelicans: influence of food supply on reproduction. Oikos 39:23–31.

Arthur, S. C. 1931. The birds of Louisiana. Louisiana Dept. of Conserv. Bull. 20. Dept. of Conserv., New Orleans, Louisiana. 598 pp.

Blus, L. J. 1982. Further interpretation of the relationship of organochlorine residues in Brown Pelican eggs to reproductive success. Environ. Pollut. (Series A) 28:15–33.

Blus, L. J., and J. R. Keahey. 1978. Variation in reproductivity with age in the Brown Pelican. Auk 95:128–134.

Blus, L. J., T. G. Lamont, and B. S. Neely, Jr. 1979. Effects of organochlorine residues on eggshell thickness, reproduction, and population status of Brown Pelicans (*Pelecanus occidentalis*) in South Carolina and Florida, 1969–76. Pestic. Monit. Jour. 12:122–184.

Carson, R. 1962. Silent spring. Fawcett Public., Inc. Greenwich, Connecticut. 304 pp.

Courtney, C. H., III, and D. J. Forrester. 1974. Helminth parasites of the Brown Pelican in Florida and Louisiana. Proc. Helminthol. Soc. Wash. 41:89–93.

Federal Register. 1970. 35FR:16047.

Federal Register. 1972. 37FR:13369–13376.

Federal Register. 1985. 50FR:4938–4945.

Fogarty, M. J., S. A. Nesbitt, and C. R. Gilbert. 1981. Diet of nestling Brown Pelicans in Florida. Fla. Field Nat. 9:38–40.

Gmelin, J.F. 1789. Syst. Nat. #1 (Pt2):571.

Henny, C. J. 1972. An analysis of the population dynamics of selected avian species, with special references to changed during the modern pesticide era. Wildlife Research Report 1, Bureau of Sport Fisheries and Wildlife, Washington, D.C. 99 pp.

Humphrey, S. R., C. H. Courtney, and D. J. Forrester. 1978. Community ecology of the helminth parasites of the Brown Pelican. Wilson Bull. 90:587–598.

Johnson, R. F., Jr., and N. F. Sloan. 1975. Fishing gear—a deadly hazard. Inland Bird Banding News 47:16–17.

King, K. A., E. L. Flickinger, and H. H. Hildebrand. 1977a. The decline of Brown Pelicans on the Louisiana and Texas Gulf Coast. SW Natural. 21:417–431.

King, K. A., D. R. Blankenship, R. T. Paul, and R. C. A. Rice. 1977b. Ticks as a factor in the 1975 nesting failure of Texas Brown Pelicans. Wilson Bull. 89:157–158.

King, K. A., D. R. Blankenship, E. Payne, A. J. Krynitsky, and G. L. Hensler. 1985. Brown Pelican populations and pollutants in Texas 1975–1981. Wilson Bull. 97:201–214.

Kushlan, J. A., and P. C. Frohring. 1985. Decreases in the Brown Pelican population in southern Florida. Colon. Waterbirds 8:83–95.

McNease, L., T. Joanen, D. Richards, J. Shepard, and S. A. Nesbitt. 1984. The Brown Pelican restocking program in Louisiana. Proc. Annu. Conf. Southeast. Assoc. Fish and Wildl. Agencies 38:165–173.

Murphy, R. C. 1936. Oceanic birds of South America, Vol. 2. American Museum of Nat. History, New York. Pp. 807–827.

Nesbitt, S. A., M. J. Fogarty, and L. E. Williams, Jr. 1977. Status of Florida nesting Brown Pelicans, 1971-1976. Bird Banding 48:138–144.

Nesbitt, S. A., L. E. Williams, Jr., L. McNease, and T. Joanen. 1978. Brown Pelican restocking efforts in Louisiana. Wilson Bull. 90:443–445.

Nesbitt, S. A., B. A. Harris, S. A. Fenelon, and D. M. King. 1980. Reproduction of Brown Pelicans in captivity. Wildl. Soc. Bull. 83:259–262.

Nesbitt, S. A., P. E. Cowan, P. W. Rankin, N. P. Thompson, and L. E. Williams, Jr. 1981. Chlorinated hydrocarbon residues in Florida Brown Pelicans. Colon. Waterbirds 4:77–84.

Peters, J. L. 1931. Check-list of birds of the world, vol I. Harvard Univ. Press, Cambridge, Massachusetts. 345 pp.

Schreiber, R. W. 1976a. Growth and development of nestling Brown Pelicans. Bird-Banding 47:19–39.

Schreiber, R. W. 1976b. Movements of color-marked Brown Pelicans in Florida. Bird-Banding 47:101–111.

Schreiber, R. W. 1977. Maintenance behavior and communication in the Brown Pelican. A.O.U. Ornithol. Monogr. no. 22.

Schreiber, R. W. 1978. Eastern Brown Pelican. Pg. 23-25 in Rare and Endangered Biota of Florida, Vol. 2 (H. W. Kale, II, ed.). Univ. Presses of Florida, Gainesville, Florida.

Schreiber, R. W. 1979. Reproductive performance of the Eastern Brown Pelican. Contrib. Sci. Nat. Hist. Mus. Los Angeles County 317:1–43.

Schreiber, R. W. 1980. Nesting chronology of the Eastern Brown Pelican. Auk 97:491–508.

Schreiber, R. W., and E. A. Schreiber. 1982. Essential habitat of the Brown Pelican in Florida. Fla. Field Nat. 10:9–17.

Schreiber, R. W., and P. J. Mock. 1988. Eastern Brown Pelican; what does 60 years of banding tell us? Jour. Field Ornith. 39:171–182.

Schreiber, R. W., T. H. Below, and W. B. Robertson, Jr. 1975a. Nesting of Brown Pelicans (*Pelecanus occidentalis*) on the Dry Tortugas, Florida. Fla. Field Nat. 3:47–48.

Schreiber, R. W., G. E. Woolfenden, and W. E. Curtsinger. 1975b. Prey capture by the Brown Pelican. Auk 92:649–654.

Schreiber, R. W., E. A. Schreiber, D. W. Anderson, and D. W. Bradley. 1989. Plumages and molts of Brown Pelicans. Contrib. Sci. Nat. Hist. Los Angeles County 402:1–43.

Schorger, A. W. 1962. Brown Pelican. Pp. 271-280 in Handbook of North American birds. Vol. I (R. S. Palmer, ed.). Yale Univ. Press. New Haven, Connecticut.

Smith, J. P., and C. B. Goguen. 1993. Inland nesting of the Brown Pelican. Fla. Field Nat. 21:29–33.

Thompson, N. P., P. W. Rankin, P. E. Cowan, L. E. Williams, Jr., and S. A. Nesbitt. 1977. Chlorinated hydrocarbon residues in the diet and eggs of the Florida Brown Pelican. Bull. Environ. Contam. & Toxicol. 18:331–339.

Wetmore, A. 1945. A review of the forms of the Brown Pelican. Auk 62:577–586.

Williams, L. E., Jr., and T. Joanen. 1974. Age of first breeding in the Brown Pelican. Wilson Bull. 86:279–280.

Williams, L. E., Jr., L. J. Blus, K. A. King, L. McNease, B. S. Neely, S. A. Nesbitt, and R. W. Schreiber. 1980. Recovery plan for the Eastern Brown Pelican. U.S. Fish and Wildlife Service, Atlanta, Georgia. 46 pp.

PREPARED BY: Stephen A. Nesbitt, Florida Game and Fresh Water Fish Commission, Wildlife Research Laboratory, 4005 South Main Street, Gainesville, FL 32601.

Magnificent Frigatebird

Fregata magnificens

FAMILY FREGATIDAE

Order Pelecaniformes

TAXONOMY: The Magnificent Frigatebird (*Fregata magnificens*) is one of an exceedingly close-knit group of five species of tropical seabirds comprising the family Fregatidae and its one present genus, *Fregata*. The fact that four of the species (all except the Lesser Frigatebird [*F. ariel*]) were regarded as a single, widely distributed species until relatively recent years illustrates their close similarity in appearance and behavior. In sharp contrast to their close within-group homogeneity, the question of the relationships of the Fregatidae to other birds currently is vexed and unsettled. As far back as Linnaeus, frigatebirds were usually allied with the other so-called "totipalmate swimmers" in what became the order Pelecaniformes. Among the pelecaniforms, certain shared characteristics were thought to ally frigatebirds with pelicans and tropicbirds in particular (Murphy 1936; Lanham 1947; Eisenmann 1962). However, evidence from DNA–DNA hybridization (Sibley and Ahlquist 1990) has effectively dismantled the traditional order Pelecaniformes. This rearrangement tentatively placed the Fregatidae in a superfamily including the penguins, loons, and petrels, with the comment (Sibley and Ahlquist 1990) ". . . the relationships of the frigatebirds require further study." The one fossil taxon of frigatebird, *Limnofregata* from the early Eocene of the western U.S. (Olson 1977), shows that the group was ". . . once more widespread and ecologically more diverse" (Olson 1985), but contributes little to the question of broader relationships.

Relatively minor geographical variation within *F. magnificens* has at times been recognized taxonomically. Thus, outlying populations in the Galapagos Islands (*F. m. magnificens*) and the Cape Verde Islands (*F. m. lowei*) have been treated as subspecifically distinct (Peters 1931; Murphy 1936; AOU 1957) from the widespread core populations of New World coasts (*F. m. rothschildi*). Because variation is evidently limited to slight differences in average measurements, the present trend seems to be against recognition of these subspecies

Magnificent Frigatebird,
Fregata magnificens. (Photo
by Dade W. Thornton)

(e.g., Hellmayr and Conover 1948; Bourne 1957; Wetmore 1965; Cramp et al. 1977).

DESCRIPTION: The Magnificent Frigatebird is a large (total length, ca. 1 m) but lightly built (1.1–1.8 kg) seabird of New World coasts and offshore waters, with long crooked wings (expanse, 2–2.4 m), a moderately long (105–130 mm) hooked beak, and a long (340–500 mm), deeply forked tail. Females, on the average, are considerably larger and heavier than males. Remarkably specialized for flying, the frigatebird is usually seen in flight and has the largest wingspread of any bird in proportion to weight, with 40% greater wing area than any seabird of similar mass (Eisenmann 1962). Frigatebirds neither swim nor ordinarily alight on water, and because of their small feet and short legs, they take wing with difficulty from the water surface or from flat ground if not wind-aided. The description of plumage and nonfeathered parts is taken principally from Eisenmann (1962) and Cramp et al. (1977). Adult males have entirely black plumage glossed with metallic green and purple when freshly molted. The bill is dusky blue-gray, the feet and legs blackish, the iris dark brown, and the orbital ring black. The gular pouch, flesh-colored to dull orange when contracted, is inflated to form a large scarlet balloon during courtship. In adult females, the head and upper parts (slightly glossed), belly, and undertail coverts are blackish-brown, and the breast and sides of the throat are white. The grayish lesser coverts often form a distinct band across

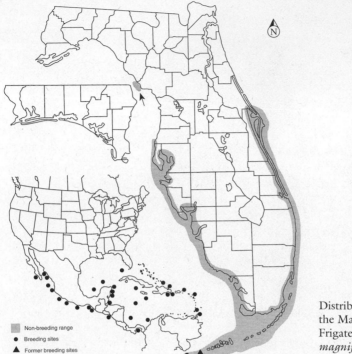

Distribution map of
the Magnificent
Frigatebird, *Fregata
magnificens.*

the top of the wing. The bill is bluish, the feet and legs reddish, the iris brown,
the orbital ring light blue, and the gular area dusky purplish and lacking a
pouch. Juveniles of either sex have the head, neck, and most of the underparts
white; the back, wings, tail, flanks, and undertail coverts, blackish-brown. New
hatchlings are naked, but they are soon covered with fluffy, whitish to buffy
down through which the juvenile feathering emerges, the scapulars and
interscapulars being first to appear. Full adult plumage may be acquired in the
fourth year of life (Cramp et al. 1977) or possibly not until the fifth year or
even later (Nelson 1975), but records from marked individuals apparently are
not available for any species of frigatebird.

POPULATION SIZE AND TRENDS: Clapp et al. (1982) summarized published records of the breeding population of Magnificent Frigatebirds at
Marquesas Keys, Florida, from 1969, when the colony was discovered, through
1979. In the nine years of record (no data for 1972 or 1973), average reported colony size was 107 nests, ranging from 25 (1974) to 250 (1976) with
no clearly time-related trend over this period. Later, an apparently declining
population continued to attempt to nest at the Marquesas Keys each year
through 1989 (Clapp and Buckley 1984; T. Wilmers, unpubl. data). Wilmers'
observations of breeding activity in the colony's last years were: 1986—13

young fledged; 1987—incubating birds were seen early in the season, but the colony was abandoned after midwinter cold spells; 1988—results uncertain, 36 nestlings were present on 19 May but the colony was empty in late July; and, 1989—the six occupied nests were deserted before early March. Frigatebirds were first confirmed nesting on the Dry Tortugas in April, 1988 (Langridge 1988), and the number nesting there has appeared to increase each year. In early March, 1993, about 70 nests were occupied in the colony on Long Key, Dry Tortugas (Robertson, pers. observ.).

Each year, principally in April through October, Magnificent Frigatebirds distribute themselves along the South Atlantic and Gulf coasts of the U.S., principally from Merritt Island, Florida, coastwise to the Chandeleur Islands, Louisiana. To our knowledge, no comprehensive survey has been attempted, but available data (e.g., Clapp et al. 1982, *American Birds*) suggest that the influx numbers in the range of 3,000–7,000 individuals. In 1968–72, Harrington et al. (1972) recorded data on sex and age class for a total of 3,739 frigatebirds in summer roosts at Tarpon Key (Tampa Bay) and Dry Tortugas, Florida. Taking these samples to be somewhat representative, about 11% of the Magnificent Frigatebirds that appear along southern U.S. coasts are in immature plumage, and about 68% of the adults are males and 32% females. Where disturbance is infrequent, even small frigatebird roosts in Florida tend to persist from year to year. In 1987–1993 (Wilmers, unpubl. data), at least 12 of 26 roosts in the lower Florida Keys (East Bahia Honda Key to Marquesas Keys) were used annually. Maximum counts at the five largest roosts of this group were from 200 to 300 individuals. Because only a small fraction of the summer frigatebirds along southern U.S. coasts can possibly belong to the population breeding in Florida, most are presumed to originate from other colonies in the Gulf-Caribbean region. The exact sources are unknown, but overall numbers in the United States suggest that individuals from several to many breeding areas must be represented. Van Halewyn and Norton (1984) estimated the Gulf-Caribbean breeding population at 8,000+ pairs. Thus, even the low estimate of summer numbers in the U.S. necessitates seasonal northward movement by about 20% of the Gulf-Caribbean population. The most recent information suggests downward population trends for frigatebird populations nesting in the Bahamas (Sprunt 1984) and in the Gulf-Caribbean (van Halewyn and Norton *loc. cit.*). Reports of decreasing numbers in Florida summer roosts, such as around Tampa Bay in the 1980s (Robertson and Woolfenden 1992), probably reflect declines farther south.

With regard to the species' overall numbers, Nelson (1975) suggested that the world population of the Magnificent Frigatebird was "possibly fewer than 500,000 pairs." A more recent estimate (del Hoyo et al. 1992) puts the figure at "several hundred thousand birds" and tags the species as "not globally threatened." These rather sanguine appraisals are difficult to reconcile with the available regional data. Thus, 8,500 pairs seems a reasonable estimate of the breeding population in the Bahamas/Gulf-Caribbean (Sprunt 1984; van Halewyn and Norton 1984). The Galapagos population is said to be 1,000 pairs (Coulter 1984); the breeding population of the Cape Verdes is very small (10–12 pairs *fide* Cramp et al. 1977); the poorly documented populations of the southern coast of Brazil reportedly number "several thousand breeding pairs" (del Hoyo et al. 1992); and, on available data, 4,000 pairs seems a liberal estimate for the Pacific coast of Central and South America. These estimates result in a combined total of about 16,500 nesting pairs. The only part of the range not accounted for in this total is the Pacific coast of Mexico. In that region from Baja California to Chiapas, about six major frigatebird colonies are said to hold (at maximum estimates) about 70,000 nesting pairs and other regional colonies of 500–1,000 pairs have been reported (Knoder et al. 1980; de la Torre 1987; Moreno and Carmona 1988; Binford 1989; Everett and Anderson 1991). An individual colony size of up to 20,000 pairs in this region is especially notable, because the largest colony of the species reported elsewhere seems to be 2,500 pairs on Barbuda, Lesser Antilles (Diamond 1973). The west coast of Mexico is undoubtedly a major population center for Magnificent Frigatebirds, but interannual movement of breeders between colonies and the inclusion of nonbreeders in estimates of colony size may have inflated population figures. For example, two Sinaloan colonies (Bahia del Pabellon, Bahia Santa Maria) that averaged 533 and 1,000 nests, respectively, on three aerial surveys in the early 1970s (Knoder et al. 1980) also have been reported to contain "10,000 to 20,000 pairs" and "about 18,000 pairs," respectively (Everett and Anderson 1991). The need for comprehensive surveys of the western Mexican breeding populations is evident.

Given the considerable uncertainty regarding present numbers, overall population trends in the species cannot be approached directly. However, it is of interest to summarize information for the specific colony sites. Rangewide, about 120 nesting locations of Magnificent Frigatebirds have been mentioned in ornithological literature (e.g., Murphy 1936; Eisenmann 1962; Cramp et al. 1977; Knoder et al. 1980; AOU 1983; Croxall et al. 1984; Everett and Anderson 1991; del Hoyo et al. 1992). It was later reported for at least 17 of these locations that frigatebirds had abandoned or probably abandoned the site (e.g., Monroe 1968; Kepler 1978; van Halewyn and Norton 1984; Sprunt 1984). In at least 41 additional instances, the information regarding frigatebird nesting is either uncertain or it dates from ≥50 years ago. From these data, it appears possible that as many as half the reported breeding colonies of Magnificent Frigatebirds may no longer exist.

DISTRIBUTION AND HISTORY OF DISTRIBUTION: The Magnificent Frigatebird primarily inhabits the coastal and offshore waters of the New

World tropics. Along the Pacific coast, it reportedly nests at about 45 locations from the west side of Baja California, Mexico, at about 25°N to the Gulf of Guayaquil, Ecuador, at about 3°S. Nesting locations include several groups of oceanic islands (Galapagos, Islas Revillagigedo) from 500 to 1,000 km offshore in the Pacific. Along the New World's Atlantic coast, the species reportedly has nested at about 75 locations from Little Abaco, Bahamas, at about 27°N, and the Marquesas Keys and Dry Tortugas, Florida, at about 25°N south through the West Indies and along continental shores to about 25°S near Sao Paulo, Brazil. St. Michael's Mount, Fernando Noronha, about 350 km off the Brazilian coast, is apparently the most isolated nesting location in the western Atlantic.

Usually in the local summer, adult and immature Magnificent Frigatebirds annually disperse along coasts as much as 1,500 km north and south of the limits of the breeding range, often in fairly large numbers. These seasonal emigrations extend more-or-less regularly to the Carolina Capes, the entire Gulf coast of the United States, Uruguay and northwestern Argentina, coastal California, and northern Peru (Murphy 1936; Eisenmann 1962; Clapp et al. 1982; AOU 1983; Harrison 1983). In addition, the Magnificent Frigatebird is prone to long-distance vagrancy, at least in its Northern Hemisphere range. With or without the intervention of storms, individuals have occurred north along coasts to southern Alaska and Newfoundland, widely in the United States and southern Canada, in Bermuda and the Azores, and several times in the British Isles and western Europe (Eisenmann 1962; Cramp et al. 1977; AOU 1983). Although the Magnificent Frigatebird probably accounts for most of the records of wandering frigatebirds in Europe and North America, other species may occur. Cramp et al. (1977) noted that *F. aquila*, *F. ariel*, and *F. minor* are potential vagrants northward in the Atlantic, and Eisenmann (1962) suggested that *F. minor* might readily occur along the Pacific coast of the United States. Notably, one occurrence of *F. ariel*, probably the least numerous Atlantic species (Murphy 1936), has been documented by photographs on the Maine coast (Snyder 1961; AOU 1983). Given the close similarity of frigatebird species, questions commonly arise as to the identity of vagrants and some observations were not definitely assigned to any species. For descriptions, diagrams, and photographs useful in field identification of the species of Fregata, see Murphy (1936), Nelson (1975), and Harrison (1983).

The regularity and extent of pelagic dispersal by the Magnificent Frigatebird remain poorly known, but such occurrences at least appear to be much more frequent than was formerly thought. Early students of seabirds, notably Murphy (1936), were strongly committed to the belief that frigatebirds were not truly pelagic, but, in fact, relatively shorebound. Assertions that they return nightly to roost on shore and that individuals seen in mid-ocean must have been driven there by storms persist in print. However, since the mid-1960s, extensive banding of several *Fregata* species and greatly increased ornithological observation at sea have made it clear that frigatebirds occur rather routinely throughout the warm oceans (see discussion in Harrington et al. 1972). The range of the Magnificent Frigatebird suggests that it indeed may be somewhat less pelagic than several other frigatebird species, but at-sea records exist from virtually all sectors of the tropical Atlantic (e.g., Cramp et al. 1977) and from far offshore in the eastern Pacific.

In Florida, Magnificent Frigatebirds occur year-round along the entire coastline, but they are much more numerous in summer and more regular in numbers (100s to [rarely] 1,000s) at summer roosts from the Cedar Key and Cape Canaveral areas south, especially in the larger Gulf coast estuaries. They are seldom seen in the interior of the peninsula in settled weather, but any severe storm may drive individuals or small flocks inland (e.g., Fellers 1988). Sparsely detailed, early reports of nesting in Florida (Howell 1932) are uncertain, in part because summer-visiting frigatebirds may form roosts on mangrove islands where other waterbirds have nested. Nesting in Florida was finally confirmed in 1969 at Marquesas Keys, Monroe County (Ogden 1969). The Florida nesting records in 1969 and later represent the only known instance of sustained breeding by Magnificent Frigatebirds in the United States. However, a published report also exists of supposed frigatebird eggs found on Ship Island, Aransas County, Texas, in 1933 (Oberholser 1974; Clapp et al. 1982; AOU 1983). This once-only occurrence, first reported 40 years after the event, appears roughly comparable to the early reports from Florida. The locality is of interest because, at about 28°10'N, it is latitudinally the most outlying report of breeding activity by the species.

HABITAT REQUIREMENTS AND HABITAT TREND: Although able to nest and roost on low vegetation, other kinds of trees, cliffs, or bare rocks (Diamond 1973; Nelson 1975), most roosting and nesting sites of Magnificent Frigatebirds in Florida and the Gulf-Caribbean are on the lee side of small islands of well-grown mangroves (usually *Rhizophora*). Location in relation to local winds may tend to determine the suitability of sites, as the heavier females in particular do not fly readily on windless days or in light breezes (Harrington et al. 1972). Frigatebirds feed opportunistically from the air in marine habitats to distances of at least 40 km from the roost or nesting colony. Over time, the quality and productivity of Florida's coastal and offshore waters have undoubtedly declined somewhat, and the array of attractive mangrove islets has undoubtedly been reduced. However, it is not evident that any shortage of basic habitat elements currently affects frigatebirds in Florida.

VULNERABILITY OF SPECIES AND HABITAT: The vulnerability of bird species that are mainly Caribbean, but also have very small, recently established, breeding populations in southern Florida must be judged on a regional basis. Florida-nesting Magnificent Frigatebirds (also Masked Boobies [*Sula dactylatra*] and Bridled Terns [*Sterna anaethetus*]) may be affected as much by changes in the status of the source populations as they are by local ambient conditions. Also, as noted above, the major summer influx of frigatebirds into Florida comes almost entirely from Gulf-Caribbean, rather than local, colonies. In general, nesting and roosting seabirds and their habitats are relatively well-protected in Florida against most threats. Most Florida colonies and roost sites are in areas where wildlife and habitats enjoy at least a degree of state and federal protection. Although protective measures have not always succeeded, seabirds that are rare in Florida have benefited from special surveillance and monitoring, vegetation management, and control of non-native predators. Conversely, although seabirds have nominal legal protection in most Gulf-Caribbean jurisdictions, few of these colonies are effectively protected other than by distance or difficulty of access. Van Halewyn and Norton (1984) point out that a large proportion of the colonies of Magnificent Frigatebirds and other seabirds are vulnerable to human exploitation of eggs and young, predation by non-native mammals, and habitat destruction by both subsistence farmers and real-estate developers.

CAUSES OF THREAT: The principal threat to Magnificent Frigatebirds in Florida is disturbance, usually negligent rather than malicious, of their vulnerable roosting and nesting sites by recreational boaters and sightseers. In the Gulf-Caribbean area, the greatest threat to seabirds is considered to be the "widespread and often large-scale collecting of eggs and, to a lesser extent, chicks" (van Halewyn and Norton 1984). Aside from the human-related threats, nesting frigatebirds also are subject to disturbance and loss of eggs and young as a result of storms. Their habit of nesting on the lee side (in relation to the prevailing southeast winds) of islands exposes colonies to winter squalls and cold fronts from the opposite direction, which tend to be more frequent and severe in southern Florida than in most of the Gulf-Caribbean. For example, a storm at Dry Tortugas on 12 March 1993 caused the failure of about 50 frigatebird nests at the Long Key colony.

RESPONSES TO HABITAT MODIFICATION: Apparently, no record exists of Magnificent Frigatebirds responding to any kind of habitat modification other than disturbance at their on-shore roosting or nesting sites. Their response to various kinds and intensities of disturbance seems to be to move and seek another site. In this way, the species has been largely evicted as a breeder from parts of its range (see Distribution above; also Kepler 1978; Sprunt 1984). Abandonment of the original Florida nesting site at Marquesas Keys after 20 years almost surely resulted from persistent, casual disturbance by aircraft tours and intrusion by boaters into the shallow waters surrounding the

colony (T. Wilmers, pers. observ.). The close coincidence of colony initiation
at Dry Tortugas and colony desertion at Marquesas Keys suggests that the
frigatebirds moved from one site to the other, but no definite evidence is
available. Modifications of the foraging habitat of frigatebirds (e.g., oil spills)
frequently occur. However, because of the species' great mobility and range,
only major events such as the IXTOC-1 oil well blowout in the Gulf of
Campeche in 1979 seem likely to have significant effects on feeding.

DEMOGRAPHIC CHARACTERISTICS: Although all five species of
frigatebirds have been the subjects of detailed life history studies, none of
these studies was based on marked birds and some demographic parameters
are estimated or unknown. From what is known or reasonably inferred, the
Fregatidae exhibit demographic characteristics common to most pelagic birds
(for a summary, see Nelson 1975). Thus, the group as a whole, and the
Magnificent Frigatebird where known, have the following characteristics: single-
egg clutches; long periods of incubation, estimated at ≥50 days in *magnificens*;
extended fledging periods, 166 days (n = 9 nests) in *magnificens* (Diamond
1973); and long periods of post-fledging care, at least 145 days in *magnificens*
(Diamond 1973). Critical demographic elements that remain uncertain are
age at first breeding, guessed to be "at least five to seven years, probably nearer
the latter" (Nelson 1975) for frigatebirds at large; and mean longevity, unknown, but probably in the range of 20–30 years (Clapp and Hackman 1969).
However, the most striking characteristic of frigatebird demography, is the
time required for successful breeding that apparently may preclude breeding
again the next year. Nelson (1967) and Schreiber and Ashmole (1970) argued
in the case of *F. minor* that the long breeding cycle, particularly the prolonged
care of young, made annual breeding impossible for successful parents. The
Magnificent Frigatebird is reported to have a similarly attenuated breeding
cycle (ca. 350–380 days), but one in which the time investment of males and
females differs greatly. In studies at a colony on Barbuda, Lesser Antilles,
Diamond (1972, 1973) found that the sexes of Magnificent Frigatebirds
shared duties equally until the chick was 6–9 weeks old. At that time, males
departed, presumably to molt, and females continued to feed the young bird
until it became independent 5–6 months later. Under such an arrangement,
successful males could breed, complete molt, and be able to initiate a new
breeding cycle in about one year, but successful females could not breed more
often than once every other year. Diamond further reported that the sex ratio
of large nestlings was 1.8 females:1 male, an imbalance that would tend to
compensate for the diminished reproductive potential of individual females.
As Diamond (1973) noted, "These points need to be investigated in greater
detail, and with marked birds." Such investigation apparently has not yet
occurred, but observations at a colony in Belize (Trivelpiece and Ferraris
1987) verified that only females appeared to feed fledged young.

KEY BEHAVIORS: Frigatebirds employ a remarkable repertoire of feeding behaviors. They are notorious for pirating food from other seabirds, especially boobies (*Sula*), but, as Nelson (1975:121) puts it, "frigatebirds obtain most of their food by honest fishing." The food obtained by Magnificent Frigatebirds consists mainly of several species of flying fishes and squids that range in length from about 5–20 cm and that are caught in the air (Nelson 1975). Besides piratical and honest fishing, Magnificent Frigatebirds also feed on offal discarded from fishing boats and other sources, on fish pirated from fishermen (Buckley and Tilger 1983; McNeil 1985), and on the eggs and young of other seabirds, including conspecific neighbors (Nelson 1975; Robertson 1978). The other well-known behavior of frigatebirds is their remarkable courtship display in which small groups of perched males indulge in a performance involving rapid vibration of the wings and inflation of the large, bright scarlet, gular pouch (see Diamond 1973; Nelson 1975). The display is directed in greatest intensity to females hovering overhead. Nelson (1975) suggested that the spectacular advertising display of males is related to the generally weak pair-bonds of frigatebirds and the near-absence of year-to-year mate and site fidelity. Finally, an often-reported, but little-understood, behavior of the Magnificent Frigatebird is its proclivity to bathe in (by aerial dunking) and drink freshwater, at times making inland excursions to considerable distances in order to do so (Murphy 1936; Keilhorn et al. 1963; Wetmore 1965).

CONSERVATION MEASURES TAKEN: National wildlife refuges, national parks, state parks, state aquatic preserves, county parks, and other protected areas in the Florida Keys and north along both coasts now include a large proportion of the mangrove-estuarine habitat attractive to Magnificent Frigatebirds. In addition, regulatory restrictions and public sentiment would seem to make it unlikely that extensive development of privately-owned estuaries in Florida will occur in the future. To limit casual disturbance by visitors, Dry Tortugas National Park has established a safe-viewing perimeter (marked with buoys) on the approach to the nesting colony. Although no survey of seabird conservation in the Gulf-Caribbean has been undertaken since van Halewyn and Norton's (1984) rather pessimistic assessment in the early 1980s, progress, if any, has doubtless been slow. Among breeding colonies of Magnificent Frigatebirds, those on Isla Contoy and Cayo Culebra (Sian Ka'an Biosphere Reserve), Mexico, and possibly also the Barbuda colony (Diamond 1973), are perhaps most likely to have effective protection. Formation of the Society of Caribbean Ornithology with study and conservation of birds and their habitats as its primary goal is probably the most hopeful development in the West Indian region in recent years.

CONSERVATION MEASURES PROPOSED: The key conservation need of the Magnificent Frigatebird in Florida is the curbing of witless disturbance at roosts and colony sites through the enforcement of safe zones and by educating boaters and the pilots of recreational aircraft. In the important Keys region, implementation of the Florida Keys National Marine Sanctuary proposal should help resolve inter-agency problems of incomplete and overlapping jurisdiction. Because the lone Florida colony at Dry Tortugas is so exposed to storms, a particular effort should be made to eliminate disturbance at Marquesas Keys in hope that frigatebirds will reoccupy their former nesting site. Surveys are needed to determine the location of important roosts in Florida and to obtain a much better grasp of total numbers, year-to-year variation, and trends of the summer population. Lastly, it is in Florida's best interests to advise and assist countries of the Gulf-Caribbean in seabird protection and other conservation initiatives.

ACKNOWLEDGMENTS: We are indebted to Roger B. Clapp of the National Museum of Natural History, Fred E. Lohrer of Archbold Biological Station, P. William Smith of Homestead, Florida, Skip Snow of Everglades National Park, and Sandy Sprunt of the National Audubon Society for information and help with references.

LITERATURE CITED:

AOU. 1957. Check-list of North American birds, 5th edition. Amer. Ornithol. Union. Lord Baltimore Press, Baltimore, Maryland.

AOU. 1983. Check-list of North American Birds, 6th edition. Amer. Ornithol. Union. Allen Press, Lawrence, Kansas.

Binford, L. C. 1989. A distributional survey of the birds of the Mexican state of Oaxaca. Ornithological Monographs No. 43, Amer. Ornithol. Union. Lawrence, Kansas.

Bourne, W. R. P. 1957. Additional notes on the birds of the Cape Verde Islands, with particular reference to *Bulweria mollis* and *Fregata magnificens*. Ibis 99:182–190.

Buckley, F. G., and G. M. Tilger. 1983. Frigatebird piracy on humans. Colon. Waterbirds 6:214–218.

Clapp, R. B., and C. D. Hackman. 1969. Longevity record for a breeding Great Frigatebird. Bird-Banding 40:47.

Clapp, R. B., R. C. Banks, D. Morgan-Jacobs, and W. A. Hoffman. 1982. Marine birds of the southeastern United States and Gulf of Mexico. Part 1. Gaviiformes through Pelecaniformes. U.S. Fish and Wildl. Serv., Washington, D.C.

Clapp, R. B., and P. A. Buckley. 1984. Status and conservation of seabirds in the southeastern United States. Pp. 135–155 in Status and conservation of the world's seabirds (J. P. Croxall, P. G. H. Evans and R. W. Schreiber, eds.). ICBP Tech. Publ. No. 2. Cambridge, United Kingdom.

Coulter, M. C. 1984. Seabird conservation in the Galapagos Islands, Ecuador. Pp. 237–244 in Status and conservation of the world's seabirds (J. P. Croxall, P. G. H. Evans, and R. W. Schreiber, eds.). ICBP Tech. Publ. No. 2. Cambridge, United Kingdom.

Cramp, S. (Chief Ed.), K. E. L. Simmons, I. J. Ferguson-Lees, R. Gilmor, P. A. D. Hollom, R. Hudson, E. M. Nicholson, M. A. Ogilvie, P. J. S. Olney, K. H. Voous, and J. Wattel. 1977. Handbook of the birds of Europe, the Middle East and North Africa. The birds of the Western Palearctic. Volume 1. Ostrich to ducks. Oxford Univ. Press, Oxford, United Kingdom.

Croxall, J. P., P. G. H. Evans, and R. W. Schreiber (eds.). 1984. Status and conservation of the world's seabirds. ICBP Tech. Publ. No. 2. Cambridge, United Kingdom.

Diamond, A. W. 1972. Sexual dimorphism in breeding cycles and unequal sex ratio in Magnificent Frigate-birds. Ibis 114:395–398.

Diamond, A. W. 1973. Notes on the breeding biology and behavior of the Magnificent Frigatebird. Condor 75:200–209.

Eisenmann, E. 1962. Fregatidae; Magnificent Frigatebird. Pp. 365–380 in Handbook of North American Birds. Volume 1. Loons through Flamingos (R. S. Palmer, ed.). Yale Univ. Press, New Haven, Connecticut.

Everett, W. T., and D. W. Anderson. 1991. Status and conservation of the breeding seabirds on offshore Pacific islands of Baja California and the Gulf of California. Pp. 115-139 in Seabird status and conservation: a supplement (J. P. Croxall, ed.). ICBP Tech. Publ. No. 11. Cambridge, United Kingdom.

Fellers, P. J. 1988. Recent occurrences of "storm waifs" in Polk County, Florida. Fla. Field Nat. 16:7.

Halewyn, R. van, and R. L. Norton. 1984. The status and conservation of seabirds in the Caribbean. Pp. 169–222 in Status and conservation of the world's seabirds (J. P. Croxall, P. G. H. Evans, and R. W. Schreiber, eds.). ICBP Tech. Publ. No. 2, Cambridge, United Kingdom.

Harrington, B. A., R. W. Schreiber, and G. E. Woolfenden. 1972. The distribution of male and female Magnificent Frigate-birds, *Fregata magnificens*, along the Gulf coast of Florida. Amer. Birds 26:927–931.

Harrison, P. 1983. Seabirds, an identification guide. Houghton Mifflin, Boston, Massachusetts.

Hellmayr, C. E., and B. Conover. 1948. Catalogue of birds of the Americas. Zool. Ser., Field Mus. of Nat. His. 13, part 1, no. 2.

Howell, A. H. 1932. Florida bird life. Coward-McCann, New York.

del Hoyo, J., A. Elliott, and J. Sargatal. 1992. Handbook of the birds of the world. Volume 1. Lynx Edicions, Barcelona, Spain.

Keilhorn, W. V., K. S. Norris, and W. E. Evans. 1963. Bathing behavior of Frigate Birds. Condor 65:240–241.

Kepler, C. B. 1978. The breeding ecology of sea birds on Monito Island, Puerto Rico. Condor 80:72–87.

Knoder, C. E., P. D. Plaza, and A. Sprunt, IV. 1980. Status and distribution of the Jabiru Stork and other water birds in western Mexico. Pp. 58-127 in Proceedings of the National Audubon Society's symposium on the birds of Mexico: their ecology and conservation (P. P. Schaeffer and S. M. Ehlers, eds.). Nat. Audubon Soc., Western Education Center.

Langridge, H. P. 1988. Florida region. Amer. Birds 42:370,424.

Lanham, U. N. 1947. Notes on the phylogeny of the Pelecaniformes. Auk 64:65–70.

McNeil, R. 1985. Another kind of frigatebird piracy on humans. Colon. Waterbirds 8:69.

Monroe, B. L., Jr. 1968. A distributional survey of the birds of Honduras. Ornithol. Monog. No. 7. Amer. Ornithol. Union. Lawrence, Kansas.

Moreno, L. A., and L. R. Carmona. 1988. Ecologia reproductiva de *Fregata magnificens* en Isla Santa Margarita, B.C.S. Univ. Auton. de Baja California Sur, Mexico (Bachelor's Thesis).

Murphy, R. C. 1936. Oceanic birds of South America. Volumes 1 & 2. Amer. Mus. Nat. Hist., New York, New York.

Nelson, J. B. 1967. Etho-ecological adaptations in the Great Frigate Bird. Nature, London, 214:318.

Nelson, J. B. 1975. The breeding biology of frigatebirds—a comparative review. Living Bird 14:113–155.

Oberholser, H. C. 1974. The bird life of Texas. Volume 1. Univ. of Texas Press, Austin, Texas.

Ogden, J. C. 1969. Florida region. Aud. Field Notes 23:651–655.

Olson, S. L. 1977. A Lower Eocene frigatebird from the Green River formation of Wyoming (Pelecaniformes: Fregatidae). Smithsonian Contrib. Paleobiology No. 35, Washington, D.C.

Olson, S. L. 1985. The fossil record of birds. Chapter 2 in Avian Biology, vol. 7 (D. S. Farner, J. R. King, and K. C. Parkes, eds.). Academic Press, Inc., Orlando, Florida.

Peters, J. L. 1931. Check-list of birds of the world. Volume 1. Harvard Univ. Press, Cambridge, Massachusetts.

Robertson, W. B., Jr. 1978. Rothchild's Magnificent Frigate-bird. Pp. 25–27 in Rare and endangered biota of Florida. Volume 2: birds (H. W. Kale, II, ed.). Univ. Presses of Florida, Gainesville, Florida.

Robertson, W. B., Jr., and G. E. Woolfenden. 1992. Florida bird species: an annotated list. Spec. Publ. No. 6. Fla. Ornith. Soc., Gainesville, Florida.

Schreiber, R. W., and N. P. Ashmole. 1970. Sea-bird breeding seasons on Christmas Island, Pacific Ocean. Ibis 112:363–394.

Sibley, C. G., and J. E. Ahlquist. 1990. Phylogeny and classification of birds. Yale Univ. Press, New Haven, Connecticut.

Snyder, D. F. 1961. First record of Least [sic] Frigate-bird (*Fregata ariel*) in North America. Auk 78:265.

Sprunt, A., IV. 1984. The status and conservation of seabirds of the Bahama Islands. Pp. 157–168 in Status and conservation of the world's seabirds (J. P. Croxall, P. M. G. Evans, and R. W. Schreiber, eds.). ICBP Tech. Publ. No. 2. Cambridge, United Kingdom.

de la Torre, G. 1987(1988). Aves de la Isabel, Nayarit, Mexico. Annales Inst. Biol. Univ. Nac. Auton. Mex., Ser. Zool. 58(2):751–812.

Trivelpiece, W. Z., and J. D. Ferraris. 1987. Notes on the behavioral ecology of the Magnificent Frigatebird *Fregata magnificens*. Ibis 129:168–174.

Wetmore, A. 1965. The birds of the Republic of Panama. Part 1. Smithsonian Misc. Collections 150. Smithsonian Inst., Washington D.C.

PREPARED BY: William B. Robertson, Jr., National Biological Survey, Everglades National Park, 40001 State Road 9336, Homestead, FL 33034-6733; and Tom Wilmers, U.S. Fish and Wildlife Service, National Key Deer Wildlife Refuge, P.O. Box 510, Big Pine Key, FL 33043.

Osprey

Pandion haliaetus

FAMILY ACCIPITRIDAE

Order Falconiformes

TAXONOMY: The Osprey (*Pandion haliaetus*) is the only species in the Subfamily Pandioninae, which is linked with the Subfamily Accipitrinae (hawks and eagles) to form the Family Accipitridae (Sibley et al. 1988). The Osprey has a nearly worldwide range, with breeding populations occurring across North America, the western Caribbean, Europe and Asia, and in coastal Australia and the adjacent southwestern Pacific region (Brown and Amadon 1968; Cramp 1980; Poole 1989). Most northern hemispere Ospreys are highly migratory, with birds wintering throughout the Caribbean, Central and South America, central and southern Africa, India, and southeastern Asia. Four (sometimes five) subspecies are recognized. The nominate race *P. h. haliaetus* is relatively larger and darker plumaged than other races and nests across northern and central Eurasia and more locally around the Mediterranean region. The large and somewhat paler North American race *P. h. carolinensis* nests from western Alaska across central and southern Canada to Nova Scotia and New Brunswick and south to Baja California and Florida. Two smaller, paler, and nonmigratory races are *P. h. ridgwayi*, which occurs in the western Caribbean region, including Cuba, the Bahamas, and the Caribbean coast of the Yucatan peninsula and Belize, and *P. h. cristatus* found around the coasts of Australia (sometimes shown as two races in Australia) and in New Guinea and adjacent regions.

DESCRIPTION: The Osprey is a large, eagle-like bird, with a 1.5 to 1.7 m wingspread (Palmer 1988). When soaring, the long, narrow wings are held with a distinct downward crook at the "wrist" (Clark and Wheeler 1987). The dorsal surface is dark brown, and the head and ventral surface is largely white. A prominent dark brown streak extends laterally behind the eye, and a small amount of dark streaking occurs on the top of the head and across the breast. The feathers on the back of the head and upper hindneck are relatively elon-

Osprey, *Pandion haliaetus.*
(Photo by Barry Mansell)

gate in shape and can be partially erected into a low, bushy crest. Females average about 10% larger than males and may have darker streaking. Immature Ospreys differ from adults by having orange irises (more yellow in adults) and in having prominent whitish margins on most dorsal feathers. Ospreys differ from other hawks and eagles in having a reversible outer toe on each foot, and the underside of the toes covered with short spines, which aids in grasping slippery fish (Cramp 1980; Palmer 1988).

POPULATION SIZE AND TREND: Most North American Osprey populations have recovered from the serious declines that occurred during the 1950s and 1960s, caused by pesticide contaminants in the environment (Henny 1983; Poole 1989). The total nesting population in the United States, excluding Alaska, was estimated at 8,000 pairs for the period 1973–1981 (Henny 1983). In eastern North America, the only recently reported declining population is the Florida Bay population in Everglades National Park (Kushlan and Bass 1983; Poole 1989).

Ospreys occur in Florida both as a nesting species and during spring and fall, when birds from more northern populations pass to and from tropical wintering regions (Poole and Agler 1987). The Ospreys that nested in Florida apparently were not seriously impacted by pesticide poisons during the DDT

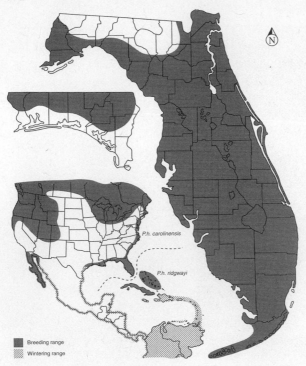

Distribution map
of the Osprey,
Pandion haliaetus.

era (Ogden 1977). Although the number of Ospreys now nesting in Florida is not known, the statewide total may be in the range of 1,500–2,000 pairs (Henny 1983). The number of pairs nesting in Florida may be about 20% of the nesting population in the lower 48 states (Henny 1983). A few to many pairs may nest together in loose aggregations. For example, 45 active Osprey nests were in a 1,620 ha swamp in Gulf County in 1979 (Eichholz 1980), and 25 active nests were on a 90 ha island in Florida Bay, Monroe County, in 1968 and 1971 (Ogden 1977).

Although Ospreys remain a common bird in many locations of Florida, regional population numbers and trends are undetermined or unreported for almost all portions of the state. Exceptions include Sanibel Island, where the population was stable between 1979 and 1981 (Westall 1983) and Florida Bay, where the number of nesting Ospreys declined 58% between 1973 and 1980 (Kushlan and Bass 1983). On the adjacent Florida Keys, the number of pairs of nesting Ospreys increased "over the last several decades" (Bowman et al. 1989). At Lake Istokpoga, Highlands County, the total number of Osprey nests surrounding the lake was 75 in 1910, down to 9 in 1973, and up to 80 by 1992 (Howell 1932; M. McMillian, pers. comm.).

DISTRIBUTION AND HISTORY OF DISTRIBUTION: In the lower 48 states, Ospreys nest most abundantly throughout Maine, along the entire

Atlantic coast (especially Chesapeake Bay), throughout Florida, in the forest and lake regions around the western Great Lakes, in a belt of northwestern forests between western Montana and western Washington, and south into northern California (Henny 1983). These regions of relatively high abundance are generally similar to those reported much earlier by Bent (1937), and thus it appears that major distributional changes have not occurred. In the remainder of the United States, excluding Alaska, Ospreys nest in only small numbers and at widely scattered locations, even in areas of seemingly good habitat in the extensive freshwater swamps and estuaries in coastal Louisiana and Texas.

Ospreys nest in all regions of Florida. They appear to be maintaining their historical distributional pattern throughout the state (Howell 1932; Sprunt 1954). They are most common as nesting birds in bays and other estuarine habitats along the coast of the Gulf of Mexico between the mouth of the Apalachicola River and Florida Bay and the Florida Keys, along the Atlantic coast between the St. Mary's River and Merritt Island, and throughout the regions of lakes and swamps in the St. Johns River and Kissimmee River basins (Henny 1983; J. Rodgers, pers. comm.). Other important nesting sites include swamps between Paynes Prairie and Orange Lake in Alachua and Marion counties, riparian swamps along Reedy Creek, Polk County, and along the Ocklawaha, Withlacoochee, and Hillsborough Rivers. Ospreys recently expanded their nesting range from the flat, prairie region of Highlands County to the ridge section, when several pairs nested for the first time on utility poles and light poles at athletic fields near Sebring and Lake Placid (F. Lohrer, pers. comm.).

HABITAT REQUIREMENTS AND HABITAT TREND: Except during migration, Ospreys spend most of their lives around bodies of open water. Nests are constructed in the tops of large living or dead trees, including cypress (*Taxodium* sp.), mangrove (*Avicennia germinans, Rhizophora mangle*), pine (*Pinus* sp.), and swamp hardwoods. Nest trees are often located in extensive stands of swamp forest, in riparian woodlands, or in belts of cypress bordering lakes or streams. Nests in Florida Bay and other coastal bays or offshore islands may be in low mangrove trees or shrubs or even on the ground (Ogden 1977). Ospreys also readily construct nests on a wide variety of manmade structures, including utility poles, radio towers, and channel markers, where human activity may be relatively high but where direct disturbance to nests is unlikely (Schreiber and Schreiber 1977). Ospreys also require open, relatively clear water in order to successfully locate and capture fish. There seems to be no overall assessment of Osprey habitat trends in Florida. Locally, and perhaps regionally, Osprey numbers appear to be limited by a lack of adequate nesting trees or other structures, if one can judge by the success of supplemental nest platform programs (Westall 1983). Construction of large numbers of lakefront homes has undoubtedly displaced Ospreys from nesting sites in shoreline trees. Logging, especially for larger trees or in limited stands of cypress and swamp hardwoods, may be eliminating nesting sites.

VULNERABILITY OF SPECIES AND HABITAT: Although Ospreys are at times remarkably tolerant of certain activities by people, they may construct nests in locations where changing patterns of human activity result in frequent disturbances and possible nesting failures. Ospreys are vulnerable to shooting because of their large size, their tolerance for relatively close approach by humans, and their occasional habit of foraging at fish farms. Osprey populations outside of Florida have in the past declined sharply due to reproductive failures induced by organochlorine pesticides in the environment (Ames 1966; Hickey and Anderson 1968; Henny and Wight 1969).

CAUSES OF THREAT: Ospreys are regularly injured or killed by striking power lines and by becoming entwined in fishing monofilament. Nests built on manmade structures, especially channel markers, may be removed if they are perceived to be interfering with the operational requirements of those structures (Schreiber and Schreiber 1977; Leenhouts 1979). Overdevelopment of coastlines and lakeshores destroys nesting habitat, while degradation of water quality can adversely impact Osprey foraging sites by reducing water clarity, changing fish populations, and promoting growth of aquatic vegetation. The number of nesting Ospreys in Florida Bay declined apparently as a result of a reduction in either the abundance or availability of food (Kushlan and Bass 1983; Bowman et al. 1989). A substantial decline in the number of nesting Ospreys on Lake Istokpoga, Highlands County, during the early 1970s was suspected to have been caused by local applications of the pesticides aldrin, toxaphene, and DDT (M. McMillian, pers. comm.).

RESPONSES TO HABITAT MODIFICATION: Ospreys readily accept nest platforms as artificial nesting sites (Reese 1970; Westall 1983). Nests located on platforms, as a group, may be more successful than nests at natural sites because the former are more secure from wind damage and ground predators.

DEMOGRAPHIC CHARACTERISTICS: Ospreys in Florida Bay begin nesting in late November, and many established pairs have laid eggs before the end of December (Ogden 1977). Most nesting begins in January on Sanibel Island (Westall 1983), in mid-February on Lake Istokpoga (M. McMillian, pers. comm.), and in late February in extreme northern Florida (Eichholz 1980). Laying by all pairs within a region may extend over a 2 to 3-month period, so that nesting is usually completed by April in south Florida, and by July in the north. Clutch size ranges between 2 and 4 eggs, with 3 being the most common. Average production of young per nest for all nesting attempts at coastal locations has been reported at 0.77–1.01 fledglings in Florida Bay from 1968 to 1972 (Ogden 1977), 0.54–0.65 in Florida Bay during 1978–1980 (Kushlan and Bass 1983), 0.50–1.61 at Sanibel Island from 1979 to 1981 (Westall 1983), and 0.73 fledglings at Seahorse Key in 1972 (Szaro 1978). These studies showed between 49 and 61% of active nests fledged one or more young on average, although the nest success rate was as low as 28% at natural nest sites (as contrasted with higher rates on nest platforms) in one year on Sanibel. Considering only successful nests, fledgling rates were 1.48–1.73 (Ogden 1977), 1.1–1.7 (Kushlan and Bass 1983), and 1.8–2.0 (Westall 1983), respectively. These studies also showed that early nests averaged larger clutches and fledged more chicks than later nests. A similar nesting success rate was documented inland at Lake Istokpoga in 1991 where 48% of the active nests produced an average of 0.7 young per active nest and 1.42 young per successful nest (M. McMillian, pers. comm.). Some tagged Ospreys in Florida Bay first laid eggs at 3 years of age and others at 4 years (Ogden 1977). Annual mortality rates and life span for the Osprey are poorly known (Palmer 1988).

KEY BEHAVIORS: Ospreys prey almost entirely on fish, which they capture by diving into the water with talons extended. Fish prey often range between 20 and 40 cm in length (Palmer 1988). Fish commonly captured in Florida include sea catfish (*Arius felis*), mullet (*Mugil* spp.), spotted trout (*Cynoscion nebulosus*), shad (*Dorosoma* spp.), crappie (*Pomoxis nigromaculatus*), and sunfish (*Lepomis* spp.) (Nesbitt 1974; Ogden 1977; Szaro 1978; Palmer 1988).

Ospreys build large, bulky nests, and commonly reuse and enlarge a nest for many consecutive years. Immature birds, generally 1–3 years old, may build small, incomplete nests later in the nesting season than when most adults build or repair nests (Ogden, unpubl. data). Ospreys perform elaborate courtship flights in the air over nest sites, with both birds of a pair participating, or a male performing alone high over a perched female (Palmer 1988). These flights are characterized by circling, downward swoops, and hovering, all accompanied by much calling. A male also will bring fish to its perched mate. The most common call is a series of shrill whistles, gradually going up the scale, with the calls of females being lower pitched and, at times, having a more nasal or raspy tone (Palmer 1988).

Although both birds of a pair participate in incubation, most is by the female (Palmer 1988). The female also remains in close attendance with the nestlings and must shade them from direct, hot sunlight. The male brings fish to the nest, which the female tears into pieces and feeds to the chicks. The young take their first flights at 52–55 days of age, but continue to be fed on or near the nest until about 90–100 days.

Ospreys in northern Florida are missing from the nesting sites during December–January, and may be migratory (Howell 1932). Ospreys in coastal, south Florida seem to be nonmigratory (Ogden 1977, Westall 1983). Marked subadults from Florida Bay tended to disperse northward into the central and southern peninsula beginning in May and returned to the Bay in November (Ogden 1977).

Bald Eagles occasionally chase Ospreys that are carrying fish, and may cause a fleeing Osprey to drop its prey (Palmer 1988). Nesting eagles may force nearby nesting Ospreys to relocate or cause nearby Ospreys to be less successful at nesting (Ogden 1975). Eagles also may occasionally prey on small nestling Ospreys (W. Robertson, pers. comm.).

CONSERVATION MEASURES TAKEN: The Osprey is protected by International Migratory Bird Treaty and by federal and Florida law. Important aggregations of nesting birds are protected in Everglades National Park, Big Cypress National Preserve, Merritt Island National Wildlife Refuge, Ocala National Forest, and other federal and state wildlife preserves. The Osprey is listed as a species of special concern only in Monroe County in the 1 June 1994 "Official Lists of Endangered and Potentially Endangered Fauna and Flora in Florida."

CONSERVATION MEASURES PROPOSED: The actual number of nesting pairs of Ospreys in Florida and the population trend are not known. Systematic censuses of nesting Ospreys should be established to estimate the current number and to determine a baseline for measuring future population and distributional changes. High priority should be given to locating major, unprotected nesting aggregations and to providing protection to these sites. Consideration should be given to implementing nest platform programs, modeled on previous efforts, in areas where an inadequate number of natural nesting sites may be severally limiting regional populations. Because Ospreys are known to be adversely impacted by certain environmental contaminants, systematic programs should be implemented to monitor for the distribution and levels of concentration of pesticides, PCBs and heavy metals in fishes and aquatic systems throughout Florida. The causes for the substantial decline in nesting Ospreys in Florida Bay are not well understood and require additional study.

ACKNOWLEDGMENTS: Various drafts of this Osprey account have been reviewed and improved by Reed Bowman, Bill Leenhouts, Steve Nesbitt, Jim Rodgers, and Mark Westall. Mike McMillian generously provided a prepublication copy of his Lake Istokpoga study. My time on this project was supported by South Florida Natural Resources, Everglades National Park.

LITERATURE CITED:

Ames, P. L. 1966. DDT residues in the eggs of the Osprey in the northeastern United States and their relationship to nesting success. Jour. Applied Ecol. 3(suppl.): 87–97.

Bent, A. C. 1937. Life histories of North American birds. Part 1. U.S. Natl. Mus. Bull. no. 167. Washington, D.C.

Bowman, R., G. V. N. Powell, J. A. Hovis, N. C. Kline, and T. Wilmers. 1989. Variation in reproductive success between subpopulations of the Osprey (Pandion haliaetus) in south Florida. Bull. Mar. Sci. 44:245–250.

Brown, L., and D. Amadon. 1968. Eagles, hawks and falcons of the World. Vol. 1. McGraw-Hill Book Co., New York, New York.

Clark, W. S., and B. K. Wheeler. 1987. A field guide to hawks of North America. Houghton Mifflin Co., Boston, Massachusetts.

Cramp, S. (Ed.). 1980. Handbook of the birds of Europe the Middle East and North Africa. Vol. 2. Oxford Univ. Press, Oxford, England.

Eichholz, N. F. 1980. Osprey nest concentration in northwest Florida. Fla. Field Nat. 8:18–19.

Henny, C. J. 1983. Distribution and abundance of nesting Ospreys in the United States. Pp. 175–186 in Biology and management of Bald Eagles and Ospreys (D. M. Bird, ed.). MacDonald Raptor Res. Ctr., McGill Univ., Harpell Press, St. Anne de Bellevue, Quebec.

Henny, C. J., and H. M. Wight. 1969. An endangered Osprey population: estimates of mortality and production. Auk 86:188–198.

Hickey, J. J., and D. W. Anderson. 1968. Chlorinated Hydrocarbons and eggshell changes in raptorial and fish-eating birds. Sci. 162: 271–273.

Howell, A. H. 1932. Florida bird life. Coward-McCann Inc., New York, New York.

Kushlan, J. A., and O. L. Bass, Jr. 1983. Decreases in the southern Florida Osprey population, a possible result of food stress. Pp. 187–200 in Biology and management of Bald Eagles and Ospreys (D. M. Bird, ed.). MacDonald Raptor Res. Ctr., McGill Univ., Harpell Press, St. Anne de Bellevue, Quebec.

Leenhouts, W. P. 1979. Osprey nest relocation at Merritt Island National Wildlife Refuge. Fla. Field Nat. 7:7–8.

Nesbitt, S. A. 1974. Foods of the Osprey at Newnan's Lake. Fla. Field Nat. 2:45.

Ogden, J. C. 1975. Effects of Bald Eagle territoriality on nesting Ospreys. Wilson Bull. 87:496–505.

Ogden, J. C. 1977. Preliminary report on a study of Florida Bay Ospreys. Pp. 143-151 in Transactions of the North American Osprey Research Conference (J. C. Ogden, ed.). U. S. Natl. Park Ser., Trans. Proc. Ser. no. two.

Palmer, R. S. 1988. Handbook of North American birds. Vol. 4. Diurnal raptors (Part 1). Yale Univ. Press, New Haven, Connecticut. Pp. 73–101.

Poole, A. F. 1989. Ospreys. A natural and unnatural history. Cambridge Univ. Press, New York, New York.

Poole, A. F., and B. Agler. 1987. Recoveries of Ospreys banded in the United States, 1914-84. Jour. Wildl. Manag. 51:148–155.

Reese, J. G. 1970. Reproduction in a Chesapeake Bay Osprey population. Auk 87:747–759.

Schreiber, R. W., and E. A. Schreiber. 1977. Observations of Ospreys nesting on artificial structures in Charlotte Harbor, Florida. Fla. Field Nat. 5:5–7.

Sibley, C. G., J. E. Ahlquist, and B. L. Monroe, Jr. 1988. A classification of the living birds of the world based on DNA-DNA hybridization studies. Auk 105:409–423.

Sprunt, A., Jr. 1954. Florida bird life. Coward-McCann Inc., New York, New York.

Szaro, R. C. 1978. Reproductive success and foraging behavior of the Osprey at Seahorse Key, Florida. Wilson Bull. 90:112–118.

Westall, M. A. 1983. An Osprey population aided by nest structures on Sanibel Island, Florida. Pp. 287–291 in Biology and management of Bald Eagles and Ospreys (D. M. Bird, ed.). MacDonald Raptor Res. Ctr., McGill Univ., Harpell Press, St. Anne de Bellevue, Quebec.

PREPARED BY: John C. Ogden, National Park Service, Everglades National Park, 40001 State Road 9336, Homestead, FL 33034-6733.

Southern Bald Eagle

Haliaeetus leucocephalus leucocephalus

FAMILY ACCIPITRIDAE

Order Falconiformes

TAXONOMY: The Bald Eagle (*Haliaeetus leucocephalus*), also known as the White-headed Eagle and the American Eagle, is the sole representative of the genus *Haliaeetus* ("sea eagle") regularly found in the western hemisphere. The division of *H. leucocephalus* into two subspecies (*H. l. leucocephalus* [Southern Bald Eagle] and *H. l. alascanus* [Northern Bald Eagle]) is based primarily on size. Bald Eagles from opposite ends of their 4,400 km (2,750 mi.) range (north-south) are distinctively different. Wing chord measurements of Alaskan females average 640 mm (males, 588 mm), whereas southeastern females (including Florida) average 576 mm (males, 529 mm). However, there is a gradient of larger to smaller birds from north to south. The gradual nature of this size gradient, and the overlap of breeding and migration ranges makes it difficult to define geographic limits of subspecies, and therefore, it should be avoided (Amadon 1983; Palmer 1988).

DESCRIPTION: The Bald Eagle is the largest raptor that breeds in Florida (total length, 0.9 m; wingspread ca. 2.1 m; females are larger than males; see wing chord measurements above). Adults are readily identified by the white head and tail, chocolate-brown wings and body, and yellow eyes, bill, and feet. First-year juveniles are nearly uniform dark-brown with variable white speckling under the wings and on the underside of the tail. Each year thereafter, molting brings about a highly variable array of dark and white patterns, with only the cere, tail, and iris following a more or less progressive change toward a definitive adult condition, normally achieved in the sixth year (McCollough 1989).

POPULATION SIZE AND TREND: During 1990, an estimated 2,933 occupied, nesting Bald Eagle territories existed in the lower 48 states (USFWS 1991). In Alaska and Canada, where nesting surveys are not as intensive, there

Southern Bald
Eagle, *Haliaeetus
leucocephalus
leucocephalus.*
(Photo by Stephen
A. Nesbitt)

are 60,000 to 70,000 individuals (Gerrard and Bortolotti 1988). In the south-eastern United States, the number of active territories has increased from 396 in 1981 to 722 in 1990. This includes an increase in Florida from 340 to 557 active territories in the same period (USFWS 1991).

The banning of DDT in 1972 halted a 30-year decline of Bald Eagle reproduction in Florida. Statewide surveys showed a steady increase in numbers of active nests from a low of about 120 in 1973 to 319 in 1978, undoubtedly influenced by a more intensive survey effort. From 1979 to 1988 numbers remained fairly steady with an average of about 367 active nests per year. Numbers of active territories have increased annually since 1989 to 623 in 1991, with an estimated population of 1,599 to 2,190 individuals (S. A. Nesbitt, unpubl. data). Population estimates, based on the 1993 statewide survey, was 1,775 to 2,450 individuals and 667 pairs in Florida (S. Nesbitt, pers. comm.). As long as environmental contaminants remain below critical levels, the population of Bald Eagles in Florida will probably continue to increase as long as there is suitable habitat available for recolonization as well.

DISTRIBUTION AND HISTORY OF DISTRIBUTION: The Bald Eagle was formerly distributed (in suitable habitat) across the North American continent from western Alaska to the Maritime Provinces of Canada south to the Florida Keys, the Gulf Coast, and Baja California. Pesticide contamination and loss of habitat have eliminated the species from most of its former breeding range south of Canada. Presently, most nesting eagles (over 90%) are found in disjunct populations in Florida, the Chesapeake Bay area, the Great Lakes, Maine, and the Pacific Northwest (Simons et al. 1988). Breeding range

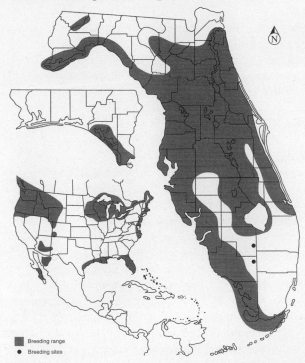

Distribution map of the Southern Bald Eagle, *Haliaeetus leucocephalus leucocephalus.*

Breeding range
Breeding sites

has increased in the southeastern United States since 1981, due to successful hacking programs and, probably, natural recolonization. Between 1981 and 1990 the number of occupied territories in the 10 southeastern states (excluding Florida) increased from 56 to 187 (USFWS 1991).

The Bald Eagle was originally found throughout Florida in great numbers. The original population was probably in excess of 1,000 nesting pairs distributed along both coasts, the Florida Keys, and inland along all larger lakes and rivers. By the early 1970s habitat loss and a declining population led to the extirpation of Bald Eagles from most of Florida, but three areas held viable nesting populations: the extreme southwest coast and Florida Bay, the Gulf coast from Pinellas County to the mouth of the Suwannee River, and the St. Johns–Oklawaha River system from Brevard County to southern Alachua County. From 1975 to 1990 numbers of active nesting territories increased in 34 of Florida's 67 counties, including 17 counties that increased from zero. Much of the increase in numbers of active nests from 1975 to 1990 occurred in two of these three nesting concentrations mentioned above. Numbers of active nests increased by more than three-fold along the St. Johns-Oklawaha River system and the surrounding counties and doubled along the Gulf coast from Tampa to the Suwannee River. The Florida Bay-southwest peninsula population, having been spared the decimation of pesticide poisoning and habitat loss that affected the rest of the state, remained stable throughout this period. Areas of nesting concentration not reported by Robertson (1978) have developed along the Kissimmee Valley (Polk and Osceola Counties) and, to a lesser extent, the northern end of the St. Johns River (Duval, Clay and St. Johns Counties). For the most part, the western panhandle remained void of nests but most of the eastern panhandle counties have shown slight increases.

HABITAT REQUIREMENTS AND HABITAT TREND: Although Bald Eagles occur in a wide variety of habitats throughout their range, proximity to water is important. Preferred habitat includes a high amount of water-to-land edge where prey is concentrated (Palmer 1988). Bald Eagles feed primarily on fish, but birds, smaller mammals, and carrion are also utilized. In north-central Florida freshwater catfish (*Ictalurus* spp.) and American Coot (*Fulica americana*) make up the bulk of the Bald Eagle's diet (McEwan and Hirth 1980), whereas in Florida Bay sea catfish (*Arius felis*), mullet (*Mugil* spp.), and assorted wading birds (up to the size of Great White Heron, *Ardea herodias*) are taken (Curnutt, unpubl. data). Nesting habitat generally consists of older, taller trees with an unimpeded view of the surrounding area. A notable exception in Florida is found on the small keys of Florida Bay where the virtual absence of both mammalian predators and tall emergent trees has led to nesting within the crowns of mangroves, on nest platforms built by Great White Herons, and nesting on the ground (Shea and Robertson 1979).

Under natural conditions habitat suitability of an area remains relatively constant so long as prey density is not diminished. The structural dynamics of undisturbed forests may lead to a decrease in the availability of emergent trees (i.e., the Gulf Coast mangrove forest of Everglades National Park), in which case eagles will occupy emergents along the inland edge of the forest if available. Much suitable Bald Eagle habitat in Florida has been developed for urban and recreational use. Recreational use of coastal areas and feeding areas, while not affecting the structural integrity of suitable habitat, may have adverse effects on eagles during the breeding season by disrupting incubation and feeding of offspring and the ability to procure prey.

VULNERABILITY OF SPECIES AND HABITAT: Surprisingly, direct persecution of adult Bald Eagles still occurs (ca. 15% of adult eagles delivered to Maitland Bird of Prey Center in 1991 were treated for gunshot wounds; T. Stemland, pers. comm.), in spite of their recognition as the national bird and as a symbol of the wilderness. Subadults, lacking the familiar white head and tail, probably suffer a higher rate of persecution. As top-level consumers in the food chain, Bald Eagles have been vulnerable to bioaccumulation of contaminants, including heavy metals and many pesticides (Krantz et al. 1970). DDT, the most well known of the organochlorines, has been banned in the United States and Canada for nearly two decades and eagles have recovered well. But, recent reports of high levels of mercury in many species of fish used as prey by Bald Eagles in Florida Bay illustrate the need for continued vigilance. Currently, a much more serious threat to Bald Eagle populations is loss of habitat to development. The continuous influx of tourists and new residents into Florida inevitably results in an increasing demand to develop wild lands for residential and recreational use.

RESPONSE TO HABITAT MODIFICATION: Bald Eagle response to habitat degradation is dependent on the type and degree of disturbance. Loss of food resources through pollution, overfishing, or habitat modification can lead to significant declines in breeding populations (i.e., Shapiro et al. 1982). Continued disturbance, especially early in the nesting cycle, can cause breeding pairs to forego nesting and perhaps abandon an area entirely (Wood et al. 1989). Changes in surrounding habitat that do not directly effect a nest tree (i.e., use of buffer zones around nests that limit disturbance during part of the year) can apparently be tolerated by a pair of eagles. However, when one or both of the nesting eagles die the territory may not be recolonized if habitat has become extremely fragmented.

DEMOGRAPHIC CHARACTERISTICS: Bald Eagles are believed to form life-long monogamous pair bonds, with defended nesting territories used year after year. Clutch size is usually 2 eggs with more 3 egg sets than singles (Palmer 1988). Replacement clutches are laid if the original is lost early in the approximately 35-day incubation period. Fledging occurs when the young are about 77 days old. Bald Eagles reach sexual maturity at 4 or 5 years, more often the latter. Life span in captivity has reached 48 years (McGehee and Crawford 1985), but little is known about longevity in the wild. Sprunt et al. (1973) reported productivity ranging from a high of 1.6 young fledged per successful nesting attempt (Alaska) to a low of 1.29 (Maine). However, the lower range was probably due to adverse effects of pesticide contamination. In Florida, productivity appears healthy with an average of 1.56 young per successful nesting attempt and 1.07 young per active territory (FGFWFC, unpubl. data). Nesting success is positively correlated with abundant food supply, early nesting, and past success at a particular territory, while inclement weather and variable and inconsistent food supply tend to reduce productivity (Gerrard and Bortolotti 1988; Curnutt 1991).

KEY BEHAVIORS: Many populations of Bald Eagles are migratory, especially those that nest in areas where food availability is seasonal (Palmer 1988). In Florida, northward migration has been documented during the nonbreeding season (summer) for eagles nesting along the Gulf coast north of Tampa (Broley 1947) and those nesting in north-central Florida (P. Wood, pers. comm.). In Everglades National Park little is known concerning migratory movements, but direct observations indicate that at least some nesting adults occupy territories year round.

Bald Eagles regularly form communal roosts near areas of concentrated prey during the nonbreeding season (e.g., Crenshaw and McClelland 1989), especially in the more northern parts of their range. In Florida, communal roosting has not often been reported, perhaps because much of the population migrates out of the state during the nonbreeding season. However, a year-round communal roost has recently been described in Everglades National Park (Curnutt 1992).

Early in the nesting season, mated pairs of Bald Eagles will perform spectacular aerial displays that include pursuit flights and high soaring, the latter often culminating in talon-locking and a cartwheeling tumble to very near the land or water, where the birds will disengage and, miraculously, not crash. Often eagles will perch high within their territory or fly around its perimeter to advertise their presence. This highly visible form of communication may help explain the disappointingly slight voice of the Bald Eagle. Its high, thin-pitched call has been described as "weak in volume and trivial in expression" (Brewster in Palmer 1988).

Foraging behavior is highly diverse. Most often, Bald Eagles soar over feeding areas and swooping down on prey to clutch it with one or both talons, usually not breaking the rhythm of flight. The sit-and-wait approach also is used, with higher success than flying, if prey is concentrated near a suitable perch (including the nest). The use of carrion and piracy from Osprey (*Pandion haliaetus*) and gulls has led many to regard the Bald Eagle with disdain (most notably Benjamin Franklin). However, the beauty and majesty of the Bald Eagle is apparent to anyone who has the opportunity to observe them.

CONSERVATION MEASURES TAKEN: The Bald Eagle is federally protected under the Endangered Species Act and the Bald Eagle Protection Act and is listed as threatened by the State of Florida. Further protection is granted under Florida's Conservation and Coastal Management Plan. In concert these laws protect individuals and, to some extent, nesting habitat during the breeding season. These laws can only be enforced where eagle nest locations are known. The FGFWFC annually monitors Bald Eagle nesting throughout the state. The USFWS is reviewing information indicating that the Bald Eagle has recovered in portions of its range to determine if it should be reclassified as threatened. In Florida, the recovery goal of 400 occupied territories (USFWS 1989) has been met. However, because this is probably less than half of the

original nesting population of the state, a critical review of the proposed reclassification should be conducted.

CONSERVATION MEASURES PROPOSED: Laws designed to protect Florida's Bald Eagle population must incorporate results of research on buffer zones around nesting territories. For example, Fraser et al. (1985) suggested limiting most human activity within a 500-meter buffer around active nests, and the USFWS (1987) suggested a 1-mile buffer zone around nests when considering general land-development projects.

Other proposals include: systematic monitoring of pesticides to determine levels of contaminants before productivity is severely affected; and research to determine the destinations of eagles migrating out of Florida during part of the year so that those areas can be protected.

ACKNOWLEDGMENTS: Data were provided by Stephen Nesbitt, Florida Game and Fresh Water Fish Commission, and the U.S. Fish and Wildlife Service, Region 4, Atlanta, Georgia. I thank Petra Wood for many informative discussions and Dr. William B. Robertson, Jr. for his comments and review of the manuscript.

LITERATURE CITED:

Amadon, D. 1983. The Bald Eagle and its relatives. Pp. 1-4 in Biology and management of Bald Eagles and Osprey (Bird, D. M., chief ed.). Harpell Press, Ste. Anne de Bellevue, Quebec.

Broley, C. L. 1947. Migration and nesting of Florida Bald Eagles. Wilson Bull. 59:30–20.

Crenshaw, J. G., and B. R. McClelland. 1989. Bald Eagle use of a communal roost. Wilson Bull. 101:626–633.

Curnutt, J. L. 1991. Population ecology of the Bald Eagle in Florida Bay, Everglades National Park, Florida, 1959–1990. M.S. thesis. Florida International Univ., Miami, Florida. 69 pages.

Curnutt, J. L. 1992. Dynamics of a year-round communal roost of Bald Eagles. Wilson Bull. 104:536–540.

Fraser, J. D., L. D. Frenzel, and J. E. Mathisen. 1985. The impact of human activities on breeding Bald Eagles in north-central Minnesota. Jour. Wildl. Manage. 49:585–592.

Gerrard, J. M., and G. R. Bortolotti. 1988. The Bald Eagle. Smithsonian Institution Press, Washington, D.C. 177 pages.

Krantz, W. C., B. M. Mulhern, G. E. Bagley, A. Sprunt, IV, F. J. Ligas, and W. B. Robertson, Jr. 1970. Organochlorine and heavy metal residues in Bald Eagle eggs. Pest. Monit. Jour. 3:136–140.

McCollough, M. A. 1989. Molting sequence and aging of Bald Eagles. Wilson Bull. 101:1–10.

McEwan, L. C., and D. H. Hirth. 1980. Food habits of the Bald Eagle in north-central Florida. Condor 82:229–231.

McGehee, s., and W. C. Crawford, Jr. 1985. Captive management and dietary requirements of eagles and osprey. Wildl. Rehabilitation 3:19–23.

Palmer, R. S. (ed.). 1988. Handbook of North American birds, vol. 4 (part 1). Yale Univ. Press, New Haven, Connecticut.

Robertson, W. B., Jr. 1978. Southern Bald Eagle. Pp. 27–30 in Rare and Endangered Biota of Florida, vol. 2 (H. W. Kale, II, ed.). Univ. Presses of Florida, Gainesville, Florida.

Shea, D. S., and W. B. Robertson, Jr. 1979. Unusual observations of nesting Bald Eagles in south Florida. Fla. Field Nat. 7:3–5.

Shapiro, A. E., F. Montalbano, III, and D. Mager. 1982. Implications of construction of a flood control project upon Bald Eagle nesting activity. Wilson Bull. 94:55–63.

Simons, T., S. K. Sherrod, M. W. Collopy, and M. A. Jenkins. 1988. Restoring the Bald Eagle. Amer. Sci. 76:253–260.

Sprunt, A., IV, W. B. Robertson, Jr., S. Postupalsky, R. J. Hensel, C. E. Knoder, and F. J. Ligas. 1973. Comparative productivity of six Bald Eagle populations. North Amer. Wildl. Conf. 38:96–106.

USFWS. 1987. Habitat management guidelines for the Bald Eagle in the southeast region. U.S. Fish and Wildlife Serv., Atlanta, Georgia. 9 pages.

USFWS. 1989. Recovery plan for the southeastern states Baid Eagle. U. S. Fish and Wildlife Serv., Atlanta, Georgia. 41 pp.

USFWS. 1991. Endangered and threatened species account: Bald eagle. U. S. Fish and Wildlife Serv., Atlanta, Georgia. 10 pp.

Wood, P. B., T. C. Edwards, Jr., and M. W. Collopy. 1989. Characteristics of Bald Eagle nesting habitat in Florida. Jour. Wildl. Manage. 53:441–449.

PREPARED BY: John L. Curnutt, National Biologial Survey, Everglades National Park, 40001 State Road 9336, Homestead, FL 33034-6733 (Current address: Department of Ecology and Evolutionary Biology, University of Tennessee, Knoxville, TN 37996-1610).

American Swallow-tailed Kite

Elanoides forficatus

FAMILY ACCIPITRIDAE

Order Falconiformes

TAXONOMY: The genus *Elanoides* is monotypic and quite distinct from the most closely related groups, *Elanus* (e.g., White-tailed Kite, *E. leucurus*) and *Pernis* (e.g., Honey-buzzard, *P. apivorus*) (Brown and Amadon 1968). The distinguishing features of the two subspecies of the American Swallow-tailed Kite (*E. f. forficatus* and *E. f. yetapa*) are poorly defined, leading some authors to question the subspecific status of *E. f. yetapa* (Robertson 1988).

DESCRIPTION: The American Swallow-tailed Kite is a medium-sized raptor distinguished by its striking black and white plumage and long, deeply forked tail. The sexes are identical in plumage and indistinguishable by size in the field. The head, neck, underside, and lower wing coverts are white. The flight feathers and back are black. On the upperside, the shoulders and the anterior secondary coverts have an iridescent sheen; the remaining black areas appear to be dusted bluish-gray in living birds, possibly due to accumulated powder from powder feathers (Robertson 1988). The feet and beak are relatively small and the tarsi are short. The cere, feet, and tarsi are bluish-gray; the beak is black. Wingspan is 120 to 130 cm, and overall length is 50 to 64 cm. Weights range from 390 to over 600 g, depending on sex and season (Brown and Amadon 1968; Robertson 1988; D. Lee, unpubl. data).

Juveniles have been described as having shorter tails, narrower wings, white-tipped flight feathers, a buffy cast to the white plumage, and fine streaking on the head and breast (Bent 1937; Skutch 1965; Clark and Wheeler 1987; Robertson 1988). However, the buff fades soon after fledging and the white feather tips, which are visible only on some prepared specimens, apparently are lost to wear. The dark streaking, which is highly variable and may persist after the first year, is not visible in the field. The short tail, in combination with a narrow wing or the absence of wing molt, is diagnostic of juvenile kites.

American
Swallow-tailed
Kite, *Elanoides
forficatus.*
(Photo by
Brian A. Millsap)

POPULATION SIZE AND TREND: No systematic count of American Swallow-tailed Kites has been made; however, based on sighting reports, Breeding Bird Atlas data, and available habitat, Meyer and Collopy (1990) estimated that there are 480–750 pairs breeding in Florida, and a total of 800–1,150 pairs in the United States. The total United States population probably numbers 3,200–4,600 birds at the end of the breeding season, which includes nonbreeding adults and young of the year.

There is no evidence of major population changes since *E. f. forficatus* reached its lowpoint in the 1940s. Whereas local reductions in parts of Florida are apparent, no clear trend emerges for the state (Meyer and Collopy 1990). Robertson (1988) cited increased extralimital sightings since the 1940s to suggest that the United States population may be slowly increasing. However, with the possible exception of limited nesting in small areas of eastern Texas (D. Boone, pers. comm.), no reoccupation or expansion of former range has occurred (Cely 1979; Robertson 1988; Meyer and Collopy 1990; Meyer 1995). Although existing data do not permit an accurate assessment of recent trends, Swallow-tailed Kites clearly are not experiencing the marked increases recently exhibited by White-tailed and Mississippi kites (*Ictinia mississippiensis*).

DISTRIBUTION AND HISTORY OF DISTRIBUTION: The current breeding range of *E. f. forficatus* includes most of Florida and small parts of South Carolina, Georgia, Alabama, Mississippi, Louisiana, and Texas (Meyer 1995).

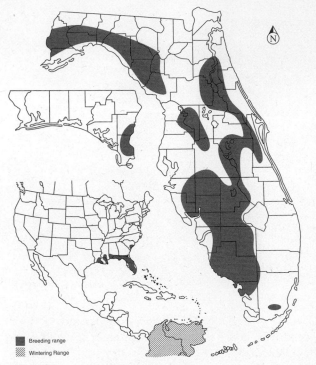

Distribution map
of the American
Swallow-tailed Kite,
Elanoides forficatus.

■ Breeding range

▨ Wintering Range

Although recent evidence is lacking, nesting is likely in the Okefenokee Swamp, Georgia (Cely 1979). *E. f. yetapa* breeds from southern Mexico to northern Argentina and southeastern Brazil (Brown and Amadon 1968; Robertson 1988). Both subspecies spend the boreal winter in South America, from southeastern Brazil northward (summarized in Robertson 1988).

The historic breeding range of *E. f. forficatus* included parts of 16 and perhaps as many as 21 states, extending up the Mississippi drainage as far north as Minnesota. Although some areas undoubtedly harbored few pairs, Swallow-tailed Kites formerly were well established in areas far removed from their current range (Meyer and Collopy 1990). Shooting and loss of habitat probably were the main causes of the decline, which occurred fairly abruptly around the turn of the century (Cely 1979; Robertson 1988).

Breeding Bird Atlas data and the results of our recent study (Meyer and Collopy 1990) indicate that nesting occurs in at least 75% of Florida's counties. Nesting kites are very rare or absent in Hillsborough, Pinellas, Pasco, Okeechobee, St. Lucie, and Martin counties. Areas with the greatest densities include Big Cypress Swamp (Big Cypress National Preserve, Fakahatchee Strand, Florida Panther National Wildlife Refuge, Golden Gate Estates south of Interstate 75, and the Okaloacoochee Slough), the Fisheating Creek drainage, Corkscrew Swamp, wetlands east of the Central Highlands in Polk and Highlands counties, ranchlands southwest of the Central Highlands and Lake Okeechobee, Long Pine Key in Everglades National Park, southwest coastal mangrove forests, St. Johns River valley, Green Swamp, Apalachicola National Forest (including adjacent areas of Liberty, Wakulla, Franklin, and Gulf Counties), and the Big Bend and Gulf Hammock regions (Jefferson, Taylor, Dixie, and Levy Counties).

HABITAT REQUIREMENTS AND HABITAT TREND: The American Swallow-tailed Kite's distribution is limited by aridity in the United States and South America (Robertson 1988). In Florida, Swallow-tailed Kites usually nest in tall pine and cypress trees that emerge from the canopy of fairly open stands. Nest and roost sites typically are within mosaics of mixed woodland-savannah habitats. Foraging ranges are a diverse array of swamp and floodplain forests: mixed pine, cypress, and hardwood stands; the vegetated margins of rivers, creeks, and lakes; hardwood hammocks; bayheads; prairies; sloughs; and mangroves. In general, nesting kites require tall, open nest trees within vegetation mosaics that are rich in small arboreal vertebrates and large flying insects. The rate of loss of critical kite habitat in Florida is accelerating.

VULNERABILITY OF SPECIES AND HABITAT: American Swallow-tailed Kites are limited by their low reproductive potential, which results from delayed breeding, small brood size, low nesting success and productivity, and failure to renest following failure. Although unmeasured for this species, first-year mortality in other long-distance migrants is high (>50%). Strong fidelity to nest and roost sites promotes social behavior and efficient foraging, thereby enhancing productivity and survival. Such site fidelity, however, concentrates nesting activity and discourages colonization of vacant habitat, thus increasing the species' vulnerability to disturbance.

The Swallow-tailed Kite's natural limiting factors help explain the species' failure to regain its former range or numbers following its abrupt decline at the beginning of this century. It is of pressing concern that these biological constraints compound the impact of the accelerating destruction of vital habitat. The effects of habitat destruction along migration routes and on the winter range are entirely unknown. Our understanding of breeding biology and the outcome of one previous attempt (J. Parker, unpubl. rept.) indicate that reintroductions probably will be difficult and prohibitively expensive.

Large communal roosts that form at the end of the breeding season probably serve to promote social facilitation of feeding, which allows the kites to exploit seasonal swarms of insects and quickly gain fat for migration (Millsap 1987; Meyer 1993). The largest of these roosts near Lake Okeechobee reached peaks of 1,500 to 2,200 birds from 1987 to 1995 (Millsap 1987; Meyer 1993, unpubl. data). Roosting Swallow-tailed Kites do not tolerate disturbance, however, and are vulnerable to disturbance and vandalism (Meyer 1995). It is likely that some communal roost sites have been used repeatedly over long periods of time; the largest are on private lands subject to disturbance and development.

CAUSES OF THREAT: At present, direct persecution of American Swallow-tailed Kites is rare in Florida. The greatest threat to Swallow-tailed Kites is the accelerating rate of habitat destruction. Most of Florida's kites nest and roost on private land in the central and southwestern regions. These areas are experiencing Florida's most rapid rate of conversion to large-scale agriculture, which comes at the expense of the habitat diversity required by Swallow-tailed Kites. In addition to drastic reductions in diversity, the inevitable changes in hydrology affect the health of the remaining natural areas.

RESPONSES TO HABITAT MODIFICATION: Responses by American Swallow-tailed Kites to changes in specific nesting areas are poorly documented. The loss of tall trees for nesting and a reduced prey base due to habitat alteration undoubtedly limit opportunities for successful nesting. Altered water periodicity and quality, and associated changes in vegetation, are evident where local nesting concentrations are known to have declined (Meyer and Collopy 1990). In southern Florida, kites frequently nest in Australian pines (*Casuarina equisetifolia*), an introduced species common along canals, edges of agricultural fields, and on dredge islands. Australian pine nests monitored during 1988 and 1989 failed at a significantly higher rate than nests in native pine or cypress (Meyer and Collopy 1990).

In 1989, Hurricane Hugo severely damaged the nesting habitat of most of South Carolina's population (about 100 pairs) of Swallow-tailed Kites (Cely and Sorrow 1990), highlighting the vulnerability of small populations to habitat disturbance. The effects of the damage are not yet known; however, virtually all of the tall trees used for nesting were leveled by the storm.

DEMOGRAPHIC CHARACTERISTICS: Age at first breeding, age-specific survival and fecundity, and sex ratios for American Swallow-tailed Kites are unknown. Average success (nests fledging at least one young) was 52% during a study of 68 nesting attempts from 1988 to 1990 (Meyer and Collopy 1990). Productivity (young fledged per clutch laid) averaged 0.85. Wind was the leading cause of nest failures; predation was rare.

KEY BEHAVIORS: The American Swallow-tailed Kite's beautiful appearance is complemented by its extraordinary aerial grace. These gregarious birds are conspicuous foragers, coursing low over the foliage in search of arboreal vertebrates, or twisting and dipping at great heights as they hawk flying insects.

Swallowtails eat while flying and perch infrequently during the day. They seldom flap their wings, except in very still air. Interactions are marked by dramatic acrobatics, persistent vocalizations, and a startling rush of parted air at the nadir of each high-speed dive.

Swallow-tailed Kites arrive in Florida in late February and early March. They are strongly site-faithful and arrival dates are consistent for specific areas. Courtship and territorial displays include diving chases of the male by the calling female and slow circling flights, usually by a single bird, over the nest area. Nests, which consist of small sticks woven into a matrix of Spanish moss (*Tillandsia usneoides*) and lichens (*Usnea* and *Ramalina* spp.), are placed near the top of one of the tallest trees in the stand. Construction takes from one day to two weeks. Females typically lay two eggs, which are incubated for about 28 days by both sexes. Young fledge in five to six weeks but continue to be fed by their parents until migration, which begins from late August to early September (Meyer and Collopy 1990). Migration routes are not clearly known. Most birds probably cross the Caribbean, perhaps pausing on Cuba or other islands, while some apparently migrate along the coast of the Gulf of Mexico (see Robertson 1988). Apart from some limited information on range (the northern half of South America), almost nothing is known about the species' winter ecology.

Nesting Swallow-tailed Kites take a great variety of prey that are relatively difficult to locate but easy to capture. The diet includes frogs (tree and true), anoles, snakes, nestling songbirds, insects (including wasp larvae), and a small number of mammals (mainly bats) (Howell 1932; Snyder 1974; Meyer and Collopy 1990). Although adults feed their developing young mainly vertebrates, insects are the mainstay of adults and the bulk of the prey captured by young during the fledgling dependency period (Snyder 1974; Meyer and Collopy 1990). It appears that insects are the principal prey for all birds during the premigratory period (Meyer and Collopy 1990; D. Lee, unpubl. data).

The species nests in loose colonies (two to five well-spaced nests) and forages in groups that may number in the hundreds. Nonbreeding adults associate with nesting kites, occasionally contributing to nest-building, offering food, and joining in group responses to predators (Meyer and Collopy 1990). Some kites gather in large communal roosts prior to migration. Social facilitation of feeding, particularly on ephemeral swarms of insects, and group defense against nest predators are the likely explanations for Swallow-tailed Kite social behavior.

The esthetic appeal of the Swallow-tailed Kite is matched by few North American birds. The species' social behavior is very unusual among raptors— colonial nesting, the behavior of nonbreeders, foraging aggregations, and communal roosts are of both theoretical and applied interest. Swallow-tailed Kites are adept at hunting a wide range of prey. Diet and habitat requirements make the species a particularly good indicator of diversity and health in Florida's natural systems.

CONSERVATION MEASURES TAKEN: In 1985, *E. f. forficatus* was listed by the United States Fish and Wildlife Service as a candidate for threatened or endangered status (Category 2) (USFWS 1985). The species' listing status was changed to Category 3c (more numerous than previously thought) as part of a broad revision of listing status in 1989; no explanation for the change was provided (USFWS 1989). The Fish and Wildlife Service is considering restoring the Category 2 status (C. Hunter, pers. comm.). The species is not listed by the Florida Game and Fresh Water Fish Commission. Swallow-tailed Kites are listed as a extirpated in Arkansas, endangered in South Carolina, and as a species of special concern in Mississippi and Louisiana (Meyer 1990). In setting priorities for wildlife research, the Florida Game and Fresh Water Fish Commission ranked the Swallow-tailed Kite as one of Florida's most vulnerable and poorly understood vertebrate species (Millsap et al. 1989).

CONSERVATION MEASURES PROPOSED: Agricultural permitting procedures in central and southwestern Florida and forestry practices in the north must consider the habitat requirements of American Swallow-tailed Kites. It is fundamentally important to maintain heterogeneity by protecting lowland forests, including the forested margins of swamps, rivers, flood-plains, prairies, and sloughs; habitat mosaics that include pine and cypress stands; bayheads and hardwood hammocks; and permanent and seasonal wetlands of all sizes. Even-aged regeneration and shorter rotations in lowland pine forests reduce the number of tall, emergent trees suitable for nesting. In all cases, it is essential that water quality and periodicity be maintained.

A study that described phenology and behavior at a large roost also developed methods for monitoring total numbers and estimating annual productivity from ratios of adults to juveniles (Meyer 1993). These monitoring methods could help to assess long term population trends. Artifical nests might increase breeding success in small, regularly used areas that are frequently affected by severe weather.

Future work on Florida's Swallow-tailed Kites should include: identifying and acquiring areas critical for nesting and roosting; developing a monitoring method; studying demographics to help predict population trends; conducting research on essential prey densities and the requirements of key prey species; and investigating migration routes and winter habitat requirements (Meyer 1995). The American Swallow-tailed Kite should be considered for listing as endangered at both state and federal levels.

ACKNOWLEDGMENTS: John Cely documented the breeding biology of South Carolina's Swallow-tailed Kites and, along with William B. Robertson, Jr., drew attention to changes in the species' United States distribution and status. David Lee provided unpublished data for this report. Florida's Nongame Wildlife Program provided the major support for studies of breeding ecology and communal roosts in Florida. Steven McGehee assisted in the field. James A. Rodgers provided a thoughtful review of an earlier draft.

LITERATURE CITED:

Bent, A. C. 1937. Life histories of North American birds of prey, part 1. Bull. no. 167, U. S. Natl. Mus. 409 pp.

Brown, L., and D. Amadon. 1968. Eagles, hawks and falcons of the world, vol. 1. Country Life Books, London. 414 pp.

Cely, J. E. 1979. Status of the swallow-tailed kite and factors affecting its distribution. Pages 144–150 in Proc. of the first South Carolina endangered species symposium. (D. M. Forsythe and W. B. Ezell, Jr., eds.). S. C. Wildl. and Mar. Resour. Dept., Columbia, South Carolina. 201 pp.

Cely, J. E., and J. A. Sorrow. 1990. The American Swallow-tailed Kite in South Carolina. Nongame and Heritage Trust Fund publication no. 1. S.C. Wildl. and Mar. Resour. Dept., Columbia, South Carolina. 160 pp.

Clark, W. S., and B. K. Wheeler. 1987. A field guide to the hawks of North America. Houghton Mifflin, Boston, Massachusetts. 198 pp.

Howell, A. H. 1932. Florida bird life. Cowan-McCann, Inc., New York, New York. 579 pp.

Meyer, K. D. 1990. The status of four species of kites in the southeastern United States. Pages 38-49 in Proc. of the southeastern raptor management symposium. (B. G. Pendleton, ed.). Natl. Wildl. Fed., Washington, D. C. 245 pp.

Meyer, K. D., and M. W. Collopy. 1990. Status, distribution, and habitat requirements of the American Swallow-tailed Kite (*Elanoides forficatus*) in Florida. Final report, Fla. Game and Fresh Water Fish Comm., Nongame Wildl. Prog., Tallahassee, Florida. 146 pp.

Meyer, K. D. 1993. Communal roosts of the American Swallow-tailed Kite in Florida: habitat associations, critical sites, and a technique for monitoring population status. Final report, Fla. Game and Fresh Water Fish Comm., Nongame Wildl. Prog., Tallahassee, Florida.

Meyer, K. D. 1995. Swallow-tailed Kite (*Elanoides forficatus*). In The Birds of North America, no. 138 (A. Poole and F. Gill, eds.). The Academy of Natural Sciences, Philadelphia, Pennsylvania.

Millsap, B. A. 1987. Summer concentrations of American Swallow-tailed Kites at Lake Okeechobee, Florida, with comments on post-breeding movements. Fla. Field Nat. 15:85–92.

Millsap, B. A., J. A. Gore, D. E. Runde, and S. I. Cerulean. 1989. Setting priorities for the conservation of fish and wildlife species in Florida. Fla. Game and Fresh Water Fish Comm., Nongame Wildl. Prog., Tallahassee, Florida. 80 pp.

Robertson, W. B., Jr. 1988. American Swallow-tailed Kite. Pp. 109-131 in Handbook of North American birds, vol. 4. (R. S. Palmer, ed.). Yale Univ. Press, New Haven, Connecticut. 429 pp.

Skutch, A. F. 1965. Life history notes on two tropical American kites. Condor 67:235–246.

Snyder, N. F. R. 1974. Breeding biology of Swallow-tailed Kites in Florida. Living Bird 13:73–97.

USFWS. 1985. Endangered and threatened wildlife and plants; review of vertebrate wildlife; notice of review. Fed. Reg. 50:37,958–37,967.

USFWS. 1989. Endangered and threatened wildlife and plants; animal notice of review. Fed. Reg. 54:554–579.

PREPARED BY: Kenneth D. Meyer and Michael W. Collopy, Department of Wildlife and Ecology and Conservation, 118 Newins-Ziegler Hall, University of Florida, Gainesville, FL 32611-0304 (Current address of KDM: National Park Service, Big Cypress National Preserve, Box 11, Ochopee, FL 33943; current address of MWC: Cooperative Research Center, Bureau of Land Management, 3200 S.W. Jefferson Way, Corvallis, OR 97331).

Crested Caracara

Caracara plancus

FAMILY FALCONIDAE

Order Falconiformes

TAXONOMY: Audubon's Crested Caracara (*Caracara plancus audubonii*) that occurs in Florida is one of three generally recognized subspecies of the Crested Caracara (Brown and Amadon 1968). It is only slightly differentiated from *C. p. cheriway,* somewhat more distinct from *C. p. pallidus,* and most clearly separable from *C. p. plancus*. Some authorities regard *C. p. plancus* as a separate species and place the other subspecies in the species *C. cheriway*. Audubon's Crested Caracara was originally described by Audubon in 1834 as *Polyborus vulgaris* from a specimen he collected in November 1831 near St. Augustine. It was renamed as *P. audubonii* by Cassin in 1865. Widely used synonyms of the scientific name include *Polyborus cheriway audubonii* and *Caracara cheriway audubonii*.

DESCRIPTION: The Crested Caracara is a large, boldly patterned raptor with a crest, naked face, heavy bill, elongate neck, and long legs. It has a body length of about 50–60 cm and a wingspan of about 124 cm. Mean measurements of wing, tail, and tarsus of 10 adult males and 10 adult females (in parentheses) from Florida, Texas, Arizona, and Mexico given by Friedman (1950) are—wing, 393.5 (391) mm; tail, 240.5 (242) mm; tarsus, 84.4 (92) mm. Mean body mass of 13 Florida adults and juveniles of both sexes was 1,042 g, with a range of 940–1,220 g (Layne, unpubl. data).

    The adult (sexes similar) is blackish-brown on the crown, upper abdomen, rump, wings, and thighs. The lower part of the head, throat, upper breast, lower abdomen, and undertail coverts are white or cream. The lower breast has blackish barring on a buffy ground color. The back also is heavily barred with black and white. The tail is white with 11–14 narrow dark crossbars and a broad terminal band. The basal region of the outer primaries is white, producing conspicuous white patches in the outer part of the wing in flight. The robust bill is bluish-gray, contrasting with the bright yellow facial skin, which

197

Crested Caracara, *Caracara plancus*. (Photo by James N. Layne)

turns reddish-orange when flushed with blood. The legs and feet are deep yellow, as is the skin on other parts of the body.

Juveniles (sexes alike) have the same basic color pattern as adults, but the dark areas are paler brown and the light-colored areas tan or buffy. The breast and back have diffuse brown streaks rather than barring. The facial skin is gray, changing to a pinkish or rosy hue when flushed with blood, and the legs and feet are pale gray.

The full adult (definitive basic) plumage is acquired at about 4 years of age after four molts. Juveniles hatched in winter or early spring undergo the post-juvenile molt, which includes the flight feathers, in late summer and fall and begin their second molt the following spring. Subsequent developmental molts as well as adult molts occur from about April to October (Layne 1986).

POPULATION SIZE AND TREND: Published accounts, field notes of naturalists, recollections of long-time residents in the central Florida prairie region, and the numbers of eggs and skins in museum collections suggest that at least up to the 1940s Caracaras were considerably more abundant than at present. The total population in the early 1950s was estimated at about 250 by Glenn Chandler (Sprunt 1954). Funderberg and Heinzman (1967) believed that the population had severely declined by the late 1960s; and Heinzman (1970)

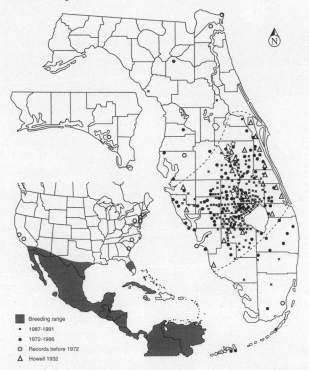

Distribution map of the Crested Caracara, *Caracara plancus.* Symbols as follows: open triangles, locality records plotted by Howell (1932); dashed line, limits of breeding range from Howell (1932); open circles, peripheral locality records prior to 1972; solid circles, locality records between 1972 and 1986; X's, locality records from 1987 to 1991. Inset map: hatched pattern, distribution of *C. p. audubonii;* cross-hatched pattern, range of other *C. plancus* subspecies; open circles, casual records.

■ Breeding range
× 1987–1991
● 1972–1986
○ Records before 1972
△ Howell 1932

reported the results of a four-year survey (1967–70) indicating fewer than 100 individuals remaining at about 58 localities. Stevenson (1975) assumed the population was close to the same number in 1974.

I gathered data on the distribution and population status of the Caracara in Florida from 1972 to 1991 by means of general road and off-road searches, systematic roadside censuses in the core area of the range, aerial surveys, compilation of published records and museum specimens, and reports of sightings from numerous cooperators (Layne 1995). Estimates of the population based on these data for the periods 1973–76 and 1973–78 were a minimum of 350 and 400 to 500 individuals, respectively (Layne 1978, 1982). Over the entire 20-year span, a total of 286 active locations was recorded. Total number of locations in which Caracaras were recorded and numbers of sites with adults (in parentheses) during 5-year periods from 1972-1991 were as follows: 1972–76, 174(130); 1977–81, 184(155); 1982–86, 122(98); 1987–91, 183(156). The slightly lower values for the 1972–76 period and the distinctly lower values for 1981–86 reflect less intense sampling effort the first year of the study and in all years of the 1981–86 period. Allowing for this effect, the data indicate an essentially stable adult population during the 20-year span, with a minimum of about 300 individuals (twice the number of sites with adults on the assumption that essentially all adults are paired). Although immatures are more difficult to census, the number present in the population at any one time during the 20-year period is estimated at about 100–200 birds. Thus, a minimum estimate of the total population during the 1972–91 interval is 400–500 individuals. Additional evidence of a stable population over the 20-year period is the similarity in the ratio of number of sites with immatures to the number with adults for each 5-year interval: 0.61 in 1972– 76, 0.53 in 1977–81, 0.55 in 1982–86, 0.55 in 1987–91. These data cast doubt on Heinzman's (1970) estimate of less than 100 birds remaining in 1967–70. In addition, a substantial number of records during 1967–70 are known from localities not shown on Heinzman's map (Layne, unpubl. data).

DISTRIBUTION AND HISTORY OF DISTRIBUTION: Audubon's Crested Caracara is the only member of the Caracara group to reach North America. The subspecies occurs from Panama to Baja California, in southern Arizona, eastern Texas, and extreme southwestern Louisiana, Florida, and Cuba and the Isle of Pines (AOU 1983). The lack of differentiation of the disjunct Florida and Cuban populations suggests that the movement from the west and subsequent isolation were relatively recent events, probably dating from the Wisconsinan glacial period. The subspecies also occurs casually north to central New Mexico and Oklahoma and on Jamaica and islands off Panama. Crested Caracaras have been reported from a number of localities well beyond the established range, including Ontario, Pennsylvania, New Jersey, North Carolina, South Carolina, New York, and Oregon (Hoyt and Hoyt 1944; Eisenmann 1947; AOU 1983). One also was captured in Fairfield, Connecticut, in December 1974 (Layne, unpubl. data). Probably most, if not all, of these records are individuals that escaped from captivity, as was confirmed in the case of the North Carolina report (Teulings 1974). As other Crested Caracara subspecies have been imported to the United States over the years (e.g., Banks and Clapp 1972), there is a good possibility that not all of these records represent *audubonii*, although reported as such.

The other subspecies of *C. plancus* occur from eastern Panama to about the Amazon River (*cheriway*), through the remainder of South America to Tierra del Fuego and the Falkland Islands (*plancus*), and on the Tres Marias Islands off the coast of Nayarit, Mexico (*pallidus*).

The breeding range in Florida is restricted to the south-central peninsular region, but Caracaras have been recorded from the Lower Keys, Monroe County, north to Fernandina, Nassau County (Carbury 1938), and as far west in the panhandle as Bay County (Loftin et al. 1987). The status of these and other peripheral occurrences, whether wandering wild individuals or escapees, is questionable.

As there had been comparatively little alteration of the state's natural habitats up to that time, Howell's (1932) map can be considered to reflect the early historical range and thus provides a valuable baseline for assessing long-term trends in the distribution of the Florida population. Howell stated that the bird was a common resident in the central Florida prairie region from northern Brevard County south to Fort Pierce, Lake Okeechobee, Rocky Lake in Hendry County, Okaloacoochee Slough, and Everglade (=Everglades City) in Collier County. He cited Audubon's record from near St. Augustine in 1831 and one from Enterprise (Volusia County) about 1858 as suggesting a somewhat wider earlier distribution. Other records well to the north of the main range during the same period include Jacksonville (Duval County) in 1925 (Grimes 1944) and Fernandina (Nassau County) in 1937 (Carbury 1938).

Sprunt (1954) noted that the range remained essentially the same as given by Howell in 1932, with the exception of fewer records south of the Tamiami Trail and north of Orlando. The Kissimmee Prairie remained the stronghold of the population.

The distribution in 1973–76 (Layne 1978) agreed with Sprunt's (1954) description. The greatest concentration of records was in the area north and west of Lake Okeechobee in Charlotte, De Soto, Glades, Highlands, Hardee, Okeechobee, Polk, and Osceola counties. The 1973–76 data also suggest that fewer Caracaras occurred in the fall and winter in the farmlands of Dade County compared with the period from the early 1950s to the early 1970s, when *Audubon Field Notes/American Birds* contained a number of such reports.

For the updated Florida range map, records for 1987–91 were selected to represent the current distribution. The isolated record from Levy County was reported during this period (Ogden 1987). As in the case of the 1973–76 period, the 1987–91 data indicate that there has been no essential change in the breeding range boundaries or the core area of the distribution since 1932.

From 1972 through 1991, Caracaras were documented at 286 locations in 28 counties (1 questionable); adults, assumed to indicate established territories, were recorded at 236 locations in 21 counties. Sixty-eight percent of all locations and 61% of adult locations were concentrated in an area including DeSoto, Glades, Hendry, Highlands, Okeechobee, and Osceola counties. Caracaras observed on Estero Island (Lee County) in 1972, 1973, and 1976, on Gasparilla Island (Charlotte County) in 1974, on Cayo Costa Island (Lee County) in 1977 and 1978, and in the Upper (Upper Matecumbe) and Lower (Big Pine, Summerland) Keys (Monroe County) in 1977 and 1978 were probably from a large group that escaped from Everglades Wonder Gardens at Bonita Springs in 1972 (J. Vanas, pers. comm.). An individual sighted on Boca Chica Key in April 1993 is less likely to have been one of these escapees (Pronty et al. 1993). Two banded individuals near Lake Tohopekaliga (Osceola County) in August 1983 and single adults in the same vicinity in July and

December 1983 were apparently from a group of four captive-raised Caracaras from the Miami Metrozoo released nearby in March of that year (Stone 1983).

HABITAT REQUIREMENTS AND HABITAT TREND: Throughout its range, the Crested Caracara is a bird of open xeric to mesic habitats. Its primary habitat in Florida was the native prairie with associated marshes and cabbage palm and cabbage palm-live oak hammocks. The core area of the distribution conforms closely to the original location of the major prairie systems (Davis 1967) in the De Soto, Okeechobee, and Osceola plains physiographic regions (White 1970). The natural prairie habitat has been greatly reduced by housing developments and conversion to improved pasture, pine or eucalyptus plantations, or citrus groves. In some cases, lack of burning has allowed former prairie communities to succeed to brushland or other more closed habitat types unfavorable to Caracaras. The bulk of the population at present is found on large cattle ranches with improved pastures (Layne 1978). Where seemingly suitable pastureland has been created by clearing of flatwoods in regions outside former prairie areas, as, for example, in parts of DeSoto, Hardee, and Manatee counties, Caracaras have either failed to become established or are rare.

Fossil records indicate that Caracaras (extinct species *C. prelutosa* and *Milvago readei*) were more widespread in Florida during the Pleistocene than in historical times (Brodkorb 1964; Pregil and Olson 1981). The subsequent restriction of the range and reduction of species diversity was probably associated with loss of arid prairie, scrubby, or savanna habitats during the post-Wisconsinan rise in sea level, as postulated for the Bahamas and Puerto Rico by Olson and Hilgartner (1982).

Suitable nest trees are an important component of Crested Caracara habitat. Cabbage palms (*Sabal palmetto*) are most frequently utilized (>90%), followed by live oaks (*Quercus virginiana*). Other species in which nests have been found include pines (*Pinus* sp.), saw palmetto (*Serenoa repens*), black gum (*Nyssa sylvatica*), and Australian pine (*Casuarina* sp.) (Nicholson 1928; Bent 1938; Layne, unpubl. data).

VULNERABILITY OF SPECIES AND HABITAT: Habitat loss is presently the primary threat to the Crested Caracara in Florida and was probably the major cause of the apparently marked decline in the population that occurred between the 1940s and 1950s or 60s. Drainage and conversion of the natural habitat to improved pastureland may have resulted in an overall reduction in the carrying capacity of the range, as improved pastures have lower diversity and fewer wetlands than the original native prairie, which may be reflected in reduced food resources. Elimination of the screw worm in the late 1950s might also have been a factor in the decline by reducing the amount of carrion available. The most extensive habitat changes in the Caracara range have occurred since the 1950s and include continuing loss of both remaining native prairie as well as improved pasture habitats to housing developments, pine and eucalyptus plantations, and more intensive types of agriculture, such as citrus groves. Citrus conversion appears to be the most serious threat to the future of the Caracara population in Florida, although at the present time actual abandonment of territories as the result of citrus planting cannot be conclusively documented. However, given continuing citrus conversion at the current rate, coupled with habitat loss from other causes, a significant decline in the population appears likely within the next 10 years.

CAUSES OF THREAT: In addition to habitat loss or degradation, several other factors may have contributed to the decline of the Florida Crested Caracara population. Egg collectors apparently exacted a heavy toll on Caracara nests in the Kissimmee Valley during the late 1800s and early 1900s. Shooting of Caracaras was probably more prevalent formerly than in recent years. Nicholson (1929) noted the belief among cattlemen at the time that Caracaras had the habit of picking out the eyes of newborn cows and sheep. Fortunately, most ranchers no longer regard Caracaras as pests and in some cases actually encourage them by putting out food. Large-scale vulture trapping, during which many Caracaras are reported to have been captured and killed along with vultures, probably had a more significant impact on the population in earlier years than either egg collecting or shooting. Although illegal vulture trapping is known to have been conducted on some ranches in recent years, it is now probably only a relatively minor threat to Caracaras.

The increase in number of paved roads and high-speed traffic over the years has presumably been accompanied by an increase in numbers of Caracaras killed or injured by vehicles, but road mortality probably did not significantly contribute to the earlier decline of the population. Pesticides would not appear to be a factor either, as typical Caracara habitats have not been subject to large-scale pesticide applications. Kiff et al. (1983) found an average reduction of eggshell thickness of 8.2%, with a decrease of 20% in 10% of the samples, in Florida Caracara eggs collected before (pre-1947) and after (post-1947) widespread use of DDT. They concluded that the relatively low frequency of severe eggshell thinning indicated that other factors were probably more important in contributing to any population decline. Johnston (1978) analyzed tissues of three specimens collected in 1975 and 1978 for levels of dieldrin and DDE. No residues of dieldrin were detected and levels of DDE in fat and uropygial glands ranged from 1.24 to 3.25 ppm and 0.48 to 2.44 ppm, respectively.

RESPONSES TO HABITAT MODIFICATION: Crested Caracaras are relatively tolerant of small-scale habitat change. They commonly hang around cattle pens, barns, and ranch houses and readily adapt to human activity if not harassed. In a number of instances, pairs have persisted in areas that became subdivisions with widely spaced homes or have continued to occupy territories where substantial blocks of row crops, citrus groves, or pine plantations were planted. In one extreme case, a territory was still occupied 8 years after an estimated 75% or more of its area, including former nest sites, was converted to citrus.

DEMOGRAPHIC CHARACTERISTICS: General features of the life history of the Crested Caracara in Florida were summarized by Bent (1938) and Layne (1978, 1982, 1985). Caracaras normally do not breed until about 4 years of age. Pairs are strongly bonded, associate closely year-round, and maintain territories. Territories tend to persist for long periods, during which they may be occupied by different individuals as a result of death and subsequent replacement of mates. Over a 20-year period, the average length of time between the first and last year adults were recorded in a given locality, assumed to be a territory, was 12 years, with 46% of the territories being active from 15 to 20 years (Layne, unpubl. data). Detailed data on territory size are not available. Maximum distances between sightings presumed to be of members of the same pair (N = 15) ranged from 4.8 km to 9.7 km, with a mean of 7.3 km (Layne, unpubl. data). Assuming the territory to be roughly circular with a diameter equal to the maximum observed distance between sightings gives a mean territory size of about 42 km^2, with a range of 18–74 km^2.

Crested Caracaras are apparently long-lived, although there is little actual information on longevity in the wild. An individual, banded as a nestling, was 9 years old when killed on a road, and an adult with a distinctively crippled leg was at least 17 years old when last observed (Layne, unpubl. data). A Florida female brought into captivity when about 4 weeks old was still (1996) in full health and vigor at 20 years of age (pers. observ.), and Palmer (1988) noted a captive that lived 30 years.

Maximum local density recorded in Florida during 1972–91 was about 1 pair/14 km^2, but average density was much less. Highest regional density was in Glades County (total area = 1,910 km^2), a large proportion of which is potential Caracara habitat. During 1987-91, 43 active territories were estimated to occur in the county, giving an overall density of about 1 pair/44 km^2 (Layne, unpubl. data).

Eggs have been recorded from September to April, with the peak of breeding from January to March. Thirty egg dates from Florida given by Bent (1938) ranged from 28 December to 7 April, with 15 of the dates falling in the period 30 January–28 February. Florida pairs are occasionally double-brooded (Layne, unpubl. data).

The nest is a bulky but well-constructed structure composed mainly of long, slender pieces of vines, dry weed stalks, and sticks. Twelve nests in cabbage palms were located an average of 8.8 m (range = 4.9–14.6 m) above ground and had a mean maximum diameter and depth of 71.1 cm and 38.1 cm, respectively (Layne, unpubl. data). Bent (1938) reported a nest only 2.1 m high in a saw palmetto clump. My observations indicate that nests are rarely reused, although pairs frequently nest in close proximity to a previous nest. Nicholson (1928) stated that Caracaras sometimes used the same tree for several years.

Clutch size is 1–4, with 2 or 3 the usual number (Bent 1938). The mean of number of eggs in eight nests (21 eggs), monitored from laying to fledging, was 2.6. Fifty-two percent (11) of the eggs hatched and 43% resulted in fledged young (9). Three (21%) of a series of 14 nests failed, resulting in a fledging rate of 1.4 young/nest for all nests and 1.8 young/nest for successful nests. Known causes of nest mortality included predation on eggs or young by Fish Crows (*Corvus ossifragus*) and raccoons (*Procyon lotor*) and loss of eggs or young as a result of nests being blown out of the tree in violent thunderstorms or dislodged by the growing fruiting stalk (Layne, unpubl. data).

Young at hatching have a mass of about 50 g, reach approximate adult mass (1,000 g) at 5 weeks, and fledge at 7–8 weeks of age. The family group typically remains together for an extended period, apparently as long as 6 months in some cases. After leaving the adults, the young are presumably nomadic and may join aggregations, which are most prevalent in fall and winter. The 9-year old individual mentioned above was recovered 54 km from where it was banded as a nestling.

KEY BEHAVIORS: With its large beak and relatively long neck the Crested Caracara appears eagle-like in flight. It is a strong flier, with a cruising speed of about 29–32 km/hr and top speed about 64 km/hr. Caracaras do not commonly soar. They spend much time on the ground. When perching they usually select a site such as mound of earth, spoil bank, fence post, utility pole, or dead stub that affords a good view of the surrounding countryside.

Crested Caracaras are highly opportunistic in their feeding behavior. The diet includes carrion as well as a wide variety of live invertebrate and vertebrate prey. They forage extensively on the ground, often scratching or digging, and will wade into shallow water in search of prey. They are attracted to fires and such activities as disking or ditch cleaning operations that promise good feeding opportunities. Insects are the chief invertebrate prey, and vertebrates taken include fish, amphibians, reptiles, birds, and mammals. They can capture birds up to the size of Cattle Egrets (*Bubulcus ibis*) (Layne et al. 1977) and small mammals up to cottontail (*Sylvilagus floridanus*) size. Caracaras frequently pursue Turkey Vultures (*Cathartes aura*) and force them to disgorge. Nicholson

(1929) also saw one cause a crow to drop a mouse it was carrying. Both members of the pair often cooperate in pursuing a vulture or attacking large prey such as Cattle Egrets or rabbits.

Road-killed animals, primarily raccoons, opossums (*Didelphis virginiana*), and armadillos (*Dasypus novemcinctus*) are an important source of carrion, and a substantial proportion of the known territories include stretches of major roads. In such cases the birds regularly patrol the roads within their range and spend much time perched along the road on utility poles or fence posts. Road-kills are probably increasingly important to Caracaras and vultures because of reduction of other sources of carrion as a result of habitat changes, elimination of the screw worm, and improved ranching practices.

Correlated with their relatively high degree of sociality, Crested Caracaras have a fairly complex vocal repertoire. The most characteristic vocalization, from which the common name "Caracara" is derived, is a dry rattle, which may be uttered with the head erect or, when the bird is more excited, with the head being tossed back and snapped forward. There is a sex difference in the Headback version of the rattle call, with the retraction of the head being more prolonged in the female (Layne, unpubl. data).

CONSERVATION MEASURES TAKEN: Efforts to protect Crested Cara-caras in the Kissimmee Prairie region go back to 1936 when National Audubon Society wardens first began to patrol the region (Sprunt 1946). The Florida population was first classified as threatened by the Florida Committee on Rare and Endangered Plants and Animals and is now included as a threatened species on both the state (Florida Game and Fresh Water Fish Commission) and federal (U. S. Fish and Wildlife Service) lists of endangered and threatened species. It received federal listing in 1987 (DOI 1987). Its inclusion on the state and federal lists of endangered and threatened species strengthens the protection provided previously by the Migratory Bird Treaty Act and Florida Administrative Code. Federal listing mandates consultation with the U. S. Fish and Wildlife Service on projects of federal agencies or supported by federal funds that may potentially impact Caracaras and provides for review by the U. S. Fish and Wildlife Service of applications for federal permits for activities that may affect Caracaras. Federal listing also includes provisions for funding of land acquisition and research directed toward recovery of the species. State listing gives state agencies and regional and local planning and governmental bodies additional authority to consider possible impacts on Caracaras in reviewing development proposals or permit applications.

Educational programs of the Nongame Program of the Florida Game and Fresh Water Fish Commission and various environmental organizations such as Florida Audubon Society and Save Our American Raptors have increased public awareness of the Crested Caracara as one of Florida's most interesting wildlife species and of its conservation needs. Wildlife rehabilitation centers have salvaged a number of injured Caracaras.

Prescribed burning for the purpose of maintaining or restoring prairie or open rangeland habitats conducted on some state and federal lands such as Myakka River State Park and the U. S. Air Force Avon Park Bombing Range is benefiting Caracaras also. The traditional practice of burning native range on cattle ranches has similarly aided in maintaining suitable Caracara habitat on private lands.

CONSERVATION MEASURES PROPOSED: Increased habitat protection is the most important need of Crested Caracaras. This should involve both actual acquisition of Caracara habitat, as well as development of means to aid in preserving the large cattle ranches that now support the bulk of Florida's Caracara population. Less than 10% of the known territories are located entirely or partly on protected public lands. Federal and state lands on which Caracaras are known to occur include Lake Kissimmee State Park, Myakka River State Park, Tosohatchee State Reserve, Three Lakes Wildlife Management Area, Cecil M. Webb Wildlife Management Area, and the Avon Park Bombing Range. Even with the most optimistic estimate of the amount of land that might be added to public ownership for Caracara protection, private cattle ranches will undoubtedly continue to be the key to maintaining a viable Florida population.

Priority in land acquisition should be given to native prairie habitats, which now rank among the most endangered of Florida's natural landscapes. But because of the large areas required to support a viable Caracara population, typical ranchland comprising a mix of native habitats and improved pasture would, of necessity, have to comprise the bulk of such acquisitions. Besides Caracaras, large-scale acquisitions of such habitats would benefit other species characteristic of the Florida prairies such as Florida Sandhill Cranes (*Grus canadensis pratensis*) and Florida Burrowing Owls (*Speotyto cunicularia*), as well as Bald Eagles (*Haliaeetus leucocephalus*), Wood Storks (*Mycteria americana*), deer (*Odocoileus virginianus*), Florida black bears (*Ursus americanus floridanus*), Florida panthers (*Felis concolor coryi*), and a host of other species.

Further research on the ecology and life history of the caracara is needed in order to provide a better basis for management. Establishment of an effective, continuing monitoring program should have high priority. There is a need for detailed studies of the effects of citrus conversion and other habitat alterations on with the objective of developing effective methods to minimize potentially deleterious impacts of such activities. The increasing trend toward more intensive agricultural practices in Caracara habitats also suggests attention should be given to the possible direct and indirect effects of pesticides and herbicides on the birds. Research to determine why Caracaras have been slow to invade newly created grassland habitats and to develop techniques to encourage occupation of such areas is warranted. An in-depth assessment of the taxonomic status of the Florida population would be useful. In addition to standard morphological characters, this study also should examine the genetic composition of the population by means of electrophoresis, mitochondrial DNA analysis, and other techniques. Such data would be important in the event that at some future time the status of the Florida population becomes so precarious as to necessitate consideration of using birds from elsewhere in the range for captive breeding or reintroduction.

ACKNOWLEDGMENTS: The many individuals who supplied sighting records or allowed access to their lands for searches are gratefully acknowledged, and I regret that space does not permit listing all of their names. Support for aerial surveys in 1973–74 was provided by the New York Zoological Society and the U.S. Fish and Wildlife Service, and the Nongame Program of the Florida Game and Fresh Water Fish Commission aided in a thorough resurvey of known territories in 1989. For their assistance in the field and laboratory, I thank Dottie Carter, Linda C. Farnsworth, Lois V. Layne, Fred Lohrer, David R. Smith, Jane Thomason, Russell Titus, Jan Watters, and Chester Winegarner.

LITERATURE CITED:

AOU. 1983. Check-list of North American birds, 6th edition. American Ornithologist's Union. Lawrence, Kansas. 877 pp.

Banks, R. C., and R. B. Clapp. 1972. Birds imported into the United States in 1969. U. S. Fish and Wildl. Serv. Spec. Sci. Rept.-Wildl. 148. Washington, D.C.

Bent, A. C. 1938. Life histories of North American birds of prey. Part 2. Bull. U. S. Natl. Mus. 170:1–482.

Brodkorb, P. 1964. Catalogue of fossil birds: Part 2 (Anseriformes through Galliformes). Bull. Fla. State Mus. 8:289–293.

Brown, L., and D. Amadon. 1968. Eagles, hawks, and falcons of the world. McGraw-Hill Book Co., New York. 945 pp.

Carbury, J. M. 1938. Caracara near Fernandina. Fla. Nat. 11:48.

Davis, J. H. 1967. General map of natural vegetation of Florida. Agr. Exp. Sta., Inst. Food and Agr. Sci., Univ. of Florida Circular S-178. Gainesville, Florida.

DOI. 1987. 50 CFR Part 17. Endangered and threatened wildlife and plants; threatened status for the Florida population of Audubon's Crested Caracara. Fed. Reg. 52 (128):25229–25232.

Eisenmann, E. 1947. Audubon's Caracara in New York. Auk 64:470.

Friedman, H. 1950. The birds of North and Middle America. Part 11. U. S. Natl. Mus. Bull. 50:1–793.

Funderberg, J. B., and G. Heinzman. 1967. Status of the caracara in Florida. Fla. Nat. 40:150–151.

Grimes, S. A. 1944. Birds of Duval County (continued). Fla. Nat. 17: 21–31.

Heinzman, G. 1970. The caracara survey, a four year report. Fla. Nat. 43:149.

Hoyt, S. F., and J. S. Y. Hoyt. 1944. First record of Audubon's Caracara in South Carolina. Auk 61:145–146.

Howell, A. H. 1932. Florida bird life. Fla. Dept. Game and Fresh Water Fish., Tallahassee, Florida. 479 pp.

Kiff, L. F., D. B. Peakall, M. L. Morrison, and S. R. Wilbur. 1983. Eggshell thickness and DDE residue levels in vulture eggs. Pp. 440–458 in Vulture biology and management (Wilbur, S. R., and J. A. Jackson, eds.). Univ. Calif. Press, Berkeley, California.

Johnston, D. W. 1978. Organochlorine pesticide residues in Florida birds of prey, 1969-76. Pesticides Monit. Jour. 12:8–15.

Layne, J. N. 1978. Audubon's Caracara (*Caracara cheriway auduboni*). Pp. 34-36 in Rare and endangered biota of Florida, Vol. 2, birds (Kale, H. W. II, ed.). Univ. Presses of Florida, Gainesville, Florida.

Layne, J. N. 1982. The caracara in Florida. ENFO (Fla. Cons. Found.) 3:10–12.

Layne, J. N. 1985. Audubon Caracara. Florida Wildl. 39:40–42.

Layne, J. N. 1986. Plumages and molts of the Crested Caracara. Prog. and Abstr. Raptor Res. Found. Ann. Mtg., Univ. Florida, Gainesville, Florida, 20-23 Nov.:27.

Layne, J. N. 1995. Audubon's Crested Caracara in Florida. pp. 82–83 *in* Our living resources (La Roe, E. T., G. S. Farris, C. E. Puckett, P. D. Doran, and M. J. Mac, eds.). U.S. Dept. Int. Nat. Biol. Serv., Washington, D.C.

Layne, J. N., F. E. Lohrer, and C. E. Winegarner. 1977. Bird and mammal predators on the Cattle Egret in Florida. Fla. Field Nat. 5:1–14.

Loftin, H., S. J. Stedman, and T. L. Francis. 1987. An annotated check-list of the birds of Bay County, Florida. Bay County Audubon Soc., Panama City, Florida. 34 pp.

Nicholson, D. J. 1928. The Audubon Caracara of Florida. Oologist 45:2–8.

Nicholson, D. J. 1929. The Audubon Caracara. Fla. Nat. 2:67–69.

Ogden, J. 1987. Florida region: continental survey, the winter season, December 1, 1986-February 28, 1987. Amer. Birds 41: 273.

Olson, S. L., and W. B. Hilgartner. 1982. Fossil and subfossil birds from the Bahamas. Pp. 22–56 in Fossil vertebrates from the Bahamas (Olson, S. L., ed.). Smithsonian Inst. Contr. Paleobiol. 48. Washington, D.C.

Palmer, R. S. (ed.). 1988. Handbook of North American birds. Vol. 5. Yale Univ. Press, New Haven, Connecticut. 465 pp.

Pranty, B., L. Cooper, J. Cox, and P. Powell. 1993. Spring report: March–May 1993. Fla. Field Nat. 21:121–128.

Pregil, G. K., and S. L. Olson. 1981. Zoogeography of West Indian vertebrates in relation to Pleistocene climatic cycles. Ann. Rev. Ecol. Syst. 12:75–98.

Sprunt, A., Jr. 1946. An avian three-in-one Audubon's Caracara. Aud. Mag. 48:42–44.

Sprunt, A., Jr. 1954. Florida bird life. Coward-McCann, Inc., New York. 527 pp.

Stevenson, H. M. 1975. Report to the Game and Fresh Water Fish Commission on avian forms of special concern in Florida. In Fla. Game and Fresh Water Fish Comm. Job Prog. Rept. W-41-22, 1 July 1974–30 June 1975. Tallahassee, Florida.

Stone, R. 1983. FAS rehabilitates, releases caracara. Fla. Nat. 56:4–5.

Teulings, R. P. 1974. Southern Atlantic Coast region. Amer. Birds 28:37-40.

White, W. A. 1970. The geomorphology of the Florida peninsula. Fla. Dept. Nat. Res. Geol. Bull. 51:1–164.

PREPARED BY: James N. Layne, Archbold Biological Station, P. O. Box 2057, Lake Placid, FL 33852.

Threatened

Southeastern American Kestrel

Falco sparverius paulus

FAMILY FALCONIDAE

Order Falconiformes

TAXONOMY: The Falconidae has six genera that occur in North America (AOU 1983). The American Kestrel (*Falco sparverius*) is a member of the genus *Falco,* a closely related group of 39 species worldwide that are considered to be "true" falcons (Cade 1982). A total of 17 subspecies of American Kestrels currently are recognized (Palmer 1988); two of these subspecies, *F. s. sparverius* and *F. s. paulus,* occur in Florida.

DESCRIPTION: The American Kestrel is the smallest species of falcon that occurs in the United States. The size of these birds varies geographically, with birds breeding at northern latitudes being larger and heavier. The resident Southeastern American Kestrel (*F. s. paulus*) is smaller than the northern subspecies (*F. s. sparverius*), which winters in Florida. Flattened wing lengths of adult male and female *paulus* averaged 173.2 mm (n = 15) and 181.9 mm (n = 10), respectively, compared with *sparverius* males (186.3 mm, n = 22) and females (193.2 mm, n = 12) measured elsewhere in eastern North America (Palmer 1988). Average body weights reported for kestrels also exhibit considerable variation, 103–112 g for males and 119–141 g for females (Roest 1957; Porter and Wiemeyer 1972; Cade 1982; Palmer 1988), with heavier birds occurring at more northern latitudes. Sexual size dimorphism in kestrels is relatively small for falcons, with male wing lengths and weights averaging about 94 and 91% of female measurements, respectively (Cade 1982).

The plumages of male and female American Kestrels differ significantly from the juvenile stage onward. The most notable differences between the sexes are found in the wing and tail feathers (Palmer 1988). The upper wing coverts and parts of the secondaries of males are slatey-blue, usually with black spots, whereas the upper wing coverts of females are rufous with black barring, similar to their back. The tail feathers of males are rufous dorsally (with no barring), have a wide, black subterminal band, and a white or gray-brownish

211

Southeastern American Kestrel, *Falco sparverius paulus.* (Photo by John A. Smallwood)

tip. Females have a rufous tail with black barring and a whitish to buff-colored tip. There also is substantial geographical variation in the color and pattern of kestrel plumage, particularly among males. For example, *paulus* males often can be distinguished from migrant *sparverius* by their reduced markings, particularly in the amount of spotting on their flanks and breast.

POPULATION SIZE AND TREND: Wiley (1978) warned that Southeastern American Kestrels in Florida were declining; however, no systematic statewide surveys to estimate current population size have been conducted. Data from the U.S. Fish and Wildlife Service Breeding Bird Survey (Fuller et al. 1987) also suggested that the kestrel population declined in Florida between 1966–1979. Even though quantitative statewide population data do not yet exist, it is expected that as *paulus* kestrel populations continue to lose foraging and nesting habitat, they will continue to experience population declines.

DISTRIBUTION AND HISTORY OF DISTRIBUTION: Most early accounts of Southeastern American Kestrels are general in nature. This may be due to the fact that most early ornithological work in the state was conducted during winter and early spring and that wintering migrants (*F. s. sparverius*), present at this time, masked the true nature of *F. s. paulus.* Unpublished oological data exist, however, which were assembled to characterize historical kestrel populations in selected regions of the state (Hoffman and Collopy 1988). Comparison of data collected in north-central Florida by Charles E. Doe with intensive surveys conducted in the same area revealed that the kestrel

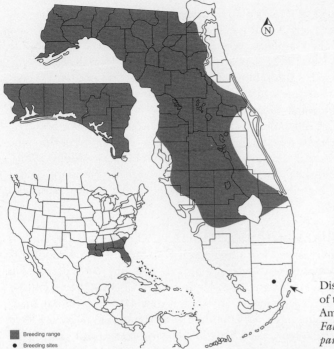

Distribution map
of the Southeastern
American Kestrel,
*Falco sparverius
paulus.*

■ Breeding range

● Breeding sites

population declined in this part of the state by at least 82% from 1938–1940 to 1981–1983.

Comparable survey data do not exist for central and south Florida; however, field notes of oologists working in these areas are available (see Hoffman and Collopy 1988). Donald and Wray Nicholson collected kestrel clutches in south-central Florida between 1909 and 1959. D. Nicholson wrote that between 1900 and 1920, the Southeastern American Kestrel "was very numerous in all of south central Florida, particularly in Orange, Lake, and Polk counties." Since 1970, efforts by ornithologists to locate *paulus* kestrels in this part of the state have resulted in relatively few sightings (Kale 1980; Paul 1982).

Data available on egg sets collected in Dade County by H. H. Bailey, between 1922 and 1932, revealed that kestrels formerly nested in the Miami Rockland pine forests. Holt and Sutton (1926) wrote that *paulus* was "abundant in certain parts of the pine-lands as far west as Long Pine Key, but never seen anywhere but in the pines." The loss of the kestrel as a breeding species in this region was likely due to the cutting of the pine forests. Robertson and Kushlan (1974) believed that breeding kestrels were gone from southeast Florida by about 1940.

Today, the range of *F. s. paulus* extends from South Carolina through Florida and west to Louisiana. It is considered rare over most of Georgia and the Piedmont of the Carolinas; very few nest in the Coastal Plain of the Carolinas (Hamel et al. 1982). A small population occurs along the Mississippi Gulf Coast. In Florida, *paulus* observations since 1980 have occurred primarily in sandhill or sand pine scrub areas, with additional observations scattered throughout south-central Florida. Southeastern American Kestrels are still widely distributed throughout much of north and central Florida; however, they are most frequently found in longleaf pine-turkey oak sandhills, sand pine scrub, and pastures with standing snags (Bohall-Wood and Collopy 1986). Scattered observations of *paulus* kestrels occur throughout the south-central part of the state. Few data have been collected on the *paulus* subspecies outside of Florida.

HABITAT REQUIREMENTS AND HABITAT TREND: American Kestrels are secondary cavity-nesters, depending on cavity excavators (e.g., woodpeckers) and natural processes to produce nesting sites. In a study of 95 nest sites in north-central Florida (Hoffman 1983; Hoffman and Collopy 1987), kestrels were found to nest predominately in longleaf pine (*Pinus palustris*) snags (53%); of the remaining nests, 32% occurred in sand pines (*P. clausa*), 12% in turkey oaks (*Quercus laevis*), 3% in live oaks (*Q. virginiana*), and <1% in post oaks (*Q. stellata*). In an area with a wide size range of potential nesting trees (8–40+ cm dbh), kestrels preferred snags that were 32–40 cm dbh (Hoffman 1983). In a comparison study area that had a smaller size range of snags available (8–32 cm dbh), 93% of the kestrels nested in the largest size class available (24–32 cm dbh).

In a longleaf pine-turkey oak sandhill study site in north-central Florida, kestrel cavities (n = 29) were most frequently old Pileated Woodpecker (*Dryocopus pileatus*) excavations (45%) or enlarged cavities of *Melanerpes* or *Colaptes* woodpeckers (38%) (Hoffman 1983). Kestrel nest cavities (n = 31) in the sand pine clearcuts of the Ocala National Forest were predominately (61%) old Northern Flicker (*C. auratus*) holes.

In addition to the presence of snags and woodpeckers to excavate cavities, kestrels require open fields to forage for food. In a roadside survey conducted in north-central Florida, *paulus* kestrels generally preferred open areas (e.g., pastures, fields, and open woodlands), and avoided hardwood stands and slash pine plantations (Bohall-Wood and Collopy 1986). Smallwood (1987) showed that the percent coverage of a kestrel's winter territory by woody canopy was negatively correlated with the foraging quality of that habitat; nearly all hunting attempts occurred in grasses and weedy forbs <25 cm in height. Nesting and foraging habitats preferred by kestrels have and are continuing to decline rapidly throughout Florida.

VULNERABILITY OF SPECIES AND HABITAT: Loss of nesting snags appears to be the dominant factor affecting American Kestrel declines in north-central Florida (Hoffman and Collopy 1988). Along the central Florida ridge, historic kestrel nesting and foraging habitats were both largely eliminated with the conversion of the original longleaf pine-turkey oak vegetation to citrus groves. The loss of nesting habitat that occurred when the pine forests in the Miami Rocklands were cut appears to coincide with the disappearance of kestrels as a breeding bird from south Florida. Although the specific factors affecting kestrels nesting in Florida vary regionally, the statewide population decline of Southeastern American Kestrels can only be reversed when both nesting sites and foraging areas are protected.

CAUSES OF THREAT: Throughout their range, American Kestrels typically are the most abundant raptor species present, are considered relatively tolerant of human disturbance, and often coexist with humans. Sizeable populations often are found in association with agricultural habitats and appear to be quite successful in human-altered environments. Kestrels often become more abundant in habitats opened up by agricultural activities. Since the turn of the century in Florida, however, millions of acres of open pine forests, particularly longleaf pine-turkey oak, have been altered for row crops, pasture land, citrus groves, residential development, or commercial timber production. Although these land uses are not necessarily incompatible with kestrels, their intensive nature requires active management to ensure that both the foraging and nesting resources needed by kestrels are protected.

RESPONSES TO HABITAT MODIFICATION: Historic records indicate that in Florida, Southeastern American Kestrel populations have declined in response to loss of both nesting and foraging habitat (Hoffman and Collopy 1988). The reduced number of longleaf pine snags left standing in agricultural fields and open pine woodlands have contributed greatly to this decline, as has widespread conversion of suitable foraging areas to intensive agriculture (e.g., citrus groves and pine plantations) and urban development.

DEMOGRAPHIC CHARACTERISTICS: Both sexes of American Kestrels are capable of breeding as yearlings, depending on the availability of mates and territories; Henny (1972) reports that about 82% of yearling kestrels breed. The clutch size of kestrels breeding in Florida averages 4.00 ± 0.71 (Henny 1972), with most nesting occurring between mid-March and early June. The incubation period is usually 28–29 days, with chicks fledging in 4–5 weeks (Palmer 1988). Data on the sex ratios of Southeastern American Kestrels are not available; however, studies elsewhere on the *sparverius* subspecies indicate that nestling and adult sex ratios approximate 1:1 (Heintzelman and Nagy

1968; Balgooyen 1976). Detailed studies of nesting success by *paulus* also have not been conducted; however, Loftin (unpubl. data) found that 20 pairs using nest boxes, from 1980–1982, fledged an average of 2.3 young per nesting attempt. Mortality rates specifically for Southeastern American Kestrels are not available; however, for the species as a whole, Henny (1972) estimated that 61% die in their first year of life, while 46% of adults die annually. The mean life expectancy of kestrels is about 1.4 years.

KEY BEHAVIORS: American Kestrels hunt for food by searching the ground from elevated perches, hovering in areas without perches, and soaring over open areas (Collopy and Koplin 1983). Although hover-hunting is the most conspicuous foraging method used by *paulus* kestrels, perch-hunting from powerlines and fence posts is the most common (81% of 2020 capture attempts: Bohall-Wood and Collopy 1987). An additional characteristic behavior of the kestrel is the exaggerated bobbing of its tail immediately after perching.

Throughout their range, kestrels are opportunistic predators, taking a wide variety of prey species. In north-central Florida, Southeastern American Kestrels captured primarily insects and reptiles (Bohall-Wood and Collopy 1987). Invertebrate prey included grasshoppers, worms, and dragonflies; lizards comprised the majority of vertebrate prey, with some frogs and a small passerine also taken.

CONSERVATION MEASURES TAKEN: The Southeastern American Kestrel is considered a threatened subspecies by the Florida Game and Fresh Water Fish Commission (FGFWFC 1990). The only other southeastern state that has a management designation for *F. s. paulus* is Mississippi, which considers it of "special concern."

CONSERVATION MEASURES PROPOSED: In light of historical and recently collected data, Wood et al. (1988) recommended a series of habitat management guidelines to the Florida Game and Fresh Water Fish Commission. These guidelines outline procedures for determining the presence of *paulus* kestrels and evaluating habitat suitability for nesting and foraging. Recommendations are made for protecting existing nest sites and for enhancing disturbed sites through snag management and nest box programs. Actions designed to protect and enhance kestrel foraging areas also are presented. The decline of this threatened subspecies will likely continue until active management is taken to protect nesting and foraging areas.

ACKNOWLEDGMENTS: Data from a variety of sources have been used in the preparation of this report. In particular, I would like to thank P. G. Wood,

M. L. Hoffman, J. N. Layne, R. W. Loftin, and J. A. Smallwood for the data and publications they have produced on Southeastern American Kestrels.

LITERATURE CITED:

AOU. 1983. Checklist of North American birds. 6th edition. American Ornithologists' Union, Allen Press, Lawrency, Kansas. 877 pp.

Balgooyen, T. G. 1976. Behavior and ecology of the American Kestrel (*Falco sparverius L.*) in the Sierra Nevada of California. University of California Publ. Zoology 103:1–83.

Bohall-Wood, P., and M. W. Collopy. 1986. Abundance and habitat selection of two American Kestrel subspecies in north-central Florida. Auk 103:557–563.

Bohall-Wood, P. G., and M. W. Collopy. 1987. Foraging behavior of Southeastern American Kestrels in relation to habitat use. Pp. 58–65 in The ancestral kestrel (D. M. Bird and R. Bowman, eds.). Raptor Research Report 6, Raptor Research Foundation, Vermillion, South Dakota. 178 pp.

Cade, T. J. 1982. The falcons of the world. Comstock-Cornell University Press, Ithaca, New York. 188 pp.

Collopy, M. W., and J. R. Koplin. 1983. Diet, capture success, and mode of hunting by female American Kestrels in winter. Condor 85:369–371.

Florida Game and Fresh Water Fish Commission. 1990. Official lists of endangered and potentially endangered fauna and flora in Florida. Tallahassee, Florida. 19 pp.

Fuller, M. R., D. Bystrak, C. S. Robbins, and R. M. Patterson. 1987. Trends in American Kestrel counts from the North American Breeding Bird Survey. Pages 22–27 in The ancestral kestrel (D. M. Bird and R. Bowman, eds.). Raptor Research Report 6, Raptor Research Foundation, Vermillion, South Dakota. 178 pp.

Hamel, P. B., H. E. LeGrand, Jr., M. R. Lennartz, and S. A Gauthreaux, Jr. 1982. Bird-habitat relationships on southeastern forest lands. USDA Forest Service, General Technical Report SE-22.

Heintzelman, D. S., and A. C. Nagy. 1968. Clutch size, hatchability rates, and sex ratios of Sparrow Hawks in eastern Pennsylvania. Wilson Bull. 80:306–311.

Henny, D. J. 1972. An analysis of the population dynamics of selected avian species. U.S. Fish and Wildlife Service Research Report No. 1. 99 pp.

Hoffman, M. L. 1983. Historical status and nest-site selection of the American Kestrel (*Falco sparverius paulus*) in Florida. Unpublished M.S. thesis, University of Florida, Gainesville, Florida. 100 pp.

Hoffman, M. L., and M. W. Collopy. 1987. Distribution and nesting ecology of the American Kestrel (*Falco sparverius paulus*) near Archer, Florida. Pages 47–57 in The ancestral kestrel (D. M. Bird and R. Bowman, eds.).

Raptor Research Report 6, Raptor Research Foundation, Vermillion, South Dakota. 178 pp.

Hoffman, M. L., and M. W. Collopy. 1988. Historical status of the American Kestrel (*Falco sparverius paulus*) in Florida. Wilson Bull. 100:91–107.

Holt, E. G., and G. M. Sutton. 1926. Notes on birds observed in southern Florida. Ann. Carnegie Museum 16:409–439.

Kale, H. W., II. 1980. Florida region. Amer. Birds 34:767–770.

Palmer, R. S. 1988. American Kestrel. Pages 253–290 in Handbook of North American birds, Volume 5 (R. S. Palmer, ed.). Yale University Press, New Haven, Connecticut. 429 pp.

Paul, R. T. 1982. Florida region. Amer. Birds 36:967–970.

Porter, R. D., and S. N. Wiemeyer. 1972. Reproductive patterns in captive American Kestrels (Sparrow Hawk). Condor 74:46–53.

Robertson, W. B., Jr., and J. A. Kushlan. 1974. The southern Florida avifauna. Pages 414–451 in Environments of south Florida: present and past (J. A. Gleason, ed.). Miami Geological Society, Coral Gables, Florida.

Roest, A. I. 1957. Notes on the American Sparrow Hawk. Auk 74:1–19.

Smallwood, J. A. 1987. Sexual segregation by American Kestrels (*Falco sparverius*) wintering in southcentral Florida: vegetative structure and responses to differential prey availability. Condor 89:842–849.

Wiley, J. W. 1978. Southeastern American Kestrel. Pages 32–34 in Rare and endangered biota of Florida. Volume 2, Birds (H. W. Kale, II, ed.). University Presses of Florida, Gainesville, Florida. 121 pp.

Wood, P. B., M. L. Hoffman, M. W. Collopy, and J. M Schaefer. 1988. Southeastern American Kestrel (*Falco sparverius paulus*) natural history, life requirements, and habitat protection guidelines. Final Report to Office of Environmental Services, Florida Game and Fresh Water Fish Commission. Tallahassee, Florida. 27 pp.

PREPARED BY: Michael W. Collopy, Forest and Rangeland Ecosystem Science Center, National Biological Service, 3200 S.W. Jefferson Way, Corvallis, OR 97331.

Florida Sandhill Crane
Grus canadensis pratensis

FAMILY GRUIDAE

Order Gruiformes

TAXONOMY: The Florida Sandhill Crane (*Grus candensis pratensis*) is one of six recognized subspecies of Sandhill Cranes, and one of three that are nonmigratory. The Savannah Crane (*Grus pratensis*—a crane of the meadows and savannahs) was named and described in 1794 (F. A. A. Meyer 1794) from the description by William Bartram of a specimen taken in 1774 during his exploration of Florida. Peters (1925) recognized that *G. pratensis* was actually a subspecies of the Sandhill Crane, but misidentified the type locality as being in Clay County. The situation was further confused when Harper (1942) gave the type locality (Alachua savannah) as near Bronson in Levy County. It was Brodkorb (1955) who corrected the type locality as being Paynes Prairie in Alachua County, south of Gainesville. The type specimen was not preserved (Peter 1925); it was eaten by Bartram and his party and made, "an excellent soup."

DESCRIPTION: The Florida Sandhill Crane, with its heavy body, long neck, and long legs, is one of Florida's largest birds. Height is about 1.2 m and wingspan about 2 m. Sexes look similar, males are usually larger; mean weight of 34 males was 4.7 kg compared to 4.1 kg for 34 females. Bill length, from posterior end of nostril, was 103.9 mm for males and 98.8 mm for females (Nesbitt et al. 1992). The Florida subspecies is slightly smaller (except in leg length) and darker (especially in the occipital and hind neck) than the Greater Sandhill Crane (*G. c. tabida*) (Peter 1925). *G. c. pratensis* is similar in size but generally a lighter color than the Mississippi Sandhill Crane (*G. c. pulla*) (Aldrich 1972).

The plumage is generally a pale mouse-gray to ashy slate-gray (plumage description follows Ridgway 1941). The occiput and hind neck are a light mouse-gray. Cheeks are paler than the occiput, blending from a pale gull-gray to white on the chin and upper throat. The extent and consistency of the

219

Florida Sandhill Crane, *Grus canadensis pratensis.* (Photo by Stephen A. Nesbitt)

coloring of the cheek, chin, and upper neck varies among individuals. Flight feathers are dark neutral-gray with lighter shafts. Feathers on the breast, abdomen, back, and upper wing coverts are margined with a light gull-gray. The tail itself is short, however, the tertials and inner secondaries are elongated giving the appearance of a plumy tail. Aldrich (1972) described a lighter to darker change in plumage from south to north through the populations. All Sandhill Cranes rub their plumage with soil (Nesbitt 1975), which in Florida produces a variation in plumage color ranging from drab clay to cinnamon-rufous depending on the color of the soil used. Stained feathers occur anywhere below the mid-neck but are particularly apparent among the primary and secondary wing coverts, the back, and upper breast feathers.

The exposed tibia, tarsi, and toes are dull greenish-black to very dark olive. The hind toe is elevated and functionally vestigial. The bill is dark drab-gray fading to an olive-gray in the mid-mandibular area, the internasal septum is perforate. Forehead, lores, and anterior crown are unfeathered and covered with a dull-reddish to begonia-rose, pappillose (raised, vascular) skin. This comb area can be extended and the color intensified during episodes of aggressive or sexual behavior. Eye color of individual adults range between spectrum-orange and scarlet, most being either chrome-orange or flame-scarlet.

Upon hatching, the downy young are a mikado-brown, darker on the rump

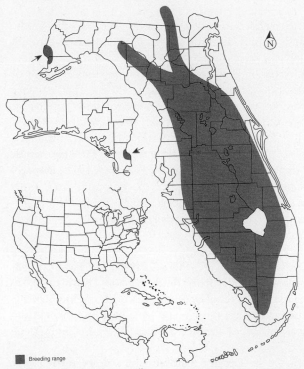

Breeding range

Distribution map of the Florida Sandhill Crane, *Grus canadensis pratensis.*

and mid-back, fading to a pale dull buffy to pale tawny underneath. As the contour and wing feathers begin to develop, the area that will become the crown remains covered with a downy feathering of ocherous-salmon. The bill is flesh colored, darker toward the tip. Eyes are dark raw umber. Legs and feet are a yellowish-flesh. As the young mature, the legs and bill darken and the eyes lighten.

After 10 to 14 months, the general appearance is adult-like (Lewis 1979). Eye color ranges from straw-yellow to buff or orange-yellow. The upper wing coverts, back feathers, and upper hind neck remain edged with a cinnamon-rufous. Some of these juvenile feathers persist through the first year, especially the outer, greater primary coverts and hind neck feathers. Beyond the first year, only wing molt patterns separate subadults from adults (Nesbitt 1987).

The other species that Sandhill Cranes are often confused with, the Great Blue Heron (*Ardea herodias*), lacks the bare, red crown. Also, unlike herons, cranes fly with neck extended. The wing stroke pattern, with a snapping upstroke and slower downstroke, also differentiates cranes from other long-legged, long-necked birds.

POPULATION SIZE AND TREND: The entire Sandhill Crane population exceeds 650,000 individuals and the species ranges from central Siberia, through western and central North America to north central Mexico into the south-eastern United States and Cuba. Throughout much of its range Sandhill Crane populations are stable or increasing.

There is no recent information that would alter the previous estimate of 4,000 Florida Sandhill Cranes (Lewis 1977; Williams 1978). That estimate was based on a mail survey, known distribution, and approximate population density. Bennett (1989) estimated a population of 403 individuals from a recent study of Okefenokee Swamp. Recent work in north Florida produced an estimate of 67 adult pairs/100 km^2 of suitable habitat (McMillen et al. 1992). The downward population trend reported by Williams (1978) may still affect the overall population, however in some areas of central and south Florida the population is sustaining itself. The two other nonmigratory populations, the Mississippi and the Cuban (*G. c. nesiotes*) are reduced, total number for either does not exceed 200 birds.

DISTRIBUTION AND HISTORY OF DISTRIBUTION: The Florida Sand-hill Crane occurs in appropriate habitat from the Everglades (Kushlan 1982) throughout the peninsula to the Okefenokee Swamp. Reports of Florida Sand-hill Cranes west of Taylor County are rare. There have been sightings in the early 1980s during July along the Apalachicola River (N. F. Eichholz, pers. comm.).

The eastern population of the Greater Sandhill Crane nests in the Great Lakes Region—primarily Michigan and Wisconsin, and winters in the south-east, occurring with *G. c. pratensis* in much of their range. There is no way to distinguish between the two subspecies in Florida. Core populations of the Florida subspecies occur in the Kissimmee and De Soto prairies (Bishop 1988). Other significant populations occur on extensive areas of appropriate habitat, especially Alachua County, northern Polk County (Dwyer 1990), and Char-lotte County (Bishop 1988).

Earlier accounts describe the subspecies nesting from southwest Louisiana (Lowery 1960) to Alabama (Imhof 1962) and Mississippi (Valentine and Noble 1970). If the hiatus between the Apalachicola River and the coastal Mississippi populations existed previously, these western gulf records could have been of the then undescribed Mississippi subspecies (Aldrich 1972).

HABITAT REQUIREMENTS AND HABITAT TREND: Mean annual home-range size for 31 Florida Sandhill Cranes was 936 ha. Home range averaged 447 ha for 20 adult pairs and 2,132 ha for 9 subadults (Nesbitt and Williams 1990). The two most frequently used habitats were pastures/prairies and emergent palustrine wetlands dominated by pickerelweed (*Pontedaria cordata*) and maidencane (*Panicum hemitomon*). Cranes also showed a preference for transition zones between wetlands and pastures/prairies and between pasture/prairies and forested habitats. During summer, to avoid the heat of the day, cranes will either stand motionless in full shade or in a marsh area.

Recently the reduction in suitable wetland habitat, pointed out by Williams (1978), may have slowed somewhat due to concern for wetland protection. However, the loss of open, upland habitat, also critical to the subspecies, continues (Bishop 1988; Nesbitt and Williams 1990) .

VULNERABILITY OF SPECIES AND HABITAT: Adult Florida Sandhill Cranes have few natural enemies. Bobcats (*Felis rufus*) do occasionally take healthy adults, and Bald Eagles (*Haliaeetus leucocephalus*) will take injured or sick individuals. Though chicks and eggs are vulnerable to most predators that frequent marshes, both are usually guarded diligently by adults. Bennett and Bennett (1987) observed an alligator (*Alligator mississippiensis*) take a juvenile crane in the Okefenokee Swamp. During periods of low water, vulnerability of nests and young increase.

Cranes are vulnerable to such manmade hazards as power lines and fences. Florida Sandhill Cranes remain in the same general area for most of their lives, becoming more familiar with the location of these potential hazards than the migratory subspecies; consequently, power lines are less of a problem. Fences that cranes cannot walk under or through present the greatest danger: they are reluctant to fly over a fence but when they do they occasionally misjudge the landing and land on the fence. Many leg injuries and deaths can be linked to encounters with fences. Death due to entanglement in fences is perhaps the single greatest source of "unnatural" mortality.

A three-strand, rather than a four-or five-strand barbed wire fence, with the bottom strand 46 cm (18 in.) from the ground is much easier for cranes to negotiate and, therefore, is less dangerous. Adult cranes will readily crouch and walk under such a fence. For woven wire/American wire fences, a framed walk-through 60 cm high by 46 cm wide placed periodically (every 0.5 km) would allow cranes to walk through the fence but still restrain livestock.

Several diseases and parasites have been identified as causes of death for cranes (Windingstad 1988). One that is singularly significant in Florida has been linked to exposure to mycotoxins (Windingstad 1988). Chronic exposure apparently produces a cancer (Allen et al. 1985) that has been diagnosed as a factor in the deaths of several older birds.

The two most important habitats (shallow freshwater marshes and adjacent uplands) are easily degraded. Even when wetlands are protected from direct loss, the pickerelweed/maidencane complex that is the key crane habitat may not be retained. This community can be altered by changes in the amount and quality of incoming water. It will quickly revert to a cattail/willow (*Typha spp./Salix spp.*) community or be overtaken by other woody plants. Such altered wetlands are of little value to cranes. The surrounding uplands are also important feeding habitat, especially during the post-nesting period. To be of value to cranes, though, these uplands must be in an open, low-growth condition. Areas of dense, high (> 0.5 m) growth are avoided. Burning, grazing, and mowing will all produce favorable upland conditions.

CAUSE OF THREAT: Shallow freshwater marshes have been altered through drainage, filling, and degradation of water quality. Upland habitats have been lost to housing and commercial development, golf courses, or intense low diversity agriculture. Although some use is made of lawns, greens, fairways, and other altered sites, the overall productivity of these habitats for Florida Sandhill Cranes is reduced. Cranes have adjusted to and may even benefit from some types of agriculture. Those that remove or modify the proximate wetlands or reduce the amount or diversity of usable uplands are ultimately detrimental. Low density housing does not, of itself, always result in habitat loss. If fencing is compatible and limited, cranes will continue to use uplands near houses. Free-ranging, domestic dogs can preclude crane use of those areas that dogs frequent. Prefledged young also are vulnerable to free-ranging dogs and cats.

RESPONSE TO HABITAT MODIFICATION: As the quality of habitat declines, the size or configuration of Florida Sandhill Crane home ranges changes. If the amount of either wetland or upland habitat is not adequate to support a pair or family group, they will leave the defended territory for extended periods (Nesbitt and Williams 1990), traveling up to 15 km to find adequate resources. These extra-territorial adults will gather with subadults and unpaired adults to exploit temporally abundant resources during the post-nesting season.

Cranes will make use of grazed or mowed pastures as well as some cultivated crop areas. Cranes also respond to burns that occur in appropriate habitat. They will begin feeding just after the fire has passed and may continue using the burned-off area for several weeks. If nesting marshes dry or become unusable, cranes will occasionally nest on dry land (Layne 1982) but more often delay or forgo nesting altogether (Williams 1978).

DEMOGRAPHIC CHARACTERISTICS: Male Sandhill Cranes may nest at 2 years of age, females at 3, rarely 2. First production (i.e., fledging of young) usually occurs at 3 years for both sexes (mean = 5.2 years; Nesbitt 1992). Egg laying usually begins in January and can extend into June if conditions remain favorable. Eggs are generally a pale brownish-buff, irregularly marked with brown and pale gray. Mean laying date in north Florida is 12 March, and 22–24 February for central Florida (Nesbitt 1989a; Walkinshaw 1982). Mean annual clutch size for 241 nests checked during 1983–1995 was 1.80 eggs (Nesbitt, unpubl. data). Mean brood size was 1.32 (1.42, Layne 1983; 1.26, Bishop and Collopy 1987; 1.29, Nesbitt unpubl. data). Average annual production for any Florida Sandhill Crane >3 years old was 0.35 young (Nesbitt 1992). If only those birds known to have successfully reproduced were considered, annual production increased to 0.54 (Nesbitt 1992). Most of the young (62%) were produced by a minority (26%) of adults (Nesbitt 1992). Annual survival probability for young from hatching to independence is 0.56 (Nesbitt 1992). Survival probability for adults is not yet known. Percentage of young in the population averages 11.1%, ranging from 7.8 to 16.5% (Bishop 1988, Nesbitt 1992); of the remainder, 63.8% were breeding age adults and the rest subadults (Nesbitt 1988).

KEY BEHAVIORS: The voice of the Sandhill Crane is one of the most distinctive bird sounds in Florida. The voice has been described as a bugling, rattling, trumpeting, or rolling croak. The typical full-voiced call, a series of 7–20 broken notes delivered at a rate of about 15 notes per second (Nesbitt and Bradley, unpubl. ms.), can be heard for several kilometers. The Unison Call (Archibald 1975) is an antiphonal vocalization given by paired cranes. It is sexually diagnostic, and the best way of determining sex in the field. Several other vocalizations are best described as purrs. The entire vocal repertoire may exceed a dozen different calls. The voice of the young, from hatching until the age of 9–10 months, is a series of high trills or variously inflected peeps, delivered several times a second lasting from 0.2 to 0.5 second.

Florida Sandhill Cranes are perennially monogamous, with established pairs remaining together for several years. Beginning in their second year, cranes form a series of dyadic relationships that eventually (perhaps after several years) result in successful reproduction (Nesbitt and Wenner 1987). When one member of an established pair dies, the surviving bird usually finds a new mate. Males more often than females will continue to occupy the same territory after repairing (Nesbitt 1989b).

Nesting and chick rearing make up a major part of the pairs' year. Incubation averages 30 days, with both members participating. If a chick or clutch of eggs is lost, the pair will renest after only 18–20 days (Nesbitt 1989a). Chicks are precocial and nidifugous, leaving the nest to follow their parents within 24 hours of hatching. Although chicks can fly by 70 days of age, they do not leave the family unit until they are about 10 months old. Chicks will continue to beg food from their parents for several months after they are capable of feeding themselves. After leaving the family unit, juveniles range widely (see subadult home range size) until they reach breeding age.

Nests are usually constructed over standing water. Depth under 70 nests averaged 32.6 cm. Nest size averaged 98 x 83 cm and were an average of 13.5

cm above the water (Nesbitt 1988). Nests constructed on dry land or floating mats of vegetation are smaller. Nest foundations are constructed of whatever vegetation is in the vicinity; the egg cup is lined with smaller, finer material.

Food habits vary greatly. Tubers, vegetative parts, and seeds of various plants are commonly eaten. Acorns are a frequent fall food, and dew berries (*Rubus* spp.) are a common summer food. Additionally, Florida Sandhill Cranes feed on agricultural crops, especially corn and peanuts. Invertebrates such as grasshoppers, dragonflies and their nymphs, and crayfish are also taken. Florida Sandhill Cranes also have been observed to feed on amphiumas (*Amphiuma means*) (Dye 1982), various snakes and frogs, young Common Moorhens (*Gallinula chloropus*), and cotton rats (*Sigmodon hispidus*) (Nesbitt 1988).

Daily activity consists of a morning feeding period beginning soon after leaving the roost, a mid-day loafing period, which may entail a return to the roost site, and an afternoon, pre-roosting feeding period. Roosting sites are almost always located in standing water (average 19.2 cm deep) usually with a firm bottoms and little vegetation. The general aspect of 11 roost sites varied; 46% were in extensive marsh (more than 200 m from the edge), 27% were in ponds, and the rest were on lake edges or in flooded pastures (Nesbitt 1988).

Florida Sandhill Cranes have a variety of conspicuous behaviors such as the unison call and various aggressive displays (Nesbitt and Archibald 1981). Perhaps the most often cited but still poorly understood behavior is Dancing. It is often assumed to be a form of courtship display, but dancing occurs at anytime throughout the year and is exhibited by all age classes. Cranes will dance when a cool wind comes up on a hot summer afternoon or when a potential predator has been spotted. Although mated pairs do dance vigorously, they do not seem to dance together to any great extent before pairing. The dance consists of Wing-dropping, Bowing and Dipping, stiff-legged vaulting, running, flaps, and tossing. During tossing bouts a bird will pick up stones, sticks, or bits of vegetation and fling it exuberantly over its back. Dancing seems to be contagious and will spread throughout a flock.

CONSERVATION MEASURES TAKEN: The Florida Sandhill Crane is listed as a threatened species by the Florida Game and Fresh Water Fish Commission. Large amounts of appropriate habitat are now in public ownership: Cecil M. Webb Wildlife Management Area, Three-Lakes Wildlife Management Area, Lake Kissimmee and Myakka River state parks, and Paynes Prairie State Preserve.

CONSERVATION MEASURES PROPOSED: The Florida Sandhill Crane may warrant listing by the U.S. Fish and Wildlife Service. The other two nonmigratory subspecies, the Cuban and the Mississippi, are federally listed as endangered. Acquisition or protection of additional habitat to ensure peninsula-wide distribution is important. To be beneficial, however, any future and all current habitat must be actively managed to ensure that the suitable vegetative type and structure are maintained.

ACKNOWLEDGMENTS: Lovett E. Williams' previous account (1978) formed the basis of this update. His research on Florida Sandhill Cranes was fundamental to what is now known about the subspecies. L. H. Walkinshaw's longstanding work on Florida Sandhill Cranes in central Florida also was an important contribution to the current "state of the art" in crane knowledge.

LITERATURE CITED:

Aldrich, J. 1972. A new subspecies of Sandhill Crane from Mississippi. Proc. Biol. Soc. Wash. 85:63–70.

Allen, J. L., H. D. Martin, and A. M. Crowley. 1985. Metastic cholangiocarcinoma in a Florida Sandhill Crane. Jour. Amer. Vet. Med. Assoc. 187:1215.

Archibald, G. W. 1975. The evolutionary and taxonomic relationship of cranes as revealed by the unison call. Ph.D. thesis, Cornell Univ. Ithaca, New York 152 pp.

Bennett, A. J. 1989. Population size and distribution of Florida Sandhill Cranes in the Okefenokee Swamp, Georgia. Jour. Field Ornith. 60:60–67.

Bennett, A. J., and L. A. Bennett. 1987. Evaluation of the Okefenokee Swamp as a site for developing a nonmigratory flock of Whooping Cranes. Unpubl. rept., Georgia Coop. Fish and Wildl. Res. Unit., Athens, Georgia. 113 pp.

Bishop, M. A. 1988. Factors affecting productivity and habitat use of Florida Sandhill Cranes (*Grus canadensis pratensis*): an evaluation of three areas in central Florida for a non-migratory population of Whooping Cranes (*Grus americana*). Ph.D. thesis, Univ. of Florida, Gainesville, Florida. 190 pp.

Bishop, M. A., and M. W. Collopy. 1987. Productivity of Florida Sandhill Cranes on three sites in central Florida. Pp. 257–263 in Proc. 1985 Crane Workshop (J. C. Lewis, ed.). Platte River Whooping Crane Maint. Trust, Grand Island, Nebraska.

Brodkorb, P. 1955. The type locality of the Florida Sandhill Crane. Auk 72:207.

Dwyer, N. 1990. Nesting ecology and nest-site selection of Florida Sandhill Cranes. M.S. thesis, Univ. of Fla., Gainesville, Florida. 85 pp.

Dye, R. L. 1982. Sandhill Cranes prey on amphiumas. Fla. Field Nat. 10:76.

Harper, F. 1942. William Bartram's names of birds. Proc. Rochester Acad. Sci. 8:208–221.

Imhof, T. A. 1962. Alabama birds. Dept. of Conser., Game and Fish Div. Univ. of Alabama Press. University, Alabama. 591 pp.

Kushlan, J. A. 1982. The Sandhill Crane in the Everglades. Fla. Field Nat. 4:74–76.

Layne, J. M. 1982. Dry ground nests of Florida Sandhill Cranes. Fla. Field Nat. 10:55–56.

Layne, J. M. 1983. Productivity of Sandhill Cranes in south central Florida. Jour. Wildl. Manage. 47:178–183.

Lewis, J. C. (Chairman). 1977. Sandhill Crane. Pp. 4–53 in Management of migratory shore and upland game birds in North America (G. C. Sanderson, ed.). Inter. Assoc. Fish Wildl. Agencies, Washington, D.C.

Lewis, J. C. 1979. Field identification of juvenile Sandhill Cranes. Jour. Wildl. Manage. 43:211–214.

Lowery, G. H. 1960. Louisiana birds. Louisiana Wildl. and Fish. Comm. Louisiana State Univ. Press. Baton Rouge, Louisiana. 567 pp.

McMillen, J. L., S. A. Nesbitt, M. A. Bishop, A. J. Bennett, and L. A. Bennett. 1992. An evaluation of three areas for potential populations of Whooping Cranes. Pp. 285–294 in Proceedings of the 1988 Crane Workshop (D. A. Wood, ed.). Nongame Wildl. Prog. Tech. Rept. #12, Tallahassee, Florida.

Meyer, F. A. A. 1794. Zool. Annal. 1:286,296.

Nesbitt, S. A. 1975. Feather staining in Florida Sandhill Cranes. Fla. Field Nat. 3:28–30.

Nesbitt, S. A. 1987. A technique for aging Sandhill Cranes using wing molt—preliminary findings. Pp. 224–229 in Proc. 1985 Crane Workshop (J. C. Lewis, ed.). Platte River Whooping Crane Habitat Maintenance Trust, Grand Island, Nebraska.

Nesbitt, S. A. 1988. An evaluation of the Florida Sandhill Crane population of peninsular Florida and its potential to support a population of non-migratory Whooping Cranes. Unpubl. rept. Florida Game and Fresh Water Fish Comm.; Bur. Wildl. Res., Gainesville, Florida. 62 pp.

Nesbitt, S. A. 1989a. Nesting, renesting, and manipulating nesting of Florida Sandhill Cranes. Jour. Wildl. Manage. 52:758–763.

Nesbitt, S. A. 1989b. The significance of mate loss in Florida Sandhill Cranes. Wilson Bull. 101:648–651.

Nesbitt, S. A. 1992. First reproductive success and individual productivity in Sandhill Cranes. Jour. Wildl. Manage. 56:573–577.

Nesbitt, S. A. and G. W. Archibald. 1981. The agonistic repertoire of Sandhill Cranes. Wilson Bull. 93:99–103.

Nesbitt, S. A., and A. S. Wenner. 1987. Pair formation and mate fidelity in Sandhill Cranes. Pp. 117–122 in Proc. 1985 Crane Workshop (J. C. Lewis, ed.). Platte River Whooping Crane Habitat Maintenance Trust, Grand Island, Nebraska.

Nesbitt, S. A., and K. S. Williams. 1990. Home range and habitat use of Florida Sandhill Cranes. Jour. Wildl. Manage. 54:92–96.

Nesbitt, S. A., C. T. Moore, and K. S. Williams. 1992. Gender prediction from body measurements of two subspecies of Sandhill Cranes. Proc. North Amer. Crane Workshop 6:38–42.

Peters, J. L. 1925. Notes on the taxonomy of *Ardea canadensis* Linn. Auk 41:120–122.

Ridgway, R. 1941. The birds of North and Middle America. Part IX. Smithsonian Institution, U.S. Nat. Museum Bull. no. 50. 254 pp.

Valentine, J. M., Jr., and R. E. Noble. 1970. A colony of Sandhill Cranes in Mississippi. Jour. Wildl. Manage. 34:761–768.

Walkinshaw, L. H. 1982. Nesting of the Florida Sandhill Crane in central Florida. Pp. 52–63 in Proc. 1981 Crane Workshop (J. C. Lewis, ed.). Natl. Audubon Soc., Tavernier, Florida.

Williams, L. E., Jr. 1978. Florida Sandhill Crane. Pp. 36–37 in Rare and endangered biota of Florida. Vol. II. Birds (H. W. Kale II, ed.). Univ. Presses of Florida. Gainesville, Florida.

Windingstad, R. M., R. R. George, and R. F. Krey. 1987. Sandhill Crane mortality at Cedar Lake, Texas—an overview. Pp. 137–139 in Proc. 1985 Crane Workshop (J. C. Lewis, ed.). Platte River Whooping Crane Habitat Maintenance Trust, Grand Island, Nebraska.

Windingstad, R. M. 1988. Nonhunting mortality in Sandhill Cranes. Jour. Wildl. Manage. 52:260–263.

PREPARED BY: Stephen A. Nesbitt, Florida Game and Fresh Water Fish Commission, Wildlife Research Laboratory, 4005 South Main Street, Gainesville, FL 32601.

American Oystercatcher

Haematopus palliatus

FAMILY HAEMATOPODIDAE

Order Charadriiformes

TAXONOMY: The American Oystercatcher (*Haematopus palliatus*) and Pied Oystercatcher (*H. bachmani*) are closely related and considered conspecific by some authors (Murphy 1936). These species are said to hybridize and form a hybrid zone about 322 km (200 miles) in width in central Baja California (Hayman et al. 1986). The European Oystercatcher (*H. ostralegus*) also is considered by some as conspecific with the preceding two species. The entire complex constitutes a superspecies. Under a single species treatment, Pied Oystercatcher may be used as the English name (AOU 1983). As *H. bachmani* is restricted to the west coast of North America (AOU 1983) the Florida population is *H. palliatus*.

DESCRIPTION: One of the largest (47 cm [18.5 in.]) and heaviest (650 g) shorebirds, the American Oystercatcher is a striking dark black-brown and white bird with bright red bill and pink legs. Males and females are similar. The head and neck are black grading into dark brown on the back and wings; the flanks and lower abdomen are white. There is a conspicuous diagonal white stripe in each wing, which with basal white of the tail, forms a V-pattern and is a good flight field mark. In immatures, the black-brown appears faded, the bill is a drabber red with the terminal end dark, and the legs are lighter pink.

POPULATION SIZE AND TREND: Christmas Bird Counts (CBCs) indicate that during the winter there are about 1,000 American Oystercatchers in Florida (*American Birds*). Although it is more difficult to document the summer population, it should be in the vicinity of 35% of the winter population (pers. observ.). Several sources (Audubon 1840; Maynard 1881; Scott 1889) indicate that oystercatchers were numerous in Florida during the 1800s, but give no numbers. Oystercatchers did not start to appear in any numbers on CBCs until 1963. Since then, the population has risen slowly to the present

American
Oystercatcher,
*Haematopus
palliatus.* (Photo
by Brian Toland)

level, but the recorded increase closely parallels the rise in the number of
CBCs documenting oystercatchers in Florida. CBCs for 1985–89 indicate that
there are probably less than 5,000 oystercatchers along the coasts of the
eastern United States, Florida and the Gulf of Mexico in winter. Seventy five
percent of these birds appeared along the eastern seaboard of the United
States, with 22% recorded in Florida and only 3% noted along the Gulf coast
(excluding Florida). What little information exists indicates that for at least the
last nine years, the numbers of oystercatchers have remained stable.

DISTRIBUTION AND HISTORY OF DISTRIBUTION: The American
Oystercatcher breeds along the Atlantic coast, from Massachusetts to south-
central Argentina, in the Bahamas, and along the Pacific coast from central
Baja California to central Chile. Wintering American Oystercatchers are ob-
served along the Atlantic from North Carolina to Honduras, and along the
Pacific from central Baja California to Guatemala. In the United States, winter
reports indicate the major part of the population is concentrated along the
southeast coast around peninsular Florida into the Gulf of Mexico, between
Cape Charles, Virginia and Cedar Key, Florida (AOU 1983). Christmas Bird
Counts, *American Birds* seasonal reports, and many observers indicate that in
Florida the American Oystercatcher is sparsely distributed along the Atlantic
coast from the north Florida line to Palm Beach County. There are few reports
of individuals and no reports of nesting south of Palm Beach County and
around the southern tip of the peninsula to Collier County. The major part of
the population inhabits the coast from Collier County north to the Suwannee
River. Continuing along the coast northwest, there are no reports until a small
population is encountered in the vicinity of Apalachee and Apalachicola bays.
The nesting distribution in Florida is similar to the above winter range. Little

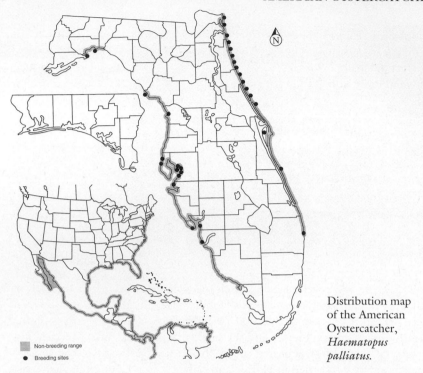

Distribution map
of the American
Oystercatcher,
*Haematopus
palliatus.*

Non-breeding range
Breeding sites

quantitative data exists on the historic range of oystercatchers in Florida, but the species probably has been eliminated from developed coastal regions of their former range, especially from West Palm Beach to Miami. With the phenomenal coastal development that has occurred in Florida it is obvious that all coastal species, including American Oystercatchers, have lost habitat and probably have declined.

HABITAT REQUIREMENTS AND HABITAT TREND: The American Oystercatcher needs extensive beach, sandbar, mudflat, and mollusk beds for feeding and roosting. Oystercatchers feed on almost any nonvegetative life that can be gleaned from wet substrates by walking and wading. Listed among their foods are bivalves, gastropods, marine worms, crustaceans, small fish, and many insects (Bent 1929; Murphy 1936). Oystercatchers prefer large, sparsely vegetated sand areas for nesting, but will use wrack and marsh grass (Lauro 1989).

VULNERABILITY OF SPECIES AND HABITAT: The American Oyster-catcher is mostly vulnerable to disturbance, habitat loss and mammalian preda-tors. The majority of predators are either man introduced (dogs and cats) or man abetted (raccoons [*Procyon lotor*]), and foxes that proliferate from feeding on garbage and generally prey on nesting birds, eggs, and chicks. In general, coastal birds deal with this problem by nesting in areas surrounded by water, as do oystercatchers. Unfortunately human use of the coast of Florida is increasing phenomenally; thus, oystercatchers (and all coastal birds) are finding it more and more difficult to maintain usual life-sustaining activities.

CAUSES OF THREAT: Man not only uses the same areas as American Oystercatchers but also alters them for his own purposes. Of special significance is the disturbance caused by the use of recreational boats and vehicles to get to isolated roosting, feeding, and nesting areas, thus causing much stress by flushing flocks of shorebirds. Shorebirds have been observed to lose as much as 10% of their body weight over a weekend on a severely disturbed sandbar (pers. observ.).

RESPONSES TO HABITAT MODIFICATION: There is little information about how the American Oystercatcher copes with the rapid changes of coastal systems, natural or man-induced. In some cases, these birds will shift from sand nesting substrate to vegetative wrack when sand areas are no longer available (Shields 1990); this has not been observed in Florida. Recently in Florida, nesting was recorded in Australian pine (*Casuarina equisetifolia*) when sand nesting areas seemed to be lacking (Toland 1992). Another response to the lack of sufficient nesting habitat recently documented was the increase of nest density and communal breeding (Lauro et al. 1992). There also are indications as to how American Oystercatchers respond to various habitats. In areas where feeding, roosting, and nesting habitat are limited, such as the Atlantic coast of Florida, the population is small and thinly spread out. Along the northern portion of the southwest coast of Florida, where typical nesting habitat is absent, oystercatchers do not breed but are numerous. Further south on the southwest coast of Florida, where there is abundant feeding habitat, but no breeding or roosting habitat, oystercatchers are not reported. This indicates that oystercatchers are able to adapt to some modifications in the shore system, but do not use or only partially use areas where major components of the three aforementioned habitats are lacking or have been changed.

DEMOGRAPHIC CHARACTERISTICS: Not much is known about American Oystercatcher nesting in Florida, but it can be assumed that it is similar to data from elsewhere (Bent 1929; Hosking 1983; Johnsgard 1981; Nol 1984). Oystercatchers nest in scrapes (shallow depressions) constructed on beaches and sandbars; the pairs nest singularly or in small colonies with distances between scrapes averaging 30 m (100 ft.). The breeding season in Virginia is from April to June. First clutch is usually 3 eggs. The effects of tides, predation, or disturbance often cause the first nest to fail. The pairs can renest at least two more times with the average clutch of 2 eggs. Eggs are ovate to elongated, light to deep olive buff, sparingly marked with black and dark brown; size is about 55.7 x 38.7 mm. Eggs are laid about 2 days apart and hatch in the same order in 24–29 days; the chicks are precocial and the young fledge in 35–40 days. Little is known about nest success or fledgling survival. Annual adult survival has been given at 90%, but life span is apparently unknown. Adults breed at 3–4 years and the female does most of the incubating.

KEY BEHAVIORS: Little has been published about American Oystercatchers in Florida, but as many of the oystercatcher species exhibit similar behaviors, it may be safe to extrapolate from the literature (Bent 1929; Hosking 1983; Johnsgard 1981). Pair formation and breeding behaviors are minimal, this is thought to be due to the establishment of long lasting pair bonds. Pair bonds lasting over years would make it unnecessary to go through elaborate breeding displays. But in Florida several investigators have noted considerable calling, wing-body posturing, and flying during pair bonding (R. T. Paul and J. A. Rodgers, pers. comm.). The Piping display, in which the pair emit high pitched calls while either walking or flying around their territory, is thought to be territorial.

Oystercatchers feed by picking over emergent mud and sand substrates, especially where mollusks are plentiful. The laterally compressed powerful bill is used to open mollusks as well as to sort through heavy shell substrates to find food. The bird prefers to roost just above high tide on nearby isolated bars. When disturbed, oystercatchers will fly around for some time emitting high pitched calls before either leaving or settling. While tending a nest the pair is extremely secretive and, when flushed, will attempt to lead a predator away from the area using the Injury-feigning behavior.

CONSERVATION MEASURES TAKEN: Other than being listed as a Species of Special Concern by the Florida Game and Fresh Water Fish Commission and safeguarded by the U. S. Migratory Bird Treaty, little protection is afforded American Oystercatchers. This probably protects oystercatchers from hunting but does nothing to protect them from disturbance caused by humans in most of their essential habitat. In recent years the Nongame Program of the Florida Game and Fresh Water Fish Commission had several sandbar locations designated Critical Wildlife Areas. This designation is not only for the benefit of nesting birds but also for roosting and feeding coastal birds; several of these areas in south Florida are now closed year round. This is an important step in the conservation of all coastal birds.

CONSERVATION MEASURES PROPOSED: A list of research needs for American Oystercatchers in Florida should include population status, seasonal fluctuation and important seasonal sites, habitat requirements for breeding, feeding, and roosting, the effects of pollution, and the significance of disturbance on breeding productivity.

ACKNOWLEDGMENTS: I would like to thank all of the respondents (too numerous to name) to my requests for information on American Oystercatchers in Florida.

LITERATURE CITED:

American Birds (Audubon Field Notes). 1948–1993. Seasonal reports. American Birds volumes 3-48.

AOU. 1983. Check-list of North American Birds. 6th. ed. American Ornithologists' Union, Washington, D.C.

Audubon, J. J. 1840. The birds of America, 1841. The MacMillan Co., New York, New York.

Bent, A. C. 1929. Life histories of North American shorebirds, part 2. Natl. Mus. Bull. no. 146.

Hayman, P., J. Marchant, and T. Prater. 1986. Shorebirds. Houghton Mifflin Co., Boston, Massachusetts.

Hosking, E., and W. G. Hale. 1983. Waders. Pelham Books Ltd., London, England.

Johnsgard, P. A. 1981. The plovers, sandpipers and snipes of the world. Univ. Nebraska Press, Lincoln, Nebraska.

Lauro, B., and J. Burger. 1989. Nest-site selection of American Oystercatchers (*Haematopus palliatus*). Auk 106:185–192.

Lauro, B., E. Nol, and M. Vicari. 1992. Nesting density and communal breeding in American Oystercatchers. Condor 94:286–289.

Maynard, C. J. 1881. The birds of eastern North America. C. J. Maynard, Newtonville, Massachusetts.

Murphy, R. C. 1936. Oceanic birds of South America, Vol. II. Amer. Mus. Nat. Hist. The MacMillan Co., New York, New York.

Nol, E., A. J. Baker, and M. D. Cadman. 1984. Clutch initiation dates, clutch size, and egg size of the American Oystercatcher in Virginia. Auk 101:855–867.

Scott, W. E. 1889. A summery of observations on the birds of the Gulf Coast of Florida. Auk 6:160.

Shields, M. A., and J. F. Parnell. 1990. Marsh Nesting by American Oystercatchers in North Carolina. Jour. Field Ornithol. 61:431–433.

Toland, B. 1992. Use of forested spoil islands by nesting American Oystercatchers in southeast Florida. Jour. Field Ornithol. 63:155–158.

PREPARED BY: Theodore H. Below, National Audubon Society, Rookery Bay Sanctuary, 3697 North Road, Naples, FL 33942.

Least Tern

Sterna antillarum

FAMILY LARIDAE

Order Charadriiformes

TAXONOMY: The Least Tern (*Sterna antillarum*) was described by Lesson in 1847 (AOU 1957) and later classified as a subspecies of the Little Tern (*S. albifrons*) of Europe. Subsequent studies identified differences in behavior and vocalizations between the two taxa (Massey 1976) and resulted in the Least Tern of the western hemisphere once again being considered a separate species (AOU 1983). Three subspecies of the Least Tern breed in North America, but this account focuses on the only one found in Florida, *S. a. antillarum*. The other two subspecies, the Interior Least Tern (*S. a. athalassos*) and the California Least Tern (*S. a. browni*), have low population sizes and separate breeding ranges.

DESCRIPTION: Least Terns have the long, pointed wings and forked tail characteristic of all terns. They also share with most other terns a distinctive plumage pattern: white underneath and light gray above, with a black cap on the head. Least Terns can be distinguished from similar species by their smaller size (length 22–24 cm, wingspan about 51 cm) and the two black outer primary feathers that form a distinctive dark edge to each wing. During the breeding season, black covers the crown and nape and a black line extends through the eyes to the bill but the forehead remains distinctly white. The feet and bill are yellowish-orange, and the bill has a black tip. By winter the bill becomes dark and the black cap disappears, except for an indistinct line through the eyes and across the nape. Juveniles are white below and mostly a mottled buff above, except for a black eye-line and leading edge of each wing. The bill and legs of juveniles are dark. First summer birds appear similar to winter adults, and both sexes are similar in appearance.

POPULATION SIZE AND TREND: Spendelow and Patton (1988) compiled estimates of Least Tern population size and identified the difficulties of

Least Tern,
Sterna antillarum.
(Photo by Jeffery
A. Gore)

collecting and interpreting population estimates for this species. According to their compilation, the breeding population of the Least Tern along the Atlantic and Gulf coasts of the United States was about 43,000 birds in nearly 300 colonies in the late 1970s. Unfortunately, the census data available for Least Tern colonies in Florida are of limited value (Clapp et al. 1983; Spendelow and Patton 1988). Some estimates from the 1970s are of about 5,000 birds in Florida (Clapp et al. 1983; Spendelow and Patton 1988), but Fisk (1975) estimated 6,400 Least Terns from the Atlantic Coast alone. These estimates probably do not include most small colonies and many colonies on roofs or at isolated locations, and it is impossible to determine what proportion of the existing colonies were censused.

Knowledge of the Least Tern population in Florida has only partially improved in recent years, but work in two regions give some indication of the current status of this species. The Florida Keys, except for the Dry Tortugas (Robertson 1964), supported few nesting Least Terns until alteration of the habitat by humans created suitable nesting sites (Hovis and Robson 1989). Surveys by Downing (1973) and Kushlan and White (1985) found that by the 1970s the number of nesting terns had increased to 1,100–1,500 birds, and in 1987 Hovis and Robson (1989) estimated that nearly 1,400 birds nested among 37 colonies. Apparently the number of nesting birds in the Keys, which increased dramatically earlier, has been relatively stable for the past two decades.

Downing (1973) found 340 nesting Least Terns in northwest Florida in 1973 and Clapp et al. (1983) estimated 500 birds in two colonies in 1978. Fisk (1978a) reported only two colonies on roofs in this area in 1976 but did not specify their size. In contrast, Gore (1991) estimated 4,700 Least Terns

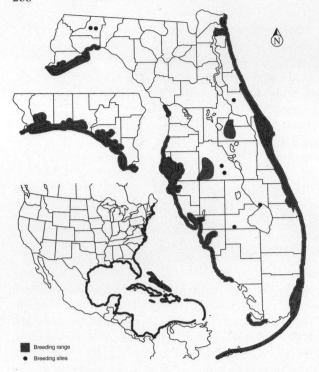

Distribution map of
the Least Tern,
Sterna antillarum.

Breeding range
Breeding sites

among 42 colonies in northwest Florida in 1990. The earlier surveys probably
did not record all colonies because they encompassed larger areas and were
necessarily less intensive than the 1990 survey. Therefore, it is risky to assume
the approximately ten-fold increase in Least Tern numbers between the 1978
and 1990 surveys is real. However, a series of more consistent observations in
coastal Mississippi also found Least Terns populations increased dramatically
starting about 1976 (Jackson and Jackson 1985).

There still is no reliable estimate of the number of breeding Least Terns in
Florida or even a trend in the population. The Keys and northwest Florida
apparently contain more nesting Least Terns now than were estimated for the
entire state in the 1970s, and that strongly suggests a statewide increase. A
conservative estimate for Florida would be 10,000 birds, but the actual size of
the population may be larger. Clearly, this species has rebounded across much
of its east coast range from very low numbers at the beginning of this century.
Trends in the last few decades are more vague; while many colonies have been
displaced by development of beaches others have formed on newly created
artificial sites.

DISTRIBUTION AND HISTORY OF DISTRIBUTION: The Least Tern is
found only in the western hemisphere, but it is one of several closely related

species (including the European Little Tern) which together comprise a nearly worldwide distribution (AOU 1983). The eastern subspecies of the Least Tern breeds along the eastern coast of the United States from Maine to Texas and south through the Caribbean to the Lesser Antilles and coastal Venezuela (Spendelow and Patton 1988). The California Least Tern breeds from central California to northern Mexico and the Interior Least Tern occurs along major rivers in the Midwest and Great Plains. The winter range of the Least Tern is not well known, but some birds winter as far as northern South America (AOU 1983). A bird banded as a chick in Bay County, Florida, was recovered in October in Guyana (J. A. Gore, unpubl. data).

Along the Atlantic and Gulf coasts, the Least Tern may be found nesting wherever suitable open, sandy habitat is available. Data from the recent Breeding Bird Atlas show Least Terns nested along nearly all of Florida's coast; notable exceptions were the salt marsh shorelines of the Big Bend region and the mangrove-lined shores of southwest Florida. Adaptation to artificial sites such as dredged-material islands, construction sites, surface-mined lands, and roofs has expanded the local distribution of Least Terns, especially to inland locations (Lohrer and Lohrer 1973; Loftin 1973; Fisk 1978a; Hovis and Robson 1989; Gore 1991). Inland colonies were recorded for the Breeding Bird Atlas in several counties including Leon, Polk, Orange, Seminole, Volusia, Glades, and Okeechobee.

HABITAT REQUIREMENTS AND HABITAT TREND: Nesting habitat of the Least Tern has been characterized in detail by several authors (Jernigan et al. 1978; Thompson and Slack 1982; Gochfeld 1983; Kotliar and Burger 1986), and Gochfeld (1983) and Carreker (1985) prepared models to evaluate potential nesting habitat. Least Terns routinely select a nesting site with a substrate of sand or gravel. Substrate composition varies among sites, but light-colored sands with less than 20% shell fragments are typical. Shell fragments make the eggs more difficult to see and may keep sand from blowing onto the nest. Clays or other fine materials are unsuitable for nesting substrate because they do not drain well and may stick to the eggs (Thompson and Slack 1982).

Most nesting sites are nearly bare and few have vegetation covering more than 20% of the area; but, as with the substrate, the amount of vegetation that will be tolerated is variable. Colonies that have been successful at a given site in past years are likely to tolerate more vegetation (Burger 1984; Kotliar and Burger 1986). Vegetation at nesting sites is usually short, thus providing cover for chicks but not for large predators.

The Least Tern historically nested along the coast on broad, sparsely vegetated, sandy beaches (Bent 1921; Gochfeld 1983). Unfortunately, as the human population has increased, many of the traditional Least Tern nesting sites have been usurped by human activities and buildings. The loss of nesting habitat apparently began earlier in the northeast (Nisbet 1973) than in the mid-Atlantic or southeast (Downing 1973; Gochfeld 1983).

The loss of traditional nesting areas has been offset somewhat by the creation of new nesting habitat. Least Terns now nest in a variety of artificial, open habitats such as dredged-material deposits (Downing 1973; Jernigan et al. 1978), gravel-covered roofs (Fisk 1975), and ground cleared by mining, construction, and other activities (Lohrer and Lohrer 1973; Loftin 1973; Maehr 1982; Gore 1991).

VULNERABILITY OF SPECIES AND HABITAT: Least Terns nest in colonies on open ground and depend on camouflaged eggs and group mobbing by adult birds for defense. This protection sometimes proves insufficient, and many birds or nests in a colony can be destroyed quickly by a single disturbance. The Least Tern's beachfront nesting habitat also is highly vulnerable because it is naturally ephemeral and subject to successional changes as well as immediate catastrophic ones. Furthermore, the beach habitat is highly desirable for human use.

CAUSES OF THREAT: In the 1800s and the early part of the 1900s, Least Terns were often killed to procure their feathers for the millinery trade. At the time, commercial hunting was the major threat to the species and almost resulted in the extirpation of the bird from the east coast (Bent 1921; Tomkins 1959; Nisbet 1973; Jackson and Jackson 1985). This threat no longer exists, but it has been replaced by others. When humans, domestic dogs, or vehicles move near or through a Least Tern colony, the adult birds usually fly up to mob the intruder. This causes the birds to expend time and energy needed to feed and tend eggs and chicks. More importantly, when the adults are off the nest the eggs and chicks are exposed to sun, wind, and predators. In addition, the cryptically-colored eggs and chicks may be crushed underfoot. This type of disturbance by humans can result in complete reproductive failure of a Least Tern colony (Burger 1984) and subsequent abandonment of the nesting site (Kotliar and Burger 1986).

The distance at which intruders cause a nesting colony to become alarmed and flush depends upon the size of the colony, the birds' line-of-sight view of approaching persons, and the frequency of disturbance and habituation of the birds to the disturbance. Rodgers and Smith (1991) recommended a buffer zone of at least 175 m to keep human activity from disturbing mixed-species colonies, including nesting Least Terns. However, because the sensitivity of the birds to disturbance varies widely among colonies, buffer zone sizes should, whenever practical, be determined for individual colonies based upon observed flushing distances.

Nesting habitat can be lost when roads or buildings are constructed near the shore, but current construction regulations and practices have made building on beaches or foredunes uncommon. Nevertheless, development of coastal property remains a major threat because construction along the coast usually leads to increased human activity on the beach regardless of where buildings are placed.

In the case of roof colonies, direct loss of nesting habitat is a serious threat. A rolled plastic roof, which is unsuitable for nesting terns, is now often used to replace the gravel-covered roofs that are so widely used as nesting sites in Florida (Gore and Kinnison 1991). Because the majority of Florida's Least Terns apparently nest on roofs (Hovis and Robson 1989; Gore 1991), loss of roof sites may soon become a major problem.

Predators can destroy all eggs and chicks in a colony and may take adults as well (Minsky 1980; Clapp et al. 1983; Burger 1984). Fish Crows (*Corvus ossifragus*), red foxes (*Vulpes vulpes*), raccoons (*Procyon lotor*), and house cats (*Felis catus*) are common predators of Least Terns in Florida (Fisk 1978b; Gore and Kinnison 1991), and many other species are known to prey on Least Terns, including ants (Formicidae) and ghost crabs (*Ocypode quadrata*) (Clapp et al. 1983). Mammals may be the most serious predators because they are most active at night, little intimidated by the terns' mobbing, and capable of taking many eggs or chicks.

Because of their exposed location near water, Least Tern colonies can be devastated by high winds, heavy rains, and high tides associated with storms (Thompson 1982; Haddon and Knight 1983; Jackson and Jackson 1985). Least Terns select higher elevation sites for nesting (Thompson and Slack 1982; Burger and Gochfeld 1990), but few coastal sites that are sparsely vegetated are high enough to prevent flooding during severe storms. Furthermore, loss of traditional nesting areas may force birds to use sites more susceptible to flooding.

Little is known of the effects of pollutants on individual Least Terns or populations. Because they feed on fish that may have accumulated toxic materials from polluted waters, Least Terns should be considered vulnerable to chemical contamination (Blus and Prouty 1979; Jackson and Jackson 1985). Spilled oil also poses a serious threat to Least Tern colonies (Hays 1980; Clapp et al. 1983), but fortunately no colony in Florida has been directly affected by an oil spill.

RESPONSES TO HABITAT MODIFICATION: Least Terns have proven remarkably adaptable to changes in their nesting habitat. This is evidenced most clearly by the widespread use of dredged-material islands (Downing 1973; Schreiber and Schreiber 1978) and gravel-covered roofs (Fisk 1975, 1978) as nesting sites. Because these sites are less susceptible to flooding,

mammalian predators, and human disturbance, they are often more productive than nesting sites on natural beaches (Jernigan et al. 1978; Gore and
Kinnison 1991). Across most of its range, the Least Tern now nests more
commonly on modified or artificial sites than natural beaches (Downing 1973;
Jernigan et al. 1978; Erwin 1980; Thompson 1982; Gochfeld 1983; Gore
1991), and data from northwest Florida and the Keys suggest that roofs
support more Least Tern nests and colonies than any other habitat in the state
(Hovis and Robson 1989; Gore 1991).

Least Terns also respond rapidly to improvements in existing habitat. For
example, since the annual removal of vegetation began a few years ago on the
causeway to St. George Island in Franklin County, the number of nesting
Least Terns has more than doubled.

DEMOGRAPHIC CHARACTERISTICS: Least Terns lay eggs as early as
mid-March (Fisk 1978b), but mid-April is a more typical date for first eggs in
south and central Florida and the first of May is usual for north Florida (Gore,
unpubl. data). One or two-egg clutches are most common, and renesting or
inexperienced birds tend to produce smaller clutches (Massey and Atwood
1981). Clapp et al. (1983) compiled data from several locations outside Florida
and found mean clutch sizes ranging from 1.7–2.2 eggs.

Eggs hatch after about 21 days and the percentage of eggs that hatch varies
widely depending on what disturbances befall the colony (Clapp et al. 1983;
Burger and Gochfeld 1990; Gore and Kinnison 1991). Only one brood is
raised to fledging, but pairs that lose eggs or chicks may renest (Massey and
Atwood 1981; Massey and Fancher 1989). The precocial young leave the nest
2–4 days after hatching and make their first flights about three weeks later
(Lohrer and Lohrer 1973; Fisk 1975; Massey and Atwood 1981). One-month-
old birds are strong fliers but they may still be fed by the parents.

In Florida, few eggs hatch after 1 August and most birds have left nesting
areas by September. Pairs nesting late in the season are usually first-time
nesters or renesting birds that lost eggs or chicks earlier (Atwood and Massey
1988). Young birds do not return to breed until at least their second year
(Atwood and Massey 1988). Adult mortality is apparently low; 5–10 year-old
Least Terns are not uncommon and some may live more than 20 years (Clapp
et al. 1983).

KEY BEHAVIORS: Least Terns migrate from their wintering grounds to
breeding sites in Florida in early spring. Pairs form soon afterwards with a
ritual in which males offer small fish to prospective mates prior to copulation
(Bent 1921; Tomkins 1959; Wolk 1974). Nests are made directly on the
ground and consist of shallow depressions scraped in the substrate and some-

times lined with small shells. Frequent disturbance during the 2–3 week period from pair formation to egg-laying can cause birds to abandon the nesting site.

Least Terns typically nest in colonies ranging in size from a few breeding pairs to many hundreds. Colonial nesting may allow Least Terns to exchange information about food sources or to produce more young than local predators can take. More importantly, colonial nesting helps the birds detect and deter or avoid predators. Nesting Least Terns mob humans or other intruders that approach the colony and dive directly toward them, often defecating with surprising accuracy (Jackson et al. 1982).

CONSERVATION MEASURES TAKEN: For many years now, individuals, private conservation groups, and natural resource agencies throughout Florida have worked to protect Least Tern colonies from disturbance, particularly from humans. At many nesting areas, signs are posted to warn people against entering colonies and to inform them about the nesting birds. In recent years, bird nesting area signs have been available from the Florida Game and Fresh Water Fish Commission (FGFWFC). Many nesting areas also have been fenced or bounded with rope or string during the breeding season to keep people out. Unfortunately, these measures have not been consistently applied each year and they have never been applied to all vulnerable colonies in Florida.

The Least Tern is listed as a threatened species by the FGFWFC (Wood 1991) and disturbing or destroying the birds, eggs, or nests is prohibited. The federal Migratory Bird Treaty Act also prohibits such activities. Some nesting areas are designated as Critical Wildlife Areas by the FGFWFC and as such receive increased protection against human intruders.

In 1988, guidelines were developed for protecting Least Tern colonies in Florida (O'Meara and Gore 1988). These guidelines have been provided to managers of public land and owners of private property where Least Terns are known or suspected to nest. The FGFWFC also produced a poster describing Least Terns and their habit of nesting on roofs. The poster is distributed to managers of buildings with roof colonies in order to inform the managers and the public about the roof-nesting birds and the need to protect them.

Because of increased interest in Least Terns and knowledge about their nesting requirements, numerous wildlife and land managers in Florida have actively improved sites for the birds. Examples of such activities include clearing vegetation, limiting vehicle access, constructing fences to deter predators, removing non-native predators, fencing roof edges, and constructing nesting platforms. In addition, increased awareness of the presence and sensitivity of nesting colonies has frequently allowed colony sites to be considered in land-use plans.

CONSERVATION MEASURES PROPOSED: Recent surveys suggest Least Tern populations are greater now than in past years, but the species remains highly vulnerable to human disturbance and warrants continued monitoring and conservation efforts. Regular monitoring of nesting colonies across Florida would help identify trends in population size and changes in colony locations. With minimal training, interested local residents could provide estimates of colony size and reproductive success, as well as educate others about the birds.

O'Meara and Gore (1988) described specific measures for protecting Least Tern colonies in Florida. Most colonies would benefit from additional efforts to reduce predation of nests, disturbance by humans, and encroachment of vegetation. Rodgers and Smith (1991) recommend restricting human activity to areas at least 175 m outside colonies to reduce disturbance. Most colonies on roofs would benefit from improved drainage, fenced edges, and additional shelter for chicks. A comprehensive management plan supported by natural resource agencies, interested volunteers, and landowners would allow more consistent protection and monitoring of nesting colonies.

ACKNOWLEDGMENTS: I thank Brian Millsap, Tim O'Meara, Jim Rodgers, and Hank Smith for their helpful comments.

LITERATURE CITED:

AOU. 1957. Check-list of North American birds. Fifth ed. Lord Baltimore Press, Baltimore, Maryland. 691 pp.

AOU. 1983. Check-list of North American birds. Sixth ed. American Ornithologists' Union, Washington, D.C. 877 pp.

Atwood, J. L. and B. W. Massey. 1988. Site fidelity of Least Terns in California. Condor 90:389–394.

Bent, A. C. 1921. Life histories of North American gulls and terns. U.S. National Mus. Bull. no. 113.

Blus, L. J., and R. M. Prouty. 1979. Organochlorine pollutants and population status of Least Terns in South Carolina. Wilson Bull. 91:62–71.

Burger, J. 1984. Colony stability in Least Terns. Condor 86:61–67.

Burger, J., and M. Gochfeld. 1990. Nest site selection in Least Terns (*Sterna antillarum*) in New Jersey and New York. Colon. Waterbirds 13:31–40.

Carreker, R. G. 1985. Habitat suitability index models: Least Tern. U.S. Fish and Wildl. Serv. Biol. Rept. 82(10.103), Washington, D.C. 29 pp.

Clapp, R. B., D. Morgan-Jacobs, and R. C. Banks. 1983. Marine birds of the southeastern United States and Gulf of Mexico. Part III: Charadriiformes. U.S. Fish and Wildl. Serv. FWS/OBS-83/30, Washington, D.C. 853 pp.

Downing, R. L. 1973. A preliminary nesting survey of Least Terns and Black Skimmers in the East. Amer. Birds 27:946–949.

Erwin, R. M. 1980. Breeding habitat use by colonially nesting waterbirds in two mid-Atlantic U.S. regions under different regimes of human disturbance. Biol. Conserv. 18:39–51.

Fisk, E. J. 1975. Least Tern: beleaguered, opportunistic and roof-nesting. Amer. Birds 29:15–16.

Fisk, E. J. 1978a. Roof-nesting terns, skimmers, and plovers in Florida. Fla. Field Nat. 6:1–8.

Fisk, E. J. 1978b. Least Tern. Pages 40–43 in Rare and endangered biota of Florida, Vol. II. Birds (H. W. Kale, II, ed.). Univ. Press of Florida, Gainesville, Florida.

Gochfeld, M. 1983. Colony site selection by Least Terns: physical attributes of sites. Colon. Waterbirds 6:205–213.

Gore, J. A. 1991. Distribution and abundance of nesting Least Terns and Black Skimmers in northwest Florida. Fla. Field Nat. 19:65–72.

Gore, J. A., and M. J. Kinnison. 1991. Hatching success in roof and ground colonies of Least Terns. Condor 93:759–762.

Haddon, P. C., and R. C. Knight. 1983. A guide to Little Tern conservation. Royal Soc. Protect. Birds, Bedfordshire, England.

Hays, M. B. 1980. Breeding biology of the Least Tern, *Sterna albifrons,* on the Gulf coast of Mississippi. M.S. thesis, Mississippi State Univ., Mississippi State, Mississippi.

Hovis, J. A., and M. S. Robson. 1989. Breeding status and distribution of the Least Tern in the Florida Keys. Fla. Field Nat. 17:61–66.

Jackson, J. A., and B. J. Jackson. 1985. Status, dispersion, and population changes of the Least Tern in coastal Mississippi. Colon. Waterbirds 8:54–62.

Jackson, J. A., B. E. Rowe, M. S. Hetrick, and B. J. Schardien. 1982. Site-specific nest defense behavior of Black Skimmers and Least Terns. Condor 8:120.

Jernigan, L. S., Jr., R. F. Soots, J. F. Parnell, and T. L. Quay. 1978. Nesting habitats and breeding populations of the Least Tern (*Sterna albifrons antillarum*) in North Carolina. Univ. North Carolina Contrib. Mar. Sci. 814, Wilmington, North Carolina. 39 pp.

Kotliar, N. B., and J. Burger. 1986. Colony site selection and abandonment by Least Terns (*Sterna antillarum*) in New Jersey, USA. Biol. Conserv. 37:1–21.

Kushlan, J. A., and D. A. White. 1985. Least and Roseate tern nesting sites in the Florida Keys. Fla. Field Nat. 13:98–99.

Loftin, R. W. 1973. Another inland colony of the Least Tern. Fla. Field Nat. 1:37.

Lohrer, F. E., and C. E. Lohrer. 1973. Inland nesting of the Least Tern in Highlands County, Florida. Fla. Field Nat. 1:3–5.

Maehr, D. S. 1982. The adaptable Least Tern. Florida Nat. 55:7–10.

Massey, B.W. 1976. Vocal differences between American Least Terns and the European Little Tern. Auk 93:760–773.

Massey, B. W., and J. L. Atwood. 1981. Second-wave nesting of the California Least Tern: age composition and reproductive success. Auk 98:596–605.

Massey, B. W., and J. M. Fancher. 1989. Renesting by California Least Terns. Jour. Field Ornithol. 60:350–357.

Minsky, D. 1980. Preventing fox predation at a Least Tern colony with an electric fence. Jour. Field. Ornithol. 51:180–181.

Nisbet, I. C. T. 1973. Terns in Massachusetts: present numbers and historical changes. Bird-Banding 44:27–55.

O'Meara, T. E., and J. A. Gore. 1988. Guidelines for conservation and management of Least Tern colonies in Florida. Fla. Game and Fresh Water Fish Comm., Tallahassee, Florida. 12 pp.

Robertson, W. B., Jr. 1964. The terns of the Dry Tortugas. Bull. Fla. State Mus. 8:1–94.

Rodgers, J. A., and H. T. Smith. 1991. Minimum buffer zone requirement to protect nesting bird colonies from human disturbance. Pp. 55–56 in Proc. Coastal Nongame Workshop, Gainesville, Florida (D. P. Jennings, compiler). U.S. Fish and Wildl. Serv., Fort Collins, Colorado. 186 pp.

Schreiber, R. W., and E. A. Schreiber. 1978. Colonial bird use and plant succession on dredged material islands in Florida. Vol. I: Sea and wading bird colonies. U.S. Army Eng. Waterways Exp. Stn. Tech. Rep. D–78–14, Vicksburg, Mississippi. 63 pp.

Spendelow, J. A., and S. R. Patton. 1988. National atlas of coastal waterbird colonies in the contiguous United States: 1976–1982. U.S. Fish and Wildl. Serv. Biol. Rep. 88(5), Washington, D.C. 326 pp.

Thompson, B. C., and R. D. Slack. 1982. Physical aspects of colony selection by Least Terns on the Texas coast. Colon. Waterbirds 5:161–168.

Thompson, S. M. 1982. Least Tern study. Pp. 72–83 in Man's impact on the vegetation, avifauna, and herpetofauna of South Carolina's barrier islands: a habitat approach to carrying capacity (L.L. Gaddy, ed.). South Carolina Wildl. and Marine Resour. Dept., Columbia, South Carolina. 168 pp.

Tomkins, I. R. 1959. Life history notes on the Least Tern. Wilson Bull. 71:313–322.

Wolk, R. G. 1974. Reproductive behavior of the Least Tern. Proc. Linn. Soc. N.Y. 72:44–62.

Wood, D. 1991. Official lists of endangered and potentially endangered fauna and flora in Florida. Fla. Game and Fresh Water Fish Comm., Tallahassee, Florida. 23 pp.

PREPARED BY: Jeffery A. Gore, Florida Game and Fresh Water Fish Commission, 3911 Highway 2321, Panama City, FL 32409.

Roseate Tern
Sterna dougallii

FAMILY LARIDAE

Order Charadriiformes

TAXONOMY: The Roseate Tern (*Sterna dougallii*) was originally described by Montagu in 1813 from a Cumbrey Islands in Firth of Clyde [Scotland] specimen (AOU 1983). Nisbet (1980) and Gochfeld (1983) discussed five subspecies that assembled a cosmopolitan breeding distribution: *S. d. dougallii*, *S. d. bangsi*, *S. d. korustes*, *S. d. arideensis*, and *S. d. gracilis*. This review primarily focuses on the population that includes the Florida Keys within its breeding range.

DESCRIPTION: The Roseate Tern is a slender, medium-sized, marine coast sea tern about 35–40 cm (15 in.) (USFWS 1989) in length. Wing length is about 23 cm (9.3 in.) (Nisbet 1989). Adults exhibit a weight range of 100–120 g (about 4 oz.) (USFWS 1989). Males and females have similar plumage. Breeding adults are gray dorsally with a black cap, creamy-white ventrally, the underparts are blushed with pink coloration, and the tail is deeply forked. Bill coloration of the northeastern population is black during the early portion of the breeding season but gradually changes to red at the base for about half of its length as breeding activities progress (Donaldson 1968). The Caribbean breeding population has more red on the bill than the northeastern breeding population (Gochfeld 1983; Nisbet 1989). The legs are red. In winter, adults develop a white forehead, have little if any pink coloration, and the legs and bill become black. Downy chicks range in base coloration from brown to gray and have dark brown or black spots. Chicks frequently exhibit a tufted or spiky appearance from the down sticking together (USFWS 1989; Nisbet 1989; W. Robertson, pers. comm.). At hatching, the legs are dull purple but become black in a few days (USFWS 1989). Juveniles are brown to gray above, light colored below, have a brown or brown-gray cap, and black bill and legs.

Roseate Tern,
Sterna dougallii.
(Photo by Mark S.
Robson)

POPULATION SIZE AND TRENDS: Roseate Terns breed in two separate major geographic areas in the Western Hemisphere. One area encompasses coastal habitats from New York through Maine and also extends along the coast of Nova Scotia (USFWS 1989). Estimates of this northeastern population were 8,500 pairs in the 1930s, 4,800 pairs in 1952, a low of 2,500 pairs in 1977, and a varying range of 2,500 to 3,300 breeding pairs from 1978 to 1988 (Nisbet 1980; USFWS 1989). By 1978, about 90% of the North American breeding pairs nested in only four major northeastern colonies (USFWS 1989). In 1988, 85% of these birds were reduced to nesting at only two small island sites (USFWS 1989).

The second area where Roseate Terns breed in the Western Hemisphere encompasses the islands throughout the Caribbean Sea. The Caribbean population breeds in the Florida Keys, the Dry Tortugas, the Bahamas, Puerto Rico, the Virgin Islands, and areas in the Lesser Antilles Islands (Bent 1921; Sprunt 1949; Robertson 1964, 1978; Nisbet 1980; Buckley and Buckley 1981; Gochfeld 1983; Clapp et al. 1983; Kushlan and White 1985; Norton 1988; Nisbet 1989; USFWS 1989). Former breeding populations on Bermuda apparently have been extirpated (Gochfeld 1983). Nisbet (1980) estimated the total West Indies population scattered among known breeding sites to be in excess of 2,000 pairs in 1976 and less than 1,500 pairs in 1979.

Previous reviews have suggested that the historical background of Caribbean Roseate Terns is poorly documented (Nisbet 1980; Clapp et al. 1983; Nisbet 1989) and early population counts for this species in Florida were not systematic. In recent times, Robertson (1978) more accurately estimated the entire Florida breeding population to be about 250–300 pairs with nesting success generally described as "poor." Nesting surveys for this species conducted in the Florida Keys during May–July 1976 by Kushlan and White

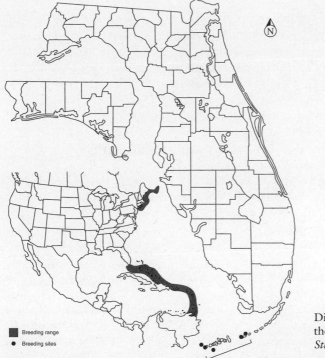

Distribution map of
the Roseate Tern,
Sterna dougallii.

■ Breeding range
● Breeding sites

(1985) identified three colonies with a June total of 370 nests. Robertson and Woolfenden (1992) reported the Florida breeding population to be about 350 pairs.

A primary breeding area at the Dry Tortugas has had irregular nesting since at least 1917 (Sprunt 1949; Robertson 1964, 1978). Locations of the colony have alternated among Bush, Long, and Hospital Keys (Robertson 1964, unpubl. ms.). Until about 1970, this colony was composed of 100–200 breeding pairs annually; however, the breeding estimates declined to a maximum of 50 pairs annually concurrent with increased nesting densities in the "Florida Keys proper" (Robertson, unpubl. ms.). The former stronghold of the Dry Tortugas had few or no Roseate Terns nesting on the "inner islands" during most of the 1980s through 1991, however, comprehensive surveys were not conducted every year during the proper season (W. Robertson, pers. comm.). The recent breeding (or suspected breeding) records for this species at various colonies in the Florida Keys were first noted in 1962 (Robertson 1962). The records for the period 1962 to 1973 ranged from 10 to approximately 400 adults and were summarized by Robertson (1978). Additional (or suspected) breeding records in Florida for the period 1974–1992 include: 17 reports in *American Birds* (1974–1989) and 11 reports by Robson et al. (FGFWFC/

NAS, unpubl. data, 1987–1992). These records range from 4 to about 600 adults and are too numerous to discuss inclusively in a review of this size. A subset of these records covering 1984–1992 suggests that Roseate Terns in the Florida Keys use a very limited, unstable, number of sites for breeding: Key West–Truman Annex rooftops, "100+ including 25–30% flying young," 1984 (Paul 1984); Key West–"Naval Air Station roof," estimated 30 pairs, 1985 (Kale 1985); Pelican Shoal, estimated 300 pairs, 1987 (FGFWFC/NAS, unpubl. data); Key West-Tank Island, 250–300 pairs-all nests failed, 1988 (Paul 1988; Robson and Hovis, unpubl. data); "Marathon condominium rooftop," 60 pairs, and Pelican Shoal, 225 pairs, 1989 (Paul 1989; Kalla and Robson, unpubl. data); Pelican Shoal, estimated 235–250 pairs, and Marathon-Casa Cayo Condominium, 6 adults and 3 fledged young, 1990 (Robson and Kalla, unpubl. data); Pelican Shoal, estimated 125–150 pairs, and Marathon-Casa Cayo, 30 pairs with eggs and chicks, 1991 (Robson and Kalla, unpubl. data); Pelican Shoal, estimated 275 pairs, Truman Annex building #289 rooftop, 5 pairs with eggs, and Vaca Rock, 6 pairs, 1992 (Robson, unpubl. data). The Key West-Truman Annex rooftops site was mentioned in the 1975–1992 records as early as 1981 (Paul 1981).

Records of migrants or wintering Roseate Terns in Florida are uncommon, with most of the reports coming from the Atlantic coast. Several records for the period 1886–1981 were summarized in Clapp et al. (1983). A dead winter specimen was collected on Key West on 6 December 1976 (Stevenson 1977).

DISTRIBUTION AND HISTORY OF DISTRIBUTION: The Roseate Tern has a patchy but cosmopolitan distribution. In the Western Hemisphere this species breeds along marine coasts from New York northward through Nova Scotia, and a second discrete population breeds on various islands dispersed throughout the Caribbean Sea (see Population Size and Trends). Nisbet (1984) analyzed 1,182 banding returns and recoveries from about 104,000 Roseate Terns banded throughout the northeastern breeding range during the period 1922–1978 and indicated that winter habitat for this population ranges from western Colombia to eastern Brazil, with a restricted latitude of 11°N–13°S. Most Caribbean Roseate Terns also migrate south during the winter and two birds banded in the Virgin Islands were later recovered in Guyana (Nisbet 1984).

HABITAT REQUIREMENTS AND HABITAT TRENDS: In Florida, Roseate Terns have an unstable breeding site distribution that is dependent on islands with open sandy or broken coral nesting areas, a lack of mammalian and avian predators, and minimal disturbance by humans. Like many other species of terns, Roseate Terns lay their eggs in shallow scrapes or depressions directly on the available substrate. Nesting substrates in Florida have included bare limestone, sand-shell mixes, rock-marl fill, broken coral (Robertson 1978), and dredge-material (Kushlan and White 1985). At sites with vegetation, nests are often located near the edge of ground cover (Robertson 1978). In some Caribbean habitats, nests may be close to rocky cover or vegetation that provide shade and shelter from inclement weather conditions or protection from predators (Burger and Gochfeld 1988). Earlier, Fisk (1978) suggested that Roseate Terns also nest on roofs of buildings in Florida. This has been confirmed by direct observations for at least two rooftop-sites (M. Robson, unpubl. data) in the Florida Keys, with other sites also reported.

A moderate amount of suitable natural breeding habitat is still available in the Caribbean population range; however, much Florida Keys natural habitat has been greatly reduced or degraded, or has otherwise suffered from anthropogenic impacts.

VULNERABILITY OF SPECIES AND HABITAT: As the breeding distribution of Roseate Terns is extremely patchy and localized, the threats of habitat conversion, predation, human disturbance, and catastrophic climatic phenomena (e.g., flooding of colony sites) all present significant hazards to the species in Florida.

CAUSES OF THREAT: Numbers of northeastern Roseate Terns were severely impacted by market hunting for the millinery trade during the 1870s and 1880s (Bent 1921; Nisbet 1980; USFWS 1989). The extent of similar impacts to the Caribbean population during the late nineteenth century are unknown.

In general, habitat conversion for human uses poses a great threat to Roseate Terns. Predation by mammals and birds upon eggs, chicks, and adults can range from a nuisance to catastrophic level depending upon site conditions. Known predators at the Dry Tortugas include black rats (*Rattus rattus*), Laughing Gulls (*Larus atricilla*), and Cattle Egrets (*Bubulcus ibis*) (Robertson, unpubl. ms.). Shealer and Burger (1992) reported that Ruddy Turnstones (*Arenaria interpres*) destroyed a colony of 154 Roseate Tern nests in Puerto Rico. Norton (1980) mentioned the Magnificent Frigatebird (*Fregata magnificens*) as a suspected predator of terns in the West Indies. The large-scale reduction in use of formerly occupied northeastern breeding colonies has been strongly attributed to expanding populations of nesting Herring Gulls (*L. argentatus*) and Great Black-backed Gulls (*L. marinus*) that co-occupy the sites (Nisbet 1980; USFWS 1989). Nisbet (1981a) identified egging as the "limiting factor" for several areas within the Caribbean range. After examining banding data, Nisbet (1984) also reported intensive sea bird hunting for local market sale at sections of wintering grounds in Guyana as a possible factor in population declines. Intrusions of humans and domestic dogs into breeding colonies, whether purposeful or inadvertent, are always problematic and can result in site abandonment or reproductive failure. Contact with spilled petroleum components in breeding or foraging areas also could result in severe impacts to a local aggregation. Discarded human artifacts such as fishing line and kite string have resulted in injuries and mortalities to various species of sea birds, including terns (Gochfeld 1973; Howe et al. 1978). In one northeastern study, the prebreeding survival rate of young Roseate Terns to age 3 years was estimated to be near 16% (Spendelow 1991).

RESPONSES TO HABITAT MODIFICATION: Manipulation of vegetation and substrates at Roseate Tern breeding sites (during the nonbreeding season) may be possible to provide preferable nesting habitat. The three Roseate Tern breeding colonies located in 1976 by Kushlan and White (1985) were on artificial dredge-material deposits. At an island site off the coast of Connecticut, creating carefully placed, sheltered nesting sites with driftwood, boards, and discarded tires was an effective technique for improving reproductive success of this species (Spendelow 1982). Roseate Terns also have nested on rooftops in the Florida Keys.

DEMOGRAPHIC CHARACTERISTICS: At the Dry Tortugas, Roseate Terns have been observed as early as April 4 (Robertson, unpubl. ms.), though they usually arrive in "late April or early May" and initiate nesting in the second half of May or very early in June (Robertson 1978). Pairs renesting after a failed initial attempt may deposit replacement clutches through early July and possibly middle July (Robertson 1964, unpubl. ms.). At the three sites in the Florida Keys located during their 1976 study, Kushlan and White (1985) observed the greatest number of active nests during surveys conducted on 15 and 26 June. Average May and June clutch sizes for Caribbean population Roseate Terns summarized from five reports during 1962–1978 ranged from 1.31–1.71 eggs per nest (Nisbet 1981a). Norton (1988) surveyed Caribbean colonies from the eastern Puerto Rico Bank to the U.S. and British Virgin Islands and reported an average of 1.49 eggs per nest during 1980 to 1985. First clutches at sites in Florida usually consist of 2 eggs while replacement clutches usually consist of 1 egg (Robertson 1978). In both the Caribbean and northeastern breeding populations clutches containing 3 or 4 eggs are occasionally (estimated <1%) observed (Norton 1988; USFWS 1989). Eggs are usually laid 2 or 3 days apart. Caribbean Roseate Tern eggs average 5–10% less in weight and volume than eggs of the northeastern population (Nisbet 1981a, 1989). Both sexes incubate the eggs. Northeastern population Roseate Tern eggs are reported to hatch in about 23 days (USFWS 1989; Nisbet 1989), whereas Robertson (1978) reported the incubation period to be 21 days. Hatching of eggs is asynchronous and northeastern birds usually fledge between 22 and 29 days of age (USFWS 1989). Juveniles are accompanied and fed by adults for many weeks (Nisbet 1989) and sometimes months (Robertson 1978) after fledging. At the Dry Tortugas, Roseate Terns leave the breeding grounds by early September (Robertson 1978). The latest observation at the Dry Tortugas was 3 October (Robertson, unpubl. ms.). The maximum age reported for a banded Roseate Tern is 14 years, but this probably does not represent the potential life span for the species (Nisbet 1989). Breeding ecology for various areas throughout the Caribbean Sea has been summarized previously by Nisbet (1980, 1981a).

KEY BEHAVIORS: Roseate Terns feed on small (40–100 mm) (USFWS 1989) marine fish by plunge-diving vertically into the water and capturing them within their bills. Plunges are usually conducted from altitudes of 3–6 m (Robertson, unpubl. ms.) up to as high as 20 m (USFWS 1989). Throughout much of its range, feeding frequently occurs in waters with strong currents (Nisbet 1989; USFWS 1989). Observations of adults from the Pelican Shoal breeding colony indicate that considerable foraging also occurs in nearby quiet waters, 1–2 m in depth (M. Robson, pers. comm.). Robertson (1978) also mentions nearshore foraging in Florida. Shealer and Burger (1992) suggested that foraging off southwestern Puerto Rico occurs primarily near shore, and a common prey is the dwarf herring (*Jenkinsia lamprotaenia*). Kleptoparasitism by Roseate Terns upon other species of terns as a mechanism for providing fish to chicks has been documented (Dunn 1973).

Colonial ground nesting and varying degrees of site tenacity are characteristic behavioral traits common to Roseate Terns and many other species. Constant breeding ground associates of Roseate Terns are Common Terns (*S. hirundo*) in the northeastern colonies (Nisbet 1981a, 1989; USFWS 1989), Sooty Terns (*S. fuscata*) or Bridled Terns (*S. anaethetus*) in some Caribbean colonies (Robertson 1978, unpubl. ms.; Nisbet 1981a, 1989), and Least Terns (*S. antillarum*) at some sites in the Florida Keys (Robson et al., unpubl. data). Roseate Terns will attack predatory birds in flight that enter their breeding colonies; however, their behavior toward mammalian predators is less aggressive and usually consists of circling or hovering above the animal while crying alarm calls (Nisbet 1981a). Considerable interruption of normal incubating behavior after trapping and release of breeding Roseate Terns during research has been reported (Nisbet 1981b). The distinctive calls of adults have been described as "chu-ick" and a rasping "ka-a-ak" (Peterson 1980), or a sharp "chi-vik" (flight) and a harsh "aaaach" (alarm) (USFWS 1989).

CONSERVATION MEASURES TAKEN: On December 2, 1987, the U.S. Fish and Wildlife Service effectively designated the northeastern population of the Roseate Tern as "endangered" and the Caribbean population as "threatened" pursuant to the Endangered Species Act of 1973 (16 U.S.C. 1531). The Caribbean population is similarly designated as "threatened" by the Florida Game and Fresh Water Fish Commission and protected by the Wildlife Code of the State of Florida (Chapter 39 F.A.C.). Further protection is provided to all tern species by the Migratory Bird Treaty Act (16 U.S.C. 703–711).

The Florida Game and Fresh Water Fish Commission, Florida Department of Natural Resources, and National Audubon Society worked collectively to designate the new Roseate Tern colony at Pelican Shoal (near Boca Chica Key) a "Critical Wildlife Area" on 13 July, 1990, thereby implementing the maximum protection for the colony site available under Chapter 39 F.A.C. Additional protection measures to prevent conflicting human activities also are conducted, as well as public environmental education efforts.

CONSERVATION MEASURES PROPOSED: Roseate Terns are extremely vulnerable to human disturbances at island nesting colonies in the Florida Keys. Further efforts to ensure safe nesting habitat for this species in the Keys, including additional posting, fencing, and public environmental education, should be conducted on a site-specific basis. Mechanisms to discourage avian and mammalian predators may be required at some sites. Potential new nesting habitat should be identified and evaluated for possible enhancement. Roseate Tern coastal roosting and loafing areas also may benefit from protection.

At the Dry Tortugas, surveys specifically targeting Roseate Terns during their temporal occupation of the area would improve the existing data base for the species in Florida (W. Robertson, pers. comm.). As Least Terns commonly nest on roofs of buildings in Florida (Hovis and Robson 1989; Gore 1991), the extent and success of rooftop-site nesting by Roseate Terns in the Keys should be evaluated (J. Gore, pers. comm.). Additional consolidation of the fragmented records, surveys, and literature regarding Roseate Terns in Florida also would facilitate management efforts (M. Robson, pers. comm.). General ecology and population dynamics of the Florida Keys breeding colonies should be investigated in relationship to the remainder of the Caribbean range population. Nisbet (1989) recommended that "the most important requirement for long-term maintenance of the roseate tern in the Western Hemisphere is protection on the wintering grounds."

Mechanisms to acquire additional funds to promote, develop, and implement proposed conservation measures in Florida should concurrently be explored.

ACKNOWLEDGMENTS: Much of the information cited herein from the U.S. Fish and Wildlife Service, Roseate Tern Recovery Plan Northeastern Population (USFWS 1989) was originally provided to the Service in two unpublished 1980 and 1981 reports by I. C. T. Nisbet. I also gratefully acknowledge Dr. Nisbet's unpublished work and its contributions to this report. I also thank W. B. Robertson, National Park Service, and M. Robson (et al.), Florida Game and Fresh Water Fish Commission (FGFWFC)/ National Audubon Society (NAS), for supplying me with their unpublished data and reports regarding Roseate Terns in Florida. J. A. Rodgers, M. Robson, W. B. Robertson, J. Gore, and D. Wood provided incentive to initiate the project as well as helpful comments that improved the manuscript. Y. Zola typed the manuscript.

LITERATURE CITED:

AOU. 1983. Checklist of North American birds. American Ornithologists' Union, Allen Press, Inc., Lawrence, Kansas.

Bent, A. C. 1921. Life histories of North American gulls and terns. U.S. National Mus. Bull. no. 113.

Buckley, P. A., and F. G. Buckley. 1981. The endangered status of North American Roseate Terns. Colon. Waterbirds 4:166–173.

Burger, J., and M. Gochfeld. 1988. Nest-site selection by Roseate Terns in two tropical colonies on Culebra, Puerto Rico. Condor 90:843–851.

Clapp, R. B., D. Morgan-Jacobs, and R. C. Banks. 1983. Marine birds of the southeastern United States and Gulf of Mexico. Part III: Charadriiformes. U.S. Fish Wildl. Serv., Div. Biol. Serv., FWS/OBS-83/80. Washington, D.C. 853 pp.

Donaldson, G. 1968. Bill color changes in adult Roseate Terns. Auk 85:662–668.

Dunn, E. K. 1973. Robbing behavior of Roseate Terns. Auk 90:641–651.

Fisk, E. J. 1978. Roof-nesting terns, skimmers, and plovers in Florida. Fla. Field Nat. 6:1–8.

Gochfeld, M. 1973. Effect of artefact pollution on the viability of seabird colonies on Long Island, New York. Environ. Pollut. 4:1–6.

Gochfeld, M. 1983. World status and distribution of the Roseate Tern, a threatened species. Biol. Conserv. 25:103–125.

Gore, J. A. 1991. Distribution and abundance of nesting Least Terns and Black Skimmers in northwest Florida. Fla. Field Nat. 19:65–72.

Hovis, J. A., and M. S. Robson. 1989. Breeding status and distribution of the Least Tern in the Florida Keys. Fla. Field Nat. 17:61–66.

Howe, M. A., R. B. Clapp, and J. S. Weske. 1978. Marine and coastal birds. MESA New York Bight Atlas Monogr. no. 31. New York Sea Grant Institute. Albany, New York. 87 pp.

Kale, H. W., II. 1985. Florida region. Amer. Birds 39:288–291.

Kushlan, J. A., and D. White. 1985. Least and Roseate tern nesting in the Florida Keys. Fla. Field Nat. 13:98–99.

Nisbet, I. C. T. 1980. Status and trends of the Roseate Tern *Sterna dougallii* in North America and the Caribbean. Unpubl. rept. to the U.S. Fish and Wildl. Serv., Office of Endangered Species. Massachusetts Aud. Soc. Lincoln, Massachusetts.

Nisbet, I. C. T. 1981a. Biological characteristics of the Roseate Tern *Sterna dougallii*. Unpubl. rept. to the U.S. Fish and Wildlife Service, Office of Endangered Species. Massachusetts Audubon Society. Lincoln, Massachusetts.

Nisbet, I. C. T. 1981b. Behavior of Common and Roseate terns after trapping. Colon. Waterbirds 4:44–46.

Nisbet, I. C. T. 1984. Migration and winter quarters of North American Roseate Terns as shown by banding recoveries. Jour. Field Ornithol. 55:1–17.

Nisbet, I. C. T. 1989. The Roseate Tern. Pp. 478–497 *in* Audubon Wildlife Report 1989/1990 (W. J. Chandler and L. Labate, eds.). Academic Press, Inc. San Diego, California.

Norton, R. L. 1980. West Indies region. Amer. Birds 34:932–933.

Norton, R. L. 1988. Extra-egg clutches and interspecific egg-dumping of the Roseate Tern (*Sterna dougallii*) in the West Indies. Fla. Field Nat. 16:67–70.

Paul, R. T. 1984. Florida region. Amer. Birds 38:1011–1013.

Paul, R. T. 1988. Florida region. Amer. Birds 42:1278–1281.

Paul, R. T. 1989. Florida region. Amer. Birds 43:1307–1310.

Peterson, R. T. 1980. A field guide to the birds. Houghton Mifflin Co., Boston, Massachusetts.

Robertson, W. B., Jr. 1962. Florida region. Aud. Field Notes 16:468–473.

Robertson, W. B., Jr. 1964. The terns of the Dry Tortugas. Bull. Fla. State Mus. 8(1):1–94.

Robertson, W. B., Jr. 1978. Roseate Tern. Pp. 39–40 *in* Rare and endangered biota of Florida, vol. II: birds (H. W. Kale, II, ed.). Univ. Presses Fla., Gainesville, Florida. 121 pp.

Robertson, W. B., Jr. Ms. Roseate Tern. Unpubl. rept. U.S. Natl. Park Serv., Everglades National Park, Homestead, Florida.

Roberston, W. B., Jr., and G. E. Woolfenden. 1992. Florida bird species—an annotated list. Fla. Ornithol. Soc. Spec. Publ. No. 6. Gainesville, Florida.

Shealer, D. A., and J. Burger. 1992. A "good" versus a "bad" year for Roseate Terns breeding in Puerto Rico. Abstract *in* Ann. meeting Colon. Waterbird Soc., 14–18 October 1992. Univ. Miss., Oxford, Mississippi.

Spendelow, J. A. 1982. An analysis of temporal variation in, and the effects of, habitat modification on reproductive success of Roseate Terns. Colon. Waterbirds 5:19–31.

Spendelow, J. A. 1991. Postfledging survival and recruitment of known-origin Roseate Terns (*Sterna dougallii*) at Falkner Island, Connecticut. Colon.

Waterbirds 14:108–115.

Sprunt, A., Jr. 1949. Status of Roseate Tern as a breeding species in southern United States. Auk 66:206–207.

Stevenson, H. M. 1977. Florida region. Amer. Birds 31:322–325.

USFWS. 1989. Roseate Tern Recovery Plan Northeastern Population. U.S. Fish and Wildl. Serv., Newton Corner, Massachusetts. 78 pp.

PREPARED BY: Henry T. Smith, Florida Department of Natural Resources, Office of Environmental Services, 3900 Commonwealth Blvd., Tallahassee, FL 32399 (Current address: Florida Department of Environmental Protection, Florida Park Service, 13798 S.E. Federal Highway, Hobe Sound, FL 33455).

White-crowned Pigeon

Columba leucocephala

FAMILY COLUMBIDAE

Order Columbiformes

TAXONOMY: The White-crowned Pigeon (*Columba leucocephala*) is one of 18 species of the genus *Columba* found in the New World (Goodwin 1983). No subspecies of White-crowned Pigeons have been recognized (AOU 1957).

DESCRIPTION: White-crowned Pigeons are approximately the size and shape of Rock Doves (*Columba livia*). They are dark slate-gray with a white top to the head. Females are noticeably less slate-gray than males and often have a brownish cast in their feathers. The female's crown is usually a duller white. On both sexes, feathers on the back of the head often have chestnut-brown tips. The nape and sides of the neck are greenish-black. In males this area is highly iridescent, less so in females. The iris is yellowish-white with a dark pupil. The iris is surrounded by two rings of bare skin: inner black and outer white. In males the white ring is often larger than that of females. The bill is red with a white tip. The bill and legs of males become bright red during the breeding season. Juvenal plumage is more brownish-gray and juveniles lack a white crown. However, they quickly begin the first prebasic molt and attain a more slate-gray plumage by early fall and a "dirty" white crown. Because of the resin on poisonwood (*Metopium toxiferum*) leaves, branches, and fruit, pigeons feeding in these trees will often pick up brown-black stains on the crown.

POPULATION SIZE AND TREND: Arendt et al. (1979) reviewed the status of the White-crowned Pigeon and listed populations as decreasing in the Bahama Islands, Cuba, Haiti, Dominican Republic, Puerto Rico, the U.S. and British Virgin Islands, Anguilla, St. Martin, and Nicaragua. Increasing or stable populations were cited in Florida, the Cayman Islands, Jamaica, Barbuda, Antigua, Mexico, Belize, Honduras, and Panama. In 1976, the breeding popu-

White-crowned
Pigeon, *Columba
leucocephala.*
(Photo by G.
Thomas Bancroft)

lation of White-crowned Pigeons in Florida was estimated at 5,000 pairs (Reeves 1977). In 1991, about 5,000 pairs were estimated to be breeding in the upper Florida Keys (Strong et al. 1994). The total breeding population in Florida is probably around 8,000 to 9,000 pairs. The actual number of birds breeding may vary from year to year. In a six-year study of the nesting biology of this bird on Middle Butternut Key in Florida Bay, the number of nest starts on study plots varied by as much as 50% (Bancroft and Bowman, unpubl. data). This variation is thought to be a result of differences in food abundance among years.

White-crowned Pigeons are permanent residents in Florida, but their population numbers are highly seasonal (Sprunt 1954; Bancroft, unpubl. data). Pigeons begin returning to Florida in large numbers in April and the numbers increase until early June. Populations remain high through the summer with the seasonal peak occurring in September when many juvenile birds are flying. Most pigeons leave Florida between mid-September and mid-October. The winter numbers are only a small percentage of the summer population. In winter, most White-crowned Pigeons from the upper Keys fly to the Bahamas and possibly south into the Greater Antilles, but some fly directly to Cuba (Paul 1977). Pigeons from the lower Keys may fly directly to Cuba and the Greater Antilles (Paul 1977).

DISTRIBUTION AND HISTORY OF DISTRIBUTION: The breeding range of White-crowned Pigeons includes the Florida Keys, the Bahama Islands, the Greater Antilles, and the Lesser Antilles south to Antigua (Bent 1932; Goodwin 1983; AOU 1983). Small populations also breed on offshore islands on the Caribbean coasts of Mexico (Quintana Roo), Belize, Honduras, Nicaragua, and possibly Panama (Bent 1932; Wetmore 1968; AOU 1983). The

Distribution map of
the White-crowned
Pigeon, *Columba
leucocephala.*

█ Breeding range
✳ Non-breeding sites

nonbreeding range is slightly larger and includes peninsular Florida north to
Fort Pierce, the Lesser Antilles south to St. Lucia, and western Panama (AOU
1983).

In Florida, Pigeons nest on mangrove islands from Biscayne Bay south
through the Marquesas Keys. More than half the Florida population nests in
Florida Bay in the upper Keys. In Florida Bay, pigeons nest on about half of
the islands, avoiding islands that have a raccoon (*Procyon lotor*) population
(Strong et al. 1991). Nesting on mainland Florida is rare (Strong et al. 1991;
Florida Breeding Bird Atlas data)

HABITAT REQUIREMENTS AND HABITAT TREND: The continued
existence of White-crowned Pigeons in the continental United States is dependent on maintaining two distinctly different habitat needs: nesting and feeding. For nesting, pigeons require mangrove-covered islands that are free of
raccoons and human disturbance. Many of their nesting keys are within Everglades National Park in the Upper Keys or National Wildlife Refuges in the
Lower Keys. Restricted public access protects these keys from human disturbance. Expansion of raccoons onto more mangrove keys could represent a
serious threat to breeding populations (Allen 1942; Strong et al. 1991). Rac-

coon distributions on mangrove keys may be limited, in part, by the frequency of large hurricanes. Human activity on the mainline Keys could cause raccoon populations to increase and accelerate the dispersal of raccoons into the heart of the pigeon's nesting range.

Pigeons require an abundant supply of fruit. The plants that produce this fruit are found in a number of habitats on the southern tip of the peninsula and in tropical hardwood forests on the Florida Keys. Because they grow on high ground, the tropical forests in the Florida Keys are under intense development pressure. Forests are being cleared daily to allow for the building of houses and businesses. The existence of Everglades National Park probably means that some nesting populations will be maintained (Strong et al. 1991), but the continued destruction and fragmentation of the hardwood forest in the Florida Keys threatens the maintenance of a large self-sustaining population (Strong and Bancroft 1994a, b).

Because most Florida White-crowned Pigeons spend part of the year outside the United States, the conservation of tropical forests in the Caribbean will affect the status of these birds in Florida. Efforts to preserve remaining fragments of forest and mangroves throughout the Caribbean will be essential for this species' survival.

VULNERABILITY OF SPECIES AND HABITAT: White-crowned Pigeons remain threatened in Florida primarily because of continued destruction of tropical forests. Remaining fragments of forest are continually being cleared for additional buildings. Within suburban neighborhoods native fruit-producing trees, particularly poisonwood, continue to be removed. These factors seriously jeopardize the food supply for this species.

In many Caribbean countries such as the Bahama Islands, White-crowned Pigeons are important game species, and in some countries subsistence hunting occurs (Blankinship 1977; Arendt et al. 1979; Wiley 1979; Wiley and Wiley 1979). Because pigeons from the United States winter in these countries, regulation of this hunting pressure also may be important for the conservation of the species in the United States.

White-crowned Pigeons are extremely wary of humans. Pigeons are flushed easily from trees by people or vehicles. It is unknown whether this disturbance has a detrimental affect on these birds' energy budget, but increased fragmentation of the remaining tropical forest is likely to increase the disturbance rate on feeding birds.

CAUSES OF THREAT: The habitats used by White-crowned Pigeons for foraging are under intense pressure as more people continue to come to the Florida Keys to live and to visit. Increasing development continues to result in the destruction of preferred upland habitats.

RESPONSES TO HABITAT MODIFICATION: Adult White-crowned Pigeons are excellent flyers and can travel over a substantial area on daily feeding trips. They respond to disturbance and clearing of forest by moving to other places. Adult birds nesting in Florida Bay regularly fly to the mainland to feed, especially when feeding conditions are poor in the Florida Keys (A. M. Strong, unpubl. data). However, nesting success is often poor during these periods (Bancroft, unpubl. data). Thus, continued loss of foraging habitat in the Keys may have a detrimental effect on nesting success.

DEMOGRAPHIC CHARACTERISTICS: In Florida, White-crowned Pigeons laid clutches from early May through early September (Bancroft and Bowman, unpubl. data). The onset and termination of nesting were linked to fruit availability. The number of clutches laid during the season also was linked to fruit availability. The number of new clutches laid per week showed a bimodal pattern during the season. An initial peak occurred in late May to mid-June. The number of new starts per week decreased during late June to early July before increasing to the seasonal peak in late July to early August. The second major period of nesting was tied to the ripening of poisonwood fruit. Based on 987 nests followed during 5 reproductive seasons (1985-1989), 45.1% were laid during July, 30.2% in August, 16.7% in June, 7.1% in May, and 1% in September. Over the five-year period, the August peak in active nests was more than twice the June peak.

White-crowned Pigeons typically lay 2 eggs. Of 1076 clutches found in Florida, 88.1% contained 2 eggs, 11.2% contained 1 egg, and 0.7% contained 3 eggs (Bancroft and Bowman, unpubl. data). Some 1-egg clutches may have had a second egg that disappeared before the nest was found. Some of the 3-egg clutches were thought to have resulted from a second female dumping one egg in the nest, but a few probably were true 3-egg clutches. Freshly laid eggs averaged 13.1 g (N = 465). Eggs averaged 35.3 mm in length, 26.0 mm in width, and 12.1 cc in volume (N = 1802). Eggs laid in July and August had significantly larger volumes than those laid in May and June.

Incubation begins with the laying of the first egg and eggs hatch 13 to 14 days later (Wiley and Wiley 1979). Generally eggs hatch on successive days. Young will leave the nest when 16 to 22 days old but remain on the nesting key up to 40 days post-hatching. These young are fed by the adults throughout this period. When food was scarce often the youngest nestling would disappear and presumably starved.

Nesting success of White-crowned Pigeons was low with only 32.2% of 429 clutches monitored over 5 years producing fledglings (Bancroft and Bowman, unpubl. data). Between years, nesting success varied from 51.6% in 1988 to 20.4% in 1989. Nesting success also varied seasonally in many years. Variation in nesting success was correlated with general food availability. Nesting numbers, nesting success, and survivorship of young increase when poisonwood fruits ripen. Poisonwood fruit is extremely high in lipids and low in water content, making the fruit the best energy source, and pigeons often digest the seeds of poisonwood. Most losses of eggs and young were attributed to predation, but predation intensity also appeared to be inversely related to food availability.

KEY BEHAVIORS: White-crowned Pigeons are semiterritorial on the nesting Keys (Wiley and Wiley 1979; Bancroft, pers. observ.). Male White-crowned Pigeons will actively supplant and chase other males entering their territory. Males do "display" flights, give "advertisement" and "display" calls from exposed perches within their territories to defend against other males and to attract a female (Wiley and Wiley 1979). Display flights consist of an alternating sequence of slow, short wing beats and short glides that leave from an advertisement perch and return to the perch or its vicinity. Pair formation occurs on the territory after the male and female go through a series of courtship displays on exposed perches (Wiley and Wiley 1979).

Both the male and female build the nest (Wiley and Wiley 1979). Generally the male fetches nesting materials and passes them to the female who places them in the nest. The pair uses a series of "nest" and "growl" calls during nest exchanges (Wiley and Wiley 1979). Male White-crowned Pigeons care for eggs and nestlings during the day, while females care for them during the night (Wiley and Wiley 1979; A. M. Strong and R. J. Sawicki, unpubl. data). Nest exchanges generally occur during mid-morning and early evening. At about day 5 in the nestling period, attendance by the male begins to decrease and within a few days males only remain long enough to feed the young. Females continue to return to the nest key for the night, at least until young leave the nest.

While nesting, adult pigeons produce an excretion from the epithelial lining of their crop with which they feed their young. When young first hatch this material, known as crop-milk, represents 100% of the chicks' diet (Bancroft and Bowman 1994). Adults begin supplementing the crop milk diet with fruit when young are 3 days old (Bancroft and Bowman 1994). The proportion of the diet composed of fruit increases as the chicks grow.

On foraging trips from nesting islands, adults may fly only a few kilometers to over 45 km to feeding sites; however, on a given trip they usually feed in an area less than 0.5 km^2 (A. M. Strong and R. J. Sawicki, unpubl. data). Individuals often show feeding-site fidelity, returning to the same area over a period of weeks before shifting to a new site. In contrast to the long flights of adults, initial flights of young birds from nesting keys are generally to the closest land containing tropical forests (Strong and Bancroft 1994a). Young most often fledge to forest fragments that are larger than 5 ha in size. These larger fragments may be important for allowing the young to learn to forage without excessive human disturbance.

In the Florida Keys, White-crowned Pigeons feed on fruit of at least 35 species of trees and shrubs (Bancroft, unpubl. data). For most of these species, pigeons digest only the pulp and either pass or regurgitate the seed. The fruits of four species of trees are extremely important for successful nesting (Bancroft and Bowman 1994): poisonwood, blolly (*Guapira discolor*), strangler fig (*Ficus aurea*), and short-leaf fig (*F. citrifolia*). Poisonwood is by far the most important. Outside of the breeding season, pigeons also feed heavily on fruits of sea grape (*Coccoloba uvifera*), pigeon plum (*C. diversifolia*), strongbark (*Bourreria ovata*), snowberry (*Chiococca alba*), mastic (*Mastichodendron foetidissimum*), and gumbo-limbo (*Bursera simaruba*).

CONSERVATION MEASURES TAKEN: In Florida, the White-crowned Pigeon is listed as a "threatened" species by the Florida Game and Fresh Water Fish Commission (Wood 1990) and is under consideration for federal listing by the U. S. Fish and Wildlife Service. Because of the continued destruction and fragmentation of forests in the Florida Keys, the health of the White-crowned Pigeon population in Florida will continue to be threatened into the foreseeable future.

CONSERVATION MEASURES PROPOSED: Five major steps need to be taken to ensure that the White-crowned Pigeon will remain a bird of the Florida Keys. The Florida Game and Fresh Water Fish Commission, U. S. Fish and Wildlife Service, Monroe County, and the Florida Department of Environmental Protection should work together to have these recommendations implemented.

(1). An accelerated acquisition program should be undertaken immediately for remaining hardwood forests in the Florida Keys (Strong and Bancroft 1994a; Bancroft et al. 1995). This program should immediately attempt to acquire as many of the remaining fragments (> 5 ha) of hardwood forest as possible. A management plan for these forest fragments that will help maintain species diversity in the Keys will benefit White-crowned Pigeons.

(2). Educational and regulatory programs should be implemented that encourage people to plant native, fruit-producing trees in their yards. Blolly and strongbark should be high on the list of suggested plants because these plants provide fruit during the nesting season.

(3). Fruit of poisonwood is extremely important for successful nesting by large numbers of pigeons (Bancroft and Bowman 1994). Poisonwood, however, causes severe dermatitis on many people and as a result this species is typically removed from people's yards. Currently, this tree is abundant and needs to remain abundant throughout the Keys. Poisonwood should be allowed to grow on habitat preserves and encouraged to grow in places where it does not threaten human activities.

(4). Collisions with high-power lines represent a major source of mortality for White-crowned Pigeons in south Florida (Bancroft, pers. obs.). Multiple lines on a pole that are at different elevations above the ground probably represent a greater risk to flying birds than multiple lines that are at the same elevation above the ground. This hazard needs to be studied and dealt with.

(5). Maintaining a population of White-crowned Pigeons in Florida will require that migratory and wintering habitat also be maintained for this species. The Florida Game and Fresh Water Fish Commission and the U.S. Fish and Wildlife Service should work closely with conservation and management personnel in the natural resources departments of Caribbean governments to ensure the conservation of critical habitats for White-crowned Pigeons and to prevent over harvesting and illegal taking of White-crowned Pigeons. The Bahamas, Cuba, and Hispaniola probably are especially important for birds from Florida.

ACKNOWLEDGMENTS: I thank R. Bowman, M. Carrington, R. J. Sawicki, and A. M. Strong for sharing their insights into White-crowned Pigeon biology with me. Our work on White-crowned Pigeons has been supported by grants from the Florida Game and Fresh Water Fish Commission and from the John D. and Catherine T. MacArthur Foundation. R. J. Sawicki and A. M. Strong read and improved an earlier version of this manuscript.

LITERATURE CITED:

Allen, R. P. 1942. The Roseate Spoonbill. Dover Publications, Inc., New York, New York.

AOU. 1957. Check-list of North American birds. 5th ed. American Ornithologists' Union, Washington, D. C.

AOU. 1983. Check-list of North American birds. 6th ed. American Ornithologists' Union, Washington, D.C.

Arendt, W. J., T. A. Vargas Mora, and J. W. Wiley. 1979. White-crowned Pigeon: status rangewide and in the Dominican Republic. Proc. Ann. Conf. S.E. Assoc. Fish & Wildl. Agencies 33:111–122.

Bancroft, G. T., and R. Bowman. 1994. Temporal patterns in diet of nestling White-crowned Pigeons: implications for conservation of frugivorous columbids. Auk 111:842-850.

Bancroft, G. T., A. M. Strong, and M. Carrington. 1995. Deforestation and its effects on forest-nesting birds in the Florida Keys. Conserv. Biol. 9:835-844.

Bent, A. C. 1932. Life histories of North American gallinaceous birds. U. S. Nat. Mus. Bull. no. 162.

Blankinship, D. R. 1977. Studies of White-crowned Pigeon populations, natural history and hunting in the Bahamas. Pp. 36–39 in Proceedings of the International White-crowned Pigeon Conference. Bahamas National Trust, Nassau, Bahamas.

Goodwin, D. 1983. Pigeons and doves of the world. Third edition. Cornell Univ. Press, Ithaca, New York.

Paul, R. T. 1977. Banding studies of the White-crowned Pigeon in Florida and the Bahamas. Pg. 25–35 in Proceedings of the International White-crowned Pigeon Conference. Bahamas National Trust, Nassau, Bahamas.

Reeves, H. M. 1977. White-crowned Pigeons in the United States. Pg. 10 in Proceedings of the International White-crowned Pigeon Conference. Bahamas National Trust, Nassau, Bahamas.

Sprunt, A., Jr. 1954. Florida bird life. Coward-McCann, Inc., New York. 527 pp.

Strong, A. M., and G. T. Bancroft. 1994a. Postfledging dispersal of White-crowned Pigeons: implications for conservation of deciduous seasonal forests in the Florida Keys. Conserv. Biol. 8:770–779.

Strong, A. M., and G. T. Bancroft. 1994b. Patterns of deforestation and fragmentation of mangrove and deciduous seasonal forests in the upper Florida Keys. Bull. Mar. Sci. 54:795–804.

Strong, A. M., R. J. Sawicki, and G. T. Bancroft. 1991. Effects of predator presence on the nesting distribution of White-crowned Pigeons in Florida Bay. Wilson Bull. 103:414–425.

Strong, A. M., R. J. Sawicki, and G. T. Bancroft. 1994. Estimating White-crowned Pigeon population size from flight-line counts. Jour. Wild. Manage. 58:156–162.

Wetmore, A. 1968. The birds of the Republic of Panama. Part 2. Columbidae (pigeons) to Picidae (woodpeckers). Smithsonian Misc. Coll. Vol. 150. Smithsonian Inst. Press, Washington, D.C.

Wetmore, A., and B. H. Swales. 1931. The birds of Haiti and the Dominican Republic. U.S. Natl. Mus. Bull. no. 155. Washington, D.C.

Wiley, J. W. 1979. The White-crowned Pigeon in Puerto Rico: status, distribution and movements. Jour. Wildl. Manage. 43:402–413.

Wiley, J. W., and B. N. Wiley. 1979. The Biology of the White-crowned Pigeon. Wildl. Monogr. 64.

Wood, D. A. 1990. Official lists of endangered and potentially endangered fauna and flora in Florida. 1 August 1990. Fla. Game and Fresh Water Fish Comm., Tallahassee, Florida, 23 pp.

PREPARED BY: G. Thomas Bancroft, National Audubon Society, 115 Indian Mound Trail, Tavernier, Florida 33070 (Current address: Archbold Biological Station, P.O. Box 2057, Lake Placid, FL 33862).

Florida Scrub-Jay

Aphelocoma coerulescens

FAMILY CORVIDAE

Order Passeriformes

TAXONOMY: The Florida Scrub-Jay (*Aphelocoma coerulescens*) is a disjunct member of a species complex otherwise restricted to western North America. Described originally as a distinct species, the Florida population was considered a subspecies during the last several decades (Pitelka 1951; AOU 1944, 1957) until recently when it regained recognition as a full species (Sibley and Monroe 1990; Fitzpatrick and Woolfenden, in review; AOU, in press). Following its isolation, probably in late Pliocene or early Pleistocene times, the Florida population diverged extensively from its western counterparts. Now, important differences exist in plumage, morphology, vocalizations, display and social behavior. The Florida Scrub-Jay also is distinct genetically, with reduced genetic variation and several unique alleles that appear to be fixed (Peterson 1990, 1992; Fitzpatrick and Woolfenden, in review). Both genetic and phenotypic differences between scrub-jays from Florida and from western North America are comparable to, or greater than, those between numerous other species-pairs found in North America. For these reasons, the AOU (in press) currently recognizes three species: Western Scrub-Jay (*A. californica*), Island Scrub-Jay (*A. insularis*), and Florida Scrub-Jay (*A. coerulescens*). The Florida Scrub-Jay represents the only bird species entirely restricted to Florida.

Work in progress on nuclear DNA indicates that even within Florida, considerable genetic differentiation has occurred (W. Potts et al., in prep.). These local divergences reflect the extremely sedentary behavior of the Florida Scrub-Jay, combined with the patchy historical distribution of its habitat.

DESCRIPTION: About 26 cm (10 in.) long, the Florida Scrub-Jay is similar in size and shape to its well known and widely distributed close relative, the Blue Jay (*Cyanocitta cristata*). The predominant colors of both species are blue and white, but the two differ strikingly in color pattern. Blue Jays are bright blue above, boldly marked with many white-tipped, black-barred feath-

Florida Scrub-Jay, *Aphelocoma coerulescens*. (Photo copyright 1990 by Brian R. Toland)

ers, and have a black bridle pattern about the head and neck. They also have pure white underparts and an ample crest. Scrub-Jays have no crest and lack the white tips, black barring, and bridle. They have a pale blue head, nape, wings, and tail, and are pale gray on the back and belly. A white eyebrow blends with a frosted white forehead. (In Scrub-Jays from western North America the forehead is blue and a thin white eyebrow is more distinct.) Throat and upper breast are faintly striped and bordered by pale blue, forming a distinct bib.

In contrast to Blue Jays, Florida Scrub-Jays have longer, stronger feet, a longer tail, and shorter wings, reflecting their more terrestrial lifestyle. Whereas the forest-inhabiting Blue Jay regularly flies long distances, the Florida Scrub-Jay is extremely sedentary and rarely sustains a flight of more than a kilometer. Many Blue Jay populations (especially north of Florida) are partially migratory. Florida Scrub-Jays are entirely nonmigratory.

The sexes of Florida Scrub-Jays are nearly identical in plumage. Males on average are only slightly larger than females (Woolfenden 1978); only females develop a brood patch. Young Florida Scrub-Jays are easily distinguished from adults for approximately five months of their lives. Hatched naked, they are well feathered before they leave the nest. The lax juvenal plumage is smoky gray on the head and back, entirely lacking the blue crown and nape of adults.

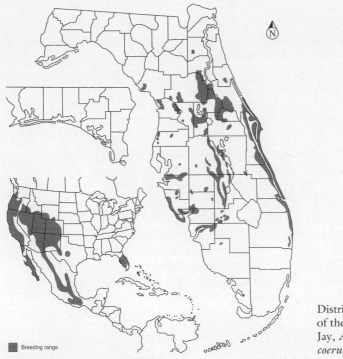

Distribution map
of the Florida Scrub-
Jay, *Aphelocoma
coerulescens.*

Breeding range

An incomplete molt during summer makes juveniles nearly indistinguishable from adults thereafter.

POPULATION SIZE AND TREND: Recently the total population of Florida Scrub-Jays was estimated to be 7,000–11,000 individuals (Breininger 1989). Supporting this figure, a 1992 compilation of estimates across the entire range yielded an overall population of approximately 4,000 pairs or about 9,500–11,000 individuals (Fitzpatrick et al., ms.). A large portion of the total population may occur on or near two large, federally owned tracts of land, Merritt Island National Wildlife Refuge (NWR) plus the adjacent Kennedy Space Center and Patrick Air Force Base, and Ocala National Forest (NF). Breininger (1989) estimated the Merritt Island population to be 1,400–3,600 jays, and Cox (1987) estimated the Ocala NF population to be 2,600–3,400 jays. We now believe that the Ocala NF population numbers about 1,500 jays or fewer. Florida Scrub-Jay populations are declining on both of these federally owned lands, and this trend will continue unless current land management practices are modified. The largest regional concentration of Florida Scrub-Jays occurs in scattered patches on the Lake Wales Ridge in Polk and, especially, Highlands Counties. The major protected population in this region is at and near Archbold Biological Station, a private ecological research station located in southern Highlands County, which manages about 2,000 ha of mostly oak scrub. About 300 jays in 100 territories are protected at Archbold, and an additional 150 jays in 50 territories exist on the adjacent, newly protected Lake Placid Scrub Preserve.

All major Florida Scrub-Jay populations are known to be declining as of 1992, and none is known to be increasing in numbers. Decline of Florida Scrub-Jays has resulted from habitat loss, habitat fragmentation, and habitat modification (mostly through the suppression of fire). Scrub soils in Florida have been used by humans for agriculture and development since the early 1900s, and conversion has accelerated during the past few decades. Cox (1987) estimated that the total population of Florida Scrub-Jays has declined at least 50% from its original level. We suspect that the decline has been considerably greater. For example, about 85% of the original scrub habitat of the Lake Wales Ridge has been destroyed (Archbold Biological Station, unpubl. data). Scrub habitat elsewhere throughout peninsular Florida has lost at least as great a proportion of its original extent (Fernald 1989). Furthermore, fire suppression in many existing tracts of scrub (e.g., Ocala NF) has caused local jay populations to decline or disappear throughout the peninsula. We conclude that as of 1993, Florida Scrub-Jay numbers represented no more than 10–20% of the original presettlement population.

DISTRIBUTION AND HISTORY OF DISTRIBUTION: The Scrub-Jay complex occurs in western North America from the state of Washington to Oaxaca, Mexico, with disjunct populations in peninsular Florida and on Santa Cruz Island off southern California. The AOU Check-list (1957) lists 13 subspecies. Pitelka (1951) recognized four discrete groups of subspecies, which are largely supported by recent genetic comparisons (Peterson 1992). (1) The "californica" group ranges from Washington through California into Baja California. Pitelka included the Santa Cruz population (*A. c. insularis*) in this group, but Peterson (1992) and the AOU (in press) treat it as a distinct species. (2) The "woodhouseii" group ranges from Nevada, Wyoming and Colorado south to central Mexico. (3) The "sumichrasti" group is restricted to Mexico and ranges from the Distrito Federal south to the Isthmus of Tehuantepec. (4) "coerulescens" is restricted to Florida.

Florida Scrub-Jays are found only in a relict, patchy habitat—the xeric oak scrub. Historically oak scrub occurred as numerous isolated patches, which were concentrated along both the Atlantic and Gulf coasts and on the central ridges of the peninsula (Davis 1967). Probably until as recently as the 1950s, Florida Scrub-Jay populations occurred in the scrub habitats of 39 of the 40 counties south of, and including Levy, Gilchrist, Alachua, Clay, and Duval counties. Only the southernmost county, Monroe, lacked Florida Scrub-Jays. As of 1993, the species was functionally or completely eliminated from 10 of the 39 counties (Alachua, Broward, Clay, Dade, Duval, Gilchrist, Hernando,

Hendry, Pinellas, and St. Johns). Numbers are reduced to 10 or fewer pairs in five other counties (Flagler, Hardee, Levy, Orange, and Putnam). Populations in all counties along the Gulf coast (from Levy south to Collier) are perilously close to being eliminated. Extensive clearing of scrub in these counties has left only small and distantly isolated populations, most of which live close to or among rapidly expanding human development.

HABITAT REQUIREMENTS AND HABITAT TRENDS: The oak scrub to which Florida Scrub-Jays are restricted is a peculiar vegetation formation found only on extremely well-drained sandy soils formed by old coastal dunes or paleodunes (Laessle 1958, 1968). Davis (1967) mapped the scrubs of Florida. The indigenous plants are adapted to nutrient-poor soils, periodic drought, high seasonal rainfall, and frequent fires. The most characteristic and, for the jays, essential plants are four stunted, low-growing oaks, which occur in vary-ing percentages in scrubs around the peninsula: *Quercus geminata, Q. chapmanii, Q. myrtifolia* and *Q. inopina* (the last is endemic to the Florida interior, mainly on the Lake Wales Ridge). In optimal habitat most of the oaks and other shrubs are between 1 and 4 m tall, and interspersed with numerous, small patches of bare sand. Trees are few and scattered, with canopy cover rarely exceeding 15% in occupied habitat. Herbaceous vegetation is sparse. The dominant trees are slash pines (*Pinus elliottii*) and sand pines (*P. clausa*). Slash pines tend to occur in lower areas, sand pines and Florida rosemary (*Ceratiola ericoides*) on the highest dune tops. Along with the oaks, two palmettos (*Serenoa repens* and *Sabal etonia* [interior only]), and several woody shrubs (especially of genera *Lyonia, Vaccinium, Carya, Befaria,* and *Osmanthus*) comprise most of the remaining dominant plants.

Fire is a frequent natural event in scrub habitats. From May to September, ground strikes by lightning are common in peninsular Florida. Lightning fires probably occurred at intervals of 8–20 years in most types of scrub during presettlement times (Myers 1990; Ostertag and Menges 1994). Natural fires usually leave many patches of scrub unburned. As a result entire Florida Scrub-Jay territories (average 10 ha or 25 ac.) rarely are completely burned.

Elimination of scrub habitat through human activities has occurred through-out the Florida Scrub-Jay's native range. Conversion of scrub habitat to citrus groves and dwellings proceeded throughout the 20th century, with rapid acceleration in the 1950s and 1960s. Continued loss of habitat to rural resi-dential development, mobile-home parks, industrial construction, shopping malls, golf courses and other recreational uses closely tracked the rapid growth of the human population in Florida throughout the 1970s and 1980s. Con-version of scrub to citrus groves no doubt eliminated scrub and jays from hundreds of xeric-soil patches as early as the 1920s. Major killing freezes caused rapid southward expansion of the citrus industry in the 1970s and 1980s, especially in the interior peninsula, which resulted in the elimination of much additional scrub. Scrub land vacated by citrus growers is not restored to its natural condition and rarely reverts to a habitat suitable for Florida Scrub-Jays.

Fire suppression by humans has caused many of the remaining patches of scrub to become tall (>3 m) and dense, with a canopy of oaks and pines and a thick leaf litter. Under these conditions, death rates for breeding adults exceeds recruitment (Fitzpatrick and Woolfenden 1986). This demographic scenario inevitably causes the jays to die out. Entire local populations of Florida Scrub-Jays have disappeared as a result, despite the persistence of native xeric vegetation.

VULNERABILITY OF SPECIES AND HABITAT: The Florida Scrub-Jay is vulnerable to extinction because the scrub vegetation to which it is restricted is being eliminated. If humans decide to save scrub habitat in sizable tracts and keep these tracts in natural condition, then the Florida Scrub-Jay will persist.

At present, many of the largest existing Florida Scrub-Jay populations occur on privately owned land. Most of these tracts are scheduled to have the scrub vegetation replaced by citrus groves or residential and commercial development in the near future. Other tracts may not be converted soon, but are losing their native character, and their jays, because of fire suppression.

Fortunately, the Florida Scrub-Jay is a classic "flagship" species. It attracts public and media attention because of its beauty and charisma. More important, preservation of scrub tracts large enough to maintain viable populations of the jays around the peninsula also will help preserve the many other organisms, including the many endangered species, that are restricted to the Florida scrub (Neill 1957; Christman and Judd 1990).

CAUSES OF THREAT: The excessively drained, sandy soils of the Florida scrub are excellent for growing citrus and for constructing human dwellings, businesses, and recreational areas that are safe from flooding. In addition, with fertilizer many scrub soils can support exotic forage grasses, and therefore are converted to low-grade pastures for beef or dairy cattle.

Because the Florida Scrub-Jay is restricted to scrub habitats, and because scrub soils continue to increase in value for human use, the bird could disappear entirely except in a few isolated habitat preserves. Long-term persistence of the jays is not guaranteed on any one of these preserves. Fragmentation of the jay's native range can be corrected only by continued acquisition and management of suitable habitat as corridors or "stepping-stones" between existing preserves and by conscientious management of private lands to protect xeric habitats outside of preserves.

RESPONSES TO HABITAT MODIFICATION: So far as is known, essentially all human modifications of oak scrub cause Florida Scrub-Jay populations to decline. As discussed above, the jay cannot tolerate outright replacement of scrub vegetation with exotic plants (e.g., citrus, forage grasses, Brazilian pepper [*Schinus terebinthefolius*], lawns, etc.) or significant reduction of fire frequency. After a few decades without fire, scrub becomes pine or oak woodland with a dense layer of tall shrubs and a continuous leaf litter lacking bare sand. Florida Scrub-Jays die out in these areas, perhaps in part because of competition with Blue Jays.

Although necessary in the long term, burning has the immediate effect of temporarily reducing cover, nest sites, and acorn crops for the jays. Therefore, burns that are too frequent or too complete also may cause Florida Scrub-Jay populations to die out. Some evidence suggests that in the recent past, burning too frequently has caused oak scrub at Merritt Island NWR to convert to palmetto-dominated areas with abnormally low jay densities. Although frequent or complete fires may simplify the process of prescribed-burn management, they are not a genuine facsimile of natural fires in the oak scrub of Florida. Chopping scrub vegetation may be a viable management practice to replace fire where burning is impractical, but the long-term consequences of this approach remain untested.

Important human modifications that probably decrease Florida Scrub-Jay populations include high-speed vehicular traffic and high densities of domestic cats. Therefore, proximity to paved roads and human dwellings are factors that must be considered when designing scrub preserves.

Recent evidence from several suburban sites suggests that Florida Scrub-Jays may persist locally in otherwise marginal or unsuitable areas because they are supplied extra food by humans (Bowman, Thaxton, and Toland, unpubl. data). However, recruitment in food-supplemented populations appears to be lower than in populations occupying native habitat. Furthermore, Florida Scrub-Jays require at least some native scrub habitat for nesting. Therefore, bird-feeding by humans may postpone the elimination of Florida Scrub-Jays from residential neighborhoods but cannot ensure their persistence in the absence of protected, native oak scrub. Moreover, local densities during nonbreeding seasons are sometimes elevated by supplementary food, even though breeding densities may not be elevated. Therefore, artificial feeding may cause certain areas to act as population "sinks," trapping dispersing jays during the summer and fall but failing to supply the necessary habitat to support them during breeding season (R. Bowman, unpubl. data). Such a result could have serious long-term implications for managing wild populations in proximity to residential development.

DEMOGRAPHIC CHARACTERISTICS: In good habitat, territory size of Florida Scrub-Jays averages 9–10 ha (22–25 ac.), with a minimum size of about 5 ha (12 ac.). In extensive good habitat, territorial defense by the family groups results in a mosaic of contiguous territories, with no space left undefended.

Group size ranges from 2 to 8 jays. However, at the onset of the nesting season most groups consist of the pair alone or the pair and one or two "helpers." The helpers are offspring from the most recent breeding season, plus any nondispersers from earlier breeding seasons. Most of the nonbreeding individuals are offspring of at least one member of the resident pair.

To become a breeder, a Florida Scrub-Jay must gain a territory as well as a mate. Typically a male either replaces a lost breeder in a nearby territory or establishes sole occupancy of a portion of his natal territory. If he "buds off" a segment of his natal space, a dispersing female from another group joins him. Occasionally, a new pair establishes a territory *de novo* in previously unoccupied scrub, or a male inherits his entire natal territory following the death of his parents. Under these circumstances, as in "territorial budding," the male's mate must be a disperser from another family. A strong incest taboo makes pairing with close relatives rare. Male Florida Scrub-Jays dominate females, which prevents females from maintaining territories without a mate (Woolfenden and Fitzpatrick 1986).

Most recruits to the breeding ranks settle within two territories of their natal ground. Maximum known dispersal is 24 km (33 mi.), but all documented long-distance dispersals (>8 km or 5 mi.) have traversed some unsuitable habitat such as pastures or suburbs. Females disperse farther than males, and they make more attempts. Prebreeding females experience a higher mortality than either prebreeding males or breeding pairs, which suggests that dispersal attempts are a dangerous activity.

Almost no Florida Scrub-Jays breed before the age of 2 years. Older prebreeders that fail to acquire breeding space almost always return to their natal area, where they help the resident breeders defend the territory and rear offspring. Three years after fledging, most females are either breeding or dead. Males tend to remain longer as helpers, sometimes up to 5 or more years.

Nesting extends only from mid-March through June, and its initiation within local populations is highly synchronous. Most nests fail, almost always from predation. Renesting may occur once or twice per season, but true second-brood attempts are rare except where *ad libitum* food is supplied by humans.

Clutch size averages 3.4 eggs (Murray et al. 1989), with a known range of 1 to 5. Clutches average significantly larger at 3.7 near artificial food sources (Bowman, pers. comm.), and included a unique 6-egg clutch (Thaxton, pers. comm.). The incubation period is 18 days and fledging occurs 16–21 days after hatching.

Average production of young is about 2 fledglings per pair per year, with a population range from less than 1 to almost 3. Survival of fledglings to the age of 1 year averages 35%, normally ranging from 21 to 44%. Breeder mortality averages about 24% per year, normally ranging from 4 to 39%. Mortality of male and female breeders is equal.

Once in 26 years at Archbold, mortality of all age classes, and especially among juveniles and the oldest breeders, rose dramatically, presumably the result of an epidemic. The 1979 year class was nearly eliminated (99% mortality) and breeder mortality was abnormally high during fall and winter, 1979–1980. From spring 1979 to spring 1980, annual mortality of all breeders was 45%. Breeder density and reproductive success were extremely low in 1980.

Using known values of mean and variance for demographic variables obtained at Archbold, we developed a simulation model of the relationship between initial population size and probability of extinction caused by random demographic fluctuations. Assuming an epidemic frequency of once every 20 to 50 years, local Florida Scrub-Jay populations have better than 90% probability of surviving more than 100 years only if at least 30 territories exist within easy dispersal distance of one another. Additional information regarding demography and the conservation of viable populations is published in Fitzpatrick and Woolfenden (1986), Woolfenden and Fitzpatrick (1991), and Fitzpatrick et al. (1991).

KEY BEHAVIORS: Florida Scrub-Jays live most of their lives as members of a group and conduct most daily activities in close proximity to their group members. Five activities account for almost all their behavior: body maintenance, foraging, nesting, predator surveillance and defense, and territory defense.

Florida Scrub-Jays forage in the low-growing, open shrub habitat by hopping through the vegetation or along the ground beneath the vegetation, visually searching for prey in the shrubs, palmettos, leaf litter, or bare sand. The animal diet of the jays is broad, but consists mostly of insects gleaned from the vegetation. Orthopterans, especially crickets and grasshoppers, and lepidopteran larvae are major components. A variety of small terrestrial vertebrates and some seeds and berries constitute a lesser portion of the diet.

Acorns are by far the most important plant food. From August to November, in addition to eating many acorns, each jay caches several thousand throughout its territory, usually 1–2 cm beneath the surface of bare sand. Cached acorns are retrieved and eaten any time of the year, but mostly in winter and early spring, when animal food is scarce (DeGange et al. 1989).

Nests are built in shrubs (mostly oaks), usually about 1 m above ground, and consist of a bulky platform of twigs supporting a tight inner cup woven from cabbage palm or palmetto (mostly from *S. palmetto* or *S. etonia*) fibers. Both members of the pair build the nest. Abandoned nests last several years, but once deserted, neither the nest nor its material is used again for any purpose.

Only the female incubates and broods. During incubation the male delivers much food to his mate. The breeding female leaves the nest daily for foraging and body maintenance, at which time the nest usually is left unguarded. Nestlings and fledglings are fed by both parents and usually by all prebreeders present in the group. Once they become volent, the dependent young begin to forage on their own but also follow the foraging adults, begging frequently and loudly for food. By the age of 3 months the young probably can find sufficient food to be considered nutritionally independent.

A well-developed sentinel system exists, in which one member of the group sits on an exposed perch above the shrubbery watching for predators or territory intruders (McGowan and Woolfenden 1989; Hailman et al. 1994). When a flying predator is spotted nearby, the sentinel jay gives a distinctive warning call and all group members dive for cover in dense shrubbery. Ground predators and certain perched raptors are mobbed with harsh scolds, attack flights, and sometimes direct contact.

Predators of adults include the eastern coachwhip (*Masticophis flagellum*), indigo snake (*Drymarchon corais*), Sharp-shinned Hawk (*Accipiter striatus*), Cooper's Hawk (*A. cooperii*), Northern Harrier (*Circus cyaneus*), Merlin (*Falco columbarius*), bobcat (*Felis rufus*), and the introduced house cat (*F. catus*). Predators of eggs or small young, in addition to certain of the aforementioned species, include other snake species, the Blue Jay, two crows (*Corvus* spp.), Eastern Screech-Owls (*Otus asio*), Great Horned Owl (*Bubo virginianus*), Red-tailed Hawk (*Buteo jamaicensis*), and several mammals (probably especially the raccoon [*Procyon lotor*]).

Daily, the monogamous pair and any associated nonbreeders defend their large territories from neighboring groups by displaying, vocalizing, chasing, and sometimes fighting. Because they live in low-growing, open habitat territory, intruders are rather easily detected.

Where not persecuted, Florida Scrub-Jays can become remarkably tame to humans. At many localities, Florida Scrub-Jays routinely perch within inches or even on the hands and heads of humans. This confiding behavior, combined with the fact that they are diurnal and live in low-growing, open habitat where they are easy to see, makes the Florida Scrub-Jay a popular bird at public parks, golf courses, and residential developments that retain some native upland habitat. Woolfenden and Fitzpatrick (1984, 1990) provide much additional information on behavior and ecology.

CONSERVATION MEASURES TAKEN: The Florida Scrub-Jay was listed as threatened by the Florida Game and Fresh Water Fish Commission (FGFWFC) in 1975 and by the U. S. Fish and Wildlife Service (USFWS) in 1987. These agencies now urge or require on-site or off-site mitigation for habitat loss caused by development throughout the range of the species. The

FGFWFC has published guidelines for habitat protection in relation to commercial or residential development (Fitzpatrick et al. 1991). Habitat preserves for protection and management of Florida scrub now exist in many parts of the jay's range, and more are proposed by both state and federal agencies (see below). Private conservation groups throughout peninsular Florida (especially The Nature Conservancy and Archbold Biological Station) are actively acquiring scrub and are collaborating with public agencies to identify and acquire additional, important scrub tracts. A statewide biological framework for habitat conservation plans is being developed to help guide the USFWS in issuing permits for "incidental take" (Fitzpatrick et al., in review). The FGFWFC, Florida Audubon Society, USFWS, and Archbold have produced printed and video information as an educational campaign to increase public awareness of the unique Florida scrub habitat, including its jays.

The first experimental translocation of Florida Scrub-Jays for purposes of reintroduction was performed by R. L. Mumme and T. H. Below, with support from the FGFWFC and Archbold. Although the results are encouraging, the process still is in a research phase, as additional translocations have been performed to sustain the populations. Relocation should not be adopted as a way to mitigate for the clearing of Florida Scrub-Jay habitat, primarily because suitable but unoccupied scrub habitat is extremely rare, and because expensive long-term management and follow-up study still is required to ensure that any relocation is successful, biologically meaningful, and informative.

CONSERVATION MEASURES PROPOSED: No substitute exists for managing what remains of the oak scrub of Florida in its natural condition. The fate of the Florida Scrub-Jay depends entirely on how the few remaining tracts of scrub are managed, both on private and on public land. Enforcing existing federal laws regarding management of federal lands as natural ecosystems supporting endangered species is essential to increase and secure the Florida Scrub-Jay populations in Merritt Island NWR, Patrick Air Force Base, and Ocala NF.

On federal, state, and private lands, prescribed burning programs should be designed to replicate the natural seasons, intensities, and intervals for fires. Such programs ultimately would restore much overgrown scrub to its former natural condition, thereby increasing local jay populations and possibly even supplying suitable habitat for reintroduction.

An aggressive program to acquire and protect the few remaining high-quality tracts of scrub is urgently needed, before these tracts disappear. Florida's Conservation and Recreational Lands program (CARL) has ranked several xeric scrub tracts among the highest priority areas for acquisition in Florida, and recently has purchased several important tracts for habitat protection. The

USFWS has created a new Lake Wales Ridge National Wildlife Refuge. These programs need active public support and additional funding in order to succeed.

ACKNOWLEDGMENTS: We thank Archbold Biological Station for extensive support through the years, and we gratefully acknowledge the National Science Foundation for several grants that have helped generate information reported here (BSR-8705443, BSR-8996276, BSR-9021902). This account summarizes portions of a report recently published by the FGFWFC (Fitzpatrick et al. 1991), for which the authors received modest support from that agency.

LITERATURE CITED:

AOU. 1944. Nineteenth supplement to the American Ornithologists' Union checklist of North American birds. Auk 61:441–464.

AOU. 1957. Check-list of North American birds, 5th ed. American Ornithologists' Union, Lawrence, Kansas.

AOU. In press. Fortieth supplement to the North American Ornithologists' Union checklist of North American birds. Auk.

Breininger, D. R. 1989. A new population estimate for the Florida Scrub-Jay on Merritt Island National Wildlife Refuge. Fla. Field Nat. 17:25–31.

Christman, S. P., and W. S. Judd. 1990. Notes on plants endemic to Florida scrub. Fla. Sci. 53:52–73.

Cox, J. A. 1987. Status and distribution of the Florida Scrub-Jay. Fla. Ornithol. Soc. Spec. Pub. no. 3, 110 pp.

Davis, J. H. 1967. General map of the natural vegetation of Florida. Agricultural Exp. Sta., Inst. of Food and Agricultural Sci., Univ. of Florida, Gainesville, Florida.

DeGange, A. R., J. W. Fitzpatrick, J. N. Layne, and G. E. Woolfenden. 1989. Acorn harvesting by Florida Scrub-Jays. Ecology 70:348–356.

Fernald, R. T. 1989. Coastal xeric scrub communities of the Treasure Coast region, Florida. Nongame Wildl. Prog. Tech. Rept. no. 6, Fla. Game and Fresh Water Fish Comm., Tallahassee, Florida.

Fitzpatrick, J. W., and G. E. Woolfenden. 1986. Demographic routes to cooperative breeding in some New World jays. Pp. 137–160 in Evolution of Animal Behavior (Nitecki, M. H. and J. A. Kitchell, eds.). Oxford Univ. Press, New York, New York.

Fitzpatrick, J. W., G. E. Woolfenden, and M. T. Kopeny. 1991. Ecology and development-related habitat guidelines of the Florida Scrub-Jay (*Aphelocoma coerulescens coerulescens*). Fla. Nongame Wildl. Prog. Tech. Rept., no. 8, Tallahassee, Florida. 49 pp.

Fitzpatrick, J. W., and G. E. Woolfenden. In review. The Florida Scrub-Jay, *Aphelocoma coerulescens,* is a distinct species. Condor.

Fitzpatrick, J. W., R. Bowman, D. R. Breininger, M. A. O'Connell, B. Stith, J. Thaxton, B. Toland, and G. E. Woolfenden. In review. Habitat conservation plan for the Florida Scrub-Jay: a biological framework. Ornith. Monogr.

Fitzpatrick, J. W., B. Pranty, and B. Stith. Ms. Statewide distribution of the Florida Scrub-Jay, 1993. Final rpt., U.S. Fish and Wildl. Serv., Coop Agreement no. 14-16-0004-91-950.

Hailman, J. P., K. J. McGowan, and G. E. Woolfenden. 1994. Role of helpers in the sentinel behavior of the Florida Scrub-Jay (*Aphelocoma c. coerulescens*). Ethology 97:119–140.

Laessle, A. M. 1958. The origin and successional relationships of sandhill vegetation and sand pine scrub. Ecol. Monogr. 28:361–387.

Laessle, A. M. 1968. Relationships of sand pine scrub to former shore lines. Quart. Jour. Fla. Acad. Sci. 30:269–286.

McGowan, K. J., and G. E. Woolfenden. 1989. A sentinel system in the Florida Scrub-Jay. Anim. Behav. 37:1000–1006.

Murray, B. G., J. W. Fitzpatrick, and G. E. Woolfenden. 1989. The evolution of clutch size. Part II: a test of the Murray-Nolan equation. Evolution 43:1706–1711.

Myers, R. L. 1990. Scrub and high pine. Pp. 150–193 in Ecosystems of Florida (Myers, R. L., and J. J. Ewel, eds.). Univ. Press of Florida, Gainesville, Florida.

Neill, W. T. 1957. Historical biogeography of present-day Florida. Bull. Fla. State Mus. 2(7):175–220.

Ostertag, B., and E. S. Menges. 1994. Patterns of reproductive effort with time since last fire in Florida scrub plants. Jour. Veg. Sci. 5:303–310.

Peterson, A. T. 1990. Evolutionary relationships of the *Aphelocoma* jays. Ph.D. dissertation, Univ. Chicago, Chicago, Illinois.

Peterson, A. T. 1992. Phylogeny and rates of molecular evolution in the *Aphelocoma* jays (Corvidae). Auk 109:133–147.

Pitelka, F. A. 1951. Speciation and ecological distribution in American jays of the genus *Aphelocoma*. Univ. Calif. Publ. in Zool. 50:195–464.

Sibley, C. G., and B. L. Monroe, Jr. 1990. Distribution and taxonomy of birds of the world. Yale Univ. Press, New Haven, Connecticut.

Woolfenden, G. E. 1978. Growth and survival of young Florida Scrub-Jays. Wilson Bull. 90:1–18.

Woolfenden, G. E., and J. W. Fitzpatrick. 1984. The Florida Scrub-Jay: demography of a cooperative-breeding bird. Monogr. Popul. Biol. no. 20, Princeton Univ. Press, Princeton, New Jersey. 406 pp.

Woolfenden, G. E., and J. W. Fitzpatrick. 1986. Sexual asymmetries in the life history of the Florida Scrub-Jay. Pp. 87–107 in Ecological aspects of social evolution: birds and mammals (Rubenstein, D., and R. W. Wrangham eds.). Princeton Univ. Press, Princeton, New Jersey.

Woolfenden, G. E., and J. W. Fitzpatrick. 1990. Florida Scrub-Jays: a synopsis after 18 years of study. Pp. 240–266 in Cooperative breeding in birds: long-term studies of ecology and behavior (Stacey, P. B., and W. D. Koenig, eds.). Cambridge Univ. Press, Cambridge, England.

Woolfenden, G. E., and J. W. Fitzpatrick. 1991. Florida Scrub-Jay ecology and conservation. Pp. 542–565 in Bird population studies: relevance to conservation and management (Perrins, C. M., J-D. Lebreton, and G. J. M. Hirons, eds.). Oxford Univ. Press, Oxford, United Kingdom.

PREPARED BY: Glen E. Woolfenden, Department of Biology, University of South Florida, Tampa, FL 33620, and John W. Fitzpatrick, Archbold Biological Station, P. O. Box 2057, Lake Placid, FL 33852.

Reddish Egret

Egretta rufescens

FAMILY ARDEIDAE

Order Ciconiiformes

TAXONOMY: The Reddish Egret (*Egretta rufescens*) was originally described as "L'Aigrette rousse" by Buffon (1783), apparently on the basis of a plate by D'Aubenton about 1780. Boddaert (1783) assigned the binomial name *Ardea rufa*, which also was applied to the "Rufous Heron" of Austria (Scopoli 1769 in Hellmayr and Conover 1948; Latham 1785). Perhaps to clarify the situation, Gmelin (1789) applied the name *A. rufescens* to the present species. A century later Ridgway (1878) assigned *rufescens* to the monotypic genus *Dichromanassa,* the accepted taxon until Payne and Risley (1976) and Payne (1979) proposed its submergence in *Egretta. Egretta rufescens* is now the accepted name (AOU 1983). The white morph was first described in 1826 as "Peale's Egret" (*A. pealii*) by Bonaparte (1826). Observation of mixed broods of white and dark-morph young by several authorities in the 1870s and 1880s led to the "lumping" of *pealii* into *rufescens* (Ridgway 1878; Baird et al. 1884).

Two weakly differentiated subspecies have been described: *colorata* of the Caribbean coast of Mexico, the West Indies, and northern South America (Griscom 1926; Blake 1977), and *dickeyi* of Baja California and the Sea of Cortez (van Rossem 1926). The nominate race *E. r. rufescens* is held to occupy the remainder of the species' range: the United States, Gulf coast of Mexico, and the Pacific coast of Oaxaca and Chiapas (Binford 1989). The validity of both *colorata* and *dickeyi* has been questioned (e.g., Blake 1977; Payne 1979). Payne (1979) upheld *dickeyi* but rejected *colorata*. My own observations of museum specimens lead me to regard *colorata* as an invalid form, but to accept *dickeyi* as distinct from *rufescens*.

DESCRIPTION: Reddish Egrets are robust, medium-sized herons standing about 75 cm (30 in.) tall with a wingspread exceeding 1.2 m (4 ft.). Males are slightly larger than females. In dark-morph adults, the head and neck are

Reddish Egret, *Egretta rufescens.* (Photo copyright by Allan D. Cruickshank, courtesy of Florida Audubon Society)

chestnut, with shaggy lanceolate plumes on the crown, nape, neck, and upper breast. On some individuals (especially early in the nesting season) the head plumes appear tawny or cinnamon, giving a "golden-maned" appearance. The body (back, wings, tail, and abdomen) is dark neutral gray, with the abdomen slightly lighter. Lanceolate feathers cover much of the back and are dark neutral gray with a blackish-gray central stripe. Filamentous scapular plumes, acquired shortly before the onset of nesting, are dark neutral gray and extend well beyond the tail (up to 15 cm) when unworn. By the end of nesting, primaries, secondaries, and wing coverts may fade toward a flat brownish-gray similar to the subadult. The iris is straw yellow. During the nesting season, the bill is sharply bicolor: the basal half is pink and the distal half is black. Late in the cycle the pink fades, and the entire bill becomes quite dusky. Lores are turquoise-blue during courtship and pair formation, flesh colored during later breeding, but begin to darken before the young fledge. Adults have dusky or blackish lores when not breeding. The legs and feet are black, except during nesting when the sides and backs of the legs and bottoms of the feet, are turquoise-blue colored.

Immature dark-morphs are duller than adults, medium gray or grayish-brown throughout, with cinnamon-tipped feathers. Recently fledged young can be quite variable; occasional individuals are quite gray or rufous through-out. Yearlings can be distinguished by the dark neutral-gray feathers of the back (also upper wing coverts) and contrasting cinnamon marginal wing co-

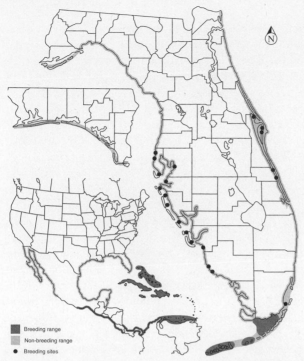

Distribution map of
the Reddish Egret,
Egretta rufescens.

■ Breeding range
■ Non-breeding range
● Breeding sites

verts, one or more short scapular plumes, and small tufts of short, cinnamon-colored occipital and breast plumes. Soft parts are dull, with legs and feet blackish and the lores and bill blackish or dark "horn"; the bill may be slightly lighter at the base but never approaches the distinctly bicolor pattern of the breeding adult.

White-morph Reddish Egrets have white plumage at all ages. Soft parts are as described above.

Occasional "pied" egrets occur. I have never seen this condition in either an immature plumage or in white-morph individuals. A typical pied bird is a dark-morph that has one or more white primaries, secondaries, and/or rec-trices, usually distributed in a bilaterally symmetrical pattern. A fine edging of white feathers along the margin of the bill and lores also may occur. More rarely, pied adults display irregular patches of white contour feathers on the body or throat (e.g., Scott 1887; Todd and Worthington 1911; Paul, pers. observ.). In recent years two individuals have been seen in Florida with an entirely white head and neck, and gray body (B. Samler, pers. comm.; Paul, pers. observ.).

POPULATION SIZE AND TREND: The U.S. breeding population of Reddish Egrets is estimated to be about 2,000 pairs (Paul 1977, 1991). About 1,500 pairs occur in Texas (Paul 1991). In Florida, 350–400 breeding pairs are believed to occur, with 100–125 pairs in Florida Bay alone (Powell et al. 1989; Paul 1991). Formerly the species was much more common in Florida, with nesting occurring in the Keys, Florida Bay, and along both coasts north to Tarpon Springs and Pelican Island or Merritt Island (Scott 1887; Howell 1932; Paul et al. 1979). Plume hunting caused the virtual extirpation of Reddish Egrets from Florida by about 1910 (Howell 1932; Allen 1954; Pierce 1962). Following the cessation of plume hunting, no nesting was known (freshwater nesting records of Baynard (1913) and Howell (1932) are probably erroneous) until a single nest was discovered in eastern Florida Bay in 1938 (Desmond 1939). Thereafter, numbers slowly increased there and in the Lower Keys (Greene 1946; Powell et al. 1989). Numbers in Florida Bay were estimated at 50 individuals in 1944 (Baker 1944), and a maximum of 150 a decade later (Allen 1954). By 1959 the population had increased to 200 birds (Allen in Palmer 1962). Robertson and Kushlan (1974) estimated the state-wide population at 300 individuals, the basis for my guess of 150 breeding pairs (Paul 1977). Censuses in the late 1970s revealed 100–125 pairs in Florida Bay alone (Powell et al. 1989) and led to the 1980 estimate of 250–300 pairs statewide (Paul 1991). Subsequently, Reddish Egrets were found nesting at a number of sites along both coasts. Currently, I estimate 350–400 breeding pairs in Florida. Based on Scott (1887, 1889, 1891) and others, I speculate the current population may be no more than 10% of the population prior to 1880, when plume hunting reached its peak.

The steady reoccupation of former range and increasing numbers recorded during the 1970s and 1980s indicate a continuing population increase on both coasts of Florida. Florida Keys and Florida Bay populations are believed to be stable or increasing, but no surveys have been conducted since 1980. Deteriorating conditions in Florida Bay (G. T. Bancroft, pers. comm.; A. Sprunt IV, pers. comm.) make resurvey of the colonies there especially important.

DISTRIBUTION AND HISTORY OF DISTRIBUTION: Reddish Egrets occur along the coastlines of Florida and the Gulf Coast states, Mexico, Caribbean countries including Belize, Venezuela, Colombia, and most Caribbean islands including Aruba, Bonaire, Curaçao and other islands off the Venezuela coast, Greater Antilles, and the Bahamas. They are accidental in the Lesser Antilles, with just two known records. Scattered sightings have been reported from Guatemala, Honduras, El Salvador, Nicaragua, Costa Rica, and Panama, where further study is needed to determine the species' status (reviewed in Paul 1991). A few individuals dispersing northward following the nesting season are now found annually north to the Carolinas on the Atlantic coast, and southern California on the Pacific coast, with occasional vagrants elsewhere.

In Florida, Reddish Egrets breed from St. Joseph Sound (Dunedin) on the west coast and Merritt Island (Haulover Canal) on the east coast, south to the Lower Keys. A few pairs also nest on the islands of Key West NWR, west of Key West (W. B. Robertson, pers. comm.). Perhaps two-thirds of the state's population occurs in Florida Bay and the Keys, where Reddish Egrets are widely distributed. Nesting is less common and generally local along peninsular coastlines. On the Gulf coast, nesting is known at Marco Island, Estero Bay, Pine Island Sound, Gasparilla Sound, Little Sarasota Bay, Roberts Bay, Sarasota Bay, Tampa Bay, and Clearwater Pass and St. Joseph Sound. On the Atlantic coast, nesting occurs on the Arsenicker Keys in southern Biscayne Bay, near Vero Beach, Pelican Island, and Merritt Island NWR. Local concentrations occur in Tampa Bay and at Merritt Island, where about 70 and 50 pairs occur, respectively.

Nonbreeding adults and immatures may be found in small numbers almost anywhere along the coast of Florida where suitable foraging habitat occurs. Such sightings are least frequent in winter. Reddish Egrets still are scarce along the Panhandle, where they may originate either from the Florida (or Cuba) colonies farther south, or possibly from the small Louisiana–Alabama population. Scattered birds, usually immatures, occur at inland locations.

The history of Reddish Egret distribution parallels population trends of the last century (see summary above). In Florida prior to the 1970s, birds were rarely seen north of the Keys and Florida Bay where they were resident. Expansion of breeding range to Pine Island Sound in 1970 (Bancroft 1971), Tampa Bay in 1974 (Paul et al. 1975), and somewhat later to the Atlantic coast (Paul et al. 1979; Rodgers and Schwikert 1986; Toland 1991) mirrored population increases and no doubt explains the increasing number of sightings along the Panhandle and north Florida coastlines.

HABITAT REQUIREMENTS AND HABITAT TREND: Reddish Egrets nest exclusively on coastal islands that are located near suitable foraging habitat and afford protection from terrestrial predators. On mangrove keys, nests are normally built in red (*Rhizophora mangle*) or black (*Avicennia germinans*) mangroves, usually 1 m or more beneath the canopy and often over water (Allen in Palmer 1962). On dredged-material islands, nests may be built in Brazilian pepper (*Schinus terebinthefolius*) or other upland vegetation. In Texas, Reddish Egrets commonly nest on the ground or in cactus (*Opuntia* sp.) on both natural and dredged-material islands (Oberholser and Kincaid 1974; Paul, unpubl. data). Rodgers and Schwikert (1986) found a nest in *Opuntia* on Pelican Island. Reddish Egrets usually nest in mixed heronries, but at some locations they nest alone or in small groups apart from most other waders. This occurs particularly in Florida Bay, where Reddish Egrets may nest in loose groups with Roseate Spoonbills (*Ajaia ajaja*) in winter, before the large colonies of small herons become active and where single pairs occasionally nest in red mangrove clumps out on the flats.

Reddish Egrets forage on broad, barren sand or mud flats, usually in water less than 15 cm deep. Examples of foraging habitat include: the extensive bank system of Florida Bay; the variably hypersaline pools and lagoons inside keys or just landward of mainland shorelines, and the scrubby, open mangrove communities nearby; tidally exposed flats on the lagoon side of undeveloped coastal barrier islands; and small "cat's eye" ponds formed between successive beach ridges at natural passes. The conditions that maintain barren substrates include high or variable salinity, temperature, and water levels (McMillan 1974; Woodhouse and Knutson 1982). Such conditions are most prevalent in coastal areas, which may help to explain why Reddish Egrets are limited to the coast.

Extensive dredge-and-fill development of Florida's coastline during the 20th century has destroyed many areas formerly important to Reddish Egrets. Important nesting sites of the 1880s (e.g., the Bird Keys of Clearwater Harbor and Sarasota; Scott 1887) are now upscale housing developments. Other former nesting sites (e.g., Bird Key at Midnight Pass) have been connected to adjacent land by filling and no longer provide isolation from terrestrial predators. Likewise, extensive foraging areas have been lost in Sarasota Bay, Boca Ciega Bay, the Florida Keys, and elsewhere as channels have been dredged, or flats filled and bulkheaded. Maynard (1881) and Scott (1887) both noted the abundance of Reddish Egrets at the important colony at Johns Pass, near St. Petersburg. Reddish Egrets no longer nest there; however, the site remains and a small colony of pelicans and herons persists, but miles of seawalls and "finger-fill" development to the north and south attest to the permanent loss of natural shorelines.

VULNERABILITY OF SPECIES AND HABITAT: Despite an apparently sustained population increase in Florida since the 1930s, the Reddish Egret remains the rarest heron both here and elsewhere in the United States. Reoccupation of nearly all former range somewhat eases the threats associated with an extremely restricted distribution, but two-thirds of the state's population still is limited to Florida Bay and the Keys. Breeding and foraging habitats occur along a very narrow coastal strip, broadening somewhat in the major bay systems. Nesting colonies are vulnerable to both chronic and catastrophic erosion, as illustrated by the impact of Hurricane Andrew on Arsenicker Keys in 1992. Individual Reddish Egrets do not appear to be as site specific as wintering Piping (*Charadrius melodus*) or Snowy (*C. alexandrinus*) Plovers (T. H. Below, pers. comm.) and seem able to exploit newly created habitats. However, extensive dredging, filling, and bulkheading of habitats in areas where important populations formerly occurred ensure that any local recovery will be very limited. Filling and other alteration of private lands to the landward edge of jurisdictional wetlands will prevent migration of coastal habitats as sea level rises over the next century, which may result in their erosion and loss. Reddish Egrets can benefit from habitat restoration efforts, especially if the requirements of the species are incorporated into project designs, but the inability of this species to exploit a wider variety of foraging habitats limits the available options.

CAUSES OF THREAT: The highly coastal distribution of Reddish Egrets places the entire population squarely in the path of past and future coastal growth and development. There is no "wilderness reservoir" that allows a portion of the population to thrive free of human influence. Primary foraging habitats have been directly affected by dredge-and-fill activities. Whereas coastal wetland protection is now fairly effective, sea-level rise now appears to be a major long-term threat to both foraging areas and nesting sites. The Reddish Egret, a habitat specialist, may have no alternative if coastal wetlands are lost. The permanent loss of intertidal flats due to dredging and filling, particularly near Sarasota, Bradenton, St. Petersburg and Clearwater, is probably the greatest single obstacle to the recovery of significant populations on the Gulf coast.

Little is known about the sensitivity of Reddish Egrets to organochlorine pesticides and other chemicals in the environment. Data reanalyzed from King et al. (1978) indicated 6.3% eggshell thinning and DDE residues of 3.7 ppm in eggs taken from Green Island, Texas in 1970. In the absence of additional information, toxic chemicals must be considered a potential threat to Reddish Egrets, as well as to other wildlife species.

A century ago, plume hunting was the major human impact on Reddish Egret populations. Habitat loss has long since supplanted direct persecution as the most important human impact, but in the last 20 years disturbance has reappeared as a significant problem. Since 1970, Florida's population has doubled to 14 million people. Eighty percent of recent growth is along the state's coasts. The popularity of coastal waters for such activities as fishing, boating, beachcombing, and picnicking has resulted in regular (and in some places, almost constant) disturbance of foraging and nesting birds. Even protected areas have come under pressure as some people, trying to "get away from it all," intentionally or unknowingly go ashore and disturb local wildlife. Airboats and jet skis offer access to extremely shallow areas that formerly were protected by their inaccessibility, and thereby pose new threats to fish and wildlife. The noise and prop wash of airboats can be very disruptive to roosting or nesting birds: one boat was observed to literally blow nesting herons out of the Rookery Bay colony (T. H. Below, pers. comm.).

Potential predators on Reddish Egrets in Florida include raccoons (*Procyon lotor*), Bald Eagles (*Haliaeetus leucocephalus*), Fish Crows (*Corvus ossifragus*), American Crows (*C. brachyrhynchos*), dogs, and, with their recent arrival in

Florida, possibly coyotes (*Canis latrans*). For the most part, predation does not represent a threat to the species, but certain aspects deserve mention. Terrestrial predators like raccoons can have profound impacts on heronries, when they can reach them. Individual Bald Eagles occasionally develop a specific prey preference (A. Sprunt, pers. comm.), and in one south Florida colony eagles took most young Reddish Egrets produced over a two-year period (Paul, unpubl. data). Crows rapidly investigate sources of disturbance in heronries and take unprotected eggs. Human disturbance increases the risk of loss. Dogs are not only potential predators, if released on colony islands, but also cause disturbances that crows may exploit.

RESPONSES TO HABITAT MODIFICATION: As noted above, extensive dredging and filling of coastal areas have caused the loss of critical nesting sites and important foraging areas. However, some projects have had unintended benefits. Channel dredging has resulted in the creation of hundreds of islands in Florida, some of which have been occupied by large mixed-species bird colonies. Two of the most important nesting sites for Reddish Egrets in Florida are spoil islands at Alafia Bank (Tampa Bay) and Haulover (Merritt Island). Nesting also occurs on spoil islands near Vero Beach (Toland 1991), Merritt Island, Sarasota, and Clearwater. Perhaps the availability of suitable nesting sites, near remnant patches of foraging habitat, has facilitated the return of nesting pairs to some areas. Likewise, Reddish Egrets have exploited new foraging areas along the shores of dredged-material islands or inside large diked disposal areas. Creation of large shallow impoundments along the Atlantic coast from Stuart north to Merritt Island, also has provided new foraging sites, although at the expense of the mangrove and high-marsh communities that may have provided suitable habitat before. In addition, construction of shallow flats as part of coastal habitat mitigation projects has provided Reddish Egrets with new foraging areas (R. R. Lewis, pers. comm.).

Recent concerns about the deterioration of Florida Bay, still the stronghold of Reddish Egrets in Florida, have centered on the lack of freshwater inputs (G. T. Bancroft, pers. comm.). Reddish Egrets must be regarded as potentially at risk. However, the same specialization that threatens the species elsewhere may allow it to escape serious harm in Florida Bay. Increasing salinities might be expected to open up new inland foraging habitats by limiting vegetational growth. In addition, the primary prey species are highly adapted to hypersaline conditions and may not be seriously affected by long-term stresses in the system.

DEMOGRAPHIC CHARACTERISTICS: Reddish Egrets first nest at 2 years of age, although banding data indicate that not all individuals do so (Paul, unpubl. data). Yearlings rarely appear in colonies and do not breed. Clutch size is typically 3–4 eggs (Bent 1926), with several Texas studies indicating averages of 3.1–3.5 (McMurry 1971; Chaney et al. 1978; Paul, unpubl. data). In Florida Bay, mean clutch size at 7 small colonies ranged from 2.33–3.00, with an overall average of 2.75 (Paul, unpubl. data). Eggs are pale bluish-green and measure 50.2 mm long by 36.3 cm breadth (Palmer 1962). Based on nests where the laying and hatching dates of the last egg was known, incubation lasts 26 days (Paul, unpubl. data).

Variable hatching and fledging rates result from the impact of predation, disturbance, and other factors (McMurry 1971; Chaney et al. 1978; Paul, unpubl. data). "Normal" hatching rate appears to be 65–85% of all eggs laid, whereas "normal" fledging rate is 60–75% of all eggs hatched. In Florida Bay, 86% of all eggs survived to hatch, with fledging success varying from 4–62% at the same colony among years (Paul, unpubl. data). Fledging occurs at 6.5–7 weeks of age, but young are fed at the colony by the parents for another 2–4 weeks (Paul, unpubl. data). Normal productivity appears to be about 1.2–1.5 fledglings per breeding pair. In Florida Bay, productivity varied from 1.8 to 0.1 young per pair; in the latter case nest failure was due to Bald Eagle predation and food shortage (Paul, unpubl. data).

Adult survivorship is unknown. The maximum known age, based on the recovery of a banded bird, is 11 years and 3 months (Kennard 1975).

KEY BEHAVIORS: Reddish Egrets feed almost exclusively on small fish. Palmer (1962) listed needlefish (*Strongylura* spp.) as a common diet item in Florida. In a Florida Bay study, 32 species of fish (n = 5,100 individuals) were found in regurgitated samples (Paul, unpubl. data). Sheepshead minnow (*Cyprinodon variegatus*), sailfin molly (*Poecilia latipinna*), goldspotted killifish (*Floridichthys carpio*), and marsh killifish (*Fundulus confluentus*) comprised 78% of the total diet. Sheepshead minnows alone accounted for 54% of all individuals. Casual observation suggests that the longnose killifish (*Fundulus similis*) is an important prey species along the Florida Gulf coast.

Unlike other herons, Reddish Egrets actively pursue their prey. Jogging erratically across shallow flats, they locate and chase small schools of fish, striking when the fish are within range. Wing-flapping and gliding are variants that exploit wind conditions or aid in rapid maneuvers, especially when the water is >15 cm deep (Rodgers 1983; Paul, unpubl. data). Active foraging techniques are probably an adaptation that allows Reddish Egrets to exploit open foraging habitats and are the critical factor in explaining why they are restricted to coastal areas. Pursuit of active prey species cannot occur in heavily vegetated coastal marshes or freshwater wetlands. Prey capture rates are higher in adult egrets than immatures (32 versus 25% in Tampa Bay; Rodgers 1983). Low foraging efficiencies may help explain why Reddish Egrets do not breed until their third year of life, probably a year later than most herons.

Reddish Egrets are considered "weakly migratory" (Cooke 1913). Banding data from Texas and Florida indicate that Reddish Egrets, particularly immatures, disperse northward after the nesting season (Paul, unpubl. data). At this time, the Florida population may be augmented by birds from Cuba and the Bahamas (Robertson 1978). In the fall, egrets return south, with Texas birds continuing into Mexico. Whether birds from south Florida leave the state is not known.

Reddish Egrets in Florida typically nest in large, mixed-species colonies among other herons, ibis, spoonbills, pelicans, cormorants, and anhingas. These aggregations allow the evolution of visual and vocal displays that serve to communicate information about the vigor and reproductive status of one bird to another. Meyerriecks (1960, in Palmer 1962) has described the agonistic and courtship behavior of the Reddish Egret, with only the briefest summary provided here. Among the most characteristic behaviors of this species are the Upright Display, in which an adult announces its presence (and which may lead to Escape or to the Aggressive Upright); Pursuit Flight, an extremely graceful flight by two birds that can extend for hundreds of yards and may end with loud bill-snaps (Audubon in Bent 1926); Head-tossing, which accompanies Stretch Displays and Greeting Ceremonies between the members of a pair; and Circle Stretch, wherein the male circles the female in a gradually tightening circle, Head-tossing with wings extended. Aerial variants include the Aerial Stretch and Circle Flight displays. My own observations are somewhat at variance with those of Meyerriecks; I regard the Stretch Display as virtually absent in this species (and replaced by extended Head-tossing), and what I (Paul, unpubl. data) have called Circling, clearly involved the female circling the male, in a high-intensity sexual interaction that in some cases was followed by copulation. More detailed study is clearly needed.

CONSERVATION MEASURES TAKEN: The Reddish Egret is protected by international treaties and state and federal laws. The species is currently listed as a "Category 2" species by the U.S. Fish and Wildlife Service, indicating "a candidate for listing, with some evidence of vulnerability, but for which not enough data exists to support listing," threatened by Texas, and a species of special concern by Florida. The species also has been included on the National Audubon Society's "Blue List" of birds needing special attention (Tate 1986).

Most of the known breeding sites of Reddish Egrets are protected within the boundaries of Everglades National Park, Biscayne National Park, and several National Wildlife Refuges (Merritt Island, Ding Darling, Pinellas, Key West, Great White Heron), or maintained as sanctuaries by the National Audubon Society. Other sites receive marginal recognition by local municipalities. Foraging areas are protected by virtue of their inclusion in federal preserves or by federal, state, and local wetlands protection regulations. Aquatic preserves also provide some additional protection. Recent actions to restrict access to seagrass meadows in the Florida Keys and other selected localities in Florida may indirectly protect foraging or breeding sites. At Audubon sanctuaries on the Florida Gulf coast, terrestrial predators annually are trapped and removed.

CONSERVATION MEASURES PROPOSED: Despite official protection, staffing at most refuges and sanctuaries is inadequate. There is a vast potential for boaters, campers, and their pets to disturb wading bird colonies and cause nesting failures. Indications that this is already happening have been observed in the Lower Keys, Estero Bay, Clearwater Harbor, and St. Joseph Sound. Increased staffing would allow more comprehensive monitoring, patrol, and educational activities. Increased survey effort is needed to locate additional nesting sites, initiate protective measures, and update population assessments. Stronger wetlands protection measures should be adopted, mandating special protections for high-marsh communities and salt barrens. Community comprehensive plans should include meaningful development setbacks to protect the habitat and hydrological function of tidal creeks, which not only are extremely important as fish nurseries, but also provide important foraging habitats for wading birds. Special land-use planning provisions should address heronry protection, including the establishment of colony buffer zones (see Rodgers and Smith 1995).

ACKNOWLEDGMENTS: Among dozens of people who provided assistance during my research on Reddish Egrets, I am especially pleased to thank T. H. Below, D. R. Blankinship, H. W. Kale, J. C. Ogden, B. W. Patty, G. W. Paulson, W. B. Robertson, Jr., and A. Sprunt, IV. J. A. Rodgers greatly improved this paper with his careful review.

LITERATURE CITED:

Allen, R. P. 1954. The Reddish Egret: bird of colors and contrasts. Audubon Mag. 56:252–255.

AOU. 1983. Check-list of North American birds, 6th edition. Amer. Ornith. Union, Washington, D.C. 877 pp.

Baird, S. F., T. M. Brewer, and R. Ridgway. 1884. The water birds of North America. 2 vols. Little, Brown, and Co., Boston, Massachusetts.

Baker, J. H. 1944. The director reports to you: good news from Florida rookeries. Audubon Mag. 46:117.

Bancroft, G. T., Jr. 1971. Northern breeding record for Reddish Egret. Auk 88:429.

Baynard, O. E. 1913. Breeding birds of Alachua County, Florida. Auk 30:240–247.

Bent, A. C. 1926. Life histories of North American marsh birds. Bull. U. S. Nat. Mus. no. 135.

Binford, L. C. 1989. A distributional survey of the birds of the Mexican state of Oaxaca. Ornithol. Monogr. 43:1–418.

Blake, E. R. 1977. Manual of neotropical birds. Vol. 1. Univ. Chicago Press, Chicago, Illinois. 674 pp.

Boddaert, P. 1783. Table des planches enlumineez d'histoire naturelle, de M. d'Aubenton. Utrecht, Netherlands. 67 pp.

Bonaparte, C. L. 1826. Further additions to the ornithology of the United States; and observations of the nomenclature of certain species. Ann. Lyc. Nat. Hist. 2:154–155.

Buffon, G. L. L. 1783. Histoire naturelle des oiseaux 7:378.

Chaney, A. H., B. R. Chapman, J. P. Karges, D. A. Nelson, R. R. Schmidt, and L. C. Thebeau. 1978. Use of dredged material islands by colonial seabirds and wading birds in Texas. U.S. Army Corps of Eng. Tech. Rept. D–78–8. Vicksburg, Mississippi. 170 pp.

Cooke, W. W. 1913. Distribution and migration of North American herons and their allies. U.S.D.A. Biol. Sur., Bull. no. 45. Washington, D.C. 70 pp.

Desmond, T. C. 1939. Reddish Egret nesting near Tavernier, Florida. Auk 56:329.

Gmelin, J. F. 1789. Systema naturae v. 1, part II:628.

Greene, E. R. 1946. Birds of the Lower Florida Keys. Quart. Jour. Fla. Acad Sci. 8:199–265.

Griscom, L. 1926. The ornithological results of the Mason-Spindon expedition to Yucatan. Amer. Mus. Novitates no. 235:1–19.

Hellmayr, C. E., and B. Conover. 1948. Catalog of birds of the Americas and the adjacent islands. Field Mus. Nat. Hist. Zool. Ser., vol. 13, part 1, no. 2:92–194.

Howell, A. H. 1932. Florida bird life. Coward-McCann, Inc., New York. 579 pp.

Kennard, J. H. 1975. Longevity records of North American birds. Bird-Banding 46:55–73.

King, K. A., E. L. Flickinger, and H. H. Hildebrand. 1978. Shell thinning and pesticide residues in Texas aquatic bird eggs, 1970. Pest. Monit. Jour. 12:16–21.

Latham, J. 1785. Gen. Syn. 3(1):88.

Maynard, C. J. 1881. The birds of eastern North America. C. J. Maynard and Co., Newtonville, Massachusetts.

McMillan, C. 1974. Salt tolerance of mangroves and submerged aquatic plants. Pp. 379–390 in Ecology of halophytes (R. J. Reimold and W. H. Queen, eds.). Academic Press, New York.

McMurry, S. L. 1971. Nesting and development of the Reddish Egret (*Dichromanassa rufescens* Gmelin) on a spoil bank chain in the Laguna Madre. Unpubl. M.S. thesis, Texas A and I Univ., Kingsville, Texas. 78 pp.

Meyerriecks, A. J. 1960. Comparative breeding behavior of four species of North American herons. Publ. Nuttall Ornithol. Club no. 2, Cambridge, Massachusetts. 158 pp.

Oberholser, H. C., and E. B. Kincaid. 1974. The bird life of Texas. Univ. Texas Press, Austin, Texas. 1070 pp.

Palmer, R. S. (Ed.). 1962. Handbook of North American birds. Vol. 1: Loons through Flamingos. Yale Univ. Press, New Haven, Connecticut. 567 pp.

Paul, R. T. 1977. History and current status of Reddish Egrets in the United States. Proc. 1977 Conf. Colon. Waterbird Group: 179–184.

Paul, R. T. 1991. Status report—*Egretta rufescens* (Gmelin) Reddish Egret. U.S. Fish & Wildl. Ser., Houston, Texas. 73 pp.

Paul, R. T., A. J. Meyerriecks, and F. M. Dunstan. 1975. Return of Reddish Egrets as breeding birds in Tampa Bay, Florida. Fla. Field Nat. 3:9–10.

Paul, R. T., H. W. Kale, II, and D. A. Nelson. 1979. Reddish Egrets nesting on Florida's east coast. Fla. Field Nat. 7:24–25.

Payne, R. B. 1979. Family Ardeidae. Pp. 193–244 in Check-list of birds of the world (E. Mayr and G. W. Cottrell, Eds.). Vol. 1. 2nd Ed. Mus. Comp. Zool., Cambridge, Massachusetts.

Payne, R. B., and C. J. Risley. 1976. Systematics and evolutionary relationships among the herons (Ardeidae). Misc. Publ. Mus. Zool., Univ. Michigan, no. 150. 115 p.

Pierce, C. W. 1962. The cruise of the Bonton. Tequesta 22:3–63.

Powell, G. V. N., R. D. Bjork, J. C. Ogden, R. T. Paul, A. H. Powell, and W. B. Robertson, Jr. 1989. Population trends in some Florida Bay wading birds. Wilson Bull. 101:436–537.

Ridgway, R. 1878. Studies of the American herodiones. Bull. U. S. Geol. & Geogr. Surv. Terr., 4:219–251.

Robertson, W. B., Jr. 1978. Reddish Egret. Pp. 51–53 in Rare and endangered biota of Florida (H. W. Kale II, ed.). Vol. 2: Birds. Fla. Game and Fresh Water Fish Comm., Gainesville, Florida.

Robertson, W. B., Jr. and J. A. Kushlan. 1974. The southern Florida avifauna. Pp. 414–451 in Environments of South Florida: present and past (P. J. Gleason, ed.). Miami Geol. Soc. Mem. no. 2, Coral Gables, Florida.

Rodgers, J. A., Jr. 1983. Foraging behavior of seven species of herons in Tampa Bay, Florida. Colon. Waterbirds 6:11–23.

Rodgers, J. A., Jr., and S. T. Schwikert. 1986. Recolonization of Pelican Island by Reddish Egrets. Fla. Field Nat. 14:76–77.

Rodgers, J. A., Jr., and H. T. Smith. 1995. Set-back distances to protect nesting bird colonies from human disturbances in Florida. Conser. Biol. 9:89–99.

Scott, W. E. D. 1887. The present condition of some of the bird rookeries of the Gulf Coast of Florida. Auk 4:135–144, 213–222, 273–284.

Scott, W. E. D. 1889. A summary of observations on the birds of the Gulf Coast of Florida. Auk 6:13–18.

Scott, W. E. D. 1891. Florida heron rookeries. Auk 8:318–319.

Tate, J., Jr. 1986. The Blue List for 1986. Amer. Birds 40:227–236.

Todd, W. E. C., and W. W. Worthington. 1911. A contribution to the ornithology of the Bahama Islands. Ann. Carnegie Mus. 7:388–464.

Toland, B. 1991. Successful nesting by Reddish Egrets at Oslo Island, Indian River County, Florida. Fla. Field Nat. 19:51–53.

van Rossem, A. J. 1926. The Lower California Reddish Egret. Condor 28:246.

Woodhouse, W. W., Jr., and P. L. Knutson. 1982. Atlantic coastal marshes. Pp. 45–70 in Creation and restoration of coastal plant communities (R. R. Lewis, III, ed.). CRC Press, Boca Raton, Florida. 219 pp.

PREPARED BY: Richard T. Paul, National Audubon Society, Tampa Bay Sanctuaries, 410 Ware Blvd., Suite 500, Tampa, FL 33619.

Roseate Spoonbill
Ajaia ajaja

FAMILY THRESKIORNITHIDAE

Order Ciconiiformes

TAXONOMY: The Roseate Spoonbill (*Ajaia ajaja*) was originally described by Linnaeus in 1758 as *Platalea Ajaia,* but in 1853 Reichenbach erected the monotypic genus *Ajaia* for its reclassification (AOU 1957, 1983), the species being differentiated from species in *Platalea* by the absence of a nuchal crest and presence of elongated lower neck feathers (Palmer 1962). Amadon and Woolfenden (Palmer 1962) have suggested the morphological differences between spoonbill genera are minor and all species should be assigned to *Platalea.* However, the AOU (1957, 1983) currently maintains the classification for Roseate Spoonbills in *Ajaia.*

DESCRIPTION: The Roseate Spoonbill, the only spoonbill native to the Western Hemisphere, is a long-legged wading bird with a spatulate bill. Spoonbills stand about 80 cm (31 in.) high, with a wingspan of 1.3 m (51 in.; Lewis 1983) and weight of 1,225–1,800 g (mean = 1,490 ± 170 g; n = 30 Florida nesting adults: R. Bjork and G. Powell, unpubl. data). Definitive alternate plumage (Palmer 1962) of an adult spoonbill (>3 years old) is a rose-pink on the back, wings, and lower breast; carmine-colored lesser wing and upper and under tail coverts; a white neck and upper breast with a patch of stiff, curly carmine feathers at the base of the neck; yellowish wash on the breast adjacent to the bend-of-wing; an unfeathered head of pale green to golden-buff, with a line of black skin around the ears and back of head that sometimes extends as a "V" down the back of the neck; and grayish-green to grayish-tan bill and orange-buff tail. Birds 1 to about 12 months old are uniformly pale pink with fully feathered, white heads and necks and dark-tipped outer primaries. Birds 1–3 years old are intermediate in color, become bare-headed, and acquire the black line on the head in their second year. Although difficult to identify in the field, a 2-year old subadult is distinguished from an adult by duller green coloration of the head, lack of horn-like excrescences at the base of the upper

Roseate Spoonbill, *Ajaia ajaja*. (Photo copyright by Allan D. Cruickshank, courtesy of Florida Audubon Society)

mandible, and absence of the curly feathers on the neck and carmine drip on the wing (Allen 1942). Allen (1942) suggested there may be a postnuptial (basic) adult plumage that resembles that of a 2-year old bird; however, there is no conclusive evidence. Sexes are morphologically similar. In flight, the spoonbill's neck is extended straight forward and the legs trail straight back with wing flaps alternating with short glides; flight is rather relaxed compared to the more rapid wing beat of White Ibis (*Eudocimus albus*).

POPULATION SIZE AND TREND: Anecdotal accounts indicate that Roseate Spoonbills existed by the thousands along the Gulf coast in Texas, Louisiana, and Florida prior to the 1850s (Allen 1942). A rapid decline, attributed to disturbance of colonies, plume hunting, and collection of nestlings and adults for food between 1850–1920, reduced U.S. populations to probably 25 breeding pairs (Allen 1942). Thereafter, recovery was fairly rapid in Texas and Louisiana, but relatively slow in Florida. The 1941 U.S. population estimate exceeded 5,000 individuals, 89% of which occurred in Texas and only 9% in Florida (Allen 1942).

Current estimates of the breeding population for the Texas coast (Texas Colonial Waterbird Society 1988, 1989, 1990) were within the range (2,200–2,700) documented in the 1970s (Chapman 1982). However, there is con-

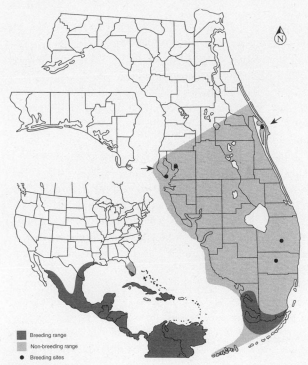

Distribution map
of the Roseate
Spoonbill, *Ajaia
ajaja*.

Breeding range
Non-breeding range
• Breeding sites

cern about a growing dependence of birds nesting along the southern coast on
agricultural drainage sites for foraging (M. Farmer, pers. comm.). In Louisiana, 1,919 nesting individuals (represents the number of nesting pairs; R.
Martin, pers. comm.) were counted in colony surveys in 1990 (Martin and
Lester 1990). This is a substantial increase from the 1,300 pairs estimated in
the 1970s (Portnoy 1977).

In Florida, travelers and naturalists reported a large population of spoonbills nesting at both inland and coastal colonies in south Florida prior to the
mid-1800s (reviewed in Allen 1942). However, fewer than 200 pairs were
thought to nest in Florida by the early 1930s, nesting sporadically in small
numbers (6–10 pairs) at Cuthbert Lake, Lane River, Shark River, and Charlotte Harbor on mainland Florida (Allen 1942) and at Bottle Key in Florida
Bay (Grimes and Sprunt 1936). Allen (1963) thought the Bottle Key colony,
comprising only 15 pairs, was the only remaining active colony in Florida by
1935. In the 1948–1949 nesting season, 100 breeding pairs in as many as 10
colonies were estimated for Florida Bay (Allen 1963). About every 10 years
during 1955–1978, the Florida Bay nesting population doubled. The population reached 1,254 nesting pairs in 18 colonies in the 1978–1979 period
(Powell et al. 1989). Two coastal mainland colonies (Madeira Rookery and

Lane River) also were active in 1978–1979, with a total of 115 nests. No information is available for 5 years after 1978–1979, but by 1984, surveys documented the nesting population of 448 pairs in 13 colonies, 64% fewer nests than the 1978–1979 peak. Surveys from 1984–1985 through 1987–1988 revealed a breeding population similar to 1984–1985 numbers (Powell et al. 1989). Since 1988–1989, nesting numbers have increased to 880 pairs in 21 colonies in 1991–1992, 50% more nests than the average for the previous 5 years (Bjork and Powell 1994).

Nesting numbers also have been increasing in other parts of Florida. Nesting has occurred annually in Hillsborough County since 1975, with numbers currently (1987–1992) reaching 50–75 pairs (R. Paul, unpubl. data). The first spoonbill nest recorded in Brevard County since the late 1800s was in 1987 (Smith and Breininger 1988). Numbers there have increased to 28 pairs in 1992 (R. Smith and D. Breininger, unpubl. data). Small numbers (3–8) of nests were found at inland nesting sites in 1992 (P. Frederick, unpubl. data; Bancroft and Sawicki 1992).

DISTRIBUTION AND HISTORY OF DISTRIBUTION: Roseate Spoonbills are resident along the Gulf coast of Texas and southwestern Louisiana, southern Florida, along both coasts of Central America, and through the Greater Antilles including Cuba, the Isle of Pines, Hispaniola and Great Inagua (AOU 1983). In South America they occur in northern and eastern Colombia, Venezuela, Guianas, Brazil, Ecuador, Peru (primarily east of the Andes), eastern Bolivia, Chile, Paraguay, Uruguay, and Argentina (Hancock et al. 1992).

In Florida, nesting spoonbills have not fully reclaimed their historic distribution. Prior to the mid-1800s, spoonbills nested north to Tampa Bay (Pinellas County) on the Gulf coast, Brevard County on the east coast and interior (17 Mile Swamp and Lake Poinsett), and south to the Marquesas and Boca Grande Keys (Allen 1942). By 1935, the nesting population was reduced in Florida to only one colony at Bottle Key in Florida Bay. Thereafter, as the population recovered, colonies were primarily established in Florida Bay, reaching a peak of 18 colonies in 1978–1979, as well as 2 colonies in the southern mangrove fringe of mainland Florida, Madeira Rookery, and Lane River (Powell et al. 1989). Nesting was noted only once at each of these mainland locations since the 1940s: six nests at Madeira Rookery in 1967 (Everglades National Park, unpubl. data) and three nests at Lane River in 1975 (Ogden 1975). Between the 1978–1979 nesting season and the mid-1980s, the Florida Bay population declined and the number of colony sites dropped to 13. However, there has been a gradual increase in colony site occupation since 1984 to a new high of 20 colonies in 1992 (Bjork and Powell 1994).

In other parts of southern Florida, spoonbills began reoccupying historic nesting areas in the 1970s. Seven pairs at Alafia Bank in 1975 (Dunstan 1976) were the first recorded in the Tampa Bay area since 1912 (Howell 1932). Numbers increased to 20–36 pairs by the mid-1980s and to about 75 pairs in 1992 (R. Paul, unpubl. data). Two nests each at Tarpon Key (first reported nesting since 1912; Howell 1932) and Terra Ceia Bird Key (a newer site) were discovered in 1992 (R. Paul, unpubl. data). In southwestern coastal Florida (Monroe County), 3 pairs nested at the Lane River colony in 1975 (Ogden 1975), the nearby East River colony contained about 10–15 spoonbill nests in 1986 (Bancroft and Jewell 1987), and 1 nest was recorded at the Rookery Branch colony in 1992 (S. Bass, unpubl. data). The first documentation of nesting in Brevard County in this century was 1 nest at Peacock's Pocket, Kennedy Space Center in 1987 (Smith and Breininger 1988), with a gradual increase in nesting and a high of 28 nests at three sites in 1992 (R. Smith and D. Breininger, unpubl. data). In 1992, eight spoonbill nests were located in a mixed-species colony (Andytown) in a freshwater marsh in Water Conservation Area 3A (P. Frederick, unpubl. data) and three nests were in a mixed-species colony in southwest Loxahatchee (Bancroft and Sawicki 1992), the first inland nesting records since 1914 (in Okaloacoochee, Kennard 1915; in Corkscrew Rookery, Allen 1942). At all of these locations outside Florida Bay, nesting was initiated three to four months later than Florida Bay colonies and may include renesters. Evidence of renesting was documented for a radio-tagged spoonbill that unsuccessfully nested in Florida Bay December 1991–January 1992 and was found at the Andytown colony in May 1992 (R. Bjork and P. Frederick, unpubl. data).

Concurrent with the growth in the nesting population has been the reoccupation of the summer range of nonbreeding and post-breeding spoonbills in Florida (reviewed in Robertson et al. 1983). Notable expansion has occurred along the Atlantic coast where flocks have been recorded regularly in Brevard County from March to October since the 1970s (Cruickshank 1980; R. Smith and D. Breininger, unpubl. data). The Gulf coast north to Tampa Bay appears to be the center of the summer population as it was historically. Mixed-age flocks, with peak numbers of about 300 birds, occur at Ding Darling National Wildlife Refuge from March–May, with small numbers of spoonbills observed there year-round. (J. N. Darling National Wildlife Refuge, unpubl. repts.). In recent years, concentrations of 700–1,100 spoonbills have been noted in interior marshes in the Water Conservation Areas and Loxahatchee National Wildlife Refuge, with highest estimated numbers in April and May (Hoffman et al. 1990; Bancroft and Sawicki 1992). As discussed in Allen (1942) and Robertson et al. (1983), a likely summering area for adults is Cuba. It is possible that the plumage of post-breeding adults has been confused with that of subadults (Robertson et al. 1983), and that a portion of the adults likely summer in peninsular Florida. However, the summer range of Florida nesting birds remains largely undetermined.

HABITAT REQUIREMENTS AND HABITAT TREND: Foraging habitat for Roseate Spoonbills consists of shallow marine, brackish, or freshwater sites, including tidal ponds and sloughs, mudflats, mangrove-dominated pools, freshwater sloughs and marshes (Palmer 1962), and human-created impoundments (Breininger and Smith 1990). Mangrove-dominated wetlands fringing the southern Florida mainland, the ecotone between marine-estuarine Florida Bay, and the freshwater Everglades are currently the primary foraging areas used by the large spoonbill colonies in northern Florida Bay.

Small fish (<30 mm, Hancock et al. 1992) constitute the major part of a spoonbill's diet (Allen 1942; Powell and Bjork 1989). Some common food items identified from stomach and nestling regurgitant samples included sheepshead minnow (*Cyprinodon variegatus*), mosquitofish (*Gambusia affinis*), sailfin molly (*Poecilia latipinna*), marsh killifish (*Fundulus confluentus*), sunfish (*Lepomis* sp.), shrimp (*Penaeus* sp.) and prawns (*Palaemonetes* sp.), with crayfish (*Cambarus* sp.), fiddler crabs (*Uca* sp.), isopods, amphipods, insects, and vegetative matter recovered less commonly.

Spoonbills in Florida nest primarily on coastal islands. In Florida Bay, nests are located in red (*Rhizophora mangle*) or black (*Avicennia germinans*) mangroves along small, inner island creeks or with shallow, pooled water below the nests. In the Tampa Bay area, they nest in Brazilian pepperbush (*Schinus terebinthefolius*) and black mangrove on a spoil island, as well as in red mangrove on natural islands (R. Paul, unpubl. data). Currently small numbers of birds, but historically to a much greater extent, nest in willow-head hammocks at inland, freshwater sites.

Though Roseate Spoonbill nesting habitat appears to be relatively stable, there has been recent die-off of mangroves in the interiors of some islands in Florida Bay. Everglades National Park ecologists have suggested that hypersalinity conditions in the Bay, brought on by reduced freshwater inflow from upstream water management and drought, has been a major factor influencing the die-off. Little is known about trends in the spoonbills' foraging habitat. However, the observed sensitivity of Florida Bay nesting spoonbills to rainfall may be related to the long-term changes in the ecotone (their primary foraging habitat) that have resulted from disruptions of natural flow patterns of freshwater into the area. The significance of these changes to primary and secondary productivity is largely unknown.

VULNERABILITY OF SPECIES AND HABITAT: Roseate Spoonbills are particularly vulnerable during the nesting period when they are restricted to foraging areas within a certain range of their colonies. In south Florida, the average distance to foraging grounds is 12 km (Powell and Bjork 1989); however, a flight distance of 65 km has been documented (R. Bjork and G. Powell, unpubl. data).

Nesting distribution can be influenced by loss of foraging habitat. Nesting abundance in eastern Florida Bay declined concurrent with a decrease in foraging habitat in the upper, mainline Florida Keys during 1955 through 1985 (Powell and Bjork 1990a). Habitat losses were due primarily to commercial and residential development. Natural expansion of mangrove vegetation accounted for some loss, as well.

Nesting success may be influenced by intraseasonal changes in availability of foraging habitat. Gradual dry-down of foraging habitat, with the resulting concentration of prey, is probably important for spoonbills particularly while raising young. Therefore, flooding events during the nesting period due to winter storms or water management could unpredictably and rapidly reduce foraging habitat availability. Almost complete nesting failure in the 1977–1978 season was attributed to an unusually wet winter that was thought to have caused frequent abrupt change in water levels and reduced food availability (Everglades National Park, unpubl. rept.). Aperiodic climatic events may also influence reproductive success directly, whereby prolonged cold temperature or precipitation may kill spoonbill nestlings due to exposure. Ogden (1978) noted that unseasonably cold weather in January 1973 resulted in nesting failure due to abandonment. Frederick and Loftus (in press) found that small fish (primary species eaten by spoonbills) tended to seek vegetation or burrow down in the marl substrate during periods of cold temperatures. Therefore, it could become difficult for adults to obtain sufficient prey for nestlings during extended periods of cold.

One direct influence on nesting wading birds is colony disturbance. Evidence of changes related to human disturbance occurred at a major spoonbill colony on a Florida Bay island. Nesting numbers declined sharply (70% decline for two consecutive years compared to the previous four-year average) concurrent with increased boating activity that caused repeated flushing of nesting birds. Nearby, more isolated colonies did not show these same trends of changes in abundance, further implicating disturbance as a factor contributing to the decline. A 100-foot no-access-zone was posted around the island and patrolling by Everglades National Park rangers was increased, and the following season nesting numbers more than doubled (Bjork and Powell 1994). The distribution of spoonbill nesting may also be restricted to areas free of raccoons (*Procyon lotor;* Allen 1942).

DEMOGRAPHIC CHARACTERISTICS: Roseate Spoonbills are thought to first nest at three years old (Allen 1942); however, birds in subadult plumage have been observed nesting in Tampa Bay (Dunstan 1976) and Florida Bay (G. Powell and R. Bjork, unpubl. data). The nesting season varies regionally: in Florida Bay, November–March; in peninsular Florida, March–July. Egg-laying occurs at a rate of 1 egg every other day, with incubation beginning with the day after the first egg is laid and lasting 22 days (White et al. 1982). Mean clutch sizes in Florida Bay colonies have ranged from 2.8 to 3.7 eggs/nest (1987–1992; Bjork and Powell 1994). Spoonbill productivity (juveniles 3–5 weeks old per nesting attempt) has been highly variable since the late 1930s, with estimates ranging from complete nesting failure to 2.2 young/nest (Allen 1963; Bjork and Powell 1994). Fledging occurs at about six weeks of age (White et al. 1982; Powell and Bjork 1990b). Fledglings disperse from the colony at about eight weeks old (Powell and Bjork 1990b).

Causes of nestling mortality are attributed to predation by Bald Eagles (*Haliaeetus leucocephalus*) and possibly Turkey Vultures (*Cathartes aura*) and to malnutrition and disease (Bjork and Powell 1994). Mercury concentrations in liver tissue of nestlings from Florida Bay colonies ranged from 0.16 to 5.38 ppm (wet weight) and showed patterns similar to other wading bird species, whereby higher concentrations occurred in eastern compared to western Florida Bay birds (Spalding and Forrester 1991).

KEY BEHAVIORS: Roseate Spoonbills are specialized, tactile foragers (Allen 1942). With spatulate bills (apparently well-supplied with sensitive nerve endings) held partially open and submerged in shallow water, they sweep their heads right and left until encountering prey that they snap up and swallow. Maximum foraging depth for spoonbills is about 20 cm (8 in.; Powell 1987). In Florida Bay, spoonbills feed primarily at night in the seagrass flats (Powell 1987). They feed actively in daylight as well, but primarily in the mangrove-dominated, ecotone habitats adjacent to the Bay.

Flocks of spoonbills participate in interesting group behaviors prevalent just prior to pair formation, referred to as Up Flights and Skygazing (Allen 1942). Up Flights refer to the act of a group of spoonbills rising up together in flight, circling a short distance and then landing. Sky Gazing refers to the action when a group of spoonbills resting on shore extend their necks full length and point their bills skyward when another spoonbill flies over them. Pairing and nesting behaviors include stick presentation and clasping bills (Allen 1942; Palmer 1962).

Spoonbills nest in mixed-species wading bird colonies or monospecific groups. In Florida Bay, where nesting occurs in the winter, the primary species nesting with spoonbills are Great White Herons (*Ardea herodias occidentalis*), Reddish Egrets (*Egretta rufescens*), and Double-crested Cormorants (*Phalacrocorax auritus*). In other parts of Florida, where nesting occurs in the spring, spoonbills nest with all the common wading bird species in mixed-species colonies.

CONSERVATION MEASURES TAKEN: Protection was initially afforded to spoonbill colonies after the turn of the century primarily by the National Audubon Society wardens (Allen 1942). Establishment of Everglades National Park in 1947, with the inclusion of Florida Bay, has since protected nesting sites of the Florida spoonbill population. Recently, additional protection from human disturbance through sign-posting and increased patrolling of selected Florida Bay colonies has benefited spoonbills. Establishment of protected areas in Hillsborough (National Audubon Society's Tampa Bay Sanctuaries) and Brevard (Kennedy Space Center/Merritt Island National Wildlife Refuge) Counties have secured other important nesting and roosting sites.

Roseate Spoonbills were listed by the State of Florida as endangered in 1972, but after the category species of special concern was added to the listings in 1979, they were moved to that category (D. Wood, pers. comm.). This designation provides the species special protection, recognition, or consideration because of its vulnerability to habitat modification, environmental alteration, and human disturbance that may result in its becoming a threatened species. This status designates that the birds or parts thereof or their nests or eggs cannot be taken, possessed, transported, or sold and requires a permit for activities that threaten the survival potential of the species.

A Habitat Suitability Index model was developed for Roseate Spoonbills from a review and synthesis of existing information to use in impact assessment and habitat management (Lewis 1983). The model provides output that would aid in evaluating potential roost and nest sites.

Wetland habitats used by spoonbills are directly and indirectly protected by a variety of Federal programs developed during the past two decades (OTA 1984). In particular, the U.S. Army Corps of Engineers' regulatory program established by Section 404 of the Clean Water Act regulates activities that involve disposal of dredged or fill material into wetlands.

CONSERVATION MEASURES PROPOSED: The Florida Bay Roseate Spoonbill population currently represents over 90% of Florida's nesting birds. Nesting numbers are about 1,000 pairs and have shown large fluctuations over the past two decades; the reasons for the variation are not clear. Many current nesting sites are protected; however, foraging habitat remains subject to human impacts.

Long-term survival of the Florida Bay population is dependent on protection of south Florida's estuaries, including the mangrove ecotone, the primary foraging grounds of the nesting birds. To achieve that goal it will be necessary to develop a better understanding of the ecological processes that once allowed the estuary to support huge populations of nesting wading birds. One major change to historic estuarine conditions in south Florida has been greatly reduced freshwater discharge (Smith et al. 1989; Walters et al. 1992). Evidence of decreased secondary productivity, correlated with reduced freshwater flow into the estuary, points to the need for restoration of more historic water-flow conditions (Browder 1985; Tilmant et al. 1989; McIvor et al. 1994). The General Design Memorandums for Shark and Taylor Sloughs, major conduits of freshwater into the south Florida estuaries, are currently being developed by the U.S. Army Corps of Engineers and must include full consideration of restoration of the estuary. There is evidence that spoonbill reproductive success is sensitive to hydropattern on their foraging grounds (Bjork and Powell 1994). Research is currently underway to determine the influence of water management of the C-111 canal on downstream hydropatterns of primary foraging habitat for northeastern Florida Bay nesting spoonbills. Recommendations forthcoming from the research should be considered in new water management policies (e.g., C-111 General Design Memorandum) for the area.

Birds nesting in some large northeastern Florida Bay colonies forage in the ecotone habitat outside Everglades National Park to the east of U.S. Highway 1 for foraging. These privately owned wetlands are subject to development pressure as well as water management practices. Through their Model Lands Program, Dade County has recommended immediate acquisition of these lands on their Environmentally Endangered Lands List and is requesting matching funds from the State of Florida through their Save Our Rivers program. In view of the importance of these wetlands to spoonbills and other wading birds, this purchase should be completed and the area's hydrologic characteristics should be restored.

Recovering colonies of spoonbills elsewhere in Florida should be given greater habitat protection. For example, mouths of tidal creeks provide primary foraging habitat for spoonbills and other wading birds in the Tampa Bay area (R. Paul, pers. comm.). Development of upland habitats threatens the integrity of these drainages. Water quality and natural hydropatterns should be monitored and protected. Management of human-created impoundments should consider wading birds' needs in addition to other wildlife species (Breininger and Smith 1990). As new nesting sites are discovered, they should be provided full protection.

Although many island colonies are protected from human access, such as those in Everglades National Park and National Audubon's Tampa Bay Sanctuaries, the adjacent waters are not closed to recreational activities. Buffer zones around the islands should be established that prohibit access of all water craft when birds are nesting. A 100 (Erwin 1989) to 125 meter (Rodgers and Smith 1991) buffer zone has been recommended for wading bird colonies.

Monitoring of mercury concentration in spoonbill nestlings should be continued, particularly in northeast Florida Bay colonies where concentrations were at levels that warrant further investigation. Concentrations in nestlings from northeastern Florida Bay colonies were higher than nestlings from the western colony and reached 5.38 ppm, which is a level associated with emaciation, disease, and weakness (Spalding and Forrester 1991). Studies directed at identifying sources of mercury contamination to wading birds should be pursued.

ACKNOWLEDGMENTS: We thank Mike Farmer for his assistance with obtaining the Texas spoonbill data. Rich T. Paul and Ann Schnapf provided many comments that greatly improved this account. Funding from the National Audubon Society, South Florida Water Management District, and Elizabeth Ordway Dunn and John and Florence Schumann Foundations supported studies that provided much of the current data on reproduction and habitat use of Roseate Spoonbills reported on in this account.

LITERATURE CITED:

Allen, R. P. 1942. The Roseate Spoonbill. Res. Rept. no. 2, Natl. Aud. Soc., New York, New York. 142 pp.

Allen, R. P. 1963. The present status of the Roseate Spoonbill, a summary of events 1943–1963. Unpubl. rept. Natl. Aud. Soc., Tavernier, Florida. 56 pp.

AOU. 1957. Checklist of North American birds. American Ornithologists' Union, Lord Baltimore Press, Inc., Baltimore, Maryland.

AOU. 1983. Checklist of North American birds. American Ornithologists' Union, Allen Press, Inc., Lawrence, Kansas.

Bancroft, G. T., and S. D. Jewell. 1987. Foraging habitat of Egretta herons relative to stage in the nest cycle and water conditions. Sec. ann. rept. to South Fla. Water Mgmt. Dist., West Palm Beach, Florida. 174 pp.

Bancroft, G. T., and R. J. Sawicki. 1992. Wading bird populations and distributions in the water conservation areas of the Everglades: the 1992 season. Ann. rept. to South Fla. Water Mgmt. Dist., West Palm Beach, Florida.

Bjork, R., and G. V. N. Powell. 1994. Relationships between hydrologic conditions and quality and quantity of foraging habitat for Roseate Spoonbills and other wading birds in the C-111 basin. Final rept. to South Fla. Res. Ctr., Everglades Natl. Park, Homestead, Florida.

Breininger, D. R., and R. B. Smith. 1990. Waterbird use of coastal impoundments and management implications in east-central Florida. Wetlands 10(2):223–241.

Browder, J. 1985. Relationship between pink shrimp production on the Tortugas grounds and water flow patterns in the Florida Everglades. Bull. Mar. Sci. 37:839–856.

Chapman, B. R. 1982. Current status of Roseate Spoonbills on the Texas

coast. Pp. 79–82 in South Texas fauna: a symposium honoring Dr. Allan
H. Chaney (Chapman, B. R. and J. W. Tunnel, Jr., eds.). Texas A & I
Univ., Kingsville, Texas.

Cruickshank, A. D. 1980. The birds of Brevard County. Florida Press, Inc.,
Orlando, Florida.

Dunstan, F. M. 1976. Roseate Spoonbill nesting in Tampa Bay, Florida. Fla.
Field Nat. 4:25–27.

Erwin, R. M. 1989. Responses to human intruders by birds nesting in colonies: experimental results and management guidelines. Colon. Waterbirds
12:104–108.

Frederick, P. F., and W. L. Loftus. In press. Responses of marsh fishes and
breeding wading birds to low temperatures: a possible behavioral link between predator and prey. Estuaries.

Grimes, S. A., and A. Sprunt, Jr. 1936. Aerial and surface inspection of the
Florida Keys in connection with the status of the Great White Heron and
spoonbill. Unpubl. rept., Natl. Aud. Soc., Tavernier, Florida.

Hancock, J. A., J. A. Kushlan, and M. P. Kahl. 1992. Storks, ibises, and
spoonbills of the World. Academic Press, San Diego, California.

Hoffman, W., R. J. Sawicki, and G. T. Bancroft. 1989. Wading bird populations and distributions in the water conservation areas of the Everglades:
the 1988–1989 season. Ann. rept. to South Fla. Water Mgmt. Dist., West
Palm Beach, Florida.

Hoffman, W., R. J. Sawicki, and G. T. Bancroft. 1990. Wading bird populations and distributions in the water conservation areas of the Everglades:
the 1989–1990 season. Ann. rept. to South Fla. Water Mgmt. Dist., West
Palm Beach, Florida.

Howell, A. H. 1932. Florida bird life. Coward-McCann, Inc., New York, New
York.

Kennard, F. G. 1915. The Oklaloacoochee Slough. Auk 32:154–166.

Lewis, J. C. 1983. Habitat suitability index models: Roseate Spoonbill. FWS/
OBS-82/10.50. U.S. Fish Wildl. Serv., Albuquerque, New Mexico. 16 pp.

Martin, R. P., and G. D. Lester. 1990. Atlas and census of wading bird and
seabird nesting colonies in Louisiana. Special publ. no. 3, U.S. Fish Wildl.
Serv. Contract no. 14–16–0004–89–963. Lafayette, Louisiana. 181 pp.

McIvor, C. C., J. A. Ley, and R. Bjork. 1994. A review of changes in freshwater inflow from the Everglades to Florida Bay including effects on biota and
biotic processes. Pp. 117–146 in Everglades: the ecosystem and its restoration (S. M. Davis and J. C. Ogden, eds.). St. Lucie Press, Delray Beach,
Florida.

Ogden, J. C. 1975. Florida region. Amer. Birds 29:960–963.

Ogden, J. C. 1978. Roseate Spoonbill. Pp. 52–54 in Rare and endangered biota of Florida, vol. II: birds (Kale, H. W.,II, ed.). Univ. Presses Fla., Gainesville, Florida.

OTS. 1984. Wetlands: their use and regulation. U.S. Congress, Office of Technology Assessment, OTA-O-206. Washington, D.C. 208 pp.

Palmer, R. S. 1962. Handbook of North American birds. Vol. 1. Yale Univ. Press, New Haven, Connecticut.

Portnoy, J. W. 1977. Nesting colonies of seabirds and wading birds—coastal Louisiana, Mississippi, and Alabama. U.S. Fish and Wildl. Serv. FWS/ OBS-77/07. 102 pp.

Powell, G. V. N. 1987. Dynamics of habitat use by wading birds in a subtropical estuary: implications of hydrography. Auk 104:740–749.

Powell, G. V. N., and R. D. Bjork. 1989. Relationships between hydrologic conditions and quality and quantity of foraging habitat for Roseate Spoonbills and other wading birds in the C-111 basin. Ann. rept. to South Fla. Res. Ctr., Everglades Natl. Park, Homestead, Florida. 106 pp.

Powell, G. V. N., and R. D. Bjork. 1990a. Studies of wading birds in Florida Bay: a biological assessment of the ecosystem. Comprehensive rept. 1987–1990 to the Elizabeth Ordway Dunn Found., Boston, Massachusetts. 59 pp.

Powell, G. V. N., and R. D. Bjork. 1990b. Relationships between hydrologic conditions and quality and quantity of foraging habitat for Roseate Spoonbills and other wading birds in the C-111 basin. Sec. ann. rept. to South Fla. Res. Ctr., Everglades Natl. Park, Homestead, Florida. 62 pp.

Powell, G. V. N., R. D. Bjork, J. C. Ogden, R. T. Paul, A. H. Powell, and W. B. Robertson. 1989. Population trends in some Florida Bay wading birds. Wilson Bull. 101:436–457.

Robertson, W. B., L. L. Breen, and B. W. Patty. 1983. Movement of marked Roseate Spoonbills in Florida with a review of present distribution. Jour. Field Ornithol. 54:225–236.

Rodgers, J. A., and H. T. Smith. 1991. Minimum buffer zone requirement to protect nesting bird colonies from human disturbance. Pp. 55–56 in Proc. Coastal Nongame Workshop. U.S. Fish Wildl. Serv. and Fla. Game Freshwater Fish Comm., Gainesville, Florida.

Smith, T. J., H. Hudson, M. B. Robblee, G. V. N. Powell, and P. J. Isdale. 1989. Freshwater flow from the Everglades to Florida Bay: a historical reconstruction based on fluorescent banding in the coral Solenastrea bournoni. Bull. Mar. Sci. 44:274–282.

Smith, R. B., and D. R. Breininger. 1988. Northern breeding range extension for the Roseate Spoonbill in Florida. Fla. Field Nat. 16:65–67.

Spalding, M. G., and D. J. Forrester. 1991. Effects of parasitism and disease on the nesting success of colonial wading birds (Ciconiiformes) in southern

Florida. Submitted as Final Rept. NG88-008 to Fla. Game and Fresh Water Fish Comm., Tallahassee, Florida.

Texas Colonial Waterbird Society. 1988. Texas colonial waterbird census-1988. Texas Parks and Wildl., Austin, Texas.

Texas Colonial Waterbird Society. 1989. Texas colonial waterbird census-1989. Texas Parks and Wildl., Austin, Texas.

Texas Colonial Waterbird Society. 1990. Texas colonial waterbird census-1990. Texas Parks and Wildl., Austin, Texas.

Tilmant, J. T., E. S. Rutherford, and E. B. Thue. 1989. Fishery harvest and population dynamics of red drum (*Sciaenops ocellatus*) from Florida Bay and adjacent waters. Bull. Mar. Sci. 44:126–138.

Walters, C., L. Gunderson, and C. S. Holling. 1992. Experimental policies for water management in the Everglades. Ecol. Appli. 2:189–202.

White, D. H., C. A. Mitchell, and E. Cromartie. 1982. Nesting ecology of Roseate Spoonbills at Nueces Bay, Texas. Auk. 99:275–284.

PREPARED BY: Robin Bjork, National Audubon Society, 115 Indian Mound Trail, Tavernier, FL 33070 (Current address: Department of Fisheries and Wildlife, Oregon State University, Corvallis, OR 97331), and George V. N. Powell, RARE Center for Tropical Conservation, 1616 Walnut Street, Suite 911, Philadelphia, PA 19103.

White-tailed Kite
Elanus leucurus

FAMILY ACCIPITRIDAE

Order Falconiformes

TAXONOMY: Several different *Elanus* species, occurring in Africa, Europe, Asia, Australia, North America, and South America were combined under *Elanus caeruleus* by Johnsgard (1990). Recently, the AOU (1993) recommended the adoption of the previous common name and scientific name *E. leucurus*. Palmer (1988) listed nine subspecies of White-tailed Kites; *Elanus l. majusculus* inhabits North and Central America, and *E. l. leucurus* occurs in South America.

DESCRIPTION: In flight, adult White-tailed Kites are distinguished by a black patch along the inner leading edge of the wing (when viewed from above), pointed wings, and a long, slightly-notched tail. A small black wrist patch contrasts with the pale gray linings on the undersides of the wings. Perched adults appear gray above and white below, with conspicuous black wing patches and a white tail. The wingtips nearly reach the tip of the tail, which may bob sporadically. The dorsum of adults varies from medium to dark blue-gray. The head and underside of the body are grayish-white, except for a narrow black eye-ring that widens toward the bill. The dorsal feathers of juveniles are brownish with narrow edges and white tips. The underside is streaked with reddish-brown. The iris is light grayish-brown in nestlings, becomes reddish-orange by 6 months, and gradually darkens thereafter to a deep scarlet. The cere and legs are yellow, and the bill and talons are black. The sexes can not be distinguished in the field (Palmer 1988; Johnsgard 1990).

Adults may appear similar to Northern Harriers (*Circus cyaneus*) when gliding, American Kestrels (*Falco sparverius*) when hovering or perching, or small gulls due to their pale gray plumage and buoyant flight. Juveniles may be confused with juvenile Mississippi Kites (*Ictinia mississippiensis*), although the latter are darker above and more heavily streaked below (Palmer 1988).

309

POPULATION SIZE AND TREND: Although there are no reports of historic numbers of White-tailed Kites, the North American population declined sharply around the turn of the century. By the 1930s, the species was extirpated from much of its range. A recovery, which began in the 1940s, continues today. Numbers generally are locally variable and trends are poorly monitored. Surveys in California indicated a decline from 1,437 in 1975 to 797 in 1978 (Pruett-Jones et al. 1980).

Sightings and nesting reports have increased recently in Florida. Kale (1974, 1978) summarized activity since the 1870s. A nest without eggs was observed in 1910 (Sprunt 1954), and a juvenile kite was seen in September 1971 (Kale 1974). One to three nests were located each year from 1986 to 1990 (King 1987; Curnutt 1989; W. B. Robertson, Jr., pers. comm.). These are the only confirmed nesting attempts for Florida this century. Although there have been no systematic counts, it is clear that White-tailed Kites are rare in Florida and have been so throughout historic times.

DISTRIBUTION AND HISTORY OF DISTRIBUTION: Prior to their sharp decline in North America around the turn of the century, White-tailed Kites were most numerous in the southern Great Plains, near the western coast of the United States, and along the western coast of the Gulf of Mexico (Brown and Amadon 1968; Toups et al. 1985; Palmer 1988).

By the 1940s, White-tailed Kites began to increase in California and Texas (Waian 1976; Larson 1980). Since the 1960s, they have reoccupied much of their former range and even expanded into areas where it did not occur historically. The species' present range extends from Washington and Oregon (since the late 1970s) south to the northwestern Baja peninsula, coastal Texas and Louisiana (since 1983) south through eastern Mexico, and includes recent breeding in Mississippi, Oklahoma, Arizona, and Florida since 1986 (Palmer 1988; Curnutt 1989; Johnsgard 1990). In Florida, nesting is restricted to portions of Broward and Dade counties.

HABITAT REQUIREMENTS AND HABITAT TRENDS: White-tailed Kites rely mainly on small grassland rodents for food (*Sigmodon* and *Oryzomys* in Florida, *Microtus* and *Mus* elsewhere) (Pickwell 1930; Dixon et al. 1957; Stendell and Myers 1973; King 1987; Curnutt 1989). They nest in a wide range of habitats that combine open areas for foraging with scattered trees for nesting. Suitable sites include riparian woodlands adjacent to open areas, edges of freshwater wetlands, semiarid grasslands, and agricultural areas (Palmer 1988; Johnsgard 1990). Nests recently located in Florida were in "open and brushy" habitat in the drier, northern portion of Water Conservation Area 3A (King 1987) and in a small cypress head surrounded by prairie and large stands of Brazilian pepper (*Schinus terebinthifolius*) in Everglades National Park (Curnutt 1989).

Distribution map of the White-tailed Kite, *Elanus leucurus.*

In the western United States, habitat changes (overgrazing, drainage, conversion to croplands) and persecution (shooting and egg collecting), which nearly extirpated the White-tailed Kite by the 1930s, were followed by favorable land-use practices that included irrigation of arid lands, more frequent fires, and forest clearing (Palmer 1988; Johnsgard 1990). Kites recently observed in Mississippi occupied fields of 60 ha or larger that were dominated by broomsedge (*Andropogon* sp.). Most of these areas had been recently clearcut but not intensively prepared for replanting, allowing scattered snags and live trees to remain as perch and nest sites (Toups et al. 1985).

VULNERABILITY OF SPECIES AND HABITAT: The White-tailed Kite's strong association with unprotected, human-altered habitats makes it highly vulnerable to changes in land use. Although Florida's kites are nesting on public lands managed at least to some degree for wildlife conservation, favorable conditions have resulted from undesirable changes in hydrology caused by human intervention. While this trend may continue in the near future, efforts to restore more natural water conditions in the southeast may make recently used sites unsuitable for nesting.

It appears that the species has not recolonized prairie and rangeland habitat in central and south-central Florida, where they once nested in at least small numbers (Kale 1974, 1978). If the few recent sightings in these areas reflect a real absence of kites (as opposed to limited opportunities for observation), it may indicate that these areas can no longer serve as productive nesting habitat.

CAUSES OF THREAT: At present, direct persecution is infrequent and probably has a negligible effect on White-tailed Kite populations. The most immediate threat to the kite's limited activity in Florida is the change in habitat that will result from efforts to restore more desirable hydrologic conditions in the southeast. Whereas small numbers may become established in the drier, disturbed margins of wetlands in Dade, Broward, and Palm Beach counties, a substantial increase in Florida's White-tailed Kite population probably will require successful reoccupation of previously used habitat to the north.

RESPONSES TO HABITAT MODIFICATION: As outlined above, the recent increase in the United States population of the White-tailed Kite, following its near extirpation in the early 1900s, has been due in large part to changes in land-use patterns.

DEMOGRAPHIC CHARACTERISTICS: Clutches are large and productivity is high in White-tailed Kites, especially in comparison with other kite species. Modal clutch size in three California studies (Dixon et al. 1957; Stendell 1972 in Johnsgard 1990; and Wright 1978) was 4 eggs (range 3–6). Productivity (young fledged per clutch) differed between two studies (1.9, Wright 1978; 3.2, Dixon et al. 1957), both of which noted second nesting attempts. Nesting success (clutches fledging ≥1 young) was 85% (Wright 1978). Wright (1978) reported that clutch size was significantly positively correlated with the density of *Microtus,* and productivity and success were significantly positively correlated with the percent of *Microtus* in the diet.

Age at first breeding and survival have not been reported for *E. l. majusculus* or *E. l. leucurus.*

KEY BEHAVIORS: This relatively small kite alternates fairly slow wingbeats with glides in which the wings are angled slightly upward. White-tailed Kites will alternate lengthy periods of hovering with brief glides in a pattern that may be repeated for several minutes (Palmer 1988).

Although White-tailed Kites do not appear to be migratory in temperate North America, they may range over a wide area outside the breeding season (Palmer 1988). Their movements and wintering behavior are poorly understood.

White-tailed Kites are social during the breeding season, often foraging in flocks and gathering in large communal roosts (Dixon et al. 1957). However, nesting pairs are territorial (Waian 1973 in Johnsgard 1990). They usually build a new nest each year and can be conspicuous while establishing territories, courting, and building (Dixon et al. 1957). Typically, the nest consists of small sticks and twigs lined with grasses and is placed on slender limbs near the top of a deciduous tree. It is usually open from above but may be well concealed from below (Palmer 1988). The birds habitually use specific trees near the nest to perch and copulate. The pair also will soar together high above the nest, occasionally diving in unison. During courtship and nest building, males display by vibrating upheld wings while emitting a chittering call (Dixon et al. 1957).

In one study (Warner and Rudd 1975), kites hunted most actively in the early morning and late afternoon. They typically foraged over open areas, hovering at about 30 m and dropping close to the ground before striking the prey. Foraging intensity and success increased late in the day.

CONSERVATION MEASURES TAKEN: Louisiana, where the White-tailed Kite is listed as a species of special concern, is the only southeastern state in which the species has a management designation (Meyer 1990). Whereas some agency personnel in Florida have followed the progress of several nesting attempts, there has been no systematic effort to locate and monitor breeding kites.

CONSERVATION MEASURES PROPOSED: Given the historic and current rarity of White-tailed Kites in Florida, and the logistic constraints on locating and observing nests, elaborate monitoring efforts probably are not justified at this time (Meyer 1990). Standardized programs, such as Christmas Bird Counts and Breeding Bird Surveys, may be the best way to track population changes. Studies focusing on a small number of birds could provide useful data on food habits and habitat selection (including the winter). Forestry practices that promote use by White-tailed Kites (Toups et al. 1985, see above) should be encouraged where the birds are active.

ACKNOWLEDGMENTS: James A. Rodgers provided a thoughtful review of an earlier draft.

LITERATURE CITED:

AOU. 1993. Thirty-ninth supplement to the American Ornithologists' Union check-list of North American birds. Auk 110:675–682.

Brown, L., and D. Amadon. 1968. Eagles, hawks and falcons of the world, vol. 1. Country Life Books, London. 414 pp.

Curnutt, J. 1989. Nesting of Black-shouldered Kite (*Elanus caeruleus*) in Everglades National Park, Florida. Fla. Field Nat. 17:77–79.

Dixon, J. B., R. E. Dixon, and J. E. Dixon. 1957. Natural history of the White-tailed Kite in San Diego County, California. Condor 59:156–165.

Johnsgard, P. A. 1990. Hawks, eagles, and falcons of North America. Smithsonian Inst. Press, Washington, D.C. 403 pp.

Kale, H. W., II. 1974. The status of the White-tailed Kite in Florida. Fla. Field Nat. 2:4–7.

Kale, H. W., II. 1978. White-tailed Kite. Rare and endangered biota of Florida, vol. 2, birds (H. W. Kale, II, ed.). Univ. Presses of Florida, Gainesville, Florida. 121 pp.

King, R. L. 1987. Successful nesting of Black-shouldered Kites in the Everglades of Broward County, Florida. Fla. Field Nat. 15:106–107.

Larson, D. 1980. Black-shouldered Kites in California and Texas. Amer. Birds 34:689–690.

Meyer, K. D. 1990. The status of four species of kites in the southeastern United States. Pp. 38–49 in Proceedings of the southeastern raptor management symposium (B. G. Pendleton, ed.). Natl. Wildl. Fed., Washington, D.C. 248 pp.

Palmer, R. S. 1988. Black-shouldered Kite. Pp. 132–147 in Handbook of North American birds, vol. 4, diurnal raptors, part 1 (R. S. Palmer, ed.). Yale Univ. Press, New Haven, Connecticut. 465 pp.

Pickwell, G. 1930. The White-tailed Kite. Condor 32:221–239.

Pruett-Jones, S. G., M. A. Pruett-Jones, and R. L. Knight. 1980. Status of the Black-shouldered Kite in North America. Amer. Birds 34:682–688.

Sprunt, A., Jr. 1954. Florida bird life. Cowan-McCann, Inc., New York. 527 pp.

Stendell, R. C. 1972. The occurrence, food habits and nesting strategy of White-tailed Kites in relation to a fluctuating vole population. Ph.D. dissertation, Univ. of California, Berkeley, California.

Stendell, R. C., and P. Myers. 1973. White-tailed Kite predation on a fluctuating vole population. Condor 75:359–360.

Toups, J. A., J. A. Jackson, and E. Johnson. 1985. Black-shouldered Kite: recent expansion into Mississippi. Amer. Birds 39:865–867.

Waian, L. B. 1973. The behavioral ecology of the North American White-tailed Kite of the Santa Barbara coastal plain. Ph.D. dissertation, Univ. of California, Santa Barbara, California.

Waian, L. B. 1976. A resurgence of kites. Nat. Hist. 85:40–47.

Warner, J. S., and R. L. Rudd. 1975. Hunting by the White-tailed Kite. Condor 77:226–230.

Wright, B. A. 1978. Ecology of the White-tailed Kite in San Diego County. M.S. thesis, San Diego State Univ., San Diego, California. 60 pp.

PREPARED BY: Kenneth D. Meyer, Department of Wildlife Ecology and Conservation, 118 Newins-Ziegler Hall, University of Florida, Gainesville, FL 32611 (current address: National Park Service, Big Cypress National Preserve, Box 110, Ochopee, FL 33943).

Short-tailed Hawk

Buteo brachyurus

FAMILY ACCIPITRIDAE

Order Falconiformes

TAXONOMY: The Short-tailed Hawk (*Buteo brachyurus*) was described in 1816 from a specimen collected in Cayenne, South America (Rand 1960). Three distinguishable populations exist, and there is ongoing debate whether one western South American population warrants status as a full species (the White-throated Hawk [*B. albigula*], Amadon et al. 1988). Florida birds have been referred to the Mexican subspecies *B. b. fuliginosus* (Rand 1960; Brown and Amadon 1968; Blake 1977), although Rand (1960) noted that the small sample of Florida specimens that he examined differed from Mexican specimens in having a rufous hindneck (in light-morph plumage) and being of larger size. The degree of differentiation between Mexican and Florida populations warrants further evaluation using modern systematic methods.

DESCRIPTION: The Short-tailed Hawk is a crow-sized, broad-winged, soaring hawk (Ogden 1973) affiliated with the prairie-savanna group of species in the genus *Buteo* (Millsap 1986). Short-tailed Hawks are 39–44 cm in length, have a wingspread of 83–103 cm, and weigh 342–560 g (Clark and Wheeler 1987); females are slightly larger than males. Light and dark plumage morphs occur in Florida, and each morph has a juvenal plumage distinguishable at close range. Ogden (1973) and Clark and Wheeler (1987) described these plumages in detail. Dark-morph adults are nearly uniformly dark brown, although the undersides of the primaries and rectrices are pale gray crossed by numerous thin, dark bars. The undersides of the secondaries are darker than the primaries. The outermost bar in the primaries and secondaries is wider than the others, giving the appearance of a dark border on the trailing edge of the wing. The terminal dark bar in the tail is wider than the others. Dark-morph juveniles are much like adults, except that the throat, abdomen, and underwing linings are variably mottled with white and light brown, and the tail (from below) shows more bars than the adult. The breast is not mottled,

315

giving the impression of a solid, dark bib. Both dark-morph plumages have a distinct white area in the lores that is sometimes visible in flight. Light-morph adults differ from dark adults in that the underside of the throat, breast, abdomen and wing linings are immaculately white; the dark face contrasts with the light throat, creating the impression of a dark hood over the head. The light-morph juvenal plumage differs from the definitive plumage on the underside in being orange- or buff-tinged at fledging, in having light streaks in the otherwise dark cheeks, and in having dark streaks along the sides of the breast. The buff fades or wears off by autumn (although some adults retain buff feathering on the legs), and juveniles at that time and in winter are difficult to distinguish from adults in the field. The cere and legs in both plumages are bright yellow in adults and paler yellow in juveniles. Adults of both morphs have dark brown irises; juveniles have beige irises.

The dark-morph plumage is more frequent in Florida than the light morph (Moore et al. 1953; Ogden 1973). Aerial surveys of the Kissimmee River and Lake Okeechobee system from 1987–1989 resulted in 16 Short-tailed Hawk sightings; 10 (63%) were dark-morph birds (B. Toland, unpubl. data).

In flight, Short-tailed Hawks appear proportionately similar to the more common and larger Red-tailed Hawk (*B. jamaicensis*). The two species can be further confused because Short-tailed Hawks can appear to have reddish tails when in flight if they are strongly backlit by the sun. Short-tails are best distinguished in flight by their slightly upswept wingtips when seen in profile; their aerial hunting technique of facing into the wind and hanging stationary, with wings and tail fully spread and head hanging down, scanning directly below; and their frequent use of *vertical* stoops to capture prey. All of these behaviors are occasionally seen in other hawks, but they are the norm for Short-tails in Florida. The dark-morph Broad-winged Hawk (*B. platypterus*), which occurs rarely in Florida in fall, closely resembles the dark-morph Short-tail, but can be distinguished from below by the even silver color of both the primaries and secondaries (i.e., Broad-wings lack the darker secondaries of the Short-tailed Hawk) and different tail pattern. Light-morph Broad-winged Hawks have distinctive streaks (juvenal plumage) or barring (adult plumage) on the breast and abdomen.

POPULATION SIZE AND TREND: Systematic statewide surveys have not been conducted for the Short-tailed Hawk, thus population size and trend are poorly known. Ogden (1988) described the Short-tailed Hawk as scarce and often overlooked; he speculated that the statewide population may total fewer than 500 individuals. Recent Florida Game and Fresh Water Fish Commission (FGFWFC) surveys and a review of historic records revealed about 36 Florida locations where Short-tailed Hawks have been reported during the breeding season since 1951 (Millsap et al. 1989). Since 1989, at least seven additional

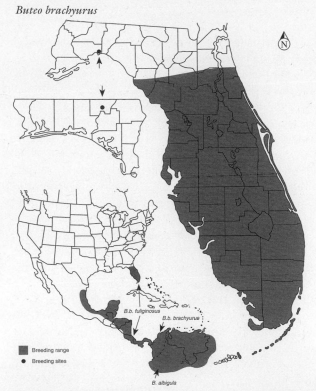

Distribution map of the Short-tailed Hawk, *Buteo brachyurus.*

locations have been documented through FGFWFC helicopter surveys and ground searches. Systematic aerial surveys of the purported winter range of the species in Everglades National Park and nearby areas were not helpful in providing information on population size; only 10 Short-tailed Hawks were detected along 789 km of transect in December 1988 (Millsap et al. 1989). Although some areas of formerly occupied habitat have been lost (e.g., swamps around Lake Istokpoga), there is no direct evidence that populations of this hawk have changed appreciably in Florida (Ogden 1988).

DISTRIBUTION AND HISTORY OF DISTRIBUTION: Short-tailed Hawks occur throughout neotropical lowlands of central and southern Mexico, Central America, and South America south to northern Argentina, southeast Brazil (east of the Andes), and Colombia and Ecuador (west of the Andes) (Brown and Amadon 1968). The disjunct U. S. population occurs widely over peninsular Florida in summer from the Lower Suwannee River on the Gulf coast (Dixie County) east to northern Putnam County, and south to Everglades National Park (Dade and Monroe counties). Short-tailed Hawks are seen in the breeding season north and south of this range periodically; historically Short-tails have nested as far north as Wakulla County (where they are still seen and may nest) and southward into the Florida Keys. During Florida's

Breeding Bird Atlas effort, Short-tailed Hawks were confirmed breeding in six, and found as probable or possible breeders in an additional 27 7.5' topographic quadrangle blocks (H. Kale II, pers. comm.).

Known important breeding areas for Short-tailed Hawks include: (1) coastal sections of Citrus, Levy, and Dixie counties; (2) the Green Swamp in Polk, Lake, and Sumter counties; (3) along and to the east of the Lake Wales, Mount Dora, and Orlando Ridges in Orange, Osceola, Seminole, Polk, and Highlands Counties; (4) along forested drainages on the Okeechobee Plain (e.g., Arbuckle Creek, Taylor Creek, Fisheating Creek, Tick Island Slough, Kissimmee River); (5) Telegraph Swamp in Charlotte County; and (6) in the Big Cypress National Preserve, Corkscrew Swamp, Fakahatchee Strand National Preserve, Collier-Seminole State Park, and Everglades National Park.

Ogden (1974) summarized sighting records that suggest Short-tailed Hawks undergo an intrapeninsular annual migration. Individuals apparently leave breeding territories in the central and northern part of the range in autumn (October–November) and winter in southern Florida (mainly south of Lake Okeechobee, and particularly in Everglades National Park). Northward movements apparently occur in February and March. The 16 Short-tailed Hawk sightings on aerial surveys of the Kissimmee River and Lake Okeechobee area between 1987–1989 were made during 1,713 km flown from March to May; no observations were made during 1,487 km flown from October to January (B. Toland, unpubl. data).

The Florida population of the Short-tailed Hawk is geographically removed from the main body of the species' range, which extends as far north as Tampico, Veracruz, in eastern Mexico. The Short-tailed Hawk perhaps colonized Florida during early-to mid-Pleistocene glacial periods when a circum-Gulf arid dispersal corridor existed (Webb 1990). Exchange of individual Short-tailed Hawks across the Gulf of Mexico is unlikely, but the similar-sized and related Broad-winged Hawk does undertake overwater crossings from the Florida Keys (MacRae 1985). In the absence of such exchange, Florida's Short-tailed Hawk population has probably been isolated since the close of the Wisconsinan stage of the Pleistocene, which was at its height 20,000 years before the present (Webb 1990).

HABITAT REQUIREMENTS AND HABITAT TREND: Based on extensive observations in Everglades National Park and Fisheating Creek, Ogden (1974) characterized the Florida habitat of the Short-tailed Hawk as mixed woodland and savanna; nesting and roosting occurred in patches, stands, or strands of forest, and foraging occurred over adjacent prairies and open country. In Polk County, Short-tailed Hawks at four sites, where nesting was confirmed or strongly suspected, used oak (*Quercus* spp.) scrub, sand pine (*Pinus clausa*) scrub, and palmetto (*Serenoa repens*) prairie ecological communities for foraging, and extensive cypress (*Taxodium distichum*) strand forests (two sites) and loblolly bay (*Gordonia lasianthus*)-mixed hardwood-slash pine (*P. elliotti*) swamps (two sites) for nesting (Millsap et al. 1989). Five nest areas located as part of ongoing FGFWFC surveys in the Big Cypress and Telegraph Swamp areas were in the interior of extensive cypress strands surrounded by wet prairies or freshwater marsh. A radio-instrumented Short-tailed Hawk from the vicinity of Rookery Bay National Estuarine Research Reserve, Collier County, spent much of its time apparently foraging along the ecotone between mangrove forest and tidal marshes and wet prairies, and roosted in mangrove forest at Collier-Seminole State Park and in a small stand of slash pine surrounded by a golf course and agricultural fields (M. Robson, unpubl. data). All 10 wintering Short-tailed Hawks detected on FGFWFC aerial surveys in Everglades National Park were soaring along the ecotone between mangrove forest and tidal or sawgrass marshes (Millsap et al. 1989).

VULNERABILITY OF SPECIES AND HABITAT: Short-tailed Hawk nesting habitat is theoretically protected through wetland protection regulations. However, timber harvest operations and land clearing have affected some nesting areas (e.g., Lake Istokpoga). Foraging habitat is unprotected in most known nesting areas, and agricultural operations and housing developments are encroaching in some cases.

CAUSES OF THREAT: The greatest threat to Short-tailed Hawks in Florida at present is loss of foraging habitat to agriculture and residential development. Loss of nesting habitat to cypress logging has occurred in some areas, most notably along Fisheating Creek in Glades County. In 1991, at least three Short-tailed Hawks were treated by Florida wildlife rehabilitators: two had been shot and one apparently had collided with a vehicle.

RESPONSES TO HABITAT MODIFICATION: Little information is available on the effects of habitat alteration on Short-tailed Hawks. Clearing of extensive cypress forests around many Florida lakes has probably resulted in the direct loss of some nesting sites, and the ongoing harvest of cypress for mulch and other uses probably threatens some existing nesting sites. Most known nesting areas are surrounded by predominately native plant communities. This suggests that large-scale landscape alterations may degrade the quality of nesting habitat. However, non-nesting Short-tailed Hawks do use suburban and agricultural areas and are seen in such habitats outside the nesting season in Dade, Collier, and Lee Counties.

DEMOGRAPHIC CHARACTERISTICS: Based on data from 24 clutches in museum collections from Florida, eggs have been found in Short-tailed Hawk nests from early March through early May (Stevenson and Anderson 1994). Incubation lasts about 34 days, but age at fledging is unknown (Ogden 1988). Young of the similarly sized and closely related Broad-winged Hawk are capable of sustained level flight at 5–6 weeks of age (Mosher 1988). Modal clutch size is 2 eggs (Ogden 1988; Stevenson and Anderson 1994). There are no substantive data on fledging success in Florida or elsewhere, although Ogden (1988) observed only one young fledge from five of six nests he monitored in South Florida; the sixth nest fledged two birds. Age at first breeding is unknown, but probably two years or older is the norm. Ogden (1988) observed an apparent one-year old female paired with an established male at a nest site in south Florida; the pair copulated but the female laid no eggs. No data are available on annual mortality rates and no substantive data are available on causes of mortality.

KEY BEHAVIORS: The Short-tailed Hawk is an extremely aerial raptor, spending much of the day soaring at altitudes up to and probably exceeding 350 m (B. Toland, unpubl. data) after thermals become active. Most hunting is done from great heights, contributing to the general inconspicuousness of the species. Short-tailed Hawks position themselves facing into the wind or over updrafts, and kite (hang motionless) on spread wings for many seconds at a time scanning the ground below. Prey is captured from nearly vertical, close-winged, high-speed dives. Dives may be interrupted one or more times as the hawk abruptly pulls out and resumes kiting. Most dives are directed at avian prey in the tops of shrubs or in trees, less frequently at prey on the ground or flying across open country (Ogden 1988).

There have been no systematic studies of Short-tailed Hawk food habits in Florida or elsewhere, but the majority of prey that have been recorded in Florida are small to medium-sized, open-country birds, especially Eastern Meadowlarks (*Sturnella magna*) and Red-winged Blackbirds (*Agelaius phoeniceus*) (Ogden 1988). Small rodents, snakes, and lizards also have been recorded in the diet in Florida (Ogden 1988; B. Millsap, unpubl. data).

The Short-tailed Hawk is generally silent, but vocally protests when humans or other raptors intrude into the immediate area of the nest. The most common protest vocalization is a high-pitched "keeeeeaa," somewhere in pitch between the whistle of a Broad-winged Hawk and the scream of a Red-tailed Hawk. Short-tailed Hawks actively dive at, and have been known to strike, humans climbing into nest trees (Ogden 1988).

CONSERVATION MEASURES TAKEN: The Short-tailed Hawk, and its nests and eggs, are protected by FGFWFC rules (Chapter 39, Florida Administrative Code) and federal rules promulgated under the Migratory Bird Treaty Act (16 U.S.C. 703–712). The FGFWFC has targeted the species for distributional surveys (Millsap et al. 1990) that are currently being conducted. Data on nest site locations are being collected and updated for eventual use in identifying and conserving essential habitat areas.

CONSERVATION MEASURES PROPOSED: Short-tailed Hawks appear to have a high degree of fidelity to breeding sites; some have been occupied for at least 16 years (Millsap et al. 1989). Given this, protection of known nesting areas should be given high priority. Currently, the known densest nesting population of this species in Florida occurs along Fisheating Creek in Glades County. This nesting area is threatened because the upland foraging habitat is being converted to cropland and the cypress are being harvested. Millsap et al. (1990) ranked the Short-tailed Hawk as one of the most vulnerable taxa to extirpation in Florida based on its apparent low population size, apparent loss of historic nesting sites, relatively small range size, tendency to concentrate its distribution during winter, and specialized diet. Given the apparent high degree of fidelity to breeding areas, increased emphasis should be placed on locating nesting sites. Nesting pairs can be located through low-elevation helicopter surveys over suitable habitat early in the morning (before thermals form and hawks begin soaring). Important nesting areas, and associated foraging habitat, should be identified and protected or brought into public ownership through whatever means are available.

ACKNOWLEDGMENTS: We would like to thank B. Cooper, C. Geanangle, T. Palmer, and R. Titus for sharing their sightings of Short-tailed Hawks with us. J. Truitt, L. Ham, and G. Weaver piloted helicopters during FGFWFC surveys. We thank D. Wood for helpful editorial comments on the manuscript. Funding for some FGFWFC surveys came from Florida's Nongame Wildlife Trust Fund.

LITERATURE CITED:

Amadon, D., J. Bull, J. T. Marshall, and B. F. King. 1988. Hawks and owls of the world: a distributional and taxonomic list. Proc. West. Found. Vert. Zool. 3(4):295–357.

Blake, E. R. 1977. Manual of neotropical birds. Univ. Chicago Press, Chicago, Illinois.

Brown, L., and D. Amadon. 1968. Eagles, hawks and falcons of the world. County Life Books, London. 945 pp.

Clark, W. S., and B. K. Wheeler. 1987. A field guide to hawks of North America. Houghton Mifflin Co., Boston, Massachussetts.

MacRae, D. 1985. Over-water migration of raptors: a review of the literature. Pp. 75–98 in Proceedings of hawk migration conference IV (M. Harwod, ed.). Hawk Migration Assoc. of North Amer. Rochester, New York.

Millsap, B. A. 1986. Biosystematics of the Gray hawk, *Buteo nitidus* (Latham). M.S. thesis, George Mason Univ., Fairfax, Virginia.

Millsap, B. A., M. Robson, and D. E. Runde. 1989. Short-tailed Hawk surveys. Fla. Game and Fresh Water Fish Comm., Nongame Wildl. Prog. Ann. Perf. Rept., Tallahassee, Florida.

Millsap, B. A., J. A. Gore, D. E. Runde, and S. I. Cerulean. 1990. Setting priorities for the conservation of fish and wildlife species in Florida. Wildl. Monog. no. 111. 57 pp.

Moore, J. C., L. A. Stimson, and W. B. Robertson. 1953. Observations of the Short-tailed Hawk in Florida. Auk 70:470–478.

Mosher, J. A. 1988. Broad-winged Hawk. Brancher stage. P. 30 in Handbook of North American birds. Volume 5. Diurnal raptors, part 2 (R. S. Palmer, ed.). Yale Univ. Press, New Haven, Connecticut.

Ogden, J. C. 1973. Field identification of difficult birds: I. Short-tailed hawk. Fla. Field Nat. 1:30–33.

Ogden, J. C. 1974. The Short-tailed Hawk in Florida. I. Migration, habitat, hunting techniques, and food habits. Auk 91:95–110.

Ogden, J. C. 1988. Short-tailed hawk. Pp. 34–47 in Handbook of North American birds. Volume 5. Diurnal raptors, part 2 (R. S. Palmer, ed). Yale Univ. Press, New Haven, Connecticut.

Rand, A. L. 1960. Races of the Short-tailed Hawk, *Buteo brachyurus*. Auk 77:448–459.

Stevenson, H. M., and B. Anderson. 1994. The birdlife of Florida. Univ. Press of Florida, Gainesville, Florida.

Webb, S. D. 1990. Historical biogeography. Pp. 70–100 in Ecosystems of Florida. (R. L. Myers and J. J. Ewel, eds.). Univ. of Central Florida Press, Orlando, Florida.

PREPARED BY: Brian A. Millsap, Nongame Wildlife Program, Florida Game and Fresh Water Fish Commission, 620 S. Meridian St., Tallahassee, FL 32399-1600; Mark S. Robson, Nongame Wildlife Program, Florida Game and Fresh Water Fish Commission, 551 North Military Trail, West Palm Beach, FL 33415; and Brian R. Toland, Florida Game and Fresh Water Fish Commission, 110 43rd Ave., S.W., Vero Beach, FL 32962 (Current address: U.S. Fish and Wildlife Service, P.O. Box 2676, Vero Beach, FL 32961-2676).

Black Rail

Laterallus jamaicensis

FAMILY RALLIDAE

Order Gruiformes

TAXONOMY: The Eastern Black Rail (*Laterallus jamaicensis*) is one of several members of the New World genus *Laterallus,* which except in North America are commonly referred to as "crakes." Other common names are Jamaican Crake and Little Black Crake. Previous synonyms are *L. j. pygmaeus* and *Cresicus jamaicensis stoddardi.*

DESCRIPTION: The Black Rail is about the size of a large sparrow (12–14 cm [5.0–5.2 in.]) with a short tail and a short black bill. The plumage is gray to black, with a chestnut collar, fine white spots on the back, and white streaks on the flanks. Males are generally larger than females. Adult males are uniformly dark gray on the head and ventral side, whereas females are lighter gray and have a white throat patch. Sexual dimorphism in juveniles is similar but less pronounced. Simultaneous wing and tail molts result in a period of flightlessness following breeding (Russell 1966; Flores and Eddleman 1990). Eye color of juveniles changes progressively from dark brown to olive-green to light brown. The scarlet eye color of the adult is gained by the first fall (Flores and Eddleman 1990).

POPULATION SIZE AND TREND: The statewide population of Black Rails is unknown and no inferences regarding population trends can be made. Extensive areas of suitable habitat are located along the north Gulf coast. Most of this area has never been surveyed for the species.

DISTRIBUTION AND HISTORY OF DISTRIBUTION: The North American range of the Black Rail is divided into five disjunct areas: (1) a threatened population is a permanent resident in southern coastal California and the lower Colorado River valley, occurring in both tidal and nontidal habitats; (2) during summer the species can be found in the upper Midwest, from Kansas to

Black Rail,
*Laterallus
jamaicensis.*
(Photo by Michael
L. Legare)

the lower Great Lakes, inhabiting the outer fringes of prairie potholes; (3) during the summer it also occurs in upper tidal marshes over a large area of the Eastern Seaboard, centered around Chesapeake Bay, and extending northward to Connecticut and southward to South Carolina; (4) Black Rails are permanent residents in upper tidal marshes along the Gulf coast from Texas to northern Florida; and (5) only slightly disjunct from the Gulf rails is a permanent resident population found on the St. Johns River marshes and Merritt Island in central Florida. Black Rails from the upper Midwest and Eastern Seaboard populations winter southward from the Gulf coast into the Caribbean, at least to the Greater Antilles. Black Rails have been reported from upland pastures in Jamaica, rooftops in Havana, and from Puerto Rico.

Howell (1932) lists a number of specific locations for the species in Florida, almost all during the migration period. The specimen records listed by Howell include locations in the Panhandle, the central Atlantic Coast, and the Keys. He states that the species "breeds in several widely separated regions." Specific breeding locations mentioned by Howell include Alachua County, St. Marks, Merritt Island, and east of Clearwater. The status of the species was updated by Sprunt (1954), who added a location in Sarasota County, based solely upon a Northern Mockingbird's imitation of the species' distinctive call. In 1989 the Florida Game and Fresh Water Fish Commission conducted extensive surveys for this species (Runde et al. 1990). These surveys detected rails at 15 locations, clustered in the upper Big Bend coast and the central St. Johns River valley. The species also has been recently reported during the breeding season in Broward County. The distribution of the Black Rail in central Florida coincides closely with the former distribution of the Dusky Seaside Sparrow (*Ammodramus maritima nigrescens*), presumably the result of these populations having similar habitat preferences and a similar history in post-Pleistocene times.

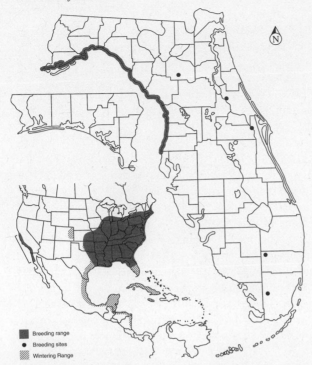

Distribution map of the Black Rail, *Laterallus jamaicensis*. Closed circles in Florida indicate recent (1980s) observations of Black Rails in the breeding season.

HABITAT REQUIREMENTS AND HABITAT TRENDS: The northern Gulf coast population of Black Rails occurs in the upper reaches of tidal marshes. The dominant vegetation in these sites is black rush (*Juncus romerianus*). In these upper marshes black rush is frequently mixed with cordgrass (*Spartina bakerii* or *S. spartinea*) and salt myrtle (*Baccharis halimifolia*). In the St. Johns River valley the species is found in freshwater marshes dominated by cordgrass. At Merritt Island it is recorded from areas where the dominant vegetation is salt grass (*Distichlis spicata*). In all these areas the species occurs in the uppermost parts of marshes. The marsh areas inhabited by these rails are typically saturated to the surface by groundwater, but are rarely inundated by surface water. Preferred habitat in Arizona (Flores and Eddleman 1990) was close to the shoreline and had water depths <2.5 cm with <25% of the substrate covered with water. Deep water appeared to preclude use of other areas of marsh.

VULNERABILITY OF SPECIES AND HABITAT: Much of the northern Gulf coast range of Black Rails is protected as publicly owned refuges or wildlife management areas. Much of the habitat in the St. Johns River valley also is within public lands. However, substantial areas in the valley are under private ownership and are used for cattle range. There is considerable development pressure on high-marsh habitat in coastal areas, although these areas receive some protection from wetland regulations. On Merritt Island large amounts of suitable habitat were destroyed by ditching of coastal marshes for mosquito control.

CAUSES OF THREAT: Conversion of habitat for development, mosquito control, and limerock mining are possible threats to Black Rail habitat, particularly in coastal areas.

RESPONSES TO HABITAT MODIFICATION: The St. Johns River Valley population of Black Rails may be susceptible to extended droughts, as a lack of recent observations suggests abandonment of known sites following the extended drought of the late 1980s. The adverse impacts from mosquito control activities have been mentioned above.

Habitat management practices likely to benefit Black Rails would maintain dense stands of perennial emergent vegetation over shallow water or moist soils. Water level manipulations in freshwater marshes must balance the need for stable, shallow water levels during nesting with the need to vary hydroperiods to maintain invertebrate populations and stands of robust emergent vegetation. The effects of fire in freshwater marshes are unknown, but use of fire must balance the need for heavy cover with any expected benefits.

DEMOGRAPHIC CHARACTERISTICS: Black Rails have a high reproductive potential, but population growth may be limited by strict requirements for shallow water habitats (Flores and Eddleman 1990). Age of first breeding has not been documented, but it is likely that Black Rails are able to reproduce in their first year. This species, as is typical of rallids, has a clutch size of 6–10 eggs. Both sexes incubate the eggs for 17–20 days and rear the brood. Double clutching or renesting is likely. Nests are cup-shaped with a canopy and ramp, all made with herbaceous materials, and placed over shallow water or moist soil. Thus, as with other rallids, this species may be vulnerable to extreme tides or floods during the nesting season.

Very little information is available regarding survival and mortality of Black Rails. Flores and Eddleman (1990) reported one adult male that was about 2.5 years old at the end of a radio-telemetry study. Evens et al. (1991) list raptors, herons, egrets, and gulls as predators of Black Rails in California marshes.

KEY BEHAVIORS: The Black Rail is very secretive, and until recently little was known about its behavior. Several different Black Rail vocalizations have been noted (Flores and Eddleman 1990; Reynard 1974). During the breeding season of April to August in Florida, a distinctive territorial call is frequently given by the male. This call is frequently rendered as "kick-kee-doo." The species will readily respond to tape recordings of this call. A growling, or "grrrr" call has been noted in aggressive responses to taped calls, and a shortened variation is given by rails guarding nests. A dove-like or cuckoo-like "croo-croo-croo-o" or "who-who-who" has been attributed to the female by Post and Enders (1969). Other vocalizations include a "tch-tch-tch" alarm call and a "churt" call note. The Black Rail, like many other rails, is active at night. However, the species also calls frequently during the day and will respond to tape recorded calls even in mid-day during the breeding season.

Radio-telemetry (Flores and Eddleman 1990) indicated very small home ranges (≤0.05 ha) and a high degree of site fidelity in a resident population.

Food habits of Black Rails in Florida are undescribed. Other studies indicate a seasonally varied diet. Bullrush (*Scirpus* spp.) and cattail (*Typha* spp.) seeds are eaten in winter. Animal foods include gastropods, amphipods, isopods, arachnids, and insects including beetles, grasshoppers, earwigs, and ants.

The Florida population is augmented in winter by migrants from the upper Midwest and Atlantic Coast populations, but nothing is known regarding the numbers of migrants wintering in Florida. Data from specimens collected at the WCTV tower in north Florida (Crawford 1981) indicates that spring movements occur from mid-March to early May. Other spring records were summarized by Stevenson and Anderson (1994) and extend from early March through early June. In the fall, Black Rails were recorded at both the WCTV tower (Crawford 1981) and Crystal River Power Plant in October (Maehr and Smith 1988). Other "fall" migration records extend from late July through early November (Stevenson and Anderson 1994).

CONSERVATION MEASURES TAKEN: No formal measures have been taken. The Florida Game and Fresh Water Fish Commission plans to conduct further surveys to determine population status and has funded research on Black Rails. The U. S. Fish and Wildlife Service (Hunter 1990) lists this bird among the highest priority "Species of Regional Concern" for the southeastern United States.

CONSERVATION MEASURES PROPOSED: The Black Rail has recently been proposed as a "Category 1" species and is being considered for possible addition to the federal "List of Endangered and Threatened Wildlife." Little management-oriented research has been conducted, but Hands et al. (1989) identified numerous information and research needs for the upper midwest population. Creation or management of impoundments with very shallow water or moist soil characteristics, and protection of coastal high marshes from dredge-and-fill operations, mosquito ditching, etc., will benefit Black Rails in Florida.

ACKNOWLEDGMENTS: W. R. Eddleman supplied unpublished reports and data.

LITERATURE CITED:

Crawford, R. L. 1981. Bird casualties at a Leon County, Florida TV tower: a 25-year migration study. Bull. Tall Timbers Res. Sta. 18:1–27.

Evens, J. G., G. W. Page, S. A. Laymon, and R. W. Stallcup. 1991. Distribution, relative abundance and status of the California Black Rail in western North America. Condor 93:952–966.

Flores, R. E., and W. R. Eddleman. 1990. Ecology of the California Black Rail in southwestern Arizona. Final report. U.S. Bur. of Reclamation. Yuma, Arizona. 68 pp.

Hands, H. M., R. D. Drobney, and M. R. Ryan. 1989. Status of the Black Rail in the northcentral United States. Unpubl. rept. U.S. Fish and Wildl. Serv. Twin Cities, Minnesota. 11 pp.

Howell, A. H. 1932. Florida bird life. Coward-McCann, Inc., New York. 579 pp.

Hunter, W. C. 1990. Handbook for nongame bird management and monitoring in the southeast region. U. S. Fish and Wildl. Serv., Southeast Region. Atlanta, Georgia. 198 pp.

Maehr, D. S., and J. Q. Smith. 1988. Bird casualties at a central Florida power plant: 1982–1986. Fla. Field Nat. 16:57–64.

Post, W., and F. Enders. 1969. Reappearance of the Black Rail on Long Island. Kingbird 19:189–191.

Reynard, G. B. 1974. Some vocalizations of the Black, Yellow and Virginia rails. Auk 91:747–756.

Runde, D. E., P. D. Southall, J. A. Hovis, R. Sullivan, and R. B. Renken. 1990. Recent records and survey methods for the Black Rail in Florida. Fla. Field Nat. 18:33–35.

Russell, S. M. 1966. Status of the Black Rail and Gray-breasted Crake in British Honduras. Condor 68:105–107.

Sprunt, A., Jr. 1954. Florida bird life. Coward-McCann, Inc., New York. 527 pp.

Stevenson, H. M., and B. H. Anderson. 1994. Birdlife of Florida. Univ. Press of Florida, Gainesville, Florida.

PREPARED BY: Douglas E. Runde, Florida Game and Fresh Water Fish Commission, Rt. 7 Box 3055, Quincy, FL 32351 (Current address: Weyerhauser Company, WTC 1A5, Federal Way, WA 98003); and Noel Wamer, 502 East Georgia Street, Tallahassee, FL 32301.

Mangrove Cuckoo

Coccyzus minor

FAMILY CUCULIDAE

Order Cuculiformes

TAXONOMY: The Mangrove Cuckoo (*Coccyzus minor*) historically has been split into 13 or more subspecies (Banks and Hole 1991), of which at least four have been claimed for Florida (Scott 1889; Howell 1932; Graves et al. 1982). Since early in this century, most authorities have designated the breeding population of Mangrove Cuckoos in Florida and the Bahamas as *C. m. maynardi* (e.g., Howell 1932). After reviewing a large series of specimens from throughout its range, Banks and Hole (1991) concluded that the Mangrove Cuckoo was best considered a somewhat variable monotypic species. They noted that the variation within each population appeared to exceed the described variation between them, although they acknowledged that their data were somewhat limited and that additional material might justify at least some subspecific recognition. This account follows Banks and Hole (1991) in considering the Mangrove Cuckoo monotypic.

DESCRIPTION: The Mangrove Cuckoo is about 30 cm long and is pale grayish-brown above. Its underparts are largely dull whitish but show a variable suffusion of buff, especially towards the ventral region. A Mangrove Cuckoo usually has a prominent black ear patch and yellow eye ring. Its tail, which is more than half the bird's length, has six large white spots on the underside. Its upper mandible is dark, its lower mandible is yellow, its iris is brown, and its legs and feet are usually described as horn-colored (Ridgway 1916). The shorter-tailed Yellow-billed Cuckoo (*C. americanus*), which breeds sympatrically with the Mangrove Cuckoo in Florida, is distinguished by the yellow base to its upper mandible and the reddish-brown inner webs to its primaries, as well as by the absence of buff on the underparts and little, if any, ear patch.

POPULATION SIZE AND TREND: Historically, the Mangrove Cuckoo has been considered a rare summer resident in Florida (Howell 1932). More

Mangrove Cuckoo, *Coccyzus minor*.
(Photo by Wes Biggs, courtesy of Florida
Audubon Society)

aggressive birdwatching techniques in recent years, including the use of song
tapes, has shown that the species is much less rare than was once believed.
However, even now its secretiveness, especially outside the breeding season,
obscures its true status. Consequently, it is difficult to assess the size and trend
of its population in the state. There is no evidence suggesting any change in
areas where its habitat has remained undisturbed.

DISTRIBUTION AND HISTORY OF DISTRIBUTION: The Mangrove
Cuckoo is found on most islands in the Caribbean basin, most of the Bahama
Islands, and parts of coastal northern South America, Central America, and
Florida (Banks and Hole 1991). It is strangely absent from nearly all of Cuba.
Banks and Hole (1991) hypothesized that it evolved in the West Indies and
then spread to the adjacent mainland portion of its range. In Florida, the
Mangrove Cuckoo was once thought confined to the Florida Keys and mainland coast north along the Gulf of Mexico to Anclote Key, Pasco County
(Howell 1932). The single May record from South Anclote Key (Scott 1888)
may merely have involved a wanderer, however, inasmuch as there appears to
be no other evidence that the species regularly occurs north of Tampa Bay. In
1994, a pair was thought to have bred at Honeymoon Island State Recreation
area, Pinellas County (D. Gagne in Pranty 1995). If true, this might represent
the northernmost breeding outpost along the Gulf. On the Atlantic coast, the
species is now known to breed regularly north at least to the vicinity of

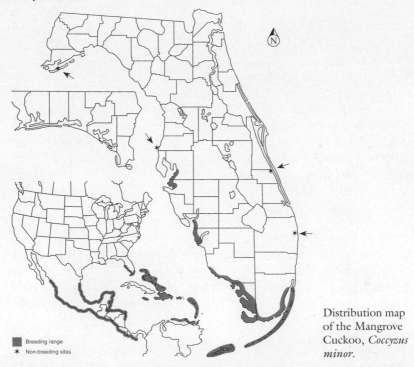

Distribution map
of the Mangrove
Cuckoo, *Coccyzus
minor*.

Virginia Key, Dade County. There also are peripheral reports at Sebastian, Indian River County (Cunningham 1966), and on Hypoluxo Island, Palm Beach County (Kale 1979, 1982, 1983). A Mangrove Cuckoo at St. George Island, Franklin County, in November 1981 was thought to be of Central American origin (Graves et al. 1982).

HABITAT REQUIREMENTS AND HABITAT TREND: The name "Mangrove" Cuckoo is possibly misleading, for in most of its Caribbean range it is found in almost any wooded habitat, in some areas even in scrublands. Although older literature suggests that in Florida it truly is confined to mangroves (Howell 1932, Bent 1940), in fact it also occupies tropical hardwood hammock in the Florida Keys and on the adjacent mainland. At least for breeding in Florida, it seems to require extensive tracts of relatively undisturbed tropical woodland, avoiding the more temperate woodlands found in most of the state away from the Keys and the southern coast. Because coastal development during this century has reduced its potential breeding habitat substantially, it might be inferred that the species has declined locally in Florida, although there is no direct evidence that it has done so. Before and after the breeding season, very limited data suggest that Mangrove Cuckoos wander into or migrate through more disturbed or temperate environments such as pinelands. There is no evidence that the species tolerates heavily developed areas here or anywhere in its range.

VULNERABILITY OF SPECIES AND HABITAT: There is apparently suitable breeding habitat for the Mangrove Cuckoo remaining in Florida in protected areas such as Everglades and Biscayne National Parks, several national wildlife refuges, Key Largo Hammocks State Botanical Preserve, and some other state-owned lands. Except for the possible impact of hurricanes or ecological change on the wooded parts of this parkland, the species and its habitat seems reasonably secure in these parts of Florida. With few exceptions, privately owned land that may once have had suitable breeding habitat has already been developed.

CAUSES OF THREAT: Outside of protected areas, especially along the Gulf coast, the Mangrove Cuckoo may be locally threatened by the prospects for development in a few remaining privately owned areas. Preservation of narrow strips of mangroves along immediate shorelines may be insufficient to provide the Mangrove Cuckoo with the continuity of tropical woodland that it seems to require, at least for breeding.

RESPONSES TO HABITAT MODIFICATION: The Mangrove Cuckoo has been found breeding in Florida only in extensive tracts of continuous tropical woodland. Its precise requirements, particularly the nature and extent of continuous forest required, have not been studied. Presumably it abandons regions as the woodland disappears or becomes too fragmented, but reoccupies them if succession to natural tropical forest is allowed to occur, as in former agricultural zones of the upper Florida Keys.

DEMOGRAPHIC CHARACTERISTICS: The reproductive biology of the Mangrove Cuckoo is poorly known in Florida and elsewhere. Nests, usually containing 2 eggs, have been found in Florida between mid-May and early July (Bent 1940). Audubon (in Howell 1932) claimed that at Key West the species was double-brooded, but there is no direct evidence to that effect. Historically the species has been considered migratory in Florida, arriving in March and departing in September (Howell 1932; Bent 1940). Since the species is virtually undetectable except when it vocalizes, and calling seems to be associated primarily with its breeding activities, its exact status as a resident or migrant in Florida is uncertain. Observations over the past thirty years or more, sometimes assisted by song tapes, show clearly that at least a portion of the population remains in Florida all year.

KEY BEHAVIORS: The Mangrove Cuckoo is so naturally secretive, especially outside the breeding season, that even determining its very presence, much less its biology, is extremely difficult. Its song consists of a distinctive series of "gaws," given mainly during its breeding period, and is often associated with the onset of rain, hence one of its vernacular names "Rain Crow." When foraging it appears to hop silently along branches through the canopy, often perching quietly for long periods. Little is known of its food requirements, but Howell (1932) mentioned that it ate caterpillars and other large insects. Langridge (1990) reported on its use of a spider in allofeeding.

CONSERVATION MEASURES TAKEN: No conservation measures have been taken specifically, but the Mangrove Cuckoo has benefited from general efforts to protect vestiges of the natural tropical ecosystems in southern Florida.

CONSERVATION MEASURES PROPOSED: Studies of the Mangrove Cuckoo's biology are sorely needed to determine more precisely its ecological requirements and status in Florida. Until such studies are undertaken, it is difficult to suggest conservation measures other than continuing to achieve the most protection possible for the remaining undisturbed tropical woodlands in the coastal regions of Florida.

ACKNOWLEDGMENTS: I thank Bill Pranty for providing draft material from the Florida Breeding Bird Atlas project, and Bill Robertson, who authored the account of the Mangrove Cuckoo in the first edition of this volume and reviewed an earlier draft of this account.

LITERATURE CITED:

Banks, R. C., and R. Hole, Jr. 1991. Taxonomic review of the Mangrove Cuckoo, *Coccyzus minor* (Gmelin). Caribbean Jour. Sci. 27:54–62.

Bent, A. C. 1940. Life histories of North American cuckoos, goatsuckers, hummingbirds, and their allies. U.S. Nat. Mus. Bull. no. 176.

Cunningham, R. L. 1966. Florida region (winter 1965-6 field notes). Aud. Field Notes 20:412–416.

Graves, G. R., R. Carter, and S. N. G. Howell. 1982. Northernmost record of the Mangrove Cuckoo on the Gulf coast. Fla. Field Nat. 10:38–39.

Howell, A. H. 1932. Florida bird life. Coward-McCann, Inc., New York.

Kale, H. W., II. 1979. Florida region (spring 1979 field notes). Amer. Birds 33:762–765.

Kale, H. W., II. 1982. Florida region (spring 1982 field notes). Amer. Birds 36:843–846.

Kale, H. W., II. 1983. Florida region (spring 1983 field notes). Amer. Birds 37:860–863.

Langridge, H. P. 1990. Courtship feeding behavior in the Mangrove Cuckoo (*Coccyzus minor*). Fla. Field Nat. 18:55–56.

Pranty, B. 1995. Field observations (summer 1994). Fla. Field Nat. 23:19–24.

Ridgway, R. 1916. The birds of North and Middle America. Part VII. U.S. Nat. Mus. Bull. no. 50.

Scott, W. E. D. 1888. Supplementary notes from the Gulf Coast of Florida, with a description of a new species of Marsh Wren. Auk 5:183–188.

Scott, W. E. D. 1889. A summary of observations of the birds of the Gulf Coast of Florida (part 4). Auk 6:245–252.

PREPARED BY: P. William Smith, Everglades National Park, 40001 State Road 9336, Homestead, FL 33034-6733.

Antillean Nighthawk
Chordeiles gundlachii
FAMILY CAPRIMULGIDAE
Order Caprimulgiformes

TAXONOMY: The Antillean Nighthawk (*Chordeiles gundlachii*) was included within the Common Nighthawk (*C. minor*) until 1982, when it was formally accorded full species rank (AOU 1982, 1983) based largely on taxonomic studies of related species by Eisenmann (1962). No detailed study of the Antillean Nighthawk and its relationships has ever been undertaken. Geographically isolated from the Common Nighthawk until only recently, it is also unclear the extent to which the Antillean Nighthawk is biologically isolated from the former species. The degree of intraspecific variation within the Antillean Nighthawk also is uncertain. Some authors (e.g., Ridgway 1914; Wetmore and Swales 1931; Peters 1940) considered the paler birds typically found in the Bahamas but also recorded elsewhere to represent a separate race (*vicinus*), distinct from *gundlachii*. Other authors (e.g., Bond 1936; Monroe 1968) believed that such differences were individual in character and that racial separation was unwarranted. Eisenmann (1962) did not discuss that issue. This account assumes that the Antillean Nighthawk is monotypic.

DESCRIPTION: The Antillean Nighthawk is similar to other nighthawks in being a long and narrow winged, aerial feeding, semidiurnal nightjar. It averages about 22 cm in length and is heavily marbled above and barred below. Both wings are crossed by patches of white about 8 cm from their tips. Males have prominent white throats and a white subterminal tail band. Females, as Common Nighthawks, usually are much buffier overall than males. Females also lack the subterminal tail band and often show a buffy rather than a white throat. The Antillean Nighthawk differs from the Common Nighthawk in several *average* characters: wing length (average <175 mm); tail length (average <98 mm); dorsal coloration (frostier ("*vicinus*") or more coarsely marked with ochre or buff); ventral coloration (buffier, especially compared to the breast); egg coloration (paler, with finer spots); clutch size (usually one rather than two eggs); and calls ("killy-ka-dick" rather than "peent") (Ridgway 1914; Eisenmann 1962; Stevenson et al. 1983). Absolute characters fail to some degree on individuals of both species within their respective core ranges and perhaps more frequently in their area of sympatry in Florida. The two examples of male Antillean Nighthawks (identified by voice and ventral coloration) in the University of Miami Research Collection taken in Florida both have longer-than-average wings, and one has a longer-than-average tail. Possibly the two species are not fully isolated genetically and some interbreeding occurs. Hybrid individuals presumably would fall within the range of variation of both species and might be difficult to detect except by genetic testing.

POPULATION SIZE AND TREND: No quantitative data is available, but the population of Antillean Nighthawks in Florida may never have exceeded a few hundred pairs. The absence of data makes it impossible to establish trends, although there are reports of recent declines in the upper Florida Keys (A. Sprunt, IV, pers. comm.).

DISTRIBUTION AND HISTORY OF DISTRIBUTION: The Antillean Nighthawk is a common breeding visitor to the Bahama Islands and Greater Antilles, where it is found north to Grand Bahama, east to the Virgin Islands, and west to Cuba and the Cayman Islands (AOU 1983). It withdraws in winter, presumably to South America (AOU 1983). The Antillean Nighthawk was first identified in Florida in 1941 at Key West (Greene 1943) and has been subsequently proven to occur in the Keys and adjacent mainland north to Virginia Key, Dade County (Stevenson et al. 1983). Published reports of Antillean Nighthawks elsewhere in Florida are mostly anecdotal and difficult to evaluate in light of the variation in both Antillean and Common nighthawks and the possibility of hybridization between them. Antillean Nighthawks probably do occur occasionally elsewhere in Florida, particularly on the southern mainland and during migration. Although the historical record is fragmentary, Stevenson et al. (1983) believed that no nighthawks bred in the Florida Keys prior to the mid-twentieth century. However, Scott (1889) stated that nighthawks were then "common . . . summer residents" at Key West. Regardless of exactly when nighthawks colonized the region, it seems unlikely that either species bred in the Keys before manmade changes to the natural environment took place. These changes would have allowed Common Nighthawks to spread southward from the Florida mainland and Antillean Nighthawks to spread northward from the West Indies.

HABITAT REQUIREMENTS AND HABITAT TREND: Over their range, Antillean Nighthawks usually nest on the ground in open areas such as little-used borrow pits, unpaved roadsides and parking lots, housing fill, airports,

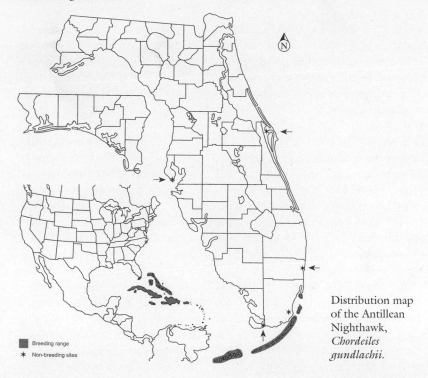

Distribution map
of the Antillean
Nighthawk,
*Chordeiles
gundlachii.*

Breeding range
Non-breeding sites

pine burns, buttonwood swashes, and marl flats. In the Florida Keys, such habitat is mostly manmade and often is transitory. Suitable areas are likely to decrease over time, either due to development or to habitat succession. However, Antillean Nighthawks appear to be acclimating to nest on flat-roofed buildings at Key West (J. Ondrejko, pers. comm.), as have Common Nighthawks on the Florida mainland. If such acclimation continues, habitat for the species should be available for the foreseeable future.

VULNERABILITY OF SPECIES AND HABITAT: It seems best to consider the Antillean Nighthawk as a recent colonist to Florida that maintains a presence here largely because of man's recent provision of suitable nesting habitat. While suitable ground areas for nesting are likely to diminish because of increasingly intensive human development in the Florida Keys, its fundamental habitat requirement should be met by flat-roofed buildings. However, habitat suitable for the Antillean Nighthawk is equally attractive to the Common Nighthawk. Although the relationship between the species has not been formally studied, the Florida Keys may provide an avenue for the more widespread Common Nighthawk to swamp the Antillean Nighthawk genetically, if the two species are not fully isolated biologically.

CAUSES OF THREAT: Man's activities have allowed two species formerly isolated geographically to come into breeding contact. Whether the Antillean Nighthawk is sufficiently isolated genetically to maintain its separate identity is unknown. Whether increasingly developed areas such as the Florida Keys will provide Antillean Nighthawks with adequate opportunities to breed and forage is also unknown.

RESPONSES TO HABITAT MODIFICATION: The Antillean Nighthawk's recent presence as a breeding species in Florida appears to be in response to man's elimination of much of the native vegetative cover in the Keys, coupled with dredge-and-fill operations. Together these activities have provided the species with suitable, if transitory, open ground areas for nesting. Development of most open ground areas coupled with more intensive human use of those that remain seem to be forcing Antillean Nighthawks to adapt to nesting on flat rooftops.

DEMOGRAPHIC CHARACTERISTICS: The Antillean Nighthawk returns to the Keys in April and remains at least into September. Its exact phenology is difficult to determine because of its close similarity in appearance to the Common Nighthawk, which is a common passage migrant and regular breeder in the area (Hundley and Hames 1961). Nests of Antillean Nighthawks in the Keys have been found principally in June (Nicholson 1957; Sutherland 1963). Nests usually are simply a bare scrape and most often consist of one pale, finely spotted egg. Nothing apparently has been published about the Antillean Nighthawk's breeding biology. The Common Nighthawk's incubation period is 19 days and its young become independent about 30 days after hatching (Harrison 1978).

KEY BEHAVIORS: Nighthawks nest on undisturbed open ground or equivalent flat areas such as rooftops. The nonincubating member of the pair often roosts on a nearby tree limb, but may also roost on the ground. Nighthawks typically are inactive during the day but become active as evening approaches, or sometimes during the day, especially before or after a rain shower. When active they chiefly remain on the wing, hawking for all kinds of flying insects from large moths and beetles to tiny flies and mosquitos (Bent 1940). The male also may engage in territorial activities such as calling in flight over his territory or diving from a great height with his wings bowed, producing a "booming" sound caused by the air rushing through his spread primaries (Bent 1940). There are no documented differences in behavior between Antillean and Common nighthawks, although the Antillean is said to boom more softly, and the call of its male is a distinctive "killy-ka-dick" rather than the male Common Nighthawk's "peent" (Wetmore and Swales 1931).

CONSERVATION MEASURES TAKEN: Other than protection under the United States' Migratory Bird Treaty Act and Florida's wildlife regulations, the Antillean Nighthawk receives no direct conservation management.

CONSERVATION MEASURES PROPOSED: Since a major threat to the Antillean Nighthawk may be from genetic swamping by the Common Nighthawk, a careful and thorough study of the interaction between populations of the two species in the Florida Keys seems especially warranted. It also seems appropriate to investigate the species' specific nesting and foraging requirements, and the advantages and disadvantages of rooftop nesting.

ACKNOWLEDGMENTS: I am greatful to Joe Ondrejko and Sandy Sprunt for sharing some of their recent observations of Antillean Nighthawks in the Keys. The staff at the American Museum of Natural History forwarded Gene Eisenmann's important taxonomic study. Bill Robertson, who authored the account of the Antillean Nighthawk in the first edition of this volume, kindly reviewed an earlier draft of this account.

LITERATURE CITED:

AOU. 1982. Thirty-fourth supplement to the American Ornithologists' Union check-list of North American birds. Auk 99 (3 Supp.):1CC–16CC.

AOU. 1983. Check-list of North American birds. Sixth ed. American Ornithologists' Union, Washington, D.C.

Bent, A. C. 1940. Life histories of North American cuckoos, goatsuckers, hummingbirds, and their allies. U.S. Nat. Mus. Bull. no. 176.

Bond, J. 1936. Birds of the West Indies. Academy of Natural Sciences, Philadelphia, Pennsylvania.

Eisenmann, E. 1962. Notes on nighthawks of the genus *Chordeiles* in southern Middle America, with a description of a new race of *Chordeiles minor* breeding in Panama. Amer. Mus. Novit. no. 2094.

Greene, E. R. 1943. Cuban Nighthawk breeding on Lower Florida Keys. Auk 60:105.

Harrison, C. A. 1978. Field guide to the nests, eggs, and nestlings of North American birds. Collins, London.

Hundley, M. H., and F. Hames. 1961. Birdlife of the Lower Florida Keys [Part 6]. Fla. Nat. 34:74–80.

Monroe, B. L., Jr. 1968. A distibutional survey of the birds of Honduras. American Ornithologists' Union Ornithol. Monog. no. 7.

Nicholson, D. J. 1957. The Bahaman Nighthawk (*Chordeiles minor vicinus*) on the Florida Keys. Auk 74:505–507.

Peters, J. L. 1940. Check-list of birds of the world. Volume IV. Harvard Univ. Press, Cambridge, Massachusetts.

Ridgway, R. 1914. The birds of North and Middle America. Part VI. U.S. Nat. Mus. Bull. no. 50.

Scott, W. E. D. 1889. A summary of observations of the birds of the Gulf Coast of Florida [Part 4]. Auk 6:245–252.

Stevenson, H. M., E. Eisenmann, C. Winegarner, and A. Karlin. 1983. Notes on Common and Antillean Nighthawks of the Florida Keys. Auk 100:983–988.

Sutherland, C. A. 1963. Notes on the behavior of Common Nighthawks in Florida. Living Bird 2:31–39.

Wetmore, A., and B. H. Swales. 1931. The birds of Haiti and the Dominican Republic. U.S. Nat. Mus. Bull. No. 155.

PREPARED BY: P. William Smith, Everglades National Park, 40001 State Road 9336, Homestead, FL 33034-6733.

West Indian Cave Swallow
Hirundo fulva fulva

FAMILY HIRUNDINIDAE

Order Passeriformes

TAXONOMY: The closest North American relative of the Cave Swallow (*Hirundo fulva*) is the Cliff Swallow (*H. pyrrhonota*). Some authors (e.g., Hellmayr 1935; Turner and Rose 1989) consider *H. fulva* to be conspecific with the Chestnut-collared Swallow (*H. rufocollaris*) of Ecuador and Peru; others (AOU 1983; Ridgely and Tudor 1989) treat the two as separate species. *H. fulva* and *pyrrhonota* are widely sympatric in the breeding season with little or no hybridization (Phillips 1986). The major taxonomic divisions within *H. fulva* are *H. f. fulva* of the Greater Antilles, *H. f. pelodoma* (=*H. f. pallida*, cf. Phillips 1986) of northern Mexico and the southwestern United States, and *H. f. citata* of southern Mexico. Barbour and Brooks (1917) named the Cuban birds *H. f. cavicola*, but Phillips (1986) considers them "doubtfully distinct" from *H. f. fulva*. Smith et al. (1988) suggested that *H. f. fulva* and *citata* together may constitute a species separate from *pelodoma*. Authors of some of the older literature (e.g., Hellmayr 1935; Bent 1942) refer to the various forms of the Cave Swallow by such names as Hispaniolan Cliff Swallow, Cuban Cliff Swallow, and Coahuila Cliff Swallow, among others.

DESCRIPTION: Cave Swallows are about 12 cm long overall and weigh about 14–22 g (Selander and Baker 1957; Turner and Rose 1989). Like Cliff Swallows, they have a buffy rump patch and a short tail with a shallow notch. Cave Swallows are most consistently distinguished from Cliff Swallows by their buffy throats; those of Cliff Swallows are dark chestnut to blackish. All Cave Swallows have cinnamon foreheads, and most Cliff Swallows have whitish foreheads, but Cliff Swallows of one race in Mexico and the southwestern United States also have cinnamon foreheads (Phillips 1986).

POPULATION SIZE AND TREND: Cave Swallows are common in Cuba (Garrido and Garcia Montana 1975), the Dominican Republic (de Dod 1978);

the lowlands of Jamaica (Lack 1976), and in Puerto Rico (Wetmore 1916; Raffaele 1989), where they are the most abundant swallows (Biaggi 1974). They are locally common in Texas where they are increasing in abundance (Martin and Martin 1978), locally common in New Mexico (Ligon 1961), and rare in Arizona (Huels 1984). Cave Swallows have nested in south Florida since at least 1987 and have increased steadily in numbers; in 1992 there were at least 100 adults at the primary breeding site (P. W. Smith, pers. comm.).

DISTRIBUTION AND HISTORY OF DISTRIBUTION: Cave Swallows breed in Jamaica, Puerto Rico, Hispaniola, and Cuba (*H. f. fulva*); on the Yucatan Peninsula and in the interior valley of Chiapas (*citata*); from north-central and northeastern Mexico north to southeastern New Mexico and west-central Texas (*pelodoma*); and in southeastern Florida (apparently *H. f. fulva*). Cave Swallows are permanent residents in southern Mexico, Jamaica, Puerto Rico, and perhaps on Hispaniola. The wintering range of the migratory forms is basically unknown (Phillips 1986). The Cave Swallow has recently expanded its range in the southwestern United States and Florida.

The first records of Cave Swallows in Florida are two specimens collected in the spring of 1890 in the Dry Tortugas. From then until the mid-1960s the species was represented in Florida by fewer than a half dozen sight and specimen records, all from the Dry Tortugas. Since then it has become a regular visitor to the Dry Tortugas from March to June, and has appeared rarely, with no seasonal pattern, along the entire Gulf coast and on the Atlantic coast north to Palm Beach County (Robertson and Woolfenden 1992; Stevenson and Anderson 1994).

In April of 1987, P. W. Smith found the first Cave Swallow nests known in Florida (Smith et al. 1988). All nests were under highway bridges in southern Dade County. Smith et al. (1988) gave general descriptions of the nesting localities; maps with the precise localities are in the Florida Ornithological Society Archives (FOSA 71) at the Florida Museum of Natural History. In 1987 there were at least 16 active nests and at least 40 birds at the two sites. The number of birds at the original sites has increased each year since then; it is not known whether they have colonized other sites (P. W. Smith, pers. comm.).

Cave Swallows may reach Florida from the Caribbean or around the Gulf coast from the west. Three specimens from the Dry Tortugas have been identified as *H. f. fulva* (Stevenson and Anderson 1994), and one from a Dade County breeding site has been identified as *cavicola* (UF 21474 in the Florida Museum of Natural History; id. by A. R. Phillips). Phillips (1986) considers a specimen from Homestead to be *pelodoma*, but Smith et al. (1988) think its identity is ambiguous.

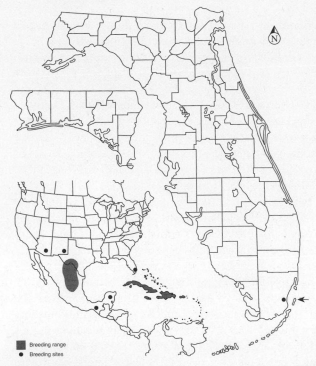

Distribution map of the West Indian Cave Swallow, *Hirundo fulva fulva*.

Breeding range
Breeding sites

HABITAT REQUIREMENTS AND HABITAT TREND: Cave Swallows require sheltered, more-or-less vertical, rock-like surfaces on which to build nests and a nearby supply of mud for nest construction. Preferred nest sites include overhanging cliffs and the twilight zone of caves, as well as buildings, bridges, and culverts (Turner and Rose 1989). All known nests in Texas were in natural caves and sinkholes until 1972, when Martin and Martin (1978) first found Cave Swallows nesting in highway culverts. The adoption of culvert nesting has allowed Cave Swallows to expand their breeding range into parts of Texas that lack caves and sinkholes (Martin and Martin 1978). All known nests in Florida are under highway bridges that cross canals. Most nests are over the middle of the canal, from 3–6 m above the water; a few are over the shore (Smith et al. 1988). Cave Swallows require flying insects for food.

VULNERABILITY OF SPECIES AND HABITAT: The major threats to Cave Swallows in Florida are likely to be competition for nests by House Sparrows (*Passer domesticus*), predation, and disturbance by humans. House Sparrows have seriously interfered with Cliff Swallow nesting in urban areas (Bent 1942; Samuel 1969). Martin (1981) found at least 14 species of vertebrate predators potentially threatening Cave Swallow nests in Texas culverts,

but found no such predators at a nearby cave. Losses due to human disturbance at the culvert nest sites in Texas are sometimes "catastrophic," yet
overall nesting success is higher in the culverts than in the caves (Martin
1981).

CAUSES OF THREAT: The Cave Swallow's status as a rarity in Florida is due
to its recent arrival in small numbers rather than reduction from former abundance. The major threat to the species' toehold in Florida may be the expansion of intense urban development that would bring with it continuous
disturbance. Some Cave Swallows do nest in towns (Turner and Rose 1989),
but there seems to be no information on their success.

RESPONSES TO HABITAT MODIFICATION: The Cave Swallow appar-
ently does not nest in any natural habitats in Florida. Its recent range expansion is due at least in part to the availability of new manmade nest sites.

DEMOGRAPHIC CHARACTERISTICS: In Texas, Cave Swallow clutch
size ranges from one to six eggs; over 95% of clutches are of three to five eggs.
Depending on the nest site (cave or culvert) and the stage of the breeding
season, mean clutch size ranges from 3.13 to 4.31, average hatching success
from 0.64 to 0.81, and mean survival to fledging from 0.11 to 0.76. At least in
some years and at some sites, clutch size, hatching success, and survival until
fledging decrease as the breeding season progresses. Most pairs are double
brooded; a few are triple brooded (Martin 1981). The incubation period is
15–18 days; the nestling period is 23–26 days (Martin et al. 1977). The most
common clutch sizes in Cuba may be 2 and 3 (Balat and Gonzalez 1982).
Most hirundines first breed when one year old, and breed for "only one or a
few seasons before dying. . ." (Turner and Rose 1989).

KEY BEHAVIORS: Like other swallows of the genus *Hirundo* (Turner and
Rose 1989), Cave Swallows build nests of mud pellets. *H. f. fulva* builds
bottle-shaped enclosed nests with a tubular entrance, whereas *pelodoma* builds
cup-shaped platforms or partially enclosed nests. The nests in Florida are
typical of *H. f. fulva* (Smith et al. 1988). Nests of *H. f. fulva* may remain half-
built during dry spells, and thus temporarily resemble those of *pelodoma,* but
when mud is again available the birds will resume construction of the nest.
Cave Swallow nests are generally not as densely clumped as those of Cliff
Swallows.

    The cave colonies in Texas described by Selander and Baker (1957) con-
tained from 3 to 1,500 nests each, with a mean of about 200 nests. The
colonies in Texas culverts surveyed by Martin (1981) had a maximum of 80
breeding pairs, with a mean of about 17 pairs. There were 14 nests along a

section of canal 300 m long at the primary Cave Swallow site in Dade County in early June of 1986 (Smith et al. 1988); the increase in the number of adults at the site since then presumably means there are more nests as well, but they have not been counted (P. W. Smith, pers. comm.).

There is little published information on the social behavior of Cave Swallows. Among migratory hirundines the male usually arrives at the colony first, selects and defends a nest site, and attempts to attract a female to it with displays and vocalizations. Hirundines nest in pairs, but males spend much time defending their mates against copulations with other males (Turner and Rose 1989). The Cave Swallow's song is about three seconds long and includes squeaks and melodic sounds. The commonest call is "weet" or "cheweet," which the birds give in choruses as they fly to and from the nest site. When disturbed they also give a high-pitched "che" or "chu" and a lower pitched "choo" (Selander and Baker 1957).

Like all swallows, Cave Swallows catch flying insects on the wing. The commonest foods are beetles, followed by diptera, ants, and other hymenoptera (Turner and Rose 1989).

CONSERVATION MEASURES TAKEN: Cave Swallows, like other native North American birds, are protected by state and federal law from unauthorized killing and harassment. The only measure taken so far to protect the Dade County swallows in particular has been to refrain from publicizing the exact location of their nest sites in order to prevent disturbance.

CONSERVATION MEASURES PROPOSED: Cave Swallow nest colonies in Florida need to be censused and mapped. Research is needed to determine whether predation, competition, harassment, and direct or indirect pesticide contamination pose threats to Cave Swallows. The agencies responsible for bridge and canal maintenance should, if possible, time their work to avoid interference with nesting. For the time being, the exact location of Cave Swallow nest sites in Florida should not be made public.

ACKNOWLEDGMENTS: I am grateful to B. H. Anderson, G. S. Morgan, W. B. Robertson, Jr., J. A. Rodgers, P. W. Smith, the late H. M. Stevenson, and G. E. Woolfenden for advice, assistance, and permission to cite unpublished information.

LITERATURE CITED:

AOU. 1983. Check-list of North American birds. 6th ed. American Ornithologists' Union, Lawrence, Kansas.

Balat, F., and J. Gonzalez. 1982. Concrete data on the breeding of Cuban birds. Acta Sc. Nat. Brno 16(8):1–46.

Barbour, T., and W. S. Brooks. 1917. Two new West Indian birds. Proc. New England Zool. Club 6:51–52.

Bent, A. C. 1942. Life histories of North American flycatchers, larks, swallows, and their allies. U.S. National Museum Bull. no. 179. Smithsonian Inst., Washington, D.C.

Biaggi, V. 1974. Las aves de Puerto Rico. Editorial Universitaria, Univ. de Puerto Rico, San Juan, Puerto Rico.

de Dod, A. S. 1978. Aves de la Republica Dominicana. Museo Nacional de Historia Natural, Santo Domingo, Dominican Republic.

Garrido, O. H., and F. Garcia Montana. 1975. Catalogo de las aves de Cuba. Academia de Ciencias de Cuba, Havana, Cuba.

Hellmayr, C. E. 1935. Catalogue of birds of the Americas and the adjacent islands in Field Museum of Natural History. Part 8. Field Mus. Nat. Hist. Publ. 347, Zool. Ser. Vol. 13.

Huels, T. R. 1984. First record of Cave Swallows breeding in Arizona. Amer. Birds 38:281–283.

Lack, D. 1976. Island biology illustrated by the land birds of Jamaica. Univ. of Calif. Press, Berkeley and Los Angeles, California.

Ligon, J. S. 1961. New Mexico birds and where to find them. Univ. of New Mexico Press, Albuquerque, New Mexico.

Martin, R. F. 1981. Reproductive correlates of environmental variation and niche expansion in the Cave Swallow in Texas. Wilson Bull. 93:506–518.

Martin, R. F., and S. R. Martin. 1978. Niche and range expansion of Cave Swallows in Texas. Amer. Birds 32:941–946.

Martin, R. F., G. O. Miller, M. R. Lewis, S. R. Martin, and W. R. Davis, II. 1977. Reproduction of the Cave Swallow: a Texas cave population. Southwestern Nat. 22:177–186.

Morgan, G. S. 1977. Late Pleistocene fossil vertebrates from the Cayman Islands, British West Indies. M.S. thesis, Univ. of Florida, Gainesville, Florida.

Phillips, A. R. 1986. The known birds of North and Middle America. Part 1. Hirundinidae to Mimidae; Certhiidae. Publ. by the author, Denver, Colorado.

Raffaele, H. A. 1989. A guide to the birds of Puerto Rico and the Virgin Islands. Rev. ed. Princeton Univ. Press, Princeton, New Jersey.

Ridgely, R. S., and G. Tudor. 1989. The birds of South America. Vol. 1, the oscine passerines. Univ. of Texas Press, Austin, Texas.

Robertson, W. B., Jr., and G. E. Woolfenden. 1992. Florida bird species: an annotated list. Spec. Publ. No. 6, Fla. Ornithol. Soc., Gainesville, Florida.

Samuel, D. E. 1969. House Sparrow occupancy of Cliff Swallow nests. Wilson Bull. 81:103–104.

Selander, R. K., and J. K. Baker. 1957. The Cave Swallow in Texas. Condor 59:345–363.

Smith, P. W., W. B. Robertson, Jr., and H. M. Stevenson. 1988. West Indian Cave Swallows nesting in Florida, with comments on the taxonomy of *Hirundo fulva*. Fla. Field Nat. 16:86–90.

Stevenson, H. M., and B. Anderson. 1994. Birdlife of Florida. Univ. Press of Florida, Gainesville, Florida.

Turner, A., and C. Rose. 1989. Swallows and martins, an identification guide and handbook. Houghton Mifflin, Boston, Massachusetts.

Wetmore, A. 1916. Birds of Porto Rico. U.S. Dept. Agriculture Bull. no. 326. Washington, D.C.

PREPARED BY: Tom Webber, Florida Museum of Natural History, University of Florida, Gainesville, FL 32611.

Black-whiskered Vireo
Vireo altiloquus

FAMILY VIREONIDAE

Order Passeriformes

TAXONOMY: The common name of the Black-whiskered Vireo (*Vireo altiloquus*) is derived from the black moustachial stripe (i.e., the "whisker") leading from the bill on each side of the throat. Ridgway (1904) recognized five subspecies in the West Indies. *V. a. barbatulus* is the typical form that breeds in southern Florida, the Bahamas, Cuba, and the Cayman Islands. *V. a. altiloquus,* which occurs from Jamaica to the northernmost Lesser Antilles, also has been recorded along the northern Gulf coast of Florida (Stevenson 1978).

DESCRIPTION: The Black-whiskered Vireo has an olive-green nape, mantle, rump, and upper tail coverts. The nape shades into the pileum that, like the forehead, is grayish-blue. The remiges are brownish-black and the outer vanes edged with yellow-green. The inner vanes are edged broadly with whitish or cream, and their tips are narrowly margined with white. A whitish superciliary line extends to the bill, and a dark streak passes through the eye. Underparts are largely whitish. The sides of the throat are bordered with a narrow, dark streak. Flanks and sides are washed with yellow-green. The brownish rectrices have the lateral vanes edged narrowly with yellow-green on their upper surfaces; inner vanes of the three lateral most rectrices are narrowly edged with white or cream. There is no discernible sexual dimorphism in plumage. *V. a. altiloquus* has a brighter olive-green back and a buffier superciliary stripe (Ridgway 1904), and a longer, more narrow bill than *V. a. barbatulus* (Stevenson 1978).

POPULATION SIZE AND TREND: Estimates of population size of the Black-whiskered Vireo are not available. However, in an analysis of Breeding Bird Survey data from 1969–1983, Cox (1987) found no significant trend for population changes in the Black-whiskered Vireo. Recent reports in *American*

348

Black-whiskered
Vireo, *Vireo
altiloquus.* (Photo
by Ken Spilios,
courtesy of Florida
Audubon Society)

Birds suggest that the population is declining in the Tampa Bay region (Paul 1988; Atherton and Atherton 1989).

DISTRIBUTION AND HISTORY OF DISTRIBUTION: The Black-whiskered Vireo breeds throughout the West Indies (AOU 1983). The two subspecies documented in Florida are migratory (Wetmore et al. 1984). They migrate through Colombia, Panama, and Venezuela and winter in the Amazon Basin from central Brazil to Peru. The species has been reported in spring at scattered locations along the Gulf coast in Alabama, Louisiana, and Texas.

Examination of unpublished breeding records obtained from the Florida Breeding Bird Atlas project (B. Pranty, pers. comm.) and sightings of the species reported in American Birds indicate that the statewide distribution of the Black-whiskered Vireo has not changed substantially from that reported by Sprunt (1954). The species breeds throughout the Florida Keys and along the coastline of the peninsula irregularly north to the Anclote Keys (Pasco County) on the west and New Smyrna Beach (Volusia County) on the east. There are scattered records of singing males from the Gulf Coast to Pensacola. The species is reported as far inland as Tallahassee in Leon County and Royal Palm Hammock in Everglades National Park.

HABITAT REQUIREMENTS AND HABITAT TREND: In Florida the Black-whiskered Vireo occurs primarily in the coastal mangrove swamps that are confined to a relatively narrow band around the southern half of the peninsula. The birds also inhabit hammocks and other hardwood areas that border the mangroves. In the past several decades, vast stretches of the coast-

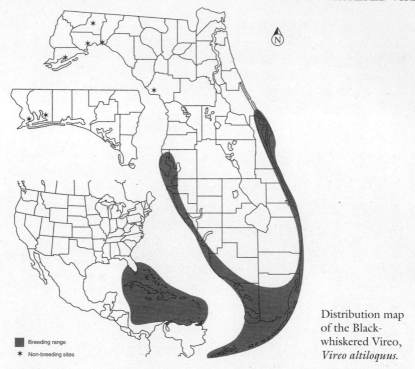

Distribution map
of the Black-
whiskered Vireo,
Vireo altiloquus.

■ Breeding range
✳ Non-breeding sites

line have been extensively modified by human development, and much of the habitat was eliminated. Today, while small amounts of mangroves are still being lost to development, most of these wetlands are protected by state and federal regulations.

VULNERABILITY OF SPECIES AND HABITAT: Population levels of the Black-whiskered Vireo may be depressed by brood parasitism from the Brown-headed Cowbird (*Molothrus ater*) and the Shiny Cowbird (*M. bonariensis*) (Paul 1987). Atherton and Atherton (1988) have suggested that the Black-whiskered Vireo may be in danger of being extirpated because of the southern range expansion of the Brown-headed Cowbird and the northern range expansion of the Shiny Cowbird. Studies of Shiny Cowbird parasitism in the West Indies indicate that the Black-whiskered Vireo is one of the main host species (Post et al. 1990), and Wiley (1988) reported that 82% of the Black-whiskered Vireo nests inspected in Puerto Rico were parasitized by Shiny Cowbirds.

CAUSES OF THREAT: The Black-whiskered Vireo would be threatened by any factors leading to an increase in the level of cowbird parasitism, or a decrease in the amount of mangrove forests along the Florida coastline.

RESPONSES TO HABITAT MODIFICATION: Freezing temperatures that have killed mangroves appear to have reduced the population of Black-whiskered Vireos in areas along the Gulf coast (R. Paul, pers. comm.). Any modification to the habitat resulting in the loss of forest canopy or the insect prey is expected to have a detrimental effect on Black-whiskered Vireos. The effects of ditching, diking, or other methods of mosquito control (e.g., aerial spraying of larvicides) in the mangroves have not been examined.

DEMOGRAPHIC CHARACTERISTICS: Most details on the reproductive variables of the Black-whiskered Vireo are unknown. Clutches are usually 2–3 eggs. The eggs are finely marked with spots of brown, purplish-brown, or reddish-brown. Information is unavailable on incubation, nestlings, fledging, or number of broods in Florida.

KEY BEHAVIORS: Black-whiskered Vireos begin arriving in Florida during the latter part of March (Sprunt 1954). Singing territorial males become conspicuous during April. Song is apparently somewhat different in various parts of the range. In Florida, the song of the Black-whiskered Vireo is chiefly three or four notes with an emphasis on the third. When perturbed, a "chirring" note may be added to the song. While on their territories, males sing for a considerable part of the day.

Information on courtship behavior and nest building is unavailable. Nests are an open cup shape similar to those of most species of the genus. The outer portion, composed of dried materials such as grasses, fibers, and seaweed, is frequently embellished with chunks of lichen, feathers, and leaves. The lining is composed of materials such as dried grass and pine needles. Nests are woven to the forks of branches; they have been reported from heights of 1.5 to more than 6 m and may overhang water.

The Black-whiskered Vireo is a canopy forager. It gleans spiders, insects, and insect larvae from the foliage. Seeds, fruits, and berries also are consumed (Bent 1950).

CONSERVATION MEASURES TAKEN: Black-whiskered Vireos are protected by Federal Migratory Bird Treaty and State wildlife regulations for take and incidental take. No specific conservation measures have been taken to protect the Black-whiskered Vireo. State and federal regulations restricting development in wetlands dominated by mangroves have helped to protect the species.

CONSERVATION MEASURES PROPOSED: Study of the Black-whiskered Vireo in both Florida and the West Indies is basic to understanding its requirements as well as its adaptations to the Florida environment. In particular, studies of its population biology and its preference of types of mangrove forests should be conducted in Florida. Also, it may be worth investigating the possible effect on the species of the various types of mosquito-control operations that are routinely conducted in mangrove forests. Significant areas of mangroves need to be preserved to afford natural habitat for the Black-whiskered Vireo, one of Florida's few native birds of tropical origin.

ACKNOWLEDGMENTS: Bill Pranty kindly provided unpublished information from the Florida Breeding Birds Atlas project. Rich Paul provided helpful comments on a draft of this species account.

LITERATURE CITED:

AOU. 1983. Check-list of North American birds, 6th ed., American Ornithologists' Union, Washington, D.C.

Atherton, L. S., and B. H. Atherton. 1988. Florida region. Amer. Birds 42:60–63.

Atherton, L. S., and B. H. Atherton. 1989. Florida region. Amer. Birds 43:90–93.

Bent, A. C. 1950. Life histories of North American wagtails, shrikes, vireos and their allies. U.S. Natl. Mus. Bull. no. 197.

Cox, J. 1987. The breeding bird survey in Florida: 1969–1983. Fla. Field Nat. 15:29–44.

Paul, R. T. 1987. Florida region. Amer. Birds 41:1425–1428.

Paul, R. T. 1988. Florida region. Amer. Birds 42:1278–1281.

Post, W., T. K. Nakamura, and A. Cruz. 1990. Patterns of Shiny Cowbird parasitism in St. Lucia and southwestern Puerto Rico. Condor 92:461–469.

Ridgway, R. 1904. Birds of North and Middle America. Part 1. Bull. U.S. Natl. Mus. no. 50.

Sprunt, A., Jr. 1954. Florida bird life. Coward-McCann, Inc., New York.

Stevenson, H. M. 1978. A probable first North American record of the Greater Antillean race of Black-whiskered Vireo. Auk 95:595.

Wetmore, A., R. F. Pasquier, and S. L. Olson. 1984. The birds of the Republic of Panama. Part 4. Passeriformes: Hirudinadae (swallows) to Fringillidae (finches). Smithsonian Inst. Press, Washington, D.C.

Wiley, J. W. 1988. Host selection by the Shiny Cowbird. Condor 90:289–303.

PREPARED BY: Peter G. Merritt, Treasure Coast Regional Planning Council, 3228 S.W. Martin Downs Blvd., Suite 205, Palm City, FL 34990; and Oscar T. Owre, Department of Biology, University of Miami, Coral Gables, FL 33124 (Deceased).

Worm-eating Warbler

Helmitheros vermivorus

FAMILY EMBERIZIDAE

Order Passeriformes

TAXONOMY: The Worm-eating Warbler (*Helmitheros vermivorus*) was originally described as *Motacilla vermivora* by Gmelin in 1789 (AOU 1983). No subspecies are recognized.

DESCRIPTION: The Worm-eating Warbler is a distinctive bird (12.5–18.8 cm, 5–5.5 in.) with two dark lateral stripes on the side of the head that contrast sharply with alternating stripes of light, buffy-orange. The throat and breast also are buffy-orange but grade into a duller whitish-gray towards the belly and remaining underparts. The upperparts are uniformly brownish-olive, except that the longer wing and tail feathers are somewhat darker. The legs are flesh toned and the bill is brown. Male, female, and immature birds are similar in appearance.

POPULATION SIZE AND TREND: Only a handful of potential breeding season records exists for the Worm-eating Warbler in Florida beginning with the record of a male in full song in 1961 (Stevenson 1961). Florida's Breeding Bird Atlas project (Kale et al. 1992) produced three "possible" breeding records along the Choctawhatchee, Escambia, and St. Marys rivers. These records were based on the presence of birds in the breeding season in suitable habitat and not actual nest records. The only other recent breeding season record comes from ravines along the eastern bank of the Apalachicola River in Liberty County (Stevenson and Anderson 1994). Needless to say, Florida's breeding population is small and no discernable trends in population size can be inferred. No effort has been made to determine whether birds occur regularly in any of these areas despite reports that this species returns to favored haunts "year after year" (Bent 1953).

Breeding Bird Survey Data (Robbins et al. 1986) spanning 1965–1979 indicate a potentially small increase in the size of the breeding population in the eastern United States. However, Stevenson and Anderson (1994) reported a decrease in the number of migrants observed in Florida in Leon, Franklin, and Wakulla Counties from 1946–1975. Decreases in the number of migrants may reflect population declines in specific regions of the eastern United States rather than broader population declines nationwide (e.g., Wiedenfeld et al. 1992). A small number of Worm-eating Warblers winters in Florida with records from as far north as Jacksonville (Stevenson and Anderson 1994), but no discernible trend in Florida's small wintering population can be seen from winter records collected to date.

DISTRIBUTION AND HISTORY OF DISTRIBUTION: The Worm-eating Warbler breeds throughout most of the eastern United States, but it is rare or absent along the Atlantic coastal plain in eastern North and South Carolina, Georgia, and Florida. The species also is missing along lower portions of the Mississippi River south of Kentucky (Stevenson 1976). The breeding range extends west of the Mississippi River to eastern Oklahoma, Texas, and Kansas, and north to northern Illinois, Indiana, Ohio, southern New York and New England.

The winter range extends from Veracruz in eastern Mexico southward through the Yucatan Peninsula and Chiapas to Panama. It is considered common in appropriate habitat in many areas of its wintering range (Rappole and Warner 1980). The species also winters in the Bahama Islands, the Greater Antilles, and casually in south and central Florida. No data are available to show any changes in the winter distribution.

HABITAT REQUIREMENTS AND HABITAT TREND: Steep, wooded ravines covered by medium-sized or larger deciduous trees and a dense undergrowth of saplings and shrubbery are appropriate breeding habitat for the Worm-eating Warbler. Preferred breeding habitat is very rare in Florida and limited to the northernmost tier of counties. Appropriate breeding habitat most often consists of beech-magnolia slope forests along tributaries of major rivers such as the Yellow, Apalachicola, Escambia, and Choctawhatchee. Habitat trends are difficult to gauge but are probably stable or declining slightly.

During migration this species prefers deciduous woods with a dense understory (Stevenson and Anderson 1994). In winter, it is common in tall evergreen tropical forests (Rappole and Werner 1980) and also may occur in second-growth woodland (Ridgely and Gwynne 1990).

VULNERABILITY OF SPECIES AND HABITAT: The Worm-eating Warbler appears to prefer large forest tracts and may be susceptible to the loss of contiguous blocks of habitat (Bond 1957; Whitcomb et al. 1981). Whereas territory size for this species averages 4–10 ha (10–25 ac.), it is rare in forest

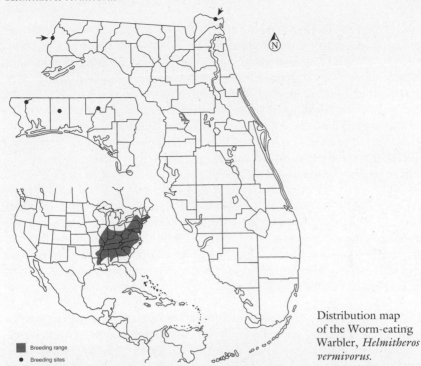

Distribution map
of the Worm-eating
Warbler, *Helmitheros
vermivorus.*

■ Breeding range
● Breeding sites

tracts that are less than 20 ha (50 ac.) in size (Whitcomb et al. 1981). However, the data used to reach this conclusion do not consider microhabitat
differences within forest patches, so it may be that absences in small forest
tracts result from a lack of suitable microhabitat conditions rather than the
small size of the tracts. A similar preference for large forest tracts was described
in wintering areas (Rappole and Werner 1980) and areas used during migration (Cox 1988).

This species is apparently not a common victim of Brown-headed Cowbird
(*Molothrus ater*) parasitism (Ehrlich et al. 1988).

CAUSES OF THREAT: Threats to Florida's small breeding population of
Worm-eating Warblers most likely stem from habitat loss, but specific causes
of habitat loss vary among the few sites where the species has been reported to
occur. In some cases the threats may stem from logging, residential development, or some other form of habitat conversion, but no generalities can be
made given the few areas where the species may nest.

A similar statement applies to Florida's small wintering population. However, habitat loss throughout a large portion of the species' wintering range in
Central America is known to stem from conversion of forested areas to agricultural activities (Sader et al. 1994).

RESPONSES TO HABITAT MODIFICATION: The responses of Worm-eating Warblers to habitat modification in Florida and elsewhere are poorly known. Bond (1957) and Whitcomb et al. (1981) consider Worm-eating Warblers to be very intolerant of large-scale forest clearing and habitat alterations. Migrants also appear to favor large forest tracts (Cox 1988) but also can be found in small forest tracts. Similar preferences for large forest tracts also have been demonstrated in wintering areas (Rappole and Werner 1980). However, all of these studies fail to account for the importance of appropriate microhabitat conditions within forest tracts, and this problem makes it difficult to pinpoint responses to deforestation and habitat modification.

DEMOGRAPHIC CHARACTERISTICS: Very little demographic data have been compiled for Worm-eating Warblers. Clutch size averages about 4–5 eggs and ranges from 3 to 6. The species is thought to be monogamous; the number of potential broods is unknown (Ehrlich et al. 1988). Average life spans have not been estimated but are likely similar to other Parulinae warblers (e.g., Kennard 1975).

KEY BEHAVIORS: Early naturalists (e.g., Brewster 1875) reported that the Worm-eating Warbler spent most of its time hopping along the ground searching for food through leaf litter, dense woody tangles, and fallen logs (Bent 1953). However, Greenberg (1987) found that Worm-eating Warblers exhibited pronounced seasonal changes in their foraging behavior. During the breeding season the species forages across all strata of deciduous woodlands. During winter the species specializes on dead curled leaves suspended in the understory of tropical forests. It may often probe a cluster of dead leaves for 15 seconds or more (Rappole and Werner 1980). Similar affinities for clusters of dead leaves can be seen during migration in Florida (J. Cox, pers. obs.).

The primary song is a rapid monotonic trill, but a varied and richer secondary song also may be given (Bent 1953). The call note is a sharp "chewt." The cup-shaped nest is usually placed on a hillside beneath low shrubs and is often concealed by dead leaves. The nest usually includes sticks, dead leaves and a soft lining made from the mycelia of the moss *Polytrichium* (Ehrlich et al. 1988, Stevenson and Anderson 1994). Most of the diet consists of spiders and insects (Kale and Maehr 1990). The name "worm-eating" is thus something of a misnomer because there are no records of it taking "worms" (Ehrlich et al. 1988). Lowery (1955) noted that this species tended to arrive slightly earlier in fall than other migrants, but its appearance in spring coincides with the bulk of spring migrants arriving in Florida in about mid-April (Stevenson and Anderson 1994). It is both a trans-Gulf migrant and a circum-Gulf migrant (Stevenson and Anderson 1994). This species also maintains a territory on its winter grounds (Rappole and Werner 1980).

CONSERVATION MEASURES TAKEN: The Worm-eating Warbler receives protection through the Migratory Bird Treaty Act, which restricts the collection of individuals and nests. In addition, two areas, where this species was reported to breed in Florida in recent years, have been protected by the land-acquisition efforts of private conservation groups and the State of Florida. Other areas along the Yellow, Choctawhatchee, and St. Marys rivers, where the species may breed, are being considered for acquisition. Timber sales on these and other state-owned lands that are not strictly dedicated to conservation may pose a threat in specific instances.

CONSERVATION MEASURES PROPOSED: Given the small size of Florida's breeding population of Worm-eating Warblers, measures to protect breeding habitat must be developed on a site-by-site basis. A more complete inventory of public land holdings in the Florida panhandle containing appropriate breeding habitat would be an important first step in this process. Migratory birds that pass through Florida could be well served by broader protection of native vegetation along coastal areas. Residential and commercial developments in coastal areas should be encouraged to protect or replant native vegetation consisting of a number of different species and structural forms (e.g., shrubs and trees).

LITERATURE CITED

AOU. 1983. A checklist of North American birds. 6th edition. American Ornithologists' Union. Allen Press. Lawrence, Kansas.

Bent, A. C. 1953. Life history of North American wood warblers. U.S. Nat. Mus. Bull. no. 203, Smithsonian Inst. Press. Washington, D.C.

Bond, R. 1957. Ecological distribution of breeding birds in the upland forests of southern Wisconsin. Ecol. Monog. 27:351–384.

Brewster, W. 1875. Some observations on the birds of Richtie County, West Virginia. Ann. Lyceum Nat. Hist., New York 22:129–146.

Cox, J. 1988. The influence of forest size on transient and resident bird species occupying maritime hammocks on northeastern Florida. Fla. Field Nat. 16:25–34.

Ehrlich, P. , D. Dobkin, and D. Wheye. 1988. The birder's handbook. Simon and Schuster. New York.

Greenberg, R. 1987. Seasonal foraging specialization in the Worm-eating Warbler. Condor 89:158–168.

Kale, H. W. II, and D. Maehr. 1990. Florida's birds. Pineapple Press. Sarasota, Florida.

Kale, H. W. II, B. Pranty, B. Stith, and W. Biggs. 1992. Florida's breeding bird atlas project. Final rept. Fla. Game and Fresh Water Fish Comm. Tallahassee, Florida.

Kennard, J. 1975. Longevity records of North American birds. Bird-Banding 46:55–73.

Lowery, G. 1955. Louisiana birds. Louisiana State Univ. Presses. Baton Rouge, Louisiana.

Rappole, J. H., and D. E. Warner. 1980. Ecological aspects of migrant bird behavior in Veracruz, Mexico. Pp. 353–393 in Migrant Birds in the Neotropics; ecology, behavior, distribution, and conservation (A. Keast and E. S. Morgon, eds.). Smithsonian Inst. Press. Washington, D.C.

Ridgely, R. S., and J. Gwynne. 1990. A guide to the birds of Panama with Costa Rica, Nicaragua, and Honduras. Second ed. Princeton Univ. Press. Princeton, New Jersey.

Robbins, C., D. Bystrak, and P. Geissler. 1986. The breeding bird survey: its first fifteen years, 1965–1979. U.S. Dept. of Int., Fish and Wildl. Serv. Res. Publ. 157. Washington, D.C.

Sadder, S. A., G. V. Powell, and J. H. Rappole. 1991. Migratory bird habitat monitoring through remote sensing. Internat. Jour. Remote. Sens. 12:363–372.

Stevenson, H. M. 1961. Possible breeding of the Worm-eating Warbler in Florida. Fla. Nat. 34:222–223.

Stevenson, H. M. 1976. Vertebrates of Florida. Univ. Presses of Florida. Gainesville, Florida.

Stevenson, H. M., and B. H. Anderson. 1994. Birdlife of Florida. Univ. Press of Florida, Gainesville, Florida.

Wiedenfeld, D., L. Messick, and F. C. James. 1992. Population trends in 65 species of North American birds. 1966–1990. U.S. Nat. Fish and Wildl. Found. Final Rept. Washington, D.C.

Whitcomb, R. F., C. S. Robbins, J. F. Lynch, B. L. Whitcomb, M. K. Klimkiewicz, and D. Bystrak. 1981. Effects of forest fragmentation on avifauna of the eastern deciduous forest. Pp. 125–205 in Forest island dynamics in man-dominated landscapes (R. L. Burgess and D. M. Sharpe, eds.). Ecological studies 41. Springer-Verlag, New York.

PREPARED BY: James Cox, Florida Game and Fresh Water Fish Commission, 620 S. Meridian Street, Tallahassee, FL 32399-1600.

Louisiana Waterthrush
Seiurus motacilla

FAMILY EMBERIZIDAE
Order Passeriformes

TAXONOMY: The Louisiana Waterthrush (*Seiurus motacilla*) was originally described as *Turdus motacilla* by Vieillot 1807 (AOU 1983). No subspecies are recognized.

DESCRIPTION: The Louisiana Waterthrush is a large warbler (14–15.5 cm, 5.75–6.25 in.) that resembles a thrush in its haunts and some of its habits. Sexes are similar both in plumage and size. The coloring is a plain olive-brown above, becoming slightly darker along the crown. The superciliary stripe, neck, and underparts are whitish with dark brown streaking along the breast. The unstreaked chin bordered by a thin, dark brown malar streak helps to distinguish this species from the Northern Waterthrush (*S. noveboracensis*), which migrates through Florida and winters in South Florida. This species also differs from the Northern Waterthrush by having light brown coloring along the flanks and brighter pink legs. Juvenile Louisiana Waterthrushes are similar to adults in appearance, except that streaking along the breast and belly is less pronounced.

POPULATION SIZE AND TREND: Florida's breeding population of the Louisiana Waterthrush is small and distributed across much of extreme northern Florida. Results of Florida's Breeding Bird Atlas project (Kale et al. 1992) show breeding records from 42 areas with an apparent concentration of records in Gadsden, Liberty, Jefferson and Leon counties. Some atlas records from late June and July should be questioned, however, because of the early dates at which this species begins to migrate (see Key Behavior). Changes in the size of Florida's breeding population cannot be determined from qualitative data sets such as breeding bird surveys (Cox 1987), and no dramatic changes in population size have been shown across the North American breeding range (Chandler et al. 1987).

Louisiana
Waterthrush,
Seiurus motacilla.
(Photo copyright
by Allan D.
Cruickshank,
courtesy of Florida
Audubon Society)

DISTRIBUTION AND HISTORY OF DISTRIBUTION: The Louisiana
Waterthrush breeds from eastern Nebraska, Kansas, Oklahoma, and Texas
north to southeastern Minnesota. The northern limit follows along the lower
Great Lakes and extends throughout much of New York, southern New
Hampshire, and Vermont. It is found throughout much of the southeast,
although somewhat localized (AOU 1983). In Florida, the species breeds
throughout the northern tier of counties with confirmed breeding records as
far south as Gainesville (Austin 1965).

The wintering range of the species includes Sonora, Nuevo Leon,
Tamaulipas, central Florida (several sight records and two specimens), the
Bahamas and Bermuda south to eastern Panama, northeast Colombia, northern Venezuela, and Trinidad (AOU 1983). It is fairly common in Puerto Rico
(Raffaele 1983). The species is rare throughout much of Florida during migration, though it appears to be more common in north Florida than in peninsular Florida (Stevenson and Anderson 1994).

Kale et al. (1988) and Stevenson and Anderson (1994) suggest that the
breeding range of this species is expanding in Florida. Recent records of birds
in new areas of Florida support this suggestion, but it is difficult to determine
whether these records constitute actual range expansion or an increase in
birding activity in little explored areas of Florida. In addition, since Florida is
at the southern limit of the breeding range, local populations may show
greater fluctuations in population size and distribution than elsewhere in the
range, and perceived range expansions may be of short duration.

HABITAT REQUIREMENTS AND HABITAT TREND: The Louisiana
Waterthrush breeds in several types of humid forests and swamps, but it

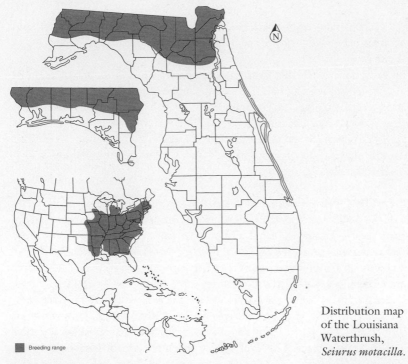

Distribution map
of the Louisiana
Waterthrush,
Seiurus motacilla.

prefers forested areas along moving streams. The species appears to favor similar areas during migration and on its wintering grounds (Morton 1980), though it may also use scrub and thicket habitats in the vicinity of water (AOU 1983) during the winter. Changes in Louisiana Waterthrush habitat are difficult to infer throughout its breeding range in Florida. Whereas trends are likely downward for a number of reasons, the rate of loss is not astronomical and appropriate habitat conditions occur locally throughout much of north Florida.

VULNERABILITY OF SPECIES AND HABITAT: Whitcomb et al. (1981) classified Louisiana Waterthrushes as a "forest interior" species that is susceptible to habitat fragmentation and reductions in the size of forested tracts. This categorization is based on very few observations, but it parallels other impressions on the birds' intolerance to deforestation (e.g., Morton 1980). Once the forest canopy along streamsides has been extensively cleared, waterthrushes tend to abandon breeding areas. Its preferred riparian habitat can thus be threatened by many types of forest-clearing operations.

The species also serves as a somewhat frequent host to Brown-headed Cowbird (*Molothrus ater*) parasitism (Ehrlich et al. 1988), at least in comparison to some other north American warblers. Although the effects of cowbird parasitism are difficult to measure, its increased frequency in fragmented and cleared areas may effectively reduce productivity on a local scale (Temple and Cary 1988).

The early date at which this species returns to Florida to breed, coupled with its streamside nesting habits, make it vulnerable to yet another calamity unrelated to habitat loss and fragmentation. Spring floods, which can occur regularly in north Florida, sometimes inundate waterthrush nests built below the high water mark (Stoddard 1978). The degree to which habitat alterations increase the magnitude of spring floods and the impact this has on waterthrushes is difficult to gauge.

CAUSES OF THREAT: Most of the forest clearing that occurs within the range of the Louisiana Waterthrush in north Florida results from commercial forestry practices rather than residential or urban development. Streamside management zones proposed as part of forestry "Best Management Practices" usually focus on major water courses and do not include the smaller streams that are most important to this species.

Residential and urban development also will decrease the habitat base available to waterthrushes. Rampant development is not occurring throughout much of north Florida, but it may be reducing habitat around some larger towns (e.g., Tallahassee). However, development need not eliminate waterthrush habitat. Protection of canopy and vegetation zones along streamsides can lessen the impacts that development and forestry practices have upon this species.

A minor threat may also stem from construction of dams that alter streamflow and may transform some areas into less favorable habitat. The Northwest Florida Water Management District currently processes about 30 permits for dam construction each year (L. Perrin, pers. comm.), but the agency has little information on the total number and distribution of dams along streams or the cumulative impacts that dam construction might pose.

RESPONSES TO HABITAT MODIFICATION: Louisiana Waterthrushes do not commonly inhabit areas that have been heavily deforested, lack overhanging vegetation along stream banks, or lack moving or standing water. One location near Tallahassee where the species was regularly seen beginning about 1982 was cleared to the edge of one side of the stream in 1987 (J. Cox, pers. obs.). The species has not been recorded along the stream since the alteration of the one side, although the other side of the stream remains forested. However, the species can apparently tolerate some moderate levels of habitat modification. A male held a territory along a small stream in a residential neighborhood in Tallahassee for two breeding seasons (1989 and 1990). Most of the homes in this neighborhood are on half-acre lots, and the neighborhood is heavily forested. The stream also flows along the edge of a conservation easement totalling 6.5 ha (16 ac.), and two passive recreation parks that span a length of about 800 m have a forested area along the stream varying from 50 to 100 m wide.

DEMOGRAPHIC CHARACTERISTICS: The Louisiana Waterthrush is single brooded (Whitcomb et al. 1981) and has a modal clutch size of 5 eggs (Bent 1953). Incubation lasts for about 12–14 days and only the female incubates (Stevenson and Anderson 1994). Both sexes feed nestlings and fledging occurs at about 9–10 (Stevenson and Anderson 1994) or 10–12 (Bent 1953) days after hatching. The species likely is sexually mature in its first breeding season, but it may become more competent with age. The maximum longevity found by Kennard (1975) was 193 months, but the average life span of post-fledgling birds has not been estimated.

KEY BEHAVIORS: The Louisiana Waterthrush is more terrestrial than other warblers, and it walks rather than hops as it forages. It also pumps its tail upwards while walking as if performing a strange dance step. The species takes many food items but adheres to a largely insectivorous diet. Howell (1932) examined stomach contents of four individuals and found dragonflies, crane fly larvae, grasshoppers, beetles, caterpillars, scale insects, spiders, as well as mollusks and one small fish.

The nest consists of wet, dead, deciduous leaves, sticks, fine grasses, and rootlets. It is held together by mud (Lowery 1955) and usually concealed amid ferns or under an exposed bank of roots.

The Louisiana Waterthrush is one of the earliest trans-Gulf migrants to appear both in fall and spring (Stevenson and Anderson 1994). Stevenson and Anderson (1994) list July as the "autumn peak" of migration. The earliest Florida record for a migrant is in late February and males may have established territories in north Florida by mid-March. The time of arrival on wintering grounds is consistently early as well (Ridgely and Gwynne 1989). Territories also are maintained in wintering areas (Morton 1980).

The song of the Louisiana Waterthrush is variable and might be confused with the song of the Hooded Warbler (*Wilsonia citrina*) or Swainson's Warbler (*Limnothlypis swainsonii*), both of which may be found in similar areas as the Louisiana Waterthrush. The song usually begins with three slurred notes (either one or two-syllable) and ends in a group of descending twitters. A flight song is occasionally given that is more elaborate (Stevenson and Anderson 1994). The call note is a sharp "chink."

CONSERVATION MEASURES TAKEN: The Louisiana Waterthrush receives some protection through the Migratory Bird Treaty Act, which protects nests, nestlings and adults from molestation, harassment, and collecting; however this act does nothing to protect the habitat that supports this species. There also are several protected areas in Florida where this species breeds. Among these are state and private conservation lands primarily along the eastern bank of the Apalachicola River, state and federal lands surrounding tributary streams of the Ochlockonee River, water management district lands along portions of the Yellow, Withlacoochee (Madison County), and Perdido Rivers, and state lands along the Chipola River.

CONSERVATION MEASURES PROPOSED: Probably the most important conservation measure that could be taken to benefit the Louisiana Waterthrush would be to extend greater protection or management to riparian zones in north Florida that are affected by silvicultural practices. Streamside management zones developed as part of "Best Management Practices" need to include smaller streams than are presently considered and also protect significant zones of deciduous vegetation along streamsides. Such activities would appear to be particularly beneficial in Gadsden, Liberty, Leon, and Jefferson counties where the bulk of Florida's breeding population appears to reside (Kale et al. 1992).

LITERATURE CITED

AOU. 1983. A checklist of North American birds. 6th Edition. American Ornithologists' Union. Allen Press. Lawrence, Kansas.

Austin, O. L. 1965. Louisiana Waterthrush (*Seiurus motacilla*) nesting in Gainesville. Fla. Nat. 38:144.

Bent, A. C. 1953. Life history of North American wood warblers. U.S. Nat. Mus. Bull. no. 203. Washington, D.C.

Cox, J. 1987. The breeding bird survey in Florida. Fla. Field Nat. 15:29–56.

Ehrlich, P. , D. Dobkin, and D. Wheye. 1988. The birder's handbook. Simon and Schuster. New York.

Howell, A. 1932. Florida bird life. Coward-McCann, Inc. New York.

Kale, H. W. II, D. Maehr, and K. Karalus. 1990. Florida's birds. A handbook and reference. Pineapple Press. Sarasota, Florida.

Kale, H. W. II, B. Pranty, B. Stith, and W. Biggs. 1992. Florida's breeding bird atlas project. Final rept. Fla. Game and Fresh Water Fish Comm. Tallahassee, Florida.

Kennard, J. 1975. Longevity record of North American birds. Bird-Banding 46:55–73.

Lowery, G. 1955. Louisiana birds. Louisiana State Univ. Presses. Baton Rouge, Louisiana.

Morton, E. S. 1980. Adaptations to seasonal changes by migrant land birds in the Panama Canal Zone. Pp. 437–453 in Migrant birds in the neotropics;

ecology, behavior, distribution, and conservation (A. Keast and E. S. Morgon, eds.). Smithsonian Inst. Press. Washington, D.C.

Raffaele, H. A. 1983. A guide to the birds of Puerto Rico and the Virgin Islands. Fondo Educativo Interamerican. San Juan, Puerto Rico.

Ridgely, R. S., and J. Gwynne. 1990. A guide to the birds of Panama with Costa Rica, Nicaragua, and Honduras. Second ed. Princeton Univ. Press. Princeton, New Jersey.

Robbins, C., D. Bystrak, and P. Geissler. 1986. The breeding bird survey: its first fifteen years, 1965–1979. U.S. Dept. of Interior, Fish and Wildl. Ser. Resour. Publ. 157. Washington, D.C.

Stevenson, H. S., and B. Anderson. 1994. Birdlife of Florida. Univ. Press of Florida, Gainesville, Florida.

Stoddard, H. 1978. The birds of Grady County, Georgia. Bull. Tall Timbers Res. Stat. no. 21. Tallahassee, Florida.

Temple, S., and J. Cary. 1988. Modeling dynamics of habitat-interior bird populations in fragmented landscapes. Cons. Biol. 2:340–347.

Whitcomb, R. F., C. S. Robbins, J. F. Lynch, B. L. Whitcomb, M. K. Klimkiewicz, and D. Bystrak. 1981. Effects of forest fragmentation on avifauna of the eastern deciduous forest. Pp. 125–205 in Forest island dynamics in man-dominated landscapes (R. L. Burgess and D. M. Sharpe, eds.). Ecological studies 41. Springer-Verlag, New York.

PREPARED BY: James Cox, Florida Game and Fresh Water Fish Commission, 620 S. Meridian Street, Tallahassee, FL 32399-1600.

American Redstart

Setophaga ruticilla

FAMILY EMBERIZIDAE

Order Passeriformes

TAXONOMY: The American Redstart (*Setophaga ruticilla*) was originally described as *Motacilla ruticilla* by Linnaeus based on information provided by Catesby (AOU 1983). Two subspecies were recognized by the AOU (1953): a northern race (*S. r. tricolora*) and the type subspecies (*S. r. ruticilla*). The validity of the *tricolora* subspecies has been questioned by Mengel (1965). Other names include flamebird, common redstart, fire-tail, redstart flycatcher, redstart warbler, and yellow-tailed warbler (Terres 1980).

DESCRIPTION: The American Redstart is an average-sized warbler (13–15 cm) with distinctive colors (Robbins et al. 1966). Males are glossy black above and white below with bright orange-red patches on the wing, tail, and sides. Females and immature males appear similar to one another with grayish or greenish-gray coloration above and yellow patches on the wing, tail, and sides instead of the orange-red patches found on adult males. Juvenile males attain the adult coloration over a two-year period with traces of the blacker adult coloration appearing first on the face and foreneck (Ficken and Ficken 1967). The American Redstart also differs from other warblers in the shape of its tail and bill. The tail is relatively long and fans out at the base. The bill is flat and similar in shape to bills found in flycatchers (Family Tyrannidae). There also are flycatcher-like rictal bristles that surround the mouth (Ehrlich et al. 1988).

POPULATION SIZE AND TREND: The breeding population of American Redstarts in Florida is localized and no definitive trends can be discerned from available datasets (e.g., Breeding Bird Surveys and Christmas Bird Counts). Weston (1965) considered the Redstart much reduced in numbers in all seasons in west Florida, and this estimation is consistent with trends reported elsewhere in the breeding range where more complete data exist. Based on a 15-year analysis of Breeding Bird Survey data, Robbins et al. (1986) reported a significant decline in numbers in the southeastern United States. Breeding

American Redstart,
Setophaga ruticilla.
(Photo by Glen M.
Wood)

season numbers elsewhere in the United States are apparently stable or increasing (Robbins et al. 1986).

Within appropriate habitat, the American Redstart can be relatively common to abundant during the breeding season. Hamel (1992) reported densities of 2.7–87 per 40 ha (100 ac.), depending on habitat type. Stevenson (1968) counted 12 birds near Laurel Hill (Walton County) in June, which provides an indication of the local abundance of the species even at the edge of its breeding range in Florida.

Robertson and Woolfenden (1992) described Florida's migratory population as uncommon to locally common. The relative abundance of birds observed during migration varies by location and season in Florida. In northwest Florida, the American Redstart is more common during fall migration than during spring migration (Stevenson and Anderson 1994). In central Florida and along the Atlantic coast, migrant American Redstarts are more common in spring than in fall (Taylor and Kershner 1986; Stevenson and Anderson 1994). Stevenson and Anderson (1994) reported a decrease in the number of individuals recorded on migration counts conducted in north-central Florida from 1952 to 1990.

American Redstarts also are regular winter visitors in Florida and become increasingly more frequent and numerous southward and near the coast (Robertson and Woolfenden 1992). Winter season records exist as far north as Gainesville (Stevenson and Anderson 1994). Winter abundances also can be fairly high with 10–51 recorded per 10 ha in Jamaica (Holmes et al. 1989). Stevenson and Anderson (1994) tabulated increasing trends on three Christmas Bird Counts and decreasing trends on one CBC in Florida.

DISTRIBUTION AND HISTORY OF DISTRIBUTION: The American Redstart breeds from southeastern Alaska east to Newfoundland; south to southern Alabama and northern Florida (AOU 1983). Within this broad area,

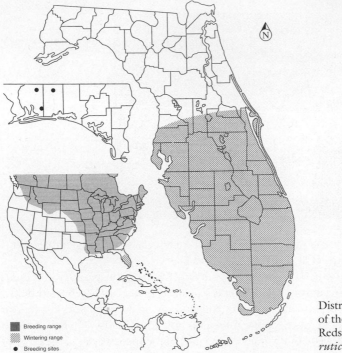

Distribution map
of the American
Redstart, *Setophaga
ruticilla.*

breeding is fairly continuous except in the Great Plains, where the species is
largely absent. The American Redstart winters from southern Baja California
and along both coasts of Mexico, southern Texas, central Florida, and the
Bahamas south to northern Ecuador and Brazil.

The breeding range in Florida is limited to the extreme northwest portion
of the state and has not likely changed dramatically in recent decades. Local
populations are found along the Yellow and Escambia Rivers and their tributaries. Stevenson (1978) described new breeding season records near Pensacola
that may represent an expanding breeding range. The Atlas of Florida Breeding Birds (Kale et al. 1992) shows one breeding season record near Pensacola
and only three other breeding season records statewide. These data indicate
the breeding population has remained very localized.

Records of migrants occur as late as mid-June in Florida (Stevenson and
Anderson 1994) and can make breeding status difficult to ascertain unless
based on direct evidence of breeding. No nest has been found in Florida
(Stevenson and Anderson 1994), and most breeding season records outside
the presumed breeding range in Florida consist of a single bird or pair of birds
(Stevenson and Anderson 1994).

HABITAT REQUIREMENTS AND HABITAT TREND: American Red-
starts prefer mature deciduous forests in Florida with a well-established under-

story of shrubs and second-growth trees (Stevenson and Anderson 1994). The preferred habitat conditions in Florida are usually associated with stream sides, but the species may be found in upland habitats farther north. DeGraaf (1985) and DeGraaf and Chadwick (1987) reported finding Redstarts in medium-aged forest stands in New England. Hamel (1992) lists preferred breeding habitat in the Southeastern Coastal Plain as extensive stands of bottomland hardwoods and swamps. Habitat trends at a coarse scale seem stable (Kautz 1993).

During migration and in winter, American Redstarts are found in a variety of habitat types. The winter habitat is described as forest borders, second-growth woodlands, broadleaf evergreen woods, scrubby thickets, and mangroves (Ridgley and Gwynne 1989; Hamel 1992). Winter habitat requirements in south Florida are not well known.

VULNERABILITY OF SPECIES AND HABITAT: American Redstarts require forest cover for breeding; thus a large-scale loss of forest cover may eliminate the American Redstart from an area. Bond (1957) reported that American Redstarts were not frequently found in forests smaller than 32 ha, and Whitcomb et al. (1981) did not find this warbler in forests smaller than 70 ha (170 ac.). However, data provided by Robbins et al. (1989) suggested the habitat requirements may not be linked to the extent of forest cover but rather to more specific habitat characteristics within forest patches. In the areas sampled by Robbins et al. (1989), abundances of Redstarts correlated most strongly with the percent coniferous canopy cover, the percent ground cover, and the number of large trees, but not forest size.

The vulnerability of wintering habitat areas are not well known. More information on winter habitat requirements is needed. Since individuals may return to specific wintering areas each year (Diamond and Smith 1973). The loss of wintering habitat may play an important role in maintaining stable populations.

CAUSES OF THREAT: Probably the primary threat to the American Redstart breeding population in Florida is large-scale timber operations along a few streams in northwest Florida. Noon et al. (1979) found populations decreased in a variety of disturbed and successional habitats, and Crawford et al. (1981) found that forestry practices that opened the canopy also decreased populations. Based on the breeding season distributions reported by Kale et al. (1992) and Stevenson and Anderson (1994), most breeding season habitat occurs on private lands.

Commercial and residential development, agricultural practices, and other human activities may pose a threat in some specific instances. American Redstarts are a frequent victim of nest parasitism by the Brown-headed Cowbird (*Molothrus ater*) (Bent 1953; Friedmann 1963; Ehrlich et al. 1988). The reduced area of forest cover and supplemental food typically found in agricultural and urban areas can favor cowbirds. The frequency of nest parasitism in forest lands surrounding such areas may be elevated and have some bearing on local populations of the American Redstart. However, American Redstarts occasionally bury cowbird eggs in the bottom of the nest (Ehrlich et al. 1988), and the long-term significance of cowbird parasitism on local populations is not well understood.

RESPONSES TO HABITAT MODIFICATION: The effects of forest clearing and other types of habitat modification are fairly well understood at a coarse scale. The American Redstart requires a closed canopy and prefers a dense midstory and understory (Bushman and Therres 1988). Total elimination of forest cover will certainly eliminate Redstarts from an area, but anything less drastic may or may not eliminate the species. Crawford et al. (1981) proposed that favorable habitat conditions were created by selected cutting and thinning of competing understory trees.

Responses to habitat modification may not be quickly evident because individuals will return to modified areas where successful breeding or overwintering occurred in previous years (Diamond and Smith 1973). Determination of response to habitat modification can be further complicated by the fact that juvenile American Redstarts occupy "sub-optimal" habitat areas (Ficken and Ficken 1967). Thus, the presence of American Redstarts during the breeding season may not provide an accurate measure of habitat quality.

Based on information presented in Bond (1957), Robbins et al. (1989), and Whitcomb et al. (1991), a conclusion would be that specific changes in the number of old trees, deciduous canopy cover, and midstory characteristics will have the most direct impact on habitat suitability. Other habitat characteristics such as forest size also may play a secondary role.

DEMOGRAPHIC CHARACTERISTICS: Longevity records for the American Redstart are around 4 to 5 years, but average lifespan is significantly less (Kennard 1975). Clutch size varies from 2 to 5 eggs with 4 being the mode in the north (Bent 1953). Clutch size in the south may be somewhat smaller (Stevenson and Anderson 1994). Whitcomb et al. (1981) estimated an average of 1.5 broods per year.

KEY BEHAVIORS: The American Redstart is a very active forager and frequently undertakes long flights in pursuit of prey. It also droops its wings and flashes its long tail frequently while foraging. Such behavior is believed to cause insects to move and disclose their positions (Ficken and Ficken 1967). Morse (1970) described foraging differences between males and females. Sherry (1979) found that the bulk (79%) of the diet consisted of dipteria, hymenoptera, and coleoptera. Homoptera and lepidoptera make up 15% of the diet. Less commonly, American Redstarts eat berries and seeds (Stevenson and Anderson 1994).

The song is rapid and a high-pitched "see, see, see, see-ah" (Stevenson and Anderson 1994). The fourth note is usually higher then the fifth note, but the fifth note may not always be given (Robbins et al. 1966).

Nesting usually occurs in the fork of a sapling, where three or more prongs intersect (Stevenson and Anderson 1994), or along a horizontal limb of a sapling or shrub (Bent 1953; Whitcomb et al. 1981). Nest height ranges 1–20 m with 3–6 m being the normal height (Bent 1953; Stevenson and Anderson 1994). The nest is shaped like a deep cup and composed of small twigs, grasses, plant down, and birch bark, with lichens placed on the outside. The nest is sometimes bounded by silk from spider webs (Lowery 1955; Stevenson and Anderson 1994), and the feathers of other birds may occasionally be used as lining. Bent (1953) listed instances where nests of other bird species (especially vireos) were used by the American Redstart.

Only the female constructs the nest and incubates eggs. Incubation last for 12–13 days. Young birds that fledge may require about 5–8 days before sustained flight is achieved.

CONSERVATION MEASURES TAKEN: The American Redstart is protected from direct threats by the Migratory Bird Treaty Act (see Wood 1991). Conservation activities relating to species of birds that nest in North America and winter in the tropics have been increasingly discussed in recent years (e.g., Bushman and Therres 1988), but no specific measures have been taken.

CONSERVATION MEASURES PROPOSED: The streamside habitats occupied by American Redstarts are the focus of silvicultural recommendations to maintain water quality (Florida Department of Agriculture and Consumer Services 1990). Some consideration for wildlife habitat also is made as part of streamside zone management recommendations, but wildlife considerations are not strongly emphasized. More specific guidelines might be emphasized for the streamside areas in Florida where this species occurs.

LITERATURE CITED

AOU. 1953. A checklist of North American birds. 6th edition. American Ornithologists' Union. Allen Press, Lawrence, Kansas.

AOU. 1983. A checklist of North American birds. 6th edition. American Ornithologists' Union. Allen Press, Lawrence, Kansas.

Bent, A. C. 1953. Life history of North American wood warblers. U.S. Nat. Mus. Bull. No. 203, Smithsonian Inst. Press, Washington, D.C.

Bond, R. 1957. Ecological distribution of breeding birds in the upland forests of southern Wisconsin. Ecol. Monog. 27:351–384.

Bushman, E., and G. Therres. 1988. Habitat management guidelines for forest interior breeding birds of coastal Maryland. Maryland Depart. of Nat. Res., Wildl. Tech. Pub. 88–1. Annapolis, Maryland.

Crawford, H. S., R. G. Hooper, and R. W. Titterington. 1981. Songbird population response to silvicultural practices in central Appalachian hardwoods. Jour. Wildl. Manage. 45:680–692.

DeGraaf, R. M. 1985. Breeding bird assemblages in New England northern hardwoods. Pp. 5–22 in Conference proceedings: the impact of timber management practices on nongame birds in Vermont (R. J. Regan and D. E. Capen, eds.). U.S. Forest Service. Montpelier, Vermont.

DeGraaf, R. M., and N. L. Chadwick. 1987. Forest type, timber size class, and New England breeding birds. Jour. Wildl. Manage. 51:212–217.

Diamond, A. W., and R. W. Smith. 1973. Returns and survival of banded warblers wintering in Jamaica. Bird Banding 44:221–24.

Ficken, M. S., and R. W. Ficken. 1967. Age-specific differences in the breeding behavior and ecology of the American Redstart. Wilson Bull. 79:188–199.

Florida Department of Agriculture and Consumer Services. 1990. Silvicultural best management practices. Div. of Forestry, Tallahassee, Florida.

Ehrlich, P. , D. Dobkin, and D. Wheye. 1988. The birder's handbook. Simon and Schuster. New York.

Friedmann, H. 1963. Host relations of the parasitic cowbirds. U. S. Natl. Mus. Bull. No. 233., Washington, D.C.

Hamel, P. 1992. The land manager's guide to the birds of the south. The Nature Conservancy, Southeast Region, Chapel Hill, North Carolina. 437 pp.

Holmes, R., T. Sherry, and L. Reitsma. 1989. Population structure, territoriality, and overwinter survival of two migrant warbler species in Jamaica. Condor 91:545–561.

Kale, H., II, B. Pranty, B. Stith, and W. Biggs. 1992. Florida's breeding bird atlas project. Final report. Fla. Game and Fresh Water Fish Comm. Tallahassee, Florida.

Kautz, R. 1993. Trends in Florida wildlife habitat 1936–1987. Fla. Sci. 56:7–24.

Kennard, J. 1975. Longevity record of North American birds. Bird-Banding 46:55–73.

Lowery, G. 1955. Louisiana birds. Louisiana State Univ. Presses. Baton Rouge, Louisiana.

Mengel, R. 1965. Birds of Kentucky. Ornithol. Mono. No. 3. American Ornithologists' Union. Allen Press, Lawrence, Kansas.

Morse, D. H. 1970. Ecological aspects of some mixed species foraging flocks of birds. Ecology 40:119–168.

Noon, B. R., V. P. Bingman, J.P. Noon. 1979. The effects of changes in habitat on northern hardwood forest bird communities. Pp 33–48 in Management of north central and northeastern forests for nongame birds (D. M. DeGraaf and K.E. Evans, eds.). U. S. For. Ser. Gen. Tech. Rept. NC-51.

Ridgely, R. S., and J. Gwynne. 1990. A guide to the birds of Panama with Costa Rica, Nicaragua, and Honduras. Second ed. Princeton Univ. Press. Princeton, New Jersey.

Robbins, C., B. Bruun, and H. Zim. 1966. Birds of North America. A guide to field identification. Golden Press, New York.

Robbins, C., D. Bystrak, and P. Geissler. 1986. The breeding bird survey: its first fifteen years, 1965–1979. U.S. Dept. of Int., Fish and Wildl. Ser. Res. Publ. 157. Washington, D.C.

Robbins, C. S., D. K. Dawson, and B. A. Dowell. 1989. Habitat area requirements of breedin forest birds of the Middle Atlantic States. Wildl. Monogr. 103.

Robertson, W., and G. Woolfenden. 1992. An annotated checklist of the birds of Florida. Spec. Publ. no. 5, Fla. Ornith. Soc., Gainesville, Florida.

Sherry, T. 1979. Competitive interactions and adaptive strategies of American Redstarts and Least flycatchers in a northern hardwoods forest. Auk 96:265–283.

Stevenson, H. S. 1968. Nesting season: Florida region. Aud. FIeld Notes 22:599–602.

Stevenson, H. S. 1978. American Redstart. *Setophaga ruticilla*, Family Parulidae, Order Passeriformes. Pp. 64–65 in Rare and endangered Biota of Florida, Vol. 2 (H. Kale, II, ed.). Univ. of Florida Presses, Gainesville, Florida.

Stevenson, H. S., and B. Anderson. 1994. Birdlife of Florida. Univ. Press of Florida, Gainesville, Florida.

Taylor, W., and M. Kershner. 1986. Migratory birds killed at the Vehicle Assembly Building (VAB), John F. Kennedy Space Center. Jour. Field Ornith. 57:142–154.

Terres, J. 1980. The Audubon Society encyclopedia of North American birds. Alfred Knopf, New York.

Weston, F. 1965. A survey of the bird life of northwestern Florida. Bull. Tall Timbers Res. Stat. 5:1–147.

Whitcomb, R. F., C. S. Robbins, J. F. Lynch, B. L. Whitcomb, M. K. Klimkiewicz, and D. Bystrak. 1981. Effects of forest fragmentation on avifauna of the eastern deciduous forest. Pp. 125–205 in Forest island dynamics in man-dominated landscapes (R. L. Burgess and D. M. Sharpe, eds.). Ecological studies 41. Springer-Verlag, New York.

Wood, D. 1991. Legal accommodation of Florida's endangered species, threatened species, and species of special concern. Fla. Game and Fresh Water Fish Comm. Tallahassee, Florida.

PREPARED BY: James Cox, Florida Game and Fresh Water Fish Commission, 620 S. Meridian Street, Tallahassee, FL 32399–1600.

Cuban Yellow Warbler

Dendroica petechia gundlachi

FAMILY EMBERIZIDAE

Order Passeriformes

TAXONOMY: The Yellow Warbler (*Dendroica petechia*) is a widespread poly-typic species with 37 subspecies currently recognized (34 subspecies by Lowery and Monroe [1968] and three additional subspecies described by Olson [1980]). These subspecies form three groups: the migratory *aestiva* group of North America and Mexico; the resident *petechia* group of the West Indies, Cozumel, and coastal Venezuela; and the resident *erithachorides* group on the coasts of Mexico, Central America, Columbia, Ecuador, Peru, and the Galapagos Islands (AOU 1983). Pashley and Hamilton (1990) distribute the South American races differently among the *petechia* and *erithachorides* groups. These three groups are sometimes considered distinct species (AOU 1983). The Cuban Yellow Warbler (*D. p. gundlachi*) is the only member of the *petechia* group to occur in the United States. Males of the *petechia* group have a red or reddish-brown cap of varying prominance; otherwise they are brighter yellow and generally more heavily streaked than members of the *aestiva* group. This cap is inconspicuous in the Cuban Yellow Warbler as the tips of the crown feathers are yellow.

DESCRIPTION: The Cuban Yellow Warbler is a medium-sized warbler of about 13 cm total length and 13 g total weight. Adult males are bright yellow with prominant red streaks on the breast and flanks; the cap is inconspicuous as mentioned above, and the back and wings are greenish-yellow. The tail also is greenish-yellow, with clear yellow patches in the outer tail feathers. Females in definitive plumage are paler yellow below and dull greenish-yellow above. Immatures are very pale below and gray or greenish-gray above in juvenal plumage, and somewhat yellower subsequently. Some winter immatures have grayish heads and much gray on the bodies, making them vaguely remniscent of immature American Redstarts (*Setophaga ruticilla*).

Cuban Yellow Warbler,
Dendroica petechia gundlachi.
(Photo courtesy of Florida
Audubon Society)

POPULATION SIZE AND TREND: No authoritative population estimates
are available for the Cuban Yellow Warbler. Densities in prime habitat in
Florida Bay have been estimated at about one singing male per hectare, with
much lower densities in less favored habitats (J. Prather, pers. comm.). A very
rough extrapolation from this figure suggests a total population for Florida of
at least a few thousand warblers. Overall, the population must have increased
substantially since the discovery of the subspecies in 1941, but no trends are
known in recent years.

DISTRIBUTION AND HISTORY OF DISTRIBUTION: Overall, Yellow
Warblers occur from Alaska and northern Canada south throughout North
and Central America and the West Indies to coastal northern South America
and to the Galapagos Islands (AOU 1983). Cuban Yellow Warblers occur in
extreme south Florida, on Cuba and the Isla de Juventud (Isle of Youth,
formerly Isle of Pines), and throughout the Bahama Islands. In Florida they
were first found in 1941 on the Bay Keys near Key West by Earle R. Greene
(Sprunt 1954). Since then, they have spread through the back-country islands
of the lower Florida Keys, through Florida Bay, and into Biscayne Bay north
to Virginia Key (Robertson 1978). Their range in Biscayne Bay seems to have
contracted (M. Wheeler, pers. comm.), but they have been spreading within
Florida Bay and up the west coast of the Everglades into the Ten Thousand
Islands area. The Florida Breeding Bird Atlas project reported probable nesting activity in the Broad River to Lostman's River area of Everglades National
Park, and possible nesting activity north to around Everglades City, with one

Distribution map of
the Cuban Yellow
Warbler, *Dendroica
petechia gundlachi.*

Breeding range

report from near Cape Romano. Members of the *aestiva* group of subspecies are uncommon to common migrants throughout Florida.

HABITAT REQUIREMENTS AND HABITAT TREND: In Florida, Cuban Yellow Warblers inhabit red (*Rhizophora mangle*) and black (*Avicennia germinans*) mangrove forests, but rarely other habitats. According to Robertson (1978) they are "almost entirely limited to . . . the dense fringing belts of red mangrove . . . of shrub to small tree size along shores." More specifically, they seem to prefer red mangroves fronting on relatively deep water, such as the channels and moats that border some small islands, but also use stands of tree-size black mangroves on some Florida Bay islands (J. Prather, pers. comm.). Presumably this preference for mangroves adjacent to deeper water is related to differences in the mangrove structure in these situations.

VULNERABILITY OF SPECIES AND HABITAT: The habitat of Cuban Yellow Warblers in Florida is relatively secure from direct human disruption in the short term. Most stands of mangroves suitable for this species are found within Everglades National Park, Biscayne National Park, and the National Wildlife Refuges of the lower Florida Keys. These habitats can be devastated by hurricanes, but the area occupied is too large to be heavily damaged by a single storm. In the longer term, rapid sea-level rise resulting from global warming potentially could lead to extensive erosion of these mangrove islands and shores (Parkinson 1989). Cuban Yellow Warblers also are vulnerable to brood parasitism by cowbirds. South Florida is currently being colonized by Brown-headed Cowbirds (*Molothrus ater*) moving south down the peninsula, and by Shiny Cowbirds (*M. bonairiensis*) from the West Indies (Hoffman and Woolfenden 1986). Members of the *petechia* group of Yellow Warblers are highly vulnerable to cowbird parasitism (Cruz et al. 1985), perhaps more so than members of the *aestiva* group.

CAUSES OF THREAT: Hurricanes are a real, but probably not severe, threat to Florida's Cuban Yellow Warbler population. Brood parasitism by cowbirds is probably the most significant threat to these populations.

RESPONSES TO HABITAT MODIFICATION: Little direct information is available. The habitat needs of Cuban Yellow Warblers appear to be very specific, so changes in the structure of the mangrove forests seem likely to displace these warblers. On Raccoon Key, off Big Torch Key in the lower Keys, Yellow Warblers apparently are absent from areas where the red mangrove fringe has been devastated by feral rhesus macaques (*Macaca mulatta*). Singing males remain in some areas where the mangroves are noticeably damaged but still alive.

DEMOGRAPHIC CHARACTERISTICS: Little definite information exists for the Cuban Yellow Warbler. J. Prather and A. Cruz (pers. comm.), in the early stages of a study of the breeding biology of the subspecies, report that the clutch size is usually 3, and sometimes 2. Nests are compact cups, typically located 1–3 m above the ground in red or black mangroves, generally at the edges of mangrove forest stands. Prather and Cruz have found birds breeding while still in immature plumage and conclude that the warblers begin breeding at age 1 year. The subspecies is presumed to be serially monogamous.

KEY BEHAVIORS: Cuban Yellow Warblers are assumed to have food habits similar to those of other Yellow Warblers, feeding mainly on insects gleaned from the twigs, flowers, and foliage of trees and shrubs. Male Cuban Yellow Warblers use a song similar to that of other Yellow Warblers to defend territories and probably to attract mates. Yellow Warblers of both sexes use short "chip" or "whit" notes as alarm calls and for maintaining contact within the territory. The Cuban Yellow Warbler population of south Florida is partially, and perhaps completely, nonmigratory. The species is found annually in Florida Bay in winter, but possibly part of the population retreats south for the winter.

Courtship, pairing, and parental behavior have not been studied in this sub-species, and it is likely that these aspects of breeding biology differ between this resident subspecies and the well-studied migratory northern subspecies.

CONSERVATION MEASURES TAKEN: Most of the habitat of Cuban Yellow Warblers in Florida is protected within national parks and wildlife refuges. Other mangrove stands enjoy substantial, although not complete, protection under Florida law. These reserves and laws, of course, were created for reasons unrelated to Cuban Yellow Warblers.

CONSERVATION MEASURES PROPOSED: Cowbird populations in the range of the Cuban Yellow Warbler should be monitored. In the event cow-birds become numerous in the warblers' habitat, intensive investigations of nest parasitism rates should be undertaken. The current study by Prather and Cruz of breeding success of Yellow Warblers and other potential cowbird hosts in south Florida should provide a valuable baseline. At some point, cowbird control may need to be considered.

ACKNOWLEDGMENTS: I thank the Florida Breeding Bird Atlas program for making their map of Yellow Warbler nesting available to me. John Prather and Alex Cruz have given me extensive access to the preliminary results of their study in Florida Bay and have provided useful comments on the manu-script.

LITERATURE CITED:

AOU. 1983. Checklist of North American Birds, 6th edition. American Orni-thologists Union. Allen Press, Inc., Lawrence, Kansas. 877 pp.

Cruz. A., T. Manolis, and J. W. Wiley. 1985. The Shiny Cowbird: a brood parasite expanding its range in the Caribbean region. Pp. 607–620 in Neotropical ornithology (Buckley, P. A., M. S. Foster, E. S. Morton, R. S. Ridgely, and F. G. Buckley, eds.). Ornithol. Monogr. no. 36. 1041 pp.

Hoffman, W., and G. E. Woolfenden. 1986. A fledgling Brown-headed Cow-bird specimen from Pinellas County. Fla. Field Nat. 14: 18–20.

Lowery, G. H., Jr., and B. L. Monroe, Jr. 1968. Family Parulidae. Pp. 3–93 in Check-list of birds of the world. Vol. 14 (R. A. Paynter, Jr., ed.). Harvard Univ. Press, Cambridge, Massachusetts.

Olson, S. L. 1980. Geogaphic variation in the Yellow Warblers (*Dendroica petechia:* Parulidae) of the Pacific coast of Middle and South America. Proc. Biol Soc. Washington 93:968–970.

Pashley, D. N. and R. B. Hamilton. 1990. Warblers of the West Indies. III. The Lesser Antilles. Carib. Jour. Sci. 26:75–97.

Parkinson, R. W. 1989. Decelerating holocene sea level rise and its influence on southwest Florida coastal evolution: a transgressive/regressive stratigraphy. Jour. Sed. Petrology 59:960–972.

Robertson, W. B., Jr. 1978. Cuban Yellow Warbler. Pp. 61–62 in Rare and endangered biota of Florida. Vol. Two: birds (Kale, H. W., II, ed.). Univ. Presses Fla., Gainesville, Florida.

Sprunt, A., Jr. 1954. Florida bird life. Coward-McCann, Inc., New York. 527 pp.

PREPARED BY: Wayne Hoffman, National Audubon Society, 115 Indian Mound Trail, Tavernier, FL 33070.

Least Bittern
Ixobrychus exilis

FAMILY ARDEIDAE

Order Ciconiiformes

TAXONOMY: Formerly *Ardea exilis* (Gmelin 1789), the Least Bittern (*Ixobrychus exilis*) was first described from Jamaican specimens. The subspecies occurring in Florida and most of North America is *I. e. exilis,* with several other subspecies occurring in Mexico and South America.

DESCRIPTION: The Least Bittern is the smallest of the North American Ardeidae, measuring about 28 cm in length, with a wingspan of about 45 cm. Compared to other herons, Least Bitterns have short legs and necks, and weak flight. The species is characterized by its small size, dark crown and back, and obvious buff-colored wing patches when in flight. This is the only North American heron in which the sexes have differing plumage. Adult males have a glossy greenish-black cap, tail, and back, with chesnut back of the neck and tips of flight feathers. In females, the black on the back and cap are replaced by a purplish-brown, and they also have narrow dark streaks on the upper throat and foreneck. Both sexes have yellowish soft-parts, bright yellow or orange iris, and brownish to yellow underparts. During breeding, the lores and gape may become reddish, particularly in males, and scarlet flushing may occur during courtship and interactions at the nest. Juveniles (into first fall) appear much as females but have a lighter mantle, streaked appearance on breast, and feathers edged with buff. Many of these characteristics may remain throughout the first year. In the range of *I. e. exilis,* melanistic forms have been regularly found with light parts replaced with dark russet (formerly called "Cory's Bittern"); these color variants are reported to have noticeably darker eggs, black chicks, and mate only with other dark bitterns.

POPULATION SIZE AND TREND: No population estimates exist for the Least Bittern in Florida, and few in other parts of its range, in part because it is so secretive and difficult to census accurately. However, its presence is often discerned by vocalizations, and most authors have previously reported the

Least Bittern,
Ixobrychus exilis.
(Photo copyright
by Allan D.
Cruickshank,
courtesy of Florida
Audubon Society)

species as common to abundant within Florida. The consistency of the common classification is bolstered somewhat by its widespread past and present distribution within the state. The Florida Breeding Bird Atlas shows a very wide distribution within the state, suggesting the species is common in peninsular Florida and confined largely to wetland sites. Kushlan (1973) found it nesting in a near-colonial situation in the Everglades, and more recently Bowman and Bancroft (1989) found evidence of several nests in Florida Bay. In 1987, Frederick et al. (1990) saw over 600 (including at least 200 adults) during airboat surveys in the central Everglades; while the distribution there was found to be quite patchy, Least Bitterns were clearly a common breeding species in the Everglades. Least Bitterns are common breeders in the littoral zone of nearly all the larger lakes in peninsular Florida, including Okeechobee, Kissimmee, Tohopekaliga, East Tohopekaliga, Tiger, Marion, Hatchineha, Orange, Cypress, and Istokpoga, as well as most of the St. Johns basin.

The lack of comprehensive census information allows no statements as to population trends. It can be assumed that considerable wetland habitat has been destroyed in the last 20 years in Florida, which cannot have helped bittern populations. However, Least Bitterns are one of the few ciconiiform birds known for their tenacity in the face of urbanization and close human habitation. In addition, the Least Bittern is one of the few wetland birds likely to benefit from the dense monocultures of cattail now replacing many wetland plant associations in the Everglades, agricultural wetlands, and residential lakes in Florida. Thus, there is no clear indication of increase or decline in populations due to the lack of information.

DISTRIBUTION AND HISTORY OF DISTRIBUTION: Least Bitterns are confined to the New World. Excepting the Appalachian Mountains, they

Distribution map
of the Least Bittern,
Ixobrychus exilis.

Breeding range

breed throughout the eastern United States, the Mississippi Valley and Midwest to Ontario and Quebec, the southeast and Gulf coastal plains, southern California, and isolated areas of the Pacific Northwest. Outside of the United States, they occur in southern Canada (Ontario and Quebec), western coastal and southern Mexico, throughout Central America, parts of Venezuela, Colombia, Suriname, Guyana, French Guyana, and much of Brazil, though the distribution in South America is not confirmed.

The *I. e. exilis* race is migratory in the United States and winters in southern Florida, Louisiana, Texas, California and the Caribbean, with wintering records from Central America and northern South America. The Least Bittern has historically been known from wetlands in nearly all parts of Florida. The Florida Breeding Bird Atlas suggests that the current distribution is still statewide, being most common in peninsular wetlands, much less so in the panhandle, and nearly absent in counties in the Big Bend region (Jefferson, Madison, Hamilton, Suwanee, Columbia, Baker, Gilchrist, Union, and Levy counties).

HABITAT REQUIREMENTS AND HABITAT TREND: Least Bitterns breed and feed in fresh and brackish wetlands, with smaller numbers occurring in salt marshes and mangrove habitats. The species seems tolerant of a wide variety of wetland habitats, including grassland such as the Everglades, lake shores, ditches, farm ponds, reservoirs, and impounded areas. The Least Bittern may continue to occupy areas until surrounded by human activity and is known even from small wetlands close to residential areas.

Least Bitterns are usually found in dense vegetation, often in a mixture of grass or reeds and shrubs. In the Everglades, Kushlan (1973) noted a dense nesting aggregation in close association with a burned area, and suggested that the association was a result of increased feeding opportunities in the burn area. Frederick et al. (1990) found that Least Bitterns were much denser in an area of the central Everglades known to be receiving nutrient-rich water, and being invaded by stands of cattail (*Typha* sp.). The birds in the central Everglades were more dense along airboat trails than in open grassland or canal edges, and were most likely to be found in edges of mixed cattail and sawgrass (*Cladium jamaicensis*). No preference was noted for burned areas, pure cattail stands, or willow ponds, although bitterns occurred in all three associations. Unlike many of the other herons, the Least Bittern usually forages from perches, and foraging does not appear to be strongly affected by water depth. Nests are typically built low over the water in cattails, grasses, sedges, low bushes such as buttonbush, and willows.

Wetland habitats are unquestionably shrinking or degrading in Florida, and to this extent, the Least Bittern is affected. However, this species may be able to benefit from some types of habitat degradation as shifts from sawgrass and other emergent vegetation to cattail does not appear to thwart nesting, and the rapid intrusion and takeover of many shallow lakes by cattail following eutrophication certainly appears to increase habitat for bitterns. It is therefore not clear whether suitable vegetative habitat for this species is showing a net increase or decrease in Florida. The preference for brackish over marine wetland environments suggests that increased salinization of estuaries will serve only to decrease suitable habitat.

VULNERABILITY OF SPECIES AND HABITAT: The Least Bittern is widely distributed in the United States, Florida, and Central and South America, and populations appear to be robust within the United States and Florida. Least Bitterns are not federally or state-listed as threatened or endangered. However, the common or abundant classification is a suggestion based solely on distribution and lack of other information; no censuses have actually been undertaken, and no population trends established. The wide habitat preferences of Least Bitterns, especially their tolerance of close human activity, eutrophic conditions, small wetlands, and dense cattail suggest that this species is not highly vulnerable to the shrinking and degradation of habitat within its North American range. However, there is very little known about the reproduction of this species in relation to habitat or about its demographics and susceptibility to contaminants. Finally, the reduction in area and degradation of wetlands of all types in Florida is sufficient to categorize any wetland-dependent species as presently vulnerable.

CAUSES OF THREAT: Outright destruction and drainage of wetlands appears to be the primary known threat to the Least Bittern, although the effect of various forms of wetland degradation are unknown. Boat traffic also may be a problem in some areas. Least Bitterns are weak fliers and flush only at very close approach. This behavior and their preference for airboat trails makes bitterns quite vulnerable to airboat collision. Even when looking explicitly for bitterns, traveling slowly in the daylight, and making every attempt to avoid collisions, Frederick et al. (1990) struck 3% of the bitterns they found in the central Everglades. Mortality from recreational airboat traffic is probably much higher than 3%, because much higher speeds, night-time travel, and lack of attention to the cryptic birds are common. In addition, bitterns are very defensive at the nest and quite unwilling to leave even when approached closely. This suggests that many adults are unwittingly killed when airboats run over their well-camouflaged nests. In dense nesting areas, heavy recreational airboat use could be a significant source of mortality.

Least Bitterns have high proportions of fish in their diets and presumably are vulnerable to infections by the *Eustrongylides ignotus* nematode parasite, which infects other ciconiiform birds in Florida. The parasite can have devastating effects on nestlings and young birds in other species. Preliminary evidence suggests that the parasite proliferates in areas receiving human sewage inputs and perhaps those receiving nutrient inputs in general. The birds seem attracted to high-nutrient conditions, and the possibility of a nutrient association for the parasite suggests that this species could be at considerable risk from this parasitic disease.

RESPONSES TO HABITAT MODIFICATION: Least Bitterns are known to be quite tenacious in the face of human encroachment of wetlands and often are found breeding in extremely small wetlands in residential areas, lakeshores next to houses, wetlands, and ditches close to roads, and wetlands impounded by dikes and canals. Whereas the species appears to be quite resilient to human habitat modification, the effect of these habitat changes on reproduction, health, and demography are unknown. There is the potential for increased risk of infection with the *Eustrongylides* nematode parasite in areas receiving treated and untreated wastewater.

DEMOGRAPHIC CHARACTERISTICS: Young Least Bitterns are fed in the vicinity of the nest for up to 4 weeks, and probably become independent soon thereafter. Young attain full adult plumage at slightly over 1 year of age;

in the absence of other information, it seems likely that first breeding is in the second spring (22–24 months of age). Clutches are 3–7 eggs (usually 4–6) in the northern part of the range, diminishing to 2 or 3 eggs in the tropics. Nesting success in studies in two northern states was between 70 and 85%, and brood sizes at hatching averaged 3 chicks (Weller 1961). Broods of 3–4 nestlings (probably 6–12 days of age) have been observed regularly in the Everglades. Whereas the species may be double-brooded in northern parts of the range, only one peak of fledglings was observed in the central Everglades. The sex ratio of adults breeding in the central Everglades was quite close to parity (1.04). No information is available on longevity or survival of young or adults.

KEY BEHAVIORS: Least Bitterns are quite secretive and stay in dense vegetation for much of the day. They may be observed most readily in early morning hours when feeding. During the breeding season, the dovelike call is distinctive and an easy identification mark; vocalizations have been used as an index of reproductive densities (Manci and Rusch 1988). Least Bitterns are weak fliers, particularly in takeoff and in damp conditions. Their legs often dangle below or behind the body when flushed. Most birds freeze or attempt to hide when disturbed, and flush only at close approach. At the nest, bitterns typically display their wings and threaten humans, and in some cases nesting birds may actually be gently picked up by humans. Bitterns move well through dense vegetation, due to their extremely thin body, and may be able to laterally compress their body. A pet bittern kept by John James Audubon was found to be able to fit through a space only one inch in width.

Feeding is usually accomplished by stabbing prey from perches very close to the water's surface, often at vegetative edges. Least Bitterns may either stand in place or walk slowly while stalking prey and often sway their neck back and forth prior to striking. Least Bitterns eat primarily small fishes, but also feed on crustaceans, amphibians, insects, and small mammals. Insects are often caught in midair, and a captive bittern once captured and devoured a pet hummingbird. Breeding appears to be monogamous with males feeding young as much or more than females. Breeding may be solitary or semicolonial, with densities of up to 40 nests/ha, and internest distances of one to several meters have been recorded. Least Bittern nests also may be found in close association with Boat-tailed Grackle (*Quiscalus major*) colonies, perhaps as a deterrent to predation (W. Post, pers. comm.).

CONSERVATION MEASURES TAKEN: Least Bitterns have no threatened or endangered status in Florida or the United States, and no specific conservation action has been directed towards this species. Programs to restore, protect, or replace wetlands in Florida and the United States will undoubtedly affect the species positively.

CONSERVATION MEASURES PROPOSED: The robust population status of the Least Bittern is an appearance generated solely from its wide distribution and lack of recent change in distribution. Aside from the Florida Breeding Bird Atlas and the sightings from the Everglades, no censuses have been undertaken in Florida, and population sizes and trends of bitterns are unknown. Population status should be assayed at a number of representative habitats within Florida on a regular basis. More importantly, the effects of various kinds of habitat degradation (salinization of estuaries, water management plans, eutrophication, vegetation change, etc.) on reproduction, demography, and distribution of this species are unknown and should be studied. In areas of high bittern density, airboat traffic should be assessed and perhaps regulated. As with nearly all of the ciconiiform birds, the magnitude and habitat correlates of the *Eustrongylides* parasite problem needs immediate attention.

LITERATURE CITED:

Bowman, R., and G. T. Bancroft. 1989. Least Bittern nesting on mangrove keys in Florida Bay. Fla. Field Nat. 16:43–46.

Frederick, P. C., N. Dwyer, S. Fitzgerald, and R. E. Bennetts. 1990. Relative abundance and habitat preferences of Least Bitterns (*Ixobrychus exilis*) in the Everglades. Fla. Field Nat. 18:1–9.

Kushlan, J. A. 1973. Least Bittern nesting colonially. Auk 90:685–686.

Manci, K. M., and D. H. Rusch. 1988. Indices to distribution and abundance of some inconspicuous waterbirds on Horicon Marsh. Jour. Field Ornith. 59:67–75.

Weller, M. W. 1961. Breeding biology of the Least Bittern. Wilson Bull. 73:11–33.

PREPARED BY: Peter C. Frederick, Department of Wildlife Ecology and Conservation, P.O. Box 110430, University of Florida, Gainesville, FL 32611.

Great White Heron
Ardea herodias occidentalis

FAMILY ARDEIDAE

Order Ciconiiformes

TAXONOMY: The "Great White Heron" (*Ardea herodias occidentalis*) is currently considered to be the white morph of the Great Blue Heron (*herodias* group), a polymorphic subspecies in the West Indies and Caribbean (AOU 1973, 1983). Originally designated as a separate species by Audubon in 1835 (AOU 1983), a classification supported by Holt (1928), its species rank was questioned by Mayr (1956) and Meyerriecks (1957). Following the rationale of these latter authors, the species was reclassified as a color morph (AOU 1973). In conflict with this decision, Zachow (1983) showed significant differences in morphology among white, resident blue, and migratory blue-morph herons through a multivariate analysis of 36 skeletal measurements of specimens of blue and white birds from museum collections and those killed by Hurricane Donna. However, because the specimens she used were, for the most part, unsexed, the question was raised whether the differences she recorded represented a possible bias due to skewed sex ratios in her samples rather than real differences between color forms.

DESCRIPTION: The Great White Heron is a large, all-white heron. The adult has a heavy, dull-yellow bill and yellowish to dull black legs, which distinguish it from the more common and widely-distributed Great Egret (*Casmerodius albus*) that has a smaller body, thinner, bright-yellow bill and shiny, black legs. The Great White Heron stands about 1.1 m (4 ft.) tall and has a wingspread to 2 m (7 ft.) (Palmer 1962). Body mass of adults from Florida Bay (captured and sexed during radio-tagging in 1988–1989) was 2,680–3,390 g (mean = 3,015 ± 256 g, n =11) for males and 1,980–3,200 g (mean = 2,570 ± 405 g, n = 8) for females (G. Powell and R. Bjork, unpubl. data). Adults have elongated plumes on the lower neck and while breeding they also develop short plumes on the back of the head, an orange to scarlet bill, reddish legs and feet and light blue coloring in the featherless (loral) area

Great White Heron, *Ardea
herodias occidentalis* (Photo
by Stephen A. Nesbitt)

around the eyes. Immature birds are similar to nonbreeding adults except the
color of the bill, legs, and feet tend to be duller and they are without chest
plumes for at least the first year. Birds intermediate between the white and
blue morphs, the result of mixed matings ("Wurdemann's Heron"), vary
greatly in color of the head, neck, bill, legs, and feet, but have a gray body and
wings and thus more resemble the blue morph. "Dark-mottled white individuals," reported for islands off Venezuela (Bond 1961), have not been
reported within the Florida population.

POPULATION SIZE AND TREND: No quantitative records exist for the
Great White Heron pre-1900s population. The only information that exists
prior to the early 1900s, when the population was nearly extirpated, were
observations by J. J. Audubon in the 1830s that referred to the species as
abundant in Florida Bay (Proby 1974). Audubon reported flocks "sometimes
a hundred or more being seen together" to be a regular occurrence. However,
as the human population grew on the mainline Keys, the use of *Ardea* as a
food source by humans had a major impact on the population (Holt 1928;
Sprunt 1935). In 1885, only a few Great White Herons were seen during a
plume-hunting trip that covered much of the heron's range (Pierce 1962).
    Sprunt (1935) made the first systematic survey of the entire Florida Bay for

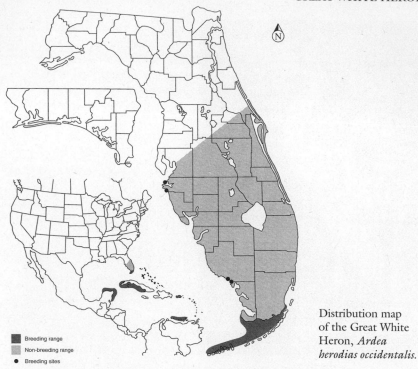

Distribution map
of the Great White
Heron, *Ardea
herodias occidentalis.*

Breeding range
Non-breeding range
● Breeding sites

Great White Herons and recorded only 56 individuals in February 1935. He concluded that this was the entire population for the area and that the species would be extirpated within 5 years due to harvesting of nestlings for food. In the fall of 1935, the Bay population was further reduced by a major hurricane that passed across the upper Keys and Florida Bay. In October, a month after the hurricane, Sprunt (1935) again surveyed the population and found only 20 Great White Herons in Florida Bay and 146 individuals throughout the species' range as far west as Key West. Over the course of the next 4 years he made four flights that each indicated a gradual recovery of the population in Florida Bay (Sprunt 1936a, 1936b, 1937, 1939). An extensive survey of the *Ardea* population in Florida Bay was next made in 1959 by the National Park Service when 809 white individuals were counted (in Powell et al. 1989). In August of 1960, Hurricane Donna passed across the upper Keys and the Bay. A survey two months after the hurricane indicated the heron population in Florida Bay had decreased by 30–40% from the previous year (Powell et al. 1989). Two years later, the Bay population had recovered to at least 90% of the prehurricane numbers. Continued surveys through the 1960s indicated stabilization of the population at between 800–900 individuals in summer and 1,200–1,400 birds in winter. The winter records include individuals that move onto the Florida peninsula during summer and recent fledglings that remain in the vicinity of their colony for one to two months after fledging (Powell and

Bjork 1990). As most of the latter group will die within six months, they cannot be considered part of the adult population. Therefore, an appropriate population estimate for Florida Bay would be 1,000–1,200 individuals. The next survey, in the winter of 1984, recorded 1,509 birds. Based on these surveys, it appears that the Great White Heron population in Florida Bay has remained relatively stable since its recovery from the mid-1960s. A complete survey of the Great White Heron population has not been conducted in the lower Keys since the early 1960s when 240 birds were recorded in August 1962 (Robertson 1978).

In Florida Bay, up to 600 nesting attempts were documented annually from 1987 to 1990 (Powell and Bjork 1990). From aerial surveys covering an estimated half of the lower Keys, up to 241 active nests were documented during the peak (December) of breeding during the late-1980s and early-1990s (T. Wilmers, pers. comm.). Based on these data, a minimum breeding population for the entire Florida Keys would be about 850 pairs.

DISTRIBUTION AND HISTORY OF DISTRIBUTION: In Florida, Great White Herons appear to occupy a range similar to their historically reported range, restricted primarily to the Florida Keys. Their status elsewhere is somewhat problematical. White *Ardea* occur in Cuba and the Isle of Pines (Bangs and Zappey 1905; Barbour 1943), on islands off Venezuela (Bond 1956, 1961; Phelps and Phelps 1958), and around the tip of the Yucatan Peninsula (Griscom 1926; Paynter 1955). They may nest in all these places, but apparently no ornithologist has seen nesting birds (except possibly in Cuba, see Bond 1965), the evidence in all cases being the testimony of fishermen. The status of Yucatan birds has not been certainly identified (AOU 1957). Reports of white *Ardea* elsewhere in the Greater Antilles possibly pertain to vagrants from elsewhere.

In Florida, the white morph nests from northwestern Florida Bay (Sandy Key) and southern Biscayne Bay (Arsenicker Keys) south through Florida Bay and the lower Florida Keys (excluding the "mainline" Keys) to the Marquesas. A few nesting occurrences have been documented in other parts of Florida. Great White Herons occasionally have been documented nesting in Great Blue Heron colonies in the Ten Thousand Islands (W. Robertson, unpubl. data). Bancroft (1969) observed a Great White Heron nesting in a colony of blue morph birds at Hemp Key, Pine Island Sound, near Fort Myers. One to two nesting attempts have been documented annually since 1981 in Cortez and Terra Ceia bays near Bradenton (R. Paul, pers. comm.). One nesting attempt has been documented on ABC Islands, Marco Island in 1976, 1979, and 1988 (T. Below, pers. comm.).

Although reports indicated that a few Great White Herons dispersed regularly to the Dry Tortugas and the southern half of peninsular Florida (i.e., Cruickshank [1980] reported sightings for every month of the year in Brevard

County from the 1950s through the 1970s), the birds were regarded as largely sedentary in Florida Bay (Robertson 1978). However, data from aerial censuses in Florida Bay showed consistent intra-annual variation of population estimates and data from wing- and radio-tagging studies indicated that a large portion of the population disperses seasonally. Intrayear variation of aerial count data showed a seasonal phenomenon, with the population being up to 50% larger in the winter, some of which could be accounted for by the presence of post-fledglings from winter nests (Powell et al. 1989). In studies involving 350 juvenile Great White Herons that were wing-tagged from 1981 through 1984, reports of sightings up to six months after tagging were from wetland sites throughout Florida with a record as far north as Atlanta, Georgia and another from Texas. Telemetry studies provided more detailed information on juvenile and adult dispersal (Powell and Bjork 1990). Ninety-five percent of the radio-tagged juveniles that survived more than one month after fledgling (n = 44) quickly left Florida Bay, and moved into a variety of habitats north of the Bay, from just south of Tampa Bay on the west coast, to Lake Okeechobee in the central peninsula, and to Melbourne on the east coast of Florida. Sightings of a few individuals in later years suggested that survivors eventually return to the Florida Bay. Migration of adult Great White Herons also was common. Twenty-seven percent (n=15) of radio-tagged adults left Florida Bay during the summer nonbreeding season, and migrated to coastal and inland locations from 5 to 300 km north of Florida Bay (Powell and Bjork 1990). Those birds returned to Florida Bay in the winter.

HABITAT REQUIREMENTS AND HABITAT TREND: The Great White Heron nests almost exclusively in coastal and estuarine habitats, primarily on isolated islands or keys. It does not nest on the mainland shore, even in far southern Florida. A report of one nest in an interior freshwater area (Howell 1921) is unique.

Great White Herons forage primarily in the shallow, open water mudflats or along shorelines that are either unvegetated or vegetated with seagrasses. Their diet consists mainly of fish. Mullet (*Mugil* sp.), Atlantic thread herring (*Opisthonema oglinum*), and Gulf toadfish (*Opsanus beta*) are common species taken by the herons (G. Powell, unpubl. data). They are visual foragers and feed both day and night and diel foraging patterns appear to vary regionally relative to tidal patterns (Powell 1987). In eastern Florida Bay, where there is little daily tidal fluctuation, most herons rest on mangove islands by day and forage on nearby grass flats at night. Powell (1987) suggested that night foraging was probably a response to the greater availability of prey, particularly Clupidae, that migrate onto the flats at night (Sogard et al. 1989a). In western Florida Bay, foraging patterns were correlated with the relatively large daily tidal fluctuation, independent of the diel cycle. In contrast to other wading bird species foraging in the eastern grass flats, Great White Herons, with relatively longer legs, were not excluded from that habitat in the summer when annual water level was consistently higher (Powell 1987). However, the absence of migratory Clupidae (Sogard et al. 1989b) may explain the propensity of Great White Herons to leave the Bay in summer.

Most of the breeding range of the Great White Heron in south Florida lies within one of four protected natural areas: Everglades National Park, the Great White Heron National Wildlife Refuge, Key West National Wildlife Refuge, and National Key Deer Refuge. However, the legal protection has not equated to *bona fide* ecological protection. Northern Florida Bay, which lies within Everglades National Park, has been heavily impacted by the loss of freshwater input as a result of drainage and redirection of historic water-flow patterns in the Everglades (Smith et al. 1989; Walters et al. 1992). The impacts of these changes on Florida Bay are poorly understood, but they have likely negatively affected secondary productivity (Browder 1985; Tilmant et al. 1989) resulting in a shortage of forage fishes for the heron population. Studies by Powell (1983) and Powell and Powell (1986) indicated that habitat quality in eastern Florida Bay had deteriorated compared to the early 1900s. The authors suggested the stability of the Great White Heron population utilizing Florida Bay may be dependent on supplemental feeding by humans. Greater reproductive success in the southern Keys (Wilmers 1990) suggests that habitat conditions have been better in that part of the breeding range.

The trends pointing toward ecological deterioration of interior Florida Bay appear to be accelerating over the last several years, with the occurrence of a massive die-off in turtle grass (*Thallassia testudinum*) beds (Robblee et al. 1991) and large algal blooms. To date, about 40,000 hectares (100,000 acres) of turtle grass die-off has occurred; many areas have recolonized with other seagrass species, but the die-off and water turbidity problems are continuing (M. Robblee, pers. comm.). These dying seagrass flats are the primary foraging areas for Great White Herons, but monitoring of the population during the early years of the die-off failed to detect any declines in reproduction. However, long-term impacts to the population may result.

In addition to the dependency of Great White Herons on estuarine and marine habitats of south Florida, Powell and Bjork (1990) documented a secondary dependency on wetland habitats throughout the central and southern Florida mainland. Virtually all juveniles that survived beyond independence from parental care left Florida Bay and moved north into a wide range of wetland habitats, including natural and artificial freshwater sites. Foraging efficiency was low among these young birds and most individuals died (38 of 42 birds, 90%) during the first 6 months while they were still in these post-dispersal habitats. In several cases, the long-term survivors depended on artificial habitats where food resources were presumably made more plentiful by management practices such as at pumping stations, drainage or irrigation operations, or fish ponds.

The Florida mainland habitats that are critical to fledgling Great White Heron survival during their first year are being heavily impacted by human development. We suggest that juveniles need dense sources of forage fish to make the transition to independence and historically, after they departed Florida Bay between February and May, they were able to take advantage of rich concentrated food resources produced by the freshwater Everglades dry-down (Powell and Bjork 1990). The birds must now depend on habitats that have experienced dramatic changes in the natural water patterns (Smith et al. 1989; Walters et al. 1992) and are subject to further manipulations from anthropogenic influences.

VULNERABILITY OF SPECIES AND HABITAT: The Great White Heron population appears most vulnerable to deterioration of its foraging habitat on the breeding grounds and in post-fledging sites. Powell and Powell (1986) demonstrated that Great White Heron reproductive success in Florida Bay is extremely low. Evaluating the significance of these data is hampered by a general lack of historical reproductive data. However, samples of Great White Heron clutches collected in the late 1800s and early 1900s indicate that, prior to human manipulation of the ecosystem, the herons laid larger clutches. In addition, a small number of nests monitored in 1923 (Holt 1928) demonstrated a higher reproductive success than recorded in modern studies of the species' reproduction in Florida Bay. However, the historical reproductive success parameters are similar to reproductive success of Great Blue Herons elsewhere in the United States (Henny 1972; Pratt 1980; Mitchell et al. 1981). These data suggest that productivity of nesting attempts has been negatively impacted in recent years by habitat deterioration. According to calculations for minimum required productivity (Henny 1972), reproductive success in Florida Bay may be too low for long-term population stability without continued food supplementation by humans.

The breeding range of Great White Herons in Florida is in estuarine habitat, which means the birds are directly dependent on a productive south Florida estuary. As an estuary, that habitat is vulnerable to disturbances in salinity balance due to changes in freshwater input and consequently, to water management practices upstream. In the case of Florida Bay, the Everglades is its historic source of freshwater. Therefore, a major factor in the long-term stability of the Great White Heron will be the ability of the relevant governmental authorities to come to grips with competing demands for freshwater in south Florida and to guarantee that the Everglades and its estuaries receive sufficient water to keep them productive as nurseries for the fish and invertebrates that provide food resources for the herons.

A potential direct threat to Great White Heron foraging habitat in Florida

Bay and the inshore waters of the Florida Keys is from the possibility of an oil spill. Currently, there is a drilling ban in effect for the southeastern Florida Gulf waters placed on the Department of the Interior by Congress, a ban that requires annual renewal. However, should drilling be permitted, the potential for damage to the Florida Bay ecosystem would be tremendous, particularly because the Gulf Loop current would carry drilling fluids into the Keys (D. Quirolo, pers. comm.).

As mentioned above, the survival of young to fledging age is one of two major survival bottlenecks that have been identified for Great White Herons. The second sensitive period that appears to be typical of Ciconiiformes, in general, is the post-fledging period. The discovery that young Great White Herons disperse from Florida Bay northward into peninsular Florida adds virtually the entire array of freshwater wetlands to the critical habitat category for the species. Outstanding among these wetlands is the Everglades. The redistribution of water in the Everglades may directly affect the stability of the heron population by reducing the accessibility of existing fish populations to foraging wading birds or negatively affecting secondary productivity. Consequently, excessive drying down or, at the other extreme, excessive dumping of water would ultimately reduce juvenile survival.

The Great White Heron's use of human-modified wetlands adds still another threat to its survival. Juvenile and adult Great White Herons that seasonally use freshwater Everglades wetlands also are subject to infection by the nematode *Eustrongylides ignotus,* which was found to be the most significant infectious disease of Ciconiiformes in Florida (Spalding and Forrester 1991). These nematodes are transmitted to the bird host when fish, infected with the nematode, are ingested by the bird. Prevalence of the infection has been linked to fish in foraging sites that have been physically altered (e.g. ditches) and to sites with high nutrient pollution.

Another threat, revealed in necropsies of radio-tagged juvenile Great White Herons that had dispersed to freshwater Everglades habitats, was from mercury contamination (Spalding and Forrester 1991; Spalding et al. 1994). Four of five (80%) first-year birds that dispersed north had accumulated levels of mercury >5 ppm (wet weight), which is a level associated with emaciation, disease, and weakness (Spalding and Forrester 1991). Herons with high concentrations of mercury died more often from multiple chronic diseases than those with relatively low levels (M. Spalding, unpubl. data).

CAUSES OF THREAT: Causes of threats to stability of Great White Herons ultimately relate to basic issues of human population growth and agricultural expansion in Florida, especially south Florida. The sensitivity of wetland ecosystems to water manipulations make modifications of hydropattern the greatest threat to their productivity. Another major threat is that of eutrophication. The threat of wetland degradation to the survival of a viable Great White

Heron population is but a small part of the threat to an entire ecosystem. We can only expect to see a stable future for the herons when balance is brought between the demands of a growing human population and the minimum requirements of viable wetland systems. Whereas Florida has made significant progress towards protecting its wetlands, the process is far from complete. In the case of the unique Everglades ecosystem, major restoration projects remain in the planning stages, generally blocked or seriously inhibited by the lack of commitment from all sides to come to grips with major adjustments that must be made to implement them. As demonstrated by the rapid deterioration of Florida Bay, these decisions must be made soon or the ramifications will be virtually irreversible. Beyond this one large wetland system, the same problems exist for the majority of wetland sites, but on a more local level. Maintaining quality habitats for herons will require land management at local, regional, and national governmental levels that allow for the coexistence of productive wetland ecosystems throughout southern Florida.

The sources of mercury contaminating wildlife in the Everglades are still being debated. The current hypotheses all relate to human activity: methylation of mercury released by oxidation of peat soils resulting from drainage for agriculture; airborne pollution from incinerators; pollution from agricultural runoff; and increased methylation of background mercury in cattail marshes that have become more prevalent with nutrient input from agriculture. As with the case of wetland deterioration, the threat of mercury contamination is one that goes well beyond the Great White Heron to include virtually all wetland vertebrates.

Another more localized threat is the cumulative impact of direct human disturbance on the survival or reproductive success of individual birds. Undetermined, though undoubtedly large (L. Quinn, unpubl. data), numbers of herons are being killed annually through collisions with human structures (wires, automobiles, etc.) and through entanglement with fishing gear (G. Powell, R. Bjork and M. Spalding, unpubl. data; L. Quinn, unpubl. data). In addition, greater recreational use of shallow-water habitats in Florida Bay and the lower "back country" Keys threatens the success of some nesting colonies.

RESPONSES TO HABITAT MODIFICATION: Little can be determined regarding responses of Great White Herons to changes in their behavior or use of habitat that have been induced by development in Florida because virtually no data exist on their historical patterns. A more recent response exhibited by the Florida Bay population, while it has recovered from the direct effect of exploitation by humans as a food source, has been to develop a heavy dependence on supplemental feeding by humans ("panhandlers"; see Powell 1983; Powell and Powell 1986). The propensity of these birds to habituate to humans is in sharp contrast to historical references to them as being an extremely secretive species (Holt 1928; Probey 1974). This adjustment has resulted in elevated reproductive success of habituated individuals, but also has resulted in a high level of fatal injuries from entanglement in fishing line and collisions with automobiles, powerlines, and other human structures.

DEMOGRAPHIC CHARACTERISTICS: The demography of the Great White Heron has attracted special interest as a key to understanding its taxonomic relationship to the sympatric blue morph. Whereas this report has been focused on the white morph of *Ardea herodius occidentalis,* it must be realized that the population of this subspecies, as currently recognized, includes substantial numbers of the blue morph (about 40%, based on data collected in 1962; Robertson 1978). Blue morphs similarly breed throughout the Keys and Florida Bay at traditional sites that they have occupied at least since the 1920s when distributional data were first collected (Holt 1928). During the 1960s, summer counts of both morphs recorded a consistently smaller number of blue morph compared to white morph birds (40% in the lower Keys and Florida Bay [Robertson 1978]). Nest counts at five major colonies in the lower Keys in 1989–1990 documented over a 2:1 ratio of white to blue morphs (Wilmers 1990). Both the blue and white morphs have their traditional colonies that include relatively few mixed pairs. Robertson (1978) concluded that only about 4% of the nests in Florida Bay contained mixed matings rather than 48% that would be expected on the basis of random mating. This low level of interbreeding was confirmed from extensive colony surveys completed between 1981 and 1984 (G. Powell, unpubl. data). These data indicate the birds exercise strong selection for similar color morphs during the mating process. The basis for this assortive mating has yet to be determined, but it is particularly interesting in light of the fact that on the foraging grounds, where individuals defend territories, agonistic behavior is illicited irrespective of color (G. Powell and R. Bjork, unpubl. data).

Great White Herons nest year round, with a marked peak in November–February. They nest primarily on isolated islands either in loosely formed colonies, with other wading birds including Roseate Spoonbills (*Ajaia ajaja*), Reddish Egrets (*Egretta refuscens*), Double-crested Cormorants (*Phalacrocorax auritus*), and Brown Pelicans (*Pelecanus occidentalis*), or as isolated pairs. The nests are solid platforms of sticks as much as 1 m (3–4 ft.) in diameter and may be more than 25 cm (1 ft.) thick. They are built over ground or water, often on top of nests of previous years. The clutch consists of 2–5, usually 3 or 4, bluish-green eggs. Incubation starts with the first egg and the incubation period is 28–30 days. Both parents incubate, brood and feed the young. Young are altricial and spend 6–8 weeks in the nest. After fledging, they spend an additional 4 weeks in the vicinity of the nest and another week venturing out to other mangrove keys, but return back to the nest where they continue to beg for food from the parents (Powell and Bjork 1990).

Nesting success (number of nests producing at least 1 fledgling/total attempts) of Great White Herons from 1981–1984 (Powell and Powell 1986) and 1987–1990 (Powell and Bjork 1990) was monitored by observation of the large, highly visible nests in monthly aerial surveys. Baywide nesting success did not vary between the two periods of study and was 48% (n = 460 for 1981–1984, n = 1,624 for 1987–1990). However, there were consistent regional differences in success documented in the later study that clearly related to differences documented in the early study between birds supplemented with food from humans (83% success) and those that were not supplemented (34% success). Birds nesting in eastern Florida Bay (adjacent to the developed mainline Keys) did better (77%) than birds in west (47%), south (36%), or northeast (43%) Florida Bay. In the lower Keys, nest success was generally higher (mean = 66%, range = 50–88% success; Wilmers 1990) than in Florida Bay.

Mortality of post-fledgling Great White Herons is high also (Powell and Bjork 1990). Of about 70 radio-tagged juveniles, 35% did not survive beyond one month after fledging and 91% died within one year (mean time from fledging to death was three months).

KEY BEHAVIORS: In eastern Florida Bay, Great White Herons consistently forage at night (Powell 1987), a behavior probably related to the diel patterns of the forage fish (Powell et al. 1987). Nocturnal foraging for *Ardea* has been noted for other environments (Willard 1975; Bayer 1978; Pratt 1980), but only Black and Collopy (1982) quantified diurnal and nocturnal occurrences. They found that *Ardea* was dependent on tidal cycle but independent of time of day. Similarly, Great White Heron activity was correlated with tidal cycle in western Florida Bay where there was a large lunar tide (Powell 1987).

The Great White Heron engages in a series of highly ritualized displays at its nest including: Stretch, Snap, Twig-shake, and Low-bow (Meyerriecks [1960] and as described for Great Blue Herons by Mock [1976]). On the foraging grounds, Great White Herons may be territorial, defending an area with short flights within the area and displays at its boundaries. One of the displays, identified as Gathering-ground dance behavior and erroneously attributed to courtship behavior (Meyerriecks 1960) was later attributed to agonistic behavior (Mock 1976; Bayer 1984). They also may forage socially, maintaining only small, individual distances (G. Powell and R. Bjork, pers. observ.). In east-central Florida Bay, groups of Great White Herons (regularly >20 and occasionally >100 birds) forage together in winter (G. Powell and R. Bjork, unpubl. data). When Great Blue and Great White Herons are startled, they utter harsh, low-pitched, croak-like calls (Palmer 1962).

CONSERVATION MEASURES TAKEN: In the 1930s, it was realized that the Great White Heron was headed toward extirpation unless greater protection was provided for its breeding sites throughout the Florida Keys (Sprunt

1935). That realization was an important force behind the establishment of Everglades National Park in 1947, which was as much an effort by conservationists to deal with the rapidly deteriorating situation in Florida Bay as in the Everglades themselves. Some of the earliest National Wildlife Refuges were established in the lower Florida Keys, as well, to protect a number of rare birds. These reserves included Key West National Wildlife Refuge in 1908 and the Great White Heron National Wildlife Refuge in 1938 (U.S. Dept. of Interior 1968). In addition, The National Key Deer Refuge established around 1957, protected important Great White Heron habitat in the lower Keys. The result was the legal protection of most of the breeding habitat of the Great White Heron in Florida. Current regulations prohibit landings on most islands within the National Park and on some islands in the refuge system. The collapse of the natural sponge industry and the resultant cessation of heron colony robbing for food by the spongers was equally important to the recovery of the species.

CONSERVATION MEASURES PROPOSED: It is absolutely necessary to develop and enact a restoration plan that incorporates quantity and timing of freshwater flow into management over the entire Everglades system, integrating the needs of the natural system and urban and agricultural users. In particular, this will require much increased freshwater flow into the historic Florida Bay drainages (Taylor and Shark sloughs), incorporation of salinity responses to freshwater flow into the hydrologic models used for management plans, and continued research on primary and secondary productivity in the estuarine habitats. Further investigation into the causes of mercury contamination in the Everglades, its effects on reproduction and behavior of animals and development of solutions to reduce the contamination should be supported.

To reduce impacts and rehabilitate the degraded shallow water, estuarine habitats adjacent to the Florida Keys, the four-point plan developed by the Boating Impact Work Group as outlined in the Monroe County Boating Impacts Management Plan (Barker and Garrett 1992) should be adopted. The plan calls for improved channel marking, increased enforcement of regulations protecting shallow water habitats, establishment of no access and restricted access areas, and development and implementation of education program for boaters to reduce prop dredging and disturbance to wildlife. Additional educational efforts should be increased to sensitize the fishing community to the dangers of discarded fishing tackle. Legislation requiring use of rapidly biodegradable fishing line in south Florida waters should be implemented. A plan should be adopted to eliminate utility lines that extend above the height of native vegetation in the Keys. In limited cases, there should be increased protection of wading bird colonies in Florida Bay and the lower Keys from human disturbance. Prohibition of petroleum extraction from coastal waters adjacent to south Florida should continue. A national energy policy with less reliance on petroleum should be encouraged, and the purchase of existing leases in Gulf waters from oil companies should be negotiated.

ACKNOWLEDGMENTS: We dedicate this species account to Don Miller, whose commitment to protecting Florida Bay started the momentum that will hopefully save that ecosystem from destruction. Also key to the momentum to protect the Bay was Nathaniel Reed, who continues the effort, undaunted. The extensive studies that provided much of the current data on reproduction and dispersal of Great White Herons reported in this account would not have been possible without the generous support of the Elizabeth Ordway Dunn Foundation. We would like to acknowledge Drs. Gary Hendrix and James Tilmant who precipitated the cooperative alignment between Everglades National Park and the National Audubon Society for Florida Bay. We acknowledge Laura Quinn and her Wild Bird Rehabilitation Center in the Florida Keys for her tremendous efforts in educating the public, providing information to museums and scientists, and rehabilitating many Great White Herons. We thank Alan Litman of StarTron who provided technical expertise and the loan of night-vision equipment that allowed us to penetrate the night-time activities of the herons. Finally, we thank William B. Robertson for contributing his extensive knowledge to this account.

LITERATURE CITED:

AOU. 1957. Check-list of North American birds. Fifth ed. American Ornithologists' Union, Washington, D.C.

AOU. 1973. Thirty-second supplement to the American Ornithologists' Union check-list of North American birds. Auk 90:411–419.

AOU. 1983. Check-list of North American birds. Sixth ed. American Ornithologists' Union, Washington, D.C.

Bancroft, G. 1969. A Great White Heron in Great Blue nesting colony. Auk 86:141–142.

Bangs, O., and W. R. Zappey. 1905. Birds of the Isle of Pines. Amer. Nat. 39:179–215.

Barbour, T. 1943. Cuban ornithology. Memoirs Nuttall Ornith. Club. no. 9. Cambridge, Massachusettes. 144 pp.

Barker, V. and G. Garrett. 1992. Boating impacts management plan. Final report, Fla. Dept. Nat. Res. contract #C-7442. Monroe Co. Dept. Mar. Res., Key West, Florida.

Bayer, R. D. 1978. Aspects of an Oregon estuarine Great Blue Heron population. Pp. 213–217 in Wading birds (A. Sprunt, IV, J. C. Ogden, and S. Winckler, eds.). Nat. Aud. Soc. Res. Rept. no. 7. New York.

Bayer, R. D. 1984. Foraging ground displays of Great Blue Herons at Yaquina Estuary, Oregon. Colonial Waterbirds 7:45–54.

Black, B. B., and M. W. Collopy. 1982. Nocturnal activity of Great Blue Herons in a north Florida saltmarsh. Jour. Field Ornithol. 53:403–406.

Bond, J. 1956. Check-list of birds of the West Indies. Acad. Nat. Sci. Philadelphia, Pennsylvania. 214 pp.

Bond, J. 1961. Sixth supplement to the check-list of birds of the West Indies (1956). Acad. Nat. Sci., Philadelphia, Pennsylvania. 12 pp.

Bond, J. 1965. Tenth supplement to the check-list of birds of the West Indies (1956). Acad. Nat. Sci., Philadelphia, Pennsylvania. 16 pp.

Browder, J. A. 1985. Relationship between pink shrimp production on the Tortugas grounds and water flow patterns in the Florida Everglades. Bull. Mar. Sci. 37:839–856.

Cruickshank, A. D. 1980. The birds of Brevard County. Florida Press, Inc., Orlando, Florida.

Griscom, L. 1926. The ornithologists results of the Mason-Spinden expedition to Yucatan. Amer. Mus. Novitates, no. 235 and no. 236.

Henny, C. J. 1972. An analysis of the population dynamics of selected avian species with special reference to changes during the modern pesticide era. U.S. Fish Wildl. Ser. Res. Rept. 1.

Holt, E. G. 1928. The status of the Great White Heron and Wurdemann's heron. Cleveland Mus. Nat. Hist. 1:1–35.

Holt, E. G., and G. M. Sutton. 1926. Notes on the birds observed in southern Florida. Ann. Carnegie Mus. 16:409–439.

Howell, A. H. 1921. A list of the birds of Royal Palm Hammock, Florida. Auk 38:250–263.

Mitchell, C. A., White D. H., and T. E. Kaiser. 1981. Reproductive success of Great Blue Herons at Nueces Bay, Corpus Christi, Texas. Bull. Texas Ornithol. Soc. 14:18–21.

Mayr, E. 1956. Is the Great White Heron a good species? Auk 73:71–77.

Meyerriecks, A. J. 1957. Field observations pertaining to the systematic status of the Great White Heron in the Florida Keys. Auk 74:469–478.

Meyerriecks, A. J. 1960. Comparative breeding behavior of four species of North American herons. Publ. Nuttall Ornith. Club no. 2. Cambridge, Massachusetts. 158 pp.

Mock, D. W. 1976. Pair-formation displays of the Great Blue Heron. Wilson Bull. 88:185–230.

Murton, R. K. 1971. Polymorphism in Ardeidae. Ibis 113:97–99.

Palmer, R. S. 1962. Handbook of North American birds. Vol. 1. Yale Univ. Press, New Haven, Connecticut. 567 pp.

Paytner, R. A., Jr. 1955. The ornithogeography of the Yucatan Peninsula. Peabody Mus. Nat. Hist. Yale Univ., Bull. 9. New Haven, Connecticut. 347 pp.

Phelps, W. H., and W. H. Phelps, Jr. 1958. Lista de las aves de Venezuela con su distribucion. Parte 2, No. Passeriformes. Editorial Cucre, Caracas, Venezuela. 317 pp.

Pierce, C. W. 1962. The cruise of the Bonton. Tequesta 22:1–78.

Powell, G. V. N. 1983. Food availability and reproduction by Great White Herons, *Ardea herodias:* a food addition study. Colon. Waterbirds 6:139–147.

Powell, G. V. N. 1987. Habitat use by wading birds in a subtropical estuary: implications of hydrography. Auk 104:740–749.

Powell, G. V. N., and A. H. Powell. 1986. Reproduction by Great White Herons Ardea herodias in Florida Bay as an indicator of habitat quality. Biol. Cons. 36:101–113.

Powell, G. V. N., and R. Bjork. 1990. Studies of wading birds in Florida Bay: a biological assessment of the ecosystem. Nat. Aud. Soc. comprehensive report to Elizabeth Ordway Dunn Found. Nat. Aud. Soc., Tavernier, Florida.

Powell, G. V. N., S. M. Sogard, and J. H. Holmquist. 1987. Ecology of shallow-water bank habitats in Florida Bay. Rept. for South Fla. Res. Ctr., contract CX5280–3–2339. Everglades Natl. Park, Homestead, Florida.

Powell, G. V. N., R. D. Bjork, J. C. Ogden, R. T. Paul, A. H. Powell, and W. B. Robertson, Jr. 1989. Population trends in some Florida Bay wading birds. Wilson Bull. 101:436–457.

Pratt, H. M. 1980. Breeding of Great Blue Herons and Common Egrets in central California. Condor 72:407–416.

Proby, K. H. 1974. Audubon in Florida, with selections from the writings of John James Audubon. Univ. Miami Press, Miami, Florida.

Robertson, W. B. 1978. Great White Heron. Pp 69–72 in Rare and endangered biota of Florida, vol. II: birds (Kale, H. W., II, ed.). Univ. Presses Fla., Gainesville, Florida.

Robblee, M. B., T. R. Barber, P. R. Carlson, Jr., M. J. Durako, J. W. Fourqurean, L. K. Muehlstein, D. Porter, L. A. Yarbro, R. T. Zieman, J. C. Zieman. 1991. Mass mortality of the tropical seagrass *Thalassia testudinum* in Florida Bay (USA). Mar. Ecol. Prog. Ser. 71:297–299.

Smith, T. J., III, J. H. Hudson, G. V. N. Powell, M. B. Robblee, and P. J. Isdale. 1989. Freshwater flow from the Everglades to Florida Bay: a historical reconstruction based on fluorescent banding in the coral *Solenastrea bournoni*. Bull. Mar. Sci. 44:274–282.

Sogard, S. M., G. V. N. Powell, and J. G. Holmquist. 1989a. Fish utilization of shallow, seagrass-covered banks in Florida Bay II. Diel and tidal patterns. Environ. Biol. Fishes. 24:81–92.

Sogard, S. M., G. V. N. Powell, and J. G. Holmquist. 1989b. Fish utilization of shallow, seagrass-covered banks in Florida Bay I. Species composition and spatial heterogeneity. Env. Biol. Fishes. 24:53–65.

Spalding, M. G., and D. J. Forrester. 1991. Effects of parasitism and disease on the nesting success of colonial wading birds (Ciconiiformes) in southern Florida. Draft report to Fla. Game Fresh Water Fish Comm. Submitted as final rept. No NG88-008. Tallahassee, Florida.

Spalding, M. S., R. Bjork, G. V. N. Powell, and S. F. Sundlof. 1994. Mercury and cause of death in Great White Herons. Jour. Wildl. Manage. 58:735–739.

Sprunt, A., Jr. 1935. The Great White Heron today. Bird Lore 37:405–411.

Sprunt, A., Jr. 1936a. Aerial inspection of the Great White Heron in Florida Bay and Keys for April 1936. Unpubl. rept., Nat. Aud. Soc., Tavernier, Florida.

Sprunt, A., Jr. 1936b. Aerial inspection of the Great White Heron in the Bay of Florida, October 1936. Unpubl. rept., Nat. Aud. Soc., Tavernier, Florida.

Sprunt, A., Jr. 1937. Aerial survey, Florida Bay. Unpubl. rept., Nat. Aud. Soc., Tavernier, Florida.

Sprunt, A., Jr. 1939. Great White Heron Survey of Florida Bay area of range, January. Unpubl. rept., Nat. Aud. Soc., Tavernier, Florida.

Tilmant, J. T., E. S. Rutherford, and E. B. Thue. 1989. Fishery harvest and population dynamics of red drum (*Sciaenops ocellatus*) from Florida Bay and adjacent waters. Bull Mar. Sci. 44:126–138.

U. S. Dept. of Interior. 1968. National Wildlife Refuges of the Florida Keys, Monroe County, Florida. U. S. Fish and Wildl. Ser. pamphlet.

Walters, C., L. Gunderson, and C. S. Holling. 1992. Experimental policies for water management in the Everglades. Ecol. Applic. 2:189–202.

Willard, D. E. 1975. The feeding behavior and ecology of five species of herons at the Brigantine National Wildlife Refuge, New Jersey. Ph. D. dissert., Princeton Univ., Princeton, New Jersey.

Wilmers, T. 1990. Great Blue Heron productivity in the lower Florida Keys, 1990. Key Deer National Wildlife Refuge Report. Big Pine Key, Florida.

Zachow, K. F. 1983. The Great Blue and Great White Heron: A multivariate morphometric analysis of skeletons. M.S. thesis, Univ. Miami, Miami, Florida.

PREPARED BY: George V. N. Powell, RARE Center for Tropical Conservation, 1616 Walnut Street, Suite 911, Philadelphia, PA 19103, and Robin Bjork, National Audubon Society, 115 Indian Mound Trail, Tavernier, FL 33070 (Current address: Department of Fisheries and Wildlife, Oregon State Universtiy, Corvallis, OR 97331).

Great Egret
Casmerodius albus

FAMILY ARDEIDAE
Order Ciconiiformes

TAXONOMY: The Great Egret *(Casmerodius albus)* is a cosmopolitan heron with four recognized subspecies. Each subspecies is geographically distinct and soft-part coloration varies in each region (see Hancock and Kushlan 1984). The subspecies *C. a. egrettus* is a permanent resident in Florida and is widespread throughout the Americas. Generic designation has been debated; Payne and Risley (1976) placed the species in *Ardea*, whereas many authors place the species in the large polytypic genus *Egretta* (e.g., Hancock and Elliot 1978; Hancock and Kushlan 1984). The AOU (1983) Checklist retains the species in *Casmerodius*.

DESCRIPTION: Great Egrets are large, all white birds with a standing height of 85–102 cm (33–40 in.) and a wingspan up to 1.5 m (59 in.) (Palmer 1962; Hancock and Kushlan 1984). Males are reportedly slightly larger than females. In *C. a. egrettus*, the legs and feet are black and bill coloration is yellow. Great Egrets lack occipital and jugular plumes, but grow exceptionally long, trailing scapular plumes during the pre-alternate molt. These "aigrettes" are shed during the latter part of the breeding season.

During courtship both sexes undergo similar morphological changes. Lore coloration changes to bright lime-green, legs become shiny black, and bill color changes to orange-yellow. Soft parts revert to nonbreeding colors soon after pair formation (Wiese 1976, 1978). Juveniles are similar to adults but lack aigrettes and their yellow bills may be tipped with black.

POPULATION SIZE AND TREND: Dramatic changes in Great Egret numbers have occurred over the past 100 years. During the latter part of the nineteenth century this species, along with Snowy egrets (*E. thula*), were prime targets for plume hunters, who supplied the millinery trade with aigrettes priced at up to 32 dollars per ounce (Bent 1926). At these prices the

Great Egret,
Casmerodius albus.
(Photo copyright
by Allan D.
Cruickshank,
courtesy of Florida
Audubon Society)

egret population in the United States was quickly decimated over its entire range. Allen (1957) reported a remnant population of only 1,400 Great Egrets distributed over 10 heronries in 1911, with 7 of these located in Florida. This slaughter and the concomitant near extinction of Great (and Snowy) Egrets was widely publicized at the turn of the century by numerous Audubon societies. This resulted in the passage of the Audubon Plumage Bill by the New York State Legislature in 1910, outlawing the sale of plumes from native birds in New York. The end of plume hunting came after passage of the Migratory Bird Treaty in 1918.

Under this protection the Great Egret population rebounded. Pennock (in Bent 1926) reported in 1917 that Great Egrets were more numerous in Florida than they had been for years. Allen (1957) estimated the Florida population of Great Egrets at 73,000 in the mid-1930s. Robertson and Kushlan (1974) attributed their quick recovery to the existence of extensive areas of intact wetlands, but also observed that "the progressive loss and deterioration of wetland habitat reduced wading bird numbers to about 10% of the reported level in the 1930s." Extensive surveys of wading bird colonies in peninsular Florida were conducted in the mid-1970s (Nesbitt et al. 1982). Data from this work indicated that about 50,000 adult Great Egrets were present in 219 colonies. Further surveys in the mid-1980s (see Runde et al. 1991; Runde

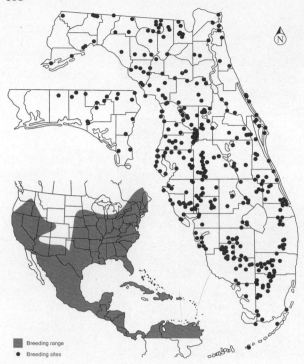

Distribution map of
the Great Egret,
Casmerodius albus.

Breeding range
Breeding sites

1991) located 393 colonies with about 39,000 Great Egrets present in peninsular Florida.

Although more breeding colonies with Great Egrets were located in the 1980s, breeding populations in peninsular Florida appeared to have declined. This apparent decline in population size was accompanied by a proportionate decline in numbers of large (>100 egrets) colonies from 64 to <24%, and a proportionate increase in numbers of small (<100 birds) colonies from 37 to 77% (Runde 1991). Thus, the recent pattern has been a splintering of the breeding population into smaller colonies accompanied by a decline in overall numbers.

Despite these recent trends, Great Egrets remain abundant in Florida. In the late-1980s, only Cattle Egrets (*Bubulcus ibis*) and White Ibis (*Eudocimus albus*) outnumbered Great Egrets in breeding colonies across the state (Runde 1991). Great Egrets were the most abundant wading birds during wet-season aerial surveys of the Water Conservation Areas north of Everglades National Park. Here, Great Egret numbers were exceeded only by White Ibis during dry-season surveys (Hoffman et al. 1990). These surveys revealed Great Egrets (along with Great Blue Herons [*A. herodius*]) were widely distributed in this area and relatively consistent in both distribution and numbers when compared to the smaller herons and ibis. In 1986 and 1987, peak wintering populations of Great Egrets were estimated to total 37,100 and 41,493, respectively in the Everglades system (Frederick and Collopy 1988). The Water Conservation Areas alone supported estimated peak wintering populations of 20,860 in 1986, 16,893 in 1987, and 18,933 in 1988 (Hoffman et al. 1990).

DISTRIBUTION AND HISTORY OF DISTRIBUTION: The Great Egret is cosmopolitan, with four subspecies distributed throughout the temperate and tropical latitudes (Hancock and Elliot 1978, Palmer 1962). *C. a. albus* is distributed across the eastern hemisphere from Europe to Siberia and Japan, wintering in northern Africa, India, and southern China. *C. a. modestus* occurs in southern Asia from India east to central China, central Japan, southern New Zealand and Australia. *C. a. melanorhynchos* is restricted to Africa, south of the Sahara, and Madagascar. Our subspecies (*C. a. egrettus*) occurs throughout most of North, Central, and South America. During the 1970s, breeding distribution along the Atlantic coast of the United States extended from Florida to Massachusetts, with Florida supporting 24% of the total U.S. coastal breeding population (Spendelow and Patton 1988). Within Florida, 80% of the Great Egret colonies were found between 25–28°N latitude (i.e., from Florida Bay to Tampa). There was little change in this figure from the 1970s to 1980s (Runde 1991). Statewide distribution is now well known with >400 active breeding colonies. In the 1980s, numerous northeastern and northwestern counties were added to the known breeding range of the Great Egret in Florida (Runde et al. 1991). Thus, the Great Egret seems secure in terms of its breeding distribution in Florida.

North American Great Egrets are migratory over most of their range. Like many ardeids, they perform extensive post-breeding dispersals into areas outside their breeding range and records along the Atlantic coast extend northward to Newfoundland. Much of the Atlantic Coast population is believed to winter in Florida (Palmer 1962). Hancock and Kushlan (1984) note that this population also moves along the coast wintering from North Carolina to the Bahamas and Antilles, and the midwestern population also may move to or through Florida in the winter.

HABITAT REQUIREMENTS AND HABITAT TRENDS: Great Egrets feed in a wide variety of habitats including coast lines, tidal creeks, seagrass flats, stream banks, lake shores, ponds, fresh and salt water marshes, wet or dry pastures, and agricultural drainage ditches. Their diet is equally varied, consisting of fishes, reptiles, amphibians, small mammals and birds, and various invertebrates (Bent 1926; Wiese 1975, 1978). Small fish dominated diets in the lower Everglades (Bancroft et al. 1990). They are considerably more specific in their nest site selection, preferring isolated, inaccessible heronries in freshwater swamps or mangrove forests.

Loss of wetlands continues to threaten much of Florida's wildlife including Great Egret populations. From the mid-1970s to mid-1980s, Florida lost an estimated 260,300 acres of wetlands (Frayer and Hefner 1991). This decline primarily affected palustrine wetlands that are major feeding and nesting habitats for all ardeids. Losses of estuarine wetlands, which also provide foraging and nesting habitat, were less severe. Overall, the annual rate of wetland loss declined during this period to nearly a third of the rate recorded during the 1950s and 1960s. But annual net losses still averaged 26,030 acres of wetlands during this period. Thus, the major trend in habitat continues to be loss of freshwater feeding and nesting habitats.

VULNERABILITY OF SPECIES AND HABITAT: Fortunately for Great Egrets, habitat losses and degradation appear to be less of an immediate threat than for other smaller or more specialized wading birds. Catholic food habits combined with the ability of the Great Egret to feed in a wide array of wetlands, deep water, and terrestrial habitats has no doubt helped to prevent the larger population declines seen in other species of Ciconiiformes (e.g., Wood Stork [*Mycteria americana*], Snowy Egret, and White Ibis). The combination of long legs and the ability to swim give this egret (and the Great Blue Heron) the advantage of feeding in deeper water than many other herons. Compared to small herons that require water depths <15 cm, Great Egrets require water depths <25 cm (Bancroft et al. 1990). This may help free them from strict dependence upon prey in naturally fluctuating wetlands and allow them to take advantage of impounded wetlands with stabilized, higher water levels. Studies in the Water Conservation Areas (Hoffman et al. 1990) noted that Great Egret distribution tracked receding water levels, as was true of other wading birds, but that this species was more consistently and widely distributed than other wading birds. Only the driest areas in low-water months and the deepest water in high-water months consistently were not used by Great Egrets.

CAUSES OF THREAT: The major causes of wetland loss (Frayer and Hefner 1991) from the mid-1970s to mid-1980s were due to agriculture (175,100 acres) and development (66,000 acres). The loss and alteration of suitable feeding and nesting habitat is the primary chronic threat to all wetland wildlife. A recently identified and potentially very serious threat to successful reproduction is excessive mortality of wading bird nestlings from parasitic infections caused by *Eustrongylides* sp. (Spalding 1990).

Less pervasive and more readily addressed threats may occur as a result of human disturbance or trespass at nesting colonies. Great Egrets require an absence of human disturbance during nest-site selection, courtship, incubation, and prior to hatching of eggs, adults will readily desert a heronry following repeated disturbances. Young nestlings will scramble from their nests to flee intruders in the colony and those unable to return to their nests may perish below the heronry. Where this has been documented as a problem, individual heronries should be afforded full protection during the nesting period, and human access should be excluded.

RESPONSES TO HABITAT MODIFICATION: Great Egrets breeding in heronries declining from natural factors (e.g., destruction of vegetative nesting substrate) may be successfully aided in some cases by the use of artificial nesting platforms, as was done at Avery Island, Louisiana (Wiese 1975, 1978). Nesting also is common in Florida on coastal spoil islands and within impoundments.

DEMOGRAPHIC CHARACTERISTICS: Many Great Egrets probably attempt nesting during their first year following hatching, but fail to nest successfully (Wiese 1975, 1978). Palmer (1962) reported that Morton concluded "it takes three years to reach maturity." There remains no conclusive evidence on age at first breeding. Pratt (1972) summarized reported Great Egret clutch sizes as ranging from 2 to 6 eggs. In a Louisiana heronry, the clutch size averaged 3.4 eggs for 68 clutches (Wiese 1975, 1978). Mean clutch size in Florida ranged from 2.2 to 3.5 (Frederick and Collopy 1978; Bancroft et al. 1990).

Louisiana Great Egrets hatched 96.6% of their eggs (Wiese 1978), whereas Teal (1965) reported a 3% hatching failure in a Georgia heronry. In California, Pratt (1972) reported hatching failures of 3–13%. Frederick and Collopy (1988) report hatching success rates >80% in the Everglades.

Despite high hatching successes, the fledging success of Great Egret nestlings is usually considerably lower. Wiese (1975, 1978) recorded fledging success of 50.3% (n = 72 nests) in Louisiana, with practically all nestling loss a result of starvation of the last hatched egret. Larger clutches suffered greater nestling losses. In Florida, Frederick and Collopy (1988) summarized nesting success from eight studies that reported values from 7.3 to 76.9%, and measured nest success rates of 14.8 and 20.6% for Great Egrets in the Everglades. Similarly, Bancroft et al. (1990) reported that nesting success from 1987 to 1989 at colonies in the lower Everglades ranged from 0 to 38.5%.

According to Pratt (1972), a fledging rate of 1–3 young per nest is the average for this species, with starvation, predation, climatic factors, and chlorinated hydrocarbon contamination accounting for sources of egg and nestling loss. Recent estimates from the Everglades range from 1.5 to 2.5 young per successful nest (Frederick and Collopy 1988; Bancroft et al. 1990). The breeding season is protracted beginning in late-January or February in the Everglades (Frederick and Collopy 1988; Bancroft et al. 1990) and extending through August in some situations. Kahl (1963) estimated a post-fledging mortality of young Great Egrets at 76% during their first year and 26% annually thereafter.

KEY BEHAVIORS: Great Egrets nests socially, most often with a variety of other ardeids, but occasionally in small, single species colonies. A well-defined interspecific stratification of nest heights is maintained in mixed species heronries, where Great Egrets (along with Great Blue Herons) consistently select the highest nest sites (Maxwell and Kale 1977; Burger 1978). This habit is of value to wildlife biologists as these tall, white birds nesting in treetops signal the presence of nesting colonies during aerial surveys.

The onset of Great Egret nesting activities is marked by shorter absences from the heronry and selection and defense of a nest site. Males cease feeding and remain in the heronry throughout the day, constructing a basic nest platform that is defended against other males, and on which all subsequent advertising takes place (Wiese 1975, 1978). Females are solicited by Stretch, Bow, and Snap displays after their return to the heronry, with the relative frequency of each display dependent on the distance between the male and female (Wiese 1976, 1978). The female is gradually accepted on the nest platform, where joint nest building, Circle-Flap Flights, and the learning of the mate's call establish the pair bond. The first egg is laid between the fourth and tenth day following pairing. Remaining eggs are laid in 2-day intervals thereafter. Length of incubation ranges from 28.5 days (first egg laid) to 26.0 days (fourth egg laid), and young Great Egrets fledge between 62–70 days following hatching (Wiese 1975, 1978).

This egret is frequently a solitary, territorial feeder, but larger foraging aggregations are common in the Everglades. They forage by standing or slowly stalking prey in a variety of wetland habitats and will feed in deep water or on dry land.

CONSERVATION MEASURES TAKEN: The Great Egret has been part of various recent research and survey projects on herons and other wading birds, but has received little specific attention (e.g., Frederick and Collopy 1988; Hoffman et al. 1990; Bancroft et al. 1990; Runde et al. 1991). This species is not officially listed by the U.S. Fish & Wildlife Service or Florida Game and Fresh Water Fish Commission.

CONSERVATION MEASURES PROPOSED: As a highly visible indicator of nesting colony locations, Great Egrets should continue to be monitored in conjunction with broad-based surveys of colonial nesting waterbirds. Wetlands protection and restoration efforts will benefit this species, as well as other wading birds.

LITERATURE CITED:

Allen, R. P. 1957. An urgent appeal for information on the wading birds. Aud. Field Notes 11:458–460.

AOU. 1983. Checklist of North American birds. American Ornithologists Union, Washington, D.C.

Bent, A. C. 1926. Life histories of North American marsh birds. Smithsonian Inst. Press, Bull. no. 135. Washington, D.C.

Bancroft, G. T., S. D. Jewel, and A. M. Strong. 1990. Foraging and nesting ecology of herons in the lower Everglades relative to water conditions. Final Rept. South Fla. Water Mgmt. Dist., West Palm Beach, Florida. 156 pp.

Burger, J. 1978. The pattern and mechanism of nesting in mixed-species heronries. Pp. 48–58 in Wading birds (A. Sprunt IV, J.C. Ogden, and S. Winckler, eds.). Nat. Aud. Soc. Res. Rept. no. 7, New York. 381 pp.

Frayer, W. E., and J. M. Hefner. 1991. Florida wetlands: status and trends, 1970's to 1980's. U.S. Fish and Wild. Serv., Atlanta, Georgia. 31 pp.

Frederick, P. C., and M. W. Collopy. 1988. Reproductive ecology of wading birds in relation to water conditions in the Florida Everglades. Tech. Rept. no. 30. Fla. Coop. Fish Wildl. Res. Unit, School For. Resour. Conserv., Univ. Florida, Gainesville, Florida. 259 pp.

Hancock, J., and H. Elliot. 1978. The herons of the world. Harper and Row, New York.

Hancock, J., and J. Kushlan. 1984. The herons handbook. Harper and Row, New York. 288 pp.

Hoffman, W., G. T. Bancroft, and R. J. Sawicki. 1990. Wading bird populations and distributions in the water conservation areas of the Everglades: 1985 through 1988. South Fla. Water Mgmt. Dist., West Palm Beach, Florida. 173 pp.

Kahl, M. P. 1963. Mortality of Common Egrets and other herons. Auk 80:295–300.

Nesbitt, S. A., J. C. Ogden, H. W. Kale, II, B. W. Patty, and L. A. Rouse. 1982. Florida atlas of breeding sites for herons and their allies: 1976–78. OBS-81/49. U.S. Fish and Wildl. Serv., Washington, D.C., 449 pp.

Maxwell, G. R., II, and H. W. Kale, II. 1977. Breeding biology of five species of herons in coastal Florida. Auk 94:689–700.

Palmer, R. S. 1962. Handbook of North American birds. Vol. 1. Yale Univ. Press, New Haven, Connecticut. 567 pp.

Payne, R. B., and C. J. Risley 1976. Systematics and evolutionary relationships among the herons (Ardeidae). Misc. Publ. Mus. Zool., Univ. of Mich., Ann Arbor, Michigan. 115 pp.

Pratt, H. M. 1972. Nesting success of Common Egrets and Great Blue Herons in the San Francisco Bay region. Condor 71:447–453.

Robertson, W. B., and J. A. Kushlan. 1974. The southern Florida avifauna. Pp. 414–452 in Environments of south Florida: past and present (P. J. Gleason, ed.). Mem. no. 2, Miami Geol. Soc., Miami, Florida. 551 pp.

Runde, D. E. 1991. Trends in wading bird nesting populations in Florida: 1976–1978 and 1986–1989. Final Perf. Rept. Fla. Game and Fresh Water Fish Comm., Tallahassee, Florida. 90 pp.

Runde, D. E., J. A. Gore, J. A. Hovis, M. S. Robson, and P. D. Southall. 1991. Florida atlas of breeding sites for herons and their allies: update 1986–89. Nongame Wildlife Tech. Rept. no. 10. Fla. Game and Fresh Water Fish Comm., Tallahassee, Florida. 147 pp.

Spalding, M. G. 1990. Antemortem diagnosis of eustrongylidosis in wading birds (Ciconiiformes). Colon. Waterbirds 13:75–77.

Spendelow, J. A., and S. R. Patton. 1988. National atlas of coastal waterbird colonies in the contiguous United States: 1976–82. U.S. Fish and Wildl. Serv. Biol. Rept. no. 88(5). Washington, D.C., 326 pp.

Teal, J. M. 1965. Nesting success of egrets and herons in Georgia. Wilson Bull. 77:257–263.

Wiese, J. H. 1975. The reproductive biology of the Great Egret (*Casmerodius albus egretta*). M.S. thesis, Fla. State Univ., Tallahassee, Florida. 83 pp.

Wiese, J. H. 1976. Courtship and pair formation in the Great Egret. Auk 93:709–724.

Wiese, J. H. 1978. Great Egret. Pp. 73–74 in Rare and endangered biota of Florida. Vol. 2. birds (H. W. Kale, II, ed.). Univ. Presses Fla., Gainesville, Florida.

PREPARED BY: Douglas E. Runde, Florida Game and Fresh Water Fish Commission, Route 7, Box 3055, Quincy, FL 32351-9807 (Current address: Weyerhauser Company, WTC 1A5, Federal Way, WA 98003).

Little Blue Heron

Egretta caerulea

FAMILY ARDEIDAE

Order Ciconiiformes

TAXONOMY: Originally described by Linnaeus in 1758 as *Ardea caerulea* from a South Carolina specimen, the Little Blue Heron was maintained in the monotypic genus *Florida* after 1858. More recently, this heron has been placed in the genus *Egretta* with the other intermediate-sized day herons (Parkes 1955; AOU 1983).

DESCRIPTION: The Little Blue Heron is a medium-size ardeid about 64–74 cm (25–29 in.) in length with a wingspread of about 1 m (40 in.). The sexes are similar in body measurements and plumage color (Palmer 1962). In the definitive adult plumage, the head and neck are purplish-maroon, there is a small whitish region on the throat and upper neck, with the rest of the plumage slaty-blue; the distal third of the bill is black, with the remainder of the bill and orbital skin dark gray (nonbreeding) to cobalt-blue (breeding); the iris is pale yellow (nonbreeding) to grayish-green (breeding); the legs are grayish-green during the nonbreeding season (S. Schwikert, pers. comm.) to black during the breeding season. Long lanceolate plumes become prominent in the crest, lower neck, and the back during the breeding season.

A unique feature among dark-plumaged ardeids, the immature Little Blue Heron is mostly white, with pale slate-gray tips on the primaries. Their legs are yellow-green. Subadults begin to acquire the dark plumage during their first spring and become "pied" or "calico" plumaged: the areas of the crest, lower neck, and back are slowly replaced with dark plumage; the secondaries and primaries are replaced in symmetry. Breeding subadults obtain the cobalt-blue soft-part colors on the bill and orbital skin, but the legs usually remain yellow-green (Rodgers 1980a). Adult plumage is attained by the second year.

POPULATION SIZE AND TREND: Because of their dark plumage and subcanopy nesting habits, Little Blue Herons cannot be surveyed as easily as the nesting white-plumaged herons (Runde 1991). The species is widespread

413

Little Blue Heron, *Egretta caerulea*. (Photo copyright by Allan D. Cruickshank, courtesy of Florida Audubon Society)

throughout Florida and the rest of its range, but with rare exceptions never as common as the other intermediate-sized day herons. Mostly because of the drainage of wetlands in Florida and some census data, Ogden (1978, et al. 1980) believed that the Little Blue Heron had declined in most of its range. Runde (1991) estimated less than 17,000 birds in 243 colonies during 1986–1989 compared to an earlier estimate by Nesbitt et al. (1982) of greater than 20,000 herons in 148 colonies, suggesting a possible decline in numbers of Little Blue Herons. Runde (1991) also noted that the proportion of small colonies of Little Blue Herons increased in frequency from 52 to 88%, while large colonies (>100 herons) declined from 48 to 11% during the 1980s. Some researchers have speculated that the Little Blue Heron has experienced greater nesting competition and interference from Cattle Egrets (*Bubulcus ibis*) than the other North American herons (Dusi and Dusi 1968; Werschkul 1977; Burger 1978).

DISTRIBUTION AND HISTORY OF DISTRIBUTION: Little Blue Herons breed in coastal and interior freshwater sites from Massachusetts to Texas, the lower Mississippi River valley, along both coasts of Mexico, much of the West Indies, and Central and northern South America (Palmer 1962; AOU 1983). In Florida, they are widely distributed from the panhandle southward

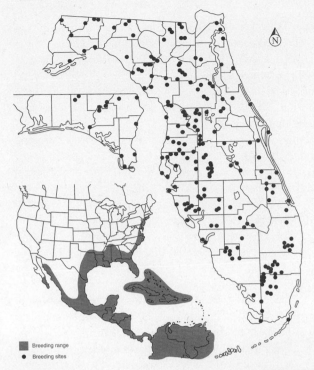

Distribution map
of the Little Blue
Heron, *Egretta
caerulea*.

Breeding range

Breeding sites

into the Keys (Runde 1991). The largest breeding colonies appear to be on
the coast and associated islands. Though the population in some areas may be
decreasing, the numbers and range may be increasing in other regions of
North America (Palmer 1962). Post-breeding dispersal is well known, especially by white-plumaged fledglings, and occurs throughout most of the eastern United States and southern Canada. Migratory Little Blue Herons move
into or through Florida in the winter as evidenced by the increased numbers of
herons seen during the nonbreeding season. The eastern population of Little
Blue Herons may migrate southward through Florida and into the West Indies;
whereas, the Mississippi River valley population may migrate southward along
the Gulf coast and into Mexico (Palmer 1962; Hancock and Kushlan 1984).

HABITAT REQUIREMENTS AND HABITAT TREND: As with other
ardeids, the Little Blue Heron requires relatively shallow freshwater, brackish,
and saltwater foraging habitats that provide access to adequate prey. The Little
Blue's diet is quite diverse and includes fishes, amphibians, and invertebrates
(Meanley 1955; Jenni 1969; Domby and McFarlane 1978; Telfair 1981;
Rodgers 1982). Little Blue Herons nesting in marine-estuarine regions often
will fly inland to forage at freshwater sites (Rodgers 1982), possibly as a
consequence of nestlings being intolerant of a high salt content of prey.

Breeding habitat requirements for Little Blue Herons are similar to other ardeids (Rodgers 1980b). Little Blue Herons nest in a variety of woody vegetation including cypress (*Taxodium distichum*), southern willow (*Salix caroliniana*), red maple (*Acer rubrum*), buttonbush (*Cephalanthus occidentalis*), red mangrove (*Rhizophora mangle*), black mangrove (*Avicennia germinans*), cabbage palm (*Sabel palmetto*), and Brazilian pepperbush (*Schinus terebenthifolius*). Little Blue Herons usually breed in mixed-species colonies located in flooded vegetation or on islands.

In Florida, much alteration of freshwater and marine-estuarine foraging habitat has had an adverse effect on the Little Blue Heron and probably has contributed to a decrease in its population. Further degradation of the foraging habitat of all ardeids probably will occur in the future.

VULNERABILITY OF SPECIES AND HABITAT: As with other ardeids, any alteration or degradation of wetland foraging habitat will have negative impacts on the population dynamics of the Little Blue Heron. Suitable nesting habitat appears stable.

CAUSES OF THREAT: The Little Blue Heron did not suffer directly from the plume trade during the early 1900s. Occasional human disturbance of breeding colonies may contribute to some reproductive failure at coastal islands used for recreational purposes. Currently, the main sources of threat to Little Blue Herons are alteration of hydrocycles of wetlands used for foraging and nesting and exposure to pesticides and heavy metal contamination. Little Blue Herons will readily forage at fish farms and hatcheries, exposing them to illegal shooting.

RESPONSES TO HABITAT MODIFICATION: The responses by Little Blue Herons to habitat modification are not accurately known, but probably include both positive and negative aspects. Little Blue Herons will forage at human-altered aquatic sites (e.g., impoundments, canals, fish ponds, drainage ditches), but this can expose them to pollutants. They also will nest on dredge-material islands with woody vegetation. Both natural and human induced changes in wetland hydrocycles have caused abandonment of breeding colonies and former foraging sites (Ogden 1978).

DEMOGRAPHIC CHARACTERISTICS: Little Blue Herons begin breeding during their first year when 11–12 months old, although they comprise only about 2% of the nesting herons (Rodgers 1980a). The pale blue eggs are laid over a period of several days at 1–2 day intervals. Incubation begins with the first egg laid and lasts for 21–24 days. Reproductive success exhibits inter- and intrayear variation (Jenni 1969; Maxwell and Kale 1977; Werschkul 1979; Rodgers 1980b, 1987). The modal clutch size is 3 eggs (range 2–5). Hatching success is generally high (ca. 91.4%), but nestling survivorship to 10–14 days of age ranges from 50.1–84.0%. Egg loss and nestling mortality result from starvation, collapse of nests, and predation. In general, early nesting Little Blue Herons exhibit larger clutch sizes and nestling survivorship.

The downy young are semialtricial at birth (McVaugh 1973). At 10–12 days, the nestlings can stand and walk out onto branches (Werschkul 1979). After 21–24 days, the young are fully feathered and independent of the parents, except for feeding. Fledging requires about 6–7 weeks. Maximun life span is unknown, but Little Blues probably attain at least 12 years.

KEY BEHAVIORS: Male Little Blue Herons initiate courtship during the spring in Florida by entering the colony site, usually in the late afternoon, establishing a territory, and engaging in courtship activities. Males possess many typical ardeid breeding behaviors (Rodgers 1980a). The primary courtship display of males, the Stretch display, consists of the heron extending the bill upward, erecting the plumes on the crest and back, and extending the wings outward as he moves up and down several times in succession, while giving several short calls. A less frequent display, the Circle Flight, is performed with the male leaping into the air, the head and neck fully extended, the legs dangling behind, and the wings beating in deep arcs as the heron flies in a large circle before returning back to the territory. Once paired, male and female herons engage in an elaborate Greeting Ceremony, with calls and Bill-nibbling, during twig-passing and nest reliefs. Though male Little Blue Herons may construct a preliminary nest structure during courtship, males generally bring nest material back to the female who then builds the nest after pair formation. Both parents incubate and feed the young.

Little Blue Herons primarily use the less active methods of foraging such as Stand and Wait and Walk Slowly (Rodgers 1983). Little Blue Herons consume a variety of species of fish, amphibians, reptiles, and invertebrates, with a high frequency of invertebrates reported in most studies (Baynard 1912; Jenni 1969; Domby and McFarlane 1978; Telfair 1981; Rodgers 1982). Rodgers (1982) reported nestling Little Blue Herons frequently regurgitated food boluses containing non-native species of fish, suggesting the parents were foraging at fish farms on the west coast of Florida.

CONSERVATION MEASURES TAKEN: Both federal and state laws protect Little Blue Herons. The establishment of sanctuaries and wetland preserves has protected some breeding and foraging habitats. Both the Florida Game and Fresh Water Fish Commission and Department of Environmental Protection currently recommend setback distances around wading bird colonies of 100 meters to prevent human disturbance to breeding colonies (Rodgers and Smith 1995).

CONSERVATION MEASURES PROPOSED: Long-term studies on the possible adverse effects of the Cattle Egret on Little Blue Heron breeding should be investigated. Reproductive rates and population dynamics in both freshwater and marine environments should be monitored during the next few decades to establish overall population status. Periodic monitoring of pesticide and heavy metal contamination should be conducted to determine if Little Blue Herons are being exposed to hazardous materials while foraging at agricultural impoundments, drainage ditches, canals, and landfill sites. Further, additional investigation should determine if significant numbers of Little Blue Herons feeding at fish farms and hatcheries are being illegally shot.

ACKNOWLEDGMENTS: I thank S. Nesbitt and D. Wood for reviewing this manuscript. The data for the distribution map of breeding colonies of Little Blue Herons that accompanies this account were supplied by D. Runde. This paper is a contribution of the Wildlife Research Laboratory, Florida Game and Fresh Water Fish Commission.

LITERATURE CITED:

AOU. 1983. Checklist of North American birds. American Ornithologists' Union, Allen Press, Inc., Lawrence, Kansas.

Baynard, O. E. 1912. Foods of herons and ibises. Wilson Bull. 24:167–169.

Burger, J. 1978. Competition between Cattle Egrets and native North American herons, egrets, and ibises. Condor 80:15–23.

Domby, A. J., and R. W. McFarlane. 1978. Feeding ecology of Little Blue Herons at a radionuclide-contaminated reservoir. Pp. 361–364 in Wading birds (A. Sprunt, IV, J. C. Odgen, and S. W. Winckler, Eds.). Research Rept. no. 7, Natl. Audubon Soc., New York.

Dusi, J. L., and R. T. Dusi. 1968. The competition between Cattle Egrets and Little Blue Herons. Alabama Birdlife 16:4–6.

Hancock, J., and J. Kushlan. 1984. The herons handbook. Harper and Row, Inc., New York.

Jenni, D. A. 1969. A study of the breeding ecology of four species of herons during the breeding season at Lake Alice, Alachua County, Florida. Ecol. Monogr. 39:245–270.

Maxwell, G. R., II, and H. W. Kale, II. 1977. Breeding biology of five species of herons in coastal Florida. Auk 94:689–700.

Meanley, B. 1955. A nesting study of the Little Blue Heron in eastern Arkansas. Wilson Bull. 67:84–99.

McVaugh, W., Jr. 1973. The development of four North American herons. Living Bird 11:155–173.

Nesbitt, S. A., J. C. Ogden, H. W. Kale, II, B. W. Patty, and L. A. Rowse. 1982. Florida atlas of breeding sites for herons and their allies: 1976–78.

U.S. Fish and Wildlife Service, Office of Biological Services. FWS/OBS-81/49.

Ogden, J. C. 1978. Recent population trends of colonial wading birds on the Atlantic and Gulf coastal plains. Pp. 137–153 in Wading birds (A. Sprunt, IV, J. C. Ogden, and S. W. Winckler, Eds.). Research Rept. no. 7, Natl. Audubon Soc., New York.

Ogden, J. C., H. W. Kale, II, and S. A. Nesbitt. 1980. The influence of annual variation in rainfall and water levels on nesting by Florida populations of wading birds. Proc. N.Y. Linn. Soc. 9:115–125.

Palmer, R. S. 1962. Handbook of North American birds. Vol. 1., Yale Univ. Press, New Haven, Connecticut.

Parkes, K. C. 1955. Systematic notes on North American birds. I. The herons and ibises (Ciconiiformes). Amer. Carneg. Mus. 33:287–293.

Rodgers, J. A., Jr. 1980a. Little Blue Heron breeding behavior. Auk 97:371–384.

Rodgers, J. A., Jr. 1980b. Breeding ecology of the Little Blue Heron on the west coast of Florida. Condor 82:164–169.

Rodgers, J. A., Jr. 1982. Food of nestling Little Blue Herons on the west coast of Florida. Fla. Field Nat. 10:25–30.

Rodgers, J. A., Jr. 1983. Foraging behavior of seven species of herons in Tampa Bay, Florida. Colon. Waterbirds 6:11–23.

Rodgers, J. A., Jr. 1987. Breeding chronology and reproductive success of Cattle Egrets and Little Blue Herons on the west coast of Florida, USA. Colon. Waterbirds 10:38–44.

Rodgers, J. A., Jr., and H. T. Smith. 1995. Set-back distances to protect nesting bird colonies from human disturbance in Florida. Conserv. Bio. 9:89–99.

Runde, D. E. 1991. Trends in wading bird nesting populations in Florida 1976–1978 and 1986–1989. Florida Game and Fresh Water Fish Commission, Tallahassee, Florida. Nongame wildlife section final performance report.

Telfair, R. C, II. 1981. Cattle Egrets, inland heronies, and the availability of crayfish. Southwest Nat. 26:37–41.

Werschkul, D. F. 1977. Changes in a southeastern heronry. Oriole 42:5–10.

Werschkul, D. F. 1979. Nestling mortality and the adaptive significance of early locomotion in the Little Blue Heron. Auk 96:116–130.

PREPARED BY: James A. Rodgers Jr., Florida Game and Fresh Water Fish Commission, Wildlife Research Laboratory, 4005 South Main Street, FL 32601.

Snowy Egret

Egretta thula

FAMILY ARDEIDAE

Order Ciconiiformes

TAXONOMY: The Snowy Egret (*Egretta thula*) is the New World counterpart of the very similar Little Egret (*E. garzetta*), which occurs throughout the tropical and warm-temperate regions of the Old World between western Europe and Australia (Palmer 1962; Cramp 1977). Two poorly differentiated races of the Snowy Egret are recognized: *E. t. thula,* the nominate race occurring in the eastern and central United States and Central and South America; and *E. t. brewsteri,* a slightly larger race in the western United States and northwestern Mexico. This species was formerly placed in the monotypic genus *Leucophoyx.*

DESCRIPTION: The Snowy Egret is a medium-small, all white wading bird, often described as "dainty" in overall appearance. The Snowy is about 60 cm (24 in.) in length and has a 1 m (39 in.) wingspread. The bill and legs are black, while the iris, lores, and feet are yellow. The skin color on the lores and feet changes to orange-red or red on adults during the courtship period. Breeding adults have prominent white plumes (aigrettes) on the head, neck, and scapulars; the latter are recurved and extend across the back to the tail. The plumes are less conspicuous or lacking on nonbreeding adults and immature birds.

POPULATION SIZE AND TREND: Snowy Egrets were intensively hunted for their plumes during the late 19th and early twentieth centuries throughout North, Central, and South America, and became rare or were locally extirpated in much of their range. Although population data for the Snowy Egret from outside the United States are practically nonexistent, the species recovered during the post-plume hunting years and is now generally considered to be fairly common to common in many regions of Central and South America (Hancock and Elliott 1978). Aerial censuses of wading birds, in the Usumacinta

420

Snowy Egret,
Egretta thula.
(Photo copyright
by Allan D.
Cruickshank,
courtesy of Florida
Audubon Society)

delta region of southeastern Mexico during the 1970s, produced a peak estimate of about 90,000 Snowy Egrets. The number of egrets that were nesting in three major colonies in the Usumaeinta region was between 5,000 and 15,000 pairs (Ogden et al. 1988).

Prior to the plume-hunting era (ca. 1880–1910) in the United States, the Snowy Egret was a common nesting species along the coast of the Gulf of Mexico, throughout Florida, and on the Atlantic coast as far north as New Jersey (Scott 1887; Bent 1926). As occurred elsewhere during the plume-hunting period, the Snowy Egret was extirpated or became rare in most parts of it's former U.S. range (Scott 1887; Bent 1926). With the prohibition of the plume trade, primarily by 1910–1913 (Doughty 1975), Snowy Egrets and other "plume birds" rapidly recovered in most regions (Bent 1926; Robertson and Kushlan 1974). Outside of Florida, this recovery resulted in the re-establishment of nesting, or first recorded nesting, by Snowy Egrets along the Atlantic coast from Virginia to Maine between 1939 and 1961; by 1975 an estimated 18,500–20,000 pairs of Snowy Egrets were nesting between coastal Georgia and Maine (Custer and Osborn 1977; Ogden 1978). The number of Snowy Egrets nesting in coastal Texas remained stable at about 3,000 pairs between 1939–1976, while the number nesting in coastal Louisiana appears to have increased substantially between 1959–1975 (Ogden 1978). It is not known if the difference between 58,250 pairs of nesting Snowy Egrets in Louisiana in 1976 (Portnoy 1980) and 13,000 pairs in 1991 (Martin 1991) reflects a population decline or differences in results between ground (1976 only) and aerial census techniques.

In Florida, Snowy Egrets recovered during the post-plume hunting era, apparently to reach peak numbers between the 1930s and early 1950s (Sprunt

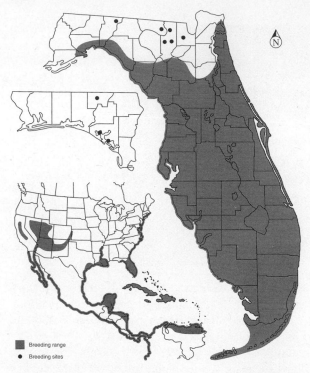

Distribution map
of the Snowy Egret,
Egretta thula.

Breeding range
Breeding sites

1954; Robertson and Kushlan 1974; Ogden 1978). Since the 1950s, the
number nesting in Florida has been declining, possibly at a more rapid rate
than other small ardeids (Robertson and Kushlan 1974). The number in the
traditional Everglades colonies recovered to an estimated 10,000 pairs by the
1930s; by the middle to late 1970s the number in Everglades colonies had
declined to 4,500 pairs, and by the late 1980s to 1,500 pairs (Frederick and
Collopy 1988; Ogden 1994). Elsewhere in Florida, one of the larger colonies
reported was 2,500 pairs at Bird Key (Pinellas County) in the late 1950s. The
number of nesting Snowy Egrets declined between the late 1950s and mid-
1970s from 2,000 to 100 pairs at Cortez (Manatee County), from 1,300 to
500 pairs at King's Bar (Okeechobee County), and from 1,000 to 500 pairs at
Alafia (Hillsborough County) (Ogden 1978; Nesbitt et al. 1982).

Snowy Egrets were nesting in 39% (114 of 295) of the colonies censused
statewide between 1976–1978 (Nesbitt et al. 1982). This three-year aerial
census located nine colonies containing 500 or more pairs, the largest being
2,500 pairs at Andytown in the Everglades (western Broward County), 1,450
pairs at the nearby L-67 levee colony one year later, 1,365 pairs at Rodgers
River Bay (Monroe County), and 1,100 pairs at Riomar (Indian River County).
A more systematic aerial census in 1986–1989 (Runde et al. 1991) found
Snowy Egrets nesting in only 22% (125 of 575) of the colonies located in the

same geographical area as was censused 10 years earlier. Although differences in the ways these two aerial censuses were conducted causes problems in interpretation, their results seem to be consistent with other data that suggest that the Snowy Egret in Florida has undergone a substantial decline in numbers since at least the 1950s. The larger Snowy Egret colonies during the 1980s, outside of the Everglades, were 500–700 pairs at Washburn (Manatee County) in 1981–1984, 725 pairs at Haulover (Brevard County) in 1987, 430 pairs at Marco Island (Collier County) in 1983, and 250–290 pairs at Alafia in 1984–1987 (Paul and Woolfenden 1985; R. Paul and T. Bancroft, pers. comm.).

DISTRIBUTION AND HISTORY OF DISTRIBUTION: Outside of the United States, the Snowy Egret occurs as a locally common to uncommon species in both interior and coastal wetlands throughout Central America, the Caribbean basin, and in South America as far south as central Chile and Argentina (De Schauensee 1966; Hancock and Elliott 1978). Major range changes by the Snowy Egret have only been documented in the United States. Generally between the end of the plume-hunting era (1910–1913) and the 1960s, this species reoccupied most of its former range north to New Jersey, Arkansas, Oklahoma, Colorado, Utah, Nevada, and central California (Bent 1926; Palmer 1962; Ogden 1978). The range recovery became a range expansion between the 1960s and 1980s, during which time Snowy Egrets first nested as far north as coastal Maine, Missouri, South Dakota, and Montana (AOU 1983).

In Florida, Snowy Egrets have shown no significant changes in distribution since the recovery following the plume-hunting period. This species occurs as a permanent resident throughout Florida, although it is relatively uncommon in interior portions of the northern peninsula and in the western panhandle, especially in winter (Bent 1926; Sprunt 1954; Palmer 1962; Robertson and Woolfenden 1992). The aerial censuses conducted during the 1970s and 1980s located Snowy Egrets nesting in 43 counties, primarily in the central and southern peninsula, but as far north as Nassau, Baker, and Columbia, and as far west as Holmes and Bay Counties (Nesbitt et al. 1982; Runde et al. 1991).

HABITAT REQUIREMENTS AND HABITAT TREND: The Snowy Egret in Florida nests in both coastal and inland wetlands, often in mangroves (*Rhizophora mangle, Avicennia germinans, Laguncularia racemosa*) or in willows (*Salix caroliniana*) (Bent 1926; Palmer 1962). Nesting also occurs in many other species of woody shrubs and small trees, including Australian pine (*Casuarina* sp.), cypress (*Taxodium* sp.), pond apple (*Annona glabra*), Brazilian pepper (*Schinus terebinthifolius*), buttonbush (*Cephalanthus occidentalis*), and elderberry (*Sambucus canadensis*) (Nesbitt et al. 1982). Almost all nesting occurs over shallow water or on islands separated from the mainland by relatively broad expanses of open water. Snowy Egrets feed in a wide variety of permanently and seasonally flooded marshes, swamps, lake and stream shorelines, and water impoundments, or even in very temporarily flooded ditches and agricultural fields, usually where the water is relatively shallow and calm (Palmer 1962; Sykes and Hunter 1978; Bancroft et al. 1990; Edelson and Collopy 1990). The Snowy Egret also feeds in upland grasslands and at the edge of the surf along beaches (Palmer 1962; Ogden, unpubl. data).

Although difficult to document, the overall impression is that significant losses of feeding habitat have been occurring for several decades in Florida, and that it is these losses rather than destruction of colony sites that has been primarily responsible for the population declines (W. Robertson and P. Frederick, pers. comm.). The pattern of population recovery prior to the 1950s, followed by several recent decades of decline, has been explained as an artificially depressed population (plume hunting) building to its regional carrying capacity, then declining as that carrying capacity diminished as wetlands were lost (Robertson and Kushlan 1974).

VULNERABILITY OF SPECIES AND HABITAT: The Snowy Egret is dependent on wetlands for nesting, feeding, and roosting sites. Wetlands may be essential as nesting habitat, in part because these habitats are less accessible to mammalian predators than are upland sites (Coulter 1986; Rodgers 1987). Feeding habitat with the proper depths of water and adequate concentrations of prey must be regionally available throughout the year and located within daily flight range of colonies for the duration of each nesting season (Kushlan 1978). A wide variety of wetland sites must be available regionally, especially sites with different depths of water and different annual hydroperiods, to provide a population of birds with options for nesting and foraging sites during a range of wet and dry rainfall conditions (Kushlan 1989a). Such conditions were more likely to exist during pre-drainage times when the overall number and variety of wetlands in Florida must have been much greater (e.g., Browder et al. 1976). The wetland sites that remain are highly susceptible to degradation as wading bird habitat, which can occur when alterations in water quality affect wetland productivity (prey composition and condition), or when altered volumes of water change the timing and availability of prey concentrations (Hynes 1960; Kushlan 1989b; M. Spalding, pers. comm.).

CAUSES OF THREAT: Although the most plausible interpretation of existing information is that the number of Snowy Egrets nesting in Florida has substantially declined during recent decades, specific data necessary to demonstrate the magnitude of this decline and the causes do not exist. However, as may be true for all native species of wading birds in Florida, chronic patterns of wetland destruction and alteration must be eliminating large areas of essential habitat. These losses in natural wetlands, at least in the Everglades basin where most historical colony sites remain protected, appear to have adversely impacted foraging habitat more severely than colony sites. The same may be true for protected coastal island colonies throughout Florida where numbers of nesting Snowy Egrets and other waders have shown long-term declines.

RESPONSES TO HABITAT MODIFICATION: The Snowy Egret regularly nests in water impoundments, on dredged-material islands, or in similarly created sites (Nesbitt et al. 1982). Although the significance of nesting by this species in artificially created sites is not known, evidence of limitations in the number of natural wetland colony sites for Wood Storks (*Mycteria americana*) in Florida (Ogden 1991) raises the question of the importance of this factor for other species of wading birds. The importance of dredged-material islands as nesting sites has previously been shown in North Carolina (Parnell and Soots 1978; Soots and Landin 1978). The creation of new nesting sites or the stabilization of existing sites through management practices may prove to benefit this species. Snowy Egrets also forage in altered or created wetland habitats and, under certain conditions, may select artificial habitats over natural wetlands as feeding sites (Edelson and Collopy 1990). Abrupt changes in water depth in impounded or managed wetlands, such as occur in the Everglades Water Conservation Areas, can adversely affect the quality of foraging habitat for wading birds (Hoffman et al. 1990).

DEMOGRAPHIC CHARACTERISTICS: Snowy Egrets almost always nest in mixed-species colonies, often with Great Egrets (*Casmerodius albus*) and Tricolored Herons (*E. tricolor*) (Nesbitt et al. 1982). Historically, the larger nesting colonies have more often been located in estuaries than in freshwater wetlands. Nests are simple platforms of twigs and usually are placed at the junction of two or more branches between 2–5 m above the ground or the surface of the water. Howell (1932) reported that egg-laying occurs primarily between late March and June, and as late as August in Florida. Snowy Egrets in southern Everglades colonies during the 1930s initiated nesting between January and May, with late February-early March being the peak period for laying (Ogden 1994). During the 1970s–1980s, laying started as early as December in Florida Bay colonies in several relative warm winters (J. Ogden and G. Powell, unpubl. data). Initiation of nesting by Snowy Egrets in the central and southern Everglades between 1986–1989 occurred during March-April (Frederick and Collopy 1988; Bancroft et al. 1990). Clutch size in Florida colonies is usually 2–5 eggs, and exhibits a wide, between-colony range of means of 2.47–4.13 eggs (Jenni 1969; Maxwell and Kale 1977; Girand and Taylor 1979; Black et al. 1984; Frederick and Collopy 1988; Bancroft et al. 1990). These same authors reported that successful nests (one or more young to an age of 2–3 weeks) also show wide intercolony variation of between 54–100% of the total active nests. Some colonies that experienced severe food shortages or climatological disturbances had all nests fail (Bancroft et al. 1990).

The incubation period is not precisely known, but presumably is about the same as the 22–25 day range known for the similar-sized Tricolored Heron (Palmer 1962; Frederick and Collopy 1988). Nestling development also has been poorly studied. Most young begin to move out of the nests and onto adjacent branches when they are between 2 and 3 weeks old (Palmer 1962; Rodgers 1980; Bancroft et al. 1990). These young return to the nest to be fed for an unknown period of time. At the Rodgers River Bay colony in 1988, most Snowy Egrets began nesting during late March-early April, and radio-instrumented young made their first foraging flights out of the colony in early June (Bancroft et al. 1990). Nest failures may be due to abandonment by the adults (usually for reasons that are difficult to determine), predation, inadequate food resources, weather-related disturbance, and human disturbance (Frederick and Collopy 1988; Bancroft et al. 1990). The age at which Snowy Egrets reach sexual maturity and the expected life span are unknown.

KEY BEHAVIORS: Although Snowy Egrets are migratory in the northern portions of their range in the United States, they are not known to be so in Florida (Palmer 1962). Snowy Egrets in Florida do move about considerably between seasons and locations in response to changing conditions at foraging and nesting sites. Typical patterns of movement by small, white herons (mostly Snowy Egrets) measured during 1985–1988 in the central and northern Everglades showed that the annual peak estimate of birds occurred in June, December, May, and January, during these 4 years, respectively (Hoffman et al. 1990). Not only were there annual differences in when the peaks occurred, the annual differences in maximum populations ranged between 1,120–8,893 birds. These seasonal and annual differences in the timing and magnitude of Snowy Egret activity in this region was in large part due to seasonal and annual differences in water depth and distribution patterns. Snowy Egrets also may change between different colony sites between years, and one radio-instrumented bird in Polk County renested in a different colony in the same year after the initial nesting effort failed (Bancroft et al. 1990; Edelson and Collopy 1990).

Snowy Egrets feed on small fishes, frogs, small rodents, prawns, crayfish, grasshoppers, worms, and a variety of other, mostly aquatic, invertebrates (Palmer 1962). Two studies in south Florida found that prawns (*Palaemonetes paludosus*) and a large number of species of fishes between 20–40 mm in length, including mosquitofish (*Gambusia affinis*), sailfin molly (*Poecilia latipinna*), flagfish (*Jordanella floridae*), least killifish (*Heterandria formosa*), and several topminnows (*Fundulus* sp.), were the most important prey (Ogden 1977; Bancroft et al. 1990). Snowy Egrets use a wide range of prey capture techniques, including such relatively specialized techniques as stirring their yellow feet in water to startle prey into movement and hovering over water that is too deep for wading (Kushlan 1978). Average flying distances between nesting colonies and foraging sites for different years and different colonies ranged from 8.2 to 21.0 km; the longest flight was 31.4 km and the flight speeds ranged between 35–39 km hour (Bancroft et al. 1990; Edelson and Collopy 1990). Snowy Egrets are more likely to forage at greater distances from colonies and to feed in large flocks than are Tricolored Herons (Jenni 1969; Ogden 1977; Bancroft et al. 1990).

Snowy Egrets have elaborate territory and courtship displays during the breeding season (Meyerriecks 1960; Palmer 1962). Males arrive in the colonies first and advertise nesting territories and attract females through a series of head stretch (Stretch Display) and head pumping (Snap Display) movements, with plumes fully erect, often performed at partially constructed nests. Initial displays are accompanied by male hostility to all other birds, which gradually wanes until a female is accepted. Snowy Egrets also perform Circle Flight and Tumbling Flight aerial displays over the colony sites during courtship. Males produce a distinctive call during courtship, a low-pitched bubbling or gurgling "wah-wah-wah." The male brings the nest material to the site while the female completes construction of the nest. Copulation occurs on or near the nest; both adults participate in incubation and feeding of the nestlings. The pair bond is maintained only through a single nesting cycle.

CONSERVATION MEASURES TAKEN: The Snowy Egret is a protected species under terms of all international, federal, and state laws and treaties that protect migratory and nongame birds. A few of the larger colonies are protected by the U.S. National Park Service, U.S. Fish and Wildlife Service, and National Audubon Society, including sites in Everglades National Park, Merritt Island NWR, and in Tampa Bay.

CONSERVATION MEASURES PROPOSED: The precise dynamics of the Snowy Egret decline in Florida, including accurate measures of population trends and a determination of the environmental factors causing the decline, remain poorly known. To fill these gaps, systematic, regional censuses of colonies must be continued, and additional research into the dynamics of nesting and foraging ecology must be undertaken. These studies must include work in the colonies to better determine when and why nesting efforts fail.

Assuming it is true that Snowy Egrets are being stressed by losses in feeding habitat, the major wetland foraging sites for this and other wading birds in Florida must be much better identified and protected. A statewide marking program, carried out over a period of years, should provide answers on total numbers of birds, seasonal movements, and important habitats for the Florida population. For example, are large numbers of Snowy Egrets that nest in the Everglades one year the same birds that nest in Tampa Bay or on Merritt Island another year? If the answer is affirmative, we may have fewer total birds in Florida than we realize.

ACKNOWLEDGMENTS: This species account was improved as a result of discussions between myself and Peter Frederick and Thomas Bancroft. Valuable comments on an earlier version of this report were provided by James Rodgers and Bill Robertson. My time on this project was supported by the South Florida Natural Resources, Everglades National Park.

LITERATURE CITED:

AOU. 1983. Check-list of North American birds. Sixth ed. American Ornithologists' Union, Washington, D.C.

Bancroft, G. T., S. D. Jewell, and A. M. Strong. 1990. Foraging and nesting ecology of herons in the lower Everglades relative to water conditions. Final rept. to South Fla. Water Mgmt. Dist. Natl. Aud. Soc., Tavernier, Florida. 140 pp.

Bent, A. C. 1926. Life histories of North American marsh birds. U.S. Natl. Mus. Bull. no. 135. Smithsonian Inst. Press, Washington, D.C.

Black, B. B., M. W. Collopy, H. F. Percival, A. A. Tiller, and P. G. Bohall. 1984. Effects of low level military training flights on wading bird colonies in Florida. Tech. Rept. no. 7, Fla. Coop. Fish and Wildl. Res. Unit, School For. Res. and Cons., Univ. Florida, Gainesville, Florida.

Browder, J. A., C. Littlejohn, and D. Young. 1976. The south Florida study. Center for Wetlands, Univ. Florida, Gainesville, Florida, and Bur. Comprehensive Planning, Fla. Dept. Admin., Tallahassee, Florida.

Coulter, M. C. 1986. Wood Storks of the Birdsville colony and swamps of the Savannah River Plant. 1985 Ann. Rept., SREL-20-UC-66e. Savannah River Ecol. Lab., Aiken, South Carolina.

Cramp, S. (Ed.). 1977. Handbook of the birds of Europe, the Middle East and North Africa. Vol. 1. Oxford Univ. Press, Oxford, England.

Custer, T. W., and R. G. Osborn. 1977. Wading birds as biological indicators: 1975 colony survey. U.S. Dept. Int., Fish and Wildl. Serv. Spec. Sci. Rept. no. 206. Washington, D.C.

De Schauensee, R. M. 1966. The species of birds of South America with their distribution. Livingston Publ. Co., Narberth, Pennsylvania.

Doughty, R. W. 1975. Feather fashions and bird preservation. Univ. California Press, Berkeley, California.

Edelson, N. A., and M. W. Collopy. 1990. Foraging ecology of wading birds using an altered landscape in central Florida. Final rept. to Fla. Inst. of Phosphate Res. Dept. Wildl. and Range Sci., Univ. Florida, Gainesville, Florida.

Frederick, P. C., and M. W. Collopy. 1988. Reproductive ecology of wading birds in relation to water conditions in the Florida Everglades. Fla. Coop. Fish and Wildl. Res. Unit, Univ. Florida. Gainesville, Florida.

Girard, G. T., and W. K. Taylor. 1979. Reproductive parameters for 9 avian species at Moore Creek, Merritt Island National Wildlife Refuge. Fla. Sci. 42:94–102.

Hancock, J., and H. Elliott. 1978. The herons of the world. Harper and Row, New York, New York.

Hoffman, W., G. T. Bancroft, and R. J. Sawicki. 1990. Wading bird populations and distributions in the water conservation areas of the Everglades: 1985 through 1988. Rept. to South Fla. Water Mgmt. Dist. Natl. Aud. Soc., Tavernier, Florida.

Howell, A. H. 1932. Florida bird life. Coward-McCann Inc., New York, New York.

Hynes, H. B. N. 1960. The biology of polluted waters. Liverpool Univ. Press. Liverpool, England.

Jenni, D. A. 1969. A study of the ecology of four species of herons during the breeding season at Lake Alice, Alachua County, Florida. Ecol. Monogr. 39:245–270.

Kushlan, J. A. 1978. Feeding ecology of wading birds. Pp. 249–297 in Wading birds (A. Sprunt, IV, J. C. Ogden, and S. Winkler, eds.). Natl. Aud. Soc. Res. Rept. no 7. New York, New York.

Kushlan, J. A. 1989a. Avian use of fluctuating wetlands. Pp. 593–604 in Freshwater wetlands and wildlife (R. R. Sharitz, and J. W. Gibbons, eds.). Dept. of Energy Symp. Ser. no. 61, Oak Ridge, Tennessee.

Kushlan, J. A. 1989b. Wetlands and wildlife, the Everglades perspective. Pp. 773–790 in Freshwater wetlands and wildlife (R. R. Sharitz, and J. W. Gibbons, eds.). Dept. of Energy Symp. Ser. no. 61, Oak Ridge, Tennessee.

Martin, R. 1991. Regional overview of wading birds in Louisiana, Mississippi and Alabama. Pp. 22–33 in Coastal nongame workshop (D. P. Jennings, ed.). U.S. Fish and Wildl. Serv., Ft. Collins, Colorado.

Maxwell, G. R., II, and H. W. Kale, II. 1977. Breeding biology of five species of herons in coastal Florida. Auk 94:689–700.

Meyerriecks, A. J. 1960. Comparative breeding behavior of four species of North American herons. Publ. Nuttall Ornithol. Club no. 2. Cambridge, Massachusetts.

Nesbitt, S. A., J. C. Ogden, H. W. Kale, II, B. W. Patty, and L. A. Rowse. 1982. Florida atlas of breeding sites for herons and their allies: 1976–78. FWS/OBS-81/49. Office Biol. Serv., U.S. Fish and Wildl. Serv., Washington, D.C.

Ogden, J. C. 1977. An evaluation of interspecific information exchange by waders on flight lines from colonies. Proc. Conf. Colon. Waterbird Group 1977:155–162.

Ogden, J. C. 1978. Population trends of colonial wading birds on the Atlantic and Gulf coastal plains. Pp. 137–153 in Wading birds (A. Sprunt, IV, J. C. Ogden, and S. Winkler, eds.). Natl. Aud. Soc. Res. Rept. no. 7. New York, New York.

Ogden, J. C. 1991. Nesting by Wood Storks in natural, altered, and artificial wetlands in central and northern Florida. Colon. Waterbirds 14:39–45.

Ogden, J. C. 1994. A comparison of wading bird nesting colony dynamics, 1931–1946 and 1974–1989, as an indication of changes in ecosystem conditions in the southern Everglades. Pp. 533–570 in Everglades. The ecosystem and its restoration (S. M. Davis and J. C. Ogden, eds.). St. Lucie Press, Delray Beach, Florida.

Ogden, J. C., C. E. Knoder, and A. Sprunt, IV. 1988. Pp. 595–605 in Colonial wading bird populations in the Usumacinta delta, Mexico. Ecologia y conservacion del Delta de los rios Usumacinta y Grijalva (Memorias). INIREB, Division Regional. Tabasco, Mexico.

Palmer, R. S. (Ed.). 1962. Handbook of North American birds. Vol. 1. Yale Univ. Press. New Haven, Connecticut.

Parnell, J. F., and R. F. Soots. 1978. The use of dredge islands by wading birds. Pp. 105–111 in Wading birds (A. Sprunt, IV, J. C. Ogden, and S. Winkler, eds.). Natl. Aud. Soc. Res. Rept. no. 7. New York, New York.

Paul, R. T., and G. E. Woolfenden. 1985. Current status and recent trends in bird populations of Tampa Bay. Pp. 426–446 in Proceedings Tampa Bay area scientific information symposium. Fla. Sea Grant College, Rept. no. 65. Sea Grant Proj. no. IR/82–2.

Portnoy, J. W. 1980. Status of colonial waterbird populations of the Louisiana, Mississippi and Alabama coasts. Pp. 10–13 in Management of colonial waterbirds (J. F. Parnell, and R. F. Soots, eds.). UNC Sea Grant Publ. UNC-SG-80-06. Wilmington, North Carolina.

Robertson, W. B., Jr., and J. A. Kushlan. 1974. The southern Florida avifauna. Pp. 414–452 in Environments of south Florida Past and present (P. J. Gleason, ed.). Memoir 2, Miami Geol. Soc., Miami, Florida.

Robertson, W. B., Jr., and G. E. Woolfenden. 1992. Florida bird species. An annotated list. Fla. Ornithol. Soc. Spec. Publ. no. 6.

Rodgers, J. A., Jr. 1980. Reproductive success of three heron species on the west coast of Florida. Fla. Field Nat. 8:37–40.

Rodgers, J. A., Jr. 1987. On the antipredator advantages of coloniality: a word of caution. Wilson Bull. 99:269–271.

Runde, D. E., J. A. Gore, J. A. Hovis, M. S. Robson, and P. D. Southall. 1991. Florida atlas of breeding sites for herons and their allies. Update 1986–89. Fla. Game and Fresh Water Fish Comm., Nongame Wildl. Prog. Tech. Rept. no. 10. Tallahassee, Florida.

Scott, W. E. D. 1887. The present condition of some of the bird rookeries of the Gulf coast of Florida. Auk 4:135–144, 213–222, 273–284.

Soots, R. F., Jr., and M. Landin. 1978. Development and management of avian habitat on dredged material islands. U.S. Army Eng. Waterways Exper. Sta. Tech. Rept. DS–78–18. Vicksburg, Mississippi.

Sprunt, A., Jr. 1954. Florida bird life. Coward-McCann, Inc. New York, New York.

Sykes, P. W., and G. S. Hunter. 1978. Bird use of flooded agricultural fields during summer and early fall and some recommendations for management. Fla. Field Nat. 6:36–43.

PREPARED BY: John C. Ogden, National Park Service, Everglades National Park, 40001 State Road 9336, Homestead, FL 33034–6733.

Tricolored Heron

Egretta tricolor

FAMILY ARDEIDAE

Order Ciconiiformes

TAXONOMY: Three races of the Tricolored Heron (*Egretta tricolor*) have been described: *E. t. ruficollis* in the United States, throughout Central America and the Caribbean, along the Pacific coast of northwestern South America, and on the coast of western Venezuela; *E. t. tricolor* along the Atlantic coast between eastern Venezuela and Brazil; and *E. t. rufimentum* confined to Trinidad (Palmer 1962; Blake 1977). The latter two races are smaller and more extensively rufous on the neck than is the more northern *ruficollis*. This species was formally placed in the monotypic genus *Hydranassa*, and was once known as the Louisiana Heron.

DESCRIPTION: The Tricolored Heron is a medium-sized heron, 65 cm (25 in.) in length, with a long, slim neck, and generally two-toned color pattern (Palmer 1962). Adults are dark slatey on the head, neck, and body except for a white rump, belly, and undertail coverts. A white and rufous streak extends down the front of the neck. Head plumes and elongate feathers on the lower neck and chest are purplish. The legs, feet, base of the bill, and bare facial skin are yellow, with the bill darkening to dusky at the tip. Breeding adults acquire long, whitish head plumes, and rufous to whitish mantle plumes. Soft parts also change color, with the bill and facial skin becoming aqua-blue, the iris turning magenta, and the legs orange-red.

Immature birds, up to about one year old, are extensively reddish-brown on the head and neck, brownish across the mantle, and white in the same areas as on adults. These young birds generally lack plumes.

POPULATION SIZE AND TREND: The dark dorsal surface of the Tricolored Herons makes this species difficult to census from the air, especially birds and nests in wooded colony sites. Thus, accurate, regional population data are

Tricolored Heron, *Egretta tricolor*.
(Photo copyright by Allan D.
Cruickshank, courtesy of Florida
Audubon Society)

relatively scarce in the United States and appear to be nonexistent elsewhere.
Historically, the race *E. t. ruficollis* was considered to be a fairly common to
very common bird throughout much of its range. It was the most common
member of its family in coastal regions of the Gulf and southern Atlantic
states, especially in Louisiana and Florida (Howell 1932; Oberholser 1938;
Palmer 1962). Some population increases may have occurred between 1941
and 1976 when Tricolored Herons expanded their nesting range into coastal
regions from Virginia to Massachusetts; by 1975 an estimated 2,500 pairs
were nesting along this coast (Ogden 1978). Also during the mid-1970s, an
estimated 10,000 pairs nested in coastal colonies between Georgia and North
Carolina (Ogden 1978), 70,000 pairs nested in coastal Louisiana (Portnoy
1977), and 8,500 pairs were nesting in coastal Texas (Ogden 1978).

Population trends for Tricolored Herons outside of Florida are not well
documented. The number nesting in coastal North Carolina remained about
1,400 pairs between 1977 and 1983 (Parnell and McCrimmon 1984). In
South Carolina, a large urban colony contained 1,500–2,000 pairs in 1975,
700–900 pairs in 1984–1986, and was deserted thereafter (Osborn and Custer
1978; Post 1990). A 1990 aerial census in Louisiana revealed only about
18,000 pairs of nesting Tricolored Herons. However, this census did not

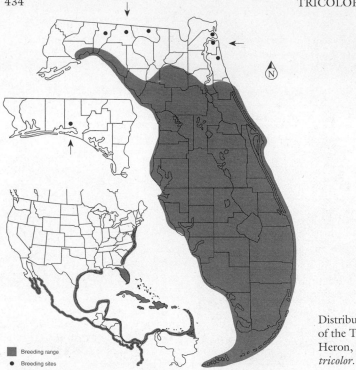

Distribution map
of the Tricolored
Heron, *Egretta
tricolor.*

Breeding range
Breeding sites

include ground counts of nests in colonies, and direct comparison with the
1976 census is not possible (Martin 1991). Tricolored Herons nesting in
Louisiana were found in 48 colonies in 1976 and in 55 colonies in 1990.

Both Howell (1932) and Sprunt (1954) considered the Tricolored Heron
to be the most abundant heron in Florida. An estimated maximum of 15,000
pairs were nesting in the central-southern Everglades and adjacent mangrove
estuarine region during the 1930s compared to an estimated 3,500 pairs in the
same region during the 1970s (Ogden 1994), and 1,100–1,400 pairs in 1986–
1987 (Frederick and Collopy 1988). Tricolored Herons were nesting in 43%
(127 of 295) of the colonies censused statewide between 1976–1978 (Nesbitt
et al. 1982). This 3-year aerial census located 9 colonies containing 500 or
more pairs, the largest being 1,200 pairs at Andytown (Broward County), 840
pairs at L-67 levee (Dade County), 700 pairs at Haulover (Brevard County),
and 600 pairs at Ft. Pierce Spoil (St. Lucie County).

Tricolored Herons were nesting only in about 24% (140 of 575 colonies)
of the colonies in a statewide census during 1986–1989 (Runde et al. 1991) in
the same geographical area that was censused 10 years earlier (Nesbitt et al.
1982). The most plausible interpretation of the census data from these different periods of time is that the number of Tricolored Herons nesting in Florida
declined substantially between the 1930s and 1970s, if one can extrapolate

from the early Everglades estimates, and that the statewide decline continued between the 1970s and 1980s.

DISTRIBUTION AND HISTORY OF DISTRIBUTION: The Tricolored Heron occurs in much of the tropical and warm temperate regions of the New World (Palmer 1962; Blake 1977; AOU 1983). Throughout most of its range, the Tricolored Heron is more common in, or largely restricted to, estuarine regions. No changes in distribution for the Tricolored Heron have been reported from outside of the United States. The range expansion in the United States was entirely coastal, with the first reported nesting in all coastal states between Virginia and New York occurring from 1941 to 1955, and in Massachusetts in 1976 (Ogden 1978). The species currently nests as far north as central Baja California, southern Sonora, southeastern New Mexico, central and eastern Texas, and along the Gulf and Atlantic coastal plains as far north as southern Maine (AOU 1983). Historically, the Tricolored Heron appears to have been most common throughout much of Florida and coastal Louisiana (Bent 1926; Palmer 1962). They also have been, and continue to be, one of the more common species in many coastal colonies located between Virginia and Texas (Bent 1926; Palmer 1962).

The Tricolored Heron occurs in all counties of Florida, although numbers are relatively low in the interior of the northern peninsula and in the panhandle away from the coast (Howell 1932; Sprunt 1954). Nesting in Florida occurs regularly in most counties in the central and southern peninsula as far north as Alachua County, much less commonly across the northern counties, and rarely west of the Apalachicola River (Nesbitt et al. 1982; Runde et al. 1991).

HABITAT REQUIREMENTS AND HABITAT TREND: Nesting colonies of the Tricolored Heron in Florida are most often located on mangrove (*Rhizophora mangle, Avicennia germinans, Laguncularia racemosa*) islands along the coast, or in willow (*Salix caroliniana*) thickets in freshwater wetlands (Bent 1926; Palmer 1962). Nesting also may occur in other woody thickets, including Australian pine (*Casuarina* sp.), cypress (*Taxodium* sp.), pond apple (*Annona glabra*), Brazilian pepper (*Schinus terebinthifolius*), saltbush (*Baccharis* sp.), and wax myrtle (*Myrica cerifera*) (Nesbitt et al. 1982). Almost all colony sites are located on islands or in woody vegetation over standing water. Tricolored Herons feed in a wide variety of permanently and seasonally flooded marshes, mangrove swamps, tidal streams, roadside ditches, and shallow edges to ponds and lakes (Bancroft et al. 1990). The long history in Florida of wetland degradation by drainage, creation of impoundments, and changes in water quality are thought to be the major cause for the population decline of Tricolored Herons. It appears that losses of wetlands essential as feeding habitats for Tricolored Herons during the nesting season may be having the greatest adverse impact on these birds. For example, water management practices in the Everglades region have altered the timing, location, and frequency of natural hydrological patterns (Johnson and Ogden 1990; Johnson et al. 1992). These hydrological changes have caused colonial nesting wading birds to abandon traditional colony sites and to have reduced levels of nesting success (Frederick and Collopy 1989; Bancroft 1989; Ogden 1994).

VULNERABILITY OF SPECIES AND HABITAT: Like most species of wading birds, Tricolored Herons show flexibility in where they nest and forage in response to seasonal and annual changes in wetland conditions (Kushlan 1978; Nesbitt et al. 1982; Hoffman et al. 1990). Thus, wading birds may deal with short-term losses of nesting and feeding habitat, due to droughts or other cyclic factors, by not nesting during a year or by relocating colony sites (Ogden et al 1980). While this strategy worked well under natural conditions when a range of nesting and foraging site options were more likely to exist, significant reductions on a regional scale in the area of viable wetlands results in a loss in habitat options, which in turn can reduce the regional carrying capacity for a population. Tricolored Heron populations certainly are highly susceptible to these kinds of limitations brought on by chronic patterns of wetland losses.

CAUSES OF THREAT: The apparent lack of stability and the long-term decline in total numbers of nesting birds in Tricolored Heron colony sites in the Everglades region (Nesbitt et al. 1982; Frederick and Collopy 1988; Ogden, unpubl. data) suggests that this species is being stressed by unstable and inadequate habitat options. No other threats, including environmental contaminents, destruction of colony sites, or shooting, have been reported.

RESPONSES TO HABITAT MODIFICATION: At least 25% (33 of 127) of the Tricolored Heron colonies found during the 1976–1978 censuses in Florida were located in manmade water impoundments or on dredge-material islands (Nesbitt et al. 1982). The importance of dredge-material islands for nesting wading birds previously had been shown in North Carolina (Parnell and Soots 1978; Soots and Landin 1978). Whereas available evidence suggests it is the lack of adequate foraging habitat rather than nesting habitat that is limiting Tricolored Herons in Florida, the creation of new nesting sites or stabilization of existing sites through site management practices may benefit this species.

DEMOGRAPHIC CHARACTERISTICS: While Tricolored Herons may nest in colonies that are small in size and Tricolored-only in composition, they much more often nest in larger, multi-species colonies. Regionally, the larger colonies are more often located in coastal areas than in the interior, although relatively large freshwater colonies of Tricolored Herons periodically form in the Everglades (Nesbitt et al. 1982; Frederick and Collopy 1988). Tricolored Herons often nest in close association with Snowy Egrets *(E. thula)*.

Nests are simple, rather flimsy platforms of twigs, often located between 2–5 m above the ground. Egg laying began in early February, and peaked during early March at Lane River, Everglades National Park in 1975 (J. Ogden, unpubl. data). Egg laying in several central and southern Everglades colonies was later during 1986–1989, generally occurring between late March and mid-May (Frederick and Collopy 1988; Bancroft et al. 1990). Statewide, Howell (1932) reported that laying occurred between the middle of March and early June, and occasionally as late as August. The most common clutch size in Florida is 3 eggs, with a range of 2–5 eggs. The mean clutch size in several Florida Bay and southern Everglades colonies between 1986–1989 ranged between 2.11 and 2.95 eggs (Bancroft et al. 1990; Powell and Bjork, ms.), and in several central Everglades colonies during 1986–1987 was 3.13–3.29 eggs (Frederick and Collopy 1988). Clutch size in the interior of central Florida had means ranging between 3.33 and 4.10 (Jenni 1969; Black et al. 1984), whereas coastal colonies in central Florida ranged from 3.0 to 3.1 (Maxwell and Kale 1977; Girand and Taylor 1979). The incubation period is 22–25 days (Frederick and Collopy 1988).

Nestling Tricolored Herons spend much of the first 2 weeks in the nests and are usually fed 4–5 times per day (Rodgers 1978). Older chicks, beginning as early as 11 days of age, move out of the nests onto adjacent branches, but return to the nests to be fed until about the age of 3–4 weeks (McVaugh 1972). Between this age and 7–8 weeks, when the chicks become independent of the adults, the young birds are fed in the colony but away from the nests. Nest success rates, often measured only through the second or third week of age for the nestlings, vary considerably among colonies and years. Florida Bay and southern Everglades colonies between 1986–1989 showed nest success rates (percent nests with one or more young up to about 3 weeks old) that ranged from 39–86%, with the exception of 1 out of 10 colonies where all nests failed (Bancroft et al. 1990; Powell and Bjork, ms.). Central Everglades colonies during 1986–1987 had nest success rates of 11–69% (Frederick and Collopy 1988). Nest success rates at several central Florida colonies ranged between 64–100% (Jenni 1969; Maxwell and Kale 1977; Black et al. 1984). Primary causes of nest failures are nestling starvation, nest abandonment by the adults, and predation (Rodgers 1978; Frederick and Collopy 1988).

KEY BEHAVIORS: Although Tricolored Herons that nest in Florida may for the most part be permanent residents, birds move about seasonally, annually, and geographically in response to changing conditions at foraging and nesting sites. For example, the number of "small dark herons" (Tricolored Herons and Little Blue Herons, [*E. caerulea*]) estimated from aerial censuses in the Water Conservation Areas of the central and north Everglades between 1985–

1988 ranged from a high of 8,067 birds during the dry season (March 1986) to 387 birds during the rainy season (August 1986) (Hoffman et al. 1990). During the next rainy season (August 1987), the dark heron estimate was a high of 5,087 birds. Tagged, adult Tricolored Herons that nested in the Lane River Rookery, Everglades National Park, in 1986 nested at different colonies (Rodgers River Bay and Frank Key in Everglades National Park) one year later (Bancroft et al. 1990).

Tricolored Herons feed on small fishes, frogs, tadpoles, crustaceans, snails, worms, and aquatic insects (Palmer 1962). Two Evergades studies have shown that small fishes, including mosquitofish (*Gambusia affinis*), sailfin molly (*Poecilia latipinna*), flagfish (*Jordanella floridae*), sheepshead killifish (*Cyprinodon variegatus*), and several topminnows (*Fundulus* sp.), mostly between 20 and 35 mm in length, were important prey (Ogden 1977; Bancroft et al. 1990). Average flying distances between nesting colonies and foraging sites, for different years and different colonies, ranged from 4.8 to 14.3 km; the maximum distance was 25.3 km (Bancroft et al. 1990). Tricolored Herons are much less likely to forage in large flocks than are Snowy Egrets and Great Egrets (*Casmerodius albus*); in one Everglades study, 74% of all Tricolored Heron feeding "aggregations" were of single birds, compared to 10% of Snowy Egrets feeding solitarily (Bancroft et al. 1990).

Tricolored Herons perform elaborate territory and mate selection displays during the breeding season (Palmer 1962; Rodgers 1977, 1978). Males arrive first in the colonies, and construct nest foundations as focal sites for territorial displays. Males perform Snap, Stretch, and Circle Flight displays to advertise the nest site and to initially attract a female; once a female approaches a Twig Shake display is added. One or more females may join a male in Circle Flights. At or near the nest site a female also utilizes a Withdrawn Crouch posture in the face of an aggressive male, and both birds perform courtship preening and a Bill-nibbling display. Copulation occurs on the nest foundation; later the female completes the construction of the nest with additional twigs collected by the male. The pair bond is maintained only until the nesting effort either fails or fledges one or more chicks.

CONSERVATION MEASURES TAKEN: The Tricolored Heron is a protected species under terms of all international, federal, and state laws and treaties that protect migratory and nongame birds. Important colony sites in Everglades National Park, Merritt Island NWR., and in Tampa Bay are protected by the National Park Service, Fish and Wildlife Service, and National Audubon Society.

CONSERVATION MEASURES PROPOSED: Additional field censuses and studies of Tricolored Herons are needed to greatly improve our understanding of regional population trends, especially to confirm the magnitude and extent of the apparent population decline in Florida, and to determine the factors responsible for the decline. The major wetland foraging habitats for this and other wading birds in Florida must be better identified as a basis for improved protection of these sites. A statewide marking program, carried out over a period of years, should be a central component of any future studies of Tricolored Herons in Florida to begin the process of measuring this species' regional population dynamics related to a range of environmental parameters.

ACKNOWLEDGMENTS: This species account was improved as a result of discussions between myself and Peter Frederick and Thomas Bancroft regarding the biology of Tricolored Herons in Florida. Valuable comments on an earlier version of this report were provided by James Rodgers. My time on this project was supported by the South Florida Natural Resources, Everglades National Park.

LITERATURE CITED:

AOU. 1983. Check-list of North American birds. Sixth ed. American Ornithologists' Union, Washington, D.C.

Bancroft, G. T. 1989. Status and conservation of wading birds in the Everglades. Amer. Birds 43:1258–1265.

Bancroft, G. T., S. D. Jewell, and A. M. Strong. 1990. Foraging and nesting ecology of herons in the lower Everglades relative to water conditions. Final rept. to South Fla. Water Manag. Dist. Natl. Aud. Soc., Tavernier, Florida. 140 pp.

Bent, A. C. 1926. Life histories of North American marsh birds. U.S. Natl. Mus. Bull. no. 135. Washington, D.C.

Black, B. B., M. W. Collopy, H. F. Percival, A. A. Tiller, and P. G. Bohall. 1984. Effects of low level military training flights on wading bird colonies in Florida. Fla. Coop. Fish and Wildl. Res. Unit, School For. Res. and Cons., Univ. Florida. Gainesville, Florida. Tech. rept. no. 7.

Blake, E. R. 1977. Manual of neotropical birds. Vol. 1. Univ. Chicago Press, Chicago, Illinois.

Frederick, P. C., and M. W. Collopy. 1988. Reproductive ecology of wading birds in relation to water conditions in the Florida Everglades. U.S. Fish and Wildl. Service, Coop. Res. Unit, Univ. Florida. Gainesville, Florida. 259 pp.

Frederick, P. C., and M. W. Collopy. 1989. Nesting success of five ciconiiform species in relation to water conditions in the Florida Everglades. Auk 106:625–634.

Girard, G. T., and W. K. Taylor. 1979. Reproductive parameters for 9 avian species at Moore Creek, Merritt Island National Wildlife Refuge. Fla. Sci. 42:94–102.

Hoffman, W., G. T. Bancroft, and R. J. Sawicki. 1990. Wading bird populations and distributions in the water conservation areas of the Everglades:
1985 through 1988. Report to South Fla. Water Manag. Dist. Natl. Aud.
Soc., Tavernier, Florida. 173 pp.

Howell, A. H. 1932. Florida bird life. Coward-McCann Inc., New York, New
York.

Jenni, D. A. 1969. A study of the ecology of four species of herons during the
breeding season at Lake Alice, Alachua County, Florida. Ecol. Monogr.
39:245–270.

Johnson, R. A., and J. C. Ogden (eds.). 1990. An assessment of hydrological
improvements and wildlife benefits from proposed alternatives for the U.S.
Army Corps of Engineers' General Design Memorandum for modified
water deliveries to Everglades National Park. Natl. Park Service, South Fla.
Res. Center, Everglades Natl. Park, Homestead, Florida. 99 pp.

Johnson, R. A., R. Fennema, and T. Bhatt. 1992. Water management and
ecosystem restoration in the Everglades. Proc. Forth Ann. Water Res. Operations Manag. Workshop. Amer. Soc. Civil Engineers.

Kushlan, J. A. 1978. Feeding ecology of wading birds. Pp. 249–297 in
Wading birds (A. Sprunt, IV, J. C. Ogden, and S. Winkler, eds.). Natl.
Aud. Soc. Res. rept. no. 7. New York, New York.

McVaugh, W., Jr. 1972. The development of four North American herons.
The Living Bird. Eleventh Ann. Lab. Ornithol., Ithaca, New York.

Martin, R. 1991. Regional overview of wading birds in Louisiana, Mississippi
and Alabama. Pp. 22–33 in Coastal nongame workshop (D. P. Jennings,
ed.). U.S. Fish and Wildl. Service, Ft. Collins, Colorado.

Maxwell, G. R., II, and H. W. Kale, II. 1977. Breeding biology of five species
of herons in coastal Florida. Auk 94:689–700.

Nesbitt, S. A., J. C. Ogden, H. W. Kale, II, B. W. Patty, and L. A. Rowse.
1982. Florida atlas of breeding sites for herons and their allies: 1976–78.
Office Biol. Serv., U.S. Fish and Wildl. Serv., FWS/OBS-81/49. Washington, D.C.

Oberholser, H. C. 1938. The bird life of Louisiana. State of Louisiana, Dept.
of Conserv., New Orleans, Louisiana.

Ogden, J. C. 1977. An evaluation of interspecific information exchange by
waders on feeding flights from colonies. Proc. 1977 Conf. Colon. Waterbird
Group. Pp. 155–162.

Ogden, J. C. 1978. Population trends of colonial wading birds on the Atlantic
and Gulf coastal plains. Pp. 137–153 in Wading birds (A. Sprunt, IV, J. C.
Ogden, and S. Winkler, eds.). Natl. Aud. Soc. Res. rept. no. 7. New York,
New York.

Ogden, J. C. 1994. A comparison of wading bird nesting colony dynamics,
1931–1946 and 1974–1989, as an indication of changes in ecosystem

conditions in the southern Everglades. Pp. 533–570 in Everglades. The ecosystem and its restoration (S. M. Davis and J. C. Ogden, eds.). St. Lucie Press, Delray Beach, Florida.

Ogden, J. C., H. W. Kale, II, and S. A. Nesbitt. 1980. The influence of annual variation in rainfall and water levels on nesting by Florida populations of wading birds. Trans. Linn. Soc. N.Y. 9:115–126.

Osborn, R. G., and T. W. Custer. 1978. Herons and their allies: atlas of Atlantic coast colonies, 1975 and 1976. U.S. Fish and Wildl. Serv., Patuxent Wildl. Res. Ctr., Laurel, Maryland. FWS/OBS-77/08.

Palmer, R. S. 1962. Handbook of North American birds. Vol. 1. Yale Univ. Press, New Haven, Connecticut.

Parnell, J. F., and R. F. Soots. 1978. The use of dredge islands by wading birds. Pp. 105–111 in Wading birds (A. Sprunt, IV, J. C. Ogden, and S. Winkler, eds.). Natl. Aud. Soc. Res. rept. no. 7. New York, New York.

Parnell, J. F., and D. A. McCrimmon, Jr. 1984. 1983 supplement to atlas of colonial waterbirds of North Carolina estuaries. Univ. North Carolina Sea Grant publ. UNC-SG-84-07.

Portnoy, J. W. 1977. Colonial waterbird population status and management on the northern Gulf of Mexico. Proc. 1977 Conf. Colon. Waterbird Group. pp. 38–43.

Post, W. 1990. Nest survival in a large ibis-heron colony during a 3-year decline to extinction. Colon. Waterbirds 13:50–61.

Powell, G., and R. Bjork. ms. Reproductive information on selected wading birds in Florida Bay in 1987. Natl. Aud. Soc. Res. Dept., Tavernier, Florida.

Rodgers, J. A., Jr. 1977. Breeding displays of the Louisiana Heron. Wilson Bull. 89:266–285.

Rodgers, J. A., Jr. 1978. Breeding behavior of the Louisiana Heron. Wilson Bull. 90:45–59.

Runde, D. E., J. A. Gore, J. A. Hovis, M. S. Robson, and P. D. Southall. 1991. Florida atlas of breeding sites for herons and their allies. Update 1986–89. Fla. Game and Fresh Water Fish Comm. Nongame Wildl. Prog., Tech. rept. no. 10. Tallahassee, Florida.

Soots, R. F., Jr., and M. Landin. 1978. Development and management of avian habitat on dredged material islands. U.S. Army Engineer Waterways Exper. Sta. Tech. rept. DS–78–18. Vicksburg, Mississippi.

Sprunt, A., Jr. 1954. Florida bird life. Coward-McCann Inc. New York, New York.

PREPARED BY: John C. Ogden, National Park Service, Everglades National Park, 40001 State Road 9336, Homestead, FL 33034–6733.

Black-crowned Night-Heron
Nycticorax nycticorax

FAMILY ARDEIDAE

Order Ciconiiformes

TAXONOMY: The Black-crowned Night-Heron (*Nycticorax nycticorax*) was described by Linnaeus in 1758. This cosmopolitan species has been divided into four subspecies: *N. n. nycticorax* in the Old World; *N. n. hoactli* in the New World, except for *N. n. obscurus* in southern South America, and *N. n. falklandicus* in the Falklands (Hancock 1984). *N. nycticorax* and *N. caledonicus* (mostly Australia) are very similar and may be a superspecies (AOU 1983). The Florida birds are *N. n. hoactli* (Palmer 1962).

DESCRIPTION: The Black-crowned Night-Heron is a stocky, medium sized ardeid about 58–66 cm (23–26 in.) in length and has a wingspan of 1.1 m (45 in.). In adult herons, the top of the head and the back are black, the wings and tail are light gray, the sides of the head, the neck, and belly are white. There are usually three white occipital plumes that extend to about the middle of the back. Sexes are mostly similar, with the female slightly smaller. The thick, black bill appears slightly down-curved. The legs and feet are light yellow and the legs and neck are shorter than day herons. The lores are shades of greenish-blue and the iris is orange to crimson-red; color intensity depends on breeding condition. Immature birds are considerably different in plumage— dark brown above with buff spots and underparts that are gray streaked with brown. The colors of the immature's eyes, lores, legs, and feet are similar to the adults but much lighter (Bent 1926; Hancock 1984).

POPULATION SIZE AND TREND: Because the species is dark-plumaged, nests below the canopy, and exhibits secretive habits, little information exists on the numbers of Black-crowned Night-Herons in either North America or Florida. About 13,000 pairs in 76 colonies were recorded in all states along the Atlantic coast of United States (Custer et al. 1980); this appears to be the only reference for this area. Spendelow and Patton (1988) summarized breeding populations (number of birds): Atlantic coast 19,560, Florida coast 1,394,

Black-crowned
Night-Heron,
*Nycticorax
nycticorax*. (Photo
copyright by Allan
D. Cruickshank,
courtesy of Florida
Audubon Society)

Gulf coast 19,110, Great Lakes coast 8,272, and California coast 1,200. Lack of early survey data and accurate recent inventories make population trends difficult. However, Erwin (1978) believed Black-crowns were declining in Massachusetts.

No statewide inventory of Black-crowned Night-Herons exists for Florida. Analysis of 37 years of Christmas Bird Counts in Florida (*American Birds* 1963–93) shows that the number of Black-crowns reported doubled, but so did the numbers of counts. The mean number of herons for the period was 632, with a range of 391–1,260 birds. Of the 293 ardeid breeding sites reported for 1976–1978 in Florida (Nesbitt et al. 1982), 28 colonies contained Black-crowned Night-Heron nests. That study recorded about 1,700 pairs in those years. In the same years there were at least three colonies with a total of about 200 nests in Collier and Lee counties that were not recorded (T. Below, pers. observ.). If this is any indication of colonies missed statewide, then it is possible that the population is considerably larger than the above data suggest. Because Black-crowned Night-Herons are active at low-light levels, use many inaccessible fresh or salt wetlands of Florida, and do not congregate in large numbers, it is not surprising that so little is known about them in Florida and elsewhere.

As with other waterbirds, Black-crowned populations probably have declined due to illegal shooting, disturbance at breeding colonies, and drainage of wetlands used for foraging. Whereas pesticide contamination is well documented for the species (Custer et al. 1983, 1991), its impact on the populations is not well understood.

DISTRIBUTION AND HISTORY OF DISTRIBUTION: The Black-crowned Night-Heron is extremely widespread, occurring in North and South America, Eurasia, and Africa. Its northern limits are uneven, reaching 53°N at their

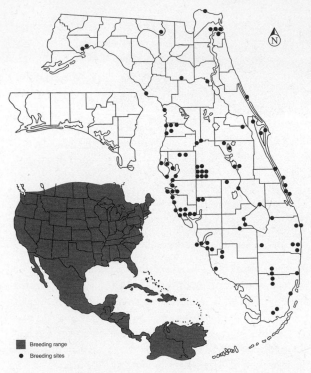

Distribution map
of the Black-
crowned Night-
Heron, *Nycticorax*
nycticorax.

Breeding range
Breeding sites

maximum. In the Western Hemisphere the range extends from Saskatchewan, Manitoba, and Quebec in Canada, south through North and South America. In Europe it occurs in patches of suitable habitat, and in Asia it extends more continuously across the continent, through Indonesia. It also occurs throughout much of Africa south of the Sahara (Hancock 1984). The nominate subspecies *N. n. nycticorax* is found throughout the Old World range. In the New World *N. n. hoactli* breeds in North and Central America and the Caribbean and in South America from the north southward to northern Chile and Argentina. *N. n. hoactli* also has reached the Galapagos and Hawaiian Islands, where it was first reported in 1891 (Hancock 1984).

A common resident in all regions of Florida (Howell 1932), the Black-crowned Night-Heron is widely distributed throughout the state. But there are considerably more records for the lower two thirds of the peninsula. Of the 99 quadrangles (9.6%) where breeding was confirmed in Florida, 86 were south of Marion County (Florida Breeding Bird Atlas, in prep.). For 31 years of Christmas Bird Counts that reported Black-crowned Night-Herons, 45 of 66 (68%) sites in Florida were located south of Marion County (*American Birds* 1963–1993). No information exists that would indicate the distribution throughout Florida is any different now than it was historically.

HABITAT REQUIREMENTS AND HABITAT TREND: The habitats used by Black-crowned Night-Herons are varied across its range. Freshwater and marine-estuarine wetlands seem to be equally used by the species. Black-crowned Night-Herons are evidently able to use all of the habitats suitable for wading birds (Palmer 1962). In Florida these elusive herons breed in ponds and sloughs in the interior and to some extent in the mangrove swamps along the coast. They breed in colonies with other ardeids, but often form a colony by themselves (Howell 1932). Black-crowned Night-Herons have been recorded nesting in a variety of woody plant species, as well as other vegetation such as grass, shrubs, and cane to 49 m (Bent 1926). The species readily nests in the non-native Brazilian pepperbush (*Schinus terebinthifolius*) on dredged-material islands along the Florida coast. Black-crowned Night-Herons need shallow fresh to salt water wetlands to feed in and adequately vegetated areas nearby to roost and nest in.

For the last 100 years, Florida's human population has been growing at a phenomenal rate and vast areas of the state have been converted for their use. About 40–50% of Florida's wetlands have been lost since the beginning of the century (Kushlan 1990). This extraordinary growth has not only impacted the areas used by man, but also has altered water flow and hydroperiods that has changed and destroyed entire ecosystems. There is no indication that this growth is slowing down even in a suppressed economy; therefore it appears reasonable to believe that the loss of wetlands, and wildlife dependent upon them, will continue. It seems impossible that these changes to wetlands have not affected the birds so dependent on them.

VULNERABILITY OF SPECIES AND HABITAT: As most of the prime habitat for human activities has already been used, more and more emphasis is being put on suboptimal land that includes wetlands. Housing developments are being built that either totally include a wetland or with other developments surrounding a wetland. A few waders use these wet areas but not many; it is obvious that the habitat is no longer suitable. As if this was not bad enough, landscaping precludes nesting and roosting habitat. Agriculture goes one step further by completely encircling wetlands and removing all natural vegetation around them. For all species of ardeids that are so dependent on wetlands and the surrounding natural vegetation, the loss of more vital habitat can only be detrimental.

CAUSES OF THREAT: Human alteration of the natural world has affected most wading birds. In Florida the destruction and alteration of more than half of the wetlands, due to the phenomenal increase in population has caused a substantial decline in ardeids. Wetlands have been filled and or impacted by housing developments, agriculture, human activity (i.e., sports, recreation), and the infrastructure that supports these activities. This not only denies Black-crowned Night-Herons and other ardeids habitat to feed, breed, or rest in, it also introduces hazardous chemicals into the environment that adversely affect wildlife.

RESPONSES TO HABITAT MODIFICATION: Apparently little is known about Black-crowned Night-Herons responses to alterations of its environment. Although Black-crowned Night-Herons will tolerate some human disturbance (Palmer 1962; Hancock 1984), this appears to be the exception and not the rule. As noted above, the species will nest on dredged-material coastal islands (Rodgers 1986). Black-crowned Night-Herons also will forage in roadside ditches and artificial wetlands.

DEMOGRAPHIC CHARACTERISTICS: Although Black-crowned Night-Herons are known to breed at 1 year, they usually breed at 2–3 years of age (Palmer 1962). The eggs are greenish-blue, oval, and average 37 X 51.5 mm (1.5 x 2 in.). Clutch size is reported as 2–5 and the eggs are laid about 2 days apart (Bent 1926). Custer and Osborn (1977) reported mean clutch sizes of 3.68 ± 0.11 and 3.72 ± 0.15 from Massachusetts and Wolford and Boag (1971a) reported average clutch sizes from 3.2 to 4.1 from Alberta. Rodgers (1986) found the average clutch size was 3.09 ± 0.16 (range 2–4 eggs) for 11 nests in Tampa Bay. Nesting starts in December in south Florida (Howell 1932) and in February–March in north Florida. Incubation starts with the first egg and takes 24-26 days (Bent 1926). Hatching success was 96.3% for a Florida colony (Rodgers 1986). Fledging success in North America is reported as 2.2–2.4 birds per successful nest, with a high (75-85%) success rate compared to other herons (Henny 1972). Rodgers (1986) reported the average number of nestlings surviving to 2 weeks of age was 2.30 ± 0.26 (range 1–3 nestlings), with 75.83% of the eggs producing large young. The nestlings fledge at about 6 weeks and first year mortality is estimated to be about 61% (Palmer 1962). Major causes of egg and nestling failure include human disturbance, predation (especially from raccoons [*Procyon lotor*] and Fish Crows [*Corvus ossifragus*]), weather (storms and related nest collapse), and insufficient food for nestlings (Palmer 1962; Burger and Hahn 1977; Burger 1982).

KEY BEHAVIORS: Black-crowned Night-Herons nest colonially with the males displaying, often at old nests. A primary advertising display of males is the Stretch that includes standing erect, swaying from foot to foot, and terminates in a hunched posture, with the bill down in Mock Preening of the belly feathers (Allen and Mangels 1940). During the display the male gives a hissing call or sometimes performs Bill Clapping. The male also exhibits Bowing and Wing Touch displays and uses Upright and Forward displays to defend the site. Allopreening is common after pairing. The Greeting Ceremony is unusual in that it does not involve a Stretch display. Both sexes lean horizontally with outstretched necks, head plumes erected, and bills touching (the pair may touch or rattle their bills together). After pairing, the male usually brings nest material to the female, who places the twigs into the nest structure. Eggs are laid every 1–2 days (Custer and Frederick 1990). The Black-crowned Night-Heron often calls in flight, has a distinctive compact silhouette and the wing-beats are faster than most herons (Hancock 1984).

Black-crowned Night-Herons typically feed during low light levels or at night, but also may feed during the day. The bird is most likely a visual feeder and uses the Standing and Walking Slowly behaviors to capture prey. It has often been reported using Hovering, Diving and Swimming feeding behaviors. Underwing Feeding also has been reported. Black-crowned Night-Herons feed in aggregations or solitarily and may defend a feeding territory (Hancock 1984). *N. n. hoactli* feeds on aquatic organisms, such as fish, frogs, snakes, salamanders, mollusks, crustaceans, marine annelids, insects, vegetable matter, and occasionally young birds and small mammals (Palmer 1962; Wolford and Boag 1971b). The following percentages are representative of the information in the literature: fish 52%, crustaceans 22%, aquatic insects 16%, frogs 6%, mice and native rats 3%. Black-crowned Night-Herons often take young of other colonial nesting waterbirds such as terns, other herons, and ibis. Thus, night herons are a very opportunistic predator.

CONSERVATION MEASURES TAKEN: Black-crowned Night-Herons are protected by both federal and state migratory bird laws. The recent general shift to the preservation of wetlands and the creation of preserved areas has helped to conserve habitat for all ardeids.

CONSERVATION MEASURES PROPOSED: Much needs to be learned about Black-crowned Night-Herons and other ardeids in Florida. No detailed studies of Black-crowns exist for Florida. A coordinated research and monitoring program should be conducted to determine the status, trends, and life histories of all these herons in the state. Statewide inventories of waterbirds should include ground counts of important colonies in order to determine the abundance of Black-crowns in Florida. This could provide information and justification for the protection and preservation of Black-crowns. This further would aid in the protection and preservation of wetlands that are so valuable to wildlife.

LITERATURE CITED:

Allen, R. P., and F. P. Mangels. 1940. Studies of the nesting behavior of the Black-crowned Night Heron. Proc. Linn. Soc. N.Y. 50–51:1–28.

American Birds (Audubon Field Notes). 1963-1993. Christmas Bird Counts. Volumes 18-48.

AOU. 1983. Check-list of North American birds. 6th. edition. American Ornithologists' Union, Washington, D.C.

Bent, A. C. 1926. Life Histories of North American marsh birds. Natl. Mus. Bull. no. 135. Smithsonian Inst. Press, Washington, D.C.

Burger, J. 1982. An overview of proximate factors affecting reproductive success in colonial birds: concluding remarks and summary of panel discussion. Colon. Waterbirds 5:58–65.

Burger, J., and C. Hahn. 1977. Crow predation on Black-crowned Night Heron eggs. Wilson Bull. 89:350–351.

Custer, T. W., and R. G. Osborn. 1977. Wading birds as biological indicators: 1975 colony survey. U.S. Fish and Wildl. Serv. Spec. Rept. Wildl. no. 206, Washington, D.C.

Custer, T. W., and P. C. Frederick. 1990. Egg size and laying order of Snowy Egrets, Great Egrets, and Black-crowned Night-Herons. Condor 92:772–775.

Custer, T. W., R. G. Osborn, and W. F. Stout. 1980. Distribution, species abundance and nest-site use of Atlantic Coast colonies of herons and their allies. Auk 97:591–600.

Custer, T. W., C. M. Bunck, and T. E. Kaiser. 1983. Organochlorine residues in Atlantic coast Black-crowned Night-Heron eggs, 1979. Colon. Waterbirds 6:160–167.

Custer, T. W., B. A. Rattner, H. M. Ohlendorf, and M. J. Melancon. 1991. Herons and egrets as proposed indicators of estuarine contamination in the United States. Proc. Internat. Ornithol. Congr. 20:2474–2479.

Erwin, R. M. 1978. Population and colony site dynamics in selected Massachusetts waterbirds. Proc. 1977 Conf. Colon. Waterbird Group 1:19–25.

Hancock, J., and J. Kushlan. 1984. The herons handbook. Harper and Row, Inc., New York.

Henny, C. J. 1972. An analysis of the population dynamics of selected avian species with special reference to changes during the modern pesticide era. Wildl. Research Rept. no. 1. U.S. Fish and Wildl. Serv., Washington, D.C.

Howell, A. H. 1932. Florida bird life. Coward-McCann, Inc. New York.

Kushlan, J. 1990. Fresh water marshes. Pp. 324-363 in Ecosystems of Florida (R. Myers and J. Ewel, Eds.). Univ. Central Fla. Press, Orlando, Florida.

Nesbitt, S. A., J. C. Ogden, H. W. Kale, II, B. W. Patty, and L. A. Rowse. 1983. Florida atlas of breeding sites for herons and their allies: 1976-78. U.S. Fish and Wildl. Serv., Office of Biol. Serv. FWS/OBS-81/49.

Palmer, R. S. 1962. Handbook of North American birds. Vol. 1. Yale Univ. Press, New Haven, Connecticut.

Rodgers, J. A., Jr. 1986. Additional observations on the reproductive success of herons on the west coast of Florida. Fla. Field Nat. 14:77–79.

Spendelow, J. A., and S. R. Patton. 1988. National atlas of coastal waterbird colonies in the contiguous United States: 1976–82. U.S. Fish and Wildl. Serv. Biol. Rept. no. 88(5), Washington, D.C.

Wolford, J. W., and D. A. Boag. 1971a. Distribution and biology of Black-crowned Night Herons in Alberta. Can. Field-Nat. 85:13–19.

Wolford, J. W., and D. A. Boag. 1971b. Food habits of Black-crowned Night Herons in southern Alberta. Auk 88:435–437.

PREPARED BY: Theodore H. Below, National Audubon Society, Rookery Bay Sanctuary, 3697 North Road, FL 33942.

Yellow-crowned Night-Heron
Nyctanassa violacea

FAMILY ARDEIDAE

Order Ciconiiformes

TAXONOMY: The Yellow-crowned Night-Heron (*Nyctanassa violacea*) is a widespread species in North and South America, and currently six subspecies are recognized. Only one subspecies (*N. v. violacea*) is found in Florida (AOU 1957). This species has been placed in the genus *Nycticorax*.

DESCRIPTION: Adult Yellow-crowned Night-Herons have a white top to the head, tinged with yellow, with white occipital plumes, and an elongated white patch on sides of the head behind the eye. The rest of the head and the bill are black. The plumage is mainly blue-gray and feathers of the back and wings are slightly darker with light edges. The iris is orange to scarlet-orange and is especially intense during the breeding season. The legs and feet are yellowish-green. The sexes are similar in plumage and size.

The juvenal plumage is dark grayish-brown. The upperparts are narrowly streaked with rust and most of the underparts are more contrastingly streaked; the tail is fuscous with white on the tips. The lesser wing coverts are deep olive with brownish edges and a small terminal spot. The greater coverts have larger whitish terminal spots. The remiges are fuscous and very narrowly tipped with white that wears off soon after molting.

Several succeeding stages of plumage occur but are poorly known. Apparently several years are needed to reach full definitive plumage, but Basic II and Alternate II are close to definitive. The subspecies are differentiated by bill dimensions and color of upperparts.

POPULATION SIZE AND TREND: Little information is available on the population of Yellow-crowned Night-Herons inhabiting Florida. Their numbers were not surveyed in the recent aerial surveys of wading birds in Florida (Runde et al. 1991) because this species is hard to see from the air. They tend to nest under vegetation and often in small colonies that make them difficult

Yellow-crowned Night-Heron, *Nyctanassa violacea*. (Photo by Dade W. Thornton)

to find. The 1976–1978 surveys of colonial wading birds in Florida found 692 birds in 7 colonies (Nesbitt et al. 1982). One colony at Alafia River contained about 600 birds and the rest were relatively small. Surveys between 1976 and 1982 found over 1,800 nests with highest numbers occurring in New Jersey, Virginia, South Carolina, Florida, and Louisiana, but little information is available on population trends in any of these areas (Spendelow and Patton 1988).

DISTRIBUTION AND HISTORY OF DISTRIBUTION: The Yellow-crowned Night-Heron occurs along the coast of South America from southern Brazil and Ecuador north through Central America and the Caribbean. Along the Pacific coast, it occurs north to central Baja California. In the United States it is found along the coast from at least as far north as Connecticut through Texas (Spendelow and Patton 1988). It breeds almost throughout Florida but is less common in the panhandle (Robertson and Woolfenden 1992). The Yellow-crowned Night-Heron has expanded its range northward since the 1930s.

HABITAT REQUIREMENTS AND HABITAT TREND: The Yellow-crowned Night-Heron feeds in a variety of wetland habitats from coastal mud-

Distribution map of
the Yellow-crowned
Night-Heron,
Nyctanassa violacea.

■ Breeding range
● Breeding sites

flats, marshes and mangrove swamps, to inland riverine forests. They nest in trees, often over water. They typically feed on crustaceans and have a deeper and broader bill than the similar Black-crowned Night-Heron (*Nycticorax nycticorax*). The loss of coastal wetlands in Florida has decreased dramatically in recent decades but the loss of freshwater wetlands continues. Alteration of hydrology in freshwater wetlands is likely to alter the productivity of coastal wetlands dependent on input from freshwater flow. Loss of feeding habitat and alteration of the productivity of feeding habitats remain the greatest threat to this species.

VULNERABILITY OF SPECIES AND HABITAT: Little is known about the population trends of the Yellow-crowned Night-Heron in Florida and elsewhere in their range. Because of their association with wetland habitats, especially coastal habitats, the species certainly has undergone population declines during the past 50 years. In a ranking system for assessment of conservation priorities for Florida, the Yellow-crowned Night-Heron received a biological score of 21 (Millsap et al. 1990). This score is near the median score of the G5 (demonstrably secure globally) and S4 (apparently secure in Florida) ranking categories (The Nature Conservancy 1986).

CAUSES OF THREAT: In Florida, the major threat to the Yellow-crowned Night-Heron is loss of wetland habitats. Secondary factors that influence the functional integrity of wetlands, such as pollutants and disruption of natural hydrology, also may threaten Yellow-crowned Night-Heron populations. In Louisiana, Yellow-crowned Night-Herons have been implicated in depredations at crawfish farms and significant illegal kills of the species have occurred.

RESPONSES TO HABITAT MODIFICATION: As with several other species of Ciconiiformes, the Yellow-crowned Night-Heron has spread north since the 1930s. Whether this is a response to deteriorating conditions in the southern part of its range (e.g., the Everglades) or recolonization of formerly occupied territories that have been afforded better protection is still being debated. Yellow-crowned Night-Herons are extremely tolerant of human activity and regularly nest in residential areas and parks where people walk under their nests.

DEMOGRAPHIC CHARACTERISTICS: Yellow-crowned Night-Herons build nests of sticks in trees (Watts 1989, Laubhan and Reid 1991). Whereas both sexes build the nest, generally males collect the sticks and the female places them in the nest (Bagley and Grau 1979). Some Yellow-crowned Night-Herons breed at one year of age in juvenal plumage, but most initiate breeding in their second year (J. A. Rodgers, pers. comm.). They lay from 3 to 6 eggs (Bent 1926; McVaugh 1976; Custer and Osborn 1977; Wischusen 1979). Both sexes incubate the eggs and care for young (Bagley and Grau 1979). Incubation bouts last from 2 to 18 hours. The adults feed young by regurgitating food into the nest (Bagley and Grau 1979). Unlike most herons, food is rarely transferred directly from the adult to a young. Nesting failure is greatest prior to egg-hatching, with most brood-reduction occurring before the nestlings are 2 weeks of age (Rodgers 1980, 1986). Young fledge at about 5–6 weeks (J. A. Rodgers, pers. comm.). Post-fledging survivorship is unknown.

KEY BEHAVIORS: Adult Yellow-crowned Night-Herons have at least six major types of vocalizations (Bagley and Grau 1979). Behaviors associated with pair formation and copulation are similar to those described for other herons including stereotypic Stretch Display, Greeting Ceremony, Forward Display, and copulatory displays (Bagley and Grau 1979).

Throughout much of its range, the Yellow-crowned Night-Heron is associated with coastal environments and feeding bouts are often synchronized with tidal cycles. Thus, the species is less nocturnal than the Black-crowned Night-Heron. Yellow-crowned Night-Herons forage by using a series of slow, stalking walks separated by motionless periods of visual searching (Rodgers 1983).

The Yellow-crowned Night-Heron's diet is relatively specialized on crustaceans (Reigner 1982a). Diet appears to vary regionally and Yellow-crowns
appear to specialize on certain species in different areas (Niethammer and
Kaiser 1983; Watts 1988). Handling time varies proportionally to prey size
and behaviors for consumption of large crabs are lengthy (>7 min) and complex (Reigner 1982b). Evidence exists that some learning may be required
before immatures become specialized on crustaceans; Laubhan et al. (1991)
found that immatures took a significantly larger proportion of tadpoles than
adults.

CONSERVATION MEASURES TAKEN: Many colony sites used by Yellow-
crowned Night-Herons within Florida have been protected within parks, refuges, and sanctuaries but other important sites may need to be protected. The
species is not listed by the Florida Game and Freshwater Fish Commission, but
is listed by Florida Natural Areas Inventory as a species of special concern.

CONSERVATION MEASURES PROPOSED: Key nesting areas of Yellow-
crowned Night-Herons within Florida need to be identified and protected.
Critical foraging areas around these sites should also be identified, protected,
and managed if necessary.

Mercury has become a serious problem throughout much of Florida. Little
information is available on the occurrence of mercury within the food chain of
Yellow-crowns or whether they experience any lethal or sublethal effects from
exposure to mercury. Careful studies of this problem need to be developed.

Parasitic infestations of wading birds has recently been documented in
Florida (Telford et al. 1992; Spalding et al. 1993). Little information is available on the occurrence or the seriousness of parasitic diseases in Yellow-
crowned Night-Herons; however, these parasites could represent a threat to
the status of this species.

LITERATURE CITED:

AOU. 1957. Check-list of North American birds, 5th edition. American Orni-
    thologists' Union. Baltimore, Lord Baltimore Press.
Bagley, F. M., and G. A. Grau. 1979. Aspects of Yellow-crowned Night-
    Heron reproductive behavior. Proc. Colon. Waterbird Group 3:165–175.
Bent, A. C. 1926. Life histories of North American marsh birds. U.S. Natl.
    Mus. Bull. no. 135. Smithsonian Inst. Press, Washington, D.C.
Custer, T. W., and R. G. Osborn. 1977. Wading birds as biological indicators:
    1975 colony survey. U.S. Dept. Inter. Spec. Rept. Wildl. no. 206, Wash-
    ington, D.C.
Laubhan, M. K., and F. A. Reid. 1991. Characteristics of Yellow-crowned

Night-Heron nests in lowland hardwood forests of Missouri. Wilson Bull. 103:486–491.

Laubhan, M. K., W. D. Runde, B. I. Swartz, and F. A. Reid. 1991. Diurnal activity patterns and foraging success of Yellow-crowned Night-Herons in seasonally flooded wetlands. Wilson Bull: 103:272–277.

McVaugh, W., Jr. 1976. The development of four North American herons. II. Living Bird 14:163–183.

Millsap, B., J. A. Gore, D. E. Runde, and S. I. Cerulean. 1990. Setting priorities for the conservation of fish and wildlife species in Florida. Wildl. Monog. 111:1–57.

Nesbitt, S. A., J. C. Ogden, H. W. Kale, B. W. Patty, L. A. Rowse. 1982. Florida atlas of breeding sites for herons and their allies: 1976–78. U.S. Fish and Wildl. Serv., Office Biol. Serv. FWS/OBS-81/49. Washington, D.C.

Niethammer, K. R., and M. S. Kaiser. 1983. Late summer food habits of three heron species in northern Louisiana. Colon. Waterbirds 6:148–153.

Riegner, M. F. 1982a. The diet of Yellow-crowned Night-Herons in the eastern and southern United States. Colon. Waterbirds 5:173–176.

Riegner, M. F. 1982b. Prey handling in Yellow-crowned Night-Herons. Auk 99:380–381.

Robertson, W. B., Jr., and G. E. Woolfenden. 1992. Florida bird species: an annotated list. Fla. Ornithol. Soc. Spec. Publ. no. 6. Gainesville, Florida.

Rodgers, J. A., Jr. 1980. Reproductive success of three heron species on the west coast of Florida. Fla. Field Nat. 8:47–40.

Rodgers, J. A., Jr. 1983. Foraging behavior of seven species of herons in Tampa Bay, Florida. Colon. Waterbirds 6:11–23.

Rodgers, J. A., Jr. 1986. Additional observations on the reproductive success of herons on the west coast of Florida. Fla. Field Nat. 14:77–79.

Runde, D. E., J. A. Gore, J. A. Hovis, M. S. Robson, and P. D. Southall. 1991. Florida atlas of breeding sites for herons and their allies. Update 1986–1989. Nongame Wildl. Prog., Tech. Rep. no. 10., Fla. Game and Freshwater Fish Comm., Tallahassee, Florida.

Spalding, M. G., G. T. Bancroft, and D. J. Forrester. 1993. An epizootic of eustrongyulidosis at a wading bird colony in Everglades. Jour. Wild. Dis. 29:237–249.

Spendelow, J. A., and S. R. Patton. 1988. National atlas of coastal waterbird colonies in the contiguous United States: 1976–82. U.S. Fish and Wildl. Serv. Biol. Rept. 88(5). 326 pp., Washington, D.C.

Telford, S. R., M. G. Spalding, and D. J. Forrester. 1992. Hemoparasites of wading birds (Ciconiiformes) in Florida. Can. Jour. Zool. 70:1397–1408.

The Nature Conservancy. 1986. Natural Heritage Program operations manual. Arlington, Virginia.

Watts, B. D. 1988. Foraging implications of food usage patterns in Yellow-crowned Night-Herons. Condor 90:860–865.
Watts, B. D. 1989. Nest-site characteristics of Yellow-crowned Night-Herons in Virginia. Condor 91:979–983.
Wischusen, E. W. 1979. The nesting success and structure of a Yellow-crowned Night-Heron colony in Alabama. Proc. Colon. Waterbird Group 3:85–86.

PREPARED BY: G. Thomas Bancroft and Allan M. Strong, National Audubon Society, 115 Indian Mound Trail, Tavernier, FL 33070 (Current address of GTB: Archbold Biological Station, P.O. Box 2057, Lake Placid, FL 33862; AMS: Department of Biology, 310 Dinwiddie Hall, Tulane University, New Orleans, LA 70118).

Glossy Ibis

Plegadis falcinellus

FAMILY THRESKIORNITHIDAE

Order Ciconiiformes

TAXONOMY: The Glossy Ibis (*Plegadis falcinellus*) has a nearly worldwide range (Cramp 1977; AOU 1983). The nominate race *P. f. falcinellus* breeds in southern Europe, northern Africa, central Asia, the eastern United States, the Caribbean, and locally in Costa Rica and Venezuela. *P. f. peregrinus* occurs in Madagascar, Indonesia, and Australia. The subspecific status of Glossy Ibis nesting between India and southern China and in eastern and southern Africa, has not been determined (Cramp 1977). The very similar appearing White-faced Ibis (*P. chihi*), nesting on the coasts of Louisiana and Texas, locally throughout much of western United States, and south through Central and South America to Argentina, has been considered by some to be conspecific with the Glossy Ibis (AOU 1983). However, the two species have been shown to nest sympatrically in Louisiana and possibly in eastern Texas.

DESCRIPTION: The Glossy Ibis is a medium-sized, long-legged wading bird with a body length of 48–66 cm (19–26 in.) and a wingspread of 80–95 cm (up to 38 in.). The bill is long, slender, and decurved. At a distance the plumage appears black; however, at close view in bright light, the adult plumage is dark chestnut with metallic green and purple iridescence on the wings, back and tail. The bill and legs are dark, slatey-blue to black in color. During the breeding season, adults show a thin, whitish margin bordering the dark blue to purplish bare facial skin anterior to the eye. The immature plumage is duller, grayish-brown on the head, neck, and underparts, with a dark, greenish sheen across the wings and back. Nonbreeding adults and immature birds may show thin, light streaking on the head and neck. The head and neck are carried outstretched during flight. Typically, flocks fly in diagonal or "V" formations.

POPULATION SIZE AND TREND: The number of Glossy Ibises nesting throughout western and central Europe and northern Africa has declined

Glossy Ibis,
*Plegadis
falcinellus.* (Photo
copyright by Allan
D. Cruickshank,
courtesy of Florida
Audubon Society)

considerably during the past 100 years (Cramp 1977). Generally, the reverse
pattern occurred in the eastern United States outside of Florida (Ogden 1978).
The number of Glossy Ibises nesting along the Atlantic coast between Georgia
and Maine increased from none prior to the late 1940s to an estimated 8,400
pairs in 1975. There is some evidence that this population growth peaked
during the 1970s; the number of pairs nesting at protected colony sites in
North Carolina subsequently declined (Parnell and McCrimmon 1984). Population growth and expansion also occurred along the central coast of the Gulf
of Mexico during this same period, with small numbers first nesting in Louisiana, Arkansas, and Alabama during the middle to late 1960s (Ogden 1978).
Numbers nesting in these Gulf coast states have remained small.

The Glossy Ibis was considered to be a rare, even casual breeding bird in
Florida prior to the late 1930s (Bent 1926; Allen 1935; Ogden 1978). Most
colonies reported during this early period were of less than 25 pairs (Baynard
1913; Ogden 1978). A surprisingly large nesting colony estimated to contain
800–900 pairs was found at Lake Okeechobee in 1937 (Ogden 1978); that
colony peaked at about 1,200 pairs by 1940 (Sprunt 1954). The general
impression was that the number nesting in Florida gradually increased during
the next three decades, with the 1970s population estimated at 3,500 birds
(Robertson and Kushlan 1974). Although no single, large colony comparable

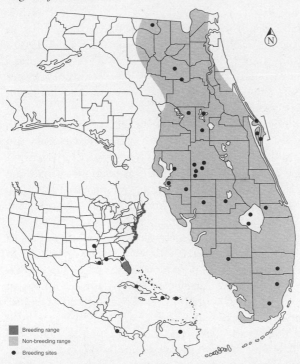

Distribution map
of the Glossy Ibis,
Plegadis falcinellus.

Breeding range
Non-breeding range
● Breeding sites

in size to that at Lake Okeechobee in the late 1930s has been reported in recent decades, several moderate-sized colonies have been documented. These have included 600 pairs in an Everglades colony in western Broward County in 1973 (Kushlan and Schortemeyer 1974), 300 pairs at Alafia (Tampa Bay) in 1976 and 500 pairs at the same location in 1987 (F. Dunstan and R. Paul, pers. comm.), 125 pairs at Moore Creek (Merritt Island) in 1975 (J. Ogden, unpubl. data), and 200 pairs in the Haulover colony (Brevard County) in 1986 (W. Leenhouts, in litt.). The population trend for Glossy Ibis nesting in Florida since the 1970s is unknown. Glossy Ibis were found in 14 of 295 (5%) active colonies found during aerial censuses in Florida between 1976–1978 (Nesbitt et al. 1982), compared to 22 of 575 (4%) colonies for a comparable geographical area censused in 1986–1989 (Runde et al. 1991).

DISTRIBUTION AND HISTORY OF DISTRIBUTION: The population decline by Glossy Ibises in western and central Europe resulted in the disappearance of nesting birds from many former colony sites throughout that region, primarily since the 1930s (Cramp 1977). In North America, the population increase produced the first Glossy Ibis nesting colonies in an extensive region along the Atlantic and Gulf of Mexico coastal plains (Ogden 1978). Nesting birds appeared in colonies between Georgia and North Carolina during the 1940s, in Virginia, Maryland, and New Jersey during the 1950s, in Delaware, New York, Alabama, Arkansas, and Louisiana during the 1960s, and in Maine in 1972 (Burger and Miller 1977; Ogden 1978). This expanded range has generally been maintained, with only local shifts in colony sites (AOU 1983). Glossy Ibis also have spread into Venezuela and Trinidad, primarily since the 1960s (Gochfeld 1973).

Glossy Ibis occur throughout Florida, most commonly in the central and southern peninsula and, least often, in the interior of northern Florida and across the panhandle (Sprunt 1954). In addition to the residents birds nesting in Florida, Glossy Ibis that breed along the Atlantic coast migrate through the state in both spring and late summer-autumn (Byrd 1978; Ogden 1981).

Throughout the 1900s, most Glossy Ibis nesting colonies in Florida have been located in the central peninsula, primarily between Lake Okeechobee and Hillsborough, Sumter, Lake, and northern Brevard Counties (Sprunt 1954; Ogden 1981; Nesbitt et al. 1982; Runde et al. 1991). Nesting in southern Florida appeared to have been sporadic prior to the 1970s but has become more regular in recent years, usually by relatively small numbers of birds (Kushlan and Schortemeyer 1974; Ogden 1981). South Florida colonies have occurred as far south as Dade and Collier counties. Glossy Ibis have been rare in Florida Bay and the Florida Keys. Few nesting colonies have been located in the northern peninsula, though one was found in Wakulla County in the panhandle in 1993 (Pranty 1994). North Florida colonies have been found in Hamilton, Alachua, and Marion counties (Baynard 1913; Sprunt 1954; Rice 1955; Runde et al. 1991).

HABITAT REQUIREMENTS AND HABITAT TREND: The Glossy Ibis in Florida is essentially a bird of freshwater wetlands, although they often nest at coastal sites if favorable feeding habitat, in fresh or brackish marshes, is located within flight range (P. Frederick, pers. comm.; W. Leenhouts, in litt.). Seasonally flooded grasslands, prairies, roadside ditches, and shallow flooded marshes and lake shorelines are the most important feeding habitats. Glossy Ibis in Florida nest in a wide variety of woody shrubs and low trees, including southern willow (*Salix caroliniana*), elderberry (*Sambucus canadensis*), wax myrtle (*Myrica cerifera*), saltbush (*Baccharis halimifolia*), mangroves (*Rhizophora mangle, Avicennia germinans*), and Brazilian pepper (*Schinus terebinthifolius*), occuring in dense thickets on islands or in standing water (Palmer 1962; Nesbitt et al. 1982). Elsewhere in the eastern United States, Glossy Ibis commonly nest in thickets of bayberry (*Iva frutescens*) and reed grass (*Phragmites communis*) (Burger and Miller 1977). The long history in Florida of drainage projects in freshwater wetlands, especially in the once numerous small, seasonally flooded sites, unquestionably has resulted in the elimination or degradation of considerable areas of feeding habitat. Conversely, the creation of large numbers of water impoundments and dredged-material islands has fortuitously provided new nesting habitat. The overall affects of these two trends on the Glossy Ibis population in Florida is unknown.

VULNERABILITY OF SPECIES AND HABITAT: The environmental factors that regulate Glossy Ibis numbers in Florida are not known. However, Glossy Ibis move about considerably between seasons and years, apparently in response to unstable habitat conditions. That the Glossy Ibis is primarily a freshwater bird suggests the Florida population, like several primarily freshwater birds now in trouble (Wood Stork [*Mycteria americana*], Snail Kite [*Rostrhamus sociabilis*], etc.), may presently be limited by the reduced extent of freshwater habitats in the state. The historical pattern of colony locations in Florida suggests that relatively large numbers of Glossy Ibises nest only where expansive, freshwater marshes exist. Examples would include the colonies in the broad littoral zone on Lake Okeechobee and on Merritt Island adjacent to the St. Johns River marshes. These colony sites may have become less supportive of large numbers of nesting Glossy Ibises if water management practices for mosquito control and water retention inside of modern levee systems have altered the natural depth and timing patterns of flooding. The total number of nests and colony sites used by Glossy Ibis in Florida are small by comparison with most other wading birds in the state. Thus, the ability of the "Florida population" to recover from an abrupt population decline caused by climatological events or the loss of major colony sites may be less than for other species.

CAUSES OF THREAT: No specific information exists on threats to Glossy Ibis in Florida. Any species in Florida that requires a variety of natural, freshwater habitats to provide feeding and nesting site options under a range of climatological and hydrological conditions is potentially being threatened by regional declines in suitable habitat.

RESPONSES TO HABITAT MODIFICATION: Several Glossy Ibis nesting sites located during the aerial censuses conducted between 1976–1978 were located in "created" habitats (Nesbitt et al. 1982). The eight created sites (57% of the total Glossy Ibis colony sites for these three years) included five that were in freshwater impoundments and three on coastal spoil islands.

DEMOGRAPHIC CHARACTERISTICS: Glossy Ibises nest in colonies, either with other wading birds or in Glossy-only colonies. Glossy Ibis in Florida have a much more prolonged nesting season than do ibis that nest along the mid-Atlantic coast (M. Byrd and J. Parnell, pers. comm.). Howell (1932) reported that Glossies in Florida may begin nesting as early as the last week in March, but that eggs are most often laid in May. Glossy Ibis in the Andytown colony (Broward County) had fledged young by 25 May 1973 (Kushlan and Schortemeyer 1974), and in the same colony in 1977 were laying eggs during mid-April (J. Ogden, unpubl. data). Glossy Ibis in the Taylor Slough colony (Dade County) laid eggs in early June in 1976, while nests of about 20 pairs of Glossy Ibis in a central Everglades colony (Broward County) contained eggs or downy young as late as early August, 1974 (J. Ogden, unpubl. data; T. Regan, pers. comm.). A large colony in the Okaloacoochee Slough (Collier County) contained nesting Glossy Ibis during the second week in October, 1974 (J. Ogden, unpubl. data). Glossy Ibis nests in the Moore Creek colony (Brevard County) contained eggs, and downy and feathered young on 8 June 1977 (J. Ogden, unpubl. data).

Clutch size is usually 3 or 4 eggs, and incubation requires 21 days (Palmer 1962; Cramp 1977). The percentage of young in a colony that survive to fledge has been reported to range between 34 and 97% (Baynard 1913; Williams 1973; Miller and Burger 1978). Food shortage, adverse weather, predation, and interspecific aggression between nesting birds are factors that have been shown to reduce nesting success rates of Glossy Ibis (Williams 1973, Burger 1978; Miller and Burger 1978). The age when the young become fully independent of the adults, and the age when birds first breed are poorly known. One ibis banded as a chick was observed building a nest one year later (Miller and Burger 1978).

KEY BEHAVIORS: Glossy Ibises occur in Florida both as breeding birds and as migrants. Although little is known of the seasonal movements of the Glossy Ibis that nest in Florida because so few have been tagged and studied, it is assumed that these birds are resident in the state (Ogden 1981). If so, then the large numbers of ibis that have recently been reported during winter, primarily in the region of phosphate mine impoundments in Polk County, may be birds from the Florida population. Examples of winter counts from the phosphate region include 750 ibises in December, 1986, and 1,180 ibises flying into an evening roost in February, 1988 (P. Fellers in Ogden 1987; Ogden 1988). Substantial numbers of Glossy Ibis that nest along the Atlantic coast north of Florida migrate through the state, primarily during the southbound flight between late June and mid-September (Ogden 1981). These birds apparently do not winter in Florida in any substantial numbers (Byrd 1978).

Relatively little information exists on Glossy Ibis food habits in Florida. Crayfish, cutworms, grasshoppers, other insects and snakes were reported from nestling reguritations at an Orange Lake (Alachua County) colony, and crayfish were the principal food in a Lake Okeechobee colony (Palmer 1962).

In other parts of their range, Glossy Ibis feed on insects and their larvae (waterbeetles, grasshoppers, dragonflies), worms and crustaceans (Cramp 1977; Kushlan 1978). Glossy Ibis search for prey, usually in small flocks, by standing or walking slowly in shallow water or at the edge of pools, probing or pecking with the tips of their bills in the water or near the surface of the ground (Kushlan 1978).

Courtship, nesting, and angonistic behaviors have not been well studied (Palmer 1962; Cramp 1977). Flocks sometimes circle to great heights over colony sites and elsewhere; the significance of this behavior is not known. The pair-bond between a male and female bird is apparently maintained only through a single nesting cycle. The adults perform mutual Bowing and allopreening at the nest site as part of the courtship ritual. Although both adults participate in incubation and feeding of the nestlings, the female may have the major role. The pair performs mutual billing and allopreening when the two adults exchange places at the nest during the incubation and small nestling periods. The young birds begin leaving the nest to walk about on adjacent branches at 2 weeks of age but return to the nest to be fed. By the seventh week, the young make flights with the adults to the feeding grounds.

CONSERVATION MEASURES TAKEN: The Glossy Ibis is a protected species under terms of all international, federal, and state laws and treaties that protect migratory and nongame birds. Important colony sites on Merritt Island and in Tampa Bay are protected by the U.S. Fish and Wildlife Service and the National Audubon Society, respectively.

CONSERVATION MEASURES PROPOSED: Baseline information on the size and distribution of the Florida population of Glossy Ibis will require a several-year combined program of aerial censuses and colony visits. A study of Glossy Ibis nesting biology also is needed to determine colony site characteristics, nesting success rates, and the factors that regulate these rates in Florida colonies. A systematic program of marking Glossy Ibis in Florida colonies is needed to determine seasonal and annual movements of birds relative to a range of environmental parameters, but in particular with the goal of learning the factors that influence the location and timing of nesting and roosting activity related to the presence and characteristics of impounded and other altered wetlands.

ACKNOWLEDGMENTS: Drafts of this Glossy Ibis species account were reviewed and improved by Peter Frederick, Richard Paul, and James Rodgers. My time on this project was supported by the South Florida Natural Resources, Everglades National Park.

LITERATURE CITED:

Allen, R. P. 1935. Notes on some bird colonies on the Gulf coast. Auk 52:198–200.

AOU 1983. Check-list of North American birds. Sixth edition. American Ornithologists' Union, Washington, D.C.

Baynard, O. E. 1913. Home life of the Glossy Ibis (*Plegadis autumnolis* Linn.). Wilson Bull. 25:103–117.

Bent, A. C. 1926. Life histories of North American marsh birds. U.S. Natl. Mus. Bull. no. 135.

Burger, J. 1978. The pattern and mechanism of nesting in mixed-species heronries. Pp. 45–58 in Wading birds (A. Sprunt, IV, J. C. Ogden, and S. Winkler, eds.). Natl. Aud. Soc. Res. Rept. no. 7. New York, New York.

Burger, J., and L. M. Miller. 1977. Colony and nest site selection in White-faced and Glossy ibises. Auk 94:664–676.

Byrd, M. A. 1978. Dispersal and movements of six North American ciconiiforms. Pp. 161–185 in Wading birds (A. Sprunt, IV, J. C. Ogden, and S. Winkler, eds.). Natl. Aud. Soc. Res. Rept. no. 7. New York, New York.

Cramp, S. (Ed.). 1977. Handbook of the birds of Europe, the Middle East and North Africa. Vol. 1. Oxford Univ. Press, Oxford, England.

Gochfeld, M. 1973. Observations on new or unusual birds from Trinidad, West Indies, and comments on the genus *Plegadis* in Venezuela. Condor 75:474–478.

Howell, A. H. 1932. Florida bird life. Coward-McCann Inc., New York, New York.

Kushlan, J. A. 1978. Feeding ecology of wading birds. Pp. 249–297 in Wading birds (A. Sprunt, IV, J. C. Ogden, and S. Winkler, eds.). Natl. Aud. Soc. Res. Rept. no. 7. New York, New York.

Kushlan, J. A., and J. L. Schortemeyer. 1974. Glossy Ibis nesting in southern Florida. Fla. Field Nat. 2:13–14.

Miller, L. M., and J. Burger. 1978. Factors affecting nesting success of the Glossy Ibis. Auk 95:353–361.

Nesbitt, S. A., J. C. Ogden, H. W. Kale, II, B. W. Patty, and L. A. Rowse. 1982. Florida atlas of breeding sites for herons and their allies: 1976–78. Office Biol. Serv., U.S. Fish and Wildl. Serv., FWS/OBS-81/49. Washington, D.C.

Ogden, J. C. 1978. Population trends of colonial wading birds on the Atlantic and Gulf coastal plains. Pp. 137–153 in Wading birds (A. Sprunt, IV, J. C. Ogden, and S. Winkler, eds.). Natl. Aud. Soc. Res. Rept. no. 7. New York, New York.

Ogden, J. C. 1981. Nesting distribution and migration of Glossy Ibis in Florida. Fla. Field Nat. 9:1–6.

Ogden, J. C. 1987. Florida region. Amer. Birds 41:272–274.

Ogden, J. C. 1988. Florida region. Amer. Birds 42:252–256.

Palmer, R. S. (Ed.). 1962. Handbook of North American birds. Vol. 1. Yale Univ. Press, New Haven, Connecticut.

Parnell, J. F., and D. A. McCrimmon. 1984. 1983 supplement to atlas of colonial waterbirds of North Carolina estuaries. UNC Sea Grant publ. UNC-SG-84-07, North Carolina State Univ., Raleigh, North Carolina.

Pranty, B. 1994. Field observations, summer report: June-July 1993. Fla. Field Nat. 22:23–28.

Rice, D. W. 1955. The Glossy Ibises of Lake Alice. Jour. Fla. Acad. Sci. 18:20.

Robertson, W. B., and J. A. Kushlan. 1974. The southern Florida avifauna. Pp. 414–452 in Environments of south Florida past and present (P. J. Gleason, ed.). Memoir 2, Miami Geol. Soc., Miami, Florida.

Runde, D. E., J. A. Gore, J. A. Hovis, M. S. Robson, and P. D. Southall. 1991. Florida atlas of breeding sites for herons and their allies. Update 1986–89. Fla. Game and Fresh Water Fish Comm. Nongame Wildl. Prog., Tech Rept. no. 10. Tallahassee, Florida.

Sprunt, A., Jr. 1954. Florida bird life. Coward-McCann Inc., New York, New York.

Williams, J. W. 1973. Growth rate and nesting aspects for the Glossy Ibis in Virginia—1972. M.S. thesis. College of William and Mary, Williamsburg, Virginia.

PREPARED BY: John C. Ogden, National Park Service, Everglades National Park, 40001 State Road 9336, Homestead, FL 33034–6733.

White Ibis
Eudocimus albus

FAMILY THRESKIORNITHIDAE

Order Ciconiiformes

TAXONOMY: The classification of the White Ibis (*Eudocimus albus*) is currently a subject of debate. Although White Ibises are listed as distinct from the Scarlet Ibis (*E. ruber*) of South America, the two could well be morphs of the same species. White and Scarlet ibises have overlapping ranges throughout much of northern South America, the Scarlet Ibis being a rare but regular vagrant in southern Florida. Scarlet and White ibises interbreed regularly in Venezuela (Ramo and Busto 1987), and White Ibises there in fact appear to pair only with Scarlet Ibises (Ramo, pers. comm.). This suggests that the two are races or morphs of the same species; Ramo and Busto (1982) have proposed that White and Scarlet ibises be given subspecific status within *E. ruber*, which has precedence in description. White Ibises in North America, however, are considerably larger than birds of the same plumage type in South America (van Wieringen and Brouwer 1990), show discernable differences in soft-part breeding coloration, and appear to be entirely allopatric with the South American congeners (unpublished band returns from Bird Banding Office of U.S. Fish and Wildlife Service). So while the Venezuelan birds of either color are by definition the same species, the status of North American White Ibises (those occurring in Florida) is not as obvious.

DESCRIPTION: The White Ibis is a medium-sized wading bird of about 56 cm total length and a 96 cm wingspan; the most distinctive feature is the long down-curved bill. Plumage of adults is white except for the black (in some light conditions iridescent dark green) extremities of the four longest primaries. Soft parts of adults are fleshy pink, becoming bright red before and during the short courtship period. A rounded, enlarged gular pouch may form under the upper throat region of females during courtship, and males develop varying amounts of black on the distal third of the bill. Irides of adults are pale blue. Considerable sexual dimorphism exists, and males may be up to 30%

White Ibis,
Eudocimus albus.
(Photo copyright
by Allan D.
Cruickshank,
courtesy of Florida
Audubon Society)

larger than females, bill length being the most noticeable difference in the field
(Kushlan 1977a). Post-fledging juveniles have dark brown wings, neck, head,
tail, and irides, white backs (apparent when flying), and gray legs during their
first year. Juveniles begin to aquire white plumage near the end of their first
year, with brown feathers remaining on the head and neck at the end of their
second year. These characteristics, together with the brown irides, are seen
throughout the summer of the third year (27 months, see Bildstein 1984),
and are presumed to have molted out by the end of the third year.

POPULATION SIZE AND TREND: Though colonial, White Ibises are extremely nomadic nesters, and many of the largest colony sites are characteristically quite unstable in size and even occupancy status from year to year.
Kushlan et al. (1984) estimated that during the first half of this century, White
Ibises never exceeded 100,000 breeding birds in the Everglades region, despite Allen's (1934) estimate of 660,000 birds breeding in Everglades National Park in 1934. Within southern Florida, numbers of breeding White
Ibises have declined by over 95% between the 1930s and the 1970s, and by an
additional 80% from the highs of the 1970s to the highs of the 1980s. A 1976
colony survey in Florida and the southeastern Atlantic states suggested there
were at least 131,900 breeding birds there. With an additional 100,000
estimated to be breeding in the Gulf coastal states (Spendelow and Patton
1988), the southeastern population may have totaled 230,000 birds. At least

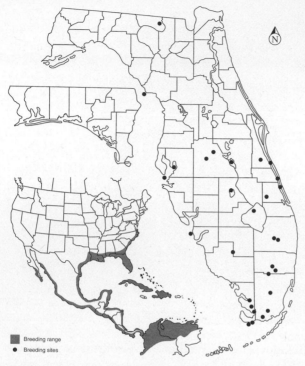

Distribution map
of the White Ibis,
Eudocimus albus.

101,000 (43%) of these ibises bred in Florida in 1976. In the 1987–1990
statewide surveys, a maximum of 34,152 birds were breeding in 1988 (D.
Runde, pers. comm.). The maximum breeding population during 1988, therefore, appears to represent a considerable decline from the estimates of 1975
(66% reduction) and 1976 (50% reduction). Seventy-nine colony locations
were occupied in the 1976–1978 survey and 60 in the 1987–1989 survey,
with 24 locations common to both surveys. Thus, 55 of the 1976–1978
colonies (70%) were not used by ibises during the later survey. Five counties
were occupied in 1976–1978 but not in 1986–1989, and six counties were
occupied in the latter period but not in the former. This level of colony-site
turnover is to some extent characteristic for this nomadic nester, and there
does not seem to have been any dramatic change in nesting range within the
state between the two statewide surveys.

DISTRIBUTION AND HISTORY OF DISTRIBUTION: White Ibises are
common as breeding species in the coastal plain of the southeastern United
States from North Carolina through Texas. Their range extends throughout
wetland habitats of Central America and northern South America to the northern coast of Brazil; congeneric Scarlet Ibises overlap in northern South America
and occur in coastal areas as far south as Rio de Janeiro in Brazil (see discus-

sion in Taxonomy above). White Ibises are common as breeding, migratory, and wintering birds throughout peninsular Florida and probably remain Florida's most common wading bird. Decreases of breeding ibises in southern Florida since the 1960s have been matched closely by a rapid breeding range extension in North and South Carolina and Louisiana. White Ibises were unknown as nesting species in North or South Carolina until the 1920s (Sprunt 1922), with up to a third of the southeastern population nesting there by 1975. Thus both the breeding range in North America and the geometric center of breeding abundance have shifted northward considerably during this century (Frederick et al., in press). White Ibises are known to migrate to Florida and Cuba in the winter; Florida probably hosts the majority of the southeastern population in the winter, as winter residents, migrants, or spring prebreeding birds. Systematic counts in the Everglades suggest that ibises become more numerous there as the winter progresses, with peak estimates of over 116,000 birds reported during March surveys in 1987. Most of these birds depart the area during March and April.

HABITAT REQUIREMENTS AND HABITAT TREND: White Ibises show very broad habitat tolerances for both foraging and nesting. The species nests and feeds commonly in freshwater, brackish, and saline environments, and adults appear to prefer foraging in freshwater areas when feeding young. Though adults are capable of excreting salt through a nasal salt gland, young will not grow when fed salty diets or denied access to fresh water (Johnston and Bildstein 1990). The success of breeding is therefore dependent on access to freshwater feeding areas, especially when nesting on marine islands. This limitation was probably the cause of the collapse of breeding by Scarlet Ibises in Trinidad's Caroni Swamp (Bildstein 1990), where an estuarine swamp became salinized through canalization of a major river. White Ibises prefer relatively shallow water depths when feeding (5–15 cm), though often they have been noted feeding on lawns and pastures. Foraging habitats include bottomland hardwood and cypress swamps, river banks, salt marsh meadows, wet prairies, floating vegetated mats, mudflats, mangrove swamps, sawgrass strand edges, hydric hammocks, canal edges, beach flats, and landfills. Ibises feed primarily on aquatic arthropods, especially crayfishes and insects, although small amphibians and reptiles also are commonly taken. Ibises will eat fish when available, but the fish must usually be extremely abundant or vulnerable for ibises to capture them. Although receding water levels in south Florida seem to be critical to the stimulation and success of nesting, this is not necessarily true of breeding in other parts of the range. In coastal South Carolina, White Ibises foraging in riparian bottomlands may nest in larger numbers during years of higher rainfall (Bildstein et al. 1990). Ibises are tactile feeders and forage effectively in turbid waters and in waters with dense vegetation.

Nesting colonies are usually surrounded by water, as this species is quite vulnerable to predation by terrestrial mammals. Ibises tend to nest in shrubby vegetation with moderate shade, although their preferences often include ground nesting on clumps of grasses and in trees to 15 m. White Ibises can travel long distances from colonies to feeding areas; regular trips to sites 30 km away have been associated with successful breeding in several locations.

Foraging and breeding habitat has declined considerably in the last 25 years, both due to the drainage or degradation of wetlands through human encroachment and through manipulation of intact wetlands. While drainage and physical destruction of habitat has been largely discontinued in the state, habitat degradation, encroachment of human development, and water management remain important sources of further habitat degradation.

VULNERABILITY OF SPECIES AND HABITAT: Although breeding populations of White Ibises in Florida are at the moment far above any endangered category, the rapidly declining population trend is extremely serious. The continued decline of over 80% in the Everglades between the 1970s and the 1980s (coming on the heels of 95% declines between the 1940s and the 1970s) is cause for genuine concern, since the Everglades has historically hosted the vast majority of breeding in the state. Statewide surveys reveal possible declines of breeding birds of over 50% in Florida as a whole during the approximately eleven-year period since the late 1970s. During 1990, White Ibises failed to breed in any aggregations of over 1,000 nests in the Carolinas and Georgia, and nearly all of Florida, suggesting that reductions might be occurring regionwide. Whereas breeding and feeding habitat is not in short supply when defined at a landscape level, the quality of foraging habitat seems quite vulnerable to changes in water quality, water management, and ultimately, the abundance and availability of prey species.

CAUSES OF THREAT: Foraging habitat destruction and degradation can result from a variety of causes in Florida. Encroachment and effects of human development on lakesides, wetlands, and rivers seems linked with wetland eutrophication, if not direct physical alteration. Increased human consumption of fresh water and lowering of the water table are, in several areas, linked with salinization of estuaries (e.g., Tampa Bay, Biscayne Bay, Florida Bay) as well as the disappearance of seasonally flooded wetlands. Both processes constitute serious degradation of foraging habitat for ibises, and neither of these effects are regulated directly, or in many cases, even monitored. In the Everglades, compartmentalization of the marsh, artificial manipulation of the normal hydrological cycle, and eutrophication of marsh waters appear to be contributing to large-scale degradation of foraging habitat, probably through reductions in prey densities. Although White Ibises feed mostly on primary and secondary consumers (and so have relatively low potential for bioaccumulation), contamination with residues of pesticides, herbicides, and heavy metals are real dangers, especially as agriculturalized wetland areas become more numerous. Ibises are common foragers at landfills even when feeding chicks, and both adults and young may ingest considerable amounts of toxic substances and refuse as a result.

White Ibises are quite vulnerable to human disturbance during courtship and egg-laying, when they may abandon nesting in large numbers. Unlike other wading bird species, ibis chicks will jump from the nest at an early age (10–18 days), and such behavior appears contagious within the usually synchronous colonies. Colony entry by humans at this stage can result in massive mortality of young due to their inability to regain the nest.

RESPONSES TO HABITAT MODIFICATION: Breeding White Ibises have declined by over 95% in southern Florida as the marshes have become compartmentalized, with marked changes in timing, flows, and distribution of waters. It is suspected that this has resulted most directly from changes in the availability of prey. Within southern Florida, the hydrological patterns in Loxahatchee NWR, and the northern third of Water Conservation Area 3 have appeared to consistently stimulate the largest nesting events in recent years, although even these aggregations are minute compared with the recent past. These two areas are characterized by rapid drying rates during the spring, and colonies are usually in close proximity to long-hydroperiod marshes. In contrast, ibises have almost completely ceased to nest in the estuarine mangrove areas of Everglades National Park, where freshwater flows have been reduced dramatically during the last 30 years.

Over a period of 20 years at Drum Island, in Charleston, South Carolina, ibises have repeatedly moved the colony site to new vegetation as alternate ends of the island have been covered with harbor dredge material. This suggests that some manipulation of colony characteristics are tolerated, when the birds are not stressed by poor food resources and good alternative nesting habitat nearby. Ibises did not nest at the otherwise extremely stable Pumpkinseed Island, South Carolina, site in 1990, possibly due to the effects of Hurricane Hugo on foraging habitat in the previous fall.

DEMOGRAPHIC CHARACTERISTICS: White Ibises attain adult plumage some time during their third year of life, and probably first breed during late spring at the end of the third year (34 months or greater). The probability of nest success (production of at least one young) is quite variable among sites and years, rarely exceeding 80%. Though clutch size ranges from 1 to 4 eggs, nesting attempts rarely bring more than one young to a fledging age. Kushlan (1977b) reported 1.03 young fledged per nest (Everglades), Frederick and

Collopy (1988) reported 0.66–1.09 for the same area, and Shields (1985) reported 0.86 and 1.30 for coastal North Carolina; all are probably generous estimates of recruitment for various reasons. Using all available band recoveries from U.S. bandings, first-year survival is estimated to be less than 30%, and it is estimated that 2.0 young must be produced per nesting attempt for adult and juvenile mortality losses to be met (Frederick, unpubl. data). These calculations, however, use outdated mortality information and may be misleading. One male White Ibis has been recorded breeding at 15 years of age; no greater longevity records were discovered in band-return records.

KEY BEHAVIORS: White Ibises are extremely gregarious and rarely found solitarily. They often feed in dense flocks, moving constantly while feeding. Feeding is accomplished mainly by rapid tactile probing into the substrate while walking; however, visual chasing, and swinging the half-open bill through the water while walking have frequently been recorded. White Ibises often fly in large flocks, characteristically in undulating skeins or V-formations. These birds often soar to and from foraging sites and make spectacular, noisy descents from high altitudes when returning to colony sites. Ibises are strong fliers, usually travelling at over 50 km/hr.

White Ibises establish a pair-bond for breeding, although extra-pair copulations are regularly seen during courtship and egg-laying (Rudegeair 1975). Unlike other colonial species with similar traits, female ibises often cooperate in, rather than protest, the extra-pair copulation attempts. Rarely, female ibises also will attempt to lay eggs in the nests of their neighbors, thereby avoiding the costs of raising the chick. A few male ibises in most colonies apparently specialize in robbing prey from the young in other nests and also have been observed pulling previously regurgitated prey from the crops of unattended young.

Large nesting aggregations of White Ibises often transport considerable quantities of nutrients in the form of guano to colony sites. These nutrients can directly alter the productivity of the waters surrounding the colony. This process can have effects throughout the local food web, with denser aquatic vegetation and fauna found near colony sites. These effects may be particularly dramatic in otherwise oligotrophic freshwater marshes. Bildstein et al. (1990) estimated that a large colony of ibises imported 9% as much nitrogen and 33% as much phosphorus to an estuary than were contributed by atmospheric sources.

CONSERVATION MEASURES TAKEN: White Ibises are currently protected from hunting by both state and federal law. The species is also listed in Florida as a state species of special concern. Since its designation as a species of special concern in Florida, the Florida Game and Fresh Water Fish Commission has instituted a colony monitoring and protection plan for the 100 largest colonies in the state, and has suggested guidelines for human activities and development near colonies. These guidelines carry almost no regulatory authority. Although no conservation activities have been directed specifically at this species, large-scale programs have been initiated to study and restore ecosystem function in the Everglades, Lake Okeechobee, and Kissimmee River. In addition, coastal wetlands and breeding sites have recieved increased protection through a ban on offshore oil drilling.

CONSERVATION MEASURES PROPOSED: The nomadic nesting habits of the White Ibis make population assessments quite difficult without regular surveys of enourmous areas. Since it is difficult to fund these at less than ten-year intervals, dramatic swings in population trend could occur undetected. Surveys should, therefore, be continued on a smaller scale and at shorter intervals. Age-related mortality is poorly understood in this species, but remains a key conservation tool, since it would allow prediction of demographic trends from reproductive success data. Studies of age-related ibis mortality are therefore of high priority as a conservation measure. The primary threat to the species is continued human alteration of wetlands through encroachment, physical alteration, pollution, salinization, and compartmentalization. Increased monitoring of wetland degradation, and restrictions on resource use are, therefore, a clear corollary to the preservation of White Ibis populations in Florida.

LITERATURE CITED:

Allen, R. P. 1934. Inspection trips. Ms. on file, National Audubon Society Res. Dept., Tavernier, Florida.

Bildstein, K. L. 1984. Age-related differences in the foraging behavior of White Ibises and the question of deferred maturity. Colon. Waterbirds 7:146–148.

Bildstein, K. L. 1990. Status, conservation and management of the Scarlet Ibis (*Eudocimus ruber*) in the Caroni Swamp, Trinidad, West Indies. Biol. Cons. 54:61–78.

Bildstein, K. L., Post, W., Frederick, P., and J. Johnston. 1990. Freshwater wetlands, rainfall, and the breeding biology of the White Ibises in coastal South Carolina. Wilson Bull. 102:84–98.

Frederick, P. C., and M. W. Collopy. 1988. Reproductive ecology of wading birds in relation to water conditions in the Florida Everglades. Florida Coop. Fish and Wildl. Res. Unit, Dept. Wild. Range Sci., Univ. Florida. Tech. Report No. 30.

Frederick, P. C., K. L. Bildstein, B. Fleury, and J. C. Ogden. In press. Conservation of large, nomadic populations of White Ibises (*Eudocimus albus*) in the United States. Conserv. Biol.

Johnston, J. W., and K. L. Bildstein. 1990. Dietary salt as a physiological constraint in White Ibises breeding in an estuary. Physiol. Zool. 63:190–207.

Kushlan, J. A. 1977a. Sexual dimorphism in the White Ibis. Wilson Bull. 89:92–98.

Kushlan, J. A. 1977b. Population energetics in the American White Ibis. Auk 94:114–122.

Kushlan, J. A., P.C. Frohring and D. Vorhees. 1984. History and status of wading birds in Everglades National Park. National Park Service report, South Florida Research Center, Everglades National Park, Homestead, Florida.

Ramo, C., and B. Busto. 1982. Son *Eudocimus ruber* y *E. albus* distintos especies? Donana Act. Vertebr. 9:404–408.

Ramo, C., and B. Busto. 1987. Hybridization between the Scarlet ibis (*Eudocimus ruber*) and the White Ibis (*Eudocimus albus*) in Venezuela. Col. Waterbirds 10:111–114.

Rudegeair, T. J., Jr. 1975. The reproductive behavior and ecology of the White Ibis (*Eudocimus albus*). Ph.D. Dissertation, University of Florida, Gainesville, Florida.

Shields, M. A. 1985. An analysis of Fish Crow predation on eggs of the White Ibis at Battery Island, North Carolina. Unpubl. Ph.D. Diss., Univ. North Carolina, Wilmington, N.C.

Spendelow, J. A., and S. R. Patton. 1988. National atlas of coastal waterbird colonies in the contiguous United States: 1976–82. U.S. Fish Wildl. Serv. Biol. Rep. 88(5). 326 pp.

Sprunt, A. Jr. 1922. Discovery of the breeding grounds of the White Ibis in South Carolina. Oologist 39:142–144.

van Wieringen, M., and K. Brouwer. 1990. Morphology and ecology of the Scarlet Ibis (*Eudocimus ruber*) and White Ibis (*E. albus*): a comparative review. In The Scarlet Ibis (*Eudocimus ruber*): status, conservation, and recent research (Frederick, P. C., L. G. Morales, A. L. Spaans, and C. S. Luthin, eds.). International Waterfowl and Wetlands Research Bureau (IWRB), Slimbridge, United Kingdom.

PREPARED BY: Peter C. Frederick, Dept. Wildlife, Ecology and Conservation, P. O. Box 110430, University of Florida, Gainesville, FL 32611.

Cooper's Hawk

Accipiter cooperii

FAMILY ACCIPITRIDAE

Order Falconiformes

TAXONOMY: The Cooper's Hawk (*Accipiter cooperii*) was described in 1828 from a specimen collected near Bordentown, New Jersey (AOU 1957). Cooper's Hawks exhibit a gradual size increase from south to north in eastern North America and from north to south in western North America (Whaley 1988), but these differences in extremes are not great enough to justify subspecies designation (Brown and Amadon 1968; Jones 1979). No close relatives of this monotypic species occur in North America; however, Amadon (1964) and Wattel (1973) regarded the Cooper's Hawk as a member of a superspecies that includes the Bicolored Hawk (*A. bicolor*) of South America and the Cuban Hawk (*A. gundlachi*) of Cuba.

Biogeographically, the Cooper's Hawk and its sister semispecies, the Bicolored Hawk and Cuban Hawk, evolved from a common stock of tropical American *Accipiter*. Wattel (1973) postulated that the ancestors of this tropical American group had a Holarctic distribution and also gave rise to the Eurasian Sparrowhawk (*A. nisus*) and its allies in the Palearctic. The Sharp-shinned Hawk (*A. striatus*), which closely resembles the Cooper's Hawk in plumage color, is actually much more closely related to *A. nisus*. Wattel (1973) further hypothesized that the Sharp-shinned Hawk evolved from a *nisus*-like ancestor that colonized the nearctic long after species from the neotropical *Accipiter* lineage were well established there.

DESCRIPTION: The Cooper's Hawk is a crow-sized accipiter, characterized by short rounded wings, a long rudder-like tail, and relatively long legs (Brown and Amadon 1968; Palmer 1988; Johnsgard 1990). Adults are dark bluish-gray above with white underparts, broadly barred with cinnamon or rufous; their tails are banded black and gray. Females have a brownish cast on the back (Clark and Wheeler 1987; Johnsgard 1990). Immatures are brown above with creamy white underparts finely streaked with dark brown (Clark and Wheeler

Cooper's Hawk, *Accipiter cooperii*. (Photo by Glen M. Wood)

1987; Palmer 1988). Immature Cooper's Hawks have pale yellow or greenish-gray irises that become progressively redder with age. Iris color is typically gray in recent fledglings, gradually changing to greenish-gray, then greenish-yellow. By the second fall, most Cooper's Hawks have light orange eyes, and eye color gradually progresses to scarlet over several years (Snyder and Snyder 1974; Mueller et al. 1981; Palmer 1988). Cooper's Hawks exhibit pronounced sexual dimorphism with females averaging 1.5 to 1.6 times heavier than males (Brown and Amadon 1968; Clark and Wheeler 1987; Palmer 1988). Males range from 37 to 41 cm in length and females are from 42 to 47 cm in length. Male wingspread and weight range from 70 to 77 cm and 302 to 402 g, respectively, compared to females with wingspreads of 79 to 87 cm and body weights of 479 to 678 g (Clark and Wheeler 1987).

The plumages and behavior of the Cooper's Hawk are similar to the smaller Sharp-shinned Hawk (*A. striatus*). There is no size overlap between the two species however, even when comparing the smaller male Cooper's Hawks with the largest female Sharp-shinned Hawks (Snyder 1978; Toland 1984; Clark and Wheeler 1987; Palmer 1988; Johnsgard 1990). Cooper's Hawks are best distinguished from Sharp-shins in flight by their more rounded tail with distinctive white terminal band, longer neck and larger head that extend beyond the wrist of the leading edge of the wing, and faster and more direct flight indicative of higher wing-loading (Toland 1984; Clark and Wheeler 1987; Palmer 1988). Adults of the two accipiters can be differentiated while perching because the Cooper's Hawk exhibits a distinct grayish-white superciliary line and a black cap that contrasts with the slate-gray dorsum. The eyes of Sharp-shinned Hawks are disproportionately larger than those of Cooper's

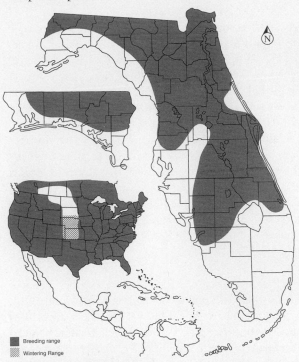

Distribution map of
the Cooper's Hawk,
Accipiter cooperii.

and give the former an almost "bug-eyed" appearance. The eye colors in immature birds are bright lemon yellow in Sharp-shins and greenish-yellow in Cooper's Hawks (Snyder 1978; Toland 1984; Palmer 1988).

POPULATION SIZE AND TREND: Over most of the Cooper's Hawk range in the eastern United States, populations are thought to have declined from the mid-1940s into the early 1970s (Henny and Wight 1972). Population declines are presumed to have resulted from decreased reproductive success due to widespread contamination by the pesticide DDT (Henny and Wight 1972) coupled with increased mortality from cyclodine pesticides like dieldrin (Newton 1979). Standardized counts of autumn migrants indicate that populations began increasing in the mid-1970s following restrictions on the use of organochlorine and cyclodine pesticides (Bednarz et al. 1990). Currently, migrant populations appear to have recovered to pre-DDT era levels (Bednarz et al. 1990). Whether Florida Cooper's Hawks were affected by DDT is unknown; if they were, it is likely that they have recovered. Florida falconers who routinely search for and monitor nesting sites have noticed no substantive changes in abundance or decrease in reproductive success over the past decade (R. Howell, pers. comm.).

Cooper's Hawks are found widely over Florida as migrants in the spring and fall and as winter residents. Systematic statewide surveys have not been conducted for the Cooper's Hawk, thus population trends and size are somewhat speculative. Cooper's Hawks were confirmed breeding in 24, and deemed probable or possible nesters in 136–7.5' topographical quadrangle blocks during Florida's Breeding Bird Atlas effort (H. Kale, pers. comm.), suggesting that breeding Cooper's Hawks are rather sparsely distributed over the interior of the peninsula, as far south as the Lake Placid area (Layne 1986; Kale and Maehr 1990). However, nesting pairs are inconspicuous and easily overlooked; falconers who are adept at finding this species have no trouble locating Cooper's Hawk nests in suitable habitat throughout the northern two-thirds of Florida (R. Howell, pers. comm.). Relatively high nesting densities have been found in some areas where thorough searches have been made. For example, in 1992 two Cooper's Hawk nests that fledged five and three young each, were found in neighboring woodlots less than 1 km apart in Suwannee County (B. Millsap, unpubl. data).

DISTRIBUTION AND HISTORY OF DISTRIBUTION: Cooper's Hawks breed from southern British Columbia, central Alberta, central Saskatchewan, southwestern Ontario, Southern Quebec, Maine, New Brunswick, Prince Edward Island, and Nova Scotia south to Baja California, Chihuahua, Nuevo Leon, southern Texas, Louisiana, central Mississippi, central Alabama, and south Florida (Brown and Amadon 1968; Palmer 1988; Johnsgard 1990). Northern birds are migratory, moving as far south as Mexico, Honduras, Guatemala, and southern Florida (Clark and Wheeler 1987; Palmer 1988).

In Florida, the Cooper's Hawk is found statewide in fall, winter, and spring and as far south as Glades and Lee counties in summer (Snyder 1978; Layne 1986). Cooper's Hawks have been found nesting in suitable habitat throughout this area. The species appears to be most frequent in elevated areas of the interior peninsula (e.g., the Southern Highlands, Brooksville Ridge, Mount Dora Ridge, Lake Wales Ridge), although several nests have been found along the Atlantic Coastal Ridge at Merritt Island, Brevard County, and elsewhere (Layne 1986; Breeding Bird Atlas data; H. Kale, pers. comm.; R. Howell, pers. comm.; S. Wise, pers. comm.). The apparent extension of the breeding range in southern Florida probably is the result of more intensive efforts to locate Cooper's Hawk nests in that area.

HABITAT REQUIREMENTS AND HABITAT TREND: During migration and winter Cooper's Hawks occur in almost any kind of habitat containing trees or shrubs and supporting concentrations of small to medium-sized birds. Nesting Cooper's Hawks prefer broad-leafed, coniferous, or mixed forest with relatively closed canopies and an interspersion of clearings or open habitats (Meng 1951; Hennessey 1978). This species nests in either deciduous or coniferous trees, usually in a densely foliaged individual of the dominant species (Millsap 1981). In Florida, Cooper's Hawks have been found nesting in a variety of habitats, including swamps, floodplain and bottomland forests, sand pine scrub, and baygalls. Whereas some accounts imply the species nests primarily in bottomland forests and swamps, falconers typically search for and find nests in hardwood forests dominated by oaks (*Quercus* spp.) (R. Howell, pers. comm.; B. Millsap, pers. obs.). The nest is placed in the crown of a tree that is close to the forest edge, a natural opening, or manmade clearing that facilitates an unimpeded flyway to the nest (Hennessey 1978; Toland 1985; Layne 1986). In such situations, nests are usually placed in relatively dense stands of moderately young (dbh< 46 cm) live (*Q. virginiana*) or laurel oak (*Q. laurifolia*) adjacent to pines, old fields, streams, marshes, or agricultural fields. Of 10 nest sites visted by Millsap (unpubl. data) in 1992, all were situated within 200 m of at least four different major habitat types. Cooper's Hawks probably have suffered from a loss of old-growth forested habitat in Florida during the 1900s.

RESPONSES TO HABITAT MODIFICATION: During nesting the Cooper's Hawk is quite secretive and rarely tolerates human disturbance in the vicinity of the nest site (Snyder 1978; Toland, pers. observ.). Males show a strong fidelity to traditional territories, and up to six old nests may be concentrated in one favored woodlot (Beebe 1974; Toland, pers. observ.). These individual nesting sites may be used for three or more years in succession by the same individuals (Reynolds and Wight 1978). Thus protection of blocks of forested habitat around the nest site are crucial to the continued survival of nesting Cooper's Hawks in Florida.

DEMOGRAPHIC CHARACTERISTICS: Cooper's Hawks nest from April through July in Florida (Layne 1986; Kale and Maehr 1990). Three to five eggs are laid and incubated for about 32 days, and young fledge at 28 to 34 days of age (Millsap 1981; Palmer 1988). Mean annual productivity is reported to range from 2.0 to 3.0 fledglings per breeding pair (Meng 1951; Hennessey 1978; Millsap 1981; Snyder and Wiley 1976; Reynolds and Wight 1978; Toland unpubl. data), but there are no data for Florida. The percentage of nests in a Cooper's Hawk population that successfully fledge at least one young can range from 50 to 80% (Meng 1951; Craighead and Craighead 1956; Henney and Wight 1972; Hennessey 1978; Reynolds and Wight 1978). Cooper's Hawk nestling sex ratios are even, and there is no differential mortality between the sexes up to the time of fledging (Rosenfield et al. 1985a). Fledglings are dependant on the adults for food for six or seven weeks after leaving the nest (Reynolds and Wight 1978). For a typical nest containing four young, adults deliver an average of six prey items per day for six weeks and feeding rates have been documented at about 0.5 prey items per hour (Snyder and Wiley 1976). Age at first breeding is at least two years for males and most females, although a small percentage of females have been documented nesting in first-year plumage (Reynolds and Wight 1978; Fischer 1986; Toland, pers. observ.).

Annual mortality of immature Cooper's Hawks has been estimated at about 80% (Henny and Wight 1972). Annual adult mortality has been reported as ranging from 34 to 44% (Henny and Wight 1972). Banding recoveries of 136 individuals suggested an average survival age of about 16 months for Cooper's Hawks less than 2 years of age (Palmer 1988). Cooper's Hawk population limiting factors include habitat loss, direct exploitation by irresponsible gun hunters, and predation, primarily by Great Horned Owls (*Bubo virginianus*), raccoons (*Procyon lotor*), and crows (*Corvus* spp.) (Meng 1951; Brown and Amadon 1968; Palmer 1988; Toland, unpubl. data).

KEY BEHAVIORS: The usual flight pattern of the Cooper's Hawk consists of several rapid wingbeats alternating with brief bouts of gliding. However, the Cooper's Hawk exhibits explosive acceleration and reckless abandon when in pursuit of prey through dense vegetation. Typical of accipitrine hawks, the Cooper's Hawk still-hunts from inconspicuous perches from where it launches aerial ambushes at unsuspecting avian quarry. When hunting, these accipiters deploy several stealthy strategies: sudden attack and pursuit from a cryptic perch site; low profile contour-hugging flight that uses trees, bushes, or other visual screens to conceal its approach; midair pursuit of quarry in a tail-chase; power dive or stoop to single out one bird from a flock, and pursuit of quarry into thick vegetation by sprinting on foot (Meng 1951; Beebe 1974; Toland 1986; Palmer 1988; Johnsgard 1990). The preponderance of prey captured by Cooper's Hawks in the eastern United States is avian, ranging from 70 to 90% by frequency of occurrence (Toland 1985; Palmer 1988; Johnsgard 1990). Birds of 50–100 g are most frequently captured, although Cooper's are adept at catching and dispatching avifauna ranging from 15 to 500 g; females take the larger size classes and males select the smaller prey items (Storer 1966; Toland 1985).

The rate of successful prey capture by Cooper's Hawks has been estimated at 30% (Toland 1986). Adult hawks are more successful on a per strike basis than are immature birds, and they also capture larger and more agile animals (Toland 1986). In Florida, Cooper's were successful during 8 of 26 hunting attempts on birds (Toland, unpubl. data). Bird species most frequently taken in Florida include: Blue Jay (*Cyanocitta cristata*), Mourning Dove (*Zenaida macroura*), Rufous-sided Towhee (*Pipilo erythrophthalmus*), Common Ground-Dove (*Columbina passerina*), Common Grackle (*Quiscalus quiscula*), Northern Flicker (*Colaptes auratus*), Red-bellied Woodpecker (*Melanerpes carolinus*),

Red-winged Blackbird (*Agelaius phoeniceus*), Northern Cardinal (*Cardinalis cardinalis*), Brown Thrasher (*Toxostoma rufum*), Northern Mockingbird (*Mimus polyglottos*), Northern Bobwhite (*Colinus virginianus*), and Rock Dove (*Columba livia*) (Layne 1986; Millsap, unpubl. data; Toland, unpubl. data).

The platter-shaped nest, which often appears shaggy around the perimeter, is invariably lined with bark flakes (Palmer 1988; Toland, pers. observ.). Most of the nest construction is performed by the male Cooper's Hawk (Meng 1951; Rosenfield and Bielefeldt 1991). Nests are typically placed in a major fork or next to the tree trunk at heights ranging from 10 to 15 m above the ground (Toland 1985; Layne 1986). Nest trees are usually in close proximity to forest edge, along trails, roads, or clearings, or at other natural or manmade openings such as stream or lake edges (Palmer 1988; Johnsgard 1990). Copulation occurs several times daily during the nest-building and egg-laying phases of breeding (Meng 1951; Palmer 1988). This typically follows an early morning period of vocal duetting by the nesting pair that may last up to an hour (Palmer 1988; Toland, pers. observ.).

Cooper's Hawks require relatively large home ranges estimated from 100 to 400 ha, averaging about 250 ha (Meng 1951; Craighead and Craighead 1956; Fitch 1958; Toland, unpubl. data). Much of this area is defended by emitting a staccatto "ca ca ca ca" protest vocalization or actively chasing away conspecifics, other hawks, owls, and crows. Cooper's Hawks may aggressively defend the nest tree from threatening humans and other mammals and are reported to administer painful blows to the head with their talons (Palmer 1988).

CONSERVATION MEASURES TAKEN: The Cooper's Hawk, and its nests and eggs, are protected by Florida Game and Fresh Water Fish Commission rules (Chapter 39, Florida Administrative Code) and federal rules promulgated under the Migratory Bird Treaty Act (16 U.S.C. 703–712).

CONSERVATION MEASURES PROPOSED: Past widespread declines in Cooper's Hawk populations appear to have been arrested through restrictions on the use of chlorinated hydrocarbon and cyclodine pesticides. Populations appear to have recovered to near historic population levels, where comparative data are available (e.g., Bednarz et al. 1990). Currently, Cooper's Hawks are widespread and probably more common as a breeding species than generally believed. Accordingly, it is questionable whether or not they warrant continued listing as a species of special concern. Because Cooper's Hawks exhibit high nest-site fidelity, increased emphasis should be placed on locating and protecting nesting habitat. Nest occupancy and breeding productivity should be monitored annually at a sample of Cooper's Hawk territories statewide. Nesting pairs can be located by implementing systematic morning auditory surveys that use tape recorded vocalizations of conspecifics or Great Horned Owls (Rosenfield et al. 1985b). Important nesting areas, roost sites, and associated foraging habitats should be identified and protected, buffered from disturbance, or acquired into public ownership through whatever means are necessary. Habitat preservation for Cooper's Hawks in Florida is contingent on protecting blocks of preferred woodland nesting habitats of from 50 to several hundred acres, and protecting them from human disturbance from March through June.

ACKNOWLEDGMENTS: We appreciate the unpublished data on nest sites contributed by R. Howell. J. Rodgers provided constructive editorial improvements to the manuscript.

LITERATURE CITED:

AOU. 1957. Checklist of North American birds. 5th Ed. American Ornithologists' Union, Washington D.C. Novit, no. 2166.

Bednarz, J. C. 1990. Migration counts of raptors at Hawk Mountain, Pennsylvania, as indicators of population trends, 1934–1986. Auk 107:96–109.

Beebe, F. L. 1974. Field studies of the falconiformes of British Columbia. Occas. Papers British Columbia Prov. Mus. 17. 163 pp.

Brown, L., and D. Amadon. 1968. Eagles, hawks, and falcons of the world. McGraw Hill, New York. 945 pp.

Clark, W. S., and B. K. Wheeler. 1987. Hawks. Houghton Mifflin Co. Boston, Massachusetts.

Craighead, J. J., and F. C. Craighead. 1956. Hawks, owls, and wildlife. Stackpole Co., Harrisburg, Pennsylvania. 443 pp.

Fischer, D. L. 1986. Daily activity patterns and habitat use of coexisting accipiter hawks in Utah. Ph.D. diss. Brigham Young Univ., Provo, Utah.

Fitch, H. S. 1958. Home ranges, territories, and seasonal movements of vertebrates in Kansas. Univ. Kansas Mus. Nat. Hist. 12:505–519.

Henny, C. J., and H. M. Wight. 1972. Population ecology and environmental pollution: Red-tailed and Cooper's hawks. Pp. 229–250 in Population ecology of migratory birds. U. S. Fish and Wildl. Serv., Wildl. Res. Rept. no 2. 278 pp.

Hennessey, S. P. 1978. Ecological relationships of accipiters in northern Utah-with special emphasis on the effects of human disturbance. M.S. thesis, Utah State Univ., Logan, Utah. 66 pp.

Johnsgard, P. A. 1990. Hawks, eagles, and falcons of North America. Smithsonian Inst. Press. Washington D. C.

Jones, S. 1979. Habitat management series for unique or endangered species. The accipiters-Goshawk, Cooper's Hawk, Sharp-shinned Hawk. U.S. Bur. Land Manag., Tech. Note 17. 51 pp.

Kale, H. W., II, and D. S. Maehr. 1990. Florida's birds. Pineapple Press, Sarasota, Florida.

Layne, J. N. 1986. Observations on Cooper's Hawk nesting in south central Florida. Fla. Field Nat. 14: 85–95.

Meng, H. K. 1951. The Cooper's Hawk. Ph.D. diss., Cornell Univ., Ithaca, New York. 216 pp.

Millsap, B. A. 1981. Distributional status of falconiformes in west-central Arizona with notes on ecology, reproductive success, and management. U.S. Dept. Int., Bur. Land Manag. Tech. Note 355. 102 pp.

Mueller, H. C., D. D. Berger, and G. Allez. 1981. Age, sex, and seasonal differences in size of Cooper's Hawks. Jour. Field Ornithol. 52:112–126.

Newton, I. 1979. Population ecology of raptors. Buteo Books, Vermillion, South Dakota.

Palmer, R. S. (ed.) 1988. Handbook of North American Birds. Vol. 4., Part 1, Diurnal raptors. Yale Univ. Press, New Haven, Connecticut.

Reynolds, R. T., and H. M. Wight. 1978. Distribution, density, and productivity of accipiter hawks breeding in Oregon. Wilson Bull. 90:182–196.

Rosenfield, R. N., J. Bielefeldt, and W. A. Smith. 1985a. Sex ratios in broods of Cooper's Hawks. Wilson Bull. 97:113–115.

Rosenfield, R. N., J. Bielefeldt, R. K. Anderson, and W. A. Smith. 1985b. Taped calls as an aid in locating Cooper's Hawk nests. Wildl. Soc. Bull. 13:62–63.

Rosenfield, R. N., and J. Bielefeldt. 1991. Reproductive investment and anti-predator behavior in Cooper's Hawks during the pre-laying period. Jour. Raptor Res. 25:113–115.

Snyder, H. A. 1978. Cooper's Hawk. Pp 85–86 in Rare and endangered biota of Florida. Vol. 2. Birds. (Kale, H. W., II, ed.) Univ. Presses Florida, Gainesville, Florida.

Snyder, N. F. R., and H. A. Snyder. 1974. Function of eye coloration in North American accipiters. Condor 76:219–222.

Snyder, N. F. R., and J. W. Wiley. 1976. Sexual size dimorphism in hawks and owls of North America. Amer. Ornithol. Union Ornithol. Monogr. No. 20.

Storer, R. W. 1966. Sexual dimorphism and food habits in three North American accipiters. The Auk 83:423–436.

Toland, B. R. 1984. Observations of the Cooper's Hawk and other accipiters in central Missouri. The Bluebird 51:25–32.

Toland, B. R. 1985. Food habits and hunting success of Cooper's Hawks in Missouri. Jour. Field Ornithol. 56:419–422.

Toland, B. R. 1986. Hunting success of some Missouri raptors. Wilson Bull. 98:116–125.

Wattel, J. 1973. Geographical differentiation in the genus *Accipiter*. Publ. Nuttal Ornithol. Club, no. 13.

Whaley, W. 1988. Trends in geographic variation of Cooper's Hawk and Northern Goshawk: a multivariate analysis. Ph.D. diss. Brigham Young Univ., Provo, Utah.

PREPARED BY: Brian R. Toland, Florida Game and Fresh Water Fish Commission, 110–43rd Ave., S.W., Vero Beach, FL 32962 (Current address: U.S. Fish and Wildlife Service, P.O. Box 2676, Vero Beach, FL 32961–2676; and Brian A. Millsap, Florida Game and Fresh Water Fish Commission, 620 South Meridian St., Tallahassee, FL 32399.

Limpkin

Aramus guarauna

FAMILY ARAMIDAE

Order Gruiformes

TAXONOMY: The Limpkin (*Aramus guarauna*) is so unusual that it has undergone at least 19 versions of classification since it was first described by Linnaeus in 1766 (Ingalls 1972). From 1854 it has been classified as monotypic in the Aramidae (Peters 1934); however, recent DNA comparisons prompted the Limpkin to be speculatively grouped with the sungrebe Family Heliornithidae (Sibley and Monroe 1990). The Limpkin is represented by four or five subspecies (Ridgway and Friedmann 1941; Palmer in Thomson 1964), with *A.g.pictus* occurring in the southeastern United States, Cuba, and Jamaica (Ridgway and Friedmann 1941).

The Limpkin is described as having characteristics and habits of both cranes (Gruidae) and rails (Rallidae). Closer relations to the rails are suggested by osteology, morphology of the bill and feet, and bird lice phylogeny; and to the cranes by feather pattern, musculature, and skull morphology (reviewed by Sibley and Ahlquist 1972). The recent DNA analysis favors the cranes (Sibley and Ahlquist 1990).

DESCRIPTION: The Limpkin is perhaps best described as a "big, brown rail-like bird" (Bent 1926); a heron-sized wader with a long neck, bill, and legs. The uniform, deep brown color exhibits a bronze iridescence and is flecked with white markings. Adults and juveniles have a slightly rusty cap and brown eyes. The bill is brownish-yellow at the base, grading to whitish-brown, and then to blackish-brown at the tip. Legs and feet also are blackish-brown. Measured specimens are 69.8–71.1 cm (27–28 in.) in length, with wing 33.0 cm (13 in.), tarsus 11.0–11.4 cm (4 in.), and bill 10.8–11.4 cm (4 in.) (Cory 1896; Chapman 1920). Wingspread is 107 cm (42 in.) (Terres 1982). The average weight for four adult males and females from Leon and Lake Counties was 1.24 kg (2.7 lbs.) and 1.08 kg (2.4 lbs.), respectively (Bryan 1981). There was a slight overlap in weights of the lightest male and heaviest female. Thirty-

Limpkin, *Aramus guarauna*. (Photo by Dana C. Bryan)

one unsexed adults in Marion County averaged 1.08 kg (2.4 lbs.) (Nesbitt et al. 1976).

Readily visible feathers, except the wing and tail feathers, have a wide white streak along the shaft that narrows to a point at the end of the feather. The overlapping of these feathers creates bright white triangles which are most prominent on the wing coverts. The wing covert triangles can be used in the field both to sex most adults and to distinguish grown first-year juveniles from adults (Bryan, pers. observ.). From a side view, adult female wing triangles typically look uniformly sized and relatively small. Male triangles appear larger and more prominent, and usually include one or more long triangles on the greater upper wing coverts, which are typically not visable in the female's folded wing. Juveniles can be distinguished up to their first pre-nuptial molt by streaked, not triangular, wing markings.

The long, slightly decurved mandible is notable because of a bend to the right in the last 2 cm or so, probably because of frequent blows and insertions into the Limpkin's preferred food, the right-handed apple snail (*Pomacea paludosa*) (Chapman 1920; Snyder and Snyder 1969). Downy young do not have the bend (Snyder and Snyder 1969; Bryan, pers. observ.), and the underlying bone of adults is usually not curved (Snyder and Snyder 1969). Also, the very tip of the mandible is twisted almost horizontally and sharpened against the tip of the maxilla (Bryan, pers. obs.). This knife-like distal end is used to wedge under the snail operculum and cut the attaching muscle.

POPULATION SIZE AND TREND: No historic or contemporary statewide population estimates of Limpkins have ever been published. Earliest accounts claim the Limpkin was common on the St. Johns River and abundant on the

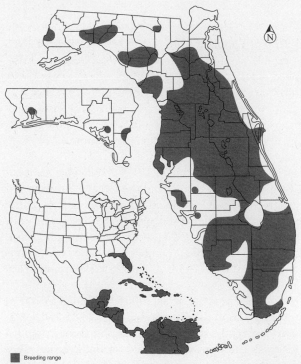

Distribution map
of the Limpkin,
Aramus guarauna.

■ Breeding range

Wekiva River (Bryant 1859) and also common around the grassy lakes and waterways from Lake Dexter southward (Allen 1871). However, Bent (1926) noted that by 1902, after a 40-year steady decline, Limpkins had practically disappeared from all areas easily visited. Its rarity prompted searches that recorded only 11 in a 3-day trip on the Oklawaha River in 1921, 41 in a 5-day trip on the Kissimmee River in 1923 (Pearson in Bent 1926), 1 along 8 miles of the Wekiva River in March, 1925, and 3 on the Weekiwachee River in mid-April (Bent 1926). Pearson (in Bent 1926) describes being told by locals that Limpkins were commonly shot for food.

In addition to hunting pressures on the Limpkin, wetlands drainage also reduced local populations, especially those of the Everglades, particularly around Okaloacoochee Slough, the southwestern shore of Lake Okeechobee, and on the eastern edge of the Everglades, west of Palm Beach (Howell 1932). Limpkins were also reduced in the lower Everglades south of the Tamiami Trail (Hall 1950).

Populations had increased by 1951 when Nicholson surveyed the St. Johns River marshes by airboat and found 250 Limpkin nests, including 76 in one day (Sprunt 1954). By 1954 Florida population strongholds were said to be at Wakulla Springs and the Kissimmee River Valley down to the west shore of Lake Okeechobee (Sprunt 1954). Sprunt (1954) also noted a building population in the Everglades around Paradise Key. Lake Okeechobee reportedly had an estimated 8,000–10,000 Limpkins in the late 1970s (Graham 1978). Long trends are not discernible from the National Audubon Society Christmas Bird Counts compiled since 1946 (Bryan, unpubl. data). Two count circles, St. Marks (Wakulla Springs) and West Palm Beach (Loxahatchee National Wildlife Refuge), dominate the numbers, yet both have historically shown large fluctuations, explained respectively by dredge-and-spoil activity (F. Fagan, pers. comm.) and drought (H. Langridge, pers. comm.).

DISTRIBUTION AND HISTORY OF DISTRIBUTION: The Limpkin ranges from southern Georgia, through Florida and the Greater Antilles, and from southern Mexico south through Central and South America to central Argentina. In the United States, the Limpkin probably breeds rarely in southeastern Georgia (Burleigh 1958; Hopkins 1975), occasionally ranging north to the Altamaha River at Darien (Hall 1950). Limpkins are noted as vagrants in many southeastern states (Oberholser 1938; Allen 1961; Wiley and Wiley 1976).

The Florida Breeding Bird Atlas project (Bryan 1995) resulted in a detailed map of the Limpkin's breeding season distribution between 1986 and 1991. The winter distribution is apparently very similar, judging from compiled Christmas Bird Count records. The distribution based on the Breeding Bird Atlas generally is very spotty throughout the panhandle and north Florida but widespread throughout the rest of the state. In the western panhandle, atlas sightings over the six years occurred only in single quadrangles (about 2,500 ha) in Bay, Gulf, and Liberty Counties. A Holmes County record also has been reported (Walkinshaw 1982). The atlas' western-most confirmed breeding record occurred in Wakulla County, where the Wakulla Springs population is large (the CBC recorded between 20 and 41 individuals in each of the last 10 years) and typically stable (Limpkins have been seen in the last 45 annual counts). On the peninsula, the population becomes more or less continuous from Levy, Alachua, and Putnam counties to southernmost Florida, excluding the Florida Keys. The current distribution is probably comparable to that of the early nineteenth century, except for the areas of Everglades that have undergone conversion to agriculture. Limpkin populations and their distribution have apparently recovered from the era of overhunting.

HABITAT REQUIREMENTS AND HABITAT TRENDS: The apple snail appears to be the most important habitat requirement of Limpkins, as their distributions are almost identical (Harper 1936). Limpkins are found along the wide and well-vegetated shallows of rivers and streams statewide, as well as around lakes in peninsular Florida and in the marshes, broad swales, strand swamps, sloughs, and impoundments in south Florida. Much natural riparian habitat has been reduced or degraded by human activities, including agricultural conversion, river channelization, wetland drainage, aquifer and surface water depletion, and the introduction of exotic aquatic plants. While the steady trend of habitat loss has certainly slowed considerably, piecemeal conversion and the spread of exotic plants continue.

Nests are built in an impressively wide variety of situations. These include on piles of slowly-sinking aquatic vegetation, among tall marsh grasses, especially bulrush (*Scirpus* spp.), between the knees of bald cypress (*Taxodium distichum*), in vine-covered shrubs, in the tops of sabal palms (*Sabal palmetto*), and on high cypress branches. An abandoned Osprey nest also was recorded to have been used and a cypress tree cavity 30 feet high was used by one individual for several years (Bryan 1992). In all these sites any usable material is pulled from nearby or, rarely, carried to construct the piled or crudely woven nest.

VULNERABILITY OF SPECIES AND HABITAT: Shooting has proven to be capable of almost extirpating Limpkins from Florida. The Limpkin's widespread distribution into very inaccessible wetland habitats protected it then, and will also protect it from most local wetland conversions and disturbances by humans. Consequently, the Limpkin's apparent dependence on the apple snail is its chief vulnerability. The Limpkin will probably remain locally common wherever apple snails are abundant.

CAUSES OF THREAT: Because apple snails depend on freshwater abundance and quality for the health of their forage plants and their own physiological needs, altered hydrology, pollution, and exotic plant proliferation are the notable threats to snail populations. Of the three, only the last needs further explanation. Throughout Florida, exotic aquatic plants are rapidly replacing the native eelgrasses (*Vallisneria americana* and *Sagittaria kurziana*), which are important forage plants for the apple snail. One of the biggest problems is water hyacinth (*Eichhornia crassipes*), which floats in large mats that shade and kill submerged plants. Subsequent frost-kill, wind-drift, or herbiciding of the water hyacinth leaves large expanses of barren riverbottom, which do not support apple snails (Bryan 1981). Furthermore, the direct effects of herbicides on snails also may be a problem; a great increase in emergent apple snail egg clutches and Limpkins along sections of Alexander Springs Creek was noted after 1970 when the herbiciding of water hyacinth during snail egg-laying season had ceased (R. G. Sheppard, pers. comm. in Ingalls 1972). Other rooted exotics, like hydrilla (*Hydrilla verticillata*) and Brazilian elodea (*Egeria densa*), crowd out the eelgrasses. Yet despite the widespread establishment of exotics, their effects on snail distributions are not clear; apple snails eat water hyacinth (Talbot in Perry 1974) and perhaps other exotics, as well. Wakulla Springs has largely been taken over by elodea, but there has been no recent Limpkin decline (Bryan, pers. obs.). Potential exotic threats include any new apple snail disease or exotic predator of the snails, which might quickly threaten the Limpkin as well.

Because the Limpkin apparently depends on apple snails, at least to establish permanent breeding sites, competition for snails may occasionally be a problem. Apple snails are important food for young American alligators (*Alligator mississippiensis*) (Fogarty and Albury 1967), Snail Kites (*Rostrhamus sociabilis*), and Boat-tailed Grackles (*Quiscalus major*) (Snyder and Snyder 1969). Snail Kites have been known to steal snails from Limpkins in drought situations (Miller and Tilson 1985); however, they normally prey on different snail size classes and apparently do not directly compete for food (Bourne 1983).

Minor and local threats such as nest loss to raccoons (*Procyon lotor*), possibly crows (*Corvus* spp.), and windstorms have been described also (Walkinshaw 1982) and flooding occasionally inundates nests (Bryan, pers. observ.). Also, downy young and juveniles can be subject to heavy or even complete predation, as occurred to the first four broods (totaling 26 chicks) at Wakulla Springs in 1979 (Bryan, unpubl. data). The specific predators or other circumstances causing the high mortality are not known. Lastly, simple increased human presence in or near Limpkin habitat also will predictably eliminate some breeding sites.

RESPONSES TO HABITAT MODIFICATION: Limpkins are known to acclimate to some human disturbance, e.g., nearby human habitation and close approach by humans and boats (Walkinshaw 1982; Bryan, pers. observ.). Also, Limpkins have been documented to move when resources are depleted (Cruickshank 1978; Walkinshaw 1982; H. Langridge, pers. comm.). Population influxes or rapid growth can be dramatic in some circumstances; for example, an 8-year population boom that occurred at Wakulla Springs was thought to have been started by the creation of long spoil piles from the dredging of boat channels in 1968–69. The spoil piles increased foraging habitat (wadable edge) and also dredged up so many snails and mussels that an abundance of Limpkins congregated (F. Fagan, pers. comm.). The Christmas Bird Count population soared from a typical 11 in 1967, to 69 in 1968, 94 in 1972, down to 45 in 1975, and 18 in 1976.

DEMOGRAPHIC CHARACTERISTICS: Egg-laying by Limpkins typically occurs from late January through March in central Florida (Walkinshaw 1982), and late February through May in north Florida (Bryan, unpubl. data); however, breeding may occur as late as October (Walkinshaw 1982). An elderly

Everglades guide reported that when the Everglades were formerly full of water, Limpkins began nesting in November and December (Sprunt 1954).

Limpkins commonly lay second clutches and occasionally third clutches (Bryan 1981). Some observers report that 5 or 6 eggs are typical (Davie 1898; Harrison 1975), whereas others claim clutches of 6 or 7 eggs are typical (Nicholson 1928; Bryan 1992). The discrepancy may in part be due to first-year birds usually having clutches of 4 or 5 eggs (Bryan, unpubl. data). Clutch size averaged 4.9 eggs (n = 11 clutches) when nesting age was not noted (Walkinshaw 1982). Nicholson (1928) reported two nests with 8 eggs and Chandler once saw 9 eggs (Walkinshaw 1982). The oval eggs are buff-colored, blotched and streaked with brown, and average 60 x 44 mm (2.4x1.8 in.) (Harrison 1975). The duration of incubation for 4 completed clutches at Fort Pierce was 26, 27, 27, and 28 days; all eggs hatched within 18–24 hours (Walkinshaw 1982). The precocial young leave the nest immediately after all eggs have hatched and are led to a new nursery location, usually a platform built of aquatic vegetation (Ingalls 1972). Juveniles lose the last of their down by the fifth week and fly at 6–7 weeks (Ingalls 1972). Both males and females breed successfully at the end of their first year, although unsuccessful pair-bonds and desertions sometimes occur on the first nesting attempt (Bryan 1981).

KEY BEHAVIORS: Limpkins can be secretive or extremely loud and prominent. Although appearing somewhat awkward, they are strong fliers, fast runners, and good, although infrequent, swimmers. Limpkins sometimes forage at night and exhibit eye-shine. Nicholson (1928) reports a Broken-wing display. A sickle-shaped outermost primary feather can produce a moderately loud, buzzing winnow (Ingalls 1972), which is used day and night apparently in territorial behavior (Bryan 1981).

Apple snails are the chief food of Limpkins, although mussels and other species of aquatic snails also are regularly eaten (Cottam 1936). Limpkins forage by sight and touch when wading on the bottom or by walking on dense mats of floating vegetation. They deftly extract the mollusks on the nearest supportive surface, leaving a characteristic scatter of empty shells.

Male limpkins give two loud call types (Bryan 1981). "Kreow" calls are given territorially, usually in a series of 4–10 vocalizations, at a uniform rate of 1 call per 1.8 seconds. "Kow" calls are used primarily in the breeding season by unpaired territorial males as solicitation for females. The vocalization is given at a uniform rate of about 1 call per second. While series of 4–8 calls are usually given, up to 80 consecutive calls have been counted (Bryan 1981). Females are often silent but have a single common call described as "gon" by Bryan (1981) or "kleow" (Ingalls 1972). When heard alone, it is usually as a single or double call. However, when a paired male starts a typical series of "kreow" or "kow" calls, the female often immediately joins in antiphonal calls, creating a distinct duet (Bryan 1981). Other adult vocalizations include alarm and challenge calls, rattles, clucks, and guttural sounds (Ingalls 1972; Bryan, unpubl. sonograms). Juveniles give "wheeee-ah" and "wheep" calls for feeding (Ingalls 1972).

The Limpkin's riparian habitats are subdivided into abutting exclusive territories arranged linearly when along rivers and lake edges. At Wakulla Springs, measured territory sizes varied widely, from an average of 0.78 ha, during a high population year (Ingalls 1972), to an average of 3.8 ha during a more typical year (Bryan 1981). Neighboring males rarely cross established boundaries; one banded juvenile male assumed his natal territory at Wakulla Springs and was censused there regularly for 12 years before disappearing (record longevity). In that time, he was never once seen outside the territory (Bryan, unpubl. data). Territories are defended with ritualistic Counter-calling, Counter-positioning, Charging/Retreating displays, occasional Feet-fighting, as well as with chasing and displacing flights (Bryan 1981). Long flights with "kreow" calls are the most common territorial behavior in the nesting season, when males challenge neighbors at territorial boundaries and chase nonterritorial birds who fly into their territories.

Pair-bonding behavior includes courtship feeding, wherein the male locates and extracts snails for the female (Ingalls 1972). Nest-building is generally initiated by the male, who may build partial nests before pair bonding. The female usually contributes to final nest-building, and the pair shares almost all other aspects of nesting and care of the young (Ingalls 1972). Only females incubate between dusk and dawn (Bryan 1981).

Color-banded pairs have been shown to have endured over two breeding seasons and the period in between, although such pair-bond longevity may occur only in relatively high-quality territories (Bryan 1981). Females stay entirely within the territories of their mates during courtship, incubation, and downy young stages. However, from 1–5 weeks after the downy stage, females often begin to forage and rest in distant parts of the territory, leaving the male to care for the young alone (Bryan 1981). Some females engage in serial polyandry, deserting their first mate and brood and mating with an unpaired territorial neighbor who is still giving repetitive "kow" calls (Bryan 1981). The notoriety of night-calling during breeding season (Nicholson 1928) as well as actual censuses (Bryan 1981) indicate that typically there are more territorial males than breeding females in good habitat.

Juveniles spend about 10 weeks in a close group, while they are still fed by the parent(s). Thereafter, male juveniles become the subject of increasing parental aggression, leave the group to feed independently, and assume a stable subterritory within the parents' territory. Female juveniles, in contrast, range throughout the parents' territory and forage and rest longer near the parents (Bryan 1981). Dispersal of juveniles from the parents' territory usually occurs at 15–17 weeks of age, after further parent and neighbor harassment. Often juveniles assume the territories of parents who disappear (Bryan 1981).

Large concentrations and seasonal movements of Limpkins occasionally have been reported. Pearson (1936) describes the gathering of thousands of Limpkins in the autumn and winter around the headwaters of the Caloosahatchee River, west of Lake Okeechobee. Whereas drought was not mentioned by Pearson (1936), it causes such concentrations today: more than 1,200 Limpkins gathered in Moonshine Bay (southwest Lake Okeechobee) in 1990 (J. Rodgers, pers. comm.). In 1961 severe drought in the Lake Worth area concentrated many Limpkins along canals, even in populated areas (H. Langridge, pers. comm.). Also, during a winter drought along the St. Johns River in 1970–71, several dozen Limpkins moved to Merritt Island and scores were seen from Georgiana north to Volusia County (Cruickshank 1978). A loose, but distinct, flock of 100 Limpkins was observed in the Horseshoe Head area of the Everglades (Broward County) during a nondrought situation in January 1994 (D. Bryan, pers. observ.). Several similarly sized, but more closely grouped, flocks were seen in the same area in December 1994 (R. Bennetts, pers. comm.).

Limpkins are typically treated as nonmigratory (e.g., Terres 1982). Although Allen (1961) states that Limpkins "apparently" migrate between Cuba and Florida, and ". . .migrating Limpkins frequently occur on the Florida Keys." Others describe Limpkins in the Keys and the Dry Tortugas as wandering (Bent 1926) or vagrant (Sibley and Ahlquist 1990). Nevertheless, a partial migration was documented with color-banded Limpkins at Alexander Springs (Lake County) and Wakulla Springs (Wakulla County) (Bryan 1981). Most females deserted their mates' year-round territories after their last broods and disappeared from mid-summer until mid-winter. At that time they returned to the same breeding territories and subsequently mated again in the second year. The destination of the migrating birds was unknown. When the females were absent from their breeding grounds, there were no other arrivals, indicating the female migrants did not simply become nonterritorial floaters in the same habitats. A few males holding low-quality territories similarly disappeared, and a very few females on high-quality territories remained, suggesting that migration from breeding sites is related to food availability.

CONSERVATION MEASURES TAKEN: No significant conservation measures have been taken for the Limpkin, except for historic wading bird anti-shooting campaigns and general bird protection legislation. The Limpkin is listed as a Species of Special Concern by FGFWFC (Wood 1991). The Florida Natural Areas Inventory lists it as G5 and S3 in their global and state element ranks. Field research has included efforts by FGFWFC to band and wing-tag Limpkins on the Oklawaha River, resulting in 6 subsequent sightings that documented movement up to 260 km (161 mi) (Nesbitt 1978). Limpkin breeding biology, ontogeny, ecology, and ethology are all well described (Snyder and Snyder 1969; Ingalls 1972; Bryan 1981; Walkinshaw 1982). Limpkins presumably have benefited indirectly from hydrological restoration and water management actions undertaken for other purposes, for example, Snail Kite (*Rostrhamus sociabilis*) management and initial Everglades and Kissimmee River restoration efforts.

CONSERVATION MEASURES PROPOSED: Protection of wetland habitats for Limpkins through zoning and restrictions on drainage and conversion will be necessary to maintain their current populations. Freshwater quality should be protected by documenting and monitoring pollution sources, recharge areas, and flow patterns. Restoration of natural wetlands also will potentially add habitat. Apple snail populations should be examined for their value in measuring and monitoring the health of Florida's freshwater wetlands. Implementation of biological control and other treatments for exotic aquatic plant populations is needed to protect native habitat for the apple snail. Statewide censusing of Limpkins to determine regional and statewide populations also would be valuable, including trying to replicate some specific census efforts like Nicholson's in 1951 (Sprunt 1954) and the Florida Breeding Bird Atlas. Limpkin migration should be further investigated to ensure that any nonbreeding season concentrations are adequately protected.

ACKNOWLEDGMENTS: I thank Tall Timbers Research Station and the Edward Ball Wildlife Foundation for their support of my Limpkin research from 1979 to 1981.

LITERATURE CITED:

Allen, J. A. 1871. On the mammals and winter birds of east Florida. Bull. Mus. Comp. Zool., Harvard Univ. II(3):362.

Allen, R. P. 1961. Birds of the Caribbean. Viking Press, New York. 256 pp.

Bent, A. C. 1926. Life histories of North American marsh birds. Smithsonian Inst., U.S. Nat. Mus. 135:254–259.

Bourne, G. R. 1983. Snail kite feeding ecology: some correlates and tests of optimal foraging. Unpubl. Ph.D. dissertation, Univ. of Michigan, Ann Arbor, Michigan. 119 pp.

Bryan, D. C. 1981. Territoriality and pairbonding in the Limpkin (*Aramus guarauna*). Unpubl. M.S. thesis. Florida State Univ., Tallahassee, Florida. 62 pp.

Bryan, D. C. 1995. Limpkin. In Atlas of the breeding birds of Florida (H. W.

Kale II, ed.). Fla. Audubon Soc. and Fla. Game and Fresh Water Fish Comm., in prep.

Bryant, H. 1859. Birds of east Florida. Proc. Boston Soc. Nat. Hist. 7:5–21.

Burleigh, T. D. 1958. Georgia birds. Univ. of Oklahoma Press, Norman, Oklahoma. 746 pp.

Chapman, F. M. 1920. Handbook of birds. D. Appleton and Co., New York, New York. 530 pp.

Cory, C. B. 1896. Water birds of Florida. Bradlee Whidden, Boston, Massachusetts. 172 pp.

Cottam, C. 1936. Food of the Limpkin. Wilson Bull. 48:11–13.

Cruickshank, A. D. 1978. The Birds of Brevard County, Florida. Privately published. 204 pp.

Davie, O. 1898. Nests and eggs of North American birds. Landon Press, Columbus, Ohio. 509 pp.

Fogarty, M. J., and J. D. Albury. 1967. Late summer foods of young alligators in Florida. Proc. Conf. S.E. Assoc. Game & Fish Comm. 21:220–222.

Graham, F., Jr. 1978. The Audubon ark. Audubon Mag. 80:2–172.

Hall, H. M. 1950. Wakulla Limpkins. Audubon Mag. 52:308–314.

Harper, F. 1936. The distribution of the Limpkin and its staple food. Oriole 1:21–23.

Harrison, H. H. 1975. Field guide to birds' nests. Houghton Mifflin Co., Boston, Massachusetts. 257 pp.

Hopkins, M. N., Jr. 1975. The birdlife of Ben Hill County, Georgia and adjacent natural areas. Occas. Publ. No. 5. Georgia Ornithol. Soc. 93 pp.

Howell, A. H. 1932. Florida bird life. Fla. Dept. Game and Fresh Water Fish Comm. and U.S. Bur. Biol. Surv. Coward-McCann, New York. 579 pp.

Ingalls, E. A. 1972. Aspects of the ethology of Limpkins (*Aramus guarauna*). Unpubl. M.S. thesis, Univ. of South Florida, Tampa, Florida. 131 pp.

Miller, B. W., and R. L. Tilson. 1985. Snail kite kleptoparasitism of Limpkins. Auk 102:170–171.

Nesbitt, S. A. 1978. Limpkin. Pp. 86–88 in Rare and endangered biota of Florida. Vol. II. Birds. (H. W. Kale II, ed.). Univ. Press Fla., Gainesville, Florida. 121 pp.

Nesbitt, S. A., D. T. Gilbert, and D. B. Barbour. 1976. Capturing and banding Limpkins in Florida. Bird-Banding 47:164–165.

Nicholson, D. J. 1928. Habits of the Limpkin in Florida. Auk 45:305–309.

Oberholser, H. C. 1938. The bird life of Louisiana. Dept. Conser., New Orleans, Louisiana. 834 pp.

Pearson, T. G. 1936. Birds of America. Doubleday, Garden City, New York. 271 pp.

Perry, M. C. 1974. Ecological studies of the apple snail at Lake Woodruff National Wildlife Refuge. Fla. Sci. 36:22–30.

Peters, J. L. 1934. Check-list of birds of the world. Vol. 2. Harvard Univ. Press, Cambridge, Massachusetts. 15 vol.

Ridgway, R., and H. Friedmann. 1941. The birds of North and Middle America. Smithsonian Inst., U.S. Nat. Mus., Bulletin 50-IX. Washington, D.C.

Sibley, C. G., and B. L. Monroe, Jr. 1990. Distribution and taxonomy of birds of the world. Yale Univ. Press, New Haven, Connecticut.

Sibley, C. G., and J. E. Ahlquist. 1972. A comparative study of the egg white proteins of non-passerine birds. Peabody Mus. Nat. Hist. 39:114–126.

Sibley, C. G., and J. E. Ahlquist. 1990. Phylogeny and classification of birds. Yale Univ. Press, New Haven.

Snyder, N. F. R., and H. A. Snyder. 1969. A comparative study of mollusc predation of Limpkins, Everglade Kites, and Boat-tailed Grackles. Living Bird 8:177–223.

Sprunt, A., Jr. 1954. Florida bird life. Coward-McCann, New York, and the National Audubon Society. 527 pp.

Terres, J. K. 1982. The Audubon Society encyclopedia of North American birds. Alfred Knopf, New York. 1110 pp.

Thomson, A. L. (ed.). 1964. A new dictionary of birds. Nelson, London. 928 pp.

Walkinshaw, L. H. 1982. Observations on Limpkin nesting. Fla. Field Nat. 10:45–54.

Wiley, R. H., and M. S. Wiley. 1976. Limpkin observed at Lake Waccamaw, N.C. Chat 40:94–95.

Wood, D. A. 1991. Official lists of endangered and potentially endangered fauna and flora in Florida. Fla. Game and Fresh Water Fish Comm., Tallahassee, Florida. 23 pp.

PREPARED BY: Dana C. Bryan, Florida Department of Environmental Protection, Division of Recreation and Parks, Tallahassee, FL 32399-3000, and Research Associate, Tall Timbers Research Station, Rt. 1 Box 678, Tallahassee, FL 32312.

Wilson's Plover

Charadrius wilsonia

FAMILY CHARADRIIDAE

Order Charadriiformes

TAXONOMY: Wilson's Plover (*Charadrius wilsonia*) was originally described by Ord in 1814 as *C. wilsonius* based on a specimen collected by Wilson from Cape May, New Jersey, but was renamed *C. wilsonia* by Peters in 1934. Linnaeus described the genus Charadrius in 1758, but the genus has had nine different names from 1830 to the present. *C. wilsonius* was the type species for the alternate genus *Ochthodromus* in 1853, but has since been merged into the currently accepted genus *Charadrius* (Stone 1937; Johnsgard 1981; AOU 1983; Sibley and Monroe 1990).

DESCRIPTION: The Wilson's Plover is a small to medium-sized plover, brown above and white below with a single, broad dark breast band and a white collar extending behind the neck. A heavier black bill, single neck band, and pinkish-gray legs distinguish it from other ringed plovers. Adults range from 16 to 20 cm (6.25 to 7.75 in.) in length, with a wing spread of 11–13 cm (4.25–5 in.) and a bill of 19–22 mm (0.8 in.) (Hayman et al. 1986).

The frontal bar, lores, and breast band are black and the forehead and supercilium are white on breeding males. Underparts are white, except for the broad black breast band. Upperparts are generally grayish-brown with white tipping on the greater wing coverts. The anterior crown is a gray-brown. Breast bands of breeding females are typically all brown or rufous. In winter plumage, adults of both sexes have a brown breast band and the anterior crown is a paler brown. Juveniles appear similar to nonbreeding adults, but they have darker brown underparts and a less distinct breast band.

Four races have been recognized. The nominate race (*wilsonius*) occurs in Florida and the eastern United States and lacks rufous on the crown. West Indian individuals, sometimes separated as *rufinucha,* are strongly rufous on the crown. The Pacific coast race (*beldingi*) is darker above and has a broader facial mask. The race *cinnamominus* (northeast Columbia to northeast Brazil,

Wilson's Plover, *Charadrius wilsonia*. (Photo copyright by Allan D. Cruickshank, courtesy of Florida Audubon Society)

Trinidad) has a rufous crown and a rufous and black breast band. Winter plumage of *rufinucha* and *cinnamominus* forms have no rufous coloration on the crown.

POPULATION SIZE AND TREND: Data about the population size of Wilson's Plover in Florida are limited. In Florida from 1980 to 1989, the average of the total for Christmas Bird Counts (CBCs) was almost 300 individuals (Sprandel 1993), but this was an incomplete census. Statewide wintering shorebird surveys in the winter of 1993-94 located an average of 282 individuals (Sprandel et al., in press). Possible flyway totals based on International Shorebird Surveys are 958 individuals (Harrington et al. 1989). Linear regression of CBC data from 1960 to 1989 in Florida showed few sites with significant trends (at P = 0.1) due to large variability in counts; however, small declines (2–4 birds a year) were detected in the Tampa Bay area and a small increase (3 birds a year) occurred in the Sanibel Island area. Numbers of wintering birds in Florida are probably greater than breeding numbers.

There has been no complete census of breeding numbers in Florida. The Breeding Bird Atlas for 1992 confirmed Wilson's Plovers in 6.1% (63 of 1036) of the quadrangles surveyed prior to 1992 (Kale et al. 1992). Decreases have undoubtedly occurred in recent years on beaches with high human populations. Cruickshank (1980) reported "a sharp decrease since 1960. . .due to man's encroachment in its habitat" in Brevard County. Weston (1965) described the species as "formerly common but now decidedly uncommon" in the Pensacola area. Howell (1932) considered Wilson's Plover as "common" statewide and noted that Audubon mentioned this bird as "more abundant than any other" wintering shorebird near St. Augustine in 1835 and noted that Scott called it "abundant" at Clearwater in 1881. From these anecdotal

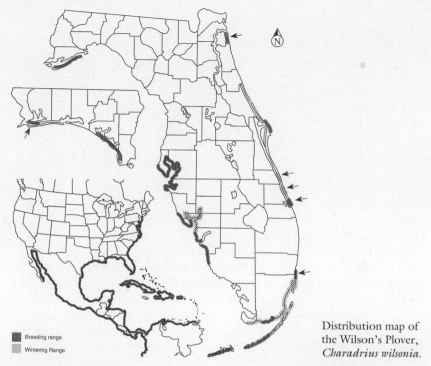

Distribution map of
the Wilson's Plover,
Charadrius wilsonia.

remarks it would be imprudent to declare a definite population status. No data are available on the population trend elsewhere within its range.

DISTRIBUTION AND HISTORY OF DISTRIBUTION: Wilson's Plovers

breed on sandy beaches, tidal mudflats, and savanna pools near the coast from central Baja California, northern Sonora, and southern New Jersey south along the Pacific and Atlantic–Gulf–Caribbean coasts of Middle America, the southeastern United States, and West Indies to Panama and northern South America east to northeastern Brazil (AOU 1983). They breed sporadically along both coasts of Florida except for the salt marsh area of the panhandle, but may be more common along the beaches of the panhandle, the Gulf coast from Tampa south, and in the Keys. Breeding distribution has no doubt been altered due to disturbances in breeding areas. The population shifts southward during the fall and northward during the spring. Spring migration in Florida begins in late February to mid-March, and during the fall most movements are in August and September (Tomkins 1944). During the winter, most Wilson's Plovers reside south of 31°N where they are regularly seen on both coasts of Florida, on the coast of Texas, and western Louisiana. These areas have a minimum January temperature of at least 7°C (45°F) and a mean ocean-surface temperature of 18°C (64°F) (Root 1988). Concentrations of wintering

Wilson's Plover occur from Tampa Bay south along the Gulf coast and into the Keys. Florida potentially hosts one-fourth of the flyway population in winter, with two-thirds of the Florida winter totals occurring in the Tampa Bay area (Sprandel et al., in press). Although there are some annual changes in distribution of wintering Wilson's Plovers in Florida, no clear pattern is evident. While Wilson's Plovers were absent in statewide wintering shorebird surveys along the East coast, historically they were "occasional" (Sprandel et al., in press). The distribution history outside of Florida is unknown.

HABITAT REQUIREMENTS AND HABITAT TREND: Wilson's Plovers nest on dry sand, bare soil, or pavement, generally within a short distance of salt or brackish water. The nests are frequently placed close to a piece of debris (Tomkins 1944), among broken shells (Bent 1929), or near clumps of vegetation (Bergstrom 1988a). This provides a windbreak and nest concealment by disrupting the outline of the nest. Nests may be in loose colonies, but usually nests are far enough apart for incubating birds to be out of sight of each other. In Texas, Wilson's Plover nests were sometimes near other nesting shorebirds, including Least Terns (*Sterna antillarum*), Common Nighthawks (*Chordeiles minor*), Snowy Plovers (*Charadrius alexandrinus*), American Avocets (*Recurvirostra americana*), and Black-necked Stilts (*Himantopus mexicanus*) (Bergstrom 1988a). In Virginia, Wilson's Plover nests always were in the same area as Least Tern and Piping Plover (*Charadrius melodus*) nests (Bergstrom and Terwilliger 1987). Howell (1932) stated that nests in Florida often were among Least Tern nests, whereas a few Wilson's Plover nests were found near Least Tern colonies in a preliminary tern survey in the panhandle during 1993 (J. Gore, pers. observ.).

The thick bill of the Wilson's Plover may be an adaptation for preying on fiddler crabs of the genus *Uca* (Tomkins 1944). A study of Wilson's Plovers wintering at the Bay of Panama in Central America found their prey to be 96% crustacean (Strauch and Abele 1979), and a study in northeastern Venezuela found that small fiddler crabs comprised 98.6% of their diet (Morrier and McNeil 1991). The Wilson's Plover diet may be more diverse in Florida. Stomachs from nine birds from Florida and Alabama included "small crabs, shrimp, crawfishes, scallop bivalves, ground beetles, leaf beetles, click beetles, ants, bugs, spiders, and crane flies" (Howell 1932).

Generally, it is not known if shorebirds are limited by habitat needs during breeding or wintering seasons (Evans and Pienkowski 1984). In Florida, increased development of coastal shoreline and disturbances on remaining shorelines will have negative impacts on both the breeding and wintering population. Wilson's Plover may be less susceptible during breeding than the Snowy Plover due to its wider tolerance of breeding conditions.

VULNERABILITY OF SPECIES AND HABITAT: As with other shore-birds, Wilson's Plover populations are adversely affected by any alteration or degradation of coastal shoreline. Because birds winter in Florida, loss of win-tering sites may affect breeding populations both in Florida and other states. On a site-by-site basis, it is generally not known if the loss of a particular site will affect wintering populations by forcing individuals to move to less favor-able environments (Goss-Custard 1979). Unfortunately, development poten-tial appears greatest in some southern Florida counties, such as Pinellas and Hillsborough, most suitable for Wilson's Plover (Fernald and Purdum 1992).

CAUSES OF THREAT: Threats to shorebirds include human disturbance, environmental contaminants, and habitat loss and degradation (Senner and Howe 1984). In a coastal setting, birds may be disturbed by people, off-road vehicles, or domestic pets. If predators are abundant, or if frequent distur-bance keeps birds off their nests, losses to predators are likely to be high. Eggs and chicks are directly vulnerable to human footsteps, vehicles, and pets. Burger (1981) considered shorebirds the avian group most vulnerable to disturbance, because they frequently vacated an area when disturbed. Burger and Gochfeld (1991) documented decreases in foraging time of Sanderlings (*Calidris alba*) as the number of people within 100 m (330 ft.) increased. Breeding Wilson's Plovers may be less susceptible to disturbance than other shorebirds because they often tend to use the backside of the beach.

Spills of crude oil pose a serious local threat to shorebirds along the coast. Wilson's Plovers wade less than other shorebirds, so oiling may be less of a problem on the belly, breast, and head. Larsen and Richardson (1990) re-ported behavioral changes and possible mortality among shorebirds caused by a major oil spill in Grays Harbor, Washington. Smith and Bleakney (1969) reported that oiled shorebirds spent a greater amount of time preening. Oil spills also may affect shorebirds by killing the crustaceans on which they, including the Wilson's Plover, feed at low tide (Jackson et al. 1989). Biologi-cal effects of spills are usually greater in lower energy environments where oil accumulates (Jackson et al. 1989); therefore, spills may have a greater impact on the lower energy Gulf coast. The ports of Fort Lauderdale (Port Ever-glades) receive large amounts of petroleum, and Tampa and Jacksonville re-ceive large amounts of pollutants (Department of Natural Resources 1988; Fernald and Purdum 1992). A variety of development and human activities result in loss of coastal habitat, including dredging and excavation, spoil disposal, impounding, and sediment diversions.

RESPONSES TO HABITAT MODIFICATION: The responses by Wilson's Plover to habitat modification are not accurately known. They are susceptible to loss of habitat at sites, but may nest on dredge-material islands. There has only been a single report of a pair nesting on a gravel roof in Florida (Fisk 1978). They may also roost on man-made habitats such as spoil islands or causeways.

DEMOGRAPHIC CHARACTERISTICS: Wilson's Plovers lay cream-colored eggs, 35 mm (1.4 in.) long, and marked with dark brown or black speckles and blotches (Bent 1929; Bergstrom 1988a). Modal clutch size is 3, with a range of 2–4 eggs. Clutches of 3 eggs are laid over 5–6 days. Mean time from nest failure to the start of a new clutch is about 8 days. Regular incubation begins after the third egg is laid and lasts for 23–27 days. Both sexes incubate, with the female being more attentive during the day and the male at night (Bergstrom 1986). During daylight, one of the pair is on the nest 77% of the time, but this is strongly affected by air temperature (Bergstrom 1989). Incubation serves roles both of heating and cooling the nest by tight sitting and shading. In hot climates (45°C, 120°F), Wilson's Plover may wet their feathers to cool the eggs, but this behavior has not been reported for Florida. Hatching success from one study in Texas (Bergstrom 1988a) was low (12–54%). Known causes of nest failure include mammalian predation, trampling by cattle, and flooding.

Egg shells are removed from the nest immediately after hatching. The downy chicks are precocial and leave the nest within 1–2 hours of hatching; then they begin following the parents and finding food. Age at fledging is not known, but 21 days is a possible minimum length (Tomkins 1944). Rates of chick survival are not known. Nesting occurs in Florida from April through July. Detailed nesting studies have not been conducted on Wilson's Plover in Florida, so variations from the above numbers are possible. Wilson's Plovers probably begin breeding in their first year, but this has not been verified. No data are available on their longevity.

KEY BEHAVIORS: Wilson's Plovers feed by standing still until food is sighted, then running directly toward it and lunging up to 1 meter (3 ft.) at it. They often actively feed at night, particularly at low tides and with sufficient moonlight (Robert et al. 1989). The nocturnal and diurnal distribution of individual Wilson's Plovers differed substantially (Thibault and McNeil 1994). Wilson's Plovers feed in mixed species flocks at low tide and also may roost at high tide in mixed flocks during winter. In winter, Wilson's Plovers spend more daylight time resting than feeding. Daylight energy intake increased appreciably during the start of the breeding season and through early fall (Morrier and McNeil 1991). These activity patterns were primarily from studies in a tropical environment, and it is unknown if the same patterns hold in Florida.

Pair-formation apparently occurs before territory establishment. Time devoted to aggression is low in winter, but increases in March–April as territories are established. The male initiates courtship, which consists of chasing other males from the female, threat displays, and scrape-making. The male makes several scrapes on the ground in his territory, and females sometimes scrape in a depression started by their mate. The female approaches the side of the male during a scrape ceremony in which the male bows in the direction of the scrape, raises and lowers his wing, and fans his tail down. Precopulatory postures include a posture in which the male lowers his head (Forward-tilt), male prancing by stamping his feet, and a behavior during which the male kicks his feet up and flicks his tail—Marking time (Bergstrom 1988b). No aerial display has been described for the Wilson's Plover as occurs in other plovers.

Territorial displays include a horizontal and hunched display in which the male rushes and chases other birds. Before and after a chase, the male fluffs the white breast feathers and holds an upright and hunched position. In the "Parallel Run," two males sometimes run parallel to each other using a horizontal-hunched position. Territories are usually no more than 30 m (100 ft.) in radius.

Alarm and distraction displays may be given in response to human intruders or predators. These displays may include a Heads-up display, Squatting, Mock-brooding, and Broken-wing displays. Wilson's Plovers show a variety of vocalizations for territorial, alarm, and brood calls. These vocalizations include: a clear "peet" as a declaration of an established territory, a clear whistled "tweet" as an alarm call, a low "dove" note used in the nest-location behavior, and a harsh guttural note used in injury-feigning (Tomkins 1944; Bergstrom 1988b).

CONSERVATION MEASURES TAKEN: Both federal (Migratory Bird Treaty Act) and state laws (Wildlife Code of the State of Florida) protect birds, eggs, or nests of Wilson's Plovers. The establishment of coastal preserves has protected some breeding and wintering habitats. Surveys of wintering shorebird distribution conducted in the winter of 1994 by the Florida Game and Fresh Water Fish Commission determined critical areas for wintering shorebirds.

CONSERVATION MEASURES PROPOSED: Local conservation efforts on breeding sites might include fencing or closing portions of beaches where Wilson's Plovers are nesting to protect them from humans, vehicles, and pets; construction of predator exclosures around nests; and vegetation control (Melvin et al. 1991). Predation can greatly influence the productivity of ground-nesting species such as the Wilson's Plover. Several techniques have been used to exclude predators from Piping Plover nests (Deblinger et al. 1992). The effects of disturbance on wintering birds should be further studied to understand if available wintering sites can limit populations. Additionally, education may cause the public to reduce disturbance by maintaining a respectful distance and by keeping pets leashed. Acquisition or restoration of beach dune habitat may be an effective means of enhancing Wilson's Plover populations, particularly in areas where developmental pressure may be greatest.

Additional monitoring of the breeding populations of Wilson's Plovers should be initiated in Florida. Continued censusing of the endangered Piping Plover in coastal areas should be expanded to include counts of both Snowy and Wilson's plovers. Statewide counts of Least Terns in coastal areas should include census of Wilson's Plover. Additional winter monitoring of sites with an average of at least 20 Wilson's Plovers would include Three Rooker Bar, Anclote Key, Lake Ingraham, Honeymoon Island, and Little Estero CWA (Sprandel et al., in press).

ACKNOWLEDGMENTS: I thank J. Gore, K. Enge, and J. Rodgers for reviewing this account. Data from Christmas Bird Counts (CBC) are from the Bird Population Studies unit at the Cornell Laboratory of Ornithology. The CBC counts are sponsored and organized by the National Audubon Society; data are collected by volunteers throughout Florida. This account is a contribution of the Bureau of Nongame Wildlife, Florida Game and Fresh Water Fish Commission.

LITERATURE CITED:

AOU. 1983. Checklist of North American birds. 6th ed. Amer. Ornithol. Union, Allen Press, Inc., Lawrence, Kansas.

Bent, A. 1929. Life histories of North American shore birds. Part 2. Bull. U.S. Nat. Mus. Bull. no. 146. Smithsonian Inst., Washington, D.C.

Bergstrom, P. W. 1986. Daylight incubation sex roles in Wilson's Plover. Condor 88:113–115.

Bergstrom, P. W. 1988a. Breeding biology of Wilson's Plover. Wilson Bull. 100:25–35.

Bergstrom, P. W. 1988b. Breeding displays and vocalizations of Wilson's Plover. Wilson Bull. 100:36–49.

Bergstrom, P .W. 1989. Incubation temperatures of Wilson's Plover and Killdeers. Condor 91:1634–1641.

Bergstrom, P. W., and K. Terwilliger. 1987. Nest sites and aggressive behavior of Piping and Wilson's plovers in Virginia: some preliminary results. Wader Study Group Bull. 50:35–39.

Burger, J. 1981. The effect of human activity on birds at a coastal bay. Biol. Conserv. 21:231–244.

Burger, J., and M. Gochfeld. 1991. Human activity influence and diurnal and nocturnal foraging of Sanderlings (Calidris alba). Condor 93:259–265.

Cruikshank, A. D. 1980. The birds of Brevard County. Ed. Helen Cruickshank, appenda Robert Barber. [privately published]

Deblinger, R. D., J. J. Vaske, and D. W. Rimmer. 1992. An evaluation of different predator exclosures used to protect Atlantic coast Piping Plover nests. Wild. Soc. Bull. 20:274–279.

Department of Natural Resources. 1988. Survey of pollutant transfers. Unpubl. report. Dept. of Nat. Res., Tallahassee, Florida.

Evans, P. R., and M. W. Pienkowski. 1984. Population dynamics of shorebirds. Pp. 83–123 in Shorebirds. Breeding behavior and populations (Burger, J. and B. L. Olla, eds.). Plenum Press, New York.

Fernald, E. A., and E. D. Purdum (eds). 1992. Atlas of Florida. Univ. Press of Florida, Gainesville, Florida.

Fisk, E. J. 1978. Roof-nesting terns, skimmers, and plovers in Florida. Fla. Field Nat. 6:1–8.

Goss-custard, J. D. 1979. Effect of habitat loss on the numbers of overwintering shorebirds. Stud. Avian Biol. 2:167–177.

Hayman, P., J. Marchant, and T. Prater. 1986. Shorebirds: an identification guide to the waders of the world. Houghton Mifflin Co., Boston, Massachusetts.

Harrington, B. A., J. P. Myers, and J. S. Grear. 1989. Coastal refueling sites for global migrants. Pp. 4293–4307 in Coastal zone '89—Proceedings of the sixth symposium on coastal and ocean management (O. T. Magoon, H. Converse, D. Miner, L. T. Tobin, and D. Clark, eds.). Amer. Soc. Civil Eng. Salem, MA.

Howell, A. H. 1932. Florida bird life. Fla. Dept. of Game and Fresh Water Fish, Tallahassee, Florida.

Jackson, J. B. C., J. D. Cubit, B. D. Keller, V. Batista, K. Burns, H. M. Caffey, R. L. Caldwell, S. D. Garrity, C. D. Getter, C. Gonzalez, H. M. Guzman, K. W. Kaufmann, A. H. Knap, S. C. Levings, M. J. Marshall, R. Steger, R. C. Thompson, and E. Weil. 1989. Ecological effects of a major oil spill on Panamanian coastal marine communities. Science 243:37–44.

Johnsgard, P. A. 1981. The plovers, sandpipers, and snipes of the world. Univ. of Nebraska Press, Lincoln, Nebraska.

Kale, H. W., II, B. M. Smith, and C. W. Biggs, eds. 1992. Atlas of breeding birds of Florida. Draft ms. submitted to the Fla. Game and Fresh Water Fish Comm., Tallahassee, Florida.

Larsen, E. M., and S. A. Richardson. 1990. Some effects of a major oil spill on wintering shorebirds at Grays Harbor, Washington. Northwest. Nat. 71:88–92.

Melvin, S. M., C. R. Griggin, L. H. MacIvor. 1991. Recovery strategies for Piping Plovers in managed coastal landscapes. Coastal Manage. 19:21–34.

Morrier, A., and R. McNeil. 1991. Time-activity budget of Wilson's and Semipalmated plovers in a tropical environment. Wilson Bull. 103:598–620.

Robert, M. , R. McNeil, and A. Leduc. 1989. Conditions and significance of night feeding in shorebirds and other water birds in a tropical lagoon. Auk 106:94–101.

Root, T. 1988. Atlas of wintering North American birds. Univ. Chicago Press, Chicago, Illinois.

Senner, S. E, and M. A. Howe. 1984. Conservation of nearctic shorebirds. Pp. 379–420 in Shorebirds. Breeding behavior and populations (Burger, J. and B. L. Olla, eds). Plenum Press, New York.

Sibley, C. G., and B. L. Monroe, Jr. 1990. Distribution and taxonomy of birds of the world. Yale Univ. Press, New Haven, Connecticut.

Smith, P. C., and J. S. Bleakney. 1969. Observations on oil pollution and wintering Purple Sandpipers *Erolia maritima* (*brunnich*), in Novia Scotia. Can. Field Nat. 83:19–22.

Sprandel, G. L. 1993. Winter shorebird survey—field techniques manual. Unpubl. rept. Fla. Game and Fresh Water Fish Comm., Tallahassee, Florida.

Sprandel, G. L., J. A. Gore, and D. T. Cobb. In Press. Winter Shorebird Survey Final Performance Report. Fla. Game and Fresh Water Fish Comm., Nongame Wildl. Prog., Tallahassee, Fla. 150 pp.

Strauch, J. G., Jr., and L. G. Abele. 1979. Feeding ecology of three species of plovers wintering on the Bay of Panama, Central America. Stud. Avian Biol. 2:217–230.

Stone, W. 1937. Bird studies at Old Cape May. Dover Publ., Inc., New York.

Thibault, M., and R. McNeil. 1994. Day/night variation in habitat use by Wilson's Plovers in northeastern Venezuela. Wilson Bull. 106:299–310.

Tomkins, I. R. 1944. Wilson's Plover in its summer home. Auk 61:259–269.

Weston, F. M. 1965. A survey of the birdlife of northwestern Florida. Bull. Tall Timbers Res. Sta. 5:1–147.

PREPARED BY: Gary L. Sprandel, Bureau of Nongame Wildlife, Florida Game and Fresh Water Fish Commission, Route 7, Box 3055, Quincy, FL 32351.

American Avocet
Recurvirostra americana
FAMILY RECURVIROSTRIDAE
Order Charadriiformes

TAXONOMY: In 1789 Gmelin based his description of the American Avocet (*Recurvirostra americana*) mainly on an account by Pennant (AOU 1983). The American Avocet is one of four species in the genus that has a worldwide distribution (Sibley and Monroe 1990) and is sometimes considered a single superspecies (AOU 1983).

DESCRIPTION: The American Avocet is a relatively large and distinctive shorebird with long legs and neck. An upcurved bill and bold black-and-white color pattern on its back and wings in flight are notable field characteristics (Palmer 1968). Sexes are alike. The avocet is 43–47 cm (17–18.5 in.) in total length including its bill of 8.3–9.5 cm (3.25–3.75 in.). Adults weigh 300–440 g with males heavier than females on average (White and Mitchell 1990). Webbing between the front toes is fairly extensive, which makes the avocet a good swimmer.

Adults have two molts: a complete postnuptial molt beginning in August and a partial prenuptial molt of the contour feathers and some scapulars and wing coverts in January (Bent 1927). Alternate plumage of the avocet lasts from February to August. During this period the avocet has a black bill and bluish legs. The head, neck, and upper breast are rusty fading into white on the lower breast and around the bill. The rest of the underparts, rump, middle of the back, and scapulars also are white. The tail is pale gray. In the definitive plumage a bluish-gray replaces the rusty color on the head, neck, and upper breast. This fades to nearly white. Wings are blackish except for the secondaries, the terminal half of greater wing coverts, and lining, which are white (Palmer 1968).

Downy young are cinnamon or creamy-buff on the upper parts, lightest on the crown and darkest on the rump. Scapulars are marked by two parallel stripes of brownish-black. The head shows narrow loral stripes and a dusky

American Avocet,
*Recurvirostra
americana*. (Photo
copyright by Allan
D. Cruickshank,
courtesy of Florida
Audubon Society)

spotted crown. Underparts are buffy-white with a nearly white throat and belly (Bent 1927).

POPULATION SIZE AND TREND: The mean number of American Avocets detected per Breeding Bird Survey (BBS) route is highest in California (1.1), followed by Alberta (0.9) and Nevada (0.5) (Robbins et al. 1986). Avocets also were detected during BBS in Colorado, Montana, New Mexico, Oregon (mean birds per route = 0.2), Washington (0.1), Arizona, Idaho, Utah, and Wyoming (<0.1). Based on the results of the BBS, the population trend for the American Avocet in the central United States and throughout its entire range is increasing significantly.

Howell (1932) described the American Avocet as "very rare and of casual occurrence" in Florida. In the early part of the century avocets were rare migrants or winter visitors. Recently, Duncan (1981) and Stevenson and Anderson (1994) commented on the increasing numbers of avocets in Florida. Winter flocks of 600 (Sykes 1980) in Tampa and nearly 700 (Sykes 1977) at Coot Bay are the highest numbers reported. Individuals in alternate plumage have been seen in spring or summer in all parts of Florida except for the panhandle during the past 50 years (Loftin et al. 1991).

In parts of Florida, avocets have been described as permanent residents

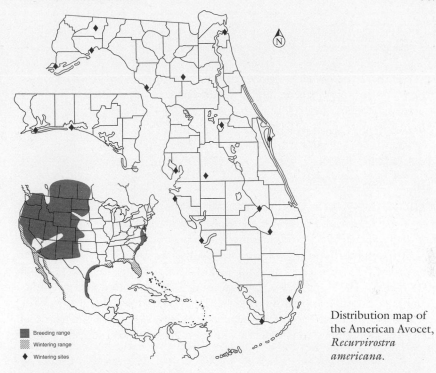

Breeding range
Wintering range
◆ Wintering sites

Distribution map of
the American Avocet,
*Recurvirostra
americana.*

with highest abundance in winter (Dinsmore 1977; Loftin et al. 1991). On 26
June 1983 "hundreds" of American Avocets, many in alternate plumage, were
seen on Hillsborough Bay (Paul 1983). Observations of courtship behavior or
copulation have been made at McKay Bay (Kale 1972) and Port Canaveral
(Ogden 1973). This evidence of pairing suggests that avocets may breed in
Florida in the future (Dinsmore 1977). A documented case of breeding among
a resident population of avocets at Pea Island, North Carolina (McVaugh
1978), supports the possibility of eventual breeding in Florida. However,
courtship behavior may occur during the winter before migration. Gibson
(1971) noted that avocets seemed to be paired when they arrived on the
breeding grounds.

DISTRIBUTION AND HISTORY OF DISTRIBUTION: The breeding distribution of the American Avocet in the United States extends from North
Dakota, southwestern Minnesota, western Nebraska, and north-central Texas
westward to California, Oregon, and Washington. The northern limits of the
distribution are southeastern British Columbia, central Alberta, and southern
Saskatchewan and Manitoba. Avocets also breed from the Texas Gulf coast
southward into Mexico and downy young were observed once in North Carolina (McVaugh 1978). Winter distribution is from coastal California and the

Salton Sea area southward to Baja California, coastal Louisiana, Mississippi, and Alabama.

The American Avocet has been observed in all parts of Florida (Lower Keys, southern and northern peninsula, and the panhandle) in all seasons over the past 50 years (Loftin et al. 1991). Although most of the observations were at coastal locations, avocets have been seen at Gainesville and Paynes Prairie (Alachua County), Lake Jackson (Leon County), Belle Glade (Palm Beach County), Zellwood (Orange County), Okaloosa County, and at phosphate mines in Polk County. A fossilized avocet bone from the late Pleistocene was collected near Haile (Alachua Co.), Florida (Ligon 1965).

HABITAT REQUIREMENT AND HABITAT TREND: The natural habitats of the American Avocet are marshes, mud flats, estuaries, alkaline lakes and ponds (Hamilton 1975; Grover and Knopf 1982; AOU 1983). Nesting avocets require very open salt or mud flats with sparse tufts of grass near water where they make nests of a simple scrape lined with grass or mud chips (Bent 1927; Gibson 1971). However, the availability of natural mud flats in Florida estuaries is becoming increasingly limited (Sykes and Hunter 1978). The availability of relatively deep freshwater ponds with islands for safe roosting may be an important component to wintering and perhaps breeding habitat (T. J. Evans, pers. comm.).

RESPONSES TO HABITAT MODIFICATION: Several manmade habitats in Florida that are used by American Avocets are probably increasing in area. Avocets are seen year round at a settling pond for material from the Tampa incinerator (Dinsmore 1977) and on a spoil island in Hillsborough Bay (Paul 1983). Flooded agricultural fields (Sykes and Hunter 1978) and phosphate mine settling ponds (Maehr 1984) also are used by avocets during migration or in the winter. Increases in wintering populations of avocets have been described after construction of sewage treatment ponds in California (Evans and Harris 1994).

DEMOGRAPHIC CHARACTERISTICS: In Oregon, American Avocets nest in loose colonies and both members of a pair defend a territory that includes the nest and area for foraging (Gibson 1971). Avocets arrived on the breeding grounds during early April. The laying period for the typical clutch of 4 eggs was 5 days. Some egg dumping occurs, but nests with extra eggs have extremely low hatching success, probably because the eggs are not well-incubated. Incubation lasts for about 3.5 weeks and parental care lasts for 4–5 weeks until the young can fly. The hatching rate of clutches of 4 eggs from 59 nests was 90% (Gibson 1971). In northern Oklahoma coyote predation and flooding were suggested as possible causes of nest failure (Grover and Knopf

(1982). Fledging success and post-fledging survivorship have not been described.

KEY BEHAVIORS: Bent (1927) described the American Avocet as having relatively little courtship activity besides frequent bows or crouching with wings widespread. Gibson (1971) identified breast preening by males or females as a precopulatory ceremony. See Hamilton (1975) for more extensive description of behaviors.

Avocets often respond as a group to intruders into nesting colonies by exibiting Dive-bombing, Circling, Crouch-running, False-incubation behaviors and erratic movements (Sordahl 1990). The alarm call of the avocet is a loud repeated "kleek" that is sometimes a more prolonged "klee-eek" (Palmer 1968). For the first three weeks after hatching, young typically hide from predators and rely on the diversionary tactics of the parents (Sordahl 1982). After 3 weeks of age, the chicks run. If they are in water, chicks will dive to escape predators.

The avocet primarily feeds by dropping its recurved bill in shallow water or mud and sweeping from side to side while moving at a half run (Bent 1927). In Texas migrant avocets fed mostly on chironomids and beetles generally in 4–16 cm deep water (Baldassarre and Gibson 1984). Behavioral and anatomical adaptations allow avocets in California to eat brine shrimp and brine flies, while maintaining relatively low stomach osmololity and sodium concentration (Mahoney and Jehl 1985). The diet of avocets also includes dragonfly nymphs, water boatmen, phyllopods, backswimmers, and various other flies and beetles and their larvae (Bent 1927; Gibson 1971). On land avocets will chase prey, such as grasshoppers, with wings partially outstretched (Bent 1927).

CONSERVATION MEASURES TAKEN: Other than protection under state and federal wildlife regulations, no conservation measures have been taken for the American Avocet in Florida.

CONSERVATION MEASURES PROPOSED: In Florida the American Avocet has increased significantly over the past 50 years in all seasons and observers have speculated that it will breed in the near future. Given these encouraging signs, inclusion of the avocet as a "Species of Special Concern" should be reexamined.

Although special conservation measures for the avocet may be unnecessary at this time, many species of migratory, wintering and resident shorebirds including the avocet would benefit from drawing down flooded agricultural fields at strategic times to provide foraging habitat (Sykes and Hunter 1978). However, agricultural drainage water used for marsh management at the Kesterson Reservoir in California contained a high concentration of selenium and caused complete reproductive failure of nesting avocets (Williams et al. 1989). Manmade habitats being used by avocets in Florida should be monitored for chemical contaminants that might be detrimental to the birds. Since the avocet is not yet a breeding bird in Florida, continued monitoring of sites where groups of avocets live year round is valuable.

ACKNOWLEDGMENTS: I thank James Rodgers and Thomas J. Evans for many helpful suggestions on the manuscript and Tall Timbers Research, Inc. for support.

LITERATURE CITED:

AOU. 1983. Check-list of North American birds, 6th ed., American Ornithologists' Union, Washington, D.C.

Baldassarre, G. A., and D. H. Fischer. 1984. Food habits of fall migrant shorebirds on the Texas high plains. Jour. Field Ornith. 55:220–229.

Bent, A. C. 1927. Life histories of North American shore birds. U.S. Nat. Mus. Bull. 142, Smithsonian Inst., Washington, D.C.

Dinsmore, J. J. 1977. Notes on avocets and stilts in Tampa Bay, Florida. Fla. Field Nat. 5:25–30.

Duncan, R. A. 1981. Some noteworthy changes in the birdlife of northwestern Florida (1965–1979). Fla. Field Nat. 9:21–27.

Evans, T. J., and S. W. Harris. 1994. Status and habitat use by American Avocets wintering at Humboldt Bay, California. Condor 96:178–189.

Gibson, F. 1971. The breeding biology of the American Avocet (*Recurvirostra americana*) in central Oregon. Condor 73:444–454.

Grover, P. B., and F. L. Knopf. 1982. Habitat requirements and breeding success of charadriiform birds nesting at Salt Plains National Wildlife Refuge, Oklahoma. Jour. Field Ornithol. 53:139–148.

Hamilton, R. B. 1975. Comparative behavior of the American Avocet and the Black-necked Stilt (Recurvirostridae). Ornithol. Monogr. No. 17, Amer. Ornithol. Union, Washington, D.C.

Howell, A. H. 1932. Florida bird life. Coward-McCann, Inc. New York.

Kale, H. W., II. 1972. The changing seasons, Florida region. Amer. Birds 26:753.

Ligon, J. D. 1965. A Pleistocene avifauna from Haile, Florida. Bull. Fla. State Mus. 10:127–158.

Loftin, R. W., G. E. Woolfenden, and J. A. Woolfenden. 1991. Florida bird records in *American Birds* and *Audubon Field Notes:* 1947–1989. Fla. Ornithol. Soc. Spec. Publ. no. 4.

Maehr, D. S. 1984. Status of birds using phosphate-mined lands in Florida. Amer. Birds 38:28–31.

Mahoney, S. A., and J. R. Jehl, Jr. 1985. Adaptations of migratory shorebirds to highly saline and alkaline lakes: Wilson's Phalarope and American Avocet. Condor 87:520–527.

McVaugh, W., Jr. 1978. American Avocet breeding at Pea Island, N.C. Chat 42:31–32.

Ogden, J. C. 1973. The changing seasons, Florida region. Amer. Birds 27:861.

Palmer, R. S. 1968. American Avocet. Pp. 150–151 in The shorebirds of North America (G. D. Stout, ed.). Viking Press, New York.

Paul, R. T. 1983. The changing seasons, Florida region. Amer. Birds 37:981.

Robbins, C. S., D. Bystrak, and P. H. Geissler. 1986. The Breeding Bird Survey: its first fifteen years, 1965–1979. U.S. Dept. Int., Fish and Wildl. Serv. Res. Publ. 157, Washington, D.C.

Sibley, C. G., and B. L. Monroe, Jr. 1990. Distribution and taxonomy of birds of the world. Yale Univ. Press, New Haven, Connecticut.

Sordahl, T. A. 1982. Antipredator behavior of American Avocet and Black-necked Stilt chicks. Jour. Field Ornith. 54:315–325.

Sordahl, T. A. 1990. Sexual differences in antipredator behavior of breeding American Avocets and Black-necked Stilts. Condor 92:530–532.

Stevenson, H. M., and B. H. Anderson. 1994. The Birdlife of Florida. Univ. Press Florida, Gainesville, Florida.

Sykes, P. W. (regional editor). 1977. The seventy-seventh Audubon Christmas Bird Count: Coot Bay. Amer. Birds 31:599.

Sykes, P. W. (regional editor). 1980. The eightieth Audubon Christmas Bird Count: Tampa. Amer. Birds 34:484.

Sykes, P. W., and G. S. Hunter. 1978. Bird use of flooded agricultural fields during summer and early fall and some recommendations for management. Fla. Field Nat. 6:36–43.

White, D. H., and C. A. Mitchell. 1990. Body mass and lipid content of shorebirds overwintering on the south Texas coast. Jour. Field Ornith. 61:445–452.

Williams, M. L., R. L. Hothem, and H. M. Ohlendorf. 1989. Recruitment failure in American Avocets and Black-necked Stilts nesting at Kesterson Reservoir, California, 1984–1985. Condor 91:797–802.

PREPARED BY: R. Todd Engstrom, Tall Timbers Research, Inc., Route 1, Box 678, Tallahassee, FL 32312.

Sooty Tern

Sterna fuscata

FAMILY LARIDAE

Order Charadriiformes

TAXONOMY: In older classifications, the Sooty Tern (*Sterna fuscata*) and other darker-mantled, more oceanic species (e.g., *S. lunata, S. anaethetus*) often were distinguished generically (as *Haliplana, Onychoprion,* and others) from the bulk of the white-winged, shore terns. Modern systems generally accommodate these species in the expanded genus *Sterna*, although, behaviorally, the Sooty at least seems to occupy an outlying location in that assemblage. All the Sooty Terns of the Atlantic belong to the nominate subspecies and, indeed, may constitute one panmictic population. Geographical variation of Sooty Terns in the Indo-Pacific evidently is much more marked with at least six subspecies described (Peters 1934; Murphy 1936; Cramp et al. 1985). But, as asserted long ago (Peters 1934), "This species is badly in need of revision."

DESCRIPTION: Adult Sooty Terns are medium-sized seabirds (length, 36–43 cm; wingspan, 82–94 cm; weight, mainly 150–240 g). The plumage is black above and white below; with long, pointed wings; a long, very deep-forked tail (forked as much as 10 cm in newly molted individuals); a black line that extends from the bill to the eye; a white forehead patch; dark brown iris; and black bill and feet. Adults in fresh plumage exhibit a remarkably sharp contrast of black and white areas that tends to become blurred as the feathers wear. New hatchlings have brownish to buffy down sparsely to heavily blotched or peppered with darker brown. Juveniles near fledging are blackish above, dark gray on the breast, whitish on the belly and undertail coverts, and have the dorsal contour feathers more-or-less broadly tipped with off-white, buff, or (less frequently) chestnut. The bills of hatchlings and younger juveniles are pinkish at the base, and the tarsi and feet also may be pink or reddish. These colors become duller with age and largely disappear by the time of fledging. The transformation from juvenile to adult dress is achieved by a series of annual molts (varying from a probable minimum of three to at least five or

Sooty Tern, *Sterna fuscata*. (Photo copyright by Allan D. Cruickshank, courtesy of Florida Audubon Society)

six), in which the sharply contrasting pattern of adults is more and more closely assumed. Intermediate immature plumages typically have smudged patterns with light markings in areas that are dark in adults and vice versa (see Clancey 1977). Unreferenced material in this section is from Robertson (1978) and Cramp et al. (1985).

POPULATION SIZE AND TRENDS: The only breeding colony of Sooty Terns in Florida and the only large (now estimated at 25,000–40,000 nesting pairs), regularly active colony in the contiguous United States is located on Bush Key, Dry Tortugas, about 110 km west of Key West. Robertson (1964) has reviewed the history of the colony. This colony's known existence almost surely dates from the area's discovery in 1513, but the first certain mention of Sooty Terns in the area was by Audubon (1835). At the time of his visit in May, 1832, the terns were reported to be abundant and tern eggs were being gathered for sale by fishermen, but no clear estimate of numbers can be derived from Audubon's account. Later 19th century records of the tern colony are sparse and undetailed, but regular exploitation for eggs probably continued, as only 5,000 Sooties were said to have been nesting in 1903 when warden protection was first provided. Thereafter, the number of Sooty Terns quickly increased. In 1907, Watson (1908) calculated about 19,000 terns based on counts of eggs on sample plots, and, by 1919, wardens' estimates placed the nesting population as high as 110,000 birds. Bird Key, the original site of the colony, eroded away rapidly during the 1920s and early 1930s. By the time the colony had completed its forced move to Bush Key in 1935, it had declined to about 30,000 individuals. On Bush Key, the colony again increased and most annual estimates of numbers from 1937 onward were in

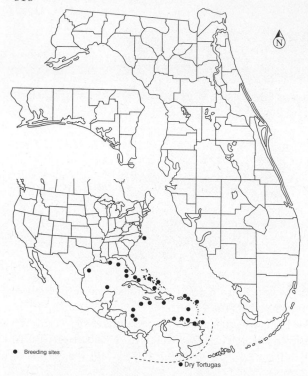

● Breeding sites

● Dry Tortugas

Distribution map of
the Sooty Tern,
Sterna fuscata.

the range of 65,000–130,000 Sooties. In nine years from the mid-1960s through the late l970s, we banded 18,000–24,000 Sooty Tern chicks each year at Dry Tortugas and judged from sample counts that those totals represented about 80% of the chicks reared. If one also assumes that not more than 65% of the eggs laid produced chicks of banding age, then the breeding population of Sooty Terns in those years ranged from 70,000 to 92,000 individuals. More recently, numbers have probably declined somewhat as shoreline erosion and denser vegetation reduced available nesting area on Bush Key.

As stated by Clapp et al. (1983), the Sooty Tern is ". . .one of the world's most abundant seabirds, and almost certainly the most abundant in tropical waters." Numerically, the species is the overwhelmingly dominant member of seabird communities in practically every part of the tropics. Thus, Sooties are thought to make up 77% of all breeding seabirds in the Gulf–Caribbean region (van Halewyn and Norton 1984) and 48% of the rich seabird fauna of the Hawaiian Leeward Islands (Harrison et al. 1983). In peak years, Sooty Tern nesting colonies on Christmas Island, Central Pacific, have been estimated to hold as many as 14 million individuals (Schreiber and Ashmole 1970). Because records are exceedingly patchy and methods of estimating have been inconsistent, no more than a crude approximation of the world population of Sooty Terns is feasible. However, based on recent regional seabird summaries (especially in Croxall et al. 1984) and other sources, it would appear that the number of adult Sooty Terns in existence somewhat exceeds 50 million. About 2.5 million of these birds inhabit the Gulf–Caribbean region plus the tropical Atlantic area (Ashmole 1963; van Halewyn and Norton 1984; Williams 1984), and the population of the Indian Ocean, including islands off Western Australia, is about 10 million (Serventy 1952; Warham 1956; Feare 1984; Cooper et al. 1984). The rest, perhaps 40 million, are in the Pacific from eastern Australian waters (Warham 1961; Hindwood et al. 1963; van Tets and Fullagar 1984), northern New Zealand (Taylor 1979; Robertson and Bell 1984), and southern Japan (Hasegawa 1984) across the wide reaches of the central and southern Pacific Ocean to islands off Mexico, Central America, and South America (Gould 1974; Garnett 1984; Harrison et al. 1984). The worldwide total would be augmented by the population of juvenile and subadult individuals, which conceivably may be several times the size of the adult population.

DISTRIBUTION AND HISTORY OF DISTRIBUTION: In its distribution, the Sooty Tern is the quintessential tropical seabird. It nests or has nested on almost every suitable oceanic island (i.e., those that are small, isolated, and not heavily forested) within the tropics. Ashmole (1963) presented an inventory of world Sooty Tern colonies and various authors have discussed particular areas and reviewed the overall range in less detail (Gould 1974; Clapp et al. 1983; regional accounts, Croxall et al. 1984; Croxall 1991). The species' regularly occupied breeding range may be described as consisting of islands in all of the world's oceans mostly within a latitudinal belt about 30°N and 30°S of the equator. The most notable departure from this pattern is the absence of nesting Sooties from the islands most affected by the cold currents that flow toward the equator along the west coast of Africa and South America. Within the cold-current regime, Sooty Tern nesting extends only slightly south of the equator (Culpepper Island, Galapagos; Tinhosas Islets, Principe); but, elsewhere in the South Pacific and South Atlantic the species nests to 20°S or beyond. Peripheral colonies in various sectors of the oceans are: North Atlantic—Walker's Cay, Bahamas, ca. 27°N (Sprunt 1984); South Atlantic—Trinidad (Olson 1972) and Martin Vas (Murphy 1936), Brazil, ca. 21°S; North Pacific—Rocas Alijos, Mexico, ca. 25°N (Everett and Anderson 1991); Kure Atoll, Hawaii, ca. 28°N (Woodward 1972); and, Bonin Islands, Japan, 27–28°N (Hasegawa 1984); South Pacific—Easter Island, Chile, 27.5°S (Johnson et al. 1970); Ilots Bass, Tubuai Islands, French Polynesia, ca. 28°S (Ashmole 1963); Kermadec Islands, New Zealand, 29–31°S (Ashmole 1963); and, Lord Howe Island, Australia, 31°S (Ashmole 1963); North Indian Ocean—Vengurla Rocks, India, 16°N (Ashmole 1963); South Indian Ocean—Houtman's Abrolhos, Australia, 28–29°S (Serventy 1952; Warham 1956); and, off southwestern Madagascar, ca. 25°S (Ashmole 1963). Dry Tortugas, the only established colony in Florida, also is located at about 25°N and thus is one of the species' more northerly breeding sites.

In addition to their established colonies, many records of nesting or attempted nesting by Sooty Terns beyond the usual range limits suggest continuing attempts towards range expansion. Typically, these efforts are ephemeral, unproductive, and involve only a few individuals (often single pairs) nesting in or near colonies of other species of Laridae. All reports of extra-Tortugan nesting by Sooties in Florida such as Key West, Tampa Bay, and Franklin County (AOU 1983; Robertson and Woolfenden 1992) seem to fit this pattern exactly, as do once-only nestings at two localities along coastal South Carolina (Wilkinson 1987; 1988) and on the lower Cape Fear River, North Carolina (Shields and Parnell 1984). However, the species has also been known to return repeatedly to attempt nesting at extralimital sites (e.g., Morgan Island, Cape Lookout, North Carolina; Fussell et al. 1981; Clapp et al. 1983) and such sequences may ultimately result in establishment. The small, but persistent, colonies on the Texas coast and the Chandeleur Islands, Louisiana (Clapp et al. 1983; H. H. Jeter, in litt.) may have originated in this manner. Sooty Terns also have frequently expanded their breeding range limits elsewhere in their range. Thus, nesting by isolated pairs in colonies of other gulls and terns has been reported in the Sine-Saloum and Senegal deltas, West Africa (Naurois 1969; Cooper et al. 1984), and on Selvagem Pequena, Salvages Islands in 1982, at about 30°N (LeGrand et al. 1984). In the Persian Gulf area, Sooties have been found nesting at several extralimital localities (Gallagher et al. 1984), and, most remarkably, on an islet near Ile St. Paul at about 39°S in the southern Indian Ocean (Jouventin et al. 1984). The latter site is by far the most peripheral record of reproductive activity by the species.

Outside the breeding season, adult Sooty Terns apparently disperse at sea, but little is known of the distribution or activity of particular populations. Gould (1974) discussed off-season records of adults marked at colonies in the central Pacific and recoveries of banded adults suggest that the Dry Tortugas population may resort mainly to the Gulf of Campeche and western Caribbean when not nesting. Banding data also indicate that the dispersal of newly fledged juveniles may consist of much more definitely programmed emigrations to oceanic "nursery areas" occupied by immatures. This movement pattern has been most clearly demonstrated for young birds of the Dry Tortugas population (Robertson 1969), but other banding records suggest that somewhat the same principles may apply for colonies in the Pacific (Lane 1967; Gould 1974) and Indian (Feare 1976) oceans. Briefly, the summer-fall movement of juvenile Sooty Terns away from Dry Tortugas appears to follow an average route via the Yucatan Channel, the extreme western and southern Caribbean, and the Guyanan coast to the area of the Intertropical Convergence, which extends across the Atlantic just south of the equator. Band recoveries have come principally from the West African and Brazilian ends of this transect (Robertson 1969, unpubl. data), but flocks of juvenile Sooties have been observed at sea in the Gulf of Guinea (Wallace 1973) and in the mid-Atlantic (W. R. P. Bourne, in litt.). Sooty Terns at sea are subject to long-distance displacement by severe storms. Thus, Sooties banded at Dry Tortugas have been carried by hurricanes to most states of the eastern United States and to regions as foreign to seabirds as western Texas (Robertsons, unpubl. data). Many similar incidents are reported for Sooty Terns in other oceans (e.g., Gould 1974; Clancey 1977).

HABITAT REQUIREMENTS AND HABITAT TREND: For successful nesting, Sooty Terns require sites that are relatively free of terrestrial predators, not densely vegetated at ground level, and within reasonable flight of fishing grounds (Robertson 1964, 1978; Dinsmore 1972; Clapp et al. 1983; Cramp et al. 1985). However, the species is highly adaptable and it probably violates all of the above conditions somewhere in its wide range. Thus, Sooties continued to nest in large numbers on Ascension in the face of heavy predation by feral cats (Ashmole 1963), and, at least for pairs feeding older chicks, commutes to feeding areas of up to about 500–750 km, one way, have been suspected or calculated from physiological data (Ashmole and Ashmole 1967; Flint 1991). The need to reach the substrate in order to make a nest scrape is perhaps the most stringent necessity, but Sooties in many colonies, including Dry Tortugas, manage to nest at sites under dense cover of trees, shrubs, or cactus as long as the ground beneath is bare. Recent trends of critical habitat factors in and around the Dry Tortugas ternery are not known in adequate detail, but no immediate threats are evident. The introduced black rat (*Rattus rattus*), historically the only mammalian predator, reached plague proportions in the early 1980s principally to the detriment of nesting Brown Noddies (*Anous stolidus*). Regular operation of a series of poison stations on Bush Key during fall and early winter has largely eliminated rat predation on the terns. However, with the shift to ever-earlier dates of colony initiation by Sooties (see Key Behaviors), predation on eggs and chicks by wintering gulls seems to have become a problem more serious, and less tractable, than rats. A possible trend of reduction of the nesting area available to Sooty Terns by erosion and overgrowth of ground-mantling plant cover (such as mats of sea purslane, *Sesuvium portulacastrum*) looms as a potentially significant change on Bush Key, but the situation is yet to be accurately analyzed. Because Sooty Terns often feed as "obligate commensals" with schools of predatory pelagic fishes (Ashmole and Ashmole 1967; Au and Pitman 1986), such as tuna and mackerel, increased commercial fishing pressure on these species in the Gulf of Mexico is of some concern. However, radio-tracking of foraging Sooties

(Robertson and Stoneburner 1980) has shown that they find their food mainly within 80 km of the Tortugas colony, a modest distance for a bird with the Sooty Tern's strength of wing.

VULNERABILITY OF SPECIES AND HABITAT: Although the Dry Tortugas colony of Sooty Terns is one of relatively few that are well-protected against most disturbances, the species' nesting and feeding habitats in Florida are vulnerable to several threats. Because the land area of Dry Tortugas is small (ca. 25 ha) and largely preempted by other uses, reduction of available nesting space on Bush Key is a continuing concern. If the number of nesting sites became severely limited, the population of Sooties, or part of it, might move to another Tortugan islet as in the past. However, options are limited and none appears to be especially satisfactory. It is doubtful whether colony sites suitable for Sooty Terns exist in Florida away from Dry Tortugas, particularly because of the abundance of raccoons (*Procyon lotor*) on islands closer to the mainland. Heavy ship traffic, much of it carrying potentially polluting cargo such as oil and chemicals, traverses the Sooty Tern fishing grounds around Dry Tortugas. Thus, the danger of local spills that could affect Sooties, either directly or by reducing marine productivity, is ever present. Moreover, year-to-year variations in the incidence of oil on the plumage of Sooties at Dry Tortugas (Robertson and Robertson 1978, unpubl. data), suggests that oil from major spills in distant parts of the Gulf of Mexico (e.g., off Louisiana, Campeche Bank) may reach the colony's feeding area in biologically significant amounts.

CAUSES OF THREAT: In addition to those discussed in the above two sections, various other natural and manmade factors constitute known or potential threats to nesting Sooty Terns at Dry Tortugas. Hurricanes, especially storms in May or June, have been known to decimate entire year-classes of chicks. Hurricane Alma in June, 1966, reduced that year's chick class by about half (Robertson, unpubl. data), and a week of rains that attended the passage of minor hurricane Agnes in June, 1972, caused heavy losses of younger chicks (White et al. 1976). Although the Tortugas' terns have become habituated to airplane noise, including sonic booms, at reasonably high altitude, overflights below about 150 m (especially by helicopters) often cause panic flights and some mortality of chicks and adults. Low overflights by jet aircraft at trans-sonic speed may be more generally threatening, but the case is not proved. Thus, several on-the-deck overflights by military jets in the spring of 1969 were thought to be the most likely cause of that year's unprecedented and virtually complete hatching failure of Sooty Terns (Mead 1971; Austin et al. 1972). A considerable variety of avian predators are known to occasionally take eggs, chicks, or adult Sooty Terns. The known predators at Dry Tortugas include Magnificent Frigatebird (*Fregata magnificens*), Cattle Egret (*Bubulcus ibis*), Yellow-crowned Night-Heron (*Nyctanassa violaceous*), Peregrine Falcon (*Falco peregrinus*), Purple Gallinule (*Porphyrula martinica;* Dinsmore 1972), Ruddy Turnstone (*Arenaria interpres;* also see Crossin and Huber 1972), Herring Gull (*Larus argentatus*), Laughing Gull (*Larus atricilla*), and Short-eared Owl (*Asio flammeus*). With the exception of gull predation on eggs in recent years, these losses are relatively minor. Ticks sometimes occur on adult and young Sooties at Dry Tortugas, but we have not noticed the adverse effects reported from several other colonies (Amerson 1966; Feare 1976b). Finally, sea-level rise, projected to be 38 cm in the next 100 years (Lidz and Shinn 1991), represents the ultimate threat to the inhabitants of Florida coasts and islands, including Sooty Terns.

RESPONSES TO HABITAT MODIFICATION: Although the history of the tern colonies (Robertson 1964) contains several reports of shifts of Sooty Tern nesting between islands at Dry Tortugas, the moves and the circumstances that prompted them were not described in detail. Beginning about 1850, many accounts refer to Sooties nesting on East Key as well as Bird Key. No specific descriptions of the East Key colony are known, but some references suggest that the two aggregations were about the same size. Around 1900 the East Key colony vanished from the record, again without comment. From what is known of contemporary events, it seems most likely that the colony was egged out of existence. What became of the survivors and whether or not the two groups were separate populations is food for speculation. Movement of the Sooty Tern colony from rapidly eroding Bird Key to Bush Key was accomplished between 1932 and 1935, and, to the extent that the estimates can be credited, it was accompanied by loss of more than 60% of the population. Early in their occupation of Bush Key in 1937, 1938, and 1947, Sooty Terns divided their numbers between Bush Key and the north end of Garden Key. Observers thought that unusually heavy vegetation and an outbreak of rats on Bush Key may have led to the move. Lastly, in 1957, 1959, 1963, and possibly other years, small numbers of Sooties (8 to 10 pairs) nested at the edges of a colony of several hundred Roseate Terns (*Sterna dougallii*) on Hospital Key. These Sooty nests were initiated much later than nests at the Bush Key colony in the same years and they probably were unproductive. Thus, they are reminiscent of many of the extralimital nesting attempts by Sooties. The scanty data thus suggest that, when nesting habitat is sufficiently modified or disturbed, Sooty Terns at Dry Tortugas shift their nesting to another island and initially may exhibit lower numbers and suffer considerable nesting failure in doing so. (See Robertson [1964] for further details.)

DEMOGRAPHIC CHARACTERISTICS: The demography of the Sooty Tern differs markedly from that of other species of *Sterna;* these differences seem to be related primarily to the Sooty's pelagic mode of life. Most terns nest at relatively hazardous, inshore sites, and adults and young-of-the-year tend to migrate and winter together. Their life parameters suggest it is advantageous to minimize time at the nesting colony and continue development of young during protracted adult–juvenile association away from the colony. Sooties nest at relatively secure, oceanic sites, and adults and young of the year probably go different ways within (at most) two or three months after leaving the colony. Based on recoveries of banded birds, adults and juveniles of the Dry Tortugas population appear to have entirely separate distributions after September or October of the year of fledging. Sooty Tern demographic evolution seemingly has emphasized production of a chick that is more competent (and much sooner independent) when it leaves the colony.

As with most pelagic birds, Sooty Terns have a clutch size of 1. At Dry Tortugas, as in other colonies studied (Brown 1975; Feare 1976a), the occurrence of 2 eggs in a nest scrape seems always to be an artifact, rather than eggs produced by one female. Sooties may be unable to rear a brood of two (Feare 1976a), but whether this results from an inadequate food supply or inflexible adult behavior seems moot. The mean incubation period (n = 17) at Dry Tortugas of 29.5 days (Dinsmore 1972) agrees well with data from Ascension Island (Ashmole 1963) and Manana Island, Hawaii (Brown 1975), but the mean (n = 234) for Bird Island, Seychelles (Feare 1976a), was substantially shorter at 28.1 days. In any case, the incubation period is long for a tern of the Sooty's size. For 14 marked chicks (M. J. Robertson, unpubl. data), the mean period from hatching to fledging was 57.5 days and from fledging to last sighting was 17.9 days. These fledging and departure periods and the associated behavioral observations agree well with Feare's data (1975, 1976a) from the Seychelles. Thus, Sooty Terns that nest successfully spend a minimum of 105 days in the colony, more than twice the colony time of successful Common Terns (*Sterna hirundo*; see Clapp et al. 1983). Although male and female parents contribute about equally to incubation and chick-rearing, records of the disappearance of 42 marked chicks of individually color-banded parents in 1980 and 1985 (M. J. Robertson, unpubl. data) suggest that males usually take the fledglings to sea. In these instances, males and fledglings were last seen at about the same time, but at least 14 of the females were seen later and some frequented the colony for several days. It is uncertain how long adults may attend fledglings, but numerous observations exist of a single adult and a juvenile at sea (Gould 1974; Ainley et al. 1986) or together on shore after storms; adults have been reported to feed juveniles both on the water (Gould 1974) and in the air (Feare 1975).

The Sooty Tern is remarkably long-lived for so small a bird, and, in the banded populations that have been studied in most detail, also remarkably late to mature. Known-age breeders (trapped on eggs) at Dry Tortugas have ranged from 4 to 32 years and Clapp and Sibley (1966) reported two individuals greater than 26 years old from Howland Island, central Pacific. The mean age of breeders at Dry Tortugas is about 15 years, and, in any year, the majority are aged 12–18 years. This age profile contrasts sharply with species such as the Common Tern (*Sterna hirundo*), in which more than half the breeders may be less than 5 years old (Austin and Austin 1956; Post and Gochfeld 1979). The age pattern of recruitment at Dry Tortugas is generally similar to the pattern Harrington (1974) described for the Sooty Terns of Johnston Atoll, central Pacific. No known-age individuals younger than the age of 3 years have returned; fewer than five individuals are known to have nested before the age of 6 years; and, some individuals may not breed for the first time until the age of 10 years or even later. In 1976–1987, a population of 112 color-banded adults at Dry Tortugas averaged 4.4 years of nesting and reared an average of 3.0 chicks. Based on known year-to-year survival, their average annual rate of mortality cannot have exceeded 11%.

In the same color-banded population, mean annual nesting success (chicks fledged as a percent of eggs laid) in 1976–1985 was 62% with extremes of 19 and 91%. Eggs laid earlier in a season tended to yield more fledglings and the youngest (and perhaps the oldest) breeders had a higher rate of failure in years of low production than did the population as a whole. These nest success data characterize the Dry Tortugas as an unusually productive Sooty Tern colony. For example, Woodward (1972) calculated success rates of 1.8, 24.2, 26.6, and 60.0% for the colony on Kure Atoll in 1965–1968. Many central Pacific colonies are subject at intervals to climatic shifts associated with the El Niño–Southern Oscillation phenomenon and may fail or be entirely deserted during the most extreme ENSO events (Schreiber and Schreiber 1984).

Finally, local Sooty Tern demography presents a puzzling dichotomy between instances of close philopatry and apparent recruitment to distant colonies. Many individuals fledged at Dry Tortugas have returned to nest within less than 5 m (exceptionally less than 1 m) of their natal nest site. Moreover, it appears doubtful that individuals change colonies once they have nested. However, banding data also suggest that movement between colonies occurs, perhaps regularly and on a large scale. The export phase of the exchange is open to little doubt. Chicks banded at Dry Tortugas have been recovered at appropriate ages and in the local breeding season in or near Sooty Tern colonies in the Bahamas, Cuba, Jamaica, Hispaniola, Puerto Rico, Virgin Islands, and, possibly, Martinique. Most of these reports do not give proof of breeding in other colonies, but a number (especially from Chandeleur Islands, Louisiana; H. H. Jeter, in litt.) were records of individuals trapped on nests. Because relatively few Sooty Terns have been banded in other Gulf-Caribbean colonies, we have no definite record of the occurrence of foreign Sooties at Dry Tortugas. However, after 20 years of intensive chick-banding, less than 60% of the breeding adults were banded. This at least suggests that many Sooties from other colonies are recruited to Dry Tortugas. Unreferenced data summarized in this section are unpublished results of the Dry Tortugas tern studies (Robertson, unpubl. data).

KEY BEHAVIORS: Throughout its range, the Sooty Tern apparently begins its breeding season by engaging in an extended period (up to 3 months) of noisy, night-time maneuvering around the colony. Robertson (1964) and Dinsmore (1972) described this behavior at Dry Tortugas, where, on the population's present schedule, the first night visitors are heard around mid-December. Near the end of the period of nocturnal swarming, Sooties begin landing in the colony at night. Pair-formation and copulation probably occur during these visits, because egg-laying generally begins almost as soon as the terns make a definitive daytime landing. Initiation of nesting in late April-early May is usual for the Sooty Terns of the northern Gulf–Caribbean. For example, Watson (1908) noted that the first Sooty Tern egg in 1907 was laid on 7 May, and, "By May 15 thousands of eggs were present." This regimen prevailed at Dry Tortugas until the late 1950s, but, since that time, nesting has tended to start earlier each year. Thus, records for 1938–1955 show 2 first-egg dates in late March, 11 in April, and 5 in early May with an average date of 23 April. The last start in May (1 May) occurred in 1958; 10 years later first eggs were laid on 1 April (Dinsmore 1972). The recession of first-egg dates has continued to the present, with 18 February 1994 and 1995 having been the earliest dates of record and the fourth and fifth consecutive starts in February. Speculations abound, but the forces driving this remarkable change remain obscure, in part because the ever-earlier nesting seems maladaptive in many respects.

As seen above and as befits the English vernacular name of Wideawake, Sooty Terns are active and vocal at all hours. Adults feeding older chicks tend to leave the colony for most of the day and often return to feed their young well after dark. It is not certain whether Sooties regularly continue to feed after nightfall, but reports suggest that they are able to do so, at least on moonlit nights. Evidence of nocturnal feeding comes from direct observations (e.g., Gould 1967) and from regurgitation of deep-sea fishes that come to the surface only at night (Morzer Bruyns and Voous 1965).

Nesting Sooty Terns are associated in "neighborhoods" within which they conduct most of their ground-based activities. Each neighborhood is a circle roughly 3–4 meters in diameter around a nest site, and consists of terns that are individually recognizable to one another, primarily by voice. Barring large changes in the local environment, neighborhoods retain considerable continuity from year to year. A major adaptive value of the neighborhood organization appears to be reduced aggression. Sooties nest in dense aggregations (often several nests per square meter) compared to most other terns, and nesting amid known birds tends to damp aggression. Study of color-banded individuals also has shown neighborhood effects upon pairing and breeding patterns. Because some adults breed intermittently and because of timing differences between former mates, few Sooty Tern pair bonds persist from one year to the next. Records suggest that males are overwhelmingly likely to choose, as mates, successful female neighbors of earlier years. Even in years when the number of color-banded breeders was highest, about one-third of the experienced adults later found to be alive were not known to breed. Most intermittent breeders have only one period of intermittency and most breaks are only one year in duration. The neighborhood system seems to accommodate these irregular appearances, in effect a time-sharing of the real estate, and available data indicate that intermittent breeders are slightly more productive on a lifetime basis than are annual breeders.

After Sooty Tern chicks are about 3 weeks old, both parents leave the colony to fish during most of the day (Dinsmore 1972). The vacated space is quickly occupied by another group of adult-plumaged individuals made up of prebreeders, intermittent breeders, and failed breeders. The prebreeders, in particular, may be returning to a place near their natal nest site and they may return in several successive years and eventually nest in the neighborhood. These unemployed Sooties stand in the same areas day after day, interact with the chicks and with one another, guard and occasionally feed chicks, and perform what seems to be a ritualized "Greeting/Advertising" display (vertical Fly-up with "wideawake" calls) to returning male parents.

Although the species is one of the most thoroughly pelagic birds, it has long been known that the Sooty Tern's feathers are easily wettable (Watson and Lashley 1915). The physical basis of this condition appears to be a deficiency of oils in the uropygial gland (Johnston 1979). Thus, where most *Sterna* species feed by plunge-diving, Sooties feed either by "dipping" in which they merely brush the water surface (Ashmole and Ashmole 1967) or by snatching in mid-air small fishes flushed by piscine predators. In addition, Sooties almost invariably take wing when a shower crosses the colony (Dinsmore 1972), because they quickly become unable to fly when wetted. At sea, Sooty Terns are well known to perch on flotsam and on the backs of surfaced sea turtles and they are able to alight on a calm sea surface briefly and take wing again (Gould 1974). However, it seems an inescapable conclusion that individuals must often fly for long periods without rest or sleep on the wing (Serventy et al. 1971). Unreferenced data summarized in this section are unpublished results of the Dry Tortugas tern studies (Robertson, unpubl. data).

CONSERVATION MEASURES TAKEN: Beginning in 1903, the tern colonies at Dry Tortugas have been protected by resident wardens in every nesting season, except perhaps in one or two Depression years of the early 1930s. Over this time, wardening was provided by the American Ornithologists' Union, the National Association of Audubon Societies, the Bureau of Biological Survey, and, since 1935, the National Park Service. Few bird colonies anywhere have a comparable record of protection. Protective measures in place include warning signs, regulations controlling operation of boats and civilian aircraft in the vicinity of the colony, a routine program of rat control, limited vegetation management, and a contingency plan for dealing with oil spills in the colony area. Frequent discussions with local military authorities attempt to keep them alerted to the need for careful operations around Dry Tortugas, particularly at lower altitudes.

CONSERVATION MEASURES PROPOSED: Protection of the Dry Tortugas tern colonies has been an unusually sustained and successful effort, now nearly a century old. The future challenge is to adapt conservation measures to the rapidly increasing public and commercial use of Dry Tortugas National Park and the surrounding seas. Specifically, need exists for more precise measurement of year-to-year changes in the area and plant cover of Bush Key and in the population size and nesting success of Sooty Terns. Developing these capabilities along with continued research to improve understanding of Sooty Tern social behavior should permit more responsive management of this major wildlife resource.

ACKNOWLEDGMENTS: Our tern studies at Dry Tortugas would have been altogether impossible without years of help, good humor, and inspiration from scores of volunteers. Their names are far too numerous to list individually and any selection is unfair. Nonetheless, we must mention Oliver Austin, Ted Below, Jim Dinsmore, Brian Harrington, Russ Mason, Ralph Schreiber, and Glen Woolfenden. For dedicated work with the color-banded population, the second author particularly thanks Bobbie Kittleson, Manny Lopez, Chet Winegarner, and Sandy Dayhoff.

LITERATURE CITED:

AOU. 1983. Check-list of North American birds. 6th ed. Allen Press, Lawrence, Kansas.

Ainley, D. G., L. B. Spear, and R. L. Boekelheide. 1986. Extended parental care in the Red-tailed Tropicbird and Sooty Tern. Condor 88:101–102.

Amerson, A. B., Jr. 1966. *Ornithodoros capensis* (Acarina: Argasidae) infesting Sooty Tern (*Sterna fuscata*) nasal cavities. Jour. Parasit. 52:1220–1221.

Ashmole, N. P. 1963. The biology of the Wideawake or Sooty Tern *Sterna fuscata* on Ascension Island. Ibis 103b:297–364.

Ashmole, N. P., and M. J. Ashmole. 1967. Comparative feeding biology of sea birds on a tropical oceanic island. Peabody Mus. Nat. Hist. Yale Univ. Bull. 24.

Au, D. W. K., and R. L. Pitman. 1986. Seabird interactions with dolphins and tuna in eastern tropical Pacific. Condor 88:304–317.

Audubon, J. J. 1835. Ornithological biography. Vol. 3.

Austin, O. L., and O. L. Austin, Jr. 1956. Some demographic aspects of the Cape Cod population of Common Terns (*Sterna hirundo*). Bird-Banding 27:55–66.

Austin, O. L., Jr., W. B. Robertson, Jr., and G. E. Woolfenden. 1972. Mass hatching failure in Dry Tortugas Sooty Terns (*Sterna fuscata*). Proc. Internat. Ornithol. Congress (1970):15:627 (Abstract only).

Brown, W. Y. 1975. Artifactual clutch size in Sooty Terns and Brown Noddies. Wilson Bull. 87:115–116.

Clancey, P. A. 1977. Data from Sooty Terns from Natal and Zululand. Ostrich 48:43–44.

Clapp, R. B., and F. C., Sibley. 1966. Longevity records of some central Pacific seabirds. Bird-Banding 38:193–197.

Clapp, R. B., D. Morgan-Jacobs, and R. C. Banks. 1983. Marine birds of the southeastern United States and Gulf of Mexico. Part III: Charadriiformes. U.S. Fish and Wildl. Serv., Div. of Biol. Services, Washington, D.C.

Cooper, J., A. J. Williams, and P. L. Britton. 1984. Distribution, population sizes and conservation of breeding seabirds in the Afrotropical region. Pp. 403–417 in Status and conservation of the world's seabirds (J. P. Croxall, G. H. Evans, and R. W. Schreiber, eds.). ICBP Tech. Publ. No. 2, Cambridge, England.

Cramp, S. (Chief Ed.), D. J. Brooks, E. Dunn, R. Gillmor, P. A. D. Hollom, R. Hudson, E. M. Nicholson, M. A. Ogilvie, P. J. S. Olney, C. S. Roselaar, K. E. L. Simmons, K, H. Voous, D. I. M. Wallace, J. Wattel, and M. G. Wilson. 1985. Handbook of the birds of Europe, the Middle East, and North Africa: the birds of the Western Paleartic. Volume 4. Terns to woodpeckers. Oxford Univ. Press, Oxford, England.

Crossin, R. S., and L. N. Huber. 1970. Sooty Tern egg predation by Ruddy Turnstones. Condor 72:372–373.

Croxall, J. P., P. G. H. Evans, and R. W. Schreiber (eds.) 1984. Status and conservation of the world's seabirds. ICBP Tech. Publ. No. 2, Cambridge, England.

Croxall, J. P. (ed.) 1991. Seabird status and conservation: a supplement. ICBP Tech. Publ. No. 11, Cambridge, England.

Dinsmore, J. J. 1972. Sooty Tern behavior. Bull. Fla. State Mus. 16:129–179.

Everett, W. T., and D. W. Anderson. 1991. Status and conservation of the breeding seabirds on offshore Pacific islands of Baja California and the Gulf of California. Pp. 115–139 in Seabird status and conservation: a supplement (J. P. Croxall, ed.). ICBP Tech. Publ. No. 11, Cambridge, England.

Feare, C. J. 1975. Post-fledging parental care in Crested and Sooty terns. Condor 77:368–370.

Feare, C. J. 1976a. The breeding of the Sooty Tern *Sterna fuscata* in the Seychelles and the effects of experimental removal of its eggs. Jour. Zool., London 179:317–360.

Feare, C. J. 1976b. Desertion and abnormal development in a colony of Sooty Terns *Sterna fuscata* infested by virus-infected ticks. Ibis 118:112–115.

Feare, C. J. 1984. Seabird status and conservation in the tropical Indian Ocean. Pp. 457–471 in Status and conservation of the world's seabirds (J. P. Croxall, P. G. H. Evans, and R. W. Schreiber, eds.). ICBP Tech. Publ. No. 2, Cambridge, England.

Flint, E. N. 1991. Time and energy limits to the foraging radius of Sooty Terns *Sterna fuscata*. Ibis 133:43–46.

Fussell, J. O., III, T. L. Quay, and R. J. Hader. 1981. Sooty Tern nest found near Cape Lookout. Amer. Birds 33:715–721.

Gallagher, M. D., D, A. Scott, R. F. G. Ormond, R. J. Conner, and M. C. Jennings. 1984. The distribution and conservation of seabirds breeding on the coasts and islands of Iran and Arabia. Pp. 421–456 in Status and conservation of the world's seabirds (J. P. Croxall, P. G. H. Evans, and R. W. Schreiber, eds.). ICBP Tech. Publ. No. 2, Cambridge, England.

Garnett, M. C. 1984. Conservation of seabirds in the South Pacific region. A review. Pp. 547–558 in Status and conservation of the world's seabirds (J. P. Croxall, P. G. H. Evans, and R. W. Schreiber, eds.). ICBP Tech. Publ. No. 2, Cambridge, England.

Gould, P. J. 1967. Nocturnal feeding of *Sterna fuscata* and *Puffinus pacificus*. Condor 69:529.

Gould, P. J. 1974. Sooty Tern (*Sterna fuscata*). Pp. 6–52 in Pelagic studies of seabirds in the central and eastern Pacific Ocean (W. B. King, ed.). Smithson. Contrib. Zool. no. 158, Smithson. Inst. Press, Washington, D.C.

Halewyn, R. van, and R. L. Norton. 1984. The status and conservation of seabirds in the Caribbean. Pp. 169–222 in Status and conservation of the world's seabirds (J. P. Croxall, P. G. H. Evans, and R. W. Schreiber, eds.). ICBP Tech. Publ. No. 2, Cambridge, England.

Harrington, B. A. 1974. Colony visitation behavior and breeding ages of Sooty Terns (*Sterna fuscata*). Bird-Banding 45:115–144.

Harrison, C. S., T. S. Hida, and M. P. Seki. 1983. Hawaiian seabird feeding ecology. Wildl. Monog. 85:1–71.

Harrison, C. S., M. B. Naughton, and S. I. Fefer. 1984. The status and conservation of seabirds in the Hawaiian Archipelago and Johnston Atoll.

Pp. 513–526 in Status and conservation of the world's seabirds (J. P. Croxall, P. G. H. Evans, and R. W. Schreiber, eds.). ICBP Tech. Publ. No. 2, Cambridge, England.

Hasegawa, H. 1984. Status and conservation of seabirds in Japan, with special attention the Short-tailed Albatross. Pp. 487–500 in Status and conservation of the world's seabirds (J. P. Croxall, P. G. H. Evans, and R. W. Schreiber, eds.). ICBP Tech. Publ. No. 2, Cambridge, England.

Hindwood, K. A., K. Keith, and D. L. Serventy. 1963. Birds of the South-West Coral Sea. CSIRO Australia, Div. Wildl. Res., Tech. Paper No. 3. 44 pp.

Johnson, A. W., W. R. Millie, and G. Moffett. 1970. Notes on the birds of Easter Island. Ibis 112:532–538.

Johnston, D. W. 1979. The uropygial gland of the Sooty Tern. Condor 81:430–432.

Jouventin, P., J. C. Stahl, H. Weimerskirch, and J. L. Mougin. 1984. The seabirds of the French subantarctic islands and Adelie Land, their status and conservation. Pp. 609–625 in Status and conservation of the world's seabirds (J. P. Croxall, P. G. H. Evans, and R. W. Schreiber, eds.). ICBP Tech. Publ. No. 2, Cambridge, England.

Lane, S. G. 1967. Sooty Tern recovery in the Philippines. Australian Bird Bander 5:57.

LeGrand, G., K. Emmerson, and A. Martin. 1984. The status and conservation of seabirds in the Macaronesian Islands. Pp. 377–391 in Status and conservation of the world's seabirds (J. P. Croxall, P. G. H. Evans, and R. W. Schreiber, eds.). ICBP Tech. Publ. No. 2, Cambridge, England.

Lidz, B. H., and E. A. Shinn. 1991. Paleoshorelines, reefs, and a rising sea: South Florida, U.S.A. Coastal Res. 7:203–229.

Mead, C. 1971. Bang go the eggs. Brit. Trust Ornithol. News 44:8.

Morzer Bruyns, W. F. J., and K. H. Voous. 1965. Night-feeding by Sooty Terns (*Sterna fuscata*). Ardea 53:79.

Murphy, R. C. 1936. Oceanic birds of South America. Volumes 1 & 2. Amer. Mus. Nat. Hist., New York, New York.

Naurois, R. de. 1969. Peuplements et cycles de reproduction des oiseaux de la cote occidentale d'Afrique. Mem. du Mus. National d'Hist. Nat., Ser. A, 56:1–312.

Peters, J. L. 1934. Check-list of birds of the world. Vol. 2. Harvard Univ. Press, Cambridge, Massachusetts.

Post, P. W., and M. Gochfeld. 1979. Recolonization by Common Terns at Breezy Point, New York. Proc. 1978 Conf. Colon. Waterbird Group 2:128–136.

Olson, S. L. 1972. Natural history of vertebrates on the Brazilian islands of the mid-South Atlantic. Natl. Geog. Soc. Res. Repts., 1972:481–492.

Robertson, C. J. R., and B. D. Bell. 1984. Seabird status and conservation in the New Zealand region. Pp. 573–586 in Status and conservation of the world's seabirds (J. P. Croxall, P. G. H. Evans, and R. W. Schreiber, eds.). ICBP Tech. Publ. No. 2, Cambridge, England.

Robertson, M. J., and W. B. Robertson, Jr. 1978. Occurrence and effects of chronic, low-level oil contamination in a population of Sooty Terns (*Sterna fuscata*). Unpubl. ms. in files of South Fla. Res. Ctr., Everglades Nat. Park, Homestead, Florida. 42 pp.

Robertson, W. B., Jr. 1964. The terns of the Dry Tortugas. Bull. Fla. State Mus. 8:1–95.

Robertson, W, B., Jr. 1969. Trans-Atlantic migration of juvenile Sooty Terns. Nature (London) 223:632–634.

Robertson, W. B., Jr. 1978. Sooty Tern. Pp. 89–91 in Rare and endangered biota of Florida. Vol. 2: Birds (H. W. Kale, II, ed.). Univ. Presses of Fla., Gainesville, Florida.

Robertson, W. B., Jr., and D. L. Stoneburner. 1980. Radio-tracking of nesting Sooty Terns (Sterna fuscata). Proc. 1979 Conf. Colonial Waterbird Group 3:260. (Abstract only).

Robertson, W. B., Jr., and G. E. Woolfenden. 1992. Florida bird species: an annotated list. Spec. Publ. No. 6, Fla. Ornithol. Soc., Gainesville, Florida.

Schreiber, R. W., and N. P. Ashmole. 1970. Sea-bird breeding seasons on Christmas Island, Pacific Ocean. Ibis 112:363–394.

Schreiber, R. W., and E. A. Schreiber. 1984. Central Pacific seabirds and the El Nino-Southern Oscillation: 1982–1983 perspectives. Science 225:713–716.

Serventy, D. L. 1952. The bird islands of the Sahul Shelf. Emu 52:33–59.

Serventy, D. L., V. Serventy, and J. Warham. 1971. The handbook of Australian seabirds. A. W. and A. H. Reed, Sydney.

Shields, M. A., and J. F. Parnell. 1984. Occurrence and nesting of the Sooty Tern in North Carolina on the lower Cape Fear River. Chat 48:73–74.

Sprunt, A., IV. 1984. The status and conservation of seabirds of the Bahama Islands. Pp. 157–168 in Status and conservation of the world's seabirds (J. P. Croxall, P. G. H. Evans, and R. W. Schreiber, eds.). ICBP Tech. Publ. No. 2, Cambridge, England.

Taylor, R. H. 1979. Predation on Sooty Terns at Raoul Island by rats and cats. Notornis 26:199–202.

van Tets, G. F., and P. J. Fullagar. 1984. Status of seabirds breeding in Australia. Pp. 559–571 in Status and conservation of the world's seabirds (J. P. Croxall, P. G. H. Evans, and R. W. Schreiber, eds.). ICBP Tech. Publ. No. 2, Cambridge, England.

Wallace, D. I. M. 1973. Sea-birds at Lagos and in the Gulf of Guinea. Ibis 115:559–571.

Warham, J. 1956. Observations on the birds of Pelsart Island. Emu 56:83–93.

Warham, J. 1961. The birds of Raine Island, Pandora Cay and Murray Island Sandbank. Emu 61:76–93.

Watson, J. B. 1908. The behavior of Noddy and Sooty terns. Carnegie Inst. Wash., Papers from the Tortugas Lab. 2:187–255.

Watson, J. B., and K. S. Lashley. 1915. Homing and related activities of birds. Carnegie Inst. Wash., Publ. 211. Papers from Dept. Marine Biol. 7:5–104.

White, S. C., W. B. Robertson, Jr., and R. E. Ricklefs. 1976. The effects of hurricane Agnes on growth and survival of tern chicks in Florida. Bird-Banding 47:54–71.

Wilkinson, P. M. 1987. First nesting of Sooty Tern in South Carolina. Chat 51:51.

Wilkinson, P, M. 1988. Second nesting of the Sooty Tern in South Carolina. Chat 52:42.

Williams, A. J. 1984. Breeding distribution, numbers and conservation of tropical seabirds on oceanic islands in the South Atlantic Ocean. Pp. 393–401 in Status and conservation of the world's seabirds (J. P. Croxall, P. G. H. Evans, and R. W. Schreiber, eds.). ICBP Tech. Publ. No. 2, Cambridge, England.

Woodward, P. W. 1972. The natural history of Kure Atoll, northwestern Hawaiian Islands. Atoll Res. Bull. No. 164.

PREPARED BY: William B. Robertson, Jr., National Biological Service, Everglades National Park, 40001 State Road 9336, Homestead, FL 33034–6733; and Mary J. Robertson, 17300 SW 300th Street, Homestead, FL 33030.

Royal Tern

Sterna maxima

FAMILY LARIDAE

Order Charadriiformes

TAXONOMY: The Royal Tern (*Sterna maxima*) was described in 1783 by Boddaert (AOU 1983). This species, along with the Elegant (*S. elegans*) and Sandwich (*S. sandvicensis*) Terns, has been placed in the genus *Thalasseus*.

DESCRIPTION: The Royal Tern is a rather large (total length 0.46–0.51 m, 18–20 in.), but typical member of the subfamily Sterninae, with long narrow wings (wing span 1.0–1.1 m, 40–44 in.), long pointed bill (63.5–69.9 mm, 2.50–2.75 in.), and deeply forked tail. The breeding plumage of males and females is similar. The pileum (crest, from the base of the bill to the nape) is dark black and extends off the back of the head; most of the remaining upper parts of the neck, back, tail, and belly are predominantly white, but with a pearl-gray tinge on the middle tail feathers; the primaries and secondaries are pearl-gray edged with white; the bill is coral or orange-red; and the feet are a dull black. Immature Royal Terns, and adults that have acquired their post-nuptial molt (by August and September), resemble birds in the breeding plumage, but there is more gray on the tail and wings. The bill is a dull orange and the pileum consists of an entire white forehead and crown streaked with black feathers. The nestlings are boldly spotted over a dusky-colored downy plumage.

POPULATION SIZE AND TREND: Spendelow and Patton (1988) compiled and synthesized earlier estimates of Florida Royal Tern breeding populations by Portnoy et al. (1981), Clapp et al. (1983), and from personal observations. The data suggest that during the period 1976–82 as many as 13,000 birds may have nested along the Atlantic coast and possibly 2,000 birds nested along the Gulf coast of Florida (Spendelow and Patton 1988). These numbers represent total numbers of breeding birds. Seven colonies ranged in size from approximately 200 to 9,000 terns.

Royal Tern, *Sterna maxima*. (Photo copyright 1976 by Allan D. Cruickshank, courtesy of Florida Audubon Society)

Unfortunately, no systematic statewide survey of the breeding population for this species was conducted in Florida from the mid-1980s through 1991. Reports from *American Birds* and unpublished data from Florida Game and Fresh Water Fish Commission files suggest lower total numbers than the figures above. Paul (1989) reported 2,250 pairs of Royals at Nassau Sound (Duval County) in 1989 and P. D. Southall (unpubl. data) reported 600 birds during 1990 in the same area. In 1987, a colony with 670 pairs was recorded on the Banana River spoil islands (Brevard County) by Paul (1987). D. Whitmore (pers. comm.) reported 452 Royal Terns in 1991 and 50 terns in 1992 on an island in the Mosquito Lagoon (Volusia County). Between 1987 and 1990, the numbers of Royal Terns found in the Tampa Bay area at Passage Key National Wildlife Refuge (Manatee County) were estimated as follows: 1,025 nests (Paul 1987), 1,825 pairs (Paul 1989), and 2,500 adult Royals (Paul 1991). Another site in Hillsborough Bay (Island 3D) had "at least 450 pairs of Royals" (Paul 1987). A small colony of 50 pairs was seen on a Florida barge canal dredged-material island in Citrus County (Paul 1987). In 1993, a colony of 139 nests with eggs was on Lanark Island in Franklin County (J. A. Gore, unpubl. data). Using these reported figures, the maximum breeding population of Royal Terns in Florida between 1987 and 1993 would be about 5,600 pairs. Multiplying this number by two in order to represent the breeding population would show a decrease by 3,800 birds from Spendelow and Patton's (1988) previous estimate of 15,000 birds. These figures, derived from several years of individual reports, are only estimates and possibly partial estimates of the actual population.

A single statewide survey is needed to accurately determine the size of the

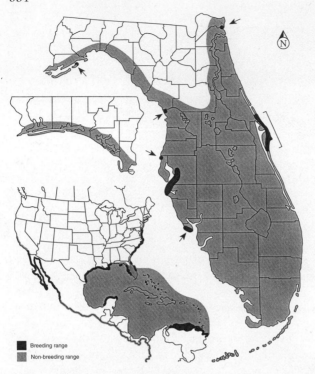

Distribution map
of the Royal Tern,
Sterna maxima.

Breeding range
Non-breeding range

current population. It is difficult to get an accurate estimate of the state
breeding population when using data collected in different years at various
sites. Many colonies fluctuate in size drastically from one year to the next. For
example, there were 9,100 birds in 1977, 2,624 in 1978, and only 239 in
1984 at Banana River spoil islands (D. Whitmore, pers. comm.). Other sites
are used intermittently over the years (R. T. Paul, pers. comm.).

DISTRIBUTION AND HISTORY OF DISTRIBUTION: The Royal Tern
breeds locally on the Pacific coast in southern California, in west-central Baja
California, along the coast of Sonora and Sinaloa, and on the Tres Marias
Islands; in the Atlantic–Gulf–Caribbean region from the Gulf coast (west to
southern Texas) and Maryland (Chesapeake Bay) south through the West
Indies to islands off the north coast of Venezuela and French Guiana; in South
America on the coast of Uruguay; and on the islands off Mauritania in West
Africa. Nonbreeding individuals in summer and winter occur in coastal and
inland freshwater areas in North America north to central California and New
York. The winter range is from central California, the Gulf coast and North
Carolina south along both coasts of the United States and Central America to
Peru, Uruguay and Argentina, and along the west coast of Africa from Mo-
rocco to Angola.

In Florida, Royal Terns breed in the marine-estuarine habitats of both the Atlantic and Gulf coasts. A recent state-wide survey for breeding Royal Terns has not been conducted. Nevertheless, we uncovered 10 breeding sites for Royal Terns in Florida from 1987 to present. These sites are: (1) Bird Island, Nassau Sound (Paul 1989; P. D. Southall unpubl. data); (2) Banana River spoil islands (Paul 1987); (3) an island in Mosquito Lagoon (D. Whitmore, pers. comm.); (4) Gasparilla Sound in Charlotte County (R. T. Paul, pers. comm.); (5) Passage Key National Wildlife Refuge in Manatee County (Paul 1987, 1989, 1991); (6) Alafia Bay in Hillsborough County (Paul, pers. comm.); (7) Island 3D in Hillsborough Bay (Paul 1987); (8) Three Rooker Bar in Pinellas County (R. T. Paul, pers. comm.); (9) barge canal spoil island in Citrus County (Paul 1987); and (10) Lanark Island in Franklin County (J. A. Gore, unpubl. data 1993). Additional small colonies may be present in Florida but it is unlikely that any large colony of Royal Terns has gone unnoticed. Royal Terns nested intermittently from 1951 to 1970 on a dredged-material island in St. Joseph Bay (Gulf County) (Hallman 1968; Stevenson 1972). This island is no longer present and no nesting seabirds have been found on recent surveys in the area (Gore 1991). Nonbreeding and wintering Royal Terns are found along the coasts and at inland, freshwater sites throughout Florida, especially the larger rivers and lakes of central and south Florida (e.g., Kissimmee River, Lake Kissimmee, St. Johns River, Lake George, Lake Okeechobee, and Lake Tohopekaliga). Recoveries of banded Royal Terns in Florida have been reviewed in Van Velzen (1968, 1971) and Smith et al. (1994).

HABITAT REQUIREMENTS AND HABITAT TRENDS: Royal Terns nest in coastal areas by making a shallow depression ("scrape") in the sand in which they place their eggs. The nesting sites are usually on islands, islets, or isolated spits along the coast (Clapp et al. 1983). The preferred substrate is sand, sometimes mixed with shell, and is located in an area devoid of vegetation (Parnell and Soots 1979; Clapp et al. 1983). Many colonies are found on dredged-material islands and these sites have become a very important breeding habitat for the Royal Tern (Soots and Parnell 1975; Schreiber and Schreiber 1978; Portnoy et al. 1981; Clapp et al. 1983). Portnoy et al. (1981) searched for seabird colonies from North Carolina to Key West, Florida and found 7 of the 11 Royal Tern colonies located on dredged-material sites.

VULNERABILITY OF SPECIES AND HABITAT: Ground nesting in coastal sites leaves Royal Tern colonies open to the destructive actions of tides and waves. Habitat destruction and human impact pose other problems for the species. Since Royal Terns tend to nest in large colonies, they can be extremely vulnerable to disturbances. In Florida, the species may be particularly at risk due to the isolated and localized breeding distribution. As ground nesters,

Royal Terns are susceptible to the actions of land predators. However, Clapp et al. (1983) reported that ground predation is not often a threat due to the absence of terrestrial predators on many of the islands on which Royal Terns nest.

CAUSES OF THREAT: Historically, Royal Terns and other terns were the subject of feather collection for the millinery trade and egg collection (Bent 1921). The former was not much of a problem since the Royal Tern's large feathers were inappropriate for ladies' hats. Egg collection was a more significant problem because the relatively large size of the eggs increased their value as a food source (Bent 1921). As with other coastal birds, Royal Terns currently face the problems of habitat destruction and increased disturbance that come with our increasing human population. For a detailed discussion of this subject refer to the Least Tern section in this text. Royal Terns may not be impacted by these issues at the same magnitude because of their more isolated nesting locations. However, because Royal Terns congregate in a few large colonies, these impacts can have a greater effect on the total population.

Extreme tides are probably the greatest natural threat to this species during the breeding season (Clapp et al. 1983). Although the nests are usually placed well above the high tide mark, extreme high tides associated with storms can cause egg-loss. Sprunt and Chamberlain (1949) reported an instance in South Carolina where unusually high tides destroyed much of a colony of 11,000 nests.

Although mammalian predators typically do not present much of a threat to Royal Terns, avian predators may cause a greater problem (Clapp et al. 1983). Buckley and Buckley (1972) believed that Laughing Gulls (*Larus atricilla*) were the only major avian predator of tern eggs in Virginia and North Carolina. Ruddy Turnstones (*Arenaria interpres*) have been seen pecking holes in eggs in a Royal Tern colony in Florida (Bird Island, Nassau Sound) eventually causing the colony to desert (Loftin and Sutton 1979). Smith et al. (1994) reported Royal Terns were frequently killed by cars at a bridge site in Florida.

Pollutants are another potential problem for Royal Terns. As fish feeders, this species may intake pesticides and other contaminants in their prey. As seen in other species of terns, this may result in deformities in young, as well as, other possible impediments to reproduction (Hays and Risebrough 1972). Catastrophic spills of contaminants such as oil are another hazard for this species (Clapp et al. 1983). Because Royal Terns congregate in large breeding colonies, there is the potential of a single disaster having an appreciable effect on a large portion of the total population.

RESPONSES TO HABITAT MODIFICATION: The creation of dredged-material islands during channel dredging has led to the creation of potential habitat for several species of seabirds (Soots and Parnell 1975). Royal Terns have taken advantage of these man-made areas to such an extent that dredged-material islands are now the predominant nesting habitat in many regions (Parnell and Soots 1979; Clapp et al. 1983). These sites are ideal as they are initially devoid of vegetation and usually isolated from ground predators. The succession of the barren island to a vegetated stage will eventually cause the birds to abandon such sites. The turnover rate for use of these sites by Royal Terns in North Carolina was estimated by Soots and Parnell (1975) to be four years. The use of these sites may be prolonged if subsequent dredging activity causes additional deposition of sand.

Toland and Gilbert (1987) found two Royal Tern nests on a gravel-covered roof in Vero Beach, Florida. This is the only reported case of roof nesting by this species that we are aware of, though the nesting attempt was unsuccessful due to the eggs cracking.

DEMOGRAPHIC CHARACTERISTICS: Royal Terns in Florida produce most of their clutches during May, June, and July; however, some late nesting occurs in August. This species nests in large, high-density colonies (see review in Clapp et al. 1983) and Schreiber and Schreiber (1978) reported that even in a small (21 nests) colony in Florida "all nests were closely packed with less than 40 cm separating each egg." The eggs of Royal Terns average 63 x 44.5 mm (Bent 1921). They are typically white (varying from light buff to ivory), with gray markings that range from small, dark-colored spots to large, bold blotches, occasionally with irregular scrawls (Bent 1921). Between 95–99% of Royal Tern clutches consist of 1 egg throughout their southeastern and Gulf coast breeding range (Clapp et al. 1983). Two, three, and even four eggs are occasionally found in nests (Barbour and Schreiber 1978; Clapp et al. 1983). The incubation period is about 30–31 days and eggs are incubated by both sexes (Buckley and Buckley 1972). At about 2–3 days of age, chicks leave the nest to form a creche and thereafter fledge at about 30 days (Buckley and Buckley 1972). The maximum age reported for a recaptured banded bird is 17 years (Clapp et al. 1982), but this probably does not represent the maximum longevity for the species.

KEY BEHAVIORS: Royal Tern pairs sometimes nest alone or in small groups (Parnell and Soots 1979; Toland and Gilbert 1987), but usually they nest in large, dense colonies (Clapp et al. 1983). Colony sizes reported by Buckley and Buckley (1972) in Virginia and North Carolina ranged from 250 to 4,500 pairs and colony sizes in excess of 10,000 breeding birds have been reported (Clapp et al. 1983; Spendelow and Patton 1988). Spendelow and Patton (1988) reported that 2,241 breeding birds was the mean colony size for Florida.

Royal Terns are known to nest with several other species of seabirds. One of the more frequent associates is the Sandwich Tern. Breeding Sandwich Terns are rare in Florida, but they have been recorded nesting with Royal Terns at Passage Key National Wildlife Refuge (Paul 1989, 1991) and at Nassau Sound (Portnoy et al. 1981). At Lanark Island, Royal Terns were nesting with Laughing Gulls in 1993 (Egensteiner and Smith, pers. obs.) and these two species have been reported nesting together at other sites in Florida (Hallman 1968; Loftin 1982). Loftin and Sutton (1979) reported Gull-billed Terns (*S. nilotica*) and Least Terns (*S. antillarum*) as nesting associates on Bird Island in Nassau Sound. At the same location, Black Skimmers (*Rynchops niger*) also were observed nesting with Royal Terns (Loftin 1982). Other species that have been reported nesting with Royal Terns are Common Terns (*S. hirundo*), Herring Gulls (*L. argentatus*), Brown Pelicans (*Pelecanus occidentalis*), and American Oystercatchers (*Haematopus palliatus*) (Buckley and Buckley 1972; Portnoy et al. 1981).

Feeding by Royal Terns is accomplished by plunge diving into the water for fish and invertebrates (Bent 1921; Clapp et al. 1983). Buckley and Buckley (1972) included silversides (*Menidia*), killifishes (*Fundulus*), anchovies (*Anchoa*), and menhaden (*Brevoortia*) in a list of common prey. They also reported that squid (*Loligo* sp.), shrimp, and blue crabs (*Callinectes sapidus*) were other food items. In Florida, Loftin (1982) listed Atlantic menhaden (*Brevoortia tyrannus*) and Atlantic croaker (*Micropogonias undulatus*) as the two most abundant prey items found in regurgitated food boluses from a colony at Nassau Sound.

CONSERVATION MEASURES TAKEN: All species of terns are protected by the Migratory Bird Treaty Act (16 U.S.C. 703–711) and the Florida Wildlife Code (Chapter 39 F.A.C.). Royal Tern breeding colonies are closed and posted annually by state and federal resource management agencies, as well as, conservation organizations such as the Audubon Society. Various wildlife and environmental education programs also are conducted by all of the above entities to promote public awareness and support for protecting colonial waterbirds in Florida. The conservation measures recommended for Least Terns by O'Meara and Gore (1988) also are applicable to Royal Terns.

CONSERVATION MEASURES PROPOSED: The number of Royal Tern colonies in Florida is limited and most locations are now known (H. W. Kale, unpubl. data). Closure of all sites prior to the start of breeding activity would reduce the likelihood of any pre-laying site abandonment caused by human disturbance. Erwin (1989) recommended a buffer of 100 meters when sign-posting Royal Tern colonies. Because Royal Terns are strongly attracted to barren substrates, dredged-material islands should be designed and maintained to encourage nesting and loafing. Mammalian predators may need to be controlled at some sites.

ACKNOWLEDGMENTS: We thank J. Gore, H. Kale, R. Paul, and D. Whitmore for their information on colonies in Florida. J. Gore and J. Morris made helpful comments on earlier versions of the manuscript.

LITERATURE CITED:

AOU. 1983. Checklist of North American birds. 6th edition. American Ornithologists' Union, Allen Press, Lawrence, Kansas.

Barbour, D. B., and R. W. Schreiber. 1978. Royal Tern. Pp. 91–92 *in* Rare and endangered biota of Florida, vol. II: Birds (H. W. Kale, II, ed.). Univ. Presses Fla., Gainesville, Florida.

Bent, A. C. 1921. Life histories of North American gulls and terns. U.S. Nat. Mus. Bull. 113.

Buckley, F. G., and P. A. Buckley. 1972. The breeding ecology of Royal Terns *Sterna* (Thalasseus) *maxima maxima*. Ibis 114:344–359.

Clapp, R. B., M. K. Klimkiewicz, and J. H. Kennard. 1982. Longevity records of North American birds: Gaviidae through Alcidae. Jour. Field Ornithol. 53:81–124.

Clapp, R. B., D. Morgan-Jacobs, and R. C. Banks. 1983. Marine birds of the southeastern United States and Gulf of Mexico. Part III: Charadriiformes. U.S. Fish and Wildl. Serv., Div. Biol. Serv., FWS/OBS-83/30. Washington, D.C. 853 pp.

Erwin, R. M. 1989. Responses to human intruders by birds nesting in colonies: experimental results and management guidelines. Colon. Waterbirds 12:104–108.

Gore, J. A. 1991. Distribution and abundance of nesting Least Terns and Black Skimmers in northwest Florida. Fla. Field Nat. 19:65–72.

Hallman, R. C. 1968. Sanctuary reports—St. Joe Island Sanctuary. Fla. Nat. 41:86.

Hays, H., and R. W. Risebrough. 1972. Pollutant concentrations in abnormal young terns from Long Island Sound. Auk 89:19–35.

Loftin, R. W. 1982. Diet of Black Skimmers and Royal Terns in northeastern Florida. Fla. Field Nat. 10:19–20.

Loftin, R. W., and S. Sutton. 1979. Ruddy Turnstones destroy Royal Tern colony. Wilson Bull. 91:133–135.

O'Meara, T. E., and J. A. Gore. 1988. Guidelines for conservation and management of Least Tern colonies in Florida. Fla. Game and Fresh Water Fish Comm., Tallahassee, Florida. 12 pp.

Parnell J. F., and R. F. Soots, Jr. 1979. Atlas of colonial waterbirds of North Carolina estuaries. N. C. Sea Grant Publ. UNC–SG–78–10. Raleigh, North Carolina. 269 pp.

Paul, R. T. 1987. Florida region. Amer. Birds 41:1425–1428.

Paul, R. T. 1989. Florida region. Amer. Birds 43:1307–1310.

Paul, R. T. 1991. Florida region. Amer. Birds 45:91–94.

Portnoy, J. W., R. M. Erwin, and T. W. Custer. 1981. Atlas of gull and tern colonies: North Carolina to Key West, Florida (including pelicans, cormorants, and skimmers). U. S. Fish and Wildl. Serv. FWS/OBS-80/05. Washington, D.C. 121 pp.

Schreiber, R. W., and E. A. Schreiber. 1978. Colonial bird use and plant succession on dredged material islands in Florida; Vol. I: sea and wading bird colonies. Tech. Rept. D–78–14. U.S. Army Eng. Waterways Exp. Sta., Vicksburg, Mississippi.

Smith, H. T., W. J. B. Miller, R. E. Roberts, C. V. Tamborski, W. W. Timmerman, and J. S. Weske. 1994. Banded Royal Terns recovered at Sebastian Inlet, Florida. Fla. Field Nat. 22:81-83.

Soots, R. F., Jr., and J. F. Parnell. 1975. Ecological succession of breeding birds in relation to plant succession on dredge islands in North Carolina. N.C. Sea Grant Publ. UNC–SG–75–27. Raleigh, North Carolina. 91 pp.

Spendelow, J. A., and S. R. Patton. 1988. National atlas of coastal waterbird colonies in the contiguous United States: 1976–1982. U.S. Fish and Wildl. Serv. Biol. Rept. no. 88(5). Washington, D.C. 326 pp.

Sprunt, Jr., A., and E. B. Chamberlain. 1949. South Carolina bird life. Univ. South Carolina Press. Columbia, South Carolina.

Stevenson, H. M. 1972. Recent breeding of the Sandwich Tern (*Thalasseus sandvicensis*) in Florida. Fla. Nat. 45:94–95.

Toland, B., and T. Gilbert. 1987. Roof nesting by Royal Terns in Vero Beach, Florida. Fla. Field Nat. 15:80–82.

Van Velzen, W. T. 1968. The status and dispersal of Virginia Royal Terns. Raven 39:55–60.

Van Velzen, W. T. 1971. Recoveries of Royal Terns banded in the Carolinas. Chat 35:64–66.

PREPARED BY: Erik D. Egensteiner, Florida Game and Fresh Water Fish Commission, Bureau of Nongame Wildlife, 3911 Highway 2321, Panama City, FL 32409 (Current address: Florida Department of Environmental Protection, Florida Park Service, 1800 Wekiwa Circle, Apopka, FL 32712); Henry T. Smith, Florida Department of Environmental Protection, Office of Environmental Services, 3900 Commonwealth Boulevard, Tallahassee, FL 32399 (Current address: Florida Department of Environmental Protection, Florida Park Service, 13798 S.E. Federal Highway, Hobe Sound, FL 33455); and James A. Rodgers, Jr., Florida Game and Fresh Water Fish Commission, Wildlife Research Laboratory, 4005 South Main Street, Gainesville, FL 32601.

Sandwich Tern

Sterna sandvicensis

FAMILY LARIDAE

Order Charadriiformes

TAXONOMY: The Sandwich Tern (*Sterna sandvicensis*) was described by Latham in 1787 (AOU 1983). Previously, the species was placed in the genus *Thalasseus*. The North American form (*S. s. acuflavidus*) also is known as Cabot's Tern, whereas, the South American form (*S. s. eurygnathus*) is sometimes referred to as the Cayenne Tern. The South American form has been regarded as a separate species (*S. eurygnatha*), but interbreeding with *S. sandvicensis* occurs and most workers now treat both forms as races of a single species (AOU 1983; Buckley and Buckley 1984). Some authors have treated the Sandwich Tern populations breeding in the Old World (*S. s. sandvicensis*) and North America and the Caribbean as separate subspecies.

DESCRIPTION: The Sandwich Tern is a typical tern with a long slender bill, long pointed wings, and long deeply forked tail. The overall length is 40 cm (15–16 in.); wingspan is about 86 cm (34 in.); tail length is about 15 cm (6 in.), with a fork about 9 cm (3.5 in.) deep. Reported mean body weights range from 191.4 to 256.6 g (reviewed in Clapp et al. 1983). The sexes of Sandwich Terns are similar in breeding plumage and soft-part coloration. The feet and legs are dull black. The bill is mostly black, with the distal 1.5 cm (1/2–3/4 in.) bright yellow. The *S. s. eurygnathus* form typically has an all yellow bill. The pileum and long occipital crest are glossy black, with a tinge of green below the eyes. The black crest is most prominent in late spring and early summer. The sides of the face below the eye, mantle, throat, belly, rump, and upper tail coverts are white. The rectrices are mostly white with a slight pearly tinge. Primaries are heavily silvered or frosted when new.

Winter adult plumage is similar to the above breeding characteristics, but the yellow bill tip is smaller and less intense; the front of the head is pure white or speckled with white; the crown is white, with distinct black shaft streaks; and the occipital crest is noticeably shorter and mostly brownish-black. Downy

Sandwich Tern, *Sterna sandvicensis.* (Photo copyright by Allan D. Cruickshank, courtesy of Florida Audubon Society)

nestlings are mottled gray above and white below. Young of the year have a noticeably brownish-black bill, with the distal portion pale yellow; the crown and short crest are brownish-black; and the upper dorsal parts are marked with irregular spots or bars of brownish-black.

POPULATION SIZE AND TREND: Spendelow and Patton (1988) compiled and synthesized regional data for the period from 1976 to 1982 and estimated about 71,460 Sandwich Terns were breeding in 32 colonies located in Virginia (1), North Carolina (5), South Carolina (1), Florida (4), Mississippi (1), Louisiana (6), and Texas (14). Colony sizes ranged from a minimum of 4 terns at an unnamed North Carolina colony to a maximum of about 40,734 breeding birds at the Chandeleur Islands in Louisiana (Spendelow and Patton 1988).

Two sites in Florida that were used intermittently by breeding Sandwich Terns during the 1970s, "a small island off Port St. Joe" (Stevenson 1972) and Little Bird Island in Nassau Sound, Duval County (Loftin and Sutton 1975), are no longer active sites for this species (H. W. Kale, unpubl. data). Spendelow and Patton (1988) reported four colonies containing a total of about 170 birds (mean = 43) for Florida during this period. More recent data compiled for the Florida Breeding Bird Atlas (H. W. Kale, unpubl. data)

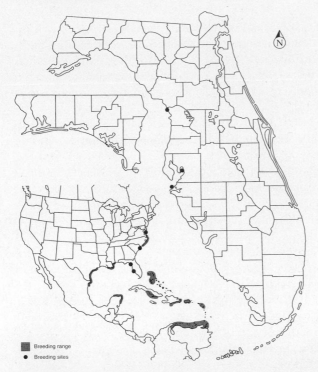

Breeding range
Breeding sites

Distribution map of
the Sandwich Tern,
Sterna sandvicensis.

during the later 1980s indicated that Sandwich Terns only bred at a few sites in the Hillsborough–Manatee County area (Tampa Bay) and along the coast of northern Citrus County. Paul (in Robertson and Woolfenden 1992) estimated the recent Sandwich Tern breeding population at about 200 pairs; most of these birds nested at Passage Key in Tampa Bay, with smaller numbers nesting at the Alafia Banks and island 3D in Hillsborough Bay and other dredged-material islands off the coast of Citrus County. The trend in the Sandwich Tern population throughout its range is not known. The Citrus County site has not been used for nesting by Sandwich Terns since 1991 (R. Paul, pers. obs.); however, the number of nests appeared relatively stable at about 200 among a few sites in the Tampa Bay region of Florida during the latter 1980s and early 1990s. An estimated 270 pairs of Sandwich Terns nested at Tampa Bay in 1994 (R. Paul, unpubl. data).

DISTRIBUTION AND HISTORY OF DISTRIBUTION: The Sandwich Tern is found at sandy beaches, flats, sea coasts, bays, and estuaries of tropical and temperate regions of the world. Sandwich Terns breed on the Atlantic coast of North America in Virginia, North Carolina, and South Carolina; along the Gulf coast from southern Texas east to southern Mississippi, and Florida; in the Bahamas, southern Cuba, and small islands in the Virgin Islands; off the coast of Yucatan; and in the eastern hemisphere from the British Isles and southern Scandinavia south to the Mediterranean, Black and Caspian Seas (AOU 1983). This species formerly bred along the coast of southern Alabama and off the coast of Belize. The *eurygnathus* subspecies breeds off the coasts of Venezuela, northern Trinidad, French Guiana, and northern Argentina.

The Sandwich Tern winters along the Pacific coast from Oaxaca to Ecuador and Peru, in the Atlantic, Gulf, and Caribbean regions from Virginia and the Gulf coast south through the West Indies, and along coasts to southern Brazil and Uruguay; and in the Old World from the southern regions of its breeding range south to the eastern Atlantic islands, southern Africa, the Persian Gulf and India (AOU 1983). The *eurygnathus* subspecies winters from the islands off Venezuela and the Columbian coast, south along the Atlantic coast to northern Argentina. This form occasionally wanders north to off the U.S. coasts (Buckley and Buckley 1984).

In Florida, Sandwich Terns formerly bred near Port St. Joe in Gulf County (Stevenson 1972) and Nassau Sound in Duval County (Loftin and Sutton 1975) during the 1970s. Currently, this species only nests at Passage Key in Manatee County, Alafia Banks Extension and island 3D in Hillsborough County, and possibly off the coast of Citrus County (R. Paul *in* Robertson and Woolfenden 1992). The breeding range of Sandwich Terns has remained along the west coast of Florida during the 1980s and 1990s.

HABITAT REQUIREMENTS AND HABITAT TREND: Little information is available regarding the specific habitat requirements of Sandwich Terns in the southeastern United States. Sandwich Terns usually nest on bare sand or sand-shell mixes on barrier beaches, isolated sandbars, natural estuarine islands, and dredged-material islands. Regional preferences for these different breeding habitats vary throughout the southeastern U.S. range of the species and appear to largely reflect local availability (see review in Clapp et al. 1983). Sandwich Terns nesting in a mixed species colony in northeastern Italy preferred bare mud and sand nesting substrates and avoided sites with vegetation, even low vegetation such as *Salicornia* sp. (Fasola and Canova 1992). Sandwich Terns especially avoided nearby tall vegetation, and nested significantly higher and farther from water than random or available sites (Fasola and Canova 1992).

Undisturbed marine/estuarine sites suitable for tern nesting are becoming rarer as the coastal zone in Florida is developed or used for recreational activities. Sandwich Terns and other tern species probably will continue to experience limited availability of nesting habitat unless natural beach and dredged-material sites are managed specifically for these species.

VULNERABILITY OF SPECIES AND HABITAT: Cochrane et al. (1991) reported that Sandwich Terns suffered mortality by colliding with electrical wires over a bay in South Africa and suggested that their intrabay habits may make them more susceptible than other more pelagic species. White et al. (1979 in Fritts et al. 1983) found that number 2 fuel oil was extremely toxic to Sandwich Tern eggs, thus suggesting that this species would be at risk to contamination from oil spills along coastal regions. We have observed other species of seabirds entangled in marine debris; Sandwich Terns probably are likewise susceptible.

CAUSES OF THREAT: The breeding ecology of Sandwich Terns in Florida makes them susceptible to the same threats as Royal Terns (*S. maxima*). These include habitat conversion, destruction of nests by extreme high tides, predation, and various environmental contaminants (see the Royal Tern account). Maintaining nesting areas with minimal vegetation and devoid of ground predators should prolong their use by breeding Sandwich Terns. Because there are so few breeding Sandwich Terns in Florida, little direct experimental information has been accumulated for the species in this state.

RESPONSES TO HABITAT MODIFICATION: As with many other species of terns, Sandwich Terns have experienced loss of their natural breeding habitat due to human activities. Sandwich Terns will abandon previously used breeding sites due to increased vegetative cover at nesting areas (Furniss 1983). Sandwich Terns often use dredged-material sites (see Clapp et al. 1983). Jackson et al. (1979) suggested the increase in the Sandwich Tern population off the Mississippi coast during the latter 1970s was the result of available spoil islands. Soots and Landin (1978) also reported Sandwich Terns nesting on dredged-material islands in North Carolina, Florida, and Texas. However, Sandwich Terns were reported nesting only on natural islands in Louisiana, not on available dredged-material islands (Portnoy 1977).

DEMOGRAPHIC CHARACTERISTICS: For a species often nesting in large colonies and relatively common along the upper Gulf coast, there is surprisingly little detailed demographic data available for the Sandwich Tern for the United States. Langham (1974) reported breeding was highly synchronized, with all nesting started within about 25 days. Sandwich Terns usually lay 1–3 eggs, with variation among years, sites, and studies (reviewed in Clapp et al. 1983). Mean clutch size reported for Sandwich Terns ranges from 1.00 to 1.90 (Clapp et al. 1983: table 48). Annual mean clutch size ranged from 1.15 to 1.41 eggs over 3 years (overall mean = 1.27, range = 1–2; n = 2,282 nests) at a colony in England (Langham 1974). Smith (1975 in Burger 1980) reported the modal clutch size was 2 eggs, whereas, Loftin and Sutton (1975) found 3 eggs in each of three nests on an island in Nassau Sound, Florida. A small sample (n = 10 nests) of nests from Tampa Bay contained only single-egg clutches (R. T. Paul, pers. observ.). Intrayear clutch size can increase, decrease, or be constant during the nesting season (Langham 1974). Incubation begins with the first egg laid and lasts 23–25 days (Langham 1974; Martin and Lester 1990). Jackson et al. (1979) found eggs in nests from early June to early July and nestlings from mid-June to mid-July at a colony in Mississippi. Langham (1974) reported annual hatching success ranged from 53.9 to 95.7%, and increased with an increase in colony size. Fledging success typically decreases during the season (Clapp et al. 1983), but Langham (1974) found little seasonal difference. Overall annual fledging success in one study was 91.1% expressed as fledgling/egg (Langham 1974). In broods of two young (i.e., two eggs hatching two nestlings), the survivorship of the second nestling ranged from 48.3 to 66.7% compared to survivorship of single nestling broods of 82.8–100.0% (Langham 1974). Age of nestlings' first flight is about 22–33 days, and the nestlings begin leaving the colony at about 32 days (Pearson 1968 in Clapp et al. 1983; Smith 1975 in Burger 1980). Sandwich Terns probably do not breed until they are about 4 years old, with a maximum reported age based on a recovered banded bird of 23 years and 7 months (Clapp et al. 1983).

Sandwich Terns face a varied source of factors that can cause death or reproductive failure (Clapp et al. 1983). Storms and high tides often wash away eggs. White et al. (1979 in Fritts et al. 1983) demonstrated that fuel oil was extremely toxic to Sandwich Tern eggs; thus, this species and their eggs may be susceptible to contamination from oil spills in coastal waters. Clapp et al. (1983) compiled the existing literature regarding predators of Sandwich Tern adults, eggs, and nestlings and listed gulls, corvids, owls, rats, mustelids, foxes, and dogs as responsible for losses. Sandwich Terns will desert a colony early in the breeding season due to heavy predation, and Langham (1974) stated that large numbers of gulls resulted in nesting failure or abandonment by Sandwich Terns at a colony in England. Cochrane et al. (1991) found Sandwich Terns were susceptible to death by colliding with aerial electric wires over a bay in South Africa. Avian and mammalian predation can be a major source of nest failure (Clapp et al. 1983). Several authors reported Sandwich Terns nest in small, compact subcolonies within larger populations of other tern species, and suggested they gain an advantage either from predator swamping or protection by more aggressive species of terns (Langham 1974; Buckley and Buckley 1980).

KEY BEHAVIORS: Sandwich Terns nest in mixed species breeding colonies, such as with Black-headed Gulls (*Larus ridibundus*), Royal Terns, Common

Terns (*S. hirundo*), and Arctic Terns (*S. paradisaea*) (Langham 1974; Portnoy 1977; Jackson et al. 1979; Buckley and Buckley 1980; Martin and Lester 1990). Sandwich Terns pair and copulate before taking up a territory at the breeding site in the colony; then they settle in synchronized subcolonies within the colony (Langham 1974). The prelaying period on the territory only lasts 2–3 days; nesting synchrony via stimulation probably occurs in prebreeding flocks and birds ready to breed then form a subcolony together. Egg-laying in the northernmost United States' colonies occurs primarily in May and June, while Sandwich Terns in the southeast United States lay earlier (Clapp et al. 1983). Incubating Sandwich Terns can be found along the northern Gulf coast between mid-April to mid-July (Portnoy 1977; Martin and Lester 1990).

Sandwich Terns nest in densely packed colonies, sometimes within the pecking distance of another Sandwich Tern (Fasola and Canova 1992). They often nest in dense, monospecific subcolonies or clusters among more numerous Royal Terns and other species of terns (Parnell and Soots 1979; Buckley and Buckley 1980). For example, within a 19 pair subcolony, Sandwich Terns were nesting at an average density of 2.1 nests/m^2 (Langham 1974). Soots and Landin (1978) reported finding maximum densities exceeding 8.0 nests/m^2. Other studies report average nesting densities as high as 5–7 nests/m^2 (reviewed in Clapp et al. 1983). Langham (1974) and Veen (1977 in Gochfeld 1980) found that Sandwich Terns exhibited high breeding synchrony within subcolonies (i.e., greater synchrony within subcolonies than among entire colony or other subcolonies). The advantages of synchronized breeding during the peak of nesting are larger clutches and reduced chick/egg loss.

Sandwich Terns most frequently (63%) forage on dense groups of near-surface small fish, mostly using the plunge-diving technique from heights ranging from 1.5 to 10.0 m (sources in Clapp et al. 1983). Duffy (1989) reported the species forages primarily in waters 6–50 meters deep off southern Africa. They mostly feed as single birds or in small groups of terns (Fritts et al. 1983; Duffy 1989), but they quickly aggregate to form large feeding flocks at concentrations of prey (Veen 1977 in Clapp et al. 1983). Off southern Africa, Duffy (1989) reported Sandwich Terns often (13%) are found scavenging on fish remains from foraging cape fur seals (*Arctocephalus pusillus*). Similar commensal behavior was observed where Sandwich Terns foraged with bottlenosed dolphins (*Tursiops truncatus*) off Cedar Key, Florida (J. Rodgers, pers. obs.). Sandwich Terns along the south Atlantic and Gulf coasts of the United States feed primarily on small shrimp (*Penaeus* sp.), anchovies (*Anchoa* spp.), silversides (*Menidia* and *Membras* sp.), and menhaden (*Brevoortia* spp.) (reviewed in Clapp et al. 1983).

Little is known about the migratory behavior of Sandwich Terns, but concentrations along the coast of the southeastern United States suggest that peak fall movement occurs during August–October, while peak spring movement occurs in April (Clapp et al. 1983). Young Sandwich Terns mostly remain on the wintering grounds through May of their third summer (Clapp et al. 1983).

CONSERVATION MEASURES TAKEN: Sandwich Terns are protected by federal and Florida wildlife laws and regulations that prohibit pursuit, capture, or killing this species. Colonies of all species of terns are closed to trespass annually by the Florida Game and Fresh Water Fish Commission and various conservation organizations, especially the National Audubon Society (NAS). Waterbird colonies in the Tampa Bay region receive special attention from the NAS. O'Meara and Gore (1988) have recommended conservation strategies for Least Terns (*S. antillarum*) that are applicable to this species.

CONSERVATION MEASURES PROPOSED: All known Sandwich Tern breeding sites should be closed to human disturbance prior to the arrival of breeding birds. This action will reduce the probability of prelaying colony abandonment by terns. Enough is known about the breeding habitat requirements of this species so that dredged-material islands can be designed and maintained to promote successful nesting. If mammalian predators have access to Sandwich Tern breeding sites, they may need to be controlled. Because breeding Sandwich Terns are frequently associated with the presence of Royal Terns, management actions targeted for Florida's Royal Terns should benefit both species. A statewide survey of all current and recently abandoned Sandwich Tern breeding colonies would greatly enhance our knowledge of the species' distribution, population size, and related trends in Florida.

ACKNOWLEDGMENTS: We thank H. W. Kale, II, for the unpublished Florida Breeding Bird Atlas data for Sandwich Terns.

LITERATURE CITED:
AOU. 1983. Check-list of North American birds. 6th edition. Amer. Ornithol. Union. Allen Press, Lawrence, Kansas.

Buckley, F. G., and P. A. Buckley. 1980. Habitat selection in marine birds. Pp. 69–112 in Behavior of marine animals. Volume 4: birds (Burger, J., B. L. Olla, and H. E. Winn, eds.). Plenum Press, New York.

Buckley, P. A., and F. G. Buckley. 1984. Cayenne Tern new to North America, with comments on its relationship to Sandwich Tern. Auk 101:396–398.

Burger, J. 1980. The transition to independence and postfledging parental care in seabirds. Pp. 367–449 in Behavior of marine animals. Volume 4: birds (Burger, J., B. L. Olla, and H. E. Winn, eds.). Plenum Press, New York.

Clapp, R. B., D. Morgan-Jacobs, and R. C. Banks. 1983. Marine birds of the southeastern United States and Gulf of Mexico. Part III. Charadriiformes. FWS/OBS-83/30. U.S. Fish and Wild. Serv., Washington, D.C.

Cochrane, K. L., R. J. M. Crawford, and F. Kriel. 1991. Tern mortality caused by collision with a cable at Table Bay, Cape Town, South Africa in 1989. Colon. Waterbirds 14:63–65.

Duffy, D. C. 1989. Seabird foraging aggregations: a comparison of two southern upwellings. Colon. Waterbirds 12:164–175.

Fasola, M., and L. Canova. 1992. Nest habitat selection by eight syntopic species of Mediterranean gulls and terns. Colon. Waterbirds 15:169–178.

Fritts, T. H., A. B. Irvine, R. D. Jennings, L. A. Collum, W. Hoffman, and M. A. McGehee. 1983. Turtles, birds, and mammals in the northern Gulf of Mexico and nearby Atlantic waters. FWS/OBS-82/65. Div. Biol. Serv., U.S. Fish Wildl. Serv., Washington, D.C.

Furniss, S. 1983. Status of the seabirds of the Culebra Archipelago, Puerto Rico. Colon. Waterbirds 6:121–125.

Gochfeld, M. 1980. Mechanisms and adaptive value of reproductive synchrony in colonial seabirds. Pp. 207–270 in Behavior of marine animals. Volume 4: birds (Burger, J., B. L. Olla, and H. E. Winn, eds.). Plenum Press, New York.

Hatch, J. J. 1970. Predation and piracy by gulls at a ternery in Maine. Auk 87:244–254.

Jackson, J. A., B. J. Schardien, and C. D. Cooley. 1979. Dispersion, phenology, and population sizes of nesting colonial seabirds on the Mississippi Gulf coast. Proc. Colon. Waterbird Group 3:145–155.

Langham, N. P. E. 1974. Comparative breeding biology of the Sandwich Tern. Auk 91:255–277.

Loftin, R. W., and S. Sutton. 1975. Sandwich Tern breeds on the Atlantic coast of Florida. Fla. Field Nat. 3:18.

Martin, R. P., and G. D. Lester. 1990. Atlas and census of wading bird and seabird nesting colonies in Louisiana 1990. Spec. Publ. No. 3. La. Dept. Wildl. and Fisheries, Baton Rouge, Louisiana.

O'Meara, T. E., and J. A. Gore. 1988. Guidelines for conservation and management of Least Tern colonies in Florida. Fla. Game and Fresh Water Fish Comm., Tallahassee, Florida.

Parnell, J. F., and R. F. Soots. 1979. Atlas of colonial waterbirds of North Carolina estuaries. Sea Grant Publ. UNC–SG–78–10. Raleigh, North Carolina.

Portnoy, J. W. 1977. Nesting colonies of seabirds and wading birds—coastal Louisiana, Mississippi, and Alabama. FWS/OBS-77/07. Off. Biol. Serv. U.S. Fish and Wildl. Serv., Washington, D.C.

Robertson, W. B., Jr., and G. E. Woolfenden. 1992. Florida bird species—an annotated list. Fla. Ornithol. Soc. Spec. Publ. No. 6, Fla. Mus. Nat. Hist., Gainesville, Florida.

Soots, R. F., Jr., and M. C. Landin. 1978. Development and management of avian habitat on dredged material islands. Tech. Rept. DS–78–18, U.S. Army Eng. Waterways Exper. Sta., Vicksburg, Mississippi.

Spendelow, J. A., and S. R. Patton. 1988. National atlas of coastal waterbird colonies in the contiguous United States: 1976–82. Biol. Rept. 88(5). U.S. Fish and Wildl. Serv., Washington, D.C.

Stevenson, H. M. 1972. Recent breeding of the Sandwich Tern (*Thalasseus sandvicensis*) in Florida. Fla. Nat. 45:94–95.

PREPARED BY: James A. Rodgers, Jr., Florida Game and Fresh Water Fish Commission, Wildlife Research Laboratory, 4005 South Main Street, Gainesville, FL 32601; Henry T. Smith, Florida Department of Environmental Protection, Florida Park Service, 13798 S.E. Federal Highway, Hobe Sound, FL 33455; and Richard T. Paul, National Audubon Society, Tampa Bay Sanctuaries, 410 Ware Blvd., Suite 500, Tampa, FL 33619.

Caspian Tern

Sterna caspia

FAMILY LARIDAE

Order Charadriiformes

TAXONOMY: The Caspian Tern (*Sterna caspia*) was described by Pallas in 1770 from the Caspian Sea of southern Russia. In the same year Lepechin renamed the species *Sterna tschegrava*. In 1829 the monotypic genus *Hydroprogne* was described by Kaup, and *H. caspia* (=*H. tschegrava*) remained the accepted name for over a century. In recent years, *Hydroprogne* was submerged in *Sterna,* and *tschegrava* rejected (Hellmayr and Conover 1948; AOU 1983). Several subspecies have been proposed, largely on the basis of size, but review of a larger series of specimens has led recent observers to reject subspecific designations (Cramp and Simmons 1985).

DESCRIPTION: The Caspian Tern is a very large, robust tern about 50 cm (20 in.) long with a wingspread of 130 cm (52 in.) (Voous 1983). Males are slightly larger than females (Quinn 1990). The following description is adapted in part from Blake (1977). The sexes are alike in plumage. In adults, the entire crown and crest feathers are black. The back and wings are pearl gray, with the tail white and slightly forked. Primaries can appear silvery, but may have dark tips. The sides of the face below the eye and underparts of the body are white. The iris is brown. The bill is a deep red with a faint tint of orange, much redder than that of the smaller Royal Tern (*S. maxima*). The legs and feet are black. In flight, the Caspian appears much more massive, with broader wings, and the bill is noticeably stouter than the Royal. In nonbreeding adults, the crown is streaked with white but remains mostly black throughout the year. Immature birds are more mottled above, and the crown is more heavily streaked with white. The bill is duller and more orange than that of the adult, with the tip blackish.

POPULATION SIZE AND TREND: Spendelow and Patton (1988) estimated the U.S. breeding population to be about 19,000 birds (9,500 breed-

Caspian Tern, *Sterna caspia*.
(Photo copyright by Allan D.
Cruickshank, courtesy of Florida
Audubon Society)

ing pairs) in the late 1970s–early 1980s, including 6,000 pairs in the western
United States, 1,700 pairs in the Great Lakes, 1,200 pairs in Texas, and 300
pairs in the southeastern states from Louisiana to Virginia.

In Florida, numbers have slowly increased since their initial discovery in
1962 (Woolfenden and Meyerriecks 1963). During the 1970s, up to 31 pairs
nested at Merritt Island NWR (Salata 1979), but the colony has not persisted.
Annual nesting has occurred in Hillsborough Bay since at least 1974 (Dunstan
et al. 1975). This is believed to be the sole Florida nesting site, with a high
count of 84 nests in 1995 (Paul, unpubl. data).

DISTRIBUTION AND HISTORY OF DISTRIBUTION: Caspian Terns are
found virtually worldwide. As breeders they occur in a patchy distribution
across North America, Eurasia, Africa, and Asia south to Australia and New
Zealand. In the Western Hemisphere, breeding occurs irregularly from north-
ern Canada to the Great Lakes and southeast Quebec, throughout the western
United States south to Baja California, Mexico, along the Atlantic coast in
Newfoundland, Virginia and the Carolinas, and on the Gulf coast in Texas,
Louisiana, Mississippi, Alabama, and Florida (AOU 1983; Clapp et al. 1983).
Nesting in Mississippi and Alabama appears to be very recent, and may not
occur in all years.

In Florida, no nesting was known until 1962, when Woolfenden and

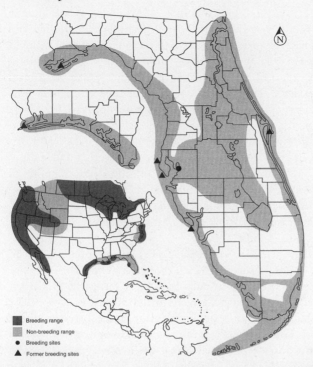

Breeding range
Non-breeding range
● Breeding sites
▲ Former breeding sites

Distribution map of
the Caspian Tern,
Sterna caspia.

Meyerriecks (1963) found one nest among a colony of Black Skimmers (*Rynchops niger*) along the Bayway Causeway in Boca Ciega Bay (Pinellas County). Since that time, nesting has been reported from scattered sites including St. Joseph Sound (Schreiber and Dinsmore 1972), Gasparilla Sound (Dunstan et al. 1975), St. George Island (Stevenson 1979) on the Gulf coast, and Merritt Island N.W.R. (Ogden 1973) on the Atlantic coast.

Caspians nested at Merritt Island NWR in 5 of the 7 years between 1973 and 1979 (Salata 1979), but no nesting has been reported there since then. Only in Tampa Bay has a permanent colony been established. In 1974, 16 nests were found on a small dredged-material island in Hillsborough Bay (Dunstan et al. 1975). Since then, nesting has occurred annually on a series of dredged-material islands nearby (Alafia Banks Extension, Island 3D, and Fantasy Island).

Wintering and nonbreeding Caspian Terns are widely distributed in Florida. They occur year round along most coastlines (but not in the western panhandle in winter), and also in the interior (Robertson and Woolfenden 1992).

HABITAT REQUIREMENTS AND HABITAT TREND: Caspian Terns breed on small barren islands that afford protection from terrestrial predators. Substrate varies from sand and shell hash to gravel (Clapp et al. 1983). Gill and Mewaldt (1983) found that Caspian Tern populations had shifted from nesting in numerous small colonies associated with interior freshwater marshes to nesting primarily in fewer large colonies on human-created habitats along the Pacific Coast. In Florida, all nesting attempts reported to date have been on dredged-material islands. There is no shortage of such sites, but most islands are heavily vegetated and do not provide the unvegetated substrates required by these terns.

Caspian Terns forage over coastal bays and rivers, inland lakes, and impoundments. Beaches, islands, and sand bars are used for roosting and loafing. Foraging habitats are not believed to be declining, although local examples of water quality (and possibly Caspian foraging habitat) deterioration may be found. Sandbars and islands suitable for roosting by terns may be limited, especially where they are easily accessible to recreational boaters.

VULNERABILITY OF SPECIES AND HABITAT: Like other terns, Caspian Terns nest on the ground and usually close to the water. Therefore, they are highly vulnerable to severe storms, unusually high tides, terrestrial predators, human disturbance and chemical spills. Caspians must be considered especially vulnerable in Florida since there is only one nesting site, and a fortuitous event could have a disproportionate impact on the "statewide" population.

Plant succession also poses a potential threat to dredged-material island nesting habitat. The higher elevations of many of these spoil islands may place nest sites beyond the reach of natural erosive forces like storms and high tides. The barren substrates preferred by terns may be replaced by grasses and later by woody shrubs, forcing the birds to move.

CAUSES OF THREAT: Human disturbance during the nesting season is the major threat to Caspian Terns in Florida. People visit islands for a variety of reasons: fishing, picnicking, shelling, camping etc., and they may bring their dogs with them. Any of these activities can cause nesting failures, if adult terns are prevented from normal care of their eggs or young.

Because Caspian Terns feed entirely on fish, they are vulnerable to chemical contamination present in aquatic and marine/estuarine food chains. Recent research by the National Oceanographic and Atmospheric Administration has begun to identify the contaminants present in "hot spots" in the Tampa Bay system (E. Long, pers. comm.). Heavy metals and organochlorine contamination are potential hazards to Caspian Terns and other species, both in Tampa Bay and elsewhere in Florida.

RESPONSES TO HABITAT MODIFICATION: Like other terns, Caspians depend on natural forces or human activities—intentional or otherwise—to provide suitable nesting habitat. They readily use managed sites, where vegetation is controlled by prescribed burning, raking, or addition of dredged material. Attempts to attract or retain nesting Caspians at a specific site are not always successful. On at least two occasions in the last decade, Caspians nesting in Tampa Bay moved to a new site despite measures intended to improve the nesting habitat at the previous year's location (R. Paul, pers. observ.). Clearly, the success of habitat management programs depends in part on other factors which may not always be obvious.

DEMOGRAPHIC CHARACTERISTICS: As a species that nests in a highly variable and unpredictable environment, the Caspian Tern should be expected to exhibit frequent nesting failures, low overall reproductive rates, delayed breeding and high adult mortality. No detailed research has been done on Caspian Terns in Florida. The following summary is drawn primarily from the compendium of Clapp et al. (1983). Clutch size is normally 1–3 eggs, with the mean varying among studies from a high of 2.81 in one Michigan study (Ludwig 1965) to a low of 1.6 in Texas (Chaney et al. 1978). Shugart et al. (1978) found clutch size averaged 2.5 eggs/nest for a large sample of 2,170 pairs in the Great Lakes. In 1993, the mean clutch size for 75 nests in Tampa Bay was 1.69 (Paul, unpubl. data). The incubation period is 26–28 days (Penland 1976 in Clapp et al. 1983). Young birds are first capable of flight at the age of 5 to 8 weeks, depending on the study. Hatching success as high as 82% has been recorded, while fledging success was 57% in one study. Nest productivity reached 1.8 young per pair in one Finnish study (Soikkeli 1973 in Clapp et al. 1983). Other studies range from 69–79% of pairs rearing at least one chick to fledging (Cuthbert 1988) to a mean fledging rate of 1.0 bird/nest (Shugart et al. 1978). In Tampa Bay, replicate counts of young Caspians during the nesting season indicated nest productivity of 0.5–1.0 young in most years since 1980 (Paul, unpubl. data).

Age at first breeding by Caspian Terns is believed to be as little as 2 years (Ludwig 1965), but Gill and Mewaldt (1983) found that they begin returning to the breeding grounds during the third summer when some breed and attain adulthood in their fourth summer. Caspian Terns are long-lived, with one banded bird reaching a minimum age of 26 years and 2 months (Clapp et al. 1982). Mean annual mortality of adult birds was estimated at 11.3 and 12% in two studies (in Clapp et al. 1983). Gill and Mewaldt (1983) found 57% of fledglings survived to their fourth year, an annual survival rate of 89% thereafter, and a mean breeding life expectancy of 8.6 years.

Egg and nestling mortality and colony desertion have been associated with investigator disburbance, military operations, nearby duck hunting, and egg-collecting (reviewed in Cuthbert 1988). Other sources of nesting failure have been due to storm and resulting wave activity and gull predation (Shugart et al. 1978).

KEY BEHAVIORS: Caspian Terns nest in colonies, often with other species of terns. Caspian Terns show a significant preference for the colony of previous breeding unless their preceding reproductive effort was unsuccessful (Cuthbert 1988). Some Caspian Tern pairs are known to remain intact from season to season, although the separation rate can be high (Cuthbert 1985). In Florida, courtship begins in March and egg laying begins in early May. Most young fledge about early July. Some nests, which may represent renesting attempts, still have eggs as late as 4 July. Males provide greater numbers and total mass of prey to young than females (Quinn 1990). Fledged young remain dependent on their parents for food for several months.

Caspian Terns primarily prey on fish. Shugart et al. (1978) found Caspian Terns feed mostly on alewives (*Alosa pseudoharengus,* 57%) and smelt (*Osmerus mordax,* 34%) in the Great Lakes (n = 1,219 fish).

The call of Caspian Terns as most often heard is a harsh, caterwauling "raaaoww" or "ra-a-aoww." This call is frequently given as the adult tern dives over a predator or human as they move through a colony. Fledged young still being cared for by the parent emit a begging call that is high, squeaky and persistent.

CONSERVATION MEASURES TAKEN: Because Caspian Terns nest in colonies and tend to use the same colony site if young were produced the previous year (Cuthbert 1988), effective protection is fairly straight forward. Annually since 1974, the Hillsborough Bay colony has been posted and patrolled by sanctuary staff of the National Audubon Society. A habitat management program, varying annually but in general consisting of prescribed burning, roto-tilling, raking, and/or pulling of sandspurs (*Cenchrus* sp.) has been carried out. Through a cooperative effort with the U.S. Army Corps of Engineers and the Tampa Port Authority, the planning process for channel maintenance dredging projects now includes a discussion of nesting populations of several larids, including Caspian Terns. Public education efforts regarding the colonial waterbird populations of Tampa Bay feature discussion of the special needs of Caspian Terns and other ground-nesting birds.

CONSERVATION MEASURES PROPOSED: The above actions should be extended, as appropriate, to new breeding colonies of Caspian Terns when they are found. Research on Florida populations of Caspian Terns and related species should be carried out to provide basic information not now available (e.g., minimum nesting and foraging habitat requirements, heavy metal and chemical contamination, etc.), and to identify new threats to these species as they arise.

ACKNOWLEDGEMENTS: I am grateful to Fred Lohrer of Archbold Biological Station and Tom Webber of the Florida Museum of Natural History for assistance in locating sources of information used in this account. I thank J. A. Rodgers for reviewing an early draft of this manuscript

LITERATURE CITED:

AOU. 1983. Check-list of North American birds, 6th edition. Amer. Ornithol. Union, Washington, D.C. 877 pp.

Blake, E. R. 1977. Manual of neotropical birds. Vol. 1. Univ. Chicago Press, Chicago, Illinois. 674 pp.

Chaney, A. H., B. R. Chapman, J. P. Karges, D. A. Nelson, R. R. Schmidt, and L. C. Thebeau. 1978. Use of dredged material islands by colonial seabirds and wading birds in Texas. Tech. Rep. D–78–8. U.S. Army Eng. Waterways Exper. Sta., Vicksburg, Mississippi.

Clapp, R. B., M. K. Klimkiewicz, and J. H. Kennard. 1982. Longevity records of North American birds: Gaviidae through Alcidae. Jour. Field Ornithol. 53:81–124.

Clapp, R. B., D. Morgan-Jacobs, and R. C. Banks. 1983. Marine birds of the southeastern United States and Gulf of Mexico. Part III: Charadriiformes. FWS/OBS-83/30. U.S. Fish and Wildl. Ser., Div. Biol. Ser., Washington, D.C. 853 pp.

Cramp, S., and K. E. L. Simmons (Eds.). 1985. Handbook of the birds of Europe, the Middle East and North Africa. Vol. IV. Terns to woodpeckers. Oxford Univ. Press. New York, New York.

Cuthbert, F. J. 1985. Mate retention in Caspian Terns. Condor 87:74–78.

Cuthbert, F. J. 1988. Reproductive success and colony-site tenacity in Caspian Terns. Auk 105:339–344.

Dunstan, F. M., R. W. Schreiber, and J. J. Dinsmore. 1975. Caspian Tern nesting in Florida, 1973 and 1974. Fla. Field Nat. 3:16–17.

Gill, R. E., Jr., and L. R. Mewaldt. 1983. Pacific coast Caspian Terns: dynamics of an expanding population. Auk 100:369–381.

Hellmayr, C. E., and B. Conover. 1948. Catalog of birds of the Americas and the adjacent islands. Field Mus. Nat. Hist. Zool. Ser., vol. 13, part 1, no. 2:92–194.

Ludwig, J. A. 1965. Biology and structure of the Caspian Tern (*Hydroprogne caspia*) population of the Great Lakes from 1896–1964. Bird-Banding 36:217–233.

Ogden, J. C. 1973. Florida region. Amer. Birds 27:859–863.

Quinn, J. S. 1990. Sexual size dimorphorism and parental care patterns in a monomorphic and a dimorphic larid. Auk 107:260–274.

Robertson, W. B., Jr., and G. E. Woolfenden. 1992. Florida bird species: an annotated list. Fla. Ornithol. Soc. Spec. Publ. No. 6. Fla. Mus. Nat. Hist. Gainesville, Florida.

Salata, L. R. 1979. Breeding bird census—Banana River spoil islands, Merritt

Island NWR, 1979. Unpubl. rept. Merritt Is. Nat. Wildl. Refuge, Titusville, Florida. 8 pp.

Schreiber, R. W., and J. J. Dinsmore. 1972. Caspian Tern nesting records in Florida. Fla. Nat. 45:161.

Shugart, G. W., W. C. Scharf, and F. J. Cuthbert. 1978. Reproductive biology of Caspian Terns in the U.S. Great Lakes. Proc. Colon. Waterbird Group 2:146–156.

Spendelow, J. A., and S. R. Patton. 1988. National atlas of coastal waterbird colonies in the contiguous United States: 1976–1982. U.S. Fish Wildl. Serv. Biol. Rept. 88(5). Washington, D.C.

Stevenson, H. M. 1979. First nesting of the Caspian Tern in the Florida Panhandle. Fla. Field Nat. 7:8.

Voous, K. H. 1983. Birds of the Netherlands Antilles. 2nd edition. De Walburg Pers, Curaçao.

Woolfenden, G. E., and A. J. Meyerriecks. 1963. Caspian Tern breeds in Florida. Auk 80:365–366.

PREPARED BY: Richard T. Paul, National Audubon Society, Tampa Bay Sanctuaries, 410 Ware Blvd., Suite 500, Tampa, FL 33619.

Brown Noddy
Anous stolidus

FAMILY LARIDAE

Order Charadriiformes

TAXONOMY: The Brown Noddy (*Anous stolidus*) represents one of a trio of tern-like genera (*Anous, Gygis, Procelsterna*) of tropical, oceanic birds. *Anous* and *Gygis* have mostly pantropical distributions, whereas, *Procelsterna* occurs only in the Pacific. Schnell's (1970) phenetic analysis of skeletal characters found that these taxa tended to form a cluster moderately removed from the more uniform, core group of terns. Moynihan's (1959) rearrangement of the Laridae united the three genera under Anous. All the Brown Noddies of the Atlantic belong to the nominate subspecies. Murphy (1936:1151), for example, quoted Saunders to the effect that a Brown Noddy shot at Inaccessible Island, Tristan da Cunha, was "absolutely identical with birds from the Dry Tortugas, Florida." The Indo-Pacific populations are considerably more variable with three or four named subspecies (Peters 1934; Cramp et al. 1985).

DESCRIPTION: The Brown Noddy is a medium-sized (length, 38–42 cm; wingspan, 75–85 cm; weight, mainly 150–200 g), dark brown seabird. Males average significantly heavier and larger in all body measurements than females (Chardine and Morris 1989). Adults (sexes similar) have a light-gray crown (white forehead grading through shades of gray on the crown and nape); a white crescent beneath the eye; black lores; black legs and feet; dark brown iris; long, pointed wings; and a long, wedge-shaped tail. Juveniles and immatures resemble adults, but the crown is dusky gray-brown and the facial markings are less distinct. At least some individuals acquire the adult head pattern at three years of age. In sharp contrast to most birds whose molting patterns are known, the molt of flight feathers by Brown Noddies is extremely attenuated (9–10 months for primaries) and continues with little slowing down through the breeding season (ffrench 1991). Hatchlings have white and black down-color morphs, with (at Dry Tortugas) relatively few intermediates. This polymorphism occurs in many (perhaps all) Brown Noddy populations, but the

Brown Noddy,
Anous stolidus.
(Photo copyright
by Allan D.
Cruickshank,
courtesy of Florida
Audubon Society)

relative proportion of the two morphs appears to vary widely among populations (Dorward and Ashmole 1963). Watson (1908) reported that about 65% of newly hatched Brown Noddy chicks at Dry Tortugas had black down and 35%, white down. At Cayo Noroeste, Culebra, Puerto Rico (Morris and Chardine 1992), numbers of the two morphs were more nearly equal averaging 56% dark and 44% light over a five-year period (n = 215). The Black Noddy (*A. minutus*), regular in very small numbers at Dry Tortugas (Robertson et al. 1961; Robertson 1964; Robertson and Woolfenden 1992), is similar in pattern, but much smaller (weight, 90–120 g) with darker body plumage; a whiter, more sharply defined crown patch; and, a longer, thinner bill. Brown Noddies are usually seen in flight or perched at the nest. The flight at times is direct, but often is slow, fluttering, and somewhat gull-like.

POPULATION SIZE AND TRENDS: Brown Noddies nest in Florida only on Dry Tortugas and the size of the Tortugas colony has been measured by means of a direct count of nests in 16 nesting seasons over a 70-year span (Robertson 1964, 1978). These counts are taken to represent minimum breeding populations, because some nests may have been overlooked and some counts may have been made before all the pairs had nested. Data from the nest counts (year, number of breeding pairs, person(s) principally responsible) were as follows; 1907: 603 (J. B. Watson); 1910: 855 (J. B. Watson); 1938: 196 (D. B. Beard); 1939: 190 (G. D. Robinson) or 227 (O. B. Taylor); 1946–48: 246, 101, and 141 (A. Sprunt, Jr.); 1949–55: 283, 245, 259, 449, 421, 485, and 554 (W. E. Dilley, J. C. Moore); 1962: 1,069 (M. J. Robertson); and 1977: 1,510 (W. B. Robertson, Jr.). In 23 additional nesting seasons

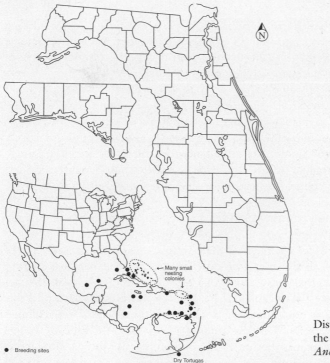

Distribution map of
the Brown Noddy,
Anous stolidus.

between 1902 and 1945, observers estimated the number of individual Brown Noddies that were in the Tortugas colony (Robertson 1964: table 4). These estimates contribute to the history of the population, but most are very sparsely detailed as to methods and some of the numbers reported (e.g., 35,000 in 1919) accord poorly with other information. In papers on aspects of the behavior of Brown Noddies, Riska (1984, 1986a, 1986b) consistently stated the size of the Tortugas population as "15,000 adults." The source of this figure is not clear, but it may be a lapsus for 1,500 pairs, the population as of the 1977 nest count. Note also that Robertson and Woolfenden (1992: 78) stated the early 1990s breeding population as "ca. 2,500–3,000 pairs." These numbers were a mere guess (one hopes, educated), which assumed that, absent serious disturbance, the population had probably increased slowly from its 1977 level.

The stable range under protection of the Dry Tortugas population of Brown Noddies appears to be in the region of 1,000–2,000+ pairs of breeding adults. Records suggest that the population has tended to reach this range whenever the colony area was free of major environmental perturbations for a few years. No ponderable evidence exists that numbers at Dry Tortugas in this century have much exceeded 2,000 breeding pairs. Fluctuations to substantially below 1,000 breeding pairs have usually been associated with known disturbances, particularly infestations of rats (*Rattus rattus*) in the nesting colony and the direct and indirect effects of hurricanes. The most extreme bottleneck known to have affected the Tortugas population—a period of severely depressed numbers extending from the late 1930s to early 1950s— was attributed to persistent plagues of rats that peaked in 1938–1940 and 1947–1948 (Robertson 1964). For 14 consecutive nesting seasons during 1938–1951, the population did not exceed 300 breeding pairs, reaching its nadir in 1947 at around 100 pairs (Sprunt 1948). A steady trend of recovery began with the 1952 nesting season. Numbers reached 500 breeding pairs in 1955, and had attained 1,000 pairs by at least 1962 (Robertson 1964). It appears that the breeding population has at least remained substantially above the 1,000-pair level up to the present time.

Van Halewyn and Norton (1984) estimated the Brown Noddy population of the Gulf–Caribbean region (presumably exclusive of the Bahamas) as "28,000+ pairs." More than half of these were located in 12–15 colonies of 500+ pairs, of which one site was Dry Tortugas. In the Bahamas, Sprunt (1984) pointed out that the existence of a large number of very small colonies made it difficult to estimate numbers, but that the entire archipelago probably harbored "50,000 to 60,000 nesting pairs." The closest neighboring colonies of Brown Noddies to Dry Tortugas are probably those in the Elbow Cay area of Cay Sal Bank, Bahamas (Sprunt 1984), and on islands off the central north coast of Cuba (van Halewyn and Norton 1984), respectively about 250 and 275 km east-southeast.

The close morphological similarity of Brown Noddies throughout the Atlantic suggests that contact and exchange of individuals must occur between the Dry Tortugas colony and at least other nearby colonies. However, the extent and nature of such linkage between populations is practically unknown. Band recoveries from the several thousand Brown Noddies banded at Dry Tortugas in 1960–1985 have yielded little information on intercolony exchange, because few have been banded elsewhere in the Gulf–Caribbean and other population studies in the region (e.g., Morris and Chardine 1992) are also few and mostly recent. It seems of obvious interest in the conservation and management of Brown Noddies at Dry Tortugas to assess the likelihood of recruitment from other populations in the event of other decimating disturbances. Available data indicate that recovery from the 1930s–1940s population bottleneck required about 15 years, which suggests that little extra-Tortugan recruitment may have occurred on that occasion.

DISTRIBUTION AND HISTORY OF DISTRIBUTION: The Brown Noddy exhibits the typical distribution pattern of a tropical, marine bird. It nests on offshore and oceanic islands around the world primarily within a latitudinal belt from about 30°N to 30°S. It rarely occurs along continental coasts except when driven there by storms. Its distribution outside the breeding season is poorly known, but it appears to leave many of its breeding outposts (probably including Dry Tortugas) in the local winter, when it presumably retreats toward warmer seas. However, by far the Brown Noddy's most striking distributional peculiarity is its occurrence as a fairly common breeder in the Tristan da Cunha-Gough Island region in the middle of the South Atlantic (Hagen 1952; Swales 1965; Watson 1966). These islands lie in relatively cold water a full 15 degrees south of the southernmost nesting station for any other species of tropical seabird in the Atlantic. Pantropical, marine distributions, such as that of the Brown Noddy, are often attributed to dispersal via the Tethys Sea, a circum-global, warm-water connection between ocean basins in the late Mesozoic and early Tertiary. However, no enlightening fossil evidence exists concerning the specific antecedents or distributional history of the Brown Noddy.

Away from Dry Tortugas, Brown Noddies occur along the entire Gulf and Atlantic coasts of Florida, but infrequently and usually in very small numbers except after onshore storms in summer and early fall (Robertson and Woolfenden 1992). North of Florida on the Atlantic coast of the United States and west along the Gulf coast, Brown Noddies are rare and most occurrences are associated with hurricanes (Clapp et al. 1983). Storm-driven individuals in Florida, particularly on the Atlantic Coast, may be as likely to originate from colonies in the Bahamas as from Dry Tortugas, but band recoveries show that Tortugan birds disperse to both coasts of Florida and are occasionally storm-blown as far north as Massachusetts (Mason and Robertson 1965).

HABITAT REQUIREMENTS AND HABITAT TREND: The Brown Noddy's breeding habitat requirements are relatively modest. It needs a nesting place free of significant mammalian predators and also requires that surrounding seas out to ca. 50 km are reasonably productive of small fishes (Harrison and Stoneburner 1981; Cramp et al. 1985). The species' off-season distribution is little known, but it probably inhabits offshore and pelagic areas, perhaps at no great distance from its nesting colonies. In its pantropical range at large, Brown Noddies use a wide variety of nesting substrates, including cliffs and ledges, barren sea stacks, flat ground, and trees and bushes, including the tops of coconut palms (Cramp et al. 1985). On the islets around Culebra, Puerto Rico, Brown Noddies reportedly "prefer steep cliffs as nest sites" and the observers saw only two "stick nests in trees" (Kepler and Kepler 1977:72). However, at Dry Tortugas (Robertson 1964, 1978), Noddies build substantial nests of twigs and marine flotsam at sites from about 10 cm to 10 m above ground in herbaceous growth, bay cedar (*Suriana*) and sea lavender (*Tournefortia*) bushes, and mangrove trees (*Laguncularia, Rhizophora*). Nesting habitat may have decreased somewhat at Dry Tortugas, because of the shore-line erosion initiated by hurricane Alma in 1966, but no evidence exists that either nesting habitat or food limits the Tortugas population at present.

VULNERABILITY OF SPECIES AND HABITAT: Although it is located near the northern edge of the species' breeding range in the Atlantic, the colony of Brown Noddies at Dry Tortugas has a long history (Audubon 1835; Watson 1908; and others cited above) and reportedly is one of the dozen or so larger colonies in the Gulf–Caribbean region (van Halewyn and Norton 1984: chart 23). Thus, as with the local Sooty Terns (*Sterna fuscata*), Florida's Brown Noddy population seems solidly established and perhaps not closely dependent upon extralimital source populations. Of course, any seabird with only one nesting colony in an area is potentially vulnerable to a wide range of disturbances that could destroy the site or decimate the breeders. Hopeful aspects in the case of the Brown Noddies of Dry Tortugas are that the colony is in a protected area and that the population has survived a variety of past environmental vicissitudes (Robertson 1964).

CAUSES OF THREAT: Brown Noddies and other breeding seabirds at Dry Tortugas, their nesting habitat, and their offshore fishing grounds are subject, potentially, to many threats. Nesting birds and their nests, eggs, and young may be disturbed or killed by careless human intrusion, by airplanes flying over or taxiing near the colony, by storms, and by predators. Storms outside the nesting season may damage or kill vegetation at the colony site and may trigger direct or secondary erosion of islands. Feeding areas and the birds themselves may be destroyed or injured by spills of oil or other toxic materials. Overharvest may deplete stocks of marine prey organisms or cause disruption of usual feeding methods.

RESPONSES TO HABITAT MODIFICATION: The history of Brown Noddies at Dry Tortugas (Robertson 1964) contains examples of the population's response to many of the disturbances and modifications of habitat mentioned above. In addition to the more "modern" sorts of disturbance, the Brown Noddy population at Dry Tortugas survived 60 or more years of frequent egging from at least the early 1840s until the colony first received warden protection in 1903. At Dry Tortugas, Brown Noddies seem invariably to have responded to major habitat modifications (erosion, vegetation change, plagues of rats) by movement of all or part of the colony to another Tortugan islet. At the level of the individual nest or local "neighborhood," Brown Noddies make vigorous (and usually successful) aerial attacks on any diurnal source of disturbance in nesting areas, including humans. However, Noddies appear to be extremely vulnerable to nocturnal predators such as rats.

DEMOGRAPHIC CHARACTERISTICS: Although band recoveries suggest that at least the Dry Tortugas population of Brown Noddies is not highly pelagic, the species has the demographics of a typical seabird. The clutch consists of one egg with a mean mass of about 35 g (Morris and Chardine 1992). Reports of 2-egg clutches (Brown 1975a,b) are usually from colonies where Noddies nest in dense aggregations on the ground and eggs may have easily been displaced. The incubation period is long for a tern. Watson (1908:212) reported the period at Dry Tortugas as "32 to 35 days" (n = 16) and Morris and Chardine (1992) reported durations of 28 to 33 days (n = 23) from laying to pipping and 33 to 36 days (n = 37) from laying to hatching in a colony at Cayo Noroeste, Culebra National Wildlife Refuge, Puerto Rico. Both parents incubate eggs and brood young. Watson (1908) reported that parental incubation stints at Dry Tortugas averaged about two hours. By contrast, individual incubation shifts at Manana Island, Hawaiian Islands, had a mean length of 23.3 hours (n = 24) and most changeovers occurred from 2000 to 0200 hours (Brown 1976b). Length of incubation shifts may be related to the distance of feeding areas from the nesting colony. Brown Noddies also replace lost eggs more readily than most seabirds. Dorward and Ashmole (1963) believed that many Brown Noddies at Ascension Island laid replacement eggs after high seas overwashed the rock stacks where they nested; ffrench (1991) noted extensive renesting after heavy rain destroyed eggs on Soldado Rock, Trinidad; and on Cayo Noroeste, Morris and Chardine (1992) found that 11 of 16 pairs that lost eggs laid replacements 12 to 35 days later (mean interval = 18.9 days). At Dry Tortugas, most juvenile Brown Noddies remain in the nest until they fly from it (38 of 44 *fide* Riska 1984) and fledging is widely reported to occur at an age of 40 to 50 days (Dorward and Ashmole 1963; Le Croy 1976; Riska 1984; Morris and Chardine 1992). However, the young birds tend to stay near the natal area and may continue to be fed at the nest more or less regularly until they are as much as 75 days old (Doward and Ashmole 1963; Riska 1984). Intermittent or occasional feeding, presumably by parents, may occur as much as three months after the young have fledged (Brown 1976a). In the absence of severe storms and mammalian predators, colonies of Brown Noddies are often remarkably productive. In most years, it is unusual at Dry Tortugas to see more than a few unhatched eggs or dead chicks in or around nests (Robertson 1964), and in two successive seasons at Cayo Noroeste, Morris and Chardine (1992) recorded success rates (chicks fledged per eggs laid) of 91% and 68%. Mean age of first breeding appears to be unknown. None of the known 2 year olds captured at Dry Tortugas had attained adult plumage, but some 3 year olds appeared identical to adults. However, acquisition of adult plumage and sexual maturity does not necessarily mean social maturity. Probably few young Noddies enter the Dry Tortugas breeding population until they are at least 5 years old. At the other end of their span, a Brown Noddy banded as a chick 25 years earlier was found breeding on Manana Island, Hawaii, and one banded as an adult 21 years earlier was caught on a nest at Dry Tortugas (Brown and Robertson 1975).

KEY BEHAVIORS: The name, *stolidus*, is apt for the Brown Noddy, because colonies of the species are unusually subdued compared to those of other terns. Adults may stand quietly at their nests for hours at a time. Interaction with neighboring pairs is usually low key, and at Dry Tortugas, Noddies seldom participate in the noisy alarms and panic flights of the Sooty Tern colony. The Brown Noddy's lack of strongly developed sociality may account for the wide variation in the size of its nesting colonies. Some aggregations in the Indo-Pacific, as at Pelsart Island, Western Australia (Warham 1956), and Necker Island, Hawaii (Clapp and Kridler 1977), reportedly include 25,000 to 50,000 pairs, but the species also nests in 'colonies' as small as "2 or 3 pairs" on outer cays and rocks in the Bahamas (Sprunt 1984). Among the more conspicuous elements in a rather limited behavioral repertoire are nodding, gaping, and high flights (Thompson 1903; Watson 1908; Murphy 1936; Le Croy 1977; Cramp et al. 1985). Nodding behavior involves repeated bowing of the head and presumably is the source of the species' name. It appears to be roughly comparable to the so-called foot-looking behavior of various gulls and terns and may serve to limit or turn aside aggression. Gaping behavior, which exposes the peach-colored mouthlining appears to be an aggressive display. High flights, also performed by many species of *Sterna*, are elaborately ritualized, circling flights by two (occasionally three or four) individuals involving intervals of very fast and very slow wingbeats and terminated by steep dives back into the colony. The exact function of the behavior is not well-understood, but it is thought to be related to pair-formation.

In the Gulf–Caribbean at large, the dates of nest initiation by Brown Noddies vary considerably among colonies, but most begin nesting in late April-early May. For example, at Cayo Noroeste (Morris and Chardine 1992), the colony was regularly reoccupied in the last week of April and dates of first eggs varied by only six days over five nesting seasons. By contrast, in a colony on Little Tobago in the extreme southeastern Caribbean (Morris 1984), Noddies began nesting in mid-February and egg-laying peaked in mid-March. From the earliest records until the 1950s, the Dry Tortugas colony followed the more common Caribbean schedule of starting nesting in early May or the last days of April (Audubon 1835; Thompson 1903; Watson 1908). In the 1950s, first-egg dates began to become earlier by a few days each year, more-or-less in phase with the changing schedule of the Sooty Tern colony, until nesting in the 1990s has routinely begun in the third or fourth week of February. No convincing explanation of this phenomenon has been suggested for either species. At many (or perhaps most) of its nesting areas, including some colonies in the central tropics (e.g., Ascension Island, see Dorward and Ashmole

1963), Brown Noddies disappear or become scarce and inconspicuous for some part of the year. Little is yet known of the whereabouts of any population during this interval and accounts suggest that great variation in the extent of seasonal movement exists among colonies within a region. Thus, "a large proportion" of the Brown Noddy population is said to leave Laysan Island, northwestern Hawaiian Islands, "from late September or October through February or March" (Ely and Clapp 1973:229), but Brown Noddies are present year-round and have nested in every month in colonies about 500 km away (and farther north) on Pearl and Hermes Reef (Amerson et al. 1974). Noddies remain at Dry Tortugas, at least in small numbers, for weeks after the Sooty Terns have departed. A few can often be seen well into October and the first heralds of the next breeding season may appear by late January. Because both the last birds to depart and the first to arrive tend to be strongly nocturnal, it is perhaps not altogether certain that a few Brown Noddies do not roost in the Dry Tortugas colony year round.

As with most tropical terns, Brown Noddies feed principally on fishes and squid that they either catch in midair or glean from the sea surface. Harrison et al. (1983: 33–35) listed a minimum of 50 prey taxa identified from 354 food samples regurgitated by Brown Noddies in the Hawaiian Islands, and their review of the available literature indicated that similarly varied fare had been reported for Noddies in other areas. Feeding appears to be highly opportunistic and wide temporal and spatial differences in diet doubtless occur. Thus, Morris and Chardine (1992) reported that 64 Brown Noddy regurgitations from Cayo Noroeste, Puerto Rico, contained only four different items of which two, a species of sardine and tiny fish larvae, made up most of the sample.

CONSERVATION MEASURES TAKEN: Brown Noddies and other seabirds at Dry Tortugas have been guarded by resident wardens and Park Rangers in all except a handful of the nesting seasons since 1903 (Robertson 1964), a record perhaps unmatched among tropical seabird colonies. In addition, studies by a succession of biologists have enlightened many aspects of the species' life history and behavior (Thompson 1903; Watson 1908; Riska 1984, 1986a, 1986b) and have suggested management measures. Thus, observations in the early 1980s verified earlier reports that nesting noddies and their eggs and young were extremely vulnerable to nocturnal predation by introduced *Rattus rattus* when the rat populations were at high levels. This led to the now-routine program of rat control on Bush Key, Dry Tortugas, during the winter off-season.

CONSERVATION MEASURES PROPOSED: As discussed in the Sooty Tern account, it is uncertain to what extent shoreline erosion and redeposition on Bush Key since the late 1960s may have affected the area of habitat available to nesting terns. This point needs to be carefully established and future changes in area and vegetation need to be closely monitored. Because the most recent complete count of nesting Brown Noddies was made in 1977, the nesting population should be censused again as soon as possible.

ACKNOWLEDGMENTS: Much of what is known about the biology of Brown Noddies at Dry Tortugas results directly from the interest, skill, and hard labor of the several hundred volunteers who participated in the Tortugas tern-banding project from 1959 into the 1980s.

LITERATURE CITED:

Amerson, A.B., Jr., R. B. Clapp, and W. O. Wirtz, II. 1974. The natural history of Pearl and Hermeo Reef, northwestern Hawaiian Islands. Atoll Research Bull., No. 174.

Audubon, J. J. 1835. Ornithological biography. Volume 3.

Brown, W. Y. 1975a. Parental feeding of young sooty terns (*Sterna fuscata* (L.)) and Brown Noddies (*Anous stolidus* (L.)) in Hawaii. Jour. Anim. Ecol. 44:731–742.

Brown, W. Y. 1975b. Artifactual clutch size in Sooty Terns and Brown Noddies. Wilson Bull. 87:115–116.

Brown, W. Y. 1976a. Prolonged parental care in the Sooty Tern and Brown Noddy. Condor 78:128–129.

Brown, W. Y. 1976b. Brown Noddy incubation shifts. Auk 93:626.

Brown, W. Y., and W. B. Robertson, Jr. 1975. Longevity of the Brown Noddy. Bird-Banding 46: 250–251.

Chardine, J. W., and R. D. Morris. 1989. Sexual size dimorphism and assortative mating in the Brown Noddy. Condor 91: 868–874.

Clapp, R. B., and E. Kridler. 1977. The natural history of Necker Island, Northwestern Hawaiian Islands. Atoll Res. Bull. 206.

Clapp, R. B., D. Morgan-Jacobs, and R. C. Banks. 1983. Marine birds of the southeastern United States and Gulf of Mexico. Part III: Charadriiformes. U.S. Fish and Wildl. Serv., Div. Biol. Ser., Washington, D.C.

Cramp, S. (Chief Ed.), D. J. Brooks, E. Dunn, R. Gillmor, P. A. D. Hollom, R. Hudson, E. M. Nicholson, M. A. Ogilvie, P. J. S. Olney, C. S. Roselaar, K. E. L. Simmons, K. H. Voous, D. I. M. Wallace, J. Wattel, and M. G. Wilson. 1985. Handbook of the birds of Europe, the Middle East, and North Africa: The birds of Western Paleartic. Volume 4. Terns to Woodpeckers. Oxford University Press, Oxford, England.

Dorward, D. F., and N. P. Ashmole. 1963. Notes on the biology of the Brown Noddy *Anous stolidus* on Ascension Island. Ibis 103b:447–457.

Ely, C. A., and R. B. Clapp. 1973. Natural history of Laysan Island, Northwestern Hawaiian Islands. Atoll Res. Bull. 171.

ffrench, R. 1991. Synchronous breeding and moult in the Brown Noddy tern on Soldado Rock, Trinidad. Living World, Jour. Trinidad and Tobago Field Naturalists' Club 1991:39–41.

Hagen, Y. 1952. Birds of Tristan da Cunha. Results Norwegian Scientific Expedition to Tristan da Cunha, No. 20. Oslo, Norway.

Harrison, C. S., T. S. Hida, and M. P. Seki. 1983. Hawaiian seabird feeding ecology. Wildl. Monogr. 85:1–71.

Harrison, C. S., and D. L. Stoneburner. 1981. Radiotelemetry of the brown noddy in Hawaii. Jour. Wildl. Manage. 45: 421–425.

Kepler, C. B., and A. K. Kepler. 1977. The sea birds of Culebra and its adjacent islands, Puerto Rico. Living Bird 16:21–50.

Le Croy, M. 1976. Bird observations in Los Roques, Venezuela. Amer. Mus. Novit. No. 2599: 1–30.

Mason, C. R., and W. B. Robertson, Jr. 1965. Noddy Tern in Massachusetts. Auk 82: 109.

Morris, R. D. 1984. Breeding chronology and reproductive success of seabirds on Little Tobago, Trinidad, 1975–76. Colon. Waterbirds 7:1–9.

Morris, R. D., and J. W. Chardine. 1992. The breeding biology and aspects of the feeding ecology of Brown Noddies *Anous stolidus* nesting near Culebra, Puerto Rico, 1985–1989. Jour. Zool., London 226: 65–79.

Moynihan, M. 1959. A revision of the family Laridae (Aves). Amer. Mus. Novit. 1928:1–42.

Murphy, R. C. 1936. Oceanic birds of South America. Volumes 1 and 2. Amer. Mus. Nat. Hist., New York.

Peters, J. L. 1934. Check-list of birds of the world. Volume 2. Harvard Univ. Press, Cambridge, Massachusetts.

Riska, D. E. 1984. Experiments on nestling recognition by Brown Noddies (*Anous stolidus*). Auk 101:605–609.

Riska, D. E. 1986a. An analysis of vocal communication in young Brown Noddies (*Anous stolidus*). Auk 103:351–358.

Riska, D. E. 1986b. An analysis of vocal communication in the adult Brown Noddy (*Anous stolidus*). Auk 103:359–369.

Robertson, W. B., Jr. 1964. The terns of the Dry Tortugas. Bull. Fla. State Mus. 8:1–95.

Robertson, W. B., Jr. 1978. Noddy Tern. Pp. 95–96 in Rare and endangered biota of Florida. Volume 2: Birds (H. W. Kale, II, ed.). Univ. Presses Fla., Gainesville, Florida.

Robertson, W. B., Jr., D. R. Paulson, and C. R. Mason. 1961. A tern new to the United States. Auk 78:423–425.

Robertson, W. B. Jr., and G. E. Woolfenden. 1992. Florida bird species: an annotated list. Spec. Publ. No. 6. Fla. Ornithol. Soc., Gainesville, Florida.

Schnell, G. D. 1970. A phenetic study of the suborder Lari (Aves). Parts I and II. Syst. Zool. 19:35–37, 264–302.

Sprunt, A., IV. 1984. The status and conservation of seabirds of the Bahama

Islands. Pp. 157–168 in Status and conservation of the world's seabirds (J. P. Croxall, P. G. H. Evans, and R. W. Schreiber, eds.). ICBP Tech. Publ. No. 2. Cambridge, England.

Sprunt, A., Jr. 1948. Population survey, tern colonies of the Dry Tortugas, Fort Jefferson National Monument, 1947. Fla. Nat. 21:25–31.

Swales, M. K. 1965. The seabirds of Gough Island. Ibis 107:17–42, 215–229.

Thompson, J. 1903. The Tortugas tern colony. Bird-Lore 5:77–84.

van Halewyn, R., and R. L. Norton. 1984. The status and conservation of seabirds in the Caribbean. Pp. 169–222 in Status and conservation of the world's seabirds (J. P. Croxall, P. G. H. Evans, and R. W. Schreiber, eds.). ICBP Tech. Bull. No. 2, Cambridge, England.

Warham, J. 1956. Observations on the birds of Pelsart Island. Emu 56:83–93.

Watson, G. E. 1966. Seabirds of the tropical Atlantic Ocean. Smithsonian Publ. 4680, Smithsonian Press, Washington, D.C.

Watson, J. B. 1908. The behavior of Noddy and Sooty terns. Carnegie Inst. Wash. Papers from the Tortugas Lab. 2:187–255.

PREPARED BY: William B. Robertson, Jr., National Biological Service, Everglades National Park, 40001 State Road 9336, Homestead, FL 33034-6733.

Black Skimmer

Rynchops niger

FAMILY LARIDAE

Order Charadriiformes

TAXONOMY: The Black Skimmer (*Rynchops niger*) is one of three species of skimmers that have sometimes been assigned their own family rank (Rynchopidae), but recent AOU (1983) classification includes them in the family Laridae composed of four subfamilies: skuas and jaegers (Stercorariinae), gulls (Larinae), terns (Sterninae), and skimmers (Rynchopinae). How closely skimmers are related to the other subfamilies has been a debated issue and probably will continue to be discussed (see Sears et al. 1976; Burger and Gochfeld 1990).

DESCRIPTION: The bill of the Black Skimmer is unique among North American birds. Both halves are laterally compressed, the lower knifelike and distinctly longer than the upper. Bill color is bright red at the base and black at the tip. The breeding plumage of both sexes is black above and immaculate white below, with a broad white stripe on the trailing edge of the wing and the outer rectrices. The body ranges from 40–50 cm long (16–20 in.) and the wingspan is about 1.1–1.3 m (42–50 in.) (Barbour 1978; Peterson 1980). Adult males weigh about 350 g and adult females average about 250 g (Clapp et al. 1983). The wings are very long in proportion to the body, permitting the bird to fly low over the water with a shallow wingbeat. The species frequently is active in the early evening and night. When it is constricted, the pupil of the eye is "oval, slit-like" (Welty 1979). Downy chicks are grayish to buffy-brown above and are sprinkled with dark spots; the underparts are white.

POPULATION SIZE AND TREND: Clapp et al. (1983) and Spendelow and Patton (1988) estimated that Florida had about 4,500 breeding Black Skimmers occupying 13 known "large" colonies during 1976–1978. There were at least 2,900 birds in Atlantic coast colonies and 1,600 in Gulf coast colonies (Clapp et al. 1983). Various small colonies probably were undetected and consequently not included in these estimated totals. An intensive survey of

571

Black Skimmer,
Rynchops niger.
(Photo by Jeffery
A. Gore)

colonies in northwest Florida from Wakulla County to the border of Alabama in 1990 located 386 Black Skimmer nests at 12 sites (Gore 1991). Colony size in that study ranged from 1 to 208 nests (mean = 32.2). Seven of the 12 sites were located on rooftops of buildings (Gore 1991). Observations of skimmer colonies throughout the state during 1990 suggested a minimum of 23 colonies containing about 1,600 breeding pairs (J. Gore, pers. comm.). An estimate of 1,500–2,000 breeding pairs of skimmers in Florida during the early 1990s appears reasonable.

DISTRIBUTION AND HISTORY OF DISTRIBUTION: The Black Skimmer breeds locally along the Atlantic coast of the United States from Massachusetts to Florida, on the Gulf coast from western Florida through Texas to Tabasco, and along the Pacific coast from southern California (recently) through Mexico to Ecuador in South America. The species also breeds along the east coast and the larger rivers of South America from Colombia to northern Argentina (AOU 1983; Clapp et al. 1983; Spendelow and Patton 1988). In winter, skimmers withdraw from the northern part of their U.S. range. They are then found from southern North Carolina to Florida, along the Gulf of Mexico and western Mexico south along both coastlines to "Middle America," and sporadically in the Caribbean (Clapp et al. 1983).

Historically in Florida, the species was known to breed no farther south than Tampa Bay along the Gulf coast and Ponce De Leon Inlet on the Atlantic coast. The Black Skimmer has more recently been documented breeding from Escambia to Collier County along the Gulf coast and from Nassau to Broward County along the Atlantic coast (H. Kale, unpubl. data). This change in the breeding range may be a result of shifting populations, a response to increased human competition at the nesting areas in the historic range of the species, a reflection of more comprehensive survey techniques, or most likely a combination of these and other factors.

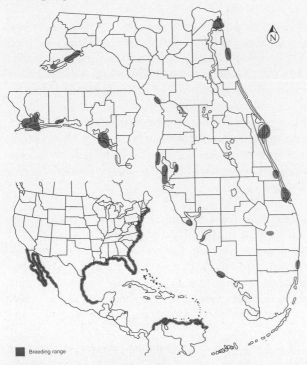

Distribution map of
Black Skimmer,
Rynchops niger.

Breeding range

HABITAT REQUIREMENTS AND HABITAT TREND: Black Skimmers depend on healthy estuaries for feeding and on undisturbed coastlines for breeding and loafing. In Florida, colonies are located on dredge-material islands, natural sandbars, small coastal islands, and beaches with little vegetation usually within sight of open water (Schreiber and Schreiber 1978; Kale 1979; Clapp et al. 1983). In some parts of their range, but not yet in Florida, Black Skimmers nest on wrack in salt marshes (see literature review in Spendelow and Patton 1988; Burger and Gochfeld 1990). This behavior is apparently of recent origin and is believed to be related to increasing human use of beaches.

Skimmers require an adequate prey base of small fish near their nesting colonies. Skimmers are opportunistic feeders, taking any small fish of suitable size. They rely heavily on silversides (*Menidia* spp.), killifishes (*Fundulus* spp.), anchovies (*Anchoa* spp.), and mullet (*Mugil* spp.) (Erwin 1977; Loftin 1982; King 1989). Most prey items are less than 100 mm long (Loftin 1982; King 1989). Prey may range in weight from about 0.5 to 14.5 g (Loftin 1982; King 1989). Shrimp also are taken "coincidentally" (Barbour 1978).

VULNERABILITY OF SPECIES AND HABITAT: The most critical need of Black Skimmers is for undisturbed, sandy beaches and islands for nesting because the adults, eggs, and nestlings are highly vulnerable to human disturbance. In addition to human disturbance, the major causes of breeding failure in Black Skimmers are predation and flooding of nesting colonies by high tides. In Florida, raccoons (*Procyon lotor*) are the major mammalian predator of eggs and chicks, and Laughing Gulls (*Larus atricilla*) are probably the most significant avian predator of eggs. Rats and foxes undoubtedly also depredate some nests. Due to the dynamic and ephemeral character of their preferred nesting habitat, Black Skimmers are not as site-tenacious as some other larids and colonies frequently fail (Schreiber and Schreiber 1978; Burger 1982). The location of colonies often shifts from year to year and those that have failed due to predation pressures are more likely to be abandoned than colonies destroyed by flooding (Burger 1982).

CAUSES OF THREAT: Because Black Skimmers are colonial nesters, they are extremely vulnerable to local disturbances by humans, predators, and domestic dogs. Many skimmer nesting areas also are under development pressure for coastal homes or other structures. Competition from humans for use of beaches, especially on islands, is great during the breeding season. Hatchling skimmers are susceptible to thermal stress in southern climates and may succumb if adults are kept away from them for even a short time (Blus and Stafford 1980; Loftin, pers. observ.).

Safina and Burger (1983) found that Black Skimmer subcolonies that were subjected to daily human disturbance exhibited greatly depressed reproductive success compared to undisturbed subcolonies. Human visitation also may result in prelaying site abandonment by adults, especially early in the breeding season (Safina and Burger 1983). Although skimmer chicks often seek shelter in nest scrapes or depressions when disturbed (Blus and Stafford 1980), those that flee a disturbance cross the nesting areas of other nearby birds and may be attacked by adults guarding their territories (Loftin, pers. observ.). While "skimming" and on the breeding grounds, skimmers may become entangled in persistent marine debris (e.g., discarded fishing line).

RESPONSES TO HABITAT MODIFICATION: The loss of natural nesting areas near the coast has resulted in attempts by Black Skimmers to nest on roofs of buildings (Greene and Kale 1976; Fisk 1978; Gore 1987) and at inland sites (Langridge and Hunter 1986). Attempts to nest on roofs usually have failed and probably represent "ecological sinks" for skimmers (Gore 1987). The species has nested successfully along bridge and causeway roadsides in Florida (Skoog 1982; Smith et al., unpubl. data). Skimmers have benefited from dredge-material island habitats, which they readily accept, and are probably as successful there as on natural islands.

DEMOGRAPHIC CHARACTERISTICS: In Florida, Black Skimmers produce clutches from about mid-May through August, with most egg laying occurring from late May through the end of June (Schreiber and Schreiber 1978). Nesting cycle initiation dates appear to be highly variable in Florida, both between colonies (Schreiber and Schreiber 1978) and in the same colony between years (Smith et al., unpubl. data). Clapp et al. (1983) reported similarly extended and variable nesting cycles for this species in a compilation of studies conducted in the southeastern United States.

Black Skimmer clutches range in size from 2 to 5 eggs (Clapp et al. 1983). Mean clutch sizes of 3.6 (Erwin 1977) and 3.8 eggs (Blus and Stafford 1980) have been reported in Virginia and South Carolina, respectively. Erwin (1977) reported an average incubation period of 22.9 days. First hatched chicks in broods have a much greater fledging success rate than their siblings; this difference is probably related to their ability to obtain more food from their parents (Erwin 1977). The fledging age of Black Skimmers in Florida is probably somewhere between 4 and 5 weeks. Skimmers can live up to 20 years (Kale and Loftin 1982).

KEY BEHAVIORS: Black Skimmers feed by "skimming" surface water with the lower bill cutting through the water. When the lower bill contacts prey, the head quickly bows forward and down to seize the item (Zusi 1962). Contrary to a popular misconception, skimmers do not scoop their prey from the water with a forward lunge; rather, when the bill strikes a small fish or crustacean, the head dips down rather than up. Because of their unique foraging method, skimmers require calm water with sufficient small prey at or near the surface (see Loftin 1982) to support contact feeding. In Florida, this translates into protected and undegraded salt marshes and estuaries.

Terrestrial display behaviors have been described by Wolk (1959), Sears et al. (1976), Burger and Gochfeld (1990), and others. An initial ground courtship display involves the presentation of a fish (or a substitute such as a small bit of wood) by a male to a female. After obtaining a fish, the male approaches the female in a posture varying between the threat posture and the submissive posture. If the female accepts the token, copulation often ensues, or nest scrape making (see Wolk 1959; Sears et al. 1976; Burger and Gochfeld 1990). The shallow nest scrape is excavated by turning round and round while seated in the scrape, kicking sand out backwards.

The Black Skimmer has an injury-feigning distraction display that sometimes serves to lure intruders away from the nest and young. This display is rather weakly developed compared to some other species, especially the plovers. The calls of adults have been described as soft, successive barks "kaup, kaup" (Peterson 1980).

CONSERVATION MEASURES TAKEN: Black Skimmers are protected by the Migratory Bird Treaty Act (16 U.S.C. 703–711) and the Wildlife Code of the State of Florida (Chapter 39 F.A.C.). The Florida Game and Fresh Water

Fish Commission has closed and posted tern nesting colonies in many areas of Florida. These efforts also have greatly benefited Black Skimmers and should be vigorously pursued. In order to avoid public resentment over closure of areas, which can result in vandalism, efforts should be continued to educate the public about the need to protect our wildlife heritage. Signs that explain the purpose of closure may be more successful than signs that take an authoritarian approach (Loftin, pers. observ.).

CONSERVATION MEASURES PROPOSED: Because so much of Florida's estuarine and marine coastline already has suffered habitat conversion or other anthropogenic disruptions, Black Skimmers frequently have been forced to disperse and relocate to new breeding sites. Consequently, all nesting colonies should be posted and protected from human interference during the breeding season. Colonies also should be monitored and data compiled on nesting success throughout the state.

Skimmers are a manageable species and readily accept dredge-material islands for nesting when these sites are available. Agencies responsible for dredging harbors and waterways are in a continuing position to be of great direct benefit to skimmers by scheduling dredging and deposition when the birds are not nesting and configuring spoil islands so that they are suitable for terns and skimmers. Annual removal of vegetative ground cover at these sites may be required to maintain their suitability for these species. Additional "critical wildlife areas" should be established to secure maximum protection for Black Skimmer breeding colonies (Robson 1991). Erwin (1989) recommended 200 m and Rodgers and Smith (1995) recommended 180 m as a buffer zone width around skimmer colonies.

ACKNOWLEDGMENTS: We would like to thank Herbert W. Kale and the Florida Breeding Bird Atlas project, Jeffery A. Gore, and Don A. Wood for providing unpublished data regarding Black Skimmer breeding colonies in Florida. James A. Rodgers and Robert G. Wolk provided helpful comments on the manuscript.

LITERATURE CITED:

AOU. 1983. Checklist of North American birds. American Ornithologists' Union, Allen Press, Inc., Lawrence, Kansas.

Barbour, D. B. 1978. Black Skimmer. Pp. 96–97 in Rare and endangered biota of Florida, vol. II: Birds (H. W. Kale, II, ed.). Univ. Presses Fla., Gainesville, Florida. 121 pp.

Blus, L. J., and C. J. Stafford. 1980. Breeding biology and relation of pollutants to Black Skimmers and Gull-billed Terns in South Carolina. U.S. Fish Wildl. Serv. Spec. Rept. no. 230. Washington, D.C. 18 pp.

Burger, J. 1982. The role of reproductive success in colony-site selection and abandonment in Black Skimmers (*Rynchops niger*). Auk 99:109–115.

Burger, J., and M. Gochfeld. 1990. The Black Skimmer: social dynamics of a colonial species. Columbia Univ. Press., New York.

Clapp, R. B., D. Morgan-Jacobs, and R. C. Banks. 1983. Marine birds of the southeastern United States and Gulf of Mexico. Part III: Charadriiformes. U.S. Fish Wildl. Serv. FWS/OBS-83/30, Washington, D.C. 853 pp.

Erwin, R. M. 1977. Black Skimmer breeding ecology and behavior. Auk 94:709–717.

Erwin, R. M. 1989. Responses to human intruders by birds nesting in colonies: experimental results and management guidelines. Colon. Waterbirds 12:104–108.

Fisk, E. J. 1978. Roof-nesting terns, skimmers and plovers in Florida. Fla. Field Nat. 6:1–8.

Gore, J. A. 1987. Black Skimmers nesting on roofs in northwestern Florida. Fla. Field Nat. 15:77–79.

Gore, J. A. 1991. Distribution and abundance of nesting Least Terns and Black Skimmers in northwest Florida. Fla. Field Nat. 19:65–72.

Greene, L. L., and H. W. Kale, II. 1976. Roof nesting by Black Skimmers. Fla. Field Nat. 4:15–17.

Kale, H. W., II. 1979. Unpublished report to Shell Oil Corp., Environmental Affairs. Florida Audubon Society, Maitland, Florida. 50 pp.

Kale, H. W., II, and R. W. Loftin. 1982. A longevity record for the Black Skimmer. North Amer. Bird Bander 7:54.

King, K. A. 1989. Food habits and organochlorine contaminants in the diet of Black Skimmers, Galveston Bay, Texas, USA. Colon. Waterbirds 12:109–112.

Langridge, H. P., and G. S. Hunter. 1986. Inland nesting of Black Skimmers. Fla. Field Nat. 14:73–74.

Loftin, R. W. 1982. Diet of Black Skimmers and Royal Terns in northeast Florida. Fla. Field Nat. 10:19–20.

Peterson, R. T. 1980. A field guide to the birds. Houghton Mifflin Co., Boston, Massachusetts.

Robson, M. 1991. Wildlife and habitat management. Ann. perf. rept. Fla. Game and Fresh Water Fish Comm., Tallahassee, Florida.

Rodgers, J. A., Jr., and H. T. Smith. 1995. Set-back distances to protect nesting bird colonies from human disturbance in Florida. Conserv. Biol. 9:89–99.

Safina, C., and J. Burger. 1983. Effects of human disturbance on reproductive success in the Black Skimmer. Condor 85:164–171.

Schreiber, R. W., and E. A. Schreiber. 1978. Colonial bird use and plant succession on dredged material islands in Florida; vol. I: Sea and wading bird colonies. Tech. rept. D–78–14. U.S. Army Eng. Waterways Exp. Sta., Vicksburg, Mississippi. 127 pp.

Sears, H. F., L. J. Moseley, and H. C. Mueller. 1976. Behavioral evidence on skimmers' evolutionary relationships. Auk 93:170–174.

Skoog, P. J. 1982. Highways and endangered wildlife in Florida; impacts and recommendations. Fla. Game and Fresh Water Fish Comm., Tallahassee, Florida. 97 pp.

Spendelow, J. A., and S. R. Patton. 1988. National atlas of coastal waterbird colonies in the contiguous United States: 1976–82. U.S. Fish Wildl. Serv. Biol. Rept. 88(5), Washington, D.C. 326 pp.

Welty, J. C. 1979. The life of birds. Saunders College Publ., Philadelphia, Pennsylvania.

Wolk, R. G. 1959. Some reproductive behavior patterns of the Black Skimmer, *Rynchops nigra nigra* Linnaeus. Ph.D. dissertation, Cornell Univ., Ithaca, New York.

Zusi, R. 1962. Structural adaptations of the head and neck in the Black Skimmer, *Rynchops nigra* L. Publ. Nuttall Ornithol. Club no. 3.

PREPARED BY: Robert W. Loftin, Department of History and Philosophy, University of North Florida, 4567 St. Johns Bluff Rd., S., Jacksonville, FL 32216 (Deceased), and Henry T. Smith, Florida Department of Environmental Protection, Office of Environmental Services, 3900 Commonwealth Blvd., Tallahassee, FL 32399 (Current address: Florida Department of Environmental Protection, Florida Park Service, 13798 S.E. Federal Highway, Hobe Sound, FL 33455).

Florida Burrowing Owl
Speotyto cunicularia floridana

FAMILY STRIGIDAE

Order Strigiformes

TAXONOMY: The Florida Burrowing Owl (*Speotyto cunicularia floridana*) was described by Ridgway in 1874 from a specimen collected in Manatee County, Florida (Ridgway 1914). The principal diagnostic characteristic of this subspecies was a darker and less buffy-brown dorsal plumage than other populations of *S. cunicularia*. Additionally, the Florida Burrowing Owl was reported to have whiter spotting, a less buffy ventral plumage, and shorter wings and tail than other Burrowing Owl races. Some authors have considered this taxon to be a full species (Baird et al. 1874), but all recent accounts treat it as conspecific with *S. cunicularia* (e.g., AOU 1983). *S. cunicularia* is highly variable, and 18 subspecies have been described (Clark et al. 1978), including several insular races within the Caribbean Basin (Ridgway 1914). The degree of differentiation among the various Caribbean races of Burrowing Owl, the mainland North American race (*S. c. hypugaea*), and *S. c. floridana* needs to be reevaluated with modern systematic methods. The Burrowing Owl is occasionally placed in the monotypic genus *Athene*.

DESCRIPTION: The Florida Burrowing Owl closely resembles other Burrowing Owls in being cryptically colored to blend in with background vegetation in their typical habitat. In Florida, the plumage blends perfectly with the herbs and forbs in grasslands and old fields. The dorsal plumage of the adult is dark brown with scattered white bars and spots. The ventral plumage is white or beige with dark brown or tan bars, mostly along the flanks. The center of the abdomen is white. The throat and upper breast are white, separated by a dark brown band. The facial disk is tan and white, and the eyebrows (superciliary line) are white. Burrowing Owls have a rounded head without ear tufts. Adults molt following the fledging of young, usually in mid to late summer (Courser 1972). Although the plumage of females is usually darker than that of males, sexes are difficult to distinguish in fresh plumage. However, by

Florida Burrowing Owl, *Speotyto cunicularia floridana*. (Photo by Allan D. Cruickshank, courtesy of Florida Audubon Society)

spring males usually appear much paler than females, presumably due to increased sun bleaching in this sex (Thomsen 1971; Butts 1973; Martin 1973; Millsap and Bear 1990) and staining of the plumage by nest contents (R. Ashton, pers. comm.). Fledged juveniles less than 10 weeks old differ from adults in that the breast is nearly solid dark brown and the abdomen solid buff with few distinct bars or spots. Fledged young and adults usually have bright lemon-yellow irises, although chocolate, olive, and straw irises are not uncommon in some populations (Millsap and Bear, unpubl. data; Julie Hovis, pers. comm.). The bill is yellow or greenish-yellow. The legs are long and relatively bare, adaptations for excavating burrows in loose soil. Burrowing Owls are about the size of soda cans, averaging around 200 mm in total length. Unlike many other owls, male Burrowing Owls average slightly larger than females (Snyder and Wiley 1976). In Florida, sexual size dimorphism is not pronounced. A series of 133 live adult females from Cape Coral, Lee County, weighed an average of 150 g and had an average wing length (unflattened chord) of 163 mm. A sample of 93 males from the same population had an average weight of 152 g and an average wing length of 166 mm (Millsap and Bear, unpubl. data). Mealey (1992) reported a statistically significant difference in mean metatarsus length between male (mean = 45.7 mm) and female (mean = 44.9 mm) Burrowing Owls from Broward and Dade counties.

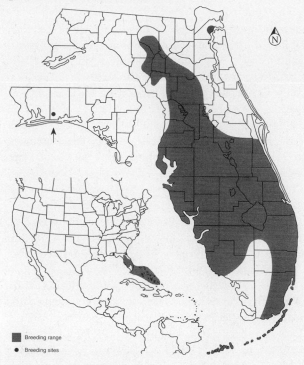

Distribution map
of the Florida
Burrowing Owl,
*Speotyto cunicularia
floridana.*

■ Breeding range
● Breeding sites

POPULATION SIZE AND TREND: Statewide surveys have not been con-
ducted for the Florida Burrowing Owl, thus population size is unknown.
However, the subspecies is relatively abundant in some local areas, and densi-
ties of up to 17.6 pairs per km² have been observed in Cape Coral, Lee County
(Wesemann and Rowe 1987); the Burrowing Owl population on the Cape
Coral peninsula alone probably exceeds 1,000 pairs (Millsap and Bear, unpubl.
data). Fairly dense local concentrations also have been reported in Monroe (J.
Hovis, pers. comm.), Sumter, Lake and Marion (R. Ashton, pers. comm.),
Broward, and Dade counties (Mealey, 1992). Using the best available information, Millsap et al. (1990) estimated the statewide population in 1987 at
between 3,000 and 10,000 pairs.

These locally flourishing populations are not necessarily secure for long
periods of time. A sizable population on and near the University of South
Florida campus in Hillsborough County studied by Courser (1976) in the mid
1970s rapidly collapsed shortly afterward (Glen Woolfenden, pers. comm.).
Similar declines have been reported in some parts of Broward County (Consiglio
and Reynolds 1987). Additionally, Burrowing Owl numbers on the Osceola
Plains have apparently declined greatly since the late 1800s, when colonies of
"hundreds of pairs" were reported around Lake Kissimmee (Rhoads 1892;

Nicholson 1954). These observations suggest an ongoing cycle of establishment and extirpation of local Burrowing Owl populations. The net status of this subspecies is a function of the relative rates of establishment and collapse of these metapopulations. Without information on the status of many more local populations, it is difficult to assess whether Burrowing Owls are increasing or decreasing statewide.

DISTRIBUTION AND HISTORY OF DISTRIBUTION: The Burrowing Owl is locally distributed throughout suitable habitat from the Great Plains westward in North America (north to southern Alberta, Saskatchewan, and Alberta), south through Central and South America to Tierra del Fuego, and on islands in the Caribbean Basin (e.g., Cuba, Hispaniola, Aruba, Margarita), nearby Atlantic (Bahama Islands), and in the Pacific Ocean off the west coast of Mexico (Isla Clarion, Revillagigedo, and Guadalupe; AOU 1983). Within these broad range limits, occurrence is variable in open, well-drained grasslands, steppes, deserts, prairies, and agricultural lands.

The Florida Burrowing Owl primarily occurs in peninsular Florida, in the Florida Keys, and in the Bahama Islands from Grand Bahama to Great Inagua (Owre 1978). In Florida, the subspecies breeds locally in open, well-drained uplands from Dixie, Lafayette, Suwannee, Columbia, and Duval Counties (Courser 1979) southward through Duck Key, Vaca Key, and Boca Chica Key in Monroe County (Julie Hovis, pers. comm.). A recently discovered breeding population, consisting of at least eight pairs, exists on Eglin Air Force Base in Okaloosa County (C. Petrick, pers. comm.). Like many other arid-adapted taxa in Florida, Burrowing Owls probably colonized the state from western North America during early to mid-Pleistocene glacial periods when a circum-Gulf arid dispersal corridor existed (Webb 1990). Florida Burrowing Owl populations have probably been isolated since the close of the Wisconsinan stage of the Pleistocene, which was at its height 20,000 years before the present (Webb 1990). Early records of Burrowing Owls in Florida were mainly from the central peninsula within the Osceola, Okeechobee, and DeSoto plains and in the Gulf coastal lowlands (Ridgway 1914; Bent 1938). Burrowing Owls appeared to have undergone a range expansion in Florida from the 1940s to 1970s. In the early 1940s Burrowing Owls were found breeding in Hernando County (MacKenzie 1944), by 1954 nesting was documented in Marion County (Neill 1954), and by 1963 breeding was reported in Levy and Alachua counties (Ligon 1963). The origin of the recently discovered population in the Florida panhandle is unknown, though presumably it is the result of further range expansion of the Florida subspecies.

HABITAT REQUIREMENTS AND HABITAT TREND: Florida Burrowing Owls typically occur in open, well-drained treeless areas where herbaceous ground cover is short. These requirements were met historically in Florida on the dry prairies of the central peninsula in the vicinity of burns and along the margins of depressional marshes during dry periods (Howell 1932; Bent 1938). Land clearing and wetland drainage have greatly expanded the amount of suitable Burrowing Owl habitat in Florida, and these activities probably played a major role in the range expansion of this species since the 1940s. Currently, Burrowing Owls still occur in dry prairies in central Florida, although they are most often associated with such unnatural elevated features as canal banks and road berms. In addition, they occur in tame-grass pastures, on airports, golf courses, athletic fields, and in partially developed residential and industrial areas where expanses of mowed lawn and ruderal grassland are maintained. The latter areas probably support the largest concentrations of Burrowing Owls in Florida at the present time. In Cape Coral, Burrowing Owls appear to prefer areas where developed lots occupy between 25 and 75% of the landscape (Wesemann and Rowe 1987). Burrowing Owl nesting density decreases under more or less intensive development (Wesemann and Rowe 1987). Although far from conclusive, these observations suggest that Burrowing Owl populations may actually thrive in some developing areas, but then decrease or collapse when the amount of developed land exceeds some critical, but unknown and probably variable, threshold. R. Ashton (pers. comm.) found Burrowing Owls in Sumter, Lake and Marion counties most likely to nest in pastures that had been cleared for at least 4 years and that were heavily grazed.

VULNERABILITY OF SPECIES AND HABITAT: Owre (1978) noted with concern that an increasing segment of the Florida Burrowing Owl population was dependant upon impermanent artificial habitat. This is perhaps even more true today. Many residential and industrial areas where Burrowing Owls currently thrive will probably not support owls 20 or more years into the future unless specific conservation efforts are undertaken. However, with forethought and planning, Burrowing Owl populations could probably persist indefinitely in many of these areas.

CAUSES OF THREAT: Intensive cultivation and development are the ultimate threats to Burrowing Owls in Florida. Proximate causes of population declines in intensively developed areas are not known, but may include an absence of suitable nesting sites and increased adult and juvenile mortality from vehicle collisions, domestic animal predation, and human harassment. R. Ashton (pers. comm.) reported that the greatest cause of death among young Burrowing Owls in his study population in improved pastures in Lake, Sumter and Marion counties was fire ant (*Solenopsis invicta*) predation.

RESPONSES TO HABITAT MODIFICATION: Burrowing Owls make extensive use of modified and disturbed areas in Florida. Historically, Burrowing Owls were probably nomadic in Florida, and followed short-term disturbances such as fires and floods. Currently, the prevalent form of disturbance is land clearing for development, which has more long-term consequences. In residential and industrial areas Burrowing Owls nest in burrows on vacant mowed lots and forage under streetlights and in landscaped yards (Wesemann and Rowe 1987). Under these conditions Burrowing Owls prey heavily on insects and vertebrates associated with disturbed areas. It is unclear if owls in less disturbed areas will adapt to encroaching human development.

DEMOGRAPHIC CHARACTERISTICS: Florida Burrowing Owls have been observed nesting from early October to early July, but most nesting activity occurs during the relatively dry period from February through late May (Owre 1978; Millsap and Bear 1990). Egg laying peaks in mid-March at Cape Coral, and fledging activity peaks 70 days later in late May (Millsap and Bear 1990). Less than 1% of pairs in Cape Coral raise two broods in the same year (Millsap and Bear 1990). A series of 14 presumably complete Florida Burrowing Owl clutches in the U.S. National Museum of Natural History ranged in size from 2 to 6 eggs (mode = 4). Median brood size at fledging from 406 Burrowing Owl nesting attempts between 1987 and 1989 in Cape Coral was 3; 77% of these nesting attempts successfully produced at least 1 fledgling. Productivity of Burrowing Owls in Broward and Dade counties from 1988 to 1990 ranged from 0.5 to 1.5 young fledged per nesting attempt (Mealey, 1992). Minimal annual survival rates (based on re-encounters of 450 banded owls) in Cape Coral have ranged from 51 to 69% for adults, and from 17 to 25% for juveniles (Millsap and Bear, unpubl. data). Adults show a high degree of fidelity to territories and mates; in Cape Coral from 1987 to 1989 an average of 78% of surviving adults remained on the same territory, and 95% of pairs where both adults survived remained together (Millsap and Bear, unpubl. data). Natal dispersal distances in Cape Coral averaged 1,596 m for females and 520 m for males (Millsap and Bear, unpubl. data).

KEY BEHAVIORS: As the name suggests, Florida Burrowing Owls make extensive use of underground burrows. Whereas their western relatives typically appropriate burrows dug by burrowing mammals, Florida Burrowing Owls most often excavate their own (although they will use burrows dug by other species, particularly gopher tortoises (*Gopherus polyphemus*): Jackson 1989; Ray Ashton, pers. comm.). Excavation is accomplished primarily with the feet, and an owl can complete a 3-meter long burrow in less than two days. Burrows typically consist of an entrance mound of waste soil, a twisting entrance tunnel 1.5–2.5 m in length, and an enlarged nest chamber at the end of the tunnel. Eggs are laid and young are brooded in the chamber. In selecting sites to dig, Burrowing Owls are attracted to areas where sod has been broken or removed. They can often be enticed to dig a burrow at a particular spot by removing a circular plug of sod 0.3 m in diameter and placing a pile of loose soil near the hole.

Burrowing Owls "decorate" burrows prior to egg laying by lining the entrance mound, tunnel, and nest chamber with clumps of grass, palm fronds, dog and cat feces, and other material. Entrance mounds of burrows that contain eggs are usually adorned with highly visible objects (e.g., shells, shredded paper, tin foil, cigarette butts, plastic, and even wayward Barbie dolls). This material disappears about the time the young begin to wander out of the burrow. Burrowing Owls use burrows extensively during the spring for nesting and winter for protection from avian predators. However, use of burrows seems to decrease during summer, when frequent heavy rains cause many to flood.

Foods of Burrowing Owls in Florida include mole crickets (*Gryllotalpa* spp.), June beetles (*Phyllophanaga* spp.) and, in south Florida, brown anoles (*Anolis sagrei*) and Cuban treefrogs (*Osteopilus septentrionalis*) (Hennemann 1980; Wesemann and Rowe 1987; Millsap and Bear, unpubl. data). In Cape Coral, Burrowing Owls also feed regularly on road-killed animals and migrant songbirds (many of which may be scavenged after colliding with glass windows in homes). Other prey reported for Florida Burrowing Owls include small rodents, crayfish (*Cambarus* spp.), various frogs (*Rana* spp.) and toads (*Bufo* spp.), spiders, and many other species of insects (Lewis 1973).

The most frequently heard calls in Florida Burrowing Owls are the primary song, a two-note call described as "coo coooo," and a series of nest defense and food solicitation calls. The latter include a "rasp" call and an "eep" call, given mainly by the female, and a series of "clucks," "chatters," and "screams," given by both sexes when mobbing predators or defending the nest.

CONSERVATION MEASURES TAKEN: The Florida Burrowing Owl is listed as a species of special concern by the FGFWFC (1990). The owls and their nests are protected by Commission rules (Chapter 39, Florida Administrative Code) and federal rules promulgated under the Migratory Bird Treaty Act (16 U. S. C. 703–712).

CONSERVATION MEASURES PROPOSED: Burrowing Owls do not appear to warrant further legal protection at this time, but continued or expanded population monitoring is warranted. Burrowing Owls can thrive in disturbed, developed areas if sufficient undeveloped but mowed land is maintained for nesting and if human harassment is minimal. In residential areas posting nest sites with informative "keep out" signs can help reduce disturbance. School-aged children account for much harassment and awareness campaigns in schools have been effective in Broward County (Consiglio and Reynolds 1987) and in Cape Coral (Cindy Bear, pers. comm.). Managing for

Burrowing Owls on existing public lands (e.g., school sites, athletic parks) can provide a measure of long-term security to some populations, but habitat set-aside programs will be needed to secure many populations. The Burrowing Owl's most consistent need is for low-height forb cover around nest sites, and any management program for this species should include mowing or prescribed burning to meet this requirement.

ACKNOWLEDGMENTS: Julie Hovis, Brian Mealey, Matt Rowe, and Ted Wesemann assisted with the preparation of this account either directly or by sharing their unpublished information. Cindy Bear and the volunteer Burrowing Owl monitoring crew in Cape Coral deserve most of the credit for the data from that owl population. Victor Heller, Julie Hovis, Timothy O'Meara and Don Wood provided many helpful suggestions on the manuscript.

LITERATURE CITED:

AOU. 1983. Check-list of North American birds. 6th ed. American Ornithologists' Union, Washington, D. C.

Baird, S. F., T. M. Brewer, and R. Ridgway. 1874. A history of North American birds. Little Brown and Co., Boston, Massachusetts.

Bent, A. C. 1938. Life histories of North American birds of prey. Part 2. U. S. Natl. Mus. Bull. no. 170. 482 pp.

Butts, K. O. 1973. Life history and habitat requirements of Burrowing Owls in western Oklahoma. M. S. thesis, Oklahoma State Univ., Stillwater, Oklahoma.

Clark, R. J., D. G. Smith, and L. H. Kelso. 1978. Working bibliography of owls of the World. Natl. Wildl. Fed., Sci. and Tech. Series no. 1. Washington, D. C. 319 p.

Consiglio, B., and G. Reynolds. 1987. Broward's Burrowing Owl watchers. Fla. Nat. 60(1):Spring:3–5.

Courser, W. D. 1972. Variability of tail molt in the Burrowing Owl. Wilson Bull. 84:93–95.

Courser, W. D. 1976. A population study of the Burrowing Owl near Tampa, Florida. M. S. thesis, Univ. of South Florida, Tampa, Florida.

Courser, W. D. 1979. Continued breeding range expansion of the Burrowing Owl in Florida. Amer. Birds 33:143–144.

FGFWFC. 1990. Official lists of endangered and potentially endangered fauna and flora in Florida. 1 August 1990. Fla. Game and Fresh Water Fish Comm., Tallahassee, Florida.

Hennemann, W. W., III. 1980. Notes on the food habits of the Burrowing Owl in Duval County, Florida. Fla. Field Nat. 8:24–25.

Howell, A. H. 1932. Florida bird life. Coward-McCann, New York. 579 pp.

Jackson, D. R. 1989. The fauna of gopher tortoise burrows. Pp. 86–98 in Gopher tortoise relocation symposium proceedings (J. E. Diemer, D. R. Jackson, J. L. Landers, J. N. Layne, and D. A. Wood, eds.). Fla. Game and

Fresh Water Fish Comm., Nongame Wildl. Prog. Tech. Rept. No. 5, Tallahassee, Florida.

Ligon, J. D. 1963. Breeding range expansion of the Burrowing Owl in Florida. Auk 80:367–368.

MacKenzie, E. S. 1944. Burrowing Owl in Hernando County. Fla. Nat. 17 (4):72.

Martin, D. J. 1973. Selected aspects of Burrowing Owl ecology and behavior. Condor 75:446–456.

Mealey, B. 1992. Reproductive ecology of the Burrowing Owl, *Athene cunicularia,* in Dade and Broward counties, Florida. M. S. thesis, Florida International Univ., Miami.

Millsap, B. A., and C. Bear. 1990. Double-brooding by Florida Burrowing Owls. Wilson Bull. 102:313–317.

Millsap, B. A., J. A. Gore, D. E. Runde, and S. I. Cerulean. 1990. Setting priorities for the conservation of fish and wildlife species in Florida. Wildl. Monogr. no. 111. 57 pp.

Neill, W. T. 1954. Notes on the Florida Burrowing Owl, and some new records for the species. Fla. Nat. 27:67–70.

Nicholson, D. J. 1954. The Florida Burrowing Owl; a vanishing species. Fla. Nat. 27 (1):3–4.

Owre, O. T. 1978. Florida Burrowing Owl. Pp. 97—99 in Rare and endangered biota of Florida. Vol. 2 birds (H. W. Kale II, ed.). Univ. Presses of Florida, Gainesville, Florida.

Rhodes, S. N. 1892. The breeding habits of the Florida Burrowing Owl (*Speotyto cunicularia floridana*). Auk 9:1–8.

Ridgway, R. 1914. The birds of North and Middle America. Part IV. Bull. U. S. Natl. Mus. no. 50.

Snyder, N. F. R., and J. Wiley. 1976. Sexual size dimorphism in hawks and owls of North America. Ornithol. Monogr. no. 20. 96 pp.

Thomsen, L. 1971. Behavior and ecology of Burrowing Owls on the Oakland Municipal Airport. Condor 73:177–192.

Webb, S. D. 1990. Historical biogeography. Pp. 70–100 in Ecosystems of Florida (R. L. Myers and J. J. Ewel, eds.). Univ. of Central Fla. Press, Orlando, Florida.

Wesemann, T., and M. Rowe. 1987. Factors influencing the distribution and abundance of Burrowing Owls in Cape Coral, Florida. Pp. 129–137 in Integrating man and nature in the metropolitan environment (L. W. Adams and D. L. Leedy, eds.). Proc. of the national symposium on urban wildlife. Natl. Inst. for Urban Wildl., Columbia, Maryland.

PREPARED BY: Brian A. Millsap, Nongame Wildlife Program, Florida Game and Fresh Water Fish Commission, 620 S. Meridian Street, Tallahassee, FL 32399.

Hairy Woodpecker

Picoides villosus

FAMILY PICIDAE

Order Piciformes

TAXONOMY: The Hairy Woodpecker (*Picoides villosus auduboni*) that is found throughout most of Florida, except on the Keys and the southern mainland, is one of 12 subspecies of the Hairy Woodpecker.

DESCRIPTION: The Hairy Woodpecker is black and white with a longitudinal white streak down the center of its back. The entire underparts and nasal tufts are white. White spottings occur on the wing coverts and remiges. A white stripe is above and below the eye. Males have a red band around the nape that may be divided medially by black. Females lack the red band that is replaced by white. The two central pairs of rectrices are black, the next pair is black proximally and white distally, and the two lateral pairs are white. The stout bill and feet are blackish; claws are horn color. Young males prior to the post-juvenal molt possess a reddish or orange crown. The crown of young females lacks any red, but often the crown is streaked with white. The similar Downy Woodpecker (*P. pubescens*) is smaller than the Hairy in all respects. The white, outer tail feathers of the Downy have faint dark bars or spots.

POPULATION SIZE AND TREND: Chapman (1888) considered the Hairy Woodpecker "common" in 1887–88 at Gainesville, but called the Pileated Woodpecker (*Dryocopus pileatus*) "rather rare." This evidently indicates that the Hairy was more abundant then than was the Pileated. Later, Howell (1932) described the Florida status of the Hairy as "rather uncommon," being generally distributed in wooded areas of the state. Based on summer counts, the Hairy Woodpecker is judged to be rare to uncommon in north Florida and occasional or rare in south Florida (Stevenson and Anderson 1994). The species is accidental on the Dry Tortugas (Sprunt 1950). Counts taken in the winter are somewhat lower; the bird is especially rare in most coastal areas

Hairy Woodpecker,
Picoides villosus. (Photo
by Barry Mansell)

(Stevenson and Anderson 1994). Based on 272 Christmas Bird Counts from all reporting stations (except those on the Florida Keys) from 1964 through 1973, 288 Hairy Woodpeckers were counted—about one bird per count-day. Compared to other woodpeckers, only the Red-cockaded Woodpecker (*P. borealis*), with a more restricted ecological range, was recorded fewer times than was the Hairy (Owre 1978). All recent criteria used to determine population trends indicate no increase during the 1900s (Stevenson and Anderson 1994). The bird has decreased in northwest Florida (Leon, Franklin, Wakulla, and Gulf counties) where regular counts and observations have been made. The species has not been recorded on a Christmas Bird Count at Pensacola since 1967 or at Coot Bay since 1962 (Stevenson and Anderson 1994).

DISTRIBUTION AND HISTORY OF DISTRIBUTION: The Southern Hairy Woodpecker is found in southern Illinois and Indiana and from southern Arkansas, Tennessee, and Virginia southward and through the Gulf-side westward to eastern Texas. In Florida the bird occurs (or had occurred) throughout the state, except for the Keys and southern mainland. Except for Florida, the Hairy Woodpecker appears to be more abundant elsewhere, including the neighboring state of Georgia (Owre 1978).

HABITAT REQUIREMENTS AND HABITAT TREND: In Florida the Hairy Woodpecker occurs in a variety of forested areas, including pinelands, sand pine scrub, cypress stands, deciduous swamp forests, and high hammocks. However, it inhabits mainly wooded bottomlands and pine flatwoods.

Distribution map
of the Hairy Wood-
pecker, *Picoides
villosus.*

Kilham (1965) reported that this woodpecker usually selects a living tree with
a rotten center. Bent (1939) and Lawrence (1967) found that most nests built
in Massachusetts and in Canada were in live trees, but the reverse is probably
true in Florida (Stevenson and Anderson 1994). Grimes (1947) remarked that
dead pines were the most common nesting sites, but live pond cypress
(*Taxodium ascendens*) also were used.

Relatively little investigation has been done on this race in Florida. Lawrence
(1967), studying in Ontario, found that the Northern Hairy occupied a "range"
from 6 to 8 acres. It may be assumed that the Florida birds require a similar
amount of acreage. The types and amount of forested habitats required by the
Hairy Woodpecker are probably decreasing within the woodpecker's range.

Insects, which may be cached, form the main diet of the Hairy Woodpecker
(Ehrlich et al. 1988). Kilham (1965) observed that birds in the northeast
United States also fed on suet and sap from maples and aspens. In the winter,
acorns, hazelnuts, beechnuts, berries, corn, and other grain may be eaten
(Owre 1978; Ehrlich et al. 1988). The Hairy in Florida has been observed to
eat figs (*Ficus*).

VULNERABILITY OF SPECIES AND HABITAT: The destruction of large
stretches of forest containing *P. v. auduboni* might prove detrimental to the

species. The ecological requirements of the species are not known, but any tract of forest designed to harbor the species must be large enough to offer adequate acreage for at least several pairs.

CAUSES OF THREAT: The precise reasons for the population decline of the Hairy Woodpecker race in Florida are unknown. Perhaps the chief reason stems from cutting large-scale tracts of mature pinelands, preferred habitats of the species.

Nests are destroyed by snakes (e.g., *Elaphe guttata, E. obsoleta*), raccoons (*Procyon lotor*), House Sparrows (*Passer domesticus*), Red-bellied Woodpeckers (*Melanerpes carolinus*), European Starlings (*Sturnus vulgaris*), and sciurid and flying squirrels (Bent 1939; Grimes 1947; Kilham 1968; Owre 1978). Squirrels have been recorded attempting to gnaw into nesting cavities containing eggs or young (Owre 1978). How much of a threat these and other predators have been to the woodpecker is not known. Nothing is known about predation of the adults.

RESPONSE TO HABITAT MODIFICATION: Detailed data on the response of Hairy Woodpeckers to habitat loss and modification are lacking. Owre (1978) mentioned a personal observation where Hairy Woodpeckers disappeared from a large tract of pinelands (*Pinus elliottii* var. *densa*), west of Perrine, Dade County, after large-scale removal of the trees. There is little doubt that large-scale removal of living trees and snags has affected this species throughout Florida.

DEMOGRAPHIC CHARACTERISTICS: Details on most aspects of the breeding cycle are unknown for the Florida populations of the Hairy Woodpecker, but probably are similar to the northern subspecies that have been studied by Lawrence (1967), Kilham (1960, 1965, 1966, 1968) and others. There are at least 16 sets of eggs from Florida in six museums; the southernmost record being from Osceola County (Stevenson and Anderson 1994). The earliest set (2 April), from Marion County, is probably an incomplete clutch as all other nests held 3–5 eggs. The latest set was taken on 4 June in Duval County (Stevenson and Anderson 1994). Other museum egg records come from Alachua, Levy, Leon, and Volusia Counties, and San Mateo (Stevenson and Anderson 1994). Stevenson and Anderson (1994) gave the average clutch size for Florida nests to be 3.6 eggs. Published records of eggs are as follows: Apopka, 3 May 1910 and 18 April 1920 (Howell 1932), Duval County, 13 April 1931 (Grimes 1947); and Pensacola, 12 April 1925 (Weston 1965). Young have been reported in Duval County, 15 May 1944 (Grimes 1947), in Santa Rosa County, 13 June 1930 (Weston 1965), and at Fort Walton on 4 May 1946 (Shannon, field notes). Stevenson found a nest with young in a fencepost near Chipley on 5 June 1962, and nests in trees near Lake Iamonia (Leon County) on 5 May 1968, and near Chaires on 6 May 1970 (Stevenson and Anderson 1994). Cruickshank (1980) observed birds at nest cavities in Brevard County on 28 March to 16 April. Eggs were not found.

Three to six white eggs may be laid, but four is the usual number. The egg-laying period may last over six days. During this time both sexes spend considerable time within the cavity, often gazing out through the entrance hole (Owre 1978).

Both sexes incubate the eggs for 11–15 days (Ehrlich et al. 1988). The male performs the duty at night and the female at day. Except for a few notes exchanged by the sexes during changeovers for incubation, Hairy Woodpeckers are subdued and silent while incubating the eggs (Kilham 1968). The nestling period may be 28 or 30 days. Both adults participate in parental care to the fledglings that occurs for several days. Once the young leave the nest cavity, they do not return to roost.

KEY BEHAVIORS: The Hairy Woodpecker is a rather wary bird and is not attracted to residential areas as is the Downy. The Hairy forages chiefly along tree trunks, although they will examine dry limbs, tree stubs, and rotting stumps. Kilham (1965, 1968), studying Hairy Woodpeckers in New Hampshire, found differences in the feeding activities of males and females, the former primarily excavating for food and the latter being more proned to forage along the bark of tree trunks and limbs. Males foraged away from the nest, whereas the female foraged near the nest. In the winter males tend to forage higher than the females (Ehrlich et al. 1988).

Hairy Woodpeckers are monogamous, and one brood is raised each year. The birds form pairs in midwinter and the female takes the lead in pair formation (Kilham 1960, 1966). She occupies the future breeding territory in the fall and attracts the male by drumming at a symbolic (unsuitable) nest site or by performing a quivering, fluttering flight (Kilham 1960, Ehrlich et al. 1988). Lawrence (1967) stated of the northern races that males play the important role in nest site selection. Excavation of the cavity takes 1–3.5 weeks (average 20 days). Both sexes excavate the cavity, but the bulk of the effort is accomplished by the male (Kilham 1960). Nest cavities are lined with chips and the cavities range in height from 8 to 60 feet.

Both sexes share in brooding (female taking the major role) and feeding the young. Unlike many woodpeckers, the Hairy does not regurgitate food to the young, but carries it in the bill. The Hairy gives a loud, sharp characteristic "peek" call among other vocalizations.

CONSERVATION MEASURES TAKEN: The Hairy Woodpecker is protected by federal and state laws. The National Audubon Society's journal,

American Birds, placed the Hairy Woodpecker in 1975–1989 on its Blue List and in 1986 the species was listed as Special Concern (Ehrlich et al 1988). The Hairy Woodpecker in Florida has been listed as a Species of Special Concern (Owre 1978). However, it is not on the "Official Lists of Endangered and Potentially Endangered Fauna and Flora in Florida" of 1 August 1990, prepared by Don A. Wood. The recommendations proposed by Owre (1978) have not been executed. Not only is the Hairy Woodpecker declining in Florida, but the species is widely reported as declining throughout its range (Ehrlich et al. 1988).

CONSERVATION MEASURES PROPOSED: A detailed ecological and breeding biology study and long-term censuses of the Hairy Woodpecker in Florida are needed. Every effort should be made to preserve mature, forested tracts (e.g., wooded bottomlands and pine flatwoods) large enough (more than 6–8 acres) for the birds to maintain themselves, especially in those areas known to contain the woodpecker. These tracts of forests should be away from residential areas and fires should not be suppressed. Removal of dead trees and snags in these forests should be prohibited.

ACKNOWLEDGMENTS: I acknowledge the late Dr. Oscar T. Owre who prepared an earlier account on the Hairy Woodpecker (Owre 1978). I thank Bruce H. Anderson for allowing me to see the account on the Hairy Woodpecker from the Stevenson and Anderson manuscript of the Birdlife of Florida prior to its publication.

LITERATURE CITED:

Bent, A. C. 1939. Life histories of North American woodpeckers. U. S. Natl. Mus. Bull. 174. 322 pp.

Chapman, F. M. 1888. A list of birds observed at Gainesville, Florida. Auk 5: 267–277.

Cruickshank, A. D. 1980. The birds of Brevard County. Florida Press, Inc. Orlando, Florida. 200 pp.

Ehrlich, P. R., D. S. Dobkin, and D. Wheye. 1988. The birders handbook. Simon and Schuster, Inc., New York, New York. 785 pp.

Grimes, S. A. 1947. Birds of Duval County. Florida Nat. 21:1–13.

Howell, A. H. 1932. Florida bird life. Coward-McCann, Inc. New York. 527 pp.

Kilham, L. 1960. Courtship and territorial behavior of Hairy Woodpeckers. Auk 77:259–270.

Kilham, L. 1965. Differences in feeding behavior of male and female Hairy Woodpeckers. Wilson Bull. 77:134–145.

Kilham, L. 1966. Reproductive behavior of Hairy Woodpeckers. I. Pair formation and courtship. Wilson Bull. 78:251–265.

Kilham, L. 1968. Reproductive behavior of Hairy Woodpeckers. II. Nesting and habitat. Wilson Bull. 80:286–305.

Lawrence, L. de K. 1967. A comparative life-history study of four species of woodpeckers. Ornithol. Monogr. no. 5, Amer. Ornithol. Union. 156 pp.

Owre, O. T. 1978. Southern Hairy Woodpecker. Pp. 99-101 in Rare and endangered biota of Florida. Vol 2. Birds (H. W. Kale, II, ed.). Univ. Presses of Florida, Gainesville, Florida. 121 pp.

Sprunt, A. Jr. 1950. A list of the birds of the Dry Tortugas Keys, 1857–1949. Florida Nat. 23:49-60, 73-78, 105–111.

Stevenson, H. M., and B. H. Anderson. 1994. Birdlife of Florida. Univ. Press of Florida, Gainesville, Florida. 892 pp.

Weston, F. M. 1965. A survey of the birdlife of northwestern Florida. Bull. Tall Timbers Res. Sta. 5:1–147.

PREPARED BY: Walter Kingsley Taylor, Department of Biology, University of Central Florida, Orlando, FL 32816.

White-breasted Nuthatch

Sitta carolinensis

FAMILY SITTIDAE

Order Passeriformes

TAXONOMY: The White-breasted Nuthatch (*Sitta carolinensis*) was named by Latham in 1790 based on prior descriptions by Brisson and Catesby (Oberholser 1917). Scott (1890) differentiated specimens taken at Tarpon Springs, Florida, from specimens taken from Massachusetts southward to North Carolina. He applied *S. c. atkinsi* to the Florida birds and noted that variation in these specimens was similar to variation in *S. c. aculeata*, a western subspecies. This is interesting because both the Florida and western nuthatches are frequently found in pine forests. The Florida subspecies was lumped with the eastern form *S.c. carolinensis* by Oberholser (1917). See Pravosudor and Grubb (1993) for additional discussion.

DESCRIPTION: The White-breasted Nuthatch is the largest North American nuthatch with a total length of 12–15 cm (5–6 in.) and a wingspan of 24–29 cm (9.5–11.5 in.) (Bent 1948; Terres 1982). It is a small, chunky bird with a straight bill and blue-gray above with a black cap, nape and upper back. The wings are dark gray-brown with white patches below. The tail is mostly black with white patches underneath. Underparts are dull white except for a ruddy brown in the vent region. Adult males have a glossy black crown and blue-gray upperparts in contrast to a dull black crown (gray tips to at least some crown feathers) with dull gray upperparts in females (Pyle et al. 1987; Wood 1992). A high frequency of females in peninsular Florida have dark crowns (Wood 1992).

Juvenile males have a dull black crown and juvenile females have a lead-colored crown. As with most nuthatches the White-breasted Nuthatch is unusual among songbirds in having "slight indication of prealternate molt" (Banks 1978).

POPULATION SIZE AND TREND: Results from the North American Breeding Bird Survey (BBS) indicate a 2.4% annual increase from 1966–1989 in the

White-breasted
Nuthatch, *Sitta
carolinensis*. (Photo
copyright by Allan D.
Cruickshank, courtesy
of Florida Audubon
Society)

White-breasted Nuthatch rangewide (Droege and Sauer 1989). Rareness of
the White-breasted Nuthatch in Florida precludes statistical analysis of BBS
results, but the population undoubtedly has declined and currently is largely
restricted to Leon and Jefferson counties. In Leon County the nuthatch is
fairly common in the older neighborhoods in Tallahassee, but rare south of
the city. Recent observations of the nuthatch at Wakulla Springs State Park in
Wakulla County are the first south of Tallahassee in several years.

DISTRIBUTION AND HISTORY OF DISTRIBUTION: The White-breasted
Nuthatch breeding distribution extends from British Columbia to southern
Quebec, southward to northern Florida and westward to Texas and southern
California (AOU 1983). The nuthatch was once described as "fairly common"
in northern and middle Florida and casual in southern Florida (Howell 1932),
but the Florida distribution of the nuthatch has diminished during this century. Stevenson and Anderson (1994) cited egg set collections from Duval,
Pinellas, Orange, St. Johns and Putnam counties and Lake Okeechobee prior
to 1936. The only confirmed breeding records from the Florida Breeding Bird
Atlas (1985–1990) were from Leon and Jefferson counties in the Tallahassee
Red Hills physiographic region. This means that the southern extent of the
breeding distribution of the nuthatch in Florida has retreated northward over
250 miles in about 50 years.

   Increased numbers during standardized bird counts and observations away
from breeding areas in fall and winter suggests some limited migration or
movement of nuthatches within or into Florida (Stevenson and Anderson
1994).

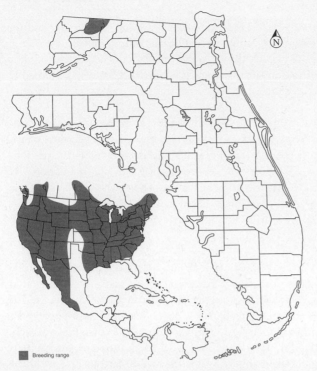

Distribution map of the White-breasted Nuthatch, *Sitta carolinensis*.

■ Breeding range

HABITAT REQUIREMENTS AND HABITAT TREND: The preferred habitat for the White-breasted Nuthatch in Florida was identified by Howell (1932) as open, mature pine woods. Upland pine forests used by the nuthatch were probably dominated by longleaf pine (*Pinus palustris*). In contrast, Weston (1965) observed that the nuthatch "seems to be confined to river swamps" in northwestern Florida. LeGrand and Hamel (1980) associated the nuthatch with hardwoods in the southeastern United States, although they do not specify where. Imhof (1976) noted that the White-breasted Nuthatch is a fairly common breeding bird in the northern part of Alabama in large hardwoods, especially oaks, uncommon and local below the Fall Line, and rare on the coast. Except for Weston (1965), a picture of the habitat affinities of the White-breasted Nuthatch seems to emerge that the nuthatch was found in pines in the coastal plains and in hardwoods farther to the north.

The pine forests used by White-breasted Nuthatches in the southeastern United States are structurally similar to the preferred habitat of the nuthatch in the western United States. This raises the interesting possibility that nuthatches of the southeastern coastal plain may be derived from western populations and isolated during a glacial epoch (Hubbard 1973). Speciation of the related Brown-headed (*S. pusilla*) and Pygmy (*S. pygmaea*) nuthatches probably developed from similar causes.

Oberholser (1974) suggested that "climatic warming and drying during the first half of the twentieth century" may have caused the retreat of the nuthatch from parts of Texas, but the exact mechanism for the decline was not stated. Elimination of mature pine forests has been suggested as a possible reason why the nuthatch disappeared from central Florida (Stevenson 1978).

VULNERABILITY OF SPECIES AND HABITAT: The key to understanding the decline of the White-breasted Nuthatch in Florida may be understanding its habitat affinities. If the White-breasted Nuthatch in Florida is dependent on mature pine trees for nesting or roosting cavities, its population will probably continue to decline in the near future. The last stronghold of the nuthatch, mature pine forest on quail hunting plantations in the Red Hills physiographic region of north Florida, is very susceptible to suburban development.

CAUSES OF THREAT: The decline of the White-breasted Nuthatch in Florida may be caused by the loss of mature pines with natural scars and cavities that provide nesting sites. However, it is interesting that even the Red-cockaded Woodpecker (*Picoides borealis*), which also is dependent on mature pines, has a larger distribution within Florida (Wood and Wenner 1983) than the nuthatch. Nuthatches frequently use abandoned Red-cockaded Woodpecker cavities. Why the woodpecker has been able to persist in peninsular Florida, while the nuthatch has declined is an important question that requires an answer in order to maintain the latter species in Florida.

RESPONSES TO HABITAT MODIFICATION: Cutting of mature longleaf pine forests in the southeastern Coastal Plain, including Florida, peaked in the 1920s (Williams 1989). Less than 600 ha of an estimated 37.4 million ha of the longleaf pine forest that dominated the uplands at the time of European settlement remains in an old-growth state (Simberloff 1993). Large portions of the original longleaf pine forest in Florida have been converted to short-rotation commercial forests and agricultural uses. Elimination of mature trees through timber harvest practices and land use changes may have largely eliminated the nuthatch from Florida. Conversion of forest to suburban land uses has an unclear effect on the nuthatch. The nuthatch is still found in suburban Tallahassee, but that may be an outgrowth of its proximity to the Red Hills hunting plantations.

Fire exclusion also may have a negative effect on the nuthatch in the few remaining pine forests with mature trees. Abundance of White-breasted Nuthatch decreased in an oldfield pine forest over a 15-year period after fire was excluded (Engstrom et al. 1984).

DEMOGRAPHIC CHARACTERISTICS: The White-breasted Nuthatch nests early in the year laying 4–7 eggs (average of 5.3 in 13 Florida egg sets) per clutch between early March and late-April (Stevenson and Anderson 1994). Incubation lasts 12 days and nestlings are fed by both parents for 14 days before fledging (Bent 1948). Nests in Florida are typically located in natural cavities in living or dead trees or in abandoned woodpecker holes, especially Red-cockaded Woodpeckers (Grimes in Bent 1948; Stevenson and Anderson 1994; Engstrom, pers. observ.).

Population density of the White-breasted Nuthatch in mature longleaf pine forest in Georgia was 12.5–17.5 pairs per 100 ha (5–6.9 pairs per 100 acres) (Engstrom 1980, 1981, 1982; Baker 1989). However, Wayne (1910) described the nuthatch as "by no means common and a forest of from one hundred to three hundred acres seldom contains more than three or four pairs."

KEY BEHAVIORS: Kilham (1972) noted that White-breasted Nuthatches "are unusual among northern hemisphere birds in their close pair bonds held over most of the year as well as in their varied forms of courtship, which can reach a crescendo in midwinter." A notable behavior during the nesting season is the habit of Bill Sweeping. One member of the pair, usually the male, will hold an insect or plant material in its beak and "sweep" the tree around the nest cavity entrance. This behavior has been hypothesized to be a defense against squirrels or a distraction display (Kilham 1968).

Kilham (1972) listed four vocalizations associated with courtship in the White-breasted Nuthatch. The courtship song of the male is a "wurp-wurp-wurp" rapidly repeated 8–11 times. Throughout the year "kun" or "quank" calls are used to express excitement.

Further north, nuthatches cache food under bark or in furrows (Petit et al. 1989). The frequency of this behavior in southern populations is unknown, but it could be an important behavior in severe winters.

CONSERVATION MEASURES TAKEN: Other than protection under state and federal wildlife regulations, no conservation measures have been taken in Florida for the White-breasted Nuthatch.

CONSERVATION MEASURES PROPOSED: A study of nesting requirements would be an important first step for the conservation of the White-breasted Nuthatch in Florida. If elimination of old trees, particularly pines, is the reason why this species has declined, then employing conservative silvicultural techniques such as single tree selection and allowing some pines to live to 150–200 years on public lands would be highly beneficial.

ACKNOWLEDGMENTS: Larry Carlile and James Rodgers provided many useful comments to the manuscript.

LITERATURE CITED:

AOU. 1983. Check-list of North American birds, 6th ed. Amer. Ornithol. Union, Washington, D.C.

Banks, R. C. 1978. Prealternate molt in nuthatches. Auk 95:179-181.

Baker, W. W. 1989. Mature longleaf pine forest. Jour. Field Ornith. 60:12.

Bent, A. C. 1948. Life histories of North American nuthatches, wrens, thrashers, and their allies. U.S. Natl. Mus. Bull. 195, Smithsonian Inst., Washington, D.C.

Droege, S., and J. R. Sauer. 1989. Annual summary of the North American Breeding Bird Survey, 1989. U.S. Fish and Wildl. Serv., Patuxent, Maryland.

Engstrom, R. T. 1980. Mature longleaf pine forest. Amer. Birds 34:29.

Engstrom, R. T. 1981. Mature longleaf pine forest. Amer. Birds 35:69.

Engstrom, R. T. 1982. Mature longleaf pine forest. Amer. Birds 36:74.

Engstrom, R. T., R. L. Crawford, and W. W. Baker. 1984. Breeding bird populations in relation to changing forest structure following fire exclusion: a 15-year study. Wilson Bull. 96:437–450.

Howell, A. H. 1932. Florida bird life. Coward-McCann, Inc., New York.

Hubbard, J. P. 1973. Avian evolution in the aridlands of North America. Living Bird 12:155–196.

Imhof, T. A. 1976. Alabama birds. Univ. Alabama Press, Birmingham, Alabama.

Kilham, L. 1968. Reproductive behavior of White-breasted Nuthatches. I. Distraction display, bill-sweeping, and nest hole defense. Auk 85:477–492.

Kilham, L. 1972. Reproductive behavior of the White-breasted Nuthatch. II. Courtship. Auk 89:115–129.

LeGrand, H. E., and P. B. Hamel. 1980. Bird-habitat associations on southeastern forest lands. Suppl. 16 to Contract No. 18–409. USDA For. Serv. S.E. For. Exper. Sta., Clemson, South Carolina.

Oberholser, H. C. 1917. Critical notes on the eastern subspecies of *Sitta carolinensis* Latham. Auk 34:181–187.

Oberholser, H. C. 1974. The bird life of Texas. Vol. 2. Univ. Texas Press, Austin, Texas.

Petit, D. R., L. J. Petit, and K. E. Petit. 1989. Winter caching ecology of deciduous woodland birds and adaptations for protection of stored food. Condor 91:766–776.

Pravosudov, V. V., and T. C. Grubb, Jr. 1993. White-breasted Nuthatch (*Sitta carolinensis*). *In* The birds of North America, no. 54 (A. Poole and F.

Gill, eds.). Amer. Ornithol. Union and Philadelphia Acad. of Nat. Sci., Washington, D.C.

Pyle, P., S. N. G. Howell, R. L. Yunick, and D. F. DeSante. 1987. Identification guide to North American passerines. Slate Creek Press, Bolinas, California.

Scott, W. E. D. 1890. A summary of observations on the birds of the Gulf coast of Florida. Auk 7:14–120.

Simberloff, D. D. 1993. Species-area relationships, fragmentation, and longleaf pine forest structure-grounds for cautious optimism. Pp. 1–13 *in* The longleaf pine ecosystem: ecology, restoration, and management (S.M. Hermann, ed.). Proc. 18th Tall Timbers Fire Ecol. Conf., Tallahassee, Florida.

Stevenson, H. M. 1978. White-breasted Nuthatch. Pp. 101–102 in Rare and endangered biota of Florida, Vol. II. Birds. (H. W. Kale, II, ed.). Univ. Presses Florida, Gainesville, Florida.

Stevenson, H .M., and B. H. Anderson. 1994. Birdlife of Florida. Univ. Press of Florida, Gainesville, Florida.

Terres, J. K. 1982. The Audubon Society handbook of North American birds. A. A. Knopf, New York.

Wayne, A. T. 1910. Birds of South Carolina. Contrib. Charleston Mus., Charleston, South Carolina.

Weston, F. M. 1965. A survey of the birdlife of northwestern Florida. Tall Timbers Res. Sta. Bull. No. 5, Tallahassee, Florida.

Williams, M. 1989. Americans and their forests. Cambridge Univ. Press, Cambridge, Great Britain.

Wood, D. A., and A. S. Wenner. 1983. Status of the Red-cockaded Woodpecker in Florida: 1983 update. Pp. 89–91 in Red-cockaded woodpecker symposium II (D. A. Wood, ed.). Fla. Game and Fresh Water Fish Comm., Tallahassee, Florida.

Wood, D. S. 1992. Color and size variation in eastern White-breasted Nuthatches. Wilson Bull. 104:599–611.

PREPARED BY: R. Todd Engstrom, Tall Timbers Research, Inc., Route 1, Box 678, Tallahassee, FL 32312.

Marsh Wrens

Cistothorus palustris

Marian's Marsh Wren, *C. p. marianae*
Worthington's Marsh Wren, *C. p. griseus*

FAMILY TROGLODYTIDAE

Order Passeriformes

TAXONOMY: The Marsh Wren (*Cistothorus palustris*) is also known as the Long-billed Marsh Wren and Grass Wren. Two subspecies of the Marsh Wren are permanent residents in Florida: Marian's Marsh Wren (*C. p. marianae*) on the Gulf coast and Worthington's Marsh Wren (*C. p. griseus*) on the Atlantic coast (Kale 1978). Several northern subspecies (*C. p. palustris, C. p. dissaeptus, C. p. waynei,* and *C. p. iliacus*) occur in marshes throughout Florida during the winter months (Kale 1975; Stevenson and Anderson 1994).

DESCRIPTION: The Marsh Wren is about the size of a House Wren (*Troglodytes aedon*), 10–12 cm (4–5 in.) in length, with a distinctive white line above the eye, and the center of the back is narrowly streaked with white (absent in juveniles). The head, neck, and foreback of Marian's Marsh Wren are dark cinnamon-brown; the back, wings, rump, and tail are dark brown, and the underparts are shaded with dusky brown. In Worthington's Marsh Wren the upper parts are grayish-brown, sometimes darker on the head, and the underparts are pale grayish. Both Florida races are darker or duller in color and lack the chestnut browns and tans of the northern subspecies of Marsh Wrens.

DISTRIBUTION AND HISTORY OF DISTRIBUTION: Marsh Wrens breed in freshwater and brackish marshes from southwestern and east-central British Columbia, northern Alberta, central Saskatchewan, southern Manitoba, western and southern New Brunswick south to southern California, northeastern Baja California, northwestern Sonora, southwestern Arizona, southern Nevada, south-central Utah, extreme northwestern New Mexico, extreme western and southern Texas, and the Gulf coast and northern Atlantic coast of Florida (AOU 1983). Marsh Wrens winter in coastal areas throughout the

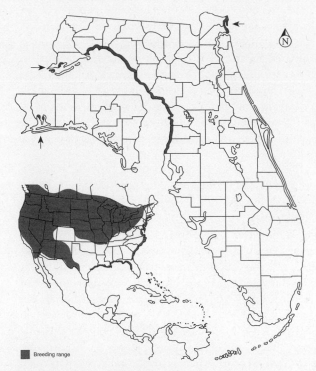

Distribution map of the
Marsh Wrens,
Cistothorus palustris spp.

Breeding range

breeding range, and the interior from southern United States south to southern Baja California, Michoacan, the State of Mexico, and Veracruz.

Marian's Marsh Wren breeds in the salt marshes along the Gulf coast of
Florida from Port Richey (Pasco Co.) to Escambia Bay (Santa Rosa Co.), and
westward to southwestern Alabama. Marsh Wrens are sparsely distributed and
less abundant along the panhandle coast west of Apalachee Bay. They occur in
the mouth of the Apalachicola River, occasionally on St. Vincent Island, and in
marshes of northwest Escambia Bay, near Mulat, and on the east side of the
Avalon peninsula between Garcon and White Points on East Bay. Until surveys of these marshes were conducted in 1979–1980, there were no summer
records of Marsh Wrens in the region (Weston 1965). Formerly, Marian's
Marsh Wrens occurred in the upper regions of Old Tampa Bay, and a nearly
completed nest was once observed in Charlotte Harbor (Howell 1932), suggesting possible breeding farther south. However, Marsh Wrens occasionally
will build courtship nests while still on wintering grounds; hence this is insufficient evidence for confirmed breeding by this species.

On the Atlantic coast Worthington's Marsh Wren is resident in the salt
marshes from South Carolina to northern Florida, where they occur from
Cumberland Sound (Nassau Co.) south to about a mile north of the St. Johns
River (Duval Co.). Formerly, they occurred south to New Smyrna, but north-

ward invasion of mangroves beginning in the early years of this century, displaced the wren's preferred salt marsh habitat (Nicholson 1950). This northward movement of mangroves has occurred on both coasts and explains in large measure the northward contraction of the wren's southern range. This most likely is the reason why no Marsh Wrens now breed south of Matanzas Inlet on the east coast; however, the disappearance of breeding wrens from Matanzas Inlet north to the St. Johns River in Duval County (Kale 1983), where extensive grass marshes still occur, must be the result of other unknown factors.

POPULATION SIZE AND TREND: Worthington's Marsh Wrens are widespread and abundant in the salt marshes of northeast Florida, probably numbering between 1,000 and 2,000 pairs between the St. Johns River in Duval County and Cumberland Sound in Nassau County. Marian's Marsh Wrens are abundant in the salt marshes between Port Richey and Apalachee Bay, probably numbering between 2,000 and 3,000 or more pairs. Wrens are spotty in distribution and little is known about the population status west of Apalachee Bay.

HABITAT REQUIREMENTS AND HABITAT TRENDS: Marsh Wrens breed in tidal marshes dominated by tall (1–2 m) vegetation, chiefly saltmarsh cordgrass (*Spartina alterniflora*) and black needlerush (*Juncus roemerianus*). *Juncus* is the dominant vegetation on the Gulf coast, and *Spartina* is dominant on the Atlantic coast. Wrens prefer the taller marsh vegetation that grows along tidal creeks. Some habitat has been lost to the northward invasion of mangroves along both coasts. During the 1950s and 1960s, some habitat was lost to coastal dredge and fill operations, but for the most part habitat for the Marsh Wrens appears stable.

VULNERABILITY OF SPECIES AND HABITAT: Dredging and filling of salt marshes up until the 1970s adversely impacted some Marsh Wren habitat. Currently, this practice is no longer permitted. A potential hazard to all salt marsh inhabitants may be the world's increasing temperature rise (the greenhouse effect), which could cause sea levels to rise at a rate greater than the ability of natural marshlands to compensate for the rise, with a consequent loss of marsh vegetation. Wrens also are vulnerable to local extirpation by hurricanes or other severe storms when tides cover all marsh vegetation.

CAUSES OF THREAT: Although salt marshes used by Marsh Wrens are now rarely subject to destruction by dredge and fill activities, these coastal habitats are vulnerable to oil and other chemical spills and impacts from nearby upland development.

RESPONSES TO HABITAT MODIFICATION: Marsh Wrens respond to invasion of their habitat by trees and shrubs by abandoning the site when the density of woody vegetation becomes too great. Prolonged impounding of marshlands for waterfowl or mariculture floods and destroys the marsh vegetation used by these wrens.

DEMOGRAPHIC CHARACTERISTICS: Marsh Wren nests are globular in shape, with a single entrance on the side, and are well secured to the tall marsh grasses or rushes, occasionally in the tops of small mangroves, or at the ends of branches of large mangroves. Nests are constructed of dead leaves of rushes and marsh grasses woven together and intertwined with green leaves of the nearby living grasses or rushes. Males build several unlined nests, called courtship or "dummy" nests, and the female lines one of these with grasses, and occasionally feathers or fur, and lays 3–5 small brown eggs. Leonard and Picman (1987) reported mean clutch sizes range from 5.6 to 5.8 eggs. Eggs hatch in 12–13 days and the young fledge after 13–15 days. Incubation and care of nestlings are primarily performed by the female, although the male assists in feeding fledglings. Egg and nestling losses occur as a result of predation by rice rats (*Oryzomys palustris*), raccoons (*Procyon lotor*), and flooding by storm driven high tides. Mammalian predation may account for as much as 44.4% of nests loss, while predation by other Marsh Wrens may cause loss of up to 23.6% of nests (Leonard and Picman 1987). Additional information on the various subspecies of Marsh Wrens in North America may be found in Wheeler (1931), Welter (1935), Bent (1948), Verner (1963, 1964), and Kroodsma and Verner (1978).

KEY BEHAVIORS: Marsh Wrens establish breeding territories in needlerush or cordgrass marshes along the edges of tidal creeks in March and April. Even though extremely territorial, the wrens tend to nest in groups or "colonies"; hence some areas of apparently suitable marsh may not be occupied during the breeding season. Because territories are small and linear along creek edges, polygamy that is characteristic of northern and insular races (Verner 1965; Verner and Engelsen 1970) rarely occurs in these two Florida subspecies.

Marsh Wrens are permanent residents in Florida coastal marshes, and except during the breeding season when the males loud bubbly song is conspicuous along creek edges, they tend to remain hidden in dense vegetation. While singing, males often perch near the tops of the grass and occasionally will fly 5–7 m above the marsh in a courtship or territorial display. Territories are extremely small, averaging 100 m^2 (ca. 300 ft.^{2}), probably the smallest territory maintained by a North American passerine (Kale 1965). Male Marsh Wrens frequently build multiple "dummy" nests on their territories, but the function of these extra nests to decoy predators from a nest used for breeding or attract females (Verner and Engelsen 1970) has recently been questioned by Metz (1991). Food consists of insects and spiders, with occasional crustaceans and mollusks—all gleaned from the marsh grass, not from the ground (Kale 1964).

CONSERVATION MEASURES TAKEN: The two resident Marsh Wren populations in Florida have been designated species of special concern by the Florida Game and Fresh Water Fish Commission (Wood 1993).

CONSERVATION MEASURES PROPOSED: The unexplained disappearance of Worthington's Marsh Wren as a breeding bird from what appears to be suitable habitat between Matanzas Inlet and the St. Johns River (a phenomena shared with the Seaside Sparrow [*Ammodramus maritimus*]) warrants conducting periodic surveys of this population in northeast Florida. Because of the sparse distribution and low numbers of Marian's Marsh Wren in the Florida panhandle, period surveys of this population should be conducted.

LITERATURE CITED:

AOU. 1983. Checklist of North American birds. 6th edition. Amer. Ornithol. Union, Allen Press, Inc., Lawrence, Kansas.

Bent, A. C. 1948. Worthington's Marsh Wren and Marian's Marsh Wren. Pp. 241–245 in Life histories of North American nuthatches, wrens, thrashers and their allies. Smithsonian Inst. U.S. Natl. Mus. Bull. No. 195. Dover Publ. reprint, New York.

Howell, A. H. 1932. Florida bird life. Coward-McCann, New York.

Kale, H. W. II. 1964. Food of the Long-billed Marsh Wren in the salt marshes of Sapelo Island, Georgia. Oriole 29:47–61.

Kale, H. W. II. 1965. Ecology and bioenergetics of the Long-billed Marsh Wren, *Telmatodytes palustris griseus,* in Georgia salt marshes. Publ. No. 5, Nuttall Ornithol. Club, 142 pp.

Kale, H. W. II. 1975. Extension of winter range of *Telmatodytes palustris waynei* to Georgia and Florida. Auk 92:806–807.

Kale, H. W. II. 1978. Marian's Marsh Wren. Pp. 102–103 in Rare and endangered biota of Florida, Vol.II. Birds (H. W. Kale II, ed.). Univ. Press of Florida, Gainesville, Florida.

Kale, H. W. II. 1978. Worthington's Marsh Wren. Pp. 103–104 in Rare and endangered biota of Florida, Vol. II. Birds (H. W. Kale II, ed.). Univ. Press of Florida, Gainesville, Florida.

Kale, H. W. II. 1983. Distribution, habitat, and status of breeding Seaside Sparrows in Florida. Pp. 41–48 in The Seaside Sparrow, its biology and management (T. L. Quay, J. B. Funderburg, Jr., D. S. Lee, E. F. Potter, and C. S. Robbins, eds.). Occas. Paps. North Carolina Biol. Surv., North Carolina State Mus. Nat. Hist. Raleigh, North Carolina.

Kroodsma, D. E., and J. Verner. 1978. Complex singing behaviors among *Cistothorus* wrens. Auk 95:703–716.

Leonard, M. L., and J. Picman. 1987. Nesting mortality and habitat selection by Marsh Wrens. Auk 104:491–495.

Metz, K. J. 1991. The enigma of multiple nest building by male Marsh Wrens. Auk 108:170–173.

Nicholson, D. J. 1950. Disappearance of Smyrna Seaside Sparrow from its former haunts. Fla. Nat. 23:104

Stevenson, H. M., and B. H. Anderson. 1994. The birdlife of Florida. Univ. Press of Florida, Gainesville, Florida.

Verner, J. 1963. Song rates and polygamy in the Long-billed Marsh Wren. Proc. 13th Intern. Ornithol. Congr., 299–307.

Verner, J. 1964. Evolution of polygamy in the Long-billed Marsh Wren. Evolution 18:252–261.

Verner, J. 1965. Breeding Biology of the Long-billed Marsh Wren. Condor 67:6–30.

Verner, J., and G. H. Engelsen. 1970. Territories, multiple nest building, and polygyny in the Long-billed Marsh Wren. Auk 87: 557–567.

Welter, W. A. 1935. The natural history of the Long-billed Marsh Wren. Wilson Bull. 47:3–34.

Weston, F. M. 1965. A survey of the bird life of northwestern Florida. Bull. Tall Timbers Res. Sta. 5:1–147.

Wheeler, H. E. 1931. The status, breeding range, and habits of Marian's Marsh Wren. Wilson Bull. 43:247–267.

Wood, D. A. 1993. Official lists of endangered and potentially endangered fauna and flora in Florida. Fla. Game and Fresh Water Fish Comm., Tallahassee, Florida.

PREPARED BY: Herbert W. Kale II, Florida Audubon Society, 460 Highway 436, Suite 200, Casselberry, FL 32707.

Species of Special Concern

Seaside Sparrows

Ammodramus maritimus

MacGillivray's Seaside Sparrow *A. m. macgillivraii*
Scott's Seaside Sparrow *A. m. peninsulae*
Louisiana Seaside Sparrow *A. m. fisheri*

FAMILY EMBERIZIDAE

Order Passeriformes

TAXONOMY: Six subspecies of the Seaside Sparrow (*Ammodramus maritimus,* formerly *Ammospiza maritima*) reside in Florida. A seventh subspecies, the Northern Seaside Sparrow (*A. m. maritimus*) occurs along the Atlantic coast of Florida only in winter. The Dusky Seaside Sparrow (*A. m. nigrescens*), formerly resident in Brevard County, is now extinct (see account in this volume). The Cape Sable Seaside Sparrow (*A. m. mirabilis*), resident in Everglades National Park and vicinity, is listed as endangered (see account in this volume). Two additional subspecies are listed by the American Ornithologists' Union (AOU 1957): the Smyrna Seaside Sparrow (*A. m. pelonota*) on the northeast Florida coast (Baker and Kale 1978), which McDonald and Kale (ms, in prep.) consider synonymous with MacGillivray's Seaside Sparrow (*A. m. macgillivraii*); and the Wakulla Seaside Sparrow (*A. m. juncicola*) on the upper Gulf coast (Stevenson et al. 1978), which McDonald and Kale consider synonymous with Scott's Seaside Sparrow (*A. m. peninsulae*). A small population of Seaside Sparrows resident on Hogtown Bayou in Choctawhatchee Bay appears to be intermediate between the Louisiana Seaside Sparrow (*A. m. fisheri*) of west Florida and Scott's Seaside Sparrow (=Wakulla Seaside) to the east (Kale 1983). On the basis of comparisons of mitochondrial DNA, Avise and Nelson (1989) concluded that the Atlantic coast Seasides and the Gulf coast Seasides comprised two phylogenetically distinct groups. They were unable to obtain samples of the Cape Sable Seaside Sparrow to determine its relationship to these populations.

DESCRIPTION: All subspecies of Seaside Sparrows are similar to the size of a House Sparrow (*Passer domesticus*), about 14–15 cm (5.5–6 in.) in length. In

Seaside Sparrow, *Ammodramus maritimus*. (Photo copyright by Allan D. Cruickshank, courtesy of Florida Audubon Society)

adults, the upperparts in fresh plumage are gray (east coast) or grayish-brown or grayish-olive (Gulf coast). Underparts are grayish-white, breast is heavily streaked with gray (east coast) or brown (Gulf coast), and washed with orange buff on breast of the Louisiana Seaside and the Choctawhatchee Bay populations. The belly is grayish-white, chin and throat are white, with a dark streak ("mustache") extending from the jaw on the throat. A prominent yellow line in front of the eye (supraloral) and at the bend of the wing, along with the mustache streak, are diagnostic of the species. Scott's Seaside Sparrow appears considerably darker brown than other races (except the Dusky, which was nearly black), especially in the northern part of its range. This is undoubtedly a result of adapting to the large amount of black needlerush (*Juncus roemerianus*) present in its habitat. Inasmuch as Seaside Sparrows molt only once annually between mid August and October, their plumage becomes worn and ragged by May and June and appears light brown in color with dark gray breast throughout its range. Juveniles are similar to adults, but are paler in color and possess finely streaked breasts.

DISTRIBUTION AND HISTORY OF DISTRIBUTION: MacGillivray's Seaside Sparrow is resident in salt marshes from Dare County, North Carolina south into Duval County, Florida. Formerly its range extended south into Volusia County (=Smyrna Seaside Sparrow). Northward invasion of mangroves into the sparrow's preferred grassy saltmarsh habitat beginning in the 1920s gradually displaced the subspecies (Nicholson 1928, 1946). By the late 1940s, Nicholson (1950) found no birds nesting near New Smyrna. Part of this decline may be attributed to heavy spraying of DDT for mosquito control in the late 1940s (Austin 1968). By 1959 no breeding sparrows were found nesting south of Matanzas Inlet (Austin 1968), and by 1975 none were found

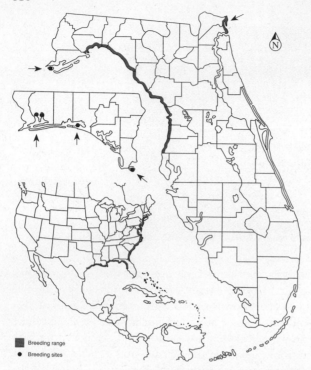

Distribution map of
the Seaside Sparrows,
*Ammodramus
maritimus* spp.

south of the St. Johns River in Duval County (Kale 1983), even though
suitable habitat still occurred southward to St. Augustine and Matanzas Inlet.

On the Gulf coast, Scott's Seaside Sparrow formerly nested southward into
upper Tampa Bay, where suitable habitat still occurs, but the southern edge of
its current range is now Port Richey, Pasco County. Here, too, mangrove
invasion of the saltmarsh habitat is occurring. Scott's Seaside Sparrows reside
in the extensive coastal saltmarshes that fringe the Gulf of Mexico northward
into Apalachee Bay and sporadically in the marshes behind barrier islands
westward to St. Vincent Island, although in some years they are absent from
these sites. Formerly, the sparrow may have nested in St. Andrews Bay (Howell
1932), but none were present in the late 1970s and early 1980s (Kale 1983).
A small population of 100 or so sparrows breeds in the saltmarshes of Hogtown
Bayou on the south side of Choctawhatchee Bay north of the town of Santa
Rosa Beach, Walton County.

The Louisiana Seaside Sparrow breeds in saltmarshes in Santa Rosa County,
near Mulat in upper Escambia Bay, on the southeast side of the Avalon peninsula in East Bay, and on the east side of Blackwater Bay in the Catfish Basin-
Weaver River marshes. Formerly, they resided in lower Escambia Bay near
Pensacola (Howell 1932), but no longer occur there. This subspecies also
breeds westward along the Gulf to the south central Texas coast.

POPULATION SIZE AND TREND: In 1975–76 Kale (1983) estimated 750–1000 pairs of MacGillivray's Seaside Sparrows in the saltmarshes of Duval and Nassau counties in northeast Florida. A resurvey of these marshes in 1987–88 indicated the distribution and densities were similar (McDonald 1988). Gulf coast surveys in 1979–80 (Kale 1983) and in 1987 (McDonald 1988) estimated between 5,000–10,000 pairs were present between Port Richey and Apalachicola Bay, with the vast majority of these birds inhabiting the marshes that open on the Gulf of Mexico between Pasco and Wakulla counties. The population of Seasides inhabiting Choctawhatchee Bay number only around 100 or so, and total numbers of Louisiana Seasides in Santa Rosa County are probably in the low hundreds.

HABITAT REQUIREMENTS AND HABITAT TRENDS: Habitat for the Seaside Sparrow consists of saltmarshes along the Atlantic and Gulf coasts. Optimal habitat on the Atlantic coast is the extensive tidal marshes that occur behind barrier islands and vegetated chiefly by saltmarsh cord grass (*Spartina alterniflora*) and (in Duval County) patches of black needlerush (*Juncus roemerianus*). On the Gulf coast optimal habitat is the mixture of dense stands of *Juncus* and *Spartina,* and scattered stands of salt grass (*Distichlis spicata*) that front on the Gulf of Mexico from Port Richey north to Apalachee Bay, and in the bays behind the barrier islands westward to Escambia Bay. Seaside Sparrows can tolerate early invasion of their grassy habitat by Red (*Rhizophora mangle*) and Black (*Avicennia germinans*) mangroves, but the sparrows abandon the site when these woody plants cover a major portion of the habitat. Nicholson (1946, 1950) documented the disappearance of Seaside Sparrows from the marshes near New Smyrna as mangroves moved northward.

In the past, dredging and filling of coastal marshlands impacted Seaside Sparrow habitat, but current governmental policy against wetland destruction now protects the habitat. The impact of rising sea level on marsh stability over the next 50–100 years may be of some concern in the future.

VULNERABILITY OF SPECIES AND HABITAT: Seaside Sparrows occupy a relatively narrow, easily fragmented coastal marsh community. Up until the 1970s, dredging and filling or impounding of saltmarshes adversely impacted Seaside Sparrow habitat. Currently, this practice rarely occurs, if at all. Future changes in conservation policy could revive this vulnerability. Up to the present, coastal wetlands were able to maintain ground elevations in relation to rising sea level. The current, or an increasing, greenhouse effect may cause sea level in the future to rise at rates greater than the ability of natural marshlands to compensate for the rise, resulting in loss of marsh vegetation. Seaside Sparrows also are vulnerable to local extirpation by hurricanes or similar storms when tides may rise so high that all the habitat is submerged. Such storms have occurred in the past and may explain the temporary absence of birds from a particular locality.

CAUSES OF THREAT: Although most coastal wetlands are now protected from dredge and fill activities, certain development of the nearby uplands can have an indirect impact on marsh habitat. For example, a proposed bridge from the Avalon peninsula in north Escambia/East bays to Gulf Breeze in southern Escambia Bay may not by itself adversely impact the Seaside Sparrow habitat on the east edge of the Avalon peninsula, but subsequent development of the uplands next to these marshes as a result of the bridge's location may have an adverse impact.

RESPONSES TO HABITAT MODIFICATION: Seaside Sparrows respond to invasion of the saltmarsh habitat by trees and shrubs by abandoning the site when the woody vegetation reaches a critical density. Climatological changes, which enable northward migration of mangroves, and man-made drainage, which enables woody vegetation to move into the marsh from uplands, are causes of these invasions. Impounding of marshes for control of mosquitos or for enhancement of waterfowl populations destroys the natural saltmarsh vegetation in which the Seaside Sparrows live, and floods the marsh floor where the birds feed, resulting in abandonment of the site by the sparrows. This was the primary cause of extirpation of the Dusky Seaside Sparrow from Merritt Island (see Dusky account in this volume). An extensive saltmarsh in East Bay, Bay County , where Seaside Sparrows had been reported to occur, was diked and converted to a fresh water marsh in the early 1970s, and no Seasides were found there in 1980 (Kale 1983).

DEMOGRAPHIC CHARACTERISTICS: Nesting by Seaside Sparrows occurs from March through August, occasionally earlier (February) in the southern part of its range, and later (June) in the panhandle. Nests are constructed of grass and are open-cupped, but occasionally domed with over-arching tops of the living cordgrass or needlerush vegetation in which they are built. Nests are located anywhere from 0.1 m up to 1 meter or so (8 in.–3+ ft.) above the ground. Occasionally a nest may be built in a mangrove or small shrub. Modal clutch size is 3 (range 2–4) eggs. The white eggs are spotted with reddish-brown. Post et al. (1983) reported only 3% of Seaside Sparrow eggs produced nestlings. While the female performs most of the nest construction and incubation, the male assists in care and feeding of the young (Post et al. 1983). Nest mortality is high in Florida, chiefly a result of predation by rice rats (*Oryzomys palustris;* Post 1981), occasionally raccoons (*Procyon lotor*), or loss by flooding during storm driven high tides.

KEY BEHAVIORS: Seaside Sparrows are permanent residents in Florida coastal marshes, and except during the breeding season when males become conspicuous while singing on exposed perches, they occur chiefly in the dense vegetation or on the marsh floor where they are rarely seen. Males sing frequently and persistently from near tops of grass, with an occasional aerial foray 5–10 m (16–30 ft.) above the marsh. The song is a weak introductory note, followed by a buzzy trill. Seaside Sparrows are monogamous and territorial, with home ranges varying from 0.1–3.6 ha (0.25–8.89 ac.) during the breeding season (Greenlaw 1992).

The diet of Seaside Sparrows consists chiefly of arthropods (mainly insects and spiders), small crabs, gastropods (Howell 1932), and seeds (chiefly *Spartina*). These food items are gleaned from the vegetation and mud substrate.

CONSERVATION MEASURES TAKEN: The Scott's and Wakulla Seaside Sparrow populations endemic to Florida's Gulf coast are listed as species of special concern, and the Cape Sable Seaside Sparrow is listed as endangered by the Florida Game and Fresh Water Fish Commission (FGFWFC). The Cape Sable Sparrow also is on the U.S. Fish and Wildlife Service's endangered list. Peripheral populations (i.e., those subspecies that also occur outside of Florida's borders such as MacGillivray's and the Louisiana Seasides) arbitrarily have been excluded from any official designation. The Florida Committee on Rare and Endangered Plants and Animals (FCREPA) in 1978 designated the Louisiana Seaside as threatened (Stevenson and Kale 1978) because of its relatively low numbers, restricted habitat in Santa Rosa County, and disappearance from former sites in Escambia County. Both the Wakulla Seaside (considered as the northern range of Scott's Seaside herein) and the Smyrna Seaside (treated as MacGillivray's Seaside herein) have been proposed as candidates for federal listing (Wood 1993).

CONSERVATION MEASURES PROPOSED: The present listing status of the endemic populations of Seaside Sparrows should be maintained. The populations of the MacGillivray's and the Louisiana Seaside Sparrows that reside within Florida's borders, and the Choctawhatchee Bay population, should be designated species of special concern by the FGFWFC for the added protection of their habitat that this listing might provide these subspecies. Although the MacGillivray's Seaside Sparrow population in the marshes north of the St. Johns River appears stable, the unexplained disappearance of breeding sparrows from what appears to be suitable habitat between Matanzas Inlet and the St. Johns in the 1970s, suggests that a close watch needs to be maintained on this population to detect any further contraction of its range.

ACKNOWLEDGMENTS: I thank M. Delany and J. Rodgers for commenting on an earlier draft of this species account.

LITERATURE CITED:

AOU. 1957 Check-list of North American Birds. 5th ed. Amer. Ornithol. Union. Lord Baltimore Press, Baltimore, Maryland.

Austin, O. L., Jr. 1968. Smyrna Seaside Sparrow. Pp. 835–838 in Life histories of North American cardinals, grosbeaks, buntings, towhees, finches, sparrows, and allies (O. L. Austin, Jr., ed.). Bull. 237, Part 2, Smithsonian Inst., U.S. Natl. Mus. Washington, D.C.

Avise, J. C., and W. S. Nelson. 1989. Molecular genetic relationships of the extinct Dusky Seaside Sparrow. Science 243:646–648.

Baker, J. L., and H. W. Kale, II. 1978. Smyrna Seaside Sparrow. Pp. 115–116 in Rare and Endangered Biota of Florida. Vol. 2: Birds (H. W. Kale, II, ed.). Univ. Presses of Florida. Gainesville, Florida.

Greenlaw, J. S. 1992. Seaside Sparrow, *Ammodramus maritimus.* Pp. 211–232 in Migratory nongame birds of management concern in the northeast (K. J. Schneider and D. M. Pence, eds.). U.S. Dept. Inter. Fish and Wildl. Serv. Newton Corners, Massachusetts.

Howell, A. H. 1932. Florida bird life. Coward-McCann Inc., New York. 579 pp.

Kale, H. W., II. 1983. Distribution, habitat, and status of breeding Seaside Sparrows in Florida. Pp. 41–48 in The Seaside Sparrow, its biology and management (T. L. Quay, J. B. Funderburg, Jr., D. S. Lee, E. F. Potter, and C. S. Robbins, eds.). Occ. Pap. North Carolina Biol. Surv., North Carolina State Mus. Nat. Hist. Raleigh, North Carolina.

McDonald, V. M. 1988. Status survey of two Florida Seaside Sparrows and taxonomic review of the Seaside Sparrow assemblage. Tech. Rept. No. 32. Fla. Coop. Fish and Wildl. Res. Unit, School For. Res. and Conserv., Univ. of Florida, Gainesville, Florida.

Nicholson, D. J. 1928. Nesting habits of the Seaside Sparrow in Florida. Wilson Bull. 40:225–237.

Nicholson, D. J. 1946. Smyrna Seaside Sparrow. Fla. Nat. 19:39–42.

Nicholson, D. J. 1950. Disappearance of Smyrna Seaside Sparrow from its former haunts. Fla. Nat. 23:104.

Post, W. 1981. The influence of rice rats *Oryzomys palustris* on the habitat use of the Seaside Sparrow *Ammospiza maritima.* Behav. Ecol. Sociobiol. 9:35–40.

Post, W., J. S. Greenlaw, T. L. Merriam, and L. A. Wood. 1983. Comparative ecology of northern and southern populations of the Seaside Sparrow. Pp. 123–136 in The Seaside Sparrow, its biology and management (T. L. Quay, J. B. Funderburg, Jr., D. S. Lee, E. F. Potter, and C. S. Robbins, eds.). Occ. Paps. North Carolina Biol. Surv., North Carolina State Mus. Nat. Hist., Raleigh, North Carolina.

Stevenson, H. M., W. W. Baker, and H. W. Kale, II. 1978. Wakulla Seaside Sparrow. P. 107 in Rare and endangered biota of Florida, Vol. 2: birds (H. W. Kale, II, ed.). Univ. Presses of Florida, Gainesville, Florida.

Stevenson, H. M., and H. W. Kale, II. 1978. Louisiana Seaside Sparrow. P. 47 in Rare and endangered biota of Florida. Vol. 2: birds (H. W. Kale, II, ed.). Univ. Presses of Florida, Gainesville, Florida.

Wood, D. A. 1993. Official Lists of Endangered and Potentially Endangered Fauna and Flora in Florida. Fla. Game and Fresh Water Fish Comm. 1 October 1993. Tallahassee, Florida.

PREPARED BY: Herbert W. Kale II, Florida Audubon Society, 460 Highway 436, Suite 200, Casselberry, FL 32707.

Status Undetermined

Merlin

Falco columbarius

FAMILY FALCONIDAE

Order Falconiformes

TAXONOMY: Three subspecies of North American Merlins (*Falco columbarius*) currently are recognized. The Taiga Merlin (*F. c. columbarius*) is the most widespread, its breeding range roughly coinciding with the northern boreal forest. The two other subspecies, the Black Merlin (*F. c. suckleyi*) and Prairie Merlin (*F. c. richardsonii*), have restricted breeding ranges along the northern Pacific coast and in the northwest prairie-boreal forest ecotone, respectively. Merlins wintering in Florida generally are considered *F. c. columbarius* (Howell 1932). Wetmore (1933) reported three records of the Western Pigeon Hawk (*F. c. béndirei*) from Key West and the Tortugas during the late 1800s. However, the former *F. c. béndirei* no longer is considered separate from *F. c. columbarius* (Brown and Amadon 1968).

DESCRIPTION: Like other falcons, the Merlin is a stocky bird of prey with long, pointed wings, compact feathering, a bony central tubercle in each circular nostril, and a tomial notch and "tooth" on each side of the short upper mandible. The cere and legs are yellow to greenish-yellow, the talons are black, and the irises are very dark brown. The bill is bluish-black and darkest toward the tip. The relatively long tail, characteristic of small falcons, is slightly rounded. Unlike many other falcons, Merlins do not have well-defined dark moustachial stripes. The dorsum of adult males is slate blue-gray to nearly black. The tail is very dark, except for three or four whitish or light blue-gray narrow bands, and a white terminal band. The feathers of the underparts are whitish, tan, or pink, and have dark shaft streaks. The streaks become wider posteriorly, especially on the flanks. The color pattern of adult females is similar to that of adult males, except that the dorsum is brownish, with tan bands on the tail. Juvenal plumage, which is worn during the first winter (Palmer 1988), resembles that of adult females, but with less defined ventral streaking. Merlins are about 25–35 cm in total length and exhibit "reversed

616

Merlin, *Falco columbarius.* (Photo by Brian A. Millsap)

sexual dimorphism" (i.e., females are larger than males). Mean measurements for 28 adult males and 32 adult females were, respectively: wing chord, 188.9 and 207.8 mm; tail length, 121.0 and 133.6 mm; and culmen length, 12.5 and 14.2 mm (Palmer 1988). Mean weights for 40 adult males and 72 adult females were 159 and 218 g (Clark 1985).

POPULATION SIZE AND TREND: Johnsgard (1990) estimated the 1986 winter population for Canada and the 48 contiguous states to be about 11,000 Merlins. Since no population count for Florida has been made, an estimation of the size of Florida's current winter population would be highly conjectural. Prairie Merlins suffered a drastic decline and range contraction during the 1950s and 1960s, but showed signs of recovery by the late 1970s (Johnsgard 1990). The apparent cause was habitat loss in the northern prairie region and reproductive failure associated with organochlorine pesticide contamination (Fox 1971). Declines in Merlin breeding populations elsewhere in North America were much less severe (Johnsgard 1990; Evans 1982; but see Oliphant and Thompson 1978).

A decline in the numbers of Merlins migrating through and wintering in Florida during "recent years" was suggested by Wiley (1978). This trend is consistent with Evans' (1982) report that breeding populations of *F. c. columbarius* appeared to be stable after slight declines. The number of Merlins seen during fall migration at Hawk Mountain, Pennsylvania, did not change significantly from 1950 to 1969; however, this was followed by a significant increase in Merlin counts from 1970 to 1988 (raw data published in Hawk Mountain News, vols. 55–71, 1981–1989). Analysis of Audubon Christmas Bird Counts (CBCs) conducted in Florida revealed a slight but not significant increase in Merlin numbers during the 1970s and 1980s (raw data published in *American Birds* vols. 25–43, 1971–1989). Although unequivocal evidence

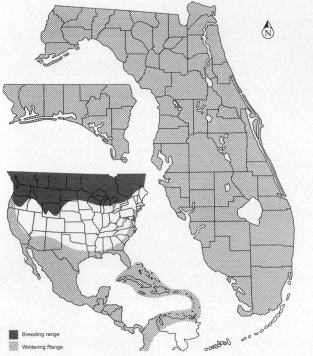

Distribution map
of the Merlin,
Falco columbarius.

Breeding range

Wintering Range

is lacking, the Merlin population in Florida appears to be stable (Smallwood 1990) or increasing slightly.

DISTRIBUTION AND HISTORY OF DISTRIBUTION: The Merlin is a circumpolar species, breeding in North America north to the treeline across Alaska, the Yukon and Northwest Territories, northern Manitoba, the Ungava Peninsula (northern Quebec), and northern Labrador, and south to Maine, the northern Great Lakes region, and the northern tier of western states to Oregon, although farther south in the plains and at higher elevations (Bent 1938; Brown and Amadon 1968). Results of a recent North American survey (Oliphant 1985) suggest that any changes in the distribution of breeding Merlins would be difficult to assess due to the fragmentary nature of available nesting data.

Merlins wintering in Florida have been observed throughout the state, but most often are encountered near the coasts. For the 22 CBC locations in Florida that were censused each year between 1970 and 1988, inland locations (all peninsular) had Merlin counts significantly lower than expected by chance. However, the relative number of Merlins counted at inland CBC locations increased significantly between the 1970s and 1980s. It is not clear whether this represents a distributional change related to the overall slightly higher

Merlin counts during the 1980s, or a change in observer awareness and ability in distinguishing Merlins from the similar but much more common American Kestrel (*F. sparverius*).

HABITAT REQUIREMENTS AND HABITAT TREND: Merlins wintering in Florida forage in a variety of habitats, including shorelines, mudflats, marshes, open parkland, pastures, and scrubby flatwoods (Smallwood 1990). In forested habitats, Merlins usually hunt along forest edges or where the woodland is discontinuous or patchy (Palmer 1988); the Merlin's preference for open habitats obviously is related to its method of prey capture. Wetlands in Florida were reduced from about 7,000,000 ha in 1954 to only 1,500,000 ha by 1982 (Mitsch and Gosselink 1986). The development of coastal wetlands, where Merlins are most numerous, accounts for much of this habitat loss.

VULNERABILITY OF SPECIES AND HABITAT: Little is known about the response of Merlin populations to changing land-use patterns in Florida. The loss or degradation of coastal wetlands probably has a negative effect by reducing the availability of shorebird prey.

CAUSES OF THREAT: Florida's wetlands currently are being destroyed at a rate of over 10,500 ha per year (Hefner 1990). The impact on coastal wetlands has been particularly severe, as much of Florida's development and urbanization is occurring along the coasts.

DDT and other organochlorine pesticides still pose a threat to Merlin populations. Although application of DDT has been banned in the United States for nearly two decades, its use is still widespread in the Caribbean and Central America (Henny et al. 1982; Gilroy and Barclay 1988) where most North American Merlins winter (Clark 1985). Furthermore, many of the bird species in the Merlin's diet are neotropical migrants (Sherrod 1978), so even the Merlins that winter in the United States still are in danger of consuming organochlorine contaminated prey during nesting or migration.

RESPONSES TO HABITAT MODIFICATION: The disappearance of a local population of Merlins breeding in shelterbelts around deserted farms in Kindersley, Saskatchewan, apparently was a response to the loss of suitable nesting trees (Fox 1971). In contrast, a population of Merlins became established in the city of Saskatoon, Saskatchewan, because of habitat modifications (Oliphant and Haug 1985). The spruce trees planted by the early residents of the city provide nest sites for crows and magpies, and ornamental fruit trees attract large flocks of waxwings in winter. Merlins now nest in abandoned crow and magpie nests, feeding primarily on the introduced House Sparrow (*Passer domesticus*). During winter the Merlins prey on waxwings. Direct evidence of Merlin responses to modification of Florida wintering habitats is lacking.

DEMOGRAPHIC CHARACTERISTICS: Merlins usually begin breeding at two years of age, but some yearlings do breed successfully (Johnsgard 1990). Mean clutch size for North American populations is 4.8 (Temple 1970). Recent reproductive success for Prairie Merlins in Canada has been 3–4 young reaching banding age per successful nest, and somewhat lower for other Merlin populations (Oliphant 1985.) First-year mortality is estimated to be 60–70% (Palmer 1988). Average life span is unknown, but the maximum age probably is about 8–10 years (Evans 1982).

KEY BEHAVIORS: Merlins feed primarily on small birds. Brown and Amadon (1968) estimated that the Merlin's diet consisted of 80% birds, 15% insects, and 5% mammals. Other estimates for the proportion of birds in the diet range from 25% (versus 74% insects by number: Snyder and Wiley 1976) to 100% (Fox 1964; Oliphant and McTaggert 1977). Sherrod (1978) summarized much of the literature on Merlin diets.

The characteristic hunting strategy of the Merlin includes a swift horizontal chase near the ground (Bent 1938; Laing 1985). A chase may be preceded by flying, often from above, directly into a dense flock of birds in order to single out an individual to pursue and capture. Bohemian Waxwings (*Bombycilla garrulus*, Servheen 1985) and small shorebirds (Page and Whitacre 1975; Boyce 1985) often are captured in this manner.

The courtship behavior of Merlins was described in detail by Feldsine and Oliphant (1985). Pairs engage in courtship feeding, in which the male makes food transfers to the female. Aerial displays include chasing, diving, gliding, fluttering, and soaring. Four distinct vocalizations were recognized. Chips are used by both sexes to communicate their location when they are near each other but not in visual contact. The "chutter" frequently precedes copulation. A food begging whine is used by females during courtship and by the young. The most common vocalization, used in a variety of contexts, has been described as a harsh, rapidly repeated "ki-ki-ki-ki-kee" or "kek-ek-ek-ek-ek" (Brown and Amadon 1968), with the male calling more rapidly and at a higher pitch (Feldsine and Oliphant 1985).

Like other falcons, Merlins do not construct nests prior to laying eggs. Instead, Merlins use the nest of another species, especially crows or magpies, or simply make a scrape directly on the ground. Cavity nesting has been reported (Bent 1938).

Merlins migrate from northern breeding grounds and arrive in Florida between mid-September and mid-October (Wiley 1978). Winter territoriality is not evident; however, some Merlins remain in a given locality in response to abundant prey resources (Palmer 1988). The northward migration back to the breeding grounds occurs in late March to mid-April (Wiley 1978).

CONSERVATION MEASURES TAKEN: Application of DDT has been banned in the United States since the early 1970s. The Merlin was on the Audubon Society's Blue List of declining species from 1972 until 1981, and was listed as a species of special concern from 1982 until 1986 (Johnsgard 1990). Merlins are included in CITES Appendix II, which limits international trade. The species is neither listed by the Florida Game and Fresh Water Fish Commission nor by the U.S. Fish and Wildlife Service.

CONSERVATION MEASURES PROPOSED: An ongoing study to determine and subsequently monitor the size of Florida's wintering Merlin population should be established. Food habits of Merlins in Florida should be more thoroughly investigated. Subsequently, an estimate of the available prey base could be made and trends in prey availability could be monitored. Another study should address the effect that recreational use of beaches and development of shoreline habitats has on the shorebird prey base. The threat of organochlorine pesticide contamination would be diminished by restricting the export of these domestically banned substances by U.S. manufacturers to foreign clients.

ACKNOWLEDGMENTS: We thank J. A. Rodgers for a thoughtful review of an earlier draft. This paper is contribution No. R-02317 of the Journal Series, Florida Agricultural Experiment Station, Gainesville.

LITERATURE CITED:

Bent, A. C. 1938. Life histories of North American birds of prey, part 2. U.S. Natl. Mus. Bull. 170.

Boyce, D. A., Jr. 1985. Merlins and the behavior of wintering shorebirds. Raptor Res. 19:94–96.

Brown, L., and D. Amadon. 1968. Eagles, hawks and falcons of the world. McGraw-Hill Book Co., New York. 945 pp.

Clark, W. S. 1985. Migration of the Merlin along the coast of New Jersey. Raptor Res. 19:85–93.

Evans, D. L. 1982. Status reports on twelve raptors. Special Scientific Rept., Wildlife, No. 238. U.S. Fish and Wildl. Serv., Washington, D.C. 68 pp.

Feldsine, J. W., and L. W. Oliphant. 1985. Breeding behavior of the Merlin: the courtship period. Raptor Res. 19:60–67.

Fox, G. A. 1964. Notes on the western race of the Pigeon Hawk. Blue Jay 22:190–192.

Fox, G. A. 1971. Recent changes in the reproductive success of the Pigeon Hawk. Jour. Wildl. Manage. 35:122–128.

Gilroy, M. J., and J. H. Barclay. 1988. DDE residues and eggshell characteristics of reestablished Peregrines in the eastern United States. Pp. 403–412 in Peregrine Falcon populations (T. J. Cade, J. H. Enderson, C. G. Thelander, and C. M. White, eds.). The Peregrine Fund, Inc., Boise, Idaho. 949 pp.

Hefner, J. 1990. Florida's wetlands fact sheet. National Wetlands Inventory, U.S. Fish and Wildlife Service, Atlanta, Georgia. 5 pp.

Henny, C. J., F. P. Ward, K. E. Riddle, and R. M. Prouty. 1982. Migratory Peregrine Falcons, *Falco peregrinus*, accumulate pesticides in Latin America during winter. Can. Field-Nat. 96:333–338.

Howell, A. H. 1932. Florida bird life. Coward-McCann, Inc., New York. 579 pp.

Johnsgard, P. A. 1990. Hawks, eagles, and falcons of North America. Smithsonian Institution Press, Washington, D.C. 403 pp.

Laing, K. 1985. Food habits and breeding biology of Merlins in Denali National Park, Alaska. Raptor Res. 19:42–51.

Mitsch, W. J., and J. G. Gosselink. 1986. Wetlands. Van Nostrand Reinhold, New York. 539 pp.

Oliphant, L. W. 1985. North American Merlin breeding survey. Raptor Res. 19:37–41.

Oliphant, L. W., and E. Haug. 1985. Productivity, population density and rate of increase of an expanding Merlin population. Raptor Res. 19:56–59.

Oliphant, L. W., and S. McTaggert. 1977. Prey species utilized by urban nesting Merlins. Can. Field-Nat. 91:190–192.

Oliphant, L. W., and W. J. P. Thompson. 1978. Recent breeding success of Richardson's Merlin in Saskatchewan. Raptor Res. 12:35–39.

Page, G., and D. F. Whitacre. 1975. Raptor predation on wintering shorebirds. Condor 77:73–83.

Palmer, R. S. 1988. Merlin. Pp. 291–314 in Handbook of North American birds, vol. 5, diurnal raptors, part 2 (R. S. Palmer, ed.). Yale University Press, New Haven, Connecticut. 465 pp.

Servheen, C. 1985. Notes on wintering Merlins in western Montana. Raptor Res. 19:97–99.

Sherrod, S. K. 1978. Diets of North American falconiformes. Raptor Res. 12:49–121.

Smallwood, J. A. 1990. American Kestrel and Merlin. Pp. 29–37 in Proceedings of the southeast raptor management symposium and workshop (B. G. Pendleton, ed.). National Wildlife Federation, Washington, D.C. 248 pp.

Snyder, N. F. R., and J. W. Wiley. 1976. Sexual size dimorphism in hawks and owls of North America. Amer. Ornith. Union Ornithol. Monogr. 20. 96 pp.

Temple, S. A. 1970. Systematics and evolution of the North American Merlins. M.S. thesis, Cornell Univ., Ithaca, New York. 62 pp.

Wetmore, A. 1933. The Western Pigeon Hawk in Florida. Auk 50:356.

Wiley, J. W. 1978. Southeastern American Kestrel. Pp. 32–34 in Rare and endangered biota of Florida, Vol. II. Birds (H. W. Kale II, ed.). University Presses of Florida, Gainesville. 121 pp.

PREPARED BY: John A. Smallwood and Kenneth D. Meyer, Department of Wildlife and Range Sciences, 118 Newins-Ziegler Hall, University of Florida, Gainesville, FL 32611 (Current address of JAS: Department of Biology, Montclair State University, Upper Montclair, NJ 07043).

Gull-billed Tern
Sterna nilotica

FAMILY LARIDAE

Order Charadriiformes

TAXONOMY: The Gull-billed Tern (*Sterna nilotica*) was originally described in 1789 by Gmelin (AOU 1983). The species has a scattered, cosmopolitan distribution (Clapp et al. 1983; Spendelow and Patton 1988). The Gull-billed Tern has sometimes been assigned to the monotypic genus *Gelochelidon*.

DESCRIPTION: The Gull-billed Tern is a stocky, medium-sized tern about 34–38 cm (14 in.) in length. Wing length is about 30 cm (12 in.) (Ridgway 1915). Adults in North America exhibit an average weight of about 170 g (6 oz.) (Clapp et al. 1983). Males and females have similar plumage. Breeding adults are pale gray dorsally, have a deep black cap, and are pure white ventrally. The legs and stout bill are black. The tail is only moderately forked. In winter, adults have a nearly white head with a dark gray-black streak through the eyeline. Downy chicks range in base coloration from buff-brown to grayish and have large dusky spots.

POPULATION SIZE AND TRENDS: Spendelow and Patton (1988) estimated that about 5,400 Gull-billed Terns composed the breeding population along the U.S. Atlantic coast (New York to east Florida) and the U.S. Gulf coast (west Florida to southern Texas). About 59% of the birds in this estimate were in colonies located along the south coast of Texas (Spendelow and Patton 1988).

The first record of Gull-billed Terns breeding in Florida cited by most authors is the single nest discovered at Pensacola (Escambia County) on 10 July 1932 (Weston 1933). However, Stevenson and Anderson (1994) recently reported an earlier record of three eggs collected at Anna Maria Island (Manatee County) on 20 May 1892. Other early breeding reports include: a colony on an island in Lake Okeechobee during June, 1939 (Sprunt 1940); a small colony at the north end of the Indian River (Haulover Canal area)

Gull-billed Tern,
Sterna nilotica.
(Photo by Jeffery
A. Gore)

during June, 1940 (Longstreet 1941); and additional colonies on several islands in Lake Okeechobee during May and June, 1943 (Nicholson 1948).

Population estimates of breeding Gull-billed Terns in Florida have varied greatly. The amount of this variation attributable to real population fluctuation versus incomplete surveys is impossible to determine. Florida region *American Birds* reports from 1975 mention "285 pairs of Gull-billed Terns" at the "Merritt I. ternery" (Brevard County), and "249 Gull-billed Tern nests" at "Little Bird I." (Duval County) (Ogden 1975). These reports suggest a minimum state-wide breeding population of more than 1,000 birds in 1975, exclusive of any undetected colonies at Florida west coast, panhandle (northwest) coast, or inland locations. Unfortunately, no sum total comparable to the 1975 report is available through the 1990 reports. The Florida Atlantic coast breeding population was estimated to be about 210 birds during 1976 (Spendelow and Patton 1988); however, those authors cautioned that the 1976 survey data was not comprehensive and therefore the state-wide breeding population total for that year was probably somewhat greater. Schreiber and Schreiber (1978) reported that "this species was not observed" during their 1977 study of 40 select dredged-material islands in Florida. The Florida population also has been estimated to be composed of about 420 birds (Clapp and Buckley 1984 *in* Spendelow and Patton 1988).

Reports in *American Birds* from 1976–1990 and the forthcoming Florida Breeding Bird Atlas maps (H. Kale, unpubl. data) indicate that "recent" Gull-billed Tern breeding sites in Florida are widely disjunct and localized throughout the state; only Duval and Brevard counties supported breeding on the east coast, Hillsborough County on the west coast, and Franklin and Bay counties on the panhandle coast. Small inland colonies also have been documented in Palm Beach, Polk, and Hillsborough counties. Most reports during this period are of small colonies usually consisting of less than 15 nests. At the St. George

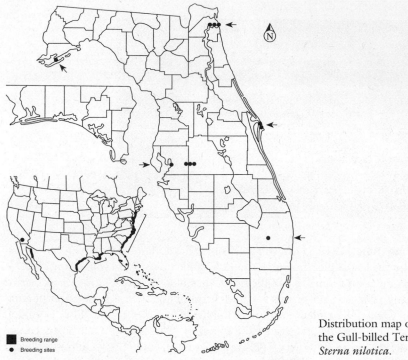

Distribution map of
the Gull-billed Tern,
Sterna nilotica.

■ Breeding range
● Breeding sites

Island Causeway colony in Franklin County, no more than three nests have
been found during each of four (1989–1992) breeding seasons (Smith et al.
1993).

DISTRIBUTION AND HISTORY OF DISTRIBUTION: The Gull-billed
Tern has a scattered distribution worldwide (Spendelow and Patton 1988). In
the eastern United States, the species breeds along the Atlantic coast (New
York to Florida) and the Gulf coast (Florida to southern Texas). Population
estimates and distribution data for breeding Gull-billed Terns in Florida have
varied considerably (see Population Size and Trends). In general, it appears
that the species has declined in abundance and range along the Atlantic coast.
Historical patterns along the Gulf coast are difficult to determine due to a lack
of early survey data for some regions.

Records of migrating and wintering Gull-billed Terns in Florida are very
limited. In the eastern United States only the Texas coast supports large
winter populations (Clapp et al. 1983). Most Gull-billed Terns breeding in
the eastern United States are believed to migrate to winter ranges in "central
and northern South America" (Clapp et al. 1983). Three birds banded in
Florida were later recovered from Guyana (Stevenson and Anderson 1994).

HABITAT REQUIREMENTS AND HABITAT TRENDS: Gull-billed Tern nesting areas have included sandy coastal beaches, natural estuary islands, coastal marshes, dredged-material islands, islands in lakes, and various disturbed inland habitats (e.g., phosphate mining areas). In general, along the U.S. southeast Atlantic coast and Gulf coast, sparsely vegetated sandy coastal habitats, dredged-material deposits, and estuary islands are most frequently used for nesting (Clapp et al. 1983; Spendelow and Patton 1988). Eggs are laid in shallow depressions ("scrapes") on substrates of sand and shell, or on coarse sand-shell-debris mixtures. The amount of dry vegetation gathered into the nest site varies considerably among breeding birds. Portnoy (1977) mentions that many nests are found near driftwood. Nest sites may be located near areas of low, dense vegetative cover to which "families" (adults and their chicks) can relocate within a few days after eggs hatch (Sears 1978). Nesting in coastal marshes occurs in North America, but much less frequently than in the Old World (Clapp et al. 1983; Spendelow and Patton 1988). In Florida, nesting on islands in Lake Okeechobee has been documented (Sprunt 1940, Nicholson 1948). The Florida Breeding Bird Atlas (H. Kale, unpubl. data) also identifies inland phosphate mining areas as recent breeding sites.

As much of Florida's marine and estuarine coastal habitat already has been greatly reduced or degraded, continuation or acceleration of this process will eventually result in additional relocation, dispersion, or loss of coastal tern colonies. General ecology and population dynamics of the inland Florida colonies of Gull-billed Terns are not well understood and trends in habitat availability are, therefore, difficult to forecast.

VULNERABILITY OF SPECIES AND HABITAT: The breeding distribution of Gull-billed Terns in Florida is widely disjunct and localized. The impacts of habitat loss, human disturbance, and flooding of colony sites all present significant dangers to the species in Florida.

CAUSES OF THREAT: With the exception of rooftop colony and feeding behavior issues, causes of threat to nesting Gull-billed Terns in Florida are similar to those for Least Terns (*Sterna antillarum*) and include coastal habitat conversion, colony disturbance by humans and domestic pets, predation by mammals and birds, and environmental contaminants. A detailed discussion of these concerns is presented in the species account on the Least Tern elsewhere in this volume. Blus and Stafford (1980) discussed extreme losses of Gull-billed Tern eggs to both flooding and predation by rats (*Rattus* sp.) and Laughing Gulls (*Larus atricilla*), at colonies in South Carolina.

RESPONSES TO HABITAT MODIFICATION: Little direct experimental information is available regarding Gull-billed Tern responses to habitat modifications. Altering breeding habitat to provide preferred species and densities of vegetative cover, or substrate types, may be beneficial. Like many other species of seabirds, Gull-billed Terns also will nest on dredged-material deposits (Portnoy 1977; Sears 1978; Soots and Landin 1978; Kale, unpubl. ms.). Gull-billed Terns were reported nesting upon sand-fills in the central Florida phosphate mining areas as early as the 1960s (Layne et al. 1977). Gull-billed Terns have nested on rooftops in Texas (P. Glass, pers. comm.). A single pair recently nested on a rooftop in Bay County, Florida (L. Coburn, pers. comm.); this may be the first such record in the state.

DEMOGRAPHIC CHARACTERISTICS: Gull-billed Terns in Florida generally deposit clutches from about the first week in May through late June (Weston 1933; Sprunt 1940; Longstreet 1941; Nicholson 1948; Hallman 1960; Paul 1983, 1986, 1988). We suspect that this species nests slightly later in the season in north Florida than in coastal central Florida, as is the latitudinal effect with Least Terns (see Least Tern account). In the southeastern and Gulf coast states Gull-billed Tern clutches range from 1 to 4 eggs with most clutches containing 2 or 3 eggs (Clapp et al. 1983). The regional modal clutch size is generally three eggs (Clapp et al. 1983). In North Carolina, Sears (1978) reported decreased clutch sizes for pairs nesting later in the breeding season. Eggs hatch in about 22–23 days. Fledging age has not been well documented in our region, but apparently ranges from 28 to 35 days (Clapp et al. 1983; Martin and Lester 1990).

KEY BEHAVIORS: Gull-billed Terns opportunistically feed on a wide variety of invertebrate and vertebrate prey captured on land and in coastal and freshwater marshes. Foraging methods include "hawking" insects during flight, capturing prey on the ground or at the surface of waters, and rarely, diving for fish. In Florida, upland foraging not only occurs over open habitats, but also over shrub-dominated fields (Rohwer and Woolfenden 1968).

A sampling of the prey items reported throughout this species' range and summarized from other reviews cited in Clapp et al. (1983) includes: insects (i.e., grasshoppers, dragonflies), mole crabs, fiddler crabs, crayfish, frogs, green anoles, racerunners, eggs and young birds of other species, and various small rodents. In Florida, food remains from the stomachs of six Gull-billed Terns collected during 1964 and 1966 in Pinellas County included: green anoles (*Anolis carolinensis*), fiddler crabs (*Uca* sp.), grasshoppers and an unidentified beetle (Rohwer and Woolfenden 1968). Densmore (1990) reported a Gull-billed Tern preying on a Least Tern chick in Mississippi. In Florida, we have observed Gull-billed Terns swooping at Least Tern chicks, but have not observed any captures.

As with other species of terns, Gull-billed Terns exhibit the common behavioral traits of colonial ground nesting (Sears 1979) and site tenacity (Blus and Stafford 1980). From Florida through the Gulf coast states, Gull-billed Terns frequently co-occupy breeding sites with Black Skimmers (*Rynchops niger*) and Least Terns, and occasionally with Royal Terns (*S. maxima*) or Laughing Gulls (Hallman 1960; Portnoy 1977; Kale, unpubl. ms.; Kunneke and Palik 1984; Paul 1988; Spendelow and Patton 1988; Hunter 1990). Associations with Black Skimmers are especially common along the northern Gulf coast states (Portnoy 1977, Smith et al. 1993); a similar relationship between these two species has been observed in South Carolina (Blus and Stafford 1980).

Gull-billed Terns will attack predatory birds and mammals that intrude into breeding colonies. Attacks against birds involve vocalizing and chasing; whereas attacks against mammals involve hovering above and diving at the predator while vocalizing (Sears 1978). Dives often culminate with the tern defecating and striking the intruder with the bill (Sears 1978). Aggressive responses toward predators generally increase in intensity as incubation progresses (Sears 1978).

The calls of adults have been described as a rasping "za-za-za" and "kay-weck, kay-weck" (Peterson 1980). Sears (1981) identified eight aerial display behaviors, eighteen terrestrial display behaviors, and five vocal displays by the species during the breeding season.

CONSERVATION MEASURES TAKEN: All tern species are protected by the federal Migratory Bird Treaty Act (16 U.S.C. 703–711). Terns in Florida also are protected by the Wildlife Code of the State of Florida (Chapter 39 F.A.C.). Establishment of "critical wildlife areas" (39–19.005 F.A.C.) provides the maximum level of security available for tern colonies under Florida law (Robson 1991). The efforts of federal and state agencies as well as conservation organizations such as Audubon Society and The Nature Conservancy have greatly improved protection for tern colonies, particularly from the threats of habitat conversion and human disturbance.

CONSERVATION MEASURES PROPOSED: Various authors have indicated that there is a paucity of information regarding both the wintering distribution and breeding distribution of Gull-billed Terns in Florida (Clapp et al. 1983; Spendelow and Patton 1988). Data collected during the Florida Breeding Bird Atlas surveys should clarify some of the questions regarding summer distribution in the state. More consistent monitoring of the location and size of Gull-billed Tern breeding colonies, in conjunction with surveys of other species, would be of great value in assessing population trends. Considerable additional survey effort would be required to define the limited Florida winter distribution of the species.

Additional posting and bounding of breeding colonies should be conducted where necessary to minimize disturbance by humans. At some locations, the activity of mammalian and avian predators may need to be controlled. Other widely applicable conservation measures for terns have been summarized by O'Meara and Gore (1988).

ACKNOWLEDGMENTS: We thank H. W. Kale for providing us with the unpublished Gull-billed Tern breeding distribution map for the forthcoming Florida Breeding Bird Atlas. P. Glass (Texas) and L. Coburn (Florida) provided unpublished data regarding Gull-billed Tern breeding activity on rooftops in their regions. J. A. Rodgers improved the manuscript with helpful review comments. W. Miley and H. L. Edmiston are project co-investigators with us at the breeding colony mentioned in Franklin County. G. Fishman typed the manuscript.

LITERATURE CITED:

AOU. 1983. Checklist of North American birds. American Ornithologists' Union, Allen Press, Inc., Lawrence, Kansas.

Blus, L. J., and C. J. Stafford. 1980. Breeding biology and relation of pollutants to Black Skimmers and Gull-billed Terns in South Carolina. U.S. Fish and Wildl. Serv. Spec. Rept. no. 230. Washington, D.C.

Clapp, R. B., D. Morgan-Jacobs, and R. C. Banks. 1983. Marine birds of the southeastern United States and Gulf of Mexico. Part III: Charadriiformes. U.S. Fish Wildl. Serv., Div. Biol. Serv., FWS/OBS-83/30. Washington, D.C. 853 pp.

Densmore, R. J. 1990. Gull-billed Tern predation on a Least Tern chick. Wilson Bull. 102:180–181.

Hallman, R. C. 1960. Gull-billed Tern (*Gelochelidon nilotica*) nesting in Gulf County, Florida. Fla. Nat. 33:224.

Hunter, W. C. 1990. Handbook for nongame bird management and monitoring in the southeast region. U.S. Fish Wildl. Serv., Atlanta, Georgia.

Kale, H. W. 1979. Unpubl. rept. to Shell Oil Corp., Environmental Affairs. Florida Audubon Society, Maitland, Florida. 50 pp.

Kunneke, J. T., and T. F. Palik. 1984. Tampa Bay environmental atlas. U.S. Fish Wildl. Serv. Biol. Rept. no. 85(15). 73 pp.

Layne, J. N., J. A. Stallcup, G. E. Woolfenden, M. N. McCauley, and D. J. Worley. 1977. Fish and wildlife inventory of the seven-county region included in the central Florida phosphate industry areawide environmental impact study. U.S. Fish Wildl. Serv., contract no. 14–16–0097–77-005. pp. 913–916.

Longstreet, R. J. 1941. Gull-billed Tern nesting in Florida. Auk 58:96.

Martin, R. P., and G. D. Lester. 1990. Atlas and census of wading bird and seabird nesting colonies in Louisiana 1990. Louisiana Dept. Wildl. and Fisheries/Louisiana Nat. Heritage Prog. Spec. Publ. no. 3.

Nicholson, D. J. 1948. Fresh-water nesting of the Gull-billed Tern in Florida. Auk 65:139–140.

Ogden, J. C. 1975. Florida region. Amer. Birds 29:960–963.

O'Meara, T. E., and J. A. Gore. 1988. Guidelines for conservation and management of Least Tern colonies in Florida. Fla. Game and Fresh Water Fish Comm., Tallahassee, Florida.

Paul, R. T. 1983. Florida region. Amer. Birds 37:980–982.

Paul, R. T. 1986. Florida region. Amer. Birds 40:1193–1197.

Paul, R. T. 1988. Florida region. Amer. Birds 42:1278–1281.

Peterson, R. T. 1980. A field guide to the birds. Houghton Mifflin Co., Boston, Massachusetts.

Portnoy, J. W. 1977. Nesting colonies of seabirds and wading birds—coastal Louisiana, Mississippi, and Alabama. FWS/OBS—77/07. U.S. Fish Wildl. Serv., Biol. Serv. Prog. 126 pp.

Ridgway, R. 1915. A manual of North American birds, fourth ed. J. B. Lippincott Co., Philadelphia, Pennsylvania.

Robson, M. 1991. Wildlife and habitat management. Ann. perf. rept. Fla. Game and Fresh Water Fish Comm., Tallahassee, Florida.

Rohwer, S. A., and G. E. Woolfenden. 1968. The varied diet of the Gull-billed Tern includes a shrub-inhabiting lizard. Wilson Bull. 80:330–331.

Schreiber, R. W., and E. A. Schreiber. 1978. Colonial bird use and plant succession on dredged material islands in Florida; Vol. I: Sea and wading bird colonies. Tech. Rept. D–78–14. U.S. Army Eng. Waterways Exp. Sta., Vicksburg, Mississippi.

Sears, H. F. 1978. Nesting behavior of the Gull-billed Tern. Bird Band. 49:1–16.

Sears, H. F. 1979. Colonial nesting as an anti-predator adaptation in the Gull-billed Tern. Auk 96:202–203.

Sears, H. F. 1981. The display behavior of the Gull-billed Tern. Jour. Field Ornithol. 52:191–209.

Smith, H. T., J. A. Gore, W. W. Miley, H. L. Edmiston, and J. A. Rodgers, Jr. 1993. Recent nesting of Gull-billed Terns in northwest Florida. Fla. Field Nat. 21:80–82.

Soots, R. F., Jr., and M. C. Landin. 1978. Development and management of avian habitat on dredged material islands. Tech. Rept. DS–78–18. U.S. Army Eng. Waterways Exp. Sta., Vicksburg, Mississippi.

Spendelow, J. A., and S. R. Patton. 1988. National atlas of coastal waterbird colonies in the contiguous United States: 1976–1982. U.S. Fish and Wildl. Serv. Biol. Rept. no. 88(5). 326 pp.

Sprunt, A., Jr. 1940. Gull-billed Tern breeding in Florida. Auk 57:251–252.

Stevenson, H. M., and B. H. Anderson. 1994. The birdlife of Florida. Univ. Press of Fla., Gainesville, Florida.
Weston, F. M. 1933. Gull-billed Tern nesting at Pensacola, Florida. Auk 50:215–216.

PREPARED BY: Henry T. Smith, Florida Department of Natural Resources, Office of Environmental Services, 3900 Commonwealth Blvd., Tallahassee, FL 32399 (Current address: Florida Department of Environmental Protection, Florida Park Service, 13798 S.E. Federal Highway, Hobe Sound, FL 33455); and Jeffery A. Gore, Florida Game and Fresh Water Fish Commission, Bureau of Nongame Wildlife, 3911 Highway 2321, Panama City, FL 32409.

Florida Prairie Warbler
Dendroica discolor paludicola

FAMILY EMBERIZIDAE

Order Passeriformes

TAXONOMY: There are two subspecies of Prairie Warblers: *Dendroica d. discolor,* which breeds across much of the eastern United States and winters in the Caribbean, and *D. d. paludicola,* which breeds on the coast of peninsular Florida and winters in Florida and the Caribbean (AOU 1957; Nolan 1978). *D. d. collinsi* is a junior synonym of *paludicola* (Van Tyne 1956). Some authors (e.g., Bent 1953) refer to *D. d. discolor* as the northern Prairie Warbler; *paludicola* is commonly called the Florida Prairie Warbler (e.g., Stevenson 1978).

The Prairie Warbler's closest relative is the Vitelline Warbler, *D. vitellina,* of the Cayman and Swan Islands. *D. vitellina* resembles a subdefinitively plumaged female Prairie Warbler (compare illustration in Griscom and Sprunt 1957 to those in Nolan 1978). *D. discolor* and *D. vitellina* may be conspecific, if not, they constitute a superspecies (Hellmayr 1935; AOU 1983).

DESCRIPTION: Prairie Warblers are of typical *Dendroica* proportions, are about 12 cm long overall, weigh about 6–8 grams (more data on weights and measurements in Nolan 1978).

In all post-juvenal plumages the underparts and throat are yellow or mostly yellow with at least a trace of darker streaking on the flanks. The rump, back, nape, crown, and ear patch are greenish. A more-or-less distinct stripe over the eye and a spot below the eye range from whitish to bright yellow. A black or olive stripe runs from the base of the bill and below the eye spot to the ear patch. All but first-fall females have at least some reddish streaks on the upper back. Most plumages include pale thin wing bars. White patches on the outer rectrices vary in extent according to age and sex. Older males in alternate plumage generally have the darker facial and flank stripes, the brighter yellow on the underparts and face markings, the more distinctive wing bars, and the more extensive red on the back. Younger females generally have the less dark,

Florida Prairie Warbler, *Dendroica discolor paludicola*. (Photo by Glen M. Wood)

bright, distinctive, and extensive states of each of these characters, but there is individual variation. See Nolan (1978) and Pyle et al. (1987) for details from which I have drawn the foregoing generalizations.

Howell (1930) distinguished *D. d. paludicola* from *D. d. discolor* as having grayer upperparts, less red on the back, and smaller black flank streaks. Male Prairie Warblers in alternate plumage should not be mistaken for any other species, but Prairie Warblers of other age and sex classes might be confused with Palm (*D. palmarum*), Pine (*D. pinus*), or Kirtland's (*D. kirtlandii*) warblers. See Pyle et al. (1987) for distinguishing warblers in the hand, and the more detailed field guides (e.g., National Geographic Society 1987) for distinguishing them in the field.

POPULATION SIZE AND TREND: There is no overall population estimate for the Florida Prairie Warbler. Its local relative abundance ranges from rare (e.g., Palm Beach and Broward counties; Stevenson and Anderson 1994) to common (e.g., about 50 pairs on Anclote Keys in July 1989; B. Pranty in Paul 1989). Average densities on small keys in Florida Bay ranged from 0.86 to 1.09 pairs/ha in 1992 and 1993 (J. W. Prather and A. Cruz, in litt.). Numbers on Breeding Bird Surveys have declined since the early 1970s (Stevenson and Anderson 1994), and since the early 1980s relative abundance has gone from common to uncommon in lower Boca Ciega Bay, including Mullet Key (R Smith in Pranty 1993; L. and B. Atherton, R. Smith, pers. comm.). Because Florida Prairie Warblers nest almost exclusively in mangroves, it is reasonable to infer that their numbers have declined somewhat as mangroves have been cleared or otherwise rendered unusable for nesting. The total amount of mangrove habitat destroyed in Florida is not known with precision; Odum et

Distribution map of the Florida Prairie Warbler, *Dendroica discolor paludicola*.

al. (1982) estimate it at about 3–5% overall, with higher losses in certain localities such as Tampa Bay, Marco Island, and the lower Atlantic coast. Mangrove trimming further reduces the amount of habitat useful to Prairie Warblers (see Responses to Habitat Modification).

DISTRIBUTION AND HISTORY OF DISTRIBUTION: The Prairie Warbler breeds from eastern Nebraska, eastern Kansas, central Wisconsin, northern Michigan, southern Ontario, southern Pennsylvania, southeastern New York, Massachusetts and southern New Hampshire south to eastern Oklahoma, extreme eastern Texas, the Gulf coast (absent from southern Mississippi and Alabama), and Florida (AOU 1983). Prairie Warblers winter from central Florida (casually from southern Texas, the Gulf coast, and Virginia) and the Bahama Islands south throughout the West Indies to islands off the coast of northern Middle America (AOU 1983).

Florida Prairie Warblers breed in a narrow strip extending from the southern keys northward to northern Pasco County on the Gulf coast, and to Brevard and probably Flagler County on the Atlantic; singing males occur farther north (Kale et al., in prep.). Breeding on the Gulf coast may once have extended as far north as Cedar Key (Stevenson and Anderson 1994). The AOU Check-list (1957), without elaboration, lists breeding localities of this subspecies as far north on the Atlantic coast as Charleston, S.C. Reports of inland breeding are doubtful (Stevenson and Anderson 1994).

Prairie Warblers are winter residents throughout most of Florida, though mainly in the peninsula (Stevenson and Anderson 1994). *D. d. discolor* is thought to winter little, if at all, in Florida (AOU 1957). This implies that the Prairie Warblers at inland sites such as Gainesville are *paludicola* that travelled north from the coast; Stevenson and Anderson (1994) are skeptical of this possibility. *D. d. paludicola* also winters in the northern West Indies (AOU 1957). Determination of the winter ranges of the two subspecies is difficult because they may not be separable in their winter plumages (Stevenson and Anderson 1994).

HABITAT REQUIREMENTS AND HABITAT TRENDS. The Prairie Warbler is found in brushy second growth, dry scrub, and low pine-juniper woodland in much of its range; in migration and winter it is also found in a variety of woodland, second growth, brush and thicket habitats (AOU 1983). Florida Prairie Warblers nest almost exclusively in mangroves, and occasionally in oak hammocks adjacent to mangroves (Stevenson and Anderson 1994). About 190,000 ha of mangroves remain in Florida; 90% of these are in Dade, Collier, Monroe, and Lee Counties (Odum et al. 1982). Development pressure will continue to be strong in the high-growth coastal zone of the southern peninsula. Though the age of wholesale dredge-and-fill seems to be over (Frayer and Hefner 1991), the widespread practice of waterfront mangrove trimming (see Responses to Habitat Modification) and other piecemeal damage continues.

VULNERABILITY OF SPECIES AND HABITAT. The state's ability to stop outright destruction of mangroves on privately owned land is subject to the vagaries of court decisions; depending upon the political climate, such regulation may be construed as an unconstitutional "taking." Mangroves are susceptible to damage from herbicides, oil spills, high concentrations of suspended solids, and permanent flooding of their aerial roots (Odum et al. 1982).

Prairie Warblers are suitable hosts for brood-parasitic cowbirds because they are small and build open nests (Friedmann 1963). Brown-headed Cowbirds (*Molothrus ater*) commonly parasitize Prairie Warblers of the northern race (Nolan 1978). Brown-headed Cowbirds and Shiny Cowbirds (*M. bonariensis*), also brood parasites, have recently invaded the breeding range of the Florida Prairie Warbler (Robertson and Woolfenden 1992; Post et al. 1993; Stevenson and Anderson 1994). It is conceivable that either or both species of cowbird will extirpate the warbler, especially if they parasitize it as heavily as the Brown-headed Cowbird has Kirtland's Warbler and the Shiny Cowbird has the Yellow-shouldered Blackbird (*Agelaius xanthomus*), and if their numbers are not controlled (Friedmann and Kiff 1985; Wiley et al. 1991; Mayfield 1992).

Florida Prairie Warblers may be vulnerable to pesticides because they are small-bodied (thus with high metabolic rates), insectivorous (Nolan 1978), and live in a habitat that produces large numbers of insects annoying to many people. Tiebout (1991) devised a model to predict the degree of risk to free-ranging birds from pesticides commonly used for controlling adult mosquitos, and concluded that Florida Prairie Warblers are at "very high risk of mortality in populations exposed to the maximal allowable applications of fenthion. . ." (H. M. Tiebout, unpubl. ms.). There has been no field test of Tiebout's (unpubl. ms.) prediction of mortality from application of maximum levels of fenthion.

The breeding range of the Florida Prairie Warbler coincides almost exactly with the zone of highest concentration of Florida bird species vulnerable to population declines, as mapped by Millsap et al. (1990).

CAUSES OF THREAT: So far there is little direct evidence that cowbirds parasitize Florida Prairie Warblers, and only plausible inference that such parasitism has reduced the size of the warbler's population. J. W. Prather and A. Cruz (in litt.) found no cowbird eggs in the 47 active Florida Prairie Warbler nests they examined in the Keys and Florida Bay from 1989 to 1993. The confirmed cases of cowbird parasitism on Florida Prairie Warblers are one each at Tierra Verde (L. Atherton in Paul 1987) and Longboat Key (Atherton and Atherton 1988), both in 1987, Flamingo in 1989 (M. Wheeler and P. W. Smith in Kale 1989), and Captiva Island in 1990 (V. McGrath, J. W. Prather and A. Cruz, in litt.). The cowbirds in the latter two instances were Brown-headed; those in the first two also were probably Brown-headed, because Shiny Cowbirds were not known to have occurred so far north by 1987 (Post et al. 1993). The seeming scarcity of cowbird parasitism on Florida Prairie Warblers is not necessarily cause for optimism. When Shiny Cowbirds arrived in Puerto Rico they at first specialized in parasitizing Yellow-shouldered Black-birds, leaving nearly unaffected a variety of other potential hosts, including Yellow Warblers (*D. petechia*). But by the early 1980s they had greatly intensi-fied use of these other hosts and parasitized 63% of Yellow Warbler nests (Cruz et al. 1989). Regular observers in lower Boca Ciega Bay and at Mullet Key note that Florida Prairie Warbler numbers there declined markedly since the influx of Brown-headed Cowbirds in the mid-1980s (L. Atherton in Paul 1987; L. and B. Atherton, pers. comm.; R. Smith, pers. comm.).

RESPONSES TO HABITAT MODIFICATION: R. Smith (pers. comm.) notes that on Mullet Key, which is bisected by roads with broad mowed shoulders, Brown-headed Cowbirds are common along the roadsides, and

Florida Prairie Warblers have become scarce since the cowbirds invaded. However, at Weedon Island where the mangroves are more nearly intact, cowbirds are few and Prairie Warblers more common. This suggests the possibility that creating openings in mangroves provides cowbirds with easier access to the nests of the warblers. Brittingham and Temple (1983) found that cowbird parasitism on a variety of eastern deciduous forest birds was highest near openings that provided habitat attractive to the cowbirds.

Many waterfront homeowners cut the mangroves between their property and the water. They may legally cut mangroves to a height of less than 2 m, create a tunnel as long as 0.4 km, and even cut on state aquatic preserves (J. Beever, pers. comm.). Mangrove cutting as typically practiced seems to render mangroves unusable for Prairie Warblers. Florida Prairie Warblers breed in four southwest Florida aquatic preserves where Beever (1989) studied the effects of mangrove cutting over a period of one year. He never found Prairie Warblers at any time of year on any of the three trimmed sites he studied in each of the four preserves (Beever 1989, pers. comm.). Cutting is widespread but varies locally in extent (J. Beever, pers. comm.). In Sarasota Bay, 33.8% of the 927 mangrove stands are trimmed to some extent. In 21.7% of these stands, the height of the trimmed portion has been reduced by more than 66%; in another 39.5% it has been reduced by 33–66%. In 39.3% of the trimmed stands, the cut portion covered more than 66% of the area of the stand, and in another 23.9% it covered from 33 to 66% (Estevez 1992).

Because of the difficulty of distinguishing between the two races of Prairie Warbler in winter (Stevenson and Anderson 1994), and therefore in determining their respective wintering grounds, it is difficult to know which changes in winter habitat affect Florida Prairie Warblers specifically. Wintering habitat of Prairie Warblers in the Caribbean is mostly abundant second growth, low shrubby vegetation, orchards, and suburbs (Nolan 1978). In some places conversion of forest to certain types of urban uses could actually increase the amount of wintering habitat attractive to Prairie Warblers (Baltz 1993).

DEMOGRAPHIC CHARACTERISTICS: Much of the following narrative is based on the demographic data presented by Nolan (1978) for his study population of Prairie Warblers in Indiana. Data for Florida Prairie Warblers, provided by J. W. Prather and A. Cruz (in litt.), are from Key Largo and Florida Bay.

Both sexes first breed at one year of age. They will attempt a second brood in a breeding season if the first brood is fledged early enough. If a nest is lost, the pair will nest again, for as many as eight replacement nestings in a single season. Mean clutch size is 3.89, range 3–5 eggs. Clutches laid in repeat and replacement nestings and perhaps those laid by yearlings are smaller; clutches begun when atmospheric temperatures are high may be larger. Mean clutch size of Florida Prairie Warblers is 2.89, range 2–4 eggs. Mean incubation is 12 days, range 10.5–14.5 days. Cool weather and perhaps cowbird parasitism prolong the incubation period; laying late in the breeding season may shorten it. The incubation period for Florida Prairie Warblers ranges from 14–19 days. Hatching success (i.e., the proportion of eggs laid that hatched) varies from 34.9% to 37.4%.

The mean nestling period is 9.4 days, range 8–11 days. Small brood size and occurrence late in the breeding season may lengthen the nestling period. The nestling period for Florida Prairie Warblers ranges from 10 to 14 days. Nolan (1978) presents nest success (i.e., production of at least one fledgling warbler or cowbird at a given nest) data from two samples. Sample 1: 22.3% of the nests succeeded; 60.1% of all nests in which at least one egg hatched succeeded; about 20% of all eggs laid and about 53.4% of those that hatched produced fledglings. Sample 2: 20.3% of the nests succeeded; 56.5% of all nests in which at least one egg hatched succeeded; about 18.5% of all eggs laid and 53.0% of those that hatched produced fledglings. Among Florida Prairie Warblers, 44% of eggs produced fledglings. Later nests were more successful than earlier ones; lower nests were more successful early in the season, and higher nests were more successful later in the season. Better concealed nests were more successful than poorly concealed ones. Mean success also may vary annually depending on the extent of cowbird parasitism, occurrence of late frosts, abundance of nest predators, and early ending of breeding season. The age of the breeding female and the density of the breeding population do not affect nest success. The laying interval, the day of hatching, and the nestling period were the riskiest parts of the nesting cycle.

Post-fledging survival of Prairie Warblers from nest-leaving to independence (ca. 32 days) is 82%, and from independence to first breeding season is about 39%. The annual survival rate for both sexes of adults is about 65%. From 14–17% of adult mortality occurs in the breeding season. Mean longevity from egg laying is about 86 days. On the first full day of independence, mean remaining longevity is 1.46 years. Those warblers that survive to 1 May of their second year have a mean longevity of 2.47 years, the highest expected longevity for any age group. The last survivor of 1,000 eggs is expected from extrapolation of life table data to die at the age of 10.5 years. The oldest known individual in the wild was 10 years and 3 months old.

Brown-headed Cowbirds parasitized 92 of 336 Prairie Warbler nests on Nolan's (1978) study site. Cowbird parasitism reduced the production of Prairie Warbler fledglings at this site by about 13% from the level expected if there had been no parasitism.

KEY BEHAVIORS: Most of the information here on Prairie Warbler behavior is derived from Nolan (1978) unless otherwise noted. With rare exceptions, only male Prairie Warblers sing. The most commonly heard song theme is a series of buzzy tones that rises gradually in pitch over a period of about two seconds. Males sing from the tops of the tallest perches in the vicinity and in flight. The commonest call is a "chek," given in a wide variety of contexts. Males defend their all-purpose territories with song, aerial and perched displays, chases, and fights. Prairie Warblers bob their tails frequently.

The types of pair bonds include season-long monogamy, polygyny, and their many variations. The great majority of pair bonds do not last from one season to another.

Only females build nests, incubate, and brood young. The nest is a cup made mostly of plant fibers and perched on or against slender branches. Nests of Florida Prairie Warblers may include palmetto fibers; most are built in mangroves about 2 to 3 m above water (Stevenson and Anderson 1994). Males occasionally feed incubating females on the nest. Males and females feed nestlings and fledglings. Prairie Warblers eat insects and spiders almost exclusively; caterpillars are important in the diet of nestlings.

CONSERVATION MEASURES TAKEN: No conservation measures have yet been undertaken specifically for Florida Prairie Warblers. They are protected from unauthorized killing or harassment by the federal Migratory Bird Treaty Act and state law. Major tracts of mangroves are at least partially protected in Everglades National Park, wildlife refuges, and state aquatic preserves. About 113,000 ha were so protected as of 1981 (Odum et al. 1982). Some mangroves may be restored in Tampa Bay as a result of studies by the Tampa Bay National Estuary Program (Hoppe et al. 1993). J. W. Prather and A. Cruz (in litt.) have been studying the breeding biology and population levels of Prairie Warblers in the Keys and Everglades since 1989; their data will provide a valuable baseline for determining the effects of any eventual cowbird parasitism.

CONSERVATION MEASURES PROPOSED. Baseline studies of Florida Prairie Warblers, such as those of J. W. Prather and A. Cruz, should be conducted at a variety of sites in Florida. These studies should include quantitative population surveys of both warblers and cowbirds, collection of basic demographic data, and determination of the extent to which cowbirds parasitize the warblers. Research should be conducted to determine whether human-created openings, including those made through trimming, increase the likelihood that cowbirds will enter mangrove forests and parasitize warblers. The effect of mangrove cutting on the overall amount of warbler breeding habitat should be determined. Field studies of fenthion spraying should be conducted to determine whether the theoretical predictions of Tiebout (unpubl. ms.) are borne out. Reliable means, perhaps biochemical, should be devised to discriminate between the two races of Prairie Warbler in winter. Such information would make possible improved understanding of the winter habitat needs of Florida Prairie Warblers.

If systematic surveys confirm that the numbers of Florida Prairie Warblers are indeed in decline, status should be upgraded from the category of Status Undetermined. If cowbirds are found to have a severe effect on warbler populations, cowbird control should be considered. Cowbird control can be effective locally (Post et al. 1991; Mayfield 1992), but the logistical problems of control throughout the mangroves of Florida may well be too great. Greater restrictions on mangrove cutting and spraying of certain pesticides may be warranted. The key to conserving Florida Prairie Warblers may be maintaining mangrove habitat in blocks undissected by roads, power lines, and other strips of habitat attractive to cowbirds, as implied by the conclusions of Brittingham and Temple (1983). Any measures that benefit Florida Prairie Warblers also should benefit other mangrove-nesting birds, such as Black-whiskered Vireos (*Vireo altiloquus*) and Mangrove Cuckoos (*Coccyzus minor*).

ACKNOWLEDGMENTS. I am indebted to B. H. Anderson, B. H. Atherton, L. S. Atherton, J. W. Beever, III, C. W. Biggs, A. Cruz, H. W. Kale, II, B. Pranty, J. W. Prather, S. P. Rowe, R. Smith, B. M. Stith, H. M. Tiebout, III, and the late H. M. Stevenson for the use of their unpublished information. I am equally indebted to E. D. Estevez, H. S. Greening, R. Hart, D. J. Levey, J. A. Rodgers, Jr., and W. Post for the generous assistance they gave me.

LITERATURE CITED:

AOU. 1957. Check-list of North American birds. 5th edition. Amer. Ornithol. Union, Washington, D.C.

AOU. 1983. Check-list of North American birds. 6th edition. Amer. Ornithol. Union, Washington, D.C.

Atherton, L. S., and B. H. Atherton. 1988. Florida region. Amer. Birds 42:60–63.

Baltz, M. E. 1993. Abundance of neotropical migrant songbirds on North Andros Island, Bahamas. Fla. Field Nat. 21:115–117.

Beever, J. W., III. 1989. The effects of fringe red mangrove trimming for view in the Southwest Florida Aquatic Preserves. Reports of the Southwest Florida Aquatic Preserves No. 5. Punta Gorda, Florida.

Bent, A. C. 1953. Life histories of North American wood warblers. U.S. Natl. Mus. Bull. 203. Washington, D.C.

Brittingham, M. C., and S. A. Temple. 1983. Have cowbirds caused forest songbirds to decline? BioScience 33:31–35.

Cruz, A., J. W. Wiley, T. K. Nakamura, and W. Post. 1989. The Shiny Cowbird *Molothrus bonariensis* in the West Indian region—biogeographical and ecological implications. Pp. 519–540 in Biogeography of the West Indies: past, present, and future (C.W. Woods, ed.). Sandhill Crane Press, Gainesville, Florida.

Estevez, E. D. 1992. Tidal wetlands. Chapter 6 in Framework for action; Sarasota Bay National Estuary Program. U.S. Environ. Prot. Agency, Sarasota, Florida.

Frayer, W. E., and J. M. Hefner. 1991. Florida wetlands. Status and trends, 1970's to 1980's. U.S. Fish Wildl. Serv., Southeast Region. Atlanta, Georgia.

Friedmann, H. 1963. Host relations of the parasitic cowbirds. U.S. Nat. Mus. Bull. no. 233. Washington, D.C.

Friedmann, H., and L. F. Kiff. 1985. The parasitic cowbirds and their hosts. Proc. West. Found. Vert. Zool. 2(4).

Griscom, L., and A. Sprunt, Jr. 1957. The warblers of North America. Devin-Adair, New York.

Hellmayr, C. E. 1935. Catalogue of the birds of the Americas and adjacent islands. Part VIII. Field Mus. Nat. Hist. Publ. 347, Zool. Ser. Vol. XIII.

Hoppe, M. K., V. Parsons, and S. Treat. 1993. Tampa Bay status and trends. Tampa Bay Natl. Estuary Prog., St. Petersburg, Florida.

Howell, A. H. 1930. Description of a new subspecies of the Prairie Warbler, with remarks on two other unrecognized Florida races. Auk 47:41–43.

Kale, H. W. II. 1989. Florida birds. Florida Nat. 62(4):14.

Kale, H. W. II, B. Pranty, B. M. Stith, and C. W. Biggs. In prep. The atlas of the breeding birds of Florida.

Mayfield, H. F. 1992. Kirtland's Warbler. No. 19 in The birds of North America (A. Poole, P. Stettenheim, and F. Gill, eds.). Philadelphia: Acad. of Nat. Sciences; Amer. Ornithol. Union, Washington, D.C.

National Geographic Society. 1987. Field guide to the birds of North America. 2nd edition. Nat. Geogr. Soc., Washington, D.C.

Nolan, V., Jr. 1978. The ecology and behavior of the Prairie Warbler Dendroica discolor. Ornithol. Monogr. No. 26. Amer. Ornithol. Union, Washington, D.C.

Odum, W. E., C. C. McIvor, and T. J. Smith, III. 1982. The ecology of the mangroves of South Florida: a community profile. FWS/OBS-81/24. U.S. Fish Wildl. Serv., Office.. of Biol. Serv., Washington, D.C.

Paul, R. T. 1987. Florida region. Amer. Birds 41:1425–1428.

Paul, R. T. 1989. Florida region. Amer. Birds 43:1307–1310.

Post, W., A. Cruz, and D. B. McNair. 1993. The North American invasion pattern of the Shiny Cowbird. Jour. Field Ornithol. 64:32–41.

Pranty, B. 1993. Field observations. Spring report: March-May 1993. Fla. Field Nat. 21:121–128.

Pyle, P., S. N. G. Howell, R. P. Yunick, D. F. DeSante. 1987. Identification guide to North American passerines. Slate Creek Press, Bolinas, California.

Robertson, W. B., Jr., and G. E. Woolfenden. 1992. Florida bird species—an annotated list. Fla. Ornithol. Soc. Spec. Publ. No. 6. Gainesville, Florida.

Stevenson, H. M. 1978. Florida Prairie Warbler. Pp. 105–106 in Rare and endangered biota of Florida, Vol. two: birds (H. W. Kale, II, ed.). Univ. Presses of Fla., Gainesville, Florida.

Stevenson, H. M., and B. H. Anderson. 1994. Birdlife of Florida. Univ. Press of Fla., Gainesville, Florida.

Tiebout, H. M., III. 1991. Adverse impacts to nontarget terrestrial vertebrates. Pp. 21–32 in Mosquito control pesticides: ecological impacts and management alternatives (T. C. Emmel and J. C. Tucker, eds.). Scientific Publ., Gainesville, Florida.

Van Tyne, J. 1956. The scientific name of the Florida Prairie Warbler. Auk 73:139.

Wiley, J. W., W. Post, and A. Cruz. 1991. Conservation of the Yellow-shouldered Blackbird *Agelaius xanthomus,* an endangered West Indian species. Biol. Conserv. 55:119–138.

PREPARED BY: Tom Webber, Florida Museum of Natural History, University of Florida, Gainesville, FL 32611.

Status Undetermined

Painted Bunting
Passerina ciris

FAMILY EMBERIZIDAE

Order Passeriformes

TAXONOMY: The Painted Bunting (*Passerina ciris*) was originally described by Linnaeus in 1758 (AOU 1953). Thompson (1991) proposed that distinctive eastern and western populations of Painted Buntings occurring in North America represented separate phylogenetic species. The breeding and wintering ranges of these two populations do not overlap (except perhaps in the Florida panhandle, see below). Eastern and western populations also differ in the timing of their feather molts and migration (Thompson 1991). Individuals in the western population initiate migration at least two months earlier than individuals in the eastern population and molt after leaving the breeding grounds. Birds in the eastern population typically complete molt on the breeding grounds prior to migration (Thompson 1991).

Two subspecies were recognized by the AOU (1953): a western race (*P. c. pallidior*) and an eastern race (*P. c. ciris*). However, the distribution of these subspecies does not match the distribution of eastern and western populations described by Thompson (1991). Other names include mariposa, Mexican canary, nonpareil, painted finch, and pope (Terres 1980).

DESCRIPTION: The Painted Bunting is a medium-sized (12–15 cm) cardinaline that is unmistakable in all plumages (Robbins et al. 1966). Males are a brilliant combination of bright colors that include a purple-blue head, red eye-ring, a yellow-green back, and red underparts and rump (Robbins et al. 1966). Females and immature males are a distinctive yellow-green color that is unique among North American cardinalines (Robbins et al. 1966). Juvenile males attain adult coloration over an extended period that lasts up to two years (Terres 1980). Birds with traces of both adult and juvenile coloration may be observed throughout the year.

POPULATION SIZE AND TREND: Painted Buntings are included in this series based in part on strong declining population trends occurring on Christ-

Painted Bunting,
Passerina ciris.
(Photo by Barry
Mansell)

mas Bird Counts (J. Cox, unpubl. data) and Breeding Bird Surveys (Robbins et al. 1986; Sauer and Droege 1992). Painted Buntings recorded along Breeding Bird Survey routes in the eastern United States have decreased at an annual rate of approximately 4.6% over the last 25 years (Sauer and Droege 1992). Significant declines also were noted on 12 of the 25 Florida Christmas Bird Counts (CBCs) on which Painted Buntings are regularly recorded, whereas only one CBC showed a significant increasing trend (J. Cox, unpubl. data). Some of the changes in numbers reported in CBCs are likely influenced by the number of flocks counted at bird feeders. However, the magnitude of declines found on many independent CBCs is striking. For example, several CBCs that once regularly reported scores or even hundreds of Painted Buntings (e.g., Coot Bay, Fort Lauderdale, Sarasota, Naples, and Fort Pierce) now report only a dozen or so individuals each year.

Within appropriate breeding habitat, the Painted Bunting can be abundant. Hamel (1992) reported densities of 5.2–9 per 40 ha (100 ac.), depending on habitat type. Stevenson and Anderson (1992) reported that Painted Buntings became less abundant in the southern portion of their Florida breeding range, as well as away from coastal areas.

In winter, Painted Buntings occur in flocks of varying sizes. The chances of overlooking small flocks in winter are good given the preference Painted Buntings have for dense vegetation (Stevenson and Anderson 1992; Wunderle and Waide 1993). These habits may make it difficult to estimate winter population densities in natural settings. Robertson and Woolfenden (1992) and Stevenson and Anderson (1992) described Florida's wintering population as fairly rare or uncommon to locally common (especially at feeders). Winter abundances appear to increase farther south and west in the Florida peninsula (Root 1988), becoming less common in the Lower Keys (Robertson and Woolfenden 1992). Painted Buntings also are a regular to uncommon spring and fall migrant throughout Florida, with highest numbers reported in coastal areas (Stevenson and Anderson 1992).

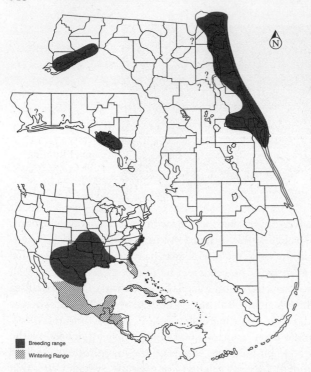

Distribution map of
the Painted Bunting,
Passerina ciris.

Sprunt (1968) suggested that most eastern Painted Buntings winter south of the United States. However, other evidence suggests that Florida may support a large portion of the eastern population. A cursory review of published Christmas Bird Counts showed that Painted Buntings were not reported in large numbers on CBCs conducted in Cuba, Jamaica, and the Bahamas, while it is frequently reported on many south Florida CBCs. Wunderle and Waide (1993) found Painted Buntings to be uncommon at point counts made in winter throughout the West Indies. In addition, most banded birds have been recovered within the continental United States rather than neighboring West Indian countries (Stevenson and Anderson 1992), although this probably reflects the distribution of bird banders as much as the distribution of birds.

DISTRIBUTION AND HISTORY OF DISTRIBUTION: The breeding range of the western population of Painted Bunting extends from northwest Florida and southwestern Alabama to southeastern New Mexico, north to central Kansas and Arkansas, throughout most of Texas, Oklahoma, Louisiana, and Arkansas, and north to southern Kansas and Missouri and southwest Tennessee (Thompson 1991; Hamel 1992). The winter range of the western population extends from southern Texas to western Panama (AOU 1983; Thompson 1991; Stevenson and Anderson 1992).

In comparison to the western population, the breeding range of the eastern population of Painted Buntings is more restricted; it extends from northeast Florida (beginning in central Brevard County) to North Carolina (AOU 1953; Thompson 1991). Although occasional reports of singing males and pairs of birds occur inland (Taylor et al. 1989; Kale et al. 1992), the bulk of the eastern population is found near coastal regions and inland along larger river systems such as the St. Johns and Savannah Rivers (Stevenson and Anderson 1992; Kale et al. 1992; Hamel 1992). The winter range of the eastern birds covers south and central Florida, Cuba, Jamaica, and the Bahamas (AOU 1983; Thompson 1991; Stevenson and Anderson 1992).

As indicated above, Florida's breeding population consists of two discrete populations whose affinities with either the eastern or western populations as described by Thompson (1991) are unclear. The Atlantic coast breeding population in northeast Florida is part of the eastern population and breeding birds in extreme northwest Florida are part of the western population as described by Thompson (1991); however, breeding birds reported in Franklin, Bay, Gulf, and Wakulla counties (Kale et al. 1992) may constitute a portion of either the eastern or western populations, or a zone of overlap (Thompson 1991). Whatever the case, the peripheral breeding populations in the panhandle are sporadic and very localized (Kale et al. 1992; Stevenson and Anderson 1992).

HABITAT REQUIREMENTS AND HABITAT TREND: Painted Buntings occupy partly open areas with scattered brush and trees. Scrub communities and the edges of maritime hammocks probably represent the key natural habitats once used, whereas hedges and yards, roadside thickets and fence rows, fallow farm fields, freeze-killed orange groves, and other weedy and shrubby areas also are used (Stevenson and Anderson 1992). Painted Buntings are found in similar habitats during migration and in the winter (Ridgley and Gwynne 1990; Stevenson and Anderson 1992; Wunderle and Waide 1993). Habitat trends at a coarse scale are probably increasing or stable (Taylor et al. 1989; Kautz 1993).

VULNERABILITY OF SPECIES AND HABITAT: The narrow geographic range of the eastern population of Painted Buntings may render this population more vulnerable to extinction than if the geographic range extended over a broader area (Soule and Simberloff 1986). The combination of a restricted range and rapidly declining population trends argue for more attention. The vulnerability of habitat seems low since birds regularly occur in urban and agricultural areas (Taylor et al. 1989; Stevenson and Anderson 1992). Large numbers of birds gathering at feeders may enhance disease transmission (e.g., aspergillosis) or collecting pressures (see Causes of Threat), but these are probably not major sources of population losses.

CAUSES OF THREAT: The reason for the population decline of Painted Buntings is unknown. Breeding success may vary among the various urban, agricultural, and natural habitats used by this species. Parasitism by Brown-headed Cowbirds (*Molothrus ater*) may be fairly common (Friedmann 1963) and has been implicated in the declines of other species with restricted geographic ranges (Robinson et al. 1993). An attraction to feeders and use of urban and agricultural habitats places Painted Buntings in frequent contact with Brown-headed Cowbirds, as well as predatory feral cats. However, the population declines in Florida appear to have begun prior to the major expansion of Brown-headed Cowbirds that occurred in Florida in the 1970s and 1980s (Robertson and Woolfenden 1992).

Painted Buntings may be trapped and sold as cage birds outside the United States (Stevenson and Anderson 1992). There are unconfirmed reports that birds are sacrificed in ceremonies performed by members of the Santa Ria religion in south Florida, Cuba, Jamaica, and the Bahamas. The degree to which these practices threaten populations is uncertain, but they are probably not the primary mechanisms behind population declines.

RESPONSES TO HABITAT MODIFICATION: Breeding Painted Buntings are often found in disturbed habitats, but productivity in modified versus natural habitats deserves study.

DEMOGRAPHIC CHARACTERISTICS: Painted Buntings can live for many years, but average life spans are not well known (Kennard 1975). Based on data from birds banded in south Florida (Fisk 1974), six birds were reported living at least 8 years in the wild, and a maximum age of at least 12 years was reported elsewhere (Kennard 1975). Clutch size varies from 2–5 eggs with most clutches in Florida consisting of 4 eggs (Stevenson and Anderson 1992). Two, occasionally three, broods may be produced in a single year, and males may feed fledglings while females initiate new nesting attempts (Stevenson and Anderson 1992).

KEY BEHAVIORS: The Painted Bunting is polygynous. Males tenaciously defend their breeding territories against conspecific males (Parmalee 1959), and intense and lengthy battles often occur that lead to permanent disfigurement or death (Parmalee 1959; Stevenson and Anderson 1992). The song is a high-pitched and variable warble (Robbins et al. 1966; Terres 1980; Stevenson and Anderson 1992). The call note is a metallic "tsick" (Stevenson and Anderson 1992). The animated courtship display performed by males involves flattening the body to the ground, fluffing feathers, spreading wings and tail, and moving in a jerky fashion (Parmalee 1959; Stevenson and Anderson 1992). Females are generally less obvious than males during the breeding season, and both sexes tend to skulk amid dense vegetation at other times of the year (Stevenson and Anderson 1992).

Sprunt (1968) lists Painted Buntings as a late migrant in spring. Males appear to arrive first on breeding grounds (Sprunt 1968). The nesting season extends from early May until late July with the peak season occurring from mid-May to early June (Stevenson and Anderson 1992; Hamel 1992). The nest is usually constructed using grass and weed stalks and situated in thick cover within 2 m of the ground (Sprunt 1968; Stevenson and Anderson 1992). The nest is shaped like a deep cup and is often placed in a clump of Spanish moss (*Tillandsia usneoides*). Only the female constructs the nest and incubates eggs. Incubation lasts for approximately 10 days, and young birds fledge within 8–10 days (Stevenson and Anderson 1992) or 11–14 days (Terres 1980) following hatching.

The diet consists mostly of seeds and, to a lesser degree, insects. Howell (1932) examined 13 stomachs and found 73% of the total volume consisted of seeds of sorrel (*Rumex* sp.), various grasses, and figs (*Ficus* sp.), whereas a variety of beetles, crickets, grasshoppers, wasps, flies, and caterpillars comprised the remaining contents.

CONSERVATION MEASURES TAKEN: The Painted Bunting is protected from direct threats by the Migratory Bird Treaty Act (Wood 1991). Additional conservation measures await a determination of the factors responsible for population declines as well as a more complete investigation of the taxonomic status of Florida's population(s).

CONSERVATION MEASURES PROPOSED: If population declines continue unabated, the eastern population of Painted Bunting may eventually reach a point where expanded conservation and management efforts are warranted. It would therefore be prudent to begin to investigate some of the factors that are likely responsible for the observed population declines in Florida and elsewhere.

LITERATURE CITED:

AOU. 1953. A checklist of North American birds. 5th ed. Amer. Ornithol. Union. Allen Press. Lawrence, Kansas.

AOU. 1983. A checklist of North American birds. 6th ed. Amer. Ornithol. Union. Allen Press. Lawrence, Kansas.

Fisk, E. J. 1974. Wintering populations of Painted Buntings in southern Florida. Bird-Banding 45:353–359.

Friedmann, H. 1963. Host relations of the parasitic cowbirds. U.S. Natl. Mus. Bull. No. 233. Washington, D.C.

Hamel, P. 1992. The land manager's guide to the birds of the south. The Nature Conservancy, Southeast Region. Chapel Hill, North Carolina. 437 pp.

Howell, A. 1932. Florida bird life. Coward-McCann. New York.

Kale, H. W. II, B. Pranty, B. Stith, and W. Biggs. 1992. Florida's breeding bird atlas project. Final report. Fla. Game and Fresh Water Fish Comm. Tallahassee, Florida.

Kautz, R. 1993. Trends in Florida wildlife habitat 1936–1987. Fla. Sci. 56:7–24.

Kennard, J. 1975. Longevity record of North American birds. Bird-Banding 46:55–73.

Parmalee, D. 1959. The breeding behavior of the Painted Bunting in southern Oklahoma. Bird-Banding 30:1–18.

Ridgely, R. S., and J. Gwynne. 1990. A guide to the birds of Panama with Costa Rico, Nicaragua, and Honduras. Second ed. Princeton Univ. Press. Princeton, New Jersey.

Robbins, C., B. Bruun, and H. Zim. 1966. Birds of North America. A guide to field identification. Golden Press. New York.

Robbins, C., D. Bystrak, and P. Geissler. 1986. The breeding bird survey: its first fifteen years, 1965–1979. U.S. Dept. of Int., Fish and Wildl. Ser. Res. Publ. 157. Washington, D.C.

Robertson, W., and G. Woolfenden. 1992. Florida bird species. An annotated list. Fla. Ornithol. Soc. Spec. Publ. 6. Gainesville, Florida.

Robinson, S., J. Grzybowski, S. Rothstein, M. Brittingham, L. Petit, and F. Thompson. 1993. Management implications of cowbird parasitism on Neotropical migrant songbirds. Pages 93–108 in Status and management of neotropical migratory birds (D. Finch and P. Stangel, eds.). U.S. Dept. of Agriculture. Ft. Collins. Colorado.

Root, T. 1988. Atlas of wintering North American birds. Univ. of Chicago Press. Chicago, Illinois.

Sauer, J., and S. Droege. 1992. Geographical patterns in population trends of Neotropical migrants in North America. Pages 24–42 in Ecology and conservation of neotropical migrant landbirds (H. M. Hagan, III, and D. W. Johnston, eds.). Smithsonian Inst. Press. Washington, D.C.

Soule, M. E., and D. Simberloff. 1986. What do genetics and ecology tell us about the design of nature preserves? Biol. Cons. 35:19–40.

Sprunt, A. 1968. Eastern Painted Bunting. Pages 137–154 in Life history of North American cardinals, grosbeaks, buntings, towhees, finches, sparrows, and allies. Part One (Bent, A. C., and collaborators). U.S. Nat. Mus. Bull. No. 237, Smithsonian Inst. Press, Washington, D.C.

Stevenson, H. S., and B. Anderson. 1992. Florida birdlife. Final Report. Fla. Game and Fresh Water Fish Comm. Tallahassee, Florida.

Taylor, W., B. H. Anderson, and H. M. Stevenson. 1989. Breeding range expansion of the Indigo Bunting, Painted Bunting, and Blue Grosbeak in Florida with new records from Seminole County. Fla. Field Nat. 17:1–10.

Terres, J. 1980. The Audubon Society encyclopedia of North American birds. Alfred Knopf, New York.

Thompson, C. 1991. Is the Painted Bunting actually two species? Problems determining species limits between allopatric populations. Condor 93:987–1000.

Wood, D. 1991. Legal accommodation of Florida's endangered species, threatened species, and species of special concern. Fla. Game and Fresh Water Fish Comm. Tallahassee, Florida.

Wunderle, J. M., Jr., and R. B. Waide. 1993. Distribution of overwinter nearctic migrants in the Bahamas and Greater Antilles. Condor 95:904–933.

PREPARED BY: James Cox, Florida Game and Fresh Water Fish Commission, 620 S. Meridian Street, Tallahassee, FL 32399-1600.

Contributors

Writers

Bruce H. Anderson, 2917 Scarlet Road, Winter Park, Florida 32792

Ray E. Ashton, Jr., Applied Technology and Management, Inc. 2770 NW 43rd Street, Gainesville, Florida 32606

G. Thomas Bancroft, National Audubon Society, 115 Indian Mound Trail, Tavernier, Florida 33070 (Current address: Archbold Biological Station, P.O. Box 2057, Lake Placid, Florida 33862)

Theodore H. Below, National Audubon Society, Rookery Bay Sanctuary, 3697 North Road, Naples, Florida 33942

Robin Bjork, National Audubon Society, 115 Indian Mound Trail, Tavernier, Florida 33070 (Current address: Department of Fisheries and Wildlife, Oregon State University, Corvallis, Oregon 97331)

Reed Bowman, Archbold Biological Station, P.O. Box 2057, Lake Placid, Florida 33862

Dana C. Bryan, Florida Park Service, Department of Environmental Protection, Tallahassee, Florida 32399, and Tall Timbers Research Station, Rt. 1 Box 678, Tallahassee, Florida 32312

Michael W. Collopy, Department of Wildlife Ecology and Conservation, University of Florida, Gainesville, Florida 32611 (Current address: Forest and Rangeland Ecosystem Science Center, National Biological Service, 3200 SW Jefferson Way, Corvallis, Oregon 97331)

James Cox, Florida Game and Fresh Water Fish Commission, 620 South Meridian Street, Tallahassee, Florida 32399

John L. Curnutt, National Biological Survey, Everglades National Park, 40001 State Road 9336, Homestead, Florida 33034 (Current address: Department of Ecology and Evolutionary Biology, University of Tennessee, Knoxville, Tennessee 37996)

Michael F. Delany, Florida Game and Fresh Water Fish Commission, Wildlife Research Laboratory, 4005 South Main Street, Gainesville, Florida 32601

Allan L. Egbert, Florida Game and Fresh Water Fish Commission, 620 South Meridian Street, Tallahassee, Florida 32399

Erik D. Egensteiner, Bureau of Nongame Wildlife, Florida Game and Fresh Water Fish Commission, 3911 Highway 2321, Panama City, Florida 32409 (Current address: Florida Park Service, Florida Department of Environmental Protection, 1800 Wekiwa Circle, Apopka, Florida 32712)

R. Todd Engstrom, Tall Timbers Research Station, Route 1, Box 678, Tallahassee, Florida 32312

John W. Fitzpatrick, Archbold Biological Station, P.O. Box 2057, Lake Placid, Florida 33862 (Current address: Cornell Laboratory of Ornithology, 159 Sapsucker Woods Road, Ithaca, New York 14850)

Peter C. Frederick, Department of Wildlife Ecology and Conservation, 118 Newins-Ziegler Hall, University of Florida, Gainesville, Florida 32611

Jeffery A. Gore, Florida Game and Fresh Water Fish Commission, 3911 Highway 2321, Panama City, Florida 32409

Bradley J. Hartman, Office of Environmental Services, Florida Game and Fresh Water Fish Commission, 620 South Meridian Street, Tallahassee, Florida 32399

Wayne Hoffman, National Audubon Society, 115 Indian Mound Trail, Tavernier, Florida 33070

Julie A. Hovis, Florida Game and Fresh Water Fish Commission, 1239 S.W. 10th Street, Ocala, Florida 34474

Herbert W. Kale, II, Florida Audubon Society, 460 Highway 435, Suite 200, Casselberry, Florida 32707 (Deceased)

Jerome A. Jackson, Department of Biological Sciences, Mississippi State University, Mississippi State, Mississippi 39762

James N. Layne, Archbold Biological Station, P.O. Box 2057, Lake Placid, Florida 33862

Ronald F. Labisky, Department of Wildlife Ecology and Conservation, University of Florida, Gainesville, Florida 32611

Robert W. Loftin, Department of History and Philosophy, University of North Florida, 4567 St. Johns Bluff Road, South, Jacksonville, Florida 32216 (Deceased)

Peter G. Merritt, Treasure Coast Regional Planning Council, 3228 S.W. Martin Downs Blvd., Suite 205, Palm City, Florida 34990

Kenneth D. Meyer, Department of Wildlife Ecology and Conservation, 118 Newins-Ziegler Hall, University of Florida, Gainesville, Florida 32611 (Current address: National Park Service, Big Cypress National Preserve, HCR 61, Box 110, Ochopee, Florida 33943)

Brian A. Millsap, Nongame Wildlife Program, Florida Game and Fresh Water Fish Commission, 620 South Meridian Street, Tallahassee, Florida 32399

Stephen A. Nesbitt, Florida Game and Fresh Water Fish Commission, Wildlife Research Laboratory, 4005 South Main Street, Gainesville, Florida 32601

Janice L. Nicholls, U.S. Fish and Wildlife Service, 75 Spring Street, Atlanta, Georgia 30303 (Current address: U.S. Fish and Wildlife Service, Asheville Field Office, 160 Zillicoa Street, Asheville, North Carolina 28801)

John C. Ogden, National Park Service, Everglades National Park, 40001 State Road 9336, Homestead, Florida 33034

Oscar T. Owre, Department of Biology, University of Miami, Coral Gables, Florida 33124 (Deceased)

Richard T. Paul, National Audubon Society, Tampa Bay Sanctuaries, 410 Ware Blvd., Suite 500, Tampa, Florida 33619

George V. N. Powell, RARE Center for Tropical Conservation, 1616 Walnut Street, Suite 911, Philadelphia, Pennsylvania 19103

Mary J. Robertson, 17300 S.W. 300th Street, Homestead, Florida 33030

William B. Robertson, Jr., National Biological Survey, Everglades National Park, 40001 State Road 9336, Homestead, Florida 33034

Mark S. Robson, Nongame Wildlife Program, Florida Game and Fresh Water Fish Commission, 551 North Military Trail, West Palm Beach, Florida 33415

James A. Rodgers, Jr., Florida Game and Fresh Water Fish Commission, Wildlife Research Laboratory, 4005 South Main Street, Gainesville, Florida 32601

Douglas E. Runde, Florida Game and Fresh Water Fish Commission, Rt. 7 Box 3055, Quincy, Florida 32351 (Current address: Weyerhaeuser Environmental Forestry Research, WTC 1A5, Federal Way, Tacoma, Washington 98477)

John A. Smallwood, Department of Wildlife Ecology and Conservation, 118 Newins-Ziegler Hall, University of Florida, Gainesville, Florida 32611 (Current address: Department of Biology, Montclair State University, Upper Montclair, New Jersey 07043)

Henry T. Smith, Florida Department of Environmental Protection, Office of Environmental Services, 3900 Commonwealth Blvd., Tallahassee, Florida 32399 (Current address: Florida Department of Environmental Protection, Florida Park Service, 13798 S.E. Federal Highway, Hobe Sound, Florida 33455)

P. William Smith, South Florida Natural Resources Center, Everglades National Park, 40001 State Road 9336, Homestead, Florida 33034

Gary L. Sprandel, Bureau of Nongame Wildlife, Florida Game and Fresh Water Fish Commission, Route 7, Box 3055, Quincy, Florida 32351

Henry M. Stevenson, Tall Timbers Research Station, Route 1, Box 678, Tallahassee, Florida 32312 (Deceased)

Allan M. Strong, National Audubon Society, 115 Indian Mound Trail, Tavernier, Florida 33070 (Current address: Department of Biology, 310 Dinwiddie Hall, Tulane University, New Orleans, Louisiana 70118)

Paul W. Sykes, Jr., National Biological Service, Warnell School of Forest Resources, The University of Georgia, Athens, Georgia 30602

Walter Kingsley Taylor, Department of Biology, University of Central Florida, Orlando, Florida 32816

Brian R. Toland, Florida Game and Fresh Water Fish Commission, 110 43rd Avenue, S.W., Vero Beach, Florida 32962 (Current address: U.S. Fish & Wildlife Service, P.O. Box 2676, Vero Beach, Florida 32961-2676)

Noel Wamer, Environmental Consulting, 502 East Georgia Street, Tallahassee, Florida 32303

Tom Webber, Florida Museum of Natural History, University of Florida, Gainesville, Florida 32611

Tom Wilmers, U.S. Fish and Wildlife Service, Florida Keys National Wildlife Refuges, P.O. Box 510, Big Pine Key, Florida 33043

Glen E. Woolfenden, Department of Biology, University of South Florida, Tampa, Florida 33620

Photographers

G. Thomas Bancroft, National Audubon Society, 115 Indian Mound Trail, Tavernier, Florida 33070 (Current address: Archbold Biological Station, P.O. Box 2057, Lake Placid, Florida 33862)

Wes Biggs, c/o Florida Nature Tours, P.O. Box 5643, Winter Park, Florida 32793

Dana C. Bryan, Florida Park Service, Department of Environmental Protection, Tallahassee, Florida 32399, and Tall Timbers Research Station, Rt. 1 Box 678, Tallahassee, Florida 32312

Allan D. Cruickshank (Deceased: photographs courtesy of Florida Audubon Society, 460 Highway 435, Suite 200, Casselberry, Florida 32707)

Florida Audubon Society, 460 Highway 435, Suite 200, Casselberry, Florida 32707

Jeffery A. Gore, Florida Game and Fresh Water Fish Commission, 3911 Highway 2321, Panama City, Florida 32409

James N. Layne, Archbold Biological Station, P.O. Box 2057, Lake Placid, Florida 33862

Michael Legare, 210B Woodward Hall, University of Rhode Island, Kingston, Rhode Island 02881

Barry Mansell, 2826 Rosselle Street, Jacksonville, Florida 32205

Brian A. Millsap, Nongame Wildlife Program, Florida Game and Fresh Water Fish Commission, 620 South Meridian Street, Tallahassee, Florida 32399

Stephen A. Nesbitt, Florida Game and Fresh Water Fish Commission, 4005 South Main Street, Gainesville, Florida 32601

Stuart L. Pimm, Department of Ecology and Evolutionary Biology, The University of Tennessee, Knoxville, Tennessee 37996

D. Bob Progulske, Jr., Avon Park Bombing Range, U.S. Air Force, 56 CSS-DEN, Avon Park, Florida 33825

Mark S. Robson, Nongame Wildlife Program, Florida Game and Fresh Water Fish Commission, 551 North Military Trail, West Palm Beach, Florida 33415

James A. Rodgers, Jr., Florida Game and Fresh Water Fish Commission, 4005 South Main Street, Gainesville, Florida 32601

John Sidle, U.S. Fish and Wildlife Service, 203 West Second Street, Federal Building, Grand Island, Nebraska 68801

John A. Smallwood, Department of Wildlife Ecology and Conservation, 118 Newins-Ziegler Hall, University of Florida, Gainesville, Florida 32611 (Current address: Department of Biology, Montclair State University, Upper Montclair, New Jersey 07043)

Lee F. Snyder, 1499 Ocean Road, Number 160, Narragansett, Rhode Island 02882

Ken Spilios, 8676 East Moccasin Slough Road, Inverness, Florida 34450

Paul W. Sykes, Jr., National Biological Service, Warnell School of Forest Resources, The University of Georgia, Athens, Georgia 30602

Dade W. Thornton, Owl's Nest Two, Number 1 Thornton Land, P.O. Box 477, Rosman, North Carolina 28772

Brian R. Toland, Florida Game and Fresh Water Fish Commission, 110 43rd Avenue, S.W., Vero Beach, Florida 32962 (Current address: U.S. Fish & Wildlife Service, P.O. Box 2676, Vero Beach, Florida 32961-2676)

Betty Wargo, 7515 Veve Lane, Tampa, Florida 33610

Glen M. Wood, Plant and Soil Science Department, University of Vermont, Burlington, Vermont 05405

Index

Note: Numbers in italic type indicate distribution maps of species.